The Palgrave Handbook of Global Citizenship and Education

Ian Davies · Li-Ching Ho · Dina Kiwan
Carla L. Peck · Andrew Peterson
Edda Sant · Yusef Waghid
Editors

The Palgrave Handbook of Global Citizenship and Education

palgrave
macmillan

Editors
Ian Davies
Department of Education
University of York
York, UK

Li-Ching Ho
University of Wisconsin-Madison
Madison, WI, USA

Dina Kiwan
Department of Education and Social
  Justice, School of Education
University of Birmingham
Birmingham, UK

Carla L. Peck
Department of Elementary Education
University of Alberta
Edmonton, AB, Canada

Andrew Peterson
Faculty of Education
Canterbury Christ Church University
Canterbury, UK

Edda Sant
Faculty of Education
Manchester Metropolitan University
Manchester, UK

Yusef Waghid
Department of Education Policy Studies,
Faculty of Education
Stellenbosch University
Stellenbosch, South Africa

ISBN 978-1-137-59732-8   ISBN 978-1-137-59733-5   (eBook)
https://doi.org/10.1057/978-1-137-59733-5

Library of Congress Control Number: 2017939879

This Palgrave Macmillan imprint is published by Springer Nature
The registered company is Macmillan Publishers Ltd.
The registered company address is: The Campus, 4 Crinan Street, London, N1 9XW, United Kingdom

CONTENTS

EDITORS AND CONTRIBUTORS

About the Editors

Ian Davies is Professor of Education in the Department of Education, University of York, UK. He is director of the Centre for Research on Education and Social Justice, deputy head of department of education and director of the Graduate School of Education at York. He is the author of many books and articles on the theme of citizenship education. He has worked as an expert for the Council of Europe on education for democratic citizenship, is a past fellow of the Japan Society for the Promotion of Science and is a visiting professor at the Hong Kong University of Education.

Li-Ching Ho is a social studies Professor at the University of Wisconsin-Madison. Her research focuses on three interrelated lines of inquiry: differentiated access to citizenship education, global issues of diversity in civic education, and environmental citizenship. She has published articles in journals such as the *Journal of Curriculum Studies*, *Teachers College Record*, and *Teaching and Teacher Education*. She is also a founding member and current President of the Singapore Association for Social Studies Education.

Dina Kiwan is a Reader in Comparative education, School of Education, University of Birmingham UK, and formerly Associate Professor in the Department of Sociology, Anthropology and Media Studies, at the American University of Beirut, since September 2012. Educated at the universities of Oxford, Harvard and London in psychology, sociology and education, her research program focuses on citizenship and civil society, which is interdisciplinary and international extending across the domains of education, gender, human rights, immigration and naturalization. Publications include Kiwan (2008). *Education for Inclusive Citizenship* (Routledge), and Kiwan, D. (ed.). (2013) *Naturalization Policies, Education and Citizenship: Multicultural and Multination Societies in International Perspective* (Palgrave Macmillan).

Carla L. Peck is Associate Professor of Social Studies Education in the Department of Elementary Education at the University of Alberta. Her research interests include students' understandings of democratic concepts, diversity, identity, citizenship and the relationship between students' ethnic identities and their understandings of history. In 2010, she was honoured with the Canadian Education Association's Pat Clifford Award for Early Career Research in Education and in the 2011 Publication Award from The History Education Network/Histoire et Education en Réseau. Dr. Peck has published widely on citizenship education and history education in prestigious journals including the Canadian Journal of Education, Curriculum Inquiry, Theory & Research in Social Education, and Citizenship Teaching and Learning. She is co-author of Education, Globalization and the Nation (Palgrave Macmillan, 2016).

Andrew Peterson is Professor of Civic and Moral Education at Canterbury Christ Church University, and Adjunct Professor of Education at the University of South Australia. He has published widely in the fields of civic and moral education, and is co-editor of the *Journal of Philosophy in Schools*. He is book reviews editor for the *British Journal of Educational Studies* and handling editor for *Citizenship Teaching and Learning*. His latest books are *The Palgrave International Handbook of Education for Citizenship and Social Justice* (Palgrave; edited with Robert Hattam, Michalinos Zembylas and James Arthur) and *Compassion and Education: Cultivating Compassionate Children, Schools and Communities*.

Edda Sant is a Senior Lecturer in the Department of Childhood, Youth and Education Studies at Manchester Metropolitan University. She has previously worked as a Teaching and Research Fellow at the Universitat Autònoma de Barcelona (Spain) and as Social science and Citizenship education teacher in different schools. Her research focuses on democratic, citizenship and history education, particularly on the topics of political participation and the education of national/global identities.

Yusef Waghid is Distinguished Professor of Philosophy of Education at Stellenbosch University in South Africa. His most recent books include, *Education, assessment and dissonance* (Co-authored with Nuraan Davids, New York: Peter Lang, 2017), and *Philosophy of education as action: Implications for teacher education* (Co-authored with Nuraan Davids, Boulder & London: Lexington Books, 2017).

Contributors

Theresa Alviar-Martin Education University of Hong Kong, Hong Kong, People's Republic of China

Jennifer M. Bondy Virginia Tech, Blacksburg, USA

Liliana Bravo Universidad Alberto Hurtado, Santiago, Chile

Stephanie Curley Manchester Metropolitan University, Manchester, UK

Ian Davies Department of Education, University of York, York, UK

Nuraan Davids Stellenbosch University, Stellenbosch, South Africa

Sandra Delgado Department of Curriculum and Pedagogy, University of British Columbia, Vancouver, Canada

Rachel Forsyth Manchester Metropolitan University, Manchester, UK

William Gaudelli Teachers College, Columbia University, New York, USA

David Geelan Griffith University, Southport Queensland, Australia

Gustavo González Valencia Universidad de Medellin, Medellin, Colombia

Annette Gough RMIT University, Melbourne, VIC, Australia

Robert Hattam School of Education, Magill Campus, University of South Australia, Magill, Australia

Reinhold Hedtke Chair of Social Science Education and Economic Sociology, Faculty of Sociology, Bielefeld University, Bielefeld, Germany

Philip Higgs University of South Africa, Pretoria, South Africa

Li-Ching Ho University of Wisconsin-Madison, Madison, USA

Kanako Ide Soka University, Tokyo, Japan

Norio Ikeno Nippon Sport Science University, Tokyo, Japan

Tracey I. Isaacs English Department, Alasala University, Dammam, Kingdom of Saudi Arabia

Aaron Johnson University of Nebraska Lincoln, Lincoln, USA

Dina Kiwan School of Education, University of Birmingham, Birmingham, UK

Allyson Larkin Western University, London, England

Sue Lewis Independent consultant, St. George, Grenada

Andrea Milligan Faculty of Education, Victoria University of Wellington, Wellington, New Zealand

Thomas Misco College of Education, Health, and Society, Miami University, Oxford, OH, USA

Amy Murillo College of Education, Lewis University, Romeoville, IL, USA

Joan Pagès Facultat de Ciències de l'Educació, Universitat Autònoma de Barcelona, Bellaterra, Spain

Marianna Papastephanou University of Cyprus, Nicosia, Cyprus; Faculty of Educational Sciences, University of Oslo, Oslo, Norway

Lynne Parmenter Centre for Tertiary Teaching and Learning, Waikato University, Hamilton, New Zealand

Karen Pashby Childhood, Youth and Education Studies, Manchester Metropolitan University, Manchester, UK

Manisha Pathak-Shelat MICA, Ahmedabad, India

Carla L. Peck Department of Elementary Education, University of Alberta, Edmonton, AB, Canada

Andrew Peterson Faculty of Education, Canterbury Christ Church University, Canterbury, Kent, England

Graham Pike Vancouver Island University, Nanaimo, Canada

Melina Porto Instituto de Investigaciones en Humanidades y Ciencias Sociales (Institute of Research in the Social Sciences and the Humanities), Facultad de Humanidades y Ciencias de la Educación (School of Humanities and Sciences of Education), Universidad Nacional de La Plata and CONICET (Consejo Nacional de Investigaciones Científicas y Técnicas), La Plata, Argentina

Alicia Prowse Manchester Metropolitan University, Manchester, UK

Laura Quaynor College of Education, Lewis University, Romeoville, IL, USA

Jeong-eun Rhee College of Education Information & Technology, New York, NY, USA

Jeong-eun Rhee College of Education, Information, & Technology, Brookville, NY, USA

Alistair Ross London Metropolitan University, London, UK

E Wayne Ross Department of Curriculum and Pedagogy, University of British Columbia, Vancouver, Canada

Edda Sant Manchester Metropolitan University, Manchester, UK

Antoni Santisteban Facultat de Ciències de l'Educació, Universitat Autònoma de Barcelona, Bellaterra, Spain

Sandra J. Schmidt Teachers College, Columbia University, New York, USA

Silke Schreiber-Barsch University of Hamburg, Hamburg, Germany

Lynette Shultz University of Alberta, Edmonton, Canada

Mackenzie Sillem Vancouver Island University, Nanaimo, Canada

Hannah Soong University of South Australia, North Adelaide, Australia

Binaya Subedi The Ohio State University at Newark, Newark, OH, USA

Sharon Subreenduth Bowling Green State University, Bowling Green, OH, USA

Vanita Sundaram University of York, York, UK

Yusef Waghid Department of Education Policy Studies, Stellenbosch University in South Africa, Matieland, South Africa

Paul Wakeling Department of Education, Derwent College, University of York, Heslington, York, UK

Jun Watanabe Nihon University, Tokyo, Japan

Bronwyn E. Wood Faculty of Education, Victoria University of Wellington, Wellington, New Zealand

List of Figures

LIST OF TABLES

Editors' Introduction

We aim in this Handbook to provide in-depth analyses of:

- Geographically based overviews of global citizenship and education (Australasia; Europe; Middle East; North America; Latin America; South East Asia; Southern Africa)
- The key ideologies that influence the meaning of global citizenship and education (globalism; nationalism; internationalism; transnationalism; cosmopolitanism, post-colonialism; indigenousness and indigeneity)
- The key concepts that underpin debates about global citizenship and education (justice; equity; diversity; identity and belonging; sustainable development)
- The principal perspectives and contexts including 'mainstream' and critical interpretations with implications for global citizenship and education (economics; politics; culture; morality; spirituality and religion; 'race'/ethnicity; gender and sexuality; migration; social class).
- Key issues in teaching about and for global citizenship through mainstream school subjects (history, geography, language, science, drama); and beyond individual school subjects (social media; service learning; study abroad; activism; and evaluation and assessment).

Global citizenship and its relationship with education is a vitally important field. This Handbook contains up-to-date contributions from leading writers in the field, providing what we hope will be a valuable international reference work. We have written and edited the Handbook principally for scholars working in higher education. We hope it will be of interest to academics, researchers and higher degree research students, and should also be of interest to students following educational studies and/or teacher preparation courses. We hope that the book will have a wide appeal, given its focus on global matters, global citizenship education and its international scope. We are also hoping to reach scholars and students in fields related to, but outside of, education—including sociology, social policy, and politics.

We know that global citizenship education is highly contested and without claiming to—or, even wishing to—have presented a completely comprehensive account around which there would be a simple consensus, we need to clarify what we mean by at least some of the key terms:

- 'Global' relates to several interlocking perspectives and contexts. There are geographically based conceptions which allow for consideration of national, international and cosmopolitan ideas to be explored. There are various characterizations of the global which encourage discussion around political matters (including a variety of matters such as affective ties as well as issues of governance). There are issues around fundamental matters such as the global economy; technology and communication; population and environment. Within these contexts, there are questions that require attention. Is globalization a new phenomenon? Is globalization the cause of growing inequality or is it establishing the conditions for a more peaceful, diverse, stable and prosperous world?
- Citizenship involves inter-related elements regarding formal membership of a politically constituted body; a sense of belonging; and, the contributions made by individuals and groups whether required or offered voluntarily to the society of which they are members. It may involve rights as well as responsibilities and reflection upon and action within private and public contexts (and as such reflects debates emerging from liberal and civic republican traditions within and beyond local, national and global communities)
- Education encompasses not just schooling but also non-formal and informal processes through which young people are prepared for their roles as citizens. This involves issues of equity and diversity for all—including issues of 'disability' and sexuality—in a wide range of contexts and requires consideration of whole school issues as well as pedagogical matters (including discrete teaching, infusion through mainstream subjects, community or service based learning and assessment)

We feel that there is a clear need for our Handbook. It is important to provide in-depth, up to date and expert consideration of these vitally important matters. There is strong international policy focus on global citizenship with debates and initiatives regarding, for example, refugee movements and conflicts of various types. Clarification is essential. The field is contested by those who are certain of their own perspective. In light of these competing assertions, there is also, on the part of some, confusion about the meaning of the key ideas and issues. For some the simple identification of the nature of high-quality education that transcends national borders is the essence of global citizenship education. For others, there is commitment to comparative education in which the similarities and differences of ideas and practices in different places is seen as providing meaning to the phrase 'global citizenship education'. We embrace, to some extent, these perspectives but our approach is rather different from both of them. In this book we focus on what we deem to require most clarity: the fundamental philosophical ideas, social and political contexts and educational issues and practices of a specific form of social studies in which people may be helped to understand and become involved in contemporary global societies, thinking and acing as global citizens. In order to understand act within that characterization, we need to explore the geographical contexts, the ideologies, concepts, perspectives and issues referred to above.

INTRODUCTORY COMMENTS ABOUT THE MAIN PARTS OF THIS HANBOOK

Geographically-Based Overviews

The purpose of this part is to describe and analyse the key features and issues regarding global citizenship education in each of our chosen areas. We have not achieved comprehensive coverage of the world but we feel that many areas are included that allow for some valuable insights to be developed into the state of play of global citizenship education around the globe. There are separate chapters on:

(i)   Southern Africa;
(ii) Australasia;
(iii) Europe;
(iv) Middle East;
(v)   North America;
(vi) Latin America;
(vii) South East Asia.

The chapters do not follow rigidly a prescribed framework but in each chapter readers will find comments about:

(i)   social, political and cultural context;
(ii) historical background;
(iii) key features of the current education system within particular locations (what general factors are relevant to educating about and for global citizenship);
(iv) what particular strategies (curricular and other) are used for educating about and for global citizenship (in curricular contexts this will involve particular consideration of social studies programmes with an emphasis on citizenship education);
(v)   likely and desirable futures.

There are very many issues that arise from a consideration of these geographical overviews. At times, of course, much more is being considered than geography. There are conceptual and ideological shifts that are implied involving, for example, differences in the characterization of citizenship. The citizenship available in the transnational European Union, for example, is not the same as citizenship(s) in, for example, Australasia. Variations in choosing from terms such as region, country, state, nation mean that simple summaries of the key issues are not possible. There are across these areas perspectives that relate to global citizenship including the economic, social, cultural and political (as well as others). North America is, for example, an economic area, a political zone in which certain common assumptions are held, a space that is culturally diverse within certain parameters and hierarchies as well as an arena for deliberation and action. These geographical divisions are as such artificial distinctions within which the key determinants of citizenship include movement and change. Migration and the status and conditions experienced by refugees and asylum seekers are crucially important to any consideration of global citizenship. The changing contexts of indigenous peoples as well as the demographics across and within countries are highly significant. The changing political contexts and perspectives in a region such as the Middle East which has recently experienced the Arab Spring in a place where more than 40% of the population is under 18 years of age raises issues about the interparts of many aspects of citizenship. The nature of sex, gender and sexuality are very important frames of reference. The competing priorities and connections associated with not only politics and economics but also values and character are central to understandings of global citizenship. And this kaleidoscope of aspects and perspectives provide a fascinating glocalised melange of people celebrating and struggling against and with and for hugely varied democratic and authoritarian contexts. Within this complex picture, educators strive to provide forms of education that promote understanding of and involvement with contemporary society. Some agreement or points of encounter are perhaps possible but only if diversity can exist without fragmentation and with resistance against uniformity.

The Key Ideologies that Influence the Meaning of Global Citizenship and Education

Global citizenship education relates to several ideological perspectives. We do not use the word 'ideology' in a pejorative sense but rather recognize the value of fundamental and particular perspectives that are relevant to globality. There are separate chapters on:

(i)   Globalism;
(ii)   Nationalism;
(iii)   Internationalism;
(iv)   Transnationalism;
(v)   Cosmopolitanism;

(vi)   Post-colonialism;
(vii) Indigenousness and indigeneity.

Although there are some differences each of these chapters has a reasonably common approach to structure:

(i)   Introduction;
(ii)   Conceptual underpinnings;
(iii) Key issues;
(iv)   Implications for education for global citizenship;
(v)   Conclusion and recommendations regarding future research.

In order to give clearer and more precise meaning to these ideologies we decided to focus on a particular part of the world. We explore in this part of the Handbook global citizenship education as a response to African higher education. This exploration of one (often relatively under-emphasised) part of the world is a deliberate effort to ensure that our global Handbook is not inappropriately from the political and economic 'west' and 'north'. And it gives us opportunities to explore the particularities of that specific context. Like the African north, political uncertainty, so endemic to sub-Saharan Africa, continues to manifest itself, and it is not unusual to find that ethnic tensions and conflict ensue unabatedly. The central concern of this anthology of chapters is whether the notion of global citizenship education can help us to think differently about higher education generally, and higher education in southern African in particular. This part of the global citizenship education Handbook has attempted to accentuate the significance of globalism, nationalism, cosmopolitanism, internationalism, transnationalism, post-coloniality and indigeneity, in cultivating global citizenship education. The possibility that such pertinent actions would ensue depends on our innovative acts of situating our localness within or encounters with globalness and *vice a versa*. The point is, that global citizenship education cannot legitimately be construed as a practice worthy of consideration and enactment if it does not bring into contestation what is both of local and global significance, especially in light of cultivating just human encounters. Unless we show that our interconnectedness and responsibilities are to ourselves and the advancement of humanity, we would not have begun to take global citizenship education seriously enough. Hence, it does not seem to be such an irrelevant idea to reconsider global citizenship education as an *active* local-cum-global educational encounter. In the context of the afore-mentioned, some of us argue in defence of drawing on cultural reasonableness as a necessary good for situating the local (Waghid 2014: 2). Perhaps it would not be inappropriate to again reiterate that cultural reasonableness—invoking local understandings in and about human encounters—is the first step towards enacting the metaphoric expression of global citizenship education.

Inasmuch as global citizenship education involves interconnecting people to address societal injustices such as poverty, famine and hunger, inequality, and forms of human oppression and exclusion, it also urges people to enlarge their moral imaginations. The latter implies that people have to begin to imagine a southern African continent where communities live under conditions of profound equality, freedom and human advancement. Only then the possibility for human flourishing would be enhanced on the basis that such a form of education would urge educators and students to imagine alternative possibilities that people have not thought of before and offer ways of building more just human relations. Hence, to talk about a global citizenship education in the context of southern African higher education is aimed at cultivating an African higher education in which 'the experience of reflective openness to the new [is] fused with reflective loyalty to the known' (Hansen 2011: 86).

The Key Concepts that Underpin Debates About Global Citizenship and Education

Global citizenship education is underpinned by several key concepts. In this part of the handbook there are five chapters to allow for consideration of the meaning of a sample of those concepts. There are separate chapters on:

(i)   Justice;
(ii)   Equity;
(iii) Diversity;
(iv)   Identity and belonging;
(v)   Sustainable development.

In all chapters, there is an emphasis on the centrality of diversity. Each of these chapters was written with some encouragement to use the following guidelines:

(i)   Introduction;
(ii)   Conceptual underpinnings;
(iii) Key issues;
(iv)   Implications for education for global citizenship;
(v)   Conclusion and recommendations regarding future research.

The relationship between social justice and global citizenship is explored to consider ways in which particular approaches to justice can inform democratic approaches to global citizenship education. It is argued that three different discourses on justice: economic, recognition and democratic justice are significant for identifying conceptual underpinnings and discussing the key implications for global citizenship education and also identifying more justice-oriented practices for global citizenship and education.

Focussing on equity may allow for insights into how global citizenship and global citizenship education may address the conditions of injustice. A global citizenship in which positionality is not acknowledged may lead only to the perpetuation of colonial relations. There is a need to explore citizenship from the perspective of those marginalized or excluded. Poverty and colonialism need to be critically examined in relation to global citizenship, where in relation to global citizenship education, colonialism continues as a problem in the exclusion of alternative (non-Western) knowledges. A plurality of knowledge may allow for cognitive justice.

Throughout these considerations of justice and equity the essential position of educating for diversity is recognized. Diversity, identity and citizenship include the local, national and global. The idea of the culturally responsive school is explored as a frame for thinking through global citizenship education and identifying six characteristics for such a school.

There is also consideration of the origins and evolution of the much debated and misunderstood concept 'sustainable development'. Achieving sustainable development may require the balancing of economic, environmental and social goals. The lack of international consensus and commitment on these issues is highlighted, and it is suggested that global citizenship education is critical for achieving sustainable development, especially as both areas struggle to find a place in the school curriculum. Increasing global inequalities require governments to take a stronger role in promoting education for sustainable development and global citizenship, as well as to achieving Sustainable Development Goals.

The Principal Perspectives and Contexts Relevant to Global Citizenship Education

In this part of the handbook we explore 'mainstream' and 'critical' interpretations of global citizenship and discuss the implications for global citizenship and education. The key words—'perspective' and 'context' provide the central characterization of this part. We provide a clear and more concrete indication of the ways in which issues are viewed and, broadly stated, how those issues are located. An economic perspective on global citizenship, for example, may highlight issues of both global systems through which capital flows as well as individual financial decision making in relation to a globalising market place. Political considerations would include reflections on the nature of formal global governance as well as the political perspectives that individuals and groups may bring to issues of power in a globalising world.

There are separate chapters on each of the following:

(i)   Economics;
(ii)   Politics;
(iii)   Culture;
(iv)   Morality;

(v)   Environment;
(vi)   Spirituality and religion;
(vii)   'Race'/ethnicity;
(viii) Gender and sexuality;
(ix)   Migration;
(x)   Social class.

Each of these chapters has, broadly, the following common structure:

(i)   Introduction;
(ii)   Conceptual underpinnings;
(iii)   Key issues;
(iv)   Implications for education for global citizenship;
(v)   Conclusion and recommendations regarding future research.

The authors in this part provide an indication of the ways in which these perspectives and issues are viewed and show how these issues are complicated by different political, social, economic, and historical contexts. The authors also explored how conditions of globalization have shaped our understandings and interpretations of ideas such as gender and sexuality, social class, 'race', and morality.

In their chapters, the authors used different theoretical lenses such as postcolonial theory to problematize the perspectives highlighted in this part and they utilize a range of conceptual understandings such as power, rights, hybridity, and social justice to frame their analyses. The authors also draw on case studies from a range of educational and national contexts, including higher education in the UK and Latina youth in US high schools, to illustrate their arguments.

Concurrently, the chapters also question the constructions of different ideas (e.g. spirituality and religion, economic systems, and culture) that assume the nation-state as the primary container. Additionally, the chapters critically examined the different dynamics that affected how these ideas are conceptualized and considered how these different perspectives and contexts have impacted global citizenship education. Finally, the authors analyze how these ideas operated at different levels, including the level of the individual citizen, the nation-state, and at the global/transnational level. More importantly, the authors also examine the relationships that occurred both within and across these levels.

Key Issues in Teaching and Learning About and for Global Citizenship

In this part of the handbook, we focus on pedagogical matters.
    There are separate chapters on each of the following:

(i)   History;
(ii)   Geography;

(iii)   Language;
(iv)   Science;
(v)   Drama;
(vi)   Social media;
(vii)   Service learning;
(viii) Study abroad;
(ix)   Activism;
(x)   Evaluation and assessment.

We explore those subjects that are relatively recently established as well as those with longer histories, and initiatives and perspectives that lie beyond formally constituted academic disciplines. Approaching things in this way allows us to explore work within different types of structure, applied in different contexts and pursued according to different social and political and academic perspectives. Each of the chapters has, in general terms, the following structure:

(i)   Introduction;
(ii)   Discussion of the issues connecting between global citizenship education and the theme of the chapter;
(iii)   Discussion including illustrative learning and teaching material;
(iv)   Discussion including illustrative assessment material;
(v)   Conclusion and future research.

In our focus on teaching and learning we recognize that global citizenship can be considered an 'empty signifier' that different concepts, perspectives and ideologies attempt to 'fill' with meaning (Mannion et al. 2011). In the context of education, the 'emptiness' of the concept offers multiple possibilities for democratic practices. However, as a consequence of this, it can represent a challenge to educators and policy-makers attempting to grasp how to bring global citizenship education into practice.

We aim to reduce the distance between theory and practice. It is our purpose here to discuss the relationship between global citizenship and educational practice. We requested the authors writing in this part to consider, 'how can global citizenship be taught, learned and assessed?' The different (and sometimes) competing answers given by these scholars illustrate the political but also the pedagogic dimension of this question. Different perspectives on global citizenship and different understandings of education have different pedagogical implications.

In this part, authors examining more holistic educational practices pay particular attention to the links between the pedagogical and the political dimension. The question here, as Geelan and Curley et al. remind us, is "are we talking about education *as* or *for* global citizenship?" To some extent, authors in this part agree that some educational practices such as activism, the use of social media, study abroad and service-learning activities seem to be often recognized *as* global citizenship. But there is an emphasis on the double dimension, of the political *and* the pedagogical of these practices. Studying abroad, for instance, can be understood as a practice of global citizenship but it is also an educative experience that can generate future processes of participation and/or identification as global citizens. Different educational practices (education *as* global citizenship) can define different present and future types of global citizens (education *for* global citizenship).

Authors writing from different subject areas emphasize the contribution of their areas to global citizenship. Here, education is essentially understood as being *for* global citizenship. Although scholars often acknowledge different perspectives on global citizenship, they commit their work to one of these perspectives and they examine their area (drama, history, science, geography and language education) in relation to this perspective. The relation here is not that much between the political and the pedagogical but rather, between the political and the subject pedagogy. Indeed, each area contributes to global citizenship with their particular disciplinary knowledge. Geography, for instance, can help to question places of citizenship, whereas Science can inform a discussion on the scientific and technological dimension of present and future challenges. Further, subject areas also make specific contribution in relation to their subject pedagogy. Previous theory and research on teaching controversial issues (in history and social studies), role plays (in drama) and processes of telecollaboration (in language) can shed some additional light to the discussion on how global citizenships can be taught and learnt.

The part finishes with an analysis on assessment and global citizenship education. The discussion illustrates how a new question needs to be added to the ones we presently presentedcurrently asked in the field. Global citizenship education, according to whom? Bringing global citizenship education into practice always represents a (explicit or implicit) commitment to certain perspective(s) on global citizenship. This is further illustrated if we are, indeed, assessing who is and who is not a 'global citizen'. To some extent, the practice necessarily requires "filling" the emptiness of the concept in itself, but in so doing, ensuring that any examination of global citizenship education is done through a critical lens.

Concluding Remarks

We have worked hard to include a variety of aspects and a range of perspectives about global citizenship education. This does not mean that we have covered everything but we hope that readers will continue to explore the vitally important issues in education that matter to all in a globalising world. We see education as the means by which a globalising world may be better understood and as a means of achieving social justice. We do not advocate a return to simplistic positions in which iniquitous colonial perspectives were celebrated. But in our search for better forms of education, we wish to avoid well-intentioned but similarly simplistic 'solutions'. There will not be one overarching policy or practice that we can urge our readers to accept. But there is a commitment to human rights that can in concrete terms be identified and strived for. And we hope this Handbook is one small contribution to that striving.

References

Hansen, D.T. (2011). *The teacher and the world: A study of cosmopolitanism as education.* London & New York: Routledge.

Mannion, G., Biesta, G., Priestley, M., & Ross, H. (2011). The global dimension in education and education for global citizenship: genealogy and critique. *Globalisation, Societies and Education, 9*(3–4), 443–456. doi:10.1080/14767724.2011.605327

Waghid, Y. (2014). *African philosophy of education reconsidered.* New York & London: Routledge.

PART I

Geographically-Based Overviews

CHAPTER 1

Global Citizenship Education in Australasia

Andrew Peterson, Andrea Milligan and Bronwyn E. Wood

INTRODUCTION AND OVERVIEW

Those residing in Australasia,[1] including *young* Australians and New Zealanders, live at a time in which the benefits and pressures of globalisation are experienced as never before, and in which global citizenship education receives a great deal of international policy attention (see most recently Citizens for Global Education 2014; see also Peterson and Warwick 2014 for an overview). Recognising this policy interest, this chapter presents an analysis of how global citizenship education (hereafter, GCED) is constructed, implemented and experienced in Australian and New Zealander policy, curricula and classrooms. Shaping these contexts is a range of contemporary public policy tensions that interact on local, national and global levels and highlight the significance of global citizenship in Australasia. These include: the impact of migration on cultural diversity; responses to, and treatment of, those seeking refuge and asylum; the recognition, reconciliation and representation of Indigenous peoples; engagement within the Asia-Pacific region; and concerns about social cohesion. Curricular documents in both Australia and New

A. Peterson (✉)
Faculty of Education, Canterbury Christ Church University, Canterbury,
Kent CT1 1QU, England
e-mail: andrew.peterson@canterbury.ac.uk

A. Milligan · B.E. Wood
Faculty of Education, Victoria University of Wellington, 15C Waiteata Road,
PO Box 600, Wellington 6140, New Zealand
e-mail: andrea.milligan@vuw.ac.nz

B.E. Wood
e-mail: bronwyn.wood@vuw.ac.nz

© The Author(s) 2018
I. Davies et al. (eds.), *The Palgrave Handbook of Global Citizenship and Education*, https://doi.org/10.1057/978-1-137-59733-5_1

3

Zealand engage in different ways with these complexities, but each requires operationalising by schools and teachers in terms of curriculum content and pedagogies employed, particularly given that global complexities are not static but are fluid and dynamic.

As other chapters within this volume attest, GCED is a term that is vital, wide-ranging and contested. In Australasia, as elsewhere, GCED sits across individual subject disciplines, providing flexibility for schools to determine their own approaches. However, such weak disciplinary boundaries (Pike 2008a; Peterson and Warwick 2014) are concomitant with a lack of clear definition for GCED in Australia and New Zealand. A whole host of themes—including globalisation, peace and conflict, social justice, cultural diversity and futures education—not only intersect with GCED in Australasia, but have been developed within contested fields in their own right (human rights education, education for sustainable development, for example).

In this chapter, we begin with some comments about how the political, economic and social context in both Australia and New Zealand informs notions of citizenship/global citizenship. We then move to examining current policy and curricular initiatives in both nations that shape GCED. In the third section, we examine teaching and learning approaches to GCED and argue that the patchy approach in both Australia and New Zealand means that students' experience of GCED are inconsistent and, at times, lack a critical edge. In the conclusion, we identify some possible futures for GCED in Australasia.

THE POLITICAL, ECONOMIC AND SOCIAL CONTEXTS

To begin to understand how the Australian and New Zealand education systems frame and enact GCED, it is necessary first to make some initial comments about the historical and contemporary social, political and cultural context of the two countries. As with other nations, sensitive, contested notions of citizenship and identity play out within public debate. How Australians and New Zealanders—including young Australians and New Zealanders—understand themselves as national and global citizens are being shaped and reshaped by the political, economic and social contexts is outlined in this section.

Approximately 3% of Australians identify as being of Aboriginal and/or Torres Strait Islander origin (Australian Bureau of Statistics 2013a), and 15% of New Zealanders identify as Māori (Statistics New Zealand 2013a). Since European colonisation, successive waves of migration have led to Australia and New Zealand being two of the most culturally diverse populations in the world. Over a quarter of both populations have been born in another country, and a further 20% of Australians have at least one overseas-born parent (Australian Bureau of Statistics 2013b), and New Zealand has more ethnicities (213) than there are nations (Statistics New Zealand 2013b). The recent, rapid growth of Asian communities has been a significant feature of this diversity, partly stimulated by shifts in immigration policy[2] from the 1970s onwards in both countries. Four Asian countries are now included in the top 10 birthplaces for Australian migrants, with India the leading birthplace of new migrants 2007–2013 (Australian Bureau of Statistics 2013b). Similarly, New Zealand's Chinese, Indian and Filipino communities have experienced substantial population increases 2006–2013 (Statistics New Zealand 2013b). Such is the extent of cultural diversity in both nations, that super-diversity now presents a significant policy challenge, and has raised questions about the institutional hegemony of majority ethnic groups (Spoonley 2015).

The political and economic rhetoric and policies of Australian and New Zealand governments over the last three decades have located both countries as Pacific Rim nations looking to forge global diplomatic and trade links across Asia, Europe, the Americas and elsewhere. Australia is a member of the G20, and both nations are part of the Commonwealth and the Asia-Pacific Economic Co-operation group. Figures for 2015 evidence widespread flows of trade, with China, USA and Japan among both country's leading bilateral trade partners (Department of Foreign Affairs and Trade 2016; New Zealand Treasury 2016). This is not to suggest that the relationship between national identity and global connections has been unproblematic or consistent. Indeed, conservative Prime Ministers like John Howard (1996–2007) and Tony Abbott (2013–2015) typically focused on traditional notions of citizenship combining economically liberal and socially conservative values central to which were Australia's colonial ties to the UK. In contrast, and for example, Labor Prime Ministers Bob Hawke (1983–1991) and Paul Keating (1991–1996) both sought to realign Australia as an outward looking nation with meaningful political and economic connections beyond the UK, in particular with both the USA and Asia (Kelly 2011). New Zealand governments have generally reflected socially liberal values since the 1980s. Policy reforms introduced in 1984 by the Labour Prime Minister David Lange (1984–1989) saw a marked shift from protectionist to neoliberal economic policy, consistent with similar shifts in economic theory in the USA and UK. However, two other key policy planks of this period saw New Zealand separate politically from its traditional alliances with Australia, USA and the UK–a nuclear-free stance and strong opposition to apartheid in South Africa.

Successive Australian governments have committed to a policy of multiculturalism, viewing cultural diversity as being 'at the heart of [Australian] national identity' and 'intrinsic to [Australian] history and character' (Australian Government 2011). Although a nation-wide report in 2014 found that 85% of Australians support multiculturalism (Markus 2014), the diverse composition of Australian society is not without tensions. Not least, there exist many tensions regarding the past and current treatment of Australia's Aboriginal and Torres Strait Islander peoples, including their continued lack of constitutional recognition. A further recent and telling example which illustrates the (re)framing of citizenship in relation to global/national identities is provided by public discourses on radicalisation and violent extremism (see Peterson and Bentley 2016 for an overview).

In contrast to Australia, successive New Zealand governments have committed to a policy of biculturalism, in which the Treaty of Waitangi is viewed as an evolving contract between Māori and New Zealand Europeans/Pākehā (Ward and Liu 2012). While New Zealand Europeans/Pākehā tend to endorse a bicultural perspective (Sibley et al. 2011), there is still considerable working through regarding the extent of recognition of customary rights. The early 2000s were particularly marked by debates over the ownership of New Zealand's foreshore and seabed, and perceptions of 'radical Māori separatism' stirred by the then Leader of the Opposition, Don Brash. This rhetoric has been somewhat mollified by subsequent coalition agreements and the economic success of several iwi (tribes) following Treaty settlements. However, the challenges of achieving structural change are never far from the surface.

While there has been little inter-racial violence other than the New Zealand Wars of the 1840s and 1860s, New Zealand has a long history of prejudice against non-whites, consistent with the experience of Australia and Canada. New Zealanders today generally have positive attitudes towards immigrants, and endorse multiculturalism more than Australians and European Union citizens (Ward and Masgoret 2008). However, an analysis of the 2009 *New Zealand Attitudes and Values Survey (NZAVS)*,[3] found that 'New Zealanders resisted a resource-specific multicultural ideology that involves race-based interventions to reduce social inequality' (Sibley and Ward 2013, p. 700), and expressed lower levels of warmth towards Asian communities. Further, results from the 2013 *NZAVS* showed that 'anti-Muslim and anti-Arab sentiments are confounded, widespread, and substantially higher than anti-immigrant sentiments' (Shaver et al. 2016, p. 1). The challenges associated with migration, such as housing and the job market, are current sites of political contention.

Within these public debates, education has become a key site of concern. In both Australia and New Zealand political forces shape conceptions of global citizenship in particular ways. One example is the considerable influence that economic policy exerts on school priorities, for example in relation to reducing educational disparity for Māori and Pacific students in New Zealand. There exists a clear policy commitment to supporting the cultural aspirations of Māori and Pacific students. The Ministry of Education's (2016a) current four-year plan, for example, envisions New Zealanders who are 'strong in their national and cultural identity' (p. 2). However, this is largely framed within a rhetoric of economic success in a global environment that relegates concepts such as diversity to a descriptive level and leaves power relationships largely unexamined (Samu 2011). Furthermore, there is some evidence to suggest a differentiated approach to Māori and Pacific students' global economic citizenship. The current Māori Education Strategy (Ministry of Education 2013a) expects students to succeed as Māori *and* as global citizens 'with the skills, knowledge and qualifications they need to achieve success in te ao Māori, New Zealand, and the wider world' (p. 13). By contrast, the Pasifika Education Plan 2013–2017 (Ministry of Education 2013b) makes no mention of this wider world, despite the globally connected nature of Pacific communities.

EDUCATION SYSTEMS AND CURRICULA

While GCED is clearly high priority at the level of global policy, the national policy and curricular contexts within Australia and New Zealand evidence a more mixed and complex picture. With this in mind, we move to examine the core features of the current education system in both nations that are relevant to educating about and for global citizenship.

Australia

It is important from the outset to understand that the organisation of education in Australia is the responsibility of both Federal and State/Territory governments. Traditionally education in Australia has mainly been the preserve of the latter, with Federal involvement being limited as far as curricular content was concerned. In 2009, the Australian Curriculum and Assessment Reporting Authority (ACARA) was established by the then Labor government to plan for the first ever Australian national curriculum. Developed in various stages, and revised following the election of the Liberal-led coalition government in 2013, the curriculum establishes the content to be taught across states and territories.

Echoing the discourses operating at the global level, GCED *has* been identified as a high priority within Australian education and schooling. The federal–state ministerial *Melbourne Declaration on Educational Goals for Young Australians* (MCEETYA 2008) establishes GCED as a key goal for Australian schooling. The declaration aims for all young Australians to 'become successful learners, confident and creative individuals and active and informed citizens', as well as 'responsible local and global citizens'. In stating this aim there is a clear intention that young Australians not only understand global issues, but come to see themselves as participating citizens within their local, national and *global* communities. Indeed, that GCED includes both cognitive and affective commitments to global citizenship is a recurring theme in policy and curricular initiatives (AusAid 2008; Oxfam 2015) and was central to the work of the Global Education Program's (Federally funded until 2014) *Framework for Global Education in Australian Schools* (ESA 2011).

The extent to which the goal of educating active, informed and responsible global citizens has been included in the new national Australian curriculum is, given the inexact nature of GCED, rather difficult to quantify. What is clear is that the Australian curriculum does not offer a clear definition of 'global citizenship', meaning that teachers have to look to the work of the now-defunct Global Education Project for any substantive framework or guidance. A simple search of the Australian Curriculum returns 31 results for 'global citizenship' and 29 results for 'global citizens', but each of these consists of learning outcomes that are presented in very general terms and without an underpinning sense of what being a global citizen may mean. For example, the Civics and Citizenship curriculum at Year 6 (11–12 years of age) requires that students understand 'the obligations citizens may consider they have beyond their own national borders as active and informed global citizens' (ACARA 2016). Other references to global citizens/citizenship come within Geography, the cross-curricular themes *Asia and Australia's engagement with Asia* and *Sustainability*, and the General Capabilities *Intercultural Understanding* and *Ethical Understanding* but again these are without any real definition. To summarise, as presented within the Australian Curriculum, GCED is fragmented and without any sense of clear definition, let alone theoretical underpinnings. Indeed, one might suggest that global dimensions were more explicit in the state/territory level combined humanities/social science (such as *Studies of Society and Environment*) which preceded the Australian Curriculum.

If we focus on particular elements of GCED, such as Human Rights Education (HRE) , there is, again, a mixed picture. HRE has no formal inclusion within the Australian Curriculum. Indeed, in a recent review of human rights across the Australian Curriculum, Burridge et al. (2014: 18–19) have argued that:

> it appears that the opportunities for delivery of effective human rights education... are fragmentary and the efforts being made to engage in discussions about our rights, particularly in schools, are limited and sporadic, across all Australian states and territories, school sectors and in each of the key school stages from the Foundation years to Year 12. Learning about human rights issues often depends on the interests and commitment of individual teachers, and is being relegated to classes in the senior, non-compulsory years of secondary school, or to optional elective subjects.

Such comments remind us that there is an essential difference between providing *possibilities* for subject teachers to draw connections to global themes such as sustainability and human rights and *explicitly supporting* (and even *requiring* them) to do so. Further, there is no real sense that the nature and meaning of human rights are themselves contested and permit a range of theoretical underpinnings, even where human rights are mentioned.

New Zealand

New Zealand has a long tradition of national-level curriculum development. Individual curricula were brought together as an outcomes-based, national framework in the early 1990s (Ministry of Education 1993), and subsequently revised and refined during the 2000s. *The New Zealand Curriculum*

(Ministry of Education 2007) is notable for a parallel, but not directly translated, curriculum for Māori-medium schools (Ministry of Education 2008a).

Similar to Australia, New Zealand does not have a curriculum as such in GCED. Instead, GCED appears as something of a *leitmotif* within the current curriculum and, echoing a long-standing lack of interrogation of conceptions of global citizenship (White and Openshaw 2005), its nature and policy status are difficult to discern directly from the text. While GCED is not directly named, it has perhaps greatest expression within the curriculum's 'future focus' principle, which expects that students will engage with issues of sustainability, citizenship, enterprise and globalisation. However, with the exception of sustainability issues, there appears a lack of shared understanding about this principle, and:

> ...some schools interpreted this principle very narrowly as "preparing students to be 21st Century learners." The scope of this principle was then limited to learning about how to use information and communications technology. (Education Review Office 2011)

Recent Ministry of Education (2011, 2016b) publications have further outlined the intent of the future focus principle and suggested that GCED can break down subject silos. However, the interconnected and contested nature of these issues, and how the tensions between them 'may be filtered out in educational contexts' (Bolstad 2011, p. 13) is not elucidated.

Two learning areas appear to have the greatest scope for GCED. The first, learning languages, has a strong emphasis on intercultural communicative competence (Newton et al. 2010) and is a new subject within the current curriculum in order 'to encourage students to participate more actively in New Zealand's diverse, multicultural society and in the global community' (Ministry of Education 2007, p. 4). The second, social sciences, hints at global perspectives and scales within senior subjects such as geography, history, economics and senior social studies (Year 11–13).

Social studies, the compulsory social sciences subject for Years 1–10, has traditionally been the main curricular vehicle for citizenship education, including GCED (Barr et al. 1997). The integrated nature of this subject, and the place of global citizenship within it, mirrors the past development of Australia's *Studies of Society and the Environment*. The current social studies curriculum statement (Ministry of Education 2007, p. 30) emphasises issues and settings within *and* beyond New Zealand, an important entry point to GCED being a strongly advocated social inquiry methodology (see also, Ministry of Education 2008b). This approach, developed in keeping with? the work on social inquiry traditions by North American and Australian educators, enables students to explore the value-laden nature of, and consider their responses to, current issues. A key series of documents exemplify the social inquiry approach, including *Taking part in global communities* (Ministry of Education 2009).

While New Zealand initial teacher education students appear predisposed towards GCED (Newton et al. 2010), the support for them enacting this curricular dimension is fragmented and devolved. As with Australia, aspects of GCED are supported through a variety of avenues. Considerable resourcing for GCED was once provided by a Ministry of Foreign Affairs and Trade funded development organisation, *Global Focus Aotearoa*. However, the organisation has recently closed as a result of funding cuts. The Ministry of Education's online portal[4] includes, for example, materials for digital citizenship, Asia knowledge, and Education for sustainability. Other agencies offer resources, programmes, and initiatives to support GCED in schools, such as *UNESCO New Zealand*, the *New Zealand Centre for Global Studies*, *World Vision*, and *Human Rights in Education*. However, in the main, there is little in the way of support for teachers make connections across, or to evaluate, these expressions of GCED—a patchy approach that is arguably exacerbated by a Ministry expectation that schools drive curriculum decision-making.

Summary: The 'Global' in Australasian Curricula

In her analysis of GCED, Davies (2006: 13–14) offers the following typology of its permutations within curricula, and this is useful in reflecting on the current formulation of GCED in Australia and New Zealand:

(a) global citizenship+education (definitions of the 'global citizen', and the implied educational framework to provide or promote this)
(b) global+citizenship education (making citizenship education more globally or internationally relevant; think global, act local)
(c) global education+citizenship (international awareness plus rights and responsibilities)
(d) education+citizenship+global (introducing 'dimensions' of citizenship and of international understanding into the school curriculum, but not necessarily connected)'.

When we consider this typology in relation to the analysis provided in this section, it would seem that, as currently expressed, Australia and New Zealand's approaches conform to the last of Davies' permutations. That is, while there is an intention for global dimensions to permeate the curriculum, these lack a unifying definition and cohesion. The reasons for this disconnect between policy rhetoric/intention and curricular content are likely varied and many. One, however, seems to be pertinent and fundamental—high-stakes testing and preparing students for economic life are increasingly prioritised when it comes to hard decisions about what to include in an over-crowded formal, compulsory curriculum and which particular initiatives to devote government funds to (at both Federal and State/Territory levels). While policy and curricular aims in Australia and New Zealand pay some attention to the importance of and need for GCED, the extent to which GCED permeates the actual curriculum is somewhat limited. In place of a clearly defined and shaped approach to GCED, global themes are included in a fragmentary and piecemeal way.

TEACHING AND LEARNING APPROACHES

Australia

At present, while there is a body of research literature focusing on the focus and directions GCED in Australia *could* and *should* take, there is much less which provides a picture of what *actually* happens in schools and classrooms. In 2015 Peterson[5] explored the perceptions of, and approaches to, GCED within a purposive sample of six[6] South Australian High Schools[7] each of which placed global citizenship as central to their school mission and ethos. Here, we summarise some key findings of the research in order to provide a sense of how these schools conceived, constructed and enacted GCED.

First and foremost, and mirroring practices in other nations (see, for example, Reid et al. 2010), none of the schools had GCED as a discrete subject, but rather employed a range of processes to educate for global citizenship. They attended to GCED through combinations of the following: integration within subject learning areas (most commonly History, Geography, Civics and Citizenship, and Languages); general school ethos and environment; student action programs; international student exchanges; extra-curricular learning; fundraising and awareness raising events; external speakers; and student representational processes.

Second, and more importantly, there were notable differences regarding the framing and orientation of global citizenship. This played out on two levels, that of the school and individual teachers. At the school level the difference was most notable in relation to the particular "global" values which were—or indeed were not—in place to frame and orientate GCED within the school. In two schools, these values were front and centre not only to GCED but to the whole of school life. A public school in metropolitan SA, for example, included *international mindedness* as one of its school values. As a senior leader in the school explained:

> So the way the values were actually developed we basically asked kids and teachers and families what do you think are the most important things that students need to be able to develop and exhibit... international mindedness... was something that came through time and time again... Now from our schools point of view it's absolutely critical and it's absolutely critical that it works with the other values as well. Now... I was really sceptical of the concept of the values and the impact they might have on kids and the impact that they have as a rallying point if you like or a focal point within a school... but I've been amazed at how successful it's been.

Similarly, an independent school in metropolitan SA drew on the values of *service* and *solidarity* to inform and structure students' engagements within GCED. By placing global values as central to the school's work, GCED is mainstreamed within these schools, providing a frame and vocabulary through which school leaders, teachers and students could make sense of their experiences, including connecting the various activities which comprised GCED.

The importance of values as a way of framing GCED within the school is highlighted further by considering other schools in which values were less central. For example, in a rural public high school, when asked what connects the various GCED activities within the school, two teachers offered the following reflections:

> *Teacher one*: I think it's dotted about… I don't think it's connected yeah, and it's probably something we should do… And I guess that's really hard, it's not exclusively taught and it's not exclusively centred … that this is global citizenship, they're certainly learning values, qualities, all the rest of it but not necessarily knowing that that's what it is.

> *Teacher two*: Yeah… they don't necessarily connect those dots.

> *Teacher one*: Yeah like I was teaching, when I teach my year 11's and 12's I always say to them "You will learn about current issues that you will have to vote on next year", but I don't say to them "These are also current global issues as well, and towards making you a global citizen". And I thought maybe I should be doing that too because then they, you know it gives them a different context as well.

There is another notable way in which GCED is framed and oriented *within* these schools. To understand this, the distinction between soft and critical global citizenship advocated by Andreotti is helpful. Andreotti (2006) warns that 'soft' global citizenship can result in the imposition of Western hegemonic discourses and a lack of critical awareness of the material and structural conditions involved. As Jefferess (2012: 33) also cautions, the precise danger is that active global citizen can be framed in ways which requires an 'Other who needs to be known, understood and ultimately uplifted or saved'. The result is that 'the ethical framework of global citizenship masks the material relationships that produce some as privileged and hence capable of being active global citizens, and some as in need of support, care, "aid"'. In contrast, 'critical' global citizenship education asks students to:

> reflect on their context and their own and others' epistemological and ontological assumptions: how we came to think/be/feel/act the way we do and the implications of our systems of belief in local/global terms in relation to power, social relationships and the distribution of labour and resources' (Andreotti 2006: 49).

Across the interviews, school leaders, teachers and students tended to move fluidly between soft and critical approaches and were frequently aware of the various tensions involved with both. Crucial here was that teachers were actively managing a range of factors (curriculum pressure, available opportunities, age and ability of students, for example) in order to try to develop appropriate, clear and meaningful GCED learning experiences.

New Zealand

While there are few extensive studies of classroom practices for teaching GCED in New Zealand, a number of studies about how aspects of GCED are taught within the social studies curriculum help to paint a picture of what is happening in classrooms. The open, conceptual nature of the New Zealand curriculum and low levels of prescription mean that social studies teachers can choose to select global or local studies and not necessarily present a range of scales, or engage with GCED with any depth. Classroom-based research[8] reveals that GCED is often used to extend or expand conceptual and citizenship knowledge in course of a unit of study. For example, many schools include an international or global focus as they study human rights, systems of government, or community decision-making, as a point of comparison or extension to a local or national context. Teachers view this 'expansion' in scale as an opportunity for deepening their students' conceptual knowledge and analysis. However, for some students who were encouraged to 'take action' in relation to their learning, there was some tension between these foci with many seeing the local as more authentic and relevant to their lives:

> *Student 1*: I'm going to sound like a heartless cow, now [laughter]… I do care about the refugees, but I do think personally we do have problems closer to home that we need to fix. I mean if you look at our unemployment rates and the people that are possibly classified as refugees and *are* struggling in New Zealand [already], I think we need to focus on them as well as the refugee crisis [in Middle East and Europe]. (Female, 18 years)

> *Student 2*: I personally think it was less rewarding [this year] because last year we did something for New Zealand… A lot of our response this year was why were we helping people in Cambodia when we have our own problems in New Zealand? And it was really our response from people because they just kept saying "Why are you doing it for them when we need help over here more? […] … we should be helping ourselves first, kind of. (Female, 16 years)

In both of these quotes, students saw the focus on international and global contexts to be in direct competition to local contexts which they viewed as more important, relevant or significant for their citizenship actions or attention.

This leads us to another pattern observed in New Zealand schools which shows evidence that GCED is reserved for students who teachers perceive to be more cosmopolitan in their outlook and experiences (Wood 2012, 2013).

Wood's study of social studies teachers and students in four New Zealand high schools found that the two schools in wealthier communities were more likely to study GCED than the two in poorer communities, which focused on local, and community issues (Wood 2012). Drawing on Bourdieu's (2000) notion of 'doxa', Wood (2012) surmised that these differences in spatial orientation reflected shared and unquestioned *doxic* ways of thinking about citizenship that in turn, closely reflected economic, social and cultural capital held by members of those school communities (teachers, students and families). Wood (2013) argues that the local/global spatial orientation of these four school communities could be explained by the concept of 'participatory capital', which related to the interrelated capitals and logic of citizenship practices within the social field of a school community. For example, students from the two wealthier schools had greater access to forms of economic capital that enabled them travel more widely and participate in international school trips to participate in acts of citizenship (offered in one school). Such students also received a more globally oriented curriculum that focused on global issues. In contrast, students at the lower socio-economic schools had less spatial mobility, less access to symbolic global capital (such as information flows and social networks) and fewer opportunities to build global awareness as a result of a curriculum which largely focused on community issues (Wood 2012).

New Zealand students often held 'soft' rather than critical perspectives when studying GCED topics, demonstrating at times quite paternalistic views about 'others' they studied and failing to explore the complexities of this (Tallon 2012; Wood 2012). For example, Tallon's (2012) research, with teachers who were using development education resources to inspire more global knowledge and action, found that some reduced the critical and 'political' content of lessons because it was perceived as too difficult for students to comprehend:

Teacher: And there's also … I'm aware and I don't teach it, but I'm aware there's some political criticism with some NGOs coming in and … not… and trying to enforce their own cultural values … on a … village … um … you know … 'we want to educate the kids in this way … for something…'

Researcher: Oh. ok,

T: It's not necessarily what the village needs or what the people need, it's what people perceive it's what they need.

Researcher: Yeah,

Teacher: But that's far too high level for these kids. (Tallon 2012, p. 14)

There is also evidence that New Zealand teachers appeared to prefer to focus on topics that highlight belonging and inclusion to themes of conflict or tension (Milligan et al. 2011). Audrey Osler's (2011) study with teachers in England had some similarities with teachers preferring a local and even global curriculum focus to one that explicitly focused on the EU, which generated tension in the classroom. Osler's (2011) research also found that higher-attaining students were offered a more 'cosmopolitan' approach to their citizenship education, which she surmised "may result in an approach where cosmopolitanism is seen as the preserve of elites" (p. 15). In sum, there is a rather patchy approach to GCED in New Zealand classrooms with some effective teaching done by passionate teachers, but many examples of lost opportunities for enriched GCED and critical thinking within these contexts.

Conclusion: Possible Futures

In this chapter, we have suggested that in Australia and New Zealand there is a disconnection between policy rhetoric that places great importance on GCED as a central component of education in and for the twenty-first century, and the disjointed, uneven and, at times, uncritical way that this aim is currently formulated within the curriculum. This tension is particularly pertinent when we remember both that 'citizens, whether local or global, are made not born: educated and socialised into their roles rather than inhabitants of those roles' (Barber 2005: 103). Within this context, GCED in Australia and New Zealand face something of an uncertain future. Clearly, and as we have suggested, there is some excellent work being undertaken within Australasian schools—work which needs greater resourcing, researching and disseminating. How such work might develop further and more widely without a more developed and explicit curricular foci remains open to question.

Of central importance in the development of GCED is the need for more sustained and widespread teacher education and professional development. Research in Australasia suggests that, despite challenges, there are a number of projects within University teacher preparation programs which seek to build the knowledge, understanding and capacity of pre-service teachers to engage with and in GCED (see, for example, Reynolds et al. 2012; Bradbery 2014; Mills and Tomas 2014). Such projects point to the benefits of collaborative, critical engagement with GCED, including dialogical engagement between teachers concerning GCED's various contested elements, as well as about more practical aspects relating to its place within the curriculum and its enactment within schools and classrooms. For GCED to develop further, such practices seem not only important, but vital.

Notes

1. While the term Australasia often includes Australia, New Zealand, New Guinea and neighbouring Pacific Islands, in this chapter our focus is on Australia and New Zealand.

2. Most significantly, the formal ending of White Australia policies in 1973, instituted following Federation in 1901, and New Zealand's 1986 immigration policy shift towards the active recruitment of Asian business migrants.
3. https://www.psych.auckland.ac.nz/en/about/our-research/research-groups/new-zealand-attitudes-and-values-study.html.
4. www.tki.org.nz.
5. Australian Research Council grant (DE150100926).
6. The six schools comprised four public high schools and two independent schools with a faith foundation. All six schools were co-educational. Two of the public high schools were in rural South Australia, with the remaining schools situated in various parts of metropolitan Adelaide.
7. South Australia is the only State or Territory which commences High School in Year 8 (13–14 years of age).
8. Undertaken by Bronwyn Wood through a New Zealand TLRI Grant 'Creating active citizens'.

References

Andreotti, V. (2006). Soft versus critical global citizenship education. *Policy & Practice—A Development Education Review*, (3). Retrieved from: http://www.developmenteducationreview.com/issue3-focus4.

Australian Agency for International Development. (2008). *Global perspectives: A framework for global education in Australian schools.* Carlton, Vic.: Education Services Australia.

Australian Bureau of Statistics (ABS). (2013a). *2011 Census counts—Aboriginal and Torres Strait islander peoples.* Retrieved from: http://www.abs.gov.au/ausstats/abs@.nsf/Lookup/2075.0main+features32011.

Australian Bureau of Statistics (ABS). (2013b). *Reflecting a nation: Stories from the 2011 census, 2012-2013.* Retrieved from: http://www.abs.gov.au/ausstats/abs@.nsf/Lookup/2071.0main+features902012-2013.

Australian Curriculum and Assessment Reporting Authority. (2016). *The Australian curriculum.* Version 8.2. Retrieved from http://www.australiancurriculum.edu.au/.

Australian Government. (2011). Fact Sheet 6—Australia's Multicultural Policy. Retrieved January 20, 2017, from https://www.mia.org.au/documents/item/232.

Barber, B. (2005). Global governance from below. In D. Held (Ed.), *Debating globalization* (pp. 93–105.). Cambridge: Polity Press.

Barr, H., Graham, J., Hunter, P., Keown, P., & McGee, J. (1997). *A position paper: Social studies in the New Zealand curriculum.* New Zealand: School of Education, University of Waikato.

Bolstad, R. (2011). *Taking a "future focus" in education—What does it mean?* An NZCER working paper from the Future-Focussed Issues in Education (FFI) project. Wellington: New Zealand Council for Educational Research.

Bourdieu, P. (2000). *Pascallian meditations* (R. Nice, Trans.). Cambridge: Polity.

Bradbery, D. (2014). Bridges to global citizenship: Ecologically sustainable futures utilising children's literature in teacher education. *Australian Journal of Environmental Education, 29*(2), 221–237.

Burridge, N., Buchanan, J., & Chodkiewicz, A. (2014). Human rights and history education: An Australian study. *The Australian Journal of Teacher Education, 39*(3), 19–36.

Citizens for Global Education. (2014). *The Brussels proposal: Towards a new direction for education.* Retrieved from: http://deeep.org/wp-content/uploads/2014/07/The_Brussels_Proposal.pdf.

Davies, L. (2006). Global citizenship: Abstraction or framework for action? *Educational Review, 58*(1), 5–25.

Department of Foreign Affairs and Trade. (2016). *Composition of Trade Australia. 2015.* Canberra: Australian Government.

Education Review Office. (2011). *Directions for learning: the New Zealand Curriculum principles, and teaching as inquiry.* Wellington: Author. Retrieved from: http://www.ero.govt.nz/publications/directions-for-learning-the-new-zealand-curriculum-principles-and-teaching-as-inquiry/.

Education Services Australia. (2011). *Global perspective: A framework for global education in Australian schools.* Carlton, VIC: Education Services Australia.

Jefferess, D. (2012). Unsettling cosmopolitanism: Global citizenship and the cultural politics of benevolence. In V. Andreotti & L. De Souza (Eds.), *Postcolonial perspectives on global citizenship education* (pp. 27–46). London: Routledge.

Kelly, P. (2011). *The march of the patriots: The struggle for modern Australia.* Carlton, VIC: Melbourne University Press.

Markus, A. (2014). *Mapping social cohesion: The Scanlon foundation surveys, 2014.* Retrieved from: http://scanlonfoundation.org.au/wp-content/uploads/2014/10/2014-Mapping-Social-Cohesion-Report.pdf.

MCEETYA. (2008). *Melbourne declaration on educational goals for young Australians.* MCEETYA.

Milligan, A., Taylor, M., & Wood, B. E. (2011). Teachers' conceptions of citizenship in New Zealand social studies education. *Citizenship Teaching and Learning, 6*(2), 287–302. doi:10.1386/ctl.6.3.287_1.

Mills, R., & Tomas, L. (2014). Integrating education for sustainability in preservice teacher education: A case study from a regional Australian University. *Australian Journal of Environmental Education, 29*(2), 152–164.

Ministry of Education. (1993). *The New Zealand curriculum framework.* Wellington, NZ: Learning.

Ministry of Education. (2007). *The New Zealand curriculum.* Wellington, NZ: Learning Media. Retrieved from: http://nzcurriculum.tki.org.nz/.

Ministry of Education. (2008a). *Te Marautanga o Aotearoa.* Wellington, NZ: Learning Media. Retrieved from: http://tmoa.tki.org.nz/Te-Marautanga-o-Aotearoa.

Ministry of Education. (2008b). *Building conceptual understandings in the social sciences: Approaches to social inquiry.* Wellington, NZ: Learning Media.

Ministry of Education. (2009). Building conceptual understandings in the social sciences: Being part of global communities. Wellington, NZ: Learning Media. Retrieved from: http://ssol.tki.org.nz/.

Ministry of Education. (2011). *The New Zealand curriculum update: The future focus principle* (Issue 15). Retrieved from: http://nzcurriculum.tki.org.nz/Curriculum-resources/NZC-Updates.

Ministry of Education. (2013a). *The Māori education strategy: ka hikitia—Accelerating success 2013–2017.* Retrieved from: http://www.education.govt.nz/ministry-of-education/overall-strategies-and-policies/the-maori-education-strategy-ka-hikitia-accelerating-success-20132017/.

Ministry of Education. (2013b). *Pasifika education plan.* Retrieved from: http://www.education.govt.nz/ministry-of-education/overall-strategies-and-policies/pasifika-education-plan-2013-2017/.

Ministry of Education. (2016a). *Ambitious for New Zealand: The Ministry of Education four year plan 2016–2020.* Retrieved from: https://www.parliament.nz/en/pb/papers-presented/current-papers/document/51DBHOH_PAP69647_1/education-ministry-of-te-t%C4%81huhu-o-te-m%C4%81tauranga-four.

Ministry of Education. (2016b). An interdependent whole: Capturing the thoughts of tomorrow's global citizens. *New Zealand Education Gazette.* March 21. Retrieved from: http://www.edgazette.govt.nz/Articles/Article.aspx?ArticleId=9244.

New Zealand Treasury. (2016). *New Zealand economic and financial overview.* Retrieved from: http://www.treasury.govt.nz/economy/overview/2015/20.htm.

Newton, J., Milligan, A., Yates, E., & Meyer, L. (2010). Global-mindedness and intercultural competence: Two responses to the challenge of educating for a linguistically and culturally diverse world. In V. Green & S. Cherrington (Eds.), *Delving into diversity: An international exploration of issues of diversity in education* (pp. 287–299). New York: Nova Science.

Newton, J., Yates, E. S., Shearn, S., & Nowitzki, W. (2010). *Intercultural communicative language teaching: Implications for effective teaching and learning. Report to the Ministry of Education.* Wellington: Ministry of Education. Retrieved from: https://www.educationcounts.govt.nz/publications/curriculum/76637/introduction.

Osler, A. (2011). Teacher interpretations of citizenship education: National identity, cosmopolitan ideals and political realities. *Journal of Curriculum Studies, 43*(1), 1–24.

Oxfam. (2015). *Resources for teachers.* https://www.oxfam.org.au/act/resources-for-teachers/. Accessed July 15, 2016.

Peterson, A., & Bentley, B. (2016). Securitisation and/or westernisation: Dominant discourses of Australian values and the implications for teacher education. *Journal of Education for Teaching, 42*(2), 239–251.

Peterson, A., & Warwick, P. (2014). *Global learning and education: Key concepts and effective practice.* London: Routledge.

Pike, G. (2008). Global education. In J. Arthur, I. Davies, & C. Hahn (Eds.), *The Sage handbook of education for citizenship and democracy.* London.: Sage.

Reid, A., Gill, J., & Sears, A. (2010). *Globalization, the nation-state and the citizen.* London: Routledge.

Reynolds, R., Brown, J., Bradbery, D., Donnelly, D., Ferguson-Patrick, K., & Macqueen, S. (2012). *Globalizing teacher training: Embedding global education perspectives in multi-disciplinary pre-service teacher programs.* Paper presented at the Joint AARE APERA International Conference, Sydney.

Samu, T. W. (2011). Understanding the lines in the sand: Diversity, its discourses and building a responsive education system. *Curriculum Matters, 7,* 175–194.

Shaver, J. H., Troughton, G., Sibley, C. G., & Bulbulia, J. A. (2016). Religion and the unmaking of prejudice toward Muslims: Evidence from a large national sample. *PLoS ONE, 11*(3), 1–25.

Sibley, C. G., & Ward, C. (2013). Measuring the preconditions for a successful multi-cultural society: A barometer test of New Zealand. *International Journal of Intercultural Relations, 37*(6), 700–713.

Sibley, C. G., Hoverd, W. J., & Liu, J. H. (2011). Pluralistic and monocultural facets of New Zealand national character and identity. *New Zealand Journal of Psychology, 40,* 19–29.

Spoonley, P. (2015). New diversity, old anxieties in New Zealand: The complex identity politics and engagement of a settler society. *Ethnic and Racial Studies, 38*(4), 650–661. doi:10.1080/01419870.2015.980292.

Statistics New Zealand. (2013a). *2013 Census QuickStats about Māori.* Retrieved from http://www.stats.govt.nz/Census/2013-census/profile-and-summary-reports/quickstats-about-maori-english.aspx.

Statistics New Zealand. (2013b). *2013 Census QuickStats about culture and identity.* Retrieved from: http://www.stats.govt.nz/Census/2013-census/profile-and-summary-reports/quickstats-culture-identity.aspx.

Tallon, R. (2012). Emotion and agency within NGO Development Education: What is at work and what is at stake in the classroom? *International Journal of Development Education and Global Learning, 4*(2), 5–22.

Ward, C., & Liu, J. H. (2012). Ethno-cultural conflict in Aotearoa/New Zealand: Balancing indigenous rights and multicultural responsibilities. In D. Landis & R. D. Albert (Eds.), *Handbook of ethnic conflict: International perspectives* (pp. 45–69). New York: Springer.

Ward, C., & Masgoret, A.-M. (2008). Attitudes toward immigrants, immigration and multiculturalism in New Zealand. *International Migration Review, 42,* 227–248.

White, C., & Openshaw, R. (Eds.). (2005). *Democracy at the crossroads: International perspectives on critical global citizenship education.* USA: Lexington Books.

Wood, B. E. (2012). Scales of citizenship: New Zealand teacher's diverse perceptions and practices. *International Journal of Progressive Education, 8*(3), 77–93. Retrieved from http://inased.org/v8n3/ijpev8n3.pdf.

Wood, B. E. (2013). Participatory capital: Bourdieu and citizenship education in diverse school communities. *British Journal of Sociology of Education, 35*(4), 578–597. doi:10.1080/01425692.2013.777209.

Authors' Biography

Andrew Peterson is Professor of Civic and Moral Education at Canterbury Christ Church University, and Adjunct Professor of Education at the University of South Australia. He has published widely in the fields of civic and moral education, and is co-editor of the *Journal of Philosophy in Schools.* He is book reviews editor for the *British Journal of Educational Studies* and handling editor for *Citizenship Teaching and Learning.* His latest books are *The Palgrave International Handbook of Education for Citizenship and Social Justice* (Palgrave; edited with Robert Hattam, Michalinos Zembylas and James Arthur) and *Compassion and Education: Cultivating Compassionate Children, Schools and Communities.*

Andrea Milligan is a Senior Lecturer at the Faculty of Education, Victoria University of Wellington, New Zealand. Her research interests include a number of intersecting themes related to social sciences and citizenship education. This includes discourses of social and environmental justice, linkages between formal and informal education, and the role of values, ethics and philosophy in education.

Bronwyn E. Wood is a Senior Lecturer at the Faculty of Education, Victoria University of Wellington, New Zealand. Her research interests lie at the intersection of sociology, geography and education and centre on issues relating to youth participation, citizenship and education. Her recent research focuses on young people's social action in schools, restorative justice in cities and education and global education policy.

CHAPTER 2

Europe and Global Citizenship

Alistair Ross and Ian Davies

INTRODUCTION AND OVERVIEW

Europe is a geographical entity, an economic trading unit, a site of cultural diversity and a political arena in which there are elements of commonality as well as the presentation of very different perspectives. This chapter will principally focus on the European Union, in part to achieve a reasonable degree of coherence, but also as a simple recognition that everything cannot be covered. European citizenship is not that of a state but of a supranational body that has a legal and political status and a commitment to common human rights values. This citizenship brings with it an expectation of shared knowledge, experiences and skills. We argue that there are very many ways in which Europe is closely aligned with and congruent with global citizenship. Following an outline of relevant historical background and contemporary social and political context we review the current education systems in place and the European strategies for and about global citizenship. We conclude by referring to the various possible futures that might exist and argue for connective citizenship.

I. Davies (✉)
Department of Education, University of York, Heslington, York YO10 5DD, UK
e-mail: ian.davies@york.ac.uk

I. Davies et al. (eds.), *The Palgrave Handbook of Global Citizenship and Education*, https://doi.org/10.1057/978-1-137-59733-5_2

21

HISTORICAL BACKGROUND

Europe has long had a global dimension. This occurred through the so-called voyages of discovery, the mapping and demarcation of the globe and the imposition of colonial empires that incorporated, exploited and manipulated every continent and the initiation and development of globalised institutions (Osterhammel 2014). The past century has seen an extensive political reconfiguration of Europe and dramatic changes in the relationship between Europe and the rest of the world.

In 1914, most of eastern Europe was divided between the large multinational empires of the Ottomans, Austria–Hungary and Russia. In the west, the UK, France, Germany, Portugal, Spain and the Netherlands had extensive global empires. The French state included Algeria as an intrinsic part of metropolitan France; the British Empire had territories in Europe, colonial 'dominions' of settlement in Canada, Australia and New Zealand, and a hotchpotch of relationships with other territories and states around the world. Germany and Italy, little more than 40 years old, were empire building, while Serbia, Romania and Bulgaria were fragile new states. None of these could be described as a nation state, though most claimed to be so, reflected in the practice of educators over much of the twentieth century (Green 1990; Reid et al. 2010) Reid, A. Fissiparous movements claimed 'national' independence. These erupted in 1914 in a 30-year European (and then global) conflict: a two-part world war, conventionally dated 1914–1918 and 1939–1945 (Kershaw 2015).

In 1918 the USA set out principles intended to settle the territorial tensions that had precipitated conflict. Wilson's Fourteen Points were designed to break up the Austria–Hungary and Ottoman empires, create independent states in the western part of the Russian Empire (including Poland and Finland) and redistribute the overseas empire of defeated Germany as League of Nations mandates. 'The relations of the several Balkan states to one another [was to be] determined by friendly counsel along historically established lines of allegiance and nationality' (USA 1918). Independent Poland's access to the sea through a free port divided East Prussia from the rest of Germany. The ethnolinguistic communities or 'nations' within the dismantled Austro-Hungarian empire meant that there were no agreed 'historically established lines' to respect, and some were thought too small to be viable. Austria and Hungary became rump nations, the northern Slavs were united through the creation of Czechoslovakia, and the southern Slavs in Yugoslavia (Hoare 2010, p. 113). The Irish Free State took much of the island out of the UK, leaving significant tensions in the north. The UK's colonial 'white' dominions became effectively autonomous—a development that led in South Africa to the eventual emergence of apartheid.

Germany was blamed and made responsible for reparations that eventually led to the Nazi state and the reigniting of the European conflict in 1939. The Nazis and their allies overran almost all of continental Europe, with a racist ideology that enabled the murder of a very large proportion of European Jewry, many Roma, homosexuals and others. On liberation, the Baltic states were reincorporated as Soviet Socialist Republics; Poland had both eastern and western borders moved westward, incorporating East Prussia and a swathe of eastern Germany; and Germany was divided into two states: the Federal Republic in the west and the Democratic Republic in the Soviet sphere. The Baltic states, Poland, Czechoslovakia, Hungary, Romania and Bulgaria had communist regimes imposed by the USSR, forming a buffer zone—the 'Warsaw Pact' bloc—to 'protect' the USSR. Gorbachev's policies of *perestroika* ('restructuring') and *glasnost* ('openness') allowed them from 1985 to determine their own internal affairs. The bloc rapidly fell apart. Polish elections in 1989 were won by the anti-communist Solidarity party, *Solidarność*; Hungary opened its border with Austria, and within weeks thousands of East Germans moved to the west. The Berlin Wall was demolished, and the other countries of the Warsaw Pact shook themselves free. The three Baltic Socialist Republics declared themselves independent of the USSR in 1991, and Yugoslavia fragmented, Serbian hegemony being contested through warfare, and now comprises seven states (Judt 2005).

In 1951 western Europe, the French, German, Benelux and Italian postwar governments created the European Coal and Steel Community with the aim of making war between France and Germany impossible (Schuman 1950). The integration of production between the member states neutralized competition, and by 1957, it became the European Common Market, based on the two principles of developing free markets, services and employment between the member states and a commitment to democracy and upholding human rights.

The colonial empires of the French, Belgians, Dutch and the UK were ending, partly because of nationalist pressures for independence and the economic (and moral) costs of oppressive empires were too high. Indonesia, French Indo-China and the Indian subcontinent became independent. A swathe of new states became independent in Africa, the Caribbean in the decade from 1956. Algeria, considered by the French to be part of France (and thus part of the EEC), was a more difficult case. The UK developed amicable associations with many of its former colonies through the Commonwealth.

The European Union was renamed the European Community (EC) in 1966, and in 1973, three new member states joined: the UK, Ireland and Denmark (a referendum in 2016 decided the UK would leave the EU). Democratic commitment meant that Greece could only join in 1981 (when the military junta had been overthrown), and Spain and Portugal in 1985, when their dictatorships had been replaced by democratic regimes (and then their remaining colonies became independent, most of which had in any case gained independence in the nineteenth century). The EC's economic progress in the period up to the mid-1970s, led to demands for labour, initially from southern Europe and Turkey to the northern states, and then from the former colonies to Europe. The reunification of East and West Germany in 1990 led to eastern Germany 'joining' the EC by default. In 1993 specific principles for future expansion were agreed in the 'Copenhagen criteria'; future members had to have stable political institutions that respected democracy, the rule of law and human rights; a robust market economies; and a commitment to political and economic union. The European Community was renamed the European Union (EU) later that year. Ten new members joined in 2004, followed by Bulgaria and Romania in 2007 and Croatia in 2013. Iceland, the remaining Balkan states and Turkey are in negotiations over membership: Norway and Switzerland currently intend to remain outside the EU.

This obviously global historical background together with many intra-European complex unifying and peripheral forces impacts on how—at both national and EU level—global citizenship education has developed.

CONTEMPORARY SOCIAL AND POLITICAL CONTEXT

The year 2013 was the 'European Year of Citizens', and various Framework Programmes for Research have focused on identities, and the most recent research initiative, Horizon 2020, is now well underway. This allows some insight into how Europeans are reacting to pressures and opportunities for global citizenship.

There is an increasing trend towards accepting an identity as a global citizen (see Grimley 2016). However, this is most apparent in developing economies with particularly strong results in Nigeria (73%), China (71%), Peru (70%) and India (67%). The situation in Europe is not straightforward. Indeed, there may be types of European identity all of which may connect with a globalism including that which sees European bodies gradually supplanting national institutions; transnationalism (particularly relevant to experiences of migration); and cosmopolitanism in which other cultures are welcomed within a European sense of tolerance and equality (EC 2012). These different identities are wrapped up with questions of standardization, desire for common action, varied personal relationships and notions of what constitutes the public sphere. National and European identities are not necessarily in conflict, and some marginalized groups find it difficult to accept the latter (Triandafyllidou and Gropas) but as Europe negotiates its way between localism, nationalism, x, transnationalism and globalism its engagement with the rest of the world is clear.

A global identity may be seen in relation to culture and religion. Baldwin (1965) argued that Europeans were unlike others in the rest of the world:

> The most illiterate among them is related, in a way that I am not, to Dante, Shakespeare, Michelangelo, Aeschylus, Da Vinci, Rembrandt, and Racine; the cathedral at Chartres says something to them which it cannot say to me (p. 162).

The Pew Research Centre (Masci 2015) estimates that by 2050 fewer Christians and more Muslims and other religious groups will live in Europe and that the overall religious composition will not dramatically change. By 2050, 65% will identify as Christian (down from 75% in 2010). Certain forms of Europeanness are seen by some as exclusive.

Europe's economic wealthy is a cause of, and expressed by, significant trade with the rest of the world. This, curiously, heightens Europe's globality with wealth that cuts it off from many in the world. The EU-28 accounted for a 23.7% share of the world's GDP in 2013 and

> Together, the EU-27, China and the USA accounted for 39.3% of global exports of goods in 2011 and 43.8% of global imports (Eurostat 2014, p. 92).

Approximately 40% of goods imported to Europe come from beyond G20 countries, but the strength of trade between Europe and other wealthy areas is obvious. There are significant fluctuations between EU countries, but there is a very clear and obvious preference by non-EU countries such as the USA to establish trading agreements with a transnational unit that can offer a market of approximately 500 million people. This is complicated by various factors including individual agreements that the EU makes with specified so-called third partner countries (such as Canada) and the complex web of connections between member states and countries beyond Europe.

The governance that is enacted in relation to European citizens is relevant to considerations of global citizenship. Few [beyond academics such as Held (1995)] argue for fully developed global governance systems, but there are some trends relevant to global citizenship. The first direct elections to the European parliament occurred in 1979. There has been a consistent apparent decline in turnout from 1979 to the most recent elections in 2015. Of course, the radical change in the size of the electorate from 1979 until today, the very different voting rules in member countries (including compulsory voting in some countries) and the inappropriateness of assuming that failure to vote is a result of lack of knowledge or commitment to the European project should make us pause before assuming that governance beyond the nation state is not accepted. There is, however, on the part of many European politicians and others civil society, recognition of a democratic deficit and there are some extremely worrying indications about the nature of European civic engagement:

> The effects of the economic crises on citizens can already be seen in terms of a loss of faith in political institutions with a dramatic reduction in trust in national and European institutions in particular in Spain, Ireland and Greece. Citizens across European countries are continuing to believe in the democratic process but consider that the current political leaders are not working for them (Hoskins et al. 2012, p. 4).

Faced by extremely difficult circumstances across much of North Africa and in parts of the Middle East (especially Syria), migration affects how Europe relates to the world (see http://globalcitizenshipalliance.org/). Research by the Pew Center (Wike et al. 2016) suggests that Europeans fear that the refugee/migrant crisis will mean more terrorism and fewer jobs (and that this is felt most strongly in south and eastern Europe).

The above suggests a mixed picture about Europe and global citizenship. Europe is an economic unit that takes its responsibilities to the less wealthy with seriousness and idealism, and it is an engine of the prosperous—and divisive—world economy. It is politically embryonic in its transnationalism. It is culturally diverse and although there are obvious aspects of democratic deficit it signals a commitment to a pluriversal engagement that is easily aligned with a progressive global citizenship.

KEY FEATURES OF THE CURRENT EDUCATION SYSTEM IN EUROPE

Each of the 28 member states retains considerable sovereignty. The EU is a mixture of being an intergovernmental institution, in which state governments negotiate, and a 'supranational' institution, where pan-EU bodies can legislate for member states. The principle of subsidiarity means that policy decisions are devolved to the most local level possible. Education was seen as an important element of a country's culture, and thus an area where policy should be determined at the state level (or even more locally), rather than by the EU. It is not easy to reconcile a common conception of citizenship and global human rights with individual state autonomy over curriculum policies, or labour mobility when each country had its own system of recording attainment and professional and vocational qualifications.

The first EU education programmes in 1987 supported trans-state university–industry exchanges. The Erasmus programme supports inter-university contacts, curricula cooperation and student study in a university of another member state. Various Socrates projects (from 1994) extended similar activities in schools (the Comenius programme), adult education (Grundtvig), and further education and vocational training (Leonardo). Together with language-learning programmes, the ambitions were to strengthen the European dimension of education at all levels. By 2000, the EU expanded its educational interests to include policy objectives; the Lisbon summit that year began coordinating educational policies in order to improve the economic strengths of the Union states. In 2004 the University Erasmus programme took on a world perspective (Erasmus Mundus programme), supporting joint programmes and exchanges with Universities on other continents.

Citizenship education in Europe was once simply 'what states in Europe do', but has subsequently developed as education *for* European citizenship. What this means has changed in concept, partly as supranationalism has waxed and waned, and partly in response to the increase in the number and nature of the member states. A relatively small group of affluent Western countries with a long tradition of democratic norms has expanded to include poorer southern states that had only recently shaken off dictatorial regimes and a much larger group of states that had been behind the Iron Curtain (poorer, with weaker infrastructure, and lacking traditions of civic participation). The EU's emerging policy in this area has focussed on European citizenship, rather than global citizenship: this represents a form of supranational citizenship education that in some ways approximates to a global element and has a clear *universal* human rights agenda (a fundamental raison d'etre of the Union itself).

A loose consensus developed that citizenship education was not national, nor European, and had a global dimension that included rights, participation and engagement, civic principles and the individual with an international dimension. The 1996 report *Accomplishing Europe through Education and Training* (EC 1996) defines European citizenship as based on a shared political culture of democracy . . . the route towards a 'post-national' model to which Europeans will feel that they belong as citizens, not because they subscribe to a common culture . . . or because of their specific origins, but because this sense of European citizenship will emerge from the new social relations that the Europeans establish between themselves. (1996, p. 21)

In 2006, the European Parliament and the Council of the European Union defined eight key competences for lifelong learning, one of which was social and civil competence:

> Civic competence, and particularly knowledge of social and political concepts and structures (democracy, justice, equality, citizenship and civil rights), equips individuals to engage in active and democratic participation. (EU 2006, p. 16)

These became increasingly reflected in national educational policies. Citizenship became a deterritorialised post-national concept of practice. Practice was centred on 'common values of European civilization' that were at least potentially more universalistic than European:

> human rights/human dignity; fundamental freedoms; democratic legitimacy; peace and the rejection of violence as a means to an end; respect for others; a spirit of solidarity (both within Europe and vis a vis the world as a whole); equitable development; equal opportunities; the principles of rational thought; the ethics of evidence and proof; personal responsibility. (EC 1996, p. 25)

Active citizenship was emphasized (see Ross 2008).

STRATEGIES FOR EDUCATING ABOUT AND FOR GLOBAL CITIZENSHIP

The Colonial Legacy

Various European states have had an intimate connection with the process of globalisation, imposing exploitative global empires, thus undermining and corrupting local agency and culture. A post-colonial analysis of contemporary European educational practices reflects the consequence of this earlier period, and reflections of imperial relationships remain in the way that global education is approached in many parts of Europe: the growth of global citizenship education is a (still emerging) response to this legacy (Mangan 2012; Sébe 2013).

The imperial 'civilising' mission of the Europeans was justified by, among others, the French historian Renan: in 1871 he explained 'the regeneration of the inferior or degenerate races, by the superior races, is part of the providential order of things for humanity' (1871: 93) Post-colonial scholars such as Bhabha (1994) and Spivak (1988) hold that European states' continuing view of the world as comprising unequal and separate cultures permeates how Europeans construct their former colonies as imaginary peoples and places. Various European school curricula, post-1960, presented the 'Third World' as impoverished, lacking agency and dependent on subventions from 'The First World' in order to survive. Even well-intentioned attempts to make the curriculum reflect the histories and origins of the growing and diverse multicultural population of western European schools were flawed: Cave (2002) notes how UK schools, focussing on the slave trade and the colonial history of these countries, 'failed to foster any sense of past achievement' (2002: 637). Errante (1998) explained that Portuguese education reduced the colonisers to the 'demonized' and the colonised as 'infantilized and idealized' (308). Textbook analyses in France (Petter 2008; Oetting 2006; Laforcade 2006), in Germany (Grindel 2008) and in Norway (Aamotsbakken 2008) confirm this. Challand (2009) analysed French, Italian and German history textbooks between 1950 and 2005, suggesting that from the early 1990s a distinct European identity was constructed around a discourse of external Other(s). Schissler and Soysal (2005) suggested that in Western Europe education 'the nation' was being increasingly reconstructed through a European lens, while in the USA Eurocentric views were being replaced by global constructions, and East European countries had other concerns about redefining the nation after the fall of communism (see also Ross 2015).

Emerging Themes of Global Citizenship

Osler and Starkey observe:

> Processes of globalisation and increased interdependence mean that no one, wherever they live in the world, can remain completely isolated within a single nation. … If democracy is now re-conceptualised as cosmopolitan, then the actors within the democracy are, by extension, cosmopolitan citizens. (Osler and Starkey 2003, 245–6)

Four Particular Trends Appear Significant

1. Developmental Citizenship

While the first world/third world dichotomy has been characterised as post-colonial, the curriculum has moved towards a more developmental approach, that stresses the agency of developing countries (Marshall 2005; Marshall and Arnot 2007). In Poland, the UK and Spain, Krzywosz-Rynkiewicz et al. (2010) found that tackling global poverty was one of the common hopes for the future expressed by young people (Minty 2010; Holden and Minty 2011). Hicks and and Holden focussed on issues of sustainable development in their 2007 collection: one of the 'issues based educations' they identify is that many young people and their teachers are concerned with 'issues to do with global inequality' (Hicks and Holden 2007, p. 5). In Norway, Nord-kvelle (1991) reported that while developmental education had expanded significantly, theoretically fostering solidarity towards the Third World, in practice teaching still depoliticised and displays a fundamental ethnocentric knowledge base.

2. Global Environmental Issues

Minty (2010) found environmental concerns featured very highly among young people in Poland and the UK. Huckle (2008) argues that part of citizenship education should include the understanding that humans have a relationship with non-human agents, and that these need to be understood on a global scale. Dobson (2003) argues strongly for environmental citizenship as a particular ecological form of cosmopolitanism: he maintains that citizenship education should focus more on communities of obligation rather than human communities, and on adopting partiality and ecological justice rather than impartiality and discussion. In some senses, because in the European context the acceptance of global warming has become very largely accepted (unlike some other parts of the world), this has become a 'safe' issue for teachers (Cowan and Maitles 2012).

3. Global Identities

Aspects of citizenship identities are now contingent and multiple, con-sciously constructed by individuals. The concept of fixed identities was chal-lenged by Foucault (1979): identity now matters more because the individual has more choice and mobility, in what Bauman (2000) describes as 'liquid modernity': he suggests that identity is constructed in a social context and located in contingent and temporal relationships. 'Self-construction of the self is, so to speak, a necessity. Self-confirmation of the self is an impossibility' (Bauman 1988: 62)

Since 1945 there have been significant changes in citizenship law in Europe. While the term citizenship is used in citizenship education largely to mean the rights that come with membership of the state, it is also used to refer to a particular status and to confer a particular identity. Joppke (2010) writes of how these elements have become part of the discourse of citizenship since 1945, which marks the beginning of the contemporary era of human rights, which establishes the individual and his or her integrity as the benchmark and ulterior constraint of state policy' (Joppke 2010: 26–27). Contemporary migration, lacking the permanence and unidirectional characteristics of earlier movement, throws this into relief. As Hall suggests, 'the concept of diaspora disrupts and unsettles our hitherto settled conceptions of culture, place and identity' (Hall 1996: 207). Acquisition of citizenship is now easier in western Europe, but in east and south-eastern Europe, it remains 'still closely linked to an ethnic interpretation of nationality, [in which] transmission to subsequent generations is exclusively based on descent, [and] there is greater hostility towards multiple nationality' (Bauböck et al. 2007: 12). In the west, citizenship has become post-national: Soysal argues that it now involves rights that transcend the boundaries of the nation state (1994: 137).

4. Universal Human Rights

A particular global conception of citizenship has emerged around human rights. Banks (2009) and Ramirez et al. (2007) Suárez, D. have written of this in a global context, but Starkey (1991) and Osler and Starkey (1999, 2005, 2010) view it as a European phenomenon. Ross (2015; in preparation) has discussed constructions of civic identity with over 2000 11- to 19-year-olds in 29 European states and notes human rights as a particular lens through which a specifically European identity (as opposed to a state identity) is constructed. In the eastern ('new') member states of the European Union, Europe was constructed as stressing democracy and human rights, unlike Russia. In western countries, freedom of speech was added to this. But young people were particularly interested in extending the human rights discourse to include areas such as the rights of those with lesbian, gay, bisexual and transgender sexual identities, and (particularly in fieldwork in 2015), the rights of migrants and refugees. Most young people broadly accepted refugees and were very critical of the racist and xenophobic attitudes they ascribed to some older people. While Russia was used as 'the other' in eastern Europeans' identification with human rights, in western Europe, the USA was also othered, particularly in respect to what they saw as racialism, particularly by the police.

THE EUROPEAN UNION'S CONTRIBUTION

The importance that many young Europeans attach to the universality of human rights derives in part to their emphasis by the European Union and to the European Convention on Human Rights and the activities of the European Court of Human Rights.[1] Survey data vary, but young Europeans may tend to express their identity, at least partially and in continental contexts, as global citizens. But the European Union itself has been slow to adopt a more global presence: even an area as relatively uncontentious as countering climate change was not addressed until 2000, when the Commission adopted the European Climate Change Programme. The EU had no equivalent to a Foreign Affairs minister until 1999, when the post of High Representative of the Common Foreign and Security Policy was created, but this was simply one of the functions of Council's Secretary General until 2009, when a specific appointment gave the post a more visible presence.

The EU's educational policy, global dimensions and conceptions of global citizenship were equally tardy. The Erasmus Programme was largely internal to the EU states until 2008, when the Erasmus Mundus initiative allowed a limited number of global exchanges of academics and projects, including the development of joint Masters programmes operated by European and non-European universities. However, this programme only operates at the level of higher education, focuses on the sciences rather than the humanities and is at least in part intended to enhance the attractiveness and visibility of European higher education worldwide.

Citizenship education has been identified as a key educational competence by the European Parliament and Council (see above), with a consensus that it was neither wholly national nor European. The implicit global dimension in this has not, on the whole, been followed by the various states in their national curricula for citizenship education. An ICCS survey on teachers' self-reported confidence in teaching citizenship education found that in European countries about 84% of teachers said they felt confident teaching about 'different cultures and ethnic groups' and 77% were confident teaching about 'the global community and international organisations (Schultz et al. 2010).

However, a pan-European survey of citizenship education provision (Eurydice 2012a, b) suggests that few countries made curricular provision for global citizenship. The Czech Republic requires 'thinking within a European and a global context' (Eurydice 2012a: 22) in primary and secondary education. In Northern Ireland (UK) there are courses on local and global citizenship' (Eurydice 2012b: 10) and in Wales (UK) 7- to 19-year-old students follow a programme 'Education for Sustainable Development and Global Citizenship', and 14- to19-year-olds also one on 'Wales, Europe and the World' (Eurydice 2012b: 10). It will be interesting to monitor developments in light of the vote on 23 June 2016 for the UK to leave the European Union. It is possible (but unlikely) that the global citizenship education emphasis in Scotland and elsewhere in the UK will be strengthened. It may be more likely that a national emphasis will become even more prominent. In Portugal global citizenship is a cross-curricular topic (Eurydice 2012b: 8) and in Spain 'Education for citizenship and human rights' was, until withdrawn by the government under pressure from the Catholic Church and others, a four year programme spread between primary and upper secondary school (Eurydice 2012b: 3). In terms of educational evaluation, the UK (Scotland) inspection guide includes international education, global citizenship and sustainability issues (Eurydice 2012a: 79). In Slovenia a study on 'Citizenship Education for the Multicultural and Globalised World' found that schools did not sufficiently address global issues and proposed adding global and multicultural content to the citizenship curricula (Eurydice 2012a: 83). Teachers have been supported in Latvia (through EU funding) to develop citizenship education competences including citizenship education in global processes and human rights (Eurydice 2012a: 91).

LIKELY AND DESIRABLE FUTURES

Given the complexities of the above in relation to ideas, perspectives, issues and events, we try to outline in very general terms what will need to be considered as the relationship between Europe and global citizenship continues to be dynamic.

The fundamental perspectives on Europe and the globe are vital. We suggest a deepening of identity around Europeanness and globality/cosmopolitanism. The question of who we are is important; the need to avoid simple exclusionary binaries is essential both for recognising empirically grounded realities as well as distancing ourselves from unpleasant characterizations of 'the other'. This focus on identity is unlikely in the short term to be developed through formal systems of government. We are arguing for characterising our lives and identities in multiple perspectives with efforts to engage with glocality or the intersections of localities, countries and elsewhere. Environmental matters, the movements of peoples, goods and ideas which are obviously all global matters mean that a failure to engage with a European global citizenship education would be negligent.

The citizenship that is likely to exist in relation to the dynamic globalising identity referred to above should be considered. Work on efficacy and participation will allow for explorations of identity congruent with global citizenship. This work relates to connective citizenship (Bennett and Segerberg 2013). Traditional institutionally based politics is still important and valid as the locus of power, even in the face of seismic social and economic shifts that have created new forms of social class. The grand narratives of conventional politics, the mechanics of party management and charismatic leadership still have their part to play in global citizenship. But there is a need to recognize the shift from macro (trade union, political party membership, voting) to micro- (individualised and personalised political actions to secure resource for oneself or those who are close). In short, we argue for a stance against the forces of neo-liberalismLiberal and populism and a more subtle but significant shift away from traditional statist collective politics to connective citizenship. In this new scenario, the role of 'new' media, emotion and the everyday actor (Bang 2010) must be part of our framework for a European global citizenship.

What then would education look like that is aligned with the European global citizenship referred to above? It should be created by and for majorities; it should be professional, and it should be about and for critically informed and socially engaged responsible action. It should not be—as it too often is—narrowly academic, left to chance and constructed narrowly around morality and law. An explicitly framed, deliberately global and conceptually based programme involving evaluation and assessment (not necessarily testing) should be developed. This would mean that the barriers that exist between school and the community, teacher and activist, and academic and practitioner should be breached.

We need research that shows us what exists and what needs to be done in order to innovate. There should be a resistance on the part of policy makers to simplistic international sources that are indicators only of nationalism. We need professionals who are educator-activists seeing themselves as connective European global citizens.

Note

1. The Convention was created by the Council of Europe (which is a much wider organisation than the European Union, with which it should not be confused): it established the Court and set out fundamental rights that all member states agree to uphold, with supra-national arrangements to allow individual citizens to have these enforced against their own state governments.

References

Aamotsbakken, B. (2008). The colonial past in Norwegian history textbooks. *International Textbook Research, 30*(3), 76–763.

Baldwin, J. (1965). *Stranger in the Village. In Notes of a Native Son*. London: Corgi.

Bang, H. (2010). Between everyday makers and expert citizens. In J. Fenwick & J. McMillan (Eds.), *Public management in the Postmodern Era: Challenges and prospects* (pp. 163–192). Cheltenham: Edward Elgar Publishing.

Banks, J. (2009). Human rights, diversity, and citizenship education. *The Educational Forum, 73*(2), 100–110.

Bauböck, R., Perching, B., & Sievers, W. (eds). (2007). *Citizenship Policies in the New Europe*. Amsterdam: Amsterdam University Press.

Bauman, Z. (1998). *Freedom*. Milton Keynes: Open University Press.

Bauman, Z. (2000). *Liquid Modernity*. Cambridge: Polity Press.

Bennett, L., & Segerberg, A. (2013). *The logic of connective action: Digital media and the personalization of contentious politics*. Cambridge: Cambridge University Press.

Bhabha, H. (1994). *The Location of Culture*. London: Routledge.

Cave, P. (2002). Teaching the history of empire in Japan and England. *International Journal of Educational Research, 37*, 41–623.

Challand, B. (2009). European identity and external others in history textbooks (1950–2005). *Journal of Educational Media, Memory, and Society, 1*(2), 60–96.

Cowan, P., & Maitles, H. (Eds.). (2012). *Teaching controversial issues in the classroom: Key issues and debates*. London: Bloomsbury.

Dobson, A. (2003). *Citizenship and the environment*. Oxford: Oxford University Press.

Errante, A. (1998). Education and National Personae in Portugal's Colonial and Post-colonial Transition. *Comparative Education Review, 42*(3), 267–308.

European Commission (1996). *Study group on education and training: Report accomplishing Europe through education and training.* Luxembourg: Office for Official Publications of the European Communities.

European Commission (2012). Directorate-General for and Innovation Socio-economic Sciences and Humanities. *The Development of European Identity/Identities: Unfinished Business A Policy Review.* Brussels: European Commission.

European Parliament and the Council of the European Union (2006). *Recommendation 2006/962/EC of the Council of 18 December 2006 on Key Competences for Lifelong Learning* [Official Journal L 394 of 30.12.2006].

Eurostat. (2014). *The EU in the world 2014. A statistical portrait.* Luxembourg: European Union.

Eurydice. (2012a). *Citizenship education in Europe.* Brussels: Education, Audiovisual and Culture Executive Agency.

Eurydice. (2012b). *Main reforms in citizenship education since 2005.* Brussels: Education, Audiovisual and Culture Executive Agency.

Foucault, M. (1979). *Discipline and Punish: The Birth of the Prison.* London: Allen Lane.

Green, A. (1990). *Education and state formation: The rise of education systems in England, France and the USA.* London: Macmillan.

Grimley, N. (2016). *Identity 2016: 'Global citizenship' rising, poll suggests.* http://www.bbc.co.uk/news/world-36139904.

Grindel, S. (2008). Deutscher Sonderweg oder europäischer Erinnerungsort? Die Darstellung des modernen Kolonialismus in neueren deutschen Schulbüchern. *International Textbook Research, 30*(3), 695–716.

Held, D. (1995). *Democracy and the global order.* Cambridge: Polity Press.

Hicks, D., & Holden, C. (Eds.). (2007). *Teaching the global dimension: Key principles and effective practice.* London: Routledge.

Hoare, M. (2010). The War of Yugoslavian Succession. In S. Ramet (Ed.), *Central and Southeast European politics since 1989* (pp. 111–135). Cambridge: Cambridge University Press.

Holden, C., & Minty, S. (2011). Going global: Young Europeans' aspirations and actions for the future. *Citizenship Teaching and Learning, 6*(2), 123–137.

Hoskins, B., et al. (2012). *Analytic Report: Participatory citizenship in the European Union, Institute of Education report for EU.* Southampton: Southampton University.

Huckle, J. (2008). Sustainable development (342–354). In J. Arthur, I. Davies, & C. Hahn (Eds.), *The SAGE handbook of education for democracy and citizenship.* London: Sage.

Joppke, C. (2010). *Citizenship and Immigration.* Cambridge: Polity Press.

Judt, T. (2005). *Postwar: A history of Europe since 1945.* London: Heinemann.

Kershaw, I. (2015). *To hell and back: Europe, 1914–1949.* London: Penguin.

Krzywosz-Rynkiewicz, B., Zalewska, A., & Ross, A. (Eds.). (2010). *Future citizens: 21st century challenges for young people.* Krakow: Impuls.

Laforcade, G. (2006). 'Foreigners', Nationalism and the 'Colonial Fracture'@ Stigmatised subjects of historical memory in France. *International Journal of Comparative Sociology, 47*(3–4), 217–233.

Mangan, J. (Ed.). (2012). *The imperial curriculum: Racial images and education in the British Colonial experience* (2nd ed.). London: Routledge.

Marshall, H. (2005). Developing the global gaze in citizenship education: Exploring the perspectives of global education NGO workers In England. *International Journal of Citizenship and Teacher Education, 1*(2), 76–92.

Marshall, H., & Arnot, M. (2007). Globalising the school curriculum (165–180). In S. Fennell & M. Arnot (Eds.), *Gender education and equality in a global context*. London: Routledge.

Masci, D. (2015). *Europe projected to retain its Christian majority, but religious minorities will grow*. http://www.pewresearch.org/fact-tank/2015/04/15/europe-projected-to-retain-its-christian-majority-but-religious-minorities-will-grow/.

Minty, S. (2010). Young people's hopes and fears for their global and local futures (p 63–88). In B. Krzywosz-Rynkiewicz, A. Zalewska, & A. Ross (Eds.), *Future citizens: 21st centrury challenges for young people*. Impuls: Krakow.

Nordkvelle, Y. (1991). Development education in Norway—context and content for the teaching of solidarity. *International Journal of Educational Development, 11*(2), 161–171.

Oetting, B. (2006). Bruch mit der kolonialen Vergangenheit? Der Algerienkrieg und die Entkolonisierung in französischen Geschichtsschulbüchern der Troisième. *International Textbook Research, 28*(1), 25–41.

Osler, A., & Starkey, H. (1999). Rights, identities and inclusion: European action programmes as political education. *Oxford Review of Education, 25*(1–2), 199–215.

Osler, A., & Starkey, H. (2003). Learning for cosmopolitan citizenship: Theoretical debates and young people's experiences. *Educational Review, 55*(3), 243–254.

Osler, A., & Starkey, H. (2005). *Changing citizenship: Democracy and inclusion in education*. Maidenhead: Open University Press/McGraw Hill.

Osler, A., & Starkey, H. (2010). *Teachers and human rights education*. Stoke on Trent: Trentham Books.

Osterhammel, J. (2014). *The transformation of the world: A global history of the nineteenth century*. Princeton, NJ: Princeton University Press.

Petter, D. (2008). Bilder imperialen Abschieds: Die französische Dekolonisation im Spiegel von öffentlichen Debatten und Geschichtsschulbüchern (1954–1962). *International Textbook Research, 30*(3), 40–717.

Ramirez, F., Suárez, D., & Meyer, J. (2007). The worldwide rise of human rights education (35–52). In A. Benavot & C. Braslavsky (Eds.), *School knowledge in comparative and historical perspective: Changing curricula in primary and secondary education*. Dordrecht: Springer.

Reid, A., Gill, J., & Sears, A. (Eds.). (2010). *Globalization, the Nation-State and the citizen: Dilemmas and directions for civics and citizenship education*. New York: Routledge.

Renan, E. (1871). *La Réforme intellectuelle et morale* Paris: Michél Leve Frères p 93. Part of this was quoted in Aimé Césaire's (1955) *Discourse on Colonialism* [*Discourse sur le colonialisme*, Paris: Editions Presence Africaine, 1955], which was translated into English by Joan Pinkham (1972, New York: Monthly Review Press): it is this translation that is used here.

Ross, A. (2008). Organising a curriculum for active citizenship education (p, 492–505). In J. Arthur, I. Davies, & C. Hahn (Eds.), *The SAGE handbook of education for democracy and citizenship*. London: Sage.

Ross, A. (2015). *Understanding the construction of identities by young New Europeans: Kaleidoscopic selves*. London: Routledge.

Schissler, H., & Soysal, Y. (Eds.). (2005). *The Nation, Europe and the World: Textbooks and curricula in transition*. New York: Berghan.

Schulz, W., Ainley, J., Fraillon, J., Kerr, D., & Losito, B. (2010). *Civic knowledge, attitudes, and engagement among lower secondary school students in 38 countries.* Amsterdam: International Association for the Evaluation of Educational Achievement (IEA).

Schuman, R. (1950) in Fontaine, P. (1990). *Europe, a fresh start: The Schuman declaration, 1950–90* (pp. 13–14). Luxembourg: Office for Official Publications of the European Communities.

Sébe, B. (2013). *Heroic imperialists in Africa: The promotion of British and French colonial heroes 1870–1939.* Manchester: Manchester University Press.

Spivak, G. (1988). Can the Subaltern Speak? In C. Nelson & L. Grossbereg (Eds.), *Marxism and the interpretation of culture* (pp. 271–313). Basingstoke: Macmillan.

Starkey, H. (1991). *Socialisation of school children and their education for democratic values and human rights.* Amsterdam: Council of Europe/Swets and Zeitlinger.

Triandafyllidou, A., & Gropas, R. (2016). European University Institute European Identity: What kind of diversity into what form of unity? Cultural Base: Social platform of cultural heritage and European identities. http://culturalbase.eu/european-identity-what-kind-of-diversity-into-what-form-of-unity/.

USA (1918). Woodrow Wilson: Speech to a Joint Session of Congress, 8 January. Washington, DC: Congressional Record.

Wike, R., Stokes, R., & Simmons, K. (2016). Europeans fear wave of refugees will mean more terrorism, fewer jobs. *Pew Research Center, Global Attitudes and Trends,* 11 July. http://www.pewglobal.org/2016/07/11/europeansfear-wave-of-refugees-will-mean-more-terrorismfewer-jobs/. Accessed 4 July 2017.

Authors' Biography

Alistair Ross is an Emeritus Professor of London Metropolitan University, holds a personal Jean Monnet chair in citizenship education in Europe, and a Fellow of the UK Academy of Social Sciences. He formerly established a European network on citizenship education and identities in Europe (CiCe), and directed the Institute for Policy Studies in Education at London Metropolitan. He continues to research and write on education and social justice and identity: his most recent book was *Understanding the Construction of Identities by young new Europeans* (2015) and he currently writing on young West Europeans.

Ian Davies is Professor of Education in the Department of Education, University of York, UK. He is director of the Centre for Research on Education and Social Justice, deputy head of department of education and director of the Graduate School of Education at York. He is the author of many books and articles on the theme of citizenship education. He has worked as an expert for the Council of Europe on education for democratic citizenship, is a past fellow of the Japan Society for the Promotion of Science and is a visiting professor at the Hong Kong University of Education.

CHAPTER 3

The Middle East

Dina Kiwan

INTRODUCTION AND OVERVIEW OF THE CHAPTER

There has been heightened consideration and debate internationally to the forms of education best suited to our changing globalising world in academia, policy and practice. Whilst the issue of access to education continues to be an important one in many parts of the world, there is now increased attention to issues of relevance and quality of education. Since 2012, Global education, and in particular global citizenship education, have been internationally prominent policy initiatives, with policy objectives and proposed outcomes being framed as responding to the new unfolding contemporary realities of our world, with Ban Ki-Moon announcing that Global Citizenship Education was to be a core pillar of the United Nations' Education First Initiative. Global Citizenship Education draws on various forms of education historically, including anti-racist education, development education, human rights education, multicultural education, peace education and education for sustainable development. UNESCO has played a leading role on work on global citizenship education (GCED) since 2013, building on its 'Learning to Live Together' work, central to its mission. It held a technical consultation on Global Citizenship Education organised by UNESCO and the Republic of Korea in Seoul in September 2013. This was followed by a further meeting in Bangkok in December 2013, and the UNESCO publication *Global Citizenship Education: preparing learners for the challenges of the twenty-first century* was launched in May 2014. This developmental work led to the publication of an international curriculum guiding framework covering all ages phases and both formal and non-formal

D. Kiwan (✉)
School of Education, University of Birmingham, Birmingham, UK
e-mail: dk32@aub.edu.lb

© The Author(s) 2018
I. Davies et al. (eds.), *The Palgrave Handbook of Global Citizenship and Education*, https://doi.org/10.1057/978-1-137-59733-5_3

education entitled *Global Citizenship Education: Topics and Learning Objectives*,[1] which was launched and well received by member states at the World Education Forum in Seoul, South Korea, in May 2015. The rationale for the publication is to provide pedagogical guidance to support member states around the world in integrating or further enhancing GCED into their education systems, addressing issues of subject matter, challenges of implementation and examples of practice and resources (UNESCO 2015).

Member states in the Arab region are also engaging with the implications of global citizenship education within their nation-states field. The UNESCO 2015 publication recognises that GCED is a contested context and that there will necessarily be regional and national particularities in conceptualization and contextualization. Approaches to citizenship education vary within the region, given the wide range of different contexts across Arab countries, from the Arab Gulf monarchies with large migrant populations, to the countries of North Africa in the aftermath of the Arab uprisings, (e.g. Egypt, Morocco, Tunisia), to countries of significant conflict (e.g. Iraq, Syria, Yemen), and highly diverse countries like Lebanon and Oman, and countries dealing with large numbers of refugee populations, like Jordan and Lebanon.

This chapter firstly situates developments in approaches to citizenship and education in historical, sociopolitical and cultural context, in order to explore and consider key features of educational systems in the region and the challenges faced. Examples of strategies and initiatives are given, and in conclusion, reflections on potential future development are considered.

HISTORICAL BACKGROUND

There is a substantive literature on education, citizenship and nation-state formation, examining how the nation-state uses educational policies in constructing and propagating a vision of national citizenship through education. In examining the history of Arab education, the framing in terms of 'modernising' or 'nationalising' projects primarily in the context of postcolonial projects has been challenged by more inclusive approaches that look historically at longstanding local and regional initiatives in the region (Abi-Mershed 2010). For example, Tamari (2010) has shown that there are strong educational and cultural continuities between pre-Ottoman and Ottoman Syria. It is of note that the production of knowledge and schools in the Arab region has a long history long predating modernity and the nation-state.

Throughout the nineteenth and twentieth centuries, in the context of colonialism, Arab educational reformers worked to develop national educational systems (Abi-Mershed 2010). Yet colonial rulers used education as a means of rule, introducing European schools and universities in the region. Some of these competing traditions continue to exist today in postcolonial states (Sbaiti 2010), where for example, the use of language and educational policies are used to construct certain visions of identity and citizenship. Schools and higher educational institutions in the region can be conceived of as sites of 'intersections' between Western (colonial/neo-colonial/post-colonial) national sociopolitical particularities and discourses on citizenship in the Arab world. For example, there is a sizable literature on the American University of Beirut (AUB), in Lebanon, including examinations of early cultural encounters between American Protestant missionaries and the Levant (Khalaf 2012), AUB's role in Arab nationalism (Anderson 2011), student politics (Rabah 2009), and accounts of women as citizens and learners in early twentieth century Beirut (Cortas 2009; Makdisi 2006).

Another theme relates to contestation of education as a nation-state bounded project. There is a literature that considers supranational initiatives, as well as for example, how 'quasi-state institutions' such as the Palestinian Authority (PA) deal with notions of citizenship through education policy. The position of Palestinian and Syrian refugees across the Arab world, notably in Lebanon and Jordan, raises interesting dilemmas about 'educating for citizenship' in the absence of any such legal status, nor with any foreseeable route to legal citizenship in these host countries. For example, Fincham (2013) has examined constructions of citizenship for Palestinian youth living in the refugee camps in Southern Lebanon, where she highlights how Palestinians are typically educated in United Nations Relief and Works Agency (UNRWA) schools through the Lebanese curriculum, yet they are invisible in this curriculum. However, through the hidden curriculum, Palestinian identity is constructed through symbols such as maps and flags, as well as rituals, clothing and school activities. I have argued that such examples illustrate Pykett's (2010) arguments about the pedagogical state, where educational spaces and interpersonal relationships challenge assumed pedagogical control of a given state curriculum (Kiwan 2013a).

CONTEMPORARY SOCIAL, POLITICAL AND CULTURAL CONTEXT

In the context of the Arab uprisings since 2011, the Arab region is grappling with contestations over citizenship. Events in the region were triggered when a street trader in Tunisia set fire to himself in protest against police confiscating his unlicensed cart in December 2010. This was followed by civil society street demonstrations, culminating in the removal of the President from Office in January 2011. Revolts subsequently erupted in Egypt, centred around Cairo's Tahrir Square, and also around the country. Protestors called for the resignation of President Mubarak, and he resigned in February 2011. Protests against Libya's Ghaddafi broke out, and by September 2011, Ghaddafi's regime had fallen and he was killed in October 2011 (Kiwan 2014a). In the Arab Gulf monarchies, protests have been limited except for Bahrain, with its Shia population. Whilst there have been protests in Morocco, Algeria and Jordan, these regimes have remained in place. In Syria, protests were initially modest calls for reform, but subsequently escalated into a civil war by July 2012 and has been ongoing since then. The conflict has become increasingly centred in terms of a battle against the Islamic State (IS, also known regionally as 'Daesh') (Kiwan 2015). This radical Islamist group has declared a caliphate across parts of Syria and Iraq, with wider regional intentions. The USA and its Western allies have been engaged in an aerial bombardment of Daesh. The Syrian conflict has resulted in what has been described as one of the "largest refugee exoduses in recent history with no end in sight" (UNHCR). In addition, millions are displaced within Syria, and 78% of registered refugees are women and children (UNHCR 2014). Yemen is also witnessing violent conflict, with President Salah resigning in 2011, and since 2014 it has descended into civil war, when Houthi Shia rebels took over the capital; this led to Saudi-led airstrikes, concerned with rising Shia power in neighbouring Yemen.

A significant feature of demography in the region is that over 40% of the population is under the age of 18 (Faour and Muasher 2012). Whilst it has not only been the youth having a significant presence on the streets throughout the uprisings, arguably youth are playing a significant leadership role in contesting traditional notions of citizenship (Kiwan 2015). This can be seen in various forms, including street protests, artistic representations and graffiti, social media and other forms of cultural expression. As in the West, public discourses and governmental policies tend to construct youth in terms of 'deficit' or as 'dangerous' (Mulderig 2013). Western governments, the EU and international organisations play a significant role in promoting youth civic participation in the Arab world, increasingly since 9/11. Yet these initiatives have been critiqued for promoting a 'depoliticised' and decontextualised citizenship (Staeheli and Nagel 2013).

It has also been argued that there are high levels of youth alienation and despair given the poor educational opportunities and high levels of unemployment. Youth unemployment is the highest in the world (on average, 25%) (IMF 2012), and commentaries on the wave of revolts in the region have been framed in terms of the 'explosive' combination of severe economic conditions under authoritarian regimes, where people have suffered from high unemployment, poor quality of life and denial of political and civil rights (Teti and Gervasio 2011). Not only is there high unemployment, but education does not meet the needs of the economy, to which political instability is in part attributed (Campante and Chor 2013). Whilst there has been public investment in education, in those countries that do not provide for labour market opportunities, we have witnessed political instability (e.g. Egypt, Tunisia, Yemen, Libya, Jordan and Morocco), in contrast to the more stable Arab Gulf countries of the UAE, Kuwait and Qatar with their strong economies (Campante and Chor 2013). In addition, those educated to degree level have higher levels of unemployment in Morocco and Jordan (Bourdarbat and Aziz 2007; European Training Foundation 2005). The educated who are unsuccessful in the labour market are more likely to protest (Kiwan 2014a).

There is also evidence of the political mobilization of youth in Islamist movements in the region (Kiwan 2015). For example, a study on religious fundamentalism in Egyptian and Saudi youth found those aged 18–25 showing higher levels of fundamentalism (Moaddel et al. 2008). Yet at the same time, given the influences of globalization and information technologies of social media, youth are subject to global influences, reformulating their identities beyond traditional nation-state boundaries (Yamani 2011).

The position of women in the region has also been the subject of commentary, given women's significant presence and indeed leadership role in the uprisings across the region, and involvement in cultural activism (Kiwan 2015). However, this civic participation has not translated into holding power in the formal political participation; indeed, the participation of women in formal politics has regressed, for example, in Egypt (Kiwan 2015). In addition, there has been an increase in human rights violations against women, and it has been argued that the Arab uprisings merely highlight women's ongoing "second-class citizenship" status (Al-Malki 2013). Despite this pessimistic appraisal, women and youth can be said to be acting politically challenging and renegotiating conceptions of citizenship and civil society (Kiwan 2015).

Key Features of the Current Education System Within Particular Locations

The educational domain—both formal and informal—is a key site for sociopolitical transformation in the context of the Arab uprisings across the region. As previously noted, this is particularly significant given the demographic that over 40% of the population in the region is under the age of eighteen (Faour and Muasher 2012). Whilst the region has made progress in primary and secondary education attendance rates, it lags behind most of the world: according to the UN Human Development Index, Libyan students have an average of 7.3 years of schooling, Tunisia, 6.5 years, Egypt, 6.4 years, Syria, 5.7 years and Yemen only 2.5 years (UNESCO 2011). Over six million primary school-aged children—mostly girls do not attend school. With regard to higher education in the Arab world, there has been significant growth in the post world war II era. In 1939, there were a total of 10 universities in the Arab world, increasing to 20 universities in 1961, 47 universities in 1975, and over 200 (Herrera 2007) universities in 2000. This 'massification' (as well as privatization) in higher education—a world-wide trend is evident in the Arab world, with 398 universities in the Arab world by 2011 (Jaramillo and Melonio 2011). Enrollment in post-secondary education is 21%—below the world average of 26%, but is increasing, with the majority enrolled in humanities and social sciences. There is also increased participation of women. However, those with higher income levels have greater access to HE. In addition, there is a mismatch between education and the needs of the marketplace, with youth unemployment rates at 25% across the region, and university graduates making up nearly 30% of the unemployed (IMF 2012).

The growing presence of refugee populations in the Arab world—also predominantly young populations—has important implications, both in terms of the practicalities of the provision of education, and also with regard to understanding citizenship through the curriculum, both formally and informally. In Lebanon, education is considered to be critically important in addressing sectarian division and promoting social cohesion and a common sense of identity (Shuayb 2012). This is in addition to the long-term Palestinian refugee population, which for several generations has lived as stateless refugees with curtailed civic, political, economic and social rights. Typically educated in United Nations Relief and Works Agency (UNRWA) schools through the Lebanese curriculum, Palestinians are invisible in the curriculum, in a context where they cannot achieve integration or equal rights as attaining Lebanese citizenship is for the most part unattainable (Fincham 2013). So, for Syrian refugees, humanitarian provision is through UNHCR, whilst for Syrian Palestinians, provision comes under the auspices of UNRWA. It is estimated that Lebanon has over 1.5 million Syrian refugees. Syrian families deeply value education, and before 2011, 93% of children in Syria were in primary education, and 67% in secondary education; in 2013 90% of Syrian children between 6 and 17 are estimated to be out of school (Ackerman 2013). Over 3,000 schools have been damaged or destroyed since 2011 (ibid., 2013). For Syrian refugee children in Lebanon, it is estimated that only 12% are in school (Watkins 2013), and they face social problems such as bullying and discrimination and post-traumatic stress, practical costs such as the cost of transportation to school, as well educational problems including accessing a curriculum being taught in a different language (French or English as opposed to Arabic), leading to high dropout rates (ibid., 2013). In addition, Lebanon's already overstretched educational system is struggling to cope, and the international humanitarian response has neglected to sufficiently support education.

Faour and Muasher (2012) have conducted research published by the Carnegie Middle East Center highlighting that school ethos across the Arab world is perceived in negative terms, with students reporting that they do not feel physically, socially or emotionally safe. With regard to teachers, salaries are typically very low, which leads to a market of private tuition for those who can afford to pay. In addition, teachers are not sufficiently trained, and there are limited resources, with pedagogical approaches tending to be didactic with a reliance on rote memorization, and a lack of focus on analytical and creative thinking, essential to higher level thinking and learning (ibid., 2012).

There has been an interest in citizenship education in the Middle East, as in other regions of the world, in particular in the last 10 years. Both policymakers and academics have highlighted the need for civic education in the region, underpinned by the development of more transformative and democratic pedagogies (Faour 2012; Faour and Muasher 2012; Kiwan 2014a; UNDP 2008a, b). However, there have been concerns that such a vision will not be implementable in a context where Islamists aim to reform education so as to include more Islamic content in schooling (Faour 2011). In the informal educational domain, civil society in the region has been characterised generally as weak and dependent on relationships with existing donors or regimes, and having weak internal governance structures, accountability or transparency (Halaseh 2012). Philanthropic support for civic change and transnational philanthropy has become a growing trend since the Arab uprisings in the region (Kiwan et al. 2014b). Initiatives focusing on youth and women are significant areas of funding, especially by international organisations, as well as in partnerships with local NGOs. Philanthropy for the education of refugees is primarily through UNRWA with education being its largest budget domain (UNRWA 2013).

Whilst traditional school environments in the Arab world might be interpreted as reflecting a notion of schooling as an extension of governmental control, the active participation of young people in the Arab uprisings across the region has illustrated that, despite negative research findings on civic education in formal school settings, there is strong civic motivation and agency for change (Kiwan 2014a). In the digital age of social media, learning global citizenship has particular pertinence, evident in the commentaries of the role of social media in the Arab uprising. In the Egyptian context, Herrara (2012) asserts that Egyptian youth are learning citizenship in new ways. Internet use has rapidly increased in Egypt from only 300,00 users in 2000–2021 million users in March 2011, with the under 35 year olds using the internet at far higher rates (ibid., 2012). In commentaries on the Arab uprising, terms such as 'Facebook revolution', 'Twitter Revolution' attest to the utilization of these technologies in these movements, and Egyptian youth are learning citizenship in more informal 'horizontal' ways, with blogging and youth citizenship journalism. In addition, with the launch of high profile initiatives such as the UNESCO (2015) *Global Citizenship Education: Topics and Learning Objectives*, there is now an international focus on global citizenship education, with increased opportunities to access resources for nation-states to develop their education systems—including curricula and teacher-training and continued professional development, as well as opportunities for developing partnerships between the formal and non-formal educational sectors in this domain. One of the stated policy aims of GCED is to better prepare learners and equip them with the skills they need in the workplace and their communities in a globalised world, of particular relevance in the Arab region with its high youth unemployment rates. In addition, it provides an opportunity to develop more transformational pedagogic approaches to learning. However, the relevance of framing citizenship education in global terms has been questioned by some in the region, with one argument put forth that, many countries in the region need to attend to their more pressing local and national issues first and foremost. There may also be concerns that global citizenship is a form of imperialism, threatening local, national or regional alliances. UNESCO's GCED initiatives has attempted to address these concerns by avoiding a precise definition of global citizenship education, but rather emphasising its complexity, and raising awareness about the interconnectedness of multiple levels of citizenship.

WHAT PARTICULAR STRATEGIES (CURRICULAR AND OTHER) ARE USED FOR EDUCATING ABOUT AND FOR GLOBAL CITIZENSHIP

Whilst there is an increased recognition of the importance of educating for citizenship in the Arab world, this is an emerging domain of policy and practice in both the formal and non-formal education settings. There is a longer tradition of more traditional forms of civic education, typically of low status in schools, and predominantly framed in national and patriotic terms, and delivered didactically, with little opportunity for democratic engagement or discussion of contemporary or controversial issues. In addition, international and Western initiatives framed in terms of democracy promotion have funded local NGOs working on youth projects and women's empowerment in the region. This is premised on the assumption that funding local NGOs to pressure their governments for reform will result in political transformation across the region. In this conception, civil society is seen as the 'magic bullet against Arab autocracy' (Yom 2005, p. 16). This has been critiqued has lacking clarity in terms of understanding the processes of social change, as well as a lack of clarity as to what constitutes civil society, and whether it is definitionally secular. Yom (2005) argues that there is no empirical evidence of a link between international funding for democracy promotion and democratization, and that paradoxically it can result in increased political control in the aid-receiving country. In addition, the impact of aid may be limited as it can tend to reflect donor priorities rather than priorities in the country receiving the aid (Altan-Oltay and Icduygu 2012).

Across the Arab world, there has been a significant increase in the number of civil society organisations in the last 20 years. For example, in Egypt, there are 14,000 registered associations, although many are not active. In Lebanon, there are about 6000 CSOs, although similarly, not all are active (Altan-Olcay and Icduygu 2012). With regard to CSOs in Egypt, the state's control over the public sphere has affected whether CSOs can function. In Lebanon, given the fragility of the state and its highly sectarian nature, CSOs take over the role of the state's declining welfare provision, and CSOs also reflect these sectarian divisions. Others have critiqued the work of NGOs as having become highly bureaucratised—what Jad (2011) has described as the 'NGO-isation of civil society'. Jad (2011) characterises the Palestinian women's movement now as having fragmented into two main groups—the Islamist women's movement, and a secular, donor-driven, professionalization and NGO-ised movement. She raises the issue of the difficulties of what civil society can achieve in the context of political instability and a quasi-state.

According to Bayat (2013), activism in the region since the 1980s has taken the form predominantly of party politics, underground Islamic organizations, student politics on university campuses, labourers striking and the middle classes being engaged in NGO work. He asserts that the majority of the poor, women and youth resorted to what he calls 'non-movements'—practices to maximise their life chances, taking on some degree of coordination, for example, in Egypt, the poor protesting against the high cost of bread, Cairo's garbage collectors striking in 2009 leaving piles of rubbish in the streets and youth becoming increasingly involved in civic activism and voluntary work. Bayat suggests that when social media as a tool became accessible to Arab youth, they began to connect and mobilise in protests. For academics and policy analysts viewing events in the Arab world through the frame of the resilience of the authoritarian state and the static nature of Arab culture, these protest actions of ordinary people did not seem a likely source of change, but rather just a series of unconnected protests (Bayat 2013).

In the remainder of this section, I highlight a few examples of educating for global citizenship in the region, including international and local initiatives. The British Council's Connecting Classrooms is one such initiative that connects learners online in different parts of the world, with the rationale of providing the opportunity to learn about another part of the world and develop skills of global citizenship, including social media expertise. One example is a partnership between a primary school in Beirut, Lebanon and a primary school in Lincolnshire, England. The school in Beirut had a sizeable population of Syrian refugees: (https://schoolsonline.britishcouncil.org/linking-programmes-worldwide/connecting-classrooms/spotlight/Lebanon).

Another international initiative of importance is the International Civic and Citizenship Education Study (ICCS), administered by the International Association for the Evaluation of Educational Achievement (IEA) (http://iccs.iea.nl/). This is an evaluation initiative in the area of civic education dating back to the 1970s covering many countries from around the world, including some countries from the Arab region. It gathers data on learners' knowledge, attitudes and behaviours relating to civics and citizenship.

In Lebanon, the National Strategy for Citizenship and Coexistence was developed by the Lebanese NGO, the Adyan Foundation, in conjunction with the Lebanese Ministry of Education. It aims to reform Lebanese education policies to promote coexistence in a framework of inclusive citizenship. However, this is predominantly a national framing, given the rationale that countries in the region have not sufficiently implemented democratic processes, which are a prerequisite for the success of global models of citizenship education. In addition, given threats of extremism, for example, ISIS, it has been argued that it is important for issues to be relative more skewed with emphasis to the national than the global.

A regional initiative called the Middle East Network on Innovative Teaching and Learning (MENIT) was launched in March 2011 on behalf of the

German Federal Ministry for Economic Cooperation (GIZ). (https://twitter.com/menitnetwork). This regional platform of more than 300 experts and practitioners of innovation and education with GIZ covers Palestine, Jordan, Syrian and Lebanon. It aims to facilitate regional educational dialogue and exchange of good practice, as well as the implementation of joint research projects. MENIT is a member of the Arab Campaign for Education for All and The regional Initiative to Promote Adult Education.

Another example comes from Tunisia, where in 2000, a competency-based approach was introduced into the curriculum, including a focus on developing competency with ICT. Tunisia has also established human rights and citizenship school-clubs in primary and secondary schools in an initiative between the government, the Arab Institute for human Rights, local NGOs and UN agencies. The focus was to link with the local community and to develop skills using participatory pedagogies. In collaboration with international and local partners, the civic education curriculum is being revised in Tunisia, Egypt and Morocco to include issues such as gender equality and sustainable development (Union for the Mediterranean 2014), in collaboration also with local NGOs in the three countries.

A final example is a newly emerging initiative—the Arab Peace Corps—an initiative of the New Arab Foundation. This foundation is a think tank serving the Arab region and the diaspora, and in particular responding to the challenges facing the region in the twenty-first century, with areas of interest being in education, health, technology and science, business, governance and political institutions, peace building and sustainable development. In the context of the challenges of conflict and extremism, the vision of the Arab Peace Corps is to provide opportunities to youth in the region, vulnerable and susceptible to being mobilised by extremists. The foundation intends to recruit college graduates from the Arab region as well as with communities in Europe to serve for 1–2 years helping to contribute to community building in the region, drawing on the model of the US Peace Corps.

LIKELY AND DESIRABLE FUTURES

Since late 2010, we have witnessed uprisings throughout the region, raising important academic and policy debates pertaining to the meaning of 'citizenship' in the Arab world. Ordinary people across the region are challenging and renegotiating constructions of citizenship in terms of its effects on their daily lives. In a globalised world, there is a growing recognition of the intersectional and multiple layers of citizenship—from the local and national, to the regional and indeed global. Examining citizenship in the different nation-state contexts in the Arab world also challenges methodological assumptions of the translatability of language and concepts in the domain of citizenship (Kiwan 2013b), and assumptions of democracy presuming secularization and liberalism (Roy 2012). Post-colonial critiques challenge the production of knowledge where Western discourses are presented as universal theories, and so the study of citizenship and its contestations and negotiations in this region will contribute to our understandings of citizenship more fully.

Of particular relevance to educating for global citizenship is the consideration of the kinds of discursive spaces that have been developing across the region. The role of social media has been widely commented on in relation to the Arab uprisings, and examining constructions of citizenship in both formal and non-formal educational settings, and their partnerships will be an important academic and policy agenda. Informal modes of citizenship learning, including the family, youth organizations, the mosque, women's organizations and social media all play an important role. In terms of practically implementing global citizenship education in the region, change will need to be incremental and build on existing curricula and initiatives. In addition, teacher-training opportunities and allocating the resources for this will be an important area of focus to equip teachers to use more participatory pedagogies necessary for embedding the transformative potentials of global citizenship education. Given the high international priority given to GCED, resources are likely to be more accessible as well as raising the status of a domain in education that has tended to hold relatively lower status, and considered less important in an educational system geared towards preparing students to pass examinations in high status subjects like maths and science.

Note

1. Dina Kiwan, American University of Beirut and Mark Evans, University of Toronto were commissioned as lead authors of this publication.

References

Abi-Mershed, O. (ed). (2010). *Trajectories of education in the Arab World: legacies and challenges.* London and New York: Routledge, published in association with contemporary Arab Studies, Georgetown University.

Ackerman, X. (2013). *Responding to Syria's education crisis: Critical points for the international community.* http://www.brookings.edu/blogs/education-plus-development/posts/2013/10/24-syria-education-crisis-ackerman. Accessed March 9, 2014.

Al-Malki, A. (2013). Why Arab Women still 'have no voice. *Aljazeera*, April 21, 2012. http://www.aljazeera.com/programmes/talktojazeera/2012/04/201242111373249723.html. Accessed May 28, 2013.

Altan-Olcay, A., & Icduygu, O. (2012). Mapping civil society in the Middle East: The cases of Egypt, Lebanon and Turkey. *British Journal of Middle East Studies, 39*(2), 157–179.

Anderson, B. (2011). *The American University of Beirut: Arab nationalism and Liberal Education.* Austin, Texas, USA: University of Texas Press.

Bayat, A. (2013). The Arab Spring and its surprises. *Development and Change, 44*(3), 587–601.

Boudarbat, B., & Aziz, A. (2007). *Youth exclusion in Morocco: context, consequences, and policies.* Wolfensohn Center for Development Middle East Youth Initiative

Working Paper Series No. 5. Wolfensohn Center for Development/Dubai School of Government, Washington, DC, cited in Mulderig, *Adulthood Denied*.

Campante, F. R., & Chor, D. (2013). The educated middle class, their economic prospects, and the Arab Spring. *The World Financial Review*. Available online at: https://www.worldfinancialreview.com/?p=2296. Accessed February 4, 2013.

Cortas, W. M. (2009). *A World I loved: The story of an Arab woman*. New York, USA: Nation Books.

European Training Foundation. (2005). *Unemployment in Jordan Pilot Study*. European Training Foundation (ETF), Torino (2005), cited in M. Chloe Mulderig, Adulthood Denied.

Faour, M. (2011). Will the Arab Spring lead to a revolution in education? *Foreign Policy*. Available online at: https://mideast.foreignpolicy.com/posts/2011/10/31/will_the_arab_spring_lead_to_a_revolution_in_education. Accessed February 4, 2013.

Faour, M. (2012). *Religious education and pluralism in Egypt and Tunisia*. Washington, D.C: Carnegie Endowment for International Peace.

Faour, M., & Muasher, M. (2012). *The Arab World's education report card: School climate and citizenship skills*. Washington, D.C: Carnegie Endowment for International Peace.

Fincham, K. (2013). Shifting youth identities and notions of 'citizenship' in the Palestinian Diaspora: The case of Lebanon. In D. Kiwan (Ed.), *Naturalisation policies, education and citizenship: Multicultural and multi-nation societies in international perspective*. London and New York: Palgrave Macmillan.

Halaseh, R. (2012). Civil society, youth and the Arab Spring. Chapter 13, pp. 254–73. Available online at: www.um.edu.mt/__data/assets/pdf_file/0012/150411/Chapter_13_-_Rama_Halaseh.pdf. Accessed February 4, 2013.

Herrera, L. (2007). Higher education in the Arab world. In J.J.F. Forest and P. Altbach (Eds.), *International Handbook of Higher Education* (pp. 409–421). Dordrecht: Springer.

Herrera, L. (2012). Youth and citizenship in the digital age: A view from Egypt. *Harvard Educational Review, 82*(3), 333–352.

IMF. (2012). Youth unemployment in the MENA Region: Determinants and challenges. Available online at: https://www.imf.org/external/np/vc/2012/061312.htm. Accessed May 30, 2013.

Jad, I. (2011). The post-Oslo Palestine and gendering Palestinian citizenship. *Ethnicities, 11*(3), 360–372.

Jaramillo, A., & Melonio, T. (2011). *Breaking even or breaking through: Reaching financial sustainability while providing high quality standards in Higher Education in the Middle East and North Africa*. Washington, D.C.: World Bank.

Khalaf, S. (2012). *Protestant missionaries in the levant: Ungodly Puritans 1820–60*. Abingdon, Oxon and New York, USA: Routledge.

Kiwan, D. (2013a). Introduction. In D. Kiwan (Ed.), *Naturalisation policies, education and citizenship: Multicultural and multi-nation societies in international perspective*. London and New York: Palgrave Macmillan.

Kiwan, D. (2013b). Conclusion. In D. Kiwan (Ed.), *Naturalisation policies, education and citizenship: Multicultural and multi-nation societies in international perspective*. London and New York: Palgrave Macmillan.

Kiwan, D. (2014a). Emerging forms of citizenship in the Arab world. In E. Isin, & P. Nyers (Eds.), *Routledge global handbook of citizenship studies* (pp. 307–316). London: Routledge.

Kiwan, D., Marshall, D., Staeheli, L., & Jalbout, M. (2014b). Education for inclusive citizenship in Lebanon: A mapping of Arab philanthropy. *Takaful 2014.* Conference, Beirut, Lebanon.

Kiwan, D. (2015). Contesting citizenship in the Arab revolutions: Youth, women and refugees. *Democracy and Security, 11*(2), 129–144.

Makdisi, J. S. (2006). *Beirut fragments: A war memoir.* New York, USA: Persea Books Inc.

Moaddel, M., & Karabenick, S. A. (2008). Religious Fundamentalism among Young. Muslims in Egypt and Saudi Arabia. *Social Forces, 86*(4), 1675–1710.

Mulderig, M. C. (2013). *Adulthood denied: Youth dissatisfaction and the Arab Spring.* Boston University: The Frederick S. Pardee Center for the Study of the Longer Range future. Available online at www.bu.edu/pardee/files/2011/10/21-IIB.pdf. Accessed February 4, 2013).

Pykett, J. (2010). Citizenship education and narratives of pedagogy. *Citizenship Studies, 14*(6), 621–635.

Rabah, M. (2009). *A campus at War: Student politics 1967–1975.* Beirut, Lebanon: Dar Nelson.

Roy, O. (2012). The transformation of the Arab World. *Journal of Democracy, 23*(3), 5–18.

Sbaiti, N. (2010). If the Devil taught French: Strategies of language learning in French mandate Beirut. In O. Abi-Mershed (Ed.), *Trajectories of education in the Arab World: Legacies and challenges.* London and New York: Routledge. (published in association with contemporary Arab Studies, Georgetown University).

Shuayb, M. (Ed.). (2012). *Rethinking education for social cohesion: International case studies.* Basingstoke: Palgrave Macmillan.

Staeheli, L., & Nagel, C. R. (2013). Whose awakening is it? Youth and the geopolitics of civic engagement in the 'Arab Awakening'. *European Urban and Regional Studies, 20*(1), 115–119.

Tamari, S. (2010). Between the "golden age" and the Renaissance: Education in eighteenth-century Damascus. In O. Abi-Mershed (Ed.), *Trajectories of education in the Arab World: legacies and challenges.* London and New York: Routledge. (published in association with contemporary Arab Studies, Georgetown University).

Teti, A., & Gervasio, G. (2011). The unbearable lightness of authoritarianism: Lessons from the Arab uprisings. *Mediterranean Politics, 16*(2), 321–327.

UNDP. (2008a). *Towards a citizen state.* Beirut: UNDP.

UNDP. (2008b). *Education and citizenship: Concepts attitudes, skills and actions: Analysis of survey results of 9th grade students in Lebanon.* Beirut: UNDP.

UNESCO. (2011). *Human development data for the Arab States. Expected years if schooling (of children) (years).* Accessed June 11, 2015. http://www.arab-hdr.org/data/indicators/2012–20.aspx.

UNESCO. (2015). *Global citizenship education: Topics and learning objectives.* Paris: UNESCO.

UNHCR. (2014). *Syria regional response plan: Strategic overview.* http://www.unhcr.org/syriarrp6/docs/Syria-rrp6-full-report.pdf. Accessed January 31, 2014.

Union for the Mediterranean. (2014). *Four new regional projects are labeled by the Union for the Mediterranean.* Accessed June 19. http://ufmsecretariat.org/four-new-regional-projects-are-labelled-by-the-union-for-the-mediterranean/.

UNRWA. (2013). *UNRWA in Figures.* http://www.unrwa.org/sites/default/files/unrwa_in_figures_new2014_10nov2014.pdf.

Watkins, K. (2013). *Education without borders: A summary.* Accessed March 9, 2014. http://s.bsd.net/awas/default/page/-/EducationWithoutBorders_KevinWatkins_Report.pdf.

Yamani, M. (2011). Saudi youth: Initiative and inertia. In S. Khalaf & R. S. Khalaf (Eds.), *Arab youth: Social mobilization in times of risk.* London: Saqi Books.

Yom, S. L. (2005). Civil society and democratization in the Arab World. *Middle East Review of International Affairs, 9*(4), 14–33.

AUTHOR BIOGRAPHY

Dina Kiwan is a Reader in Comparative education, School of Education, University of Birmingham UK, and formerly Associate Professor in the Department of Sociology, Anthropology and Media Studies, at the American University of Beirut, since September 2012. Educated at the universities of Oxford, Harvard and London in psychology, sociology and education, her research program focuses on citizenship and civil society, which is interdisciplinary and international extending across the domains of education, gender, human rights, immigration and naturalization. Publications include Kiwan (2008). *Education for Inclusive Citizenship* (Routledge), and Kiwan, D. (ed). (2013) *Naturalization Policies, Education and Citizenship: Multicultural and Multination Societies in International Perspective* (Palgrave Macmillan).

CHAPTER 4

Global Citizenship Education in North America

Carla L. Peck and Karen Pashby

INTRODUCTION

According to Pashby (2016), "Global citizenship education generally extends the idea of rights and responsibilities beyond the limits of the nation-state. It can be understood in a variety of ways and reflects different ideologies and ideas of what is and ought to be desired of citizens" (p. 70). She draws on Andreotti (2010a) who argues that it is important to recognize how a term such as global citizenship is: (a) *situated* in one context (culture, time period, geographical location, political climate); (b) *partial* in that different people will see it differently; (c) *contingent* because the context determines how it is used and understood; and (d) *provisional* based on the fact that the understanding and application of the concept perpetually changes (p. 236). The discursive aspect of GCE has been the focus of some important critiques.

Scholars have pointed to the way that GCE comprises a discursive field wherein critical analyses of citizenship, education, and globalization interact and mediate one another (e.g., Camicia and Franklin 2011). There is a very complex field of languages and processes existing in institutions and activities that relate to both globalization and citizenship, and when we begin to talk about GCE, we are "thrown into" this "complex inherited field" (Tully

C.L. Peck
Department of Elementary Education, University of Alberta, 551 Education South Tower, 11210-87 Avenue, Edmonton, AB T6G 265, Canada
e-mail: carla.peck@ualberta.ca

K. Pashby (✉)
Childhood, Youth and Education Studies, Manchester Metropolitan University, 1.43 Brooks Building, Manchester M15 6GX, UK
e-mail: k.pashby@mmu.ac.uk

© The Author(s) 2018   51
I. Davies et al. (eds.), *The Palgrave Handbook of Global Citizenship and Education*, https://doi.org/10.1057/978-1-137-59733-5_4

2008, p. 15). This includes how articulating what is going wrong in the world and in education and what actions should be taken to rectify these problems is at least in part "structured in ongoing processes of hegemony" (Steinberg 1999, 748). By adding questions about education to this matrix, GCE scholars take the broader questions about what is going wrong in the world and what should be done about it (diagnoses and prognoses) and apply them to questions of educational policy, curriculum, and pedagogy. Perhaps Mannion et al. (2011) say it best: GCE serves as "a floating signifier that different discourses attempt to cover with meaning....[and converge] within this new nexus of intentions" (p. 444). Importantly, this discursive field is also framed by wider dominant discourses and hegemonic notions of who defines what a global problem or global citizen is (Pashby 2011). Thus, in order to consider global education trends in North America, it is important to recognize the ways global education and global citizenship education function as discursive fields across contexts.

Social, Political, and Cultural Contexts

Global citizenship education has emerged as popular discourse directing education initiatives around the world as a result of the inevitable diversities that exist in all societies. In what follows below, we explore the particular contexts for global citizenship education in Canada, the USA, and Mexico. The rise of populism and neoliberalism is clearly a significant factor in all three countries. In addition, the challenges of identifying the centers and peripheries of power, policy-making and professional practice are made clear in these varied contexts.

Canada

With a population of approximately 35 million people, Canada is a highly diverse nation. Widely acknowledged as a multi-national state, the country has had deep diversity and the presence of many nations since before it became, officially, a country. National minorities (Kymlicka 1998) include Francophone Québécois and First Nations, Métis, and Inuit (FMNI) peoples, whose unique status as "nations within" with distinct rights have been recognized by law. Kymlicka (2003) argues that Canada is distinct among Western nations with regard to addressing its complex diversity and "the extent to which it has not only legislated but also *constitutionalized*, practices of accommodation" (p. 374, original emphasis). In addition to these national minorities, the population includes over 200 ethnic origins (Statistics Canada 2006). With strong levels of immigration from Asia, Africa, Caribbean, Central and South Asia as well as South American and the Middle East, the visible minority population is growing quickly. Contemporary factors related to globalization, including changing patterns of migration and citizenship, have created "a growing awareness of the multiethnic nature of most contemporary nation-states and the need to account for this aspect of pluralism in public policy" (Johnson and Joshee 2007, p. 3).

Canada has a federal government, ten provinces, and three territories. Education falls under the jurisdictions of the provinces. However, national policy does have spillover influence as is the case with multiculturalism. Canada adopted an official policy of multiculturalism in the 1970s, and the policy became law in 1988, requiring government agencies, departments and state corporations to have plans, programs, and procedures to enable and promote the full participation of all ethnic minority groups. The *Charter of Rights and Freedoms* also includes the right to maintenance of one's cultural identity, among other protections.

United States

The USA is the dominant nation on the continent, with the highest population of the three countries (approximately 324 million) and the largest economy. Like Canada, the USA is a highly diverse nation. White Americans, Black Americans, and Latino/as are the three most prominent groups, making up (approximately) 64, 13, and 16% of the population, respectively (Humes et al. 2011). Whereas Canada's approach to multiculturalism has been to support the rights of people and groups to maintain their ethnocultural identity and customs through accommodation of difference, the USA has historically taken a "melting pot" approach where immigrants are expected to (and perhaps desire to) assimilate into American society and customs.

The USA is a constitutional federal republic comprised of 50 states and 1 district. The federal Department of Education provides funding to states to improve their standards and "under the current Every Student Succeeds policy, states are required to test students annually to receive federal dollars" (Hahn 2016, p. 127). There is no national curriculum; rather, states bear the responsibility for developing curricula. Due to both state and federal accountability pressures, curriculum narrowing has occurred across the country with states focusing more and more attention and curricular time on literacy and numeracy, resulting in the reduction or complete elimination of other subject areas, including social studies, the subject most closely connected to global citizenship education (Fitchett et al. 2014).

Mexico

Mexico has a population of just over 123 million people, with approximately a quarter of the population living in and around the capital, Mexico City (CIA 2017). The country is a federal presidential republic made up of 31 states, many of which are rural. The government does not collect census data on ethnicity, however we can gain some insight into the ethnocultural diversity by looking at language statistics: In 2012, the CIA World Factbook reports that approximately 93% of population speaks Spanish only, 6% speaks Spanish and indigenous languages, and less than 2% speak indigenous language(s) only or did not specify. Young people (aged 15 or under) make up approximately 30% of the population and less than 1% of the population is foreign-born (OECD 2017).

Education policy is governed at both the national level led by the Secretaría de Educación Pública (SEP) and the state level. While the SEP sets educational policy at the national level, there remains wide variation in terms of policies, programs, and funding from state to state. According to the OECD (2013), Mexico has the "highest proportion of students in the lower level of socioeconomic status (58%), which is clearly related to poverty rates" (p. 6). The country has implemented several policies aimed at aiding low-income families and encouraging education. Mexico has compulsory, state-funded education that begins with preschool (3–5-year-olds) and continues with 6 years of primary education and 3 years of lower secondary education. Upper secondary education was made compulsory in 2012; however, by 2013, only 56% of Mexicans aged 15–19 pursued upper secondary education (OECD 2013).

In addition to sharing a continent, the USA, Canada, and Mexico are connected economically and culturally. The North American Free Trade Agreement (NAFTA), which came into force in 1994, reduces or removes trade tariffs and on balance economists consider it to have had a positive effect on the economies of all three nations. However, the agreement is not without its critics; at the time of writing the newly elected President of the United States has vowed to renegotiate the agreement with the Mexican and Canadian governments. Canadian arts and culture is heavily influenced by the USA, and people can move easily across the Canadian–US border. While the same is true for the Americans crossing into Mexico, over the years the American government has expressed concerns over the number (or perceived number) of Mexicans who cross into the USA illegally. This continues to be a tension felt by both countries.

Historical Background of GCE

Because education is under the jurisdictions of provinces in Canada, the Multicultural Act itself neither mentions education nor schools (Galczynski et al. 2011). However, multiculturalism policy has had a strong influence on education. Despite differences in program and curriculum across the provinces, there are some general trends pointing to the influence of Canada's official policy on multiculturalism. In alignment with federal multicultural policy in the 1980s, education jurisdictions shifted focus from assimilation toward more explicit recognition of ethnic minorities and issues of racism. Since the 1990s, there has been a shift away from explicit attention to systemic issues of racism and discrimination toward character education and the development of interpersonal skills. However, there remain some important policies and programs promoting equity (Joshee 2007; Pashby 2013). An important recent development is the release of the report of the Truth and Reconciliation Commission which investigated the impact of the Indian Residential School system on First Nations, Métis, and Inuit (FNMI) persons who attended these schools (the last one closed in 1996). In response, educational jurisdictions across the country are revising curricula and implementing programs to increase awareness and knowledge of FMNI history and worldviews.

Similar to multiculturalism, global education in Canada has changed with historical, social, and political developments (Pashby 2013). Specifically, global education has reflected various perceptions of Canada's international role. Richardson (2008) has mapped out three early phases: (a) one focusing on membership in the British Empire and Commonwealth, (b) a second focused on UN involvement (particularly in peace-keeping) and relationship with the USA, and (c) third, a post-Cold War period with participation in various organizations and agreements (e.g., G8, NATO). Global education in Canada followed similar development to that of multicultural education through the 1970s–1990s with a strong focus on human rights. Richardson (2008) suggests that through these different phases, social studies curricula have increasingly included more broad and sophisticated understandings of one's identity in relation to communities (p. 54). However, Pashby (2008) argues that "in order for citizenship to provide a framework for a sense of belonging and loyalty to a 'global community,' it must be flexible enough to serve as an axis to the multiple and shifting identities and allegiances that characterize the current global moment" (p. 17).

Global citizenship themes began to appear in curricula in the US as early as the 1970s (Schattle 2008). In the early 1980s, Carole Hahn, then president of the National Council for the Social Studies, highlighted the need for US educators to attend to global citizenship concerns (Previte and Sheehan 2002). Primarily the domain of social studies education (including history, geography, political science, and economics), global citizenship education themes may also appear in other curricular areas such as language arts and music. However, given the heavy focus in US schools on literacy and numeracy as well as the accountability pressures noted earlier, opportunities to teach GCE vary widely by state. Schattle (2008) identifies several overlapping themes that GCE in the USA may emphasize including: the role of international organizations in promoting human rights, respect for ethnocultural diversity, world hunger and population studies, and environmental concerns, among others. However, because GCE is not a required curriculum nor does it "live" in any one curricular area, it is difficult to say to what extent these themes are taught in US schools.

Levinson (2005) traced the development of citizenship education in Mexico and noted that by the 1990s, after years of sustained violence and economic hardship, human rights and tolerance emerged as "crucial value[s]"

(p. 261) for Mexicans and these themes found their way into secondary school curricula. This emerges from a general concern to provide education for all through legislation in 1946, 1973 and the General Law of Education in 1993, which made primary and secondary education free and compulsory. Article 7 within the General Law of Education of 1993 insists on the promotion through education of many aspects of global citizenship education including justice, equity, and diversity. According to Araujo-Olivera and Gonçalves e Silva (2009), diversity is affirmed in Article 38 as well, particularly in terms of protection of the cultures and languages of Mexico's Indigenous peoples although the authors contend that the intent of Article 38 has not been fully realized.

The determination to act inclusively of course needs to be set within a broader context. Tatto et al. (2001) note that "in the mid-1990s as the country's agenda became dominated once more by globalisation concerns, the federal government added to a nationalistic focus an emphasis on hard work, competitiveness, productivity and 'international literacy'" (p. 178). Urbina Garcia (n.d.) has referenced the work of Díaz Barriga and Rigo (2000) to point to a context in which the demands of the labor market are recognized, and there have been modifications to the content of the curricula (e.g., in 2002), and that some government reforms have occurred in a context influenced by neoliberalism.

KEY FEATURES OF GLOBAL CITIZENSHIP EDUCATION

Across North America as in Europe, there has been a rise in theory and policy work regarding the inclusion of a global dimension in citizenship education in the past three decades. This has corresponded with work in political science at the turn of the twenty-first century regarding intersections of the discourses of globalization and citizenship and the promotion of the idea of global citizenship (e.g., Delanty 2000, 2006; Tully 2000). In Canada, there has been a focus in education on civic literacy and promoting active engagement in local-to-global issues. GCE is a discourse currently evident across ministries of education, school boards, teacher education institutions, and teacher organizations (Evans et al. 2009). For the most part, across the provinces, GCE is receiving increased attention, particularly in social studies curricula (Evans et al. 2009). Pashby (2008) notes that, "as an ideal, it [GCE] encourages students to adopt a critical understanding of globalization, to reflect on how they and their nation are implicated in local and global problems, and to engage in intercultural perspectives" (p. 23).

Despite a general promotion of global education broadly and GCE more specifically, there have been some concerns raised as to some general trends. These include: a piecemeal approach to global education divorced from critical literacy or active citizenship (Mundy and Manion 2008) and a tokenistic approach to global others reinforcing superficial treatments of Canada's "good fortune" coupled with one-off fundraising events (Taylor 2012). There is a general concern as to how much transformative or critical work is going on through global education in Canadian schools considering that there have been multiple decades of work and despite the continued efforts of some dedicated educators (Pike 2008). These trends are linked with the increasing dominance of neoliberal discourses of equity and diversity focusing less on systemic issues of inequities and more on economic rationales and individual development (Joshee 2007; Pashby et al. 2014). One example is in the province of Alberta, where global citizenship is a key concept in social studies from primary to secondary curricula, and recent curriculum redesign initiatives include "cultural and global citizenship" as one of eight key competencies students will develop from Kindergarten to Grade 12 and across all subject areas (Alberta Education 2016).

According to Tye (2014), in the USA "there has been no central source for global education since the American Forum for Global Education closed in 2003" (p. 857). Nevertheless, global education and global citizenship education programs and initiatives exist across the country in the form of school programs, university research centers, degrees and courses, and programs offered by NGOs. Noting a growing trend of US social studies curricula to attend more to global and international perspectives, Rapoport (2015) argues that "globalization has profoundly influenced the very notion of citizenship and citizenship education rationales by not only infusing a more distinct global perspective but also by challenging the core principles of citizenship as an idiosyncratically nation-state-related concept" (p. 121). However, although the "home" for GCE in K-12 education is often thought of in terms of social studies, Harshman (2015) contends that global citizenship education is "the responsibility of all teachers, regardless of their areas of expertise" (p. 5).

Merryfield et al. (2008) identify and explore five aspects of global education that contribute to students' "world mindedness" (p. 6):

- Knowledge of global interconnectedness
- Inquiry into global issues
- Skills and perspectives consciousness
- Open-mindedness, recognition of bias, stereotypes, and exotica
- Intercultural experiences and intercultural competence (p. 8)

These authors provide examples of how teachers can build students' capacity in these areas across a range of subject areas and using a wide array of teaching strategies. Focusing on geography education, Gaudelli and Heilman (2009) argue that any study of the world requires knowledge of geography and they "offer a typology of global education to identify those types most congruent with democratic citizenship, namely cosmopolitan, environmental, and critical justice, and those less congruent, such as disciplinary, neoliberal, and human relations global education" (p. 2651).

Rapaport's (2015) research with teachers in Indiana found that although the teachers stated that they rarely used the terms "global citizenship" or "global citizens" in their classes, this "did not prevent them from teaching global citizenship-related themes" in their courses (p. 126). After reviewing the range of discourses that have shaped understandings of GCE, Rapaport notes that the field is surprising lacking in empirical research that investigates the strength or relative merits of the theoretical and conceptual work that has dominated the field. He attributes this lack of research to the following factors: lack of conceptual clarity about what global citizenship means, curricular insecurity, and a traditionalist (i.e., state-centered) approach to citizenship education (pp. 123–124).

In Mexico, Tatto et al. (2001) note that "the new Mexican identity evolving as part of a global economy is more open and globally interactive, reflexive and bound by two equally powerful and often contradictory forces: modernity and tradition" (p. 184). Urbina Garcia (n.d.) argues that the General Law of Education of 1993 insists upon an approach that is both personal and social in which democratic knowledge and practices improve coexistence. He summarizes key sections of that Law as follows:

> it aims at strengthening national and sovereignty awareness, recognising national history and institutions as well as patriotic symbols valuing traditions and customs from different regions of the country (Article 7; LGE). This document, seeks to promote in students, an awareness of the linguistic diversity as well as respect for indigenous communities across the country. The educational system must promote the values of justice, equity, diversity, inclusion, non-discrimination, non-violence and respect for human rights as well as young people and children's rights. It also states that the criteria which guide the education provided by the government, which will be based on the scientific progress, fighting against ignorance, fanaticism, prejudice, stereotypes, discrimination and violence specially against children and women (Article 8; LGE).

This aligns with Tatto et al.'s (2001) research on the place of values education in Mexico. They argue that,

> values concerning *social/global responsibility* in Mexico are based on the assumption that the development of reflective and autonomous personalities among young people should be accompanied by values that include ideas about the need to combat social prejudice and promote greater tolerance for ethnic, language and racial groups, respect and opportunity for girls and women, promoting pride in local communities and community life, social justice and equity, promotion of world peace and the need to combat ecological abuse. Values having to do with social/global responsibility are directed at encouraging civic consciousness and strengthening democracy. (p. 184)

García (2014) raises an important caution, however. She notes that the economic and political contexts in Mexico, including its largely centralized education system, presents barriers to achieving the aspirations noted above and asks, "how could it be possible to develop competences for global citizenship, if the cultural contexts where they take place do not offer the conditions for their development?" (p. 166). Levinson (2010) raises an additional concern related to teacher preparation and maintains that the most significant challenge in terms of the (potential) effects of democratic citizenship education in schools is teachers "have largely failed to adopt new pedagogical styles and methods. They may be discussing aspects of democracy, but not modelling it" (p. 186). (See also García 2014).

Momentum Toward a Critical Approach to GCE: Engaging the Realities of the Twenty-first Century

Much work has already been done in regard to developing a critical approach to GCE that has the potential to influence curriculum and pedagogy in all three jurisdictions. Andreotti's (2006) seminal soft versus critical GCE framework has been highly influential and highlights the need to engage with difference and complicity and to work against ethnocentrism. It distinguishes 'soft GCE' as charity-work and 'helping others over there' from 'critical GCE' which helps provide a way of thinking about how we are all—differently—part of the problems the world faces and part of creating solutions. The framework is widely cited in recent GCE literature (e.g. Bamber and Hankin 2011; Bryan et al. 2009; Bourn 2009; Edge and Khamsi 2012; Eidoo et al. 2011; Marshall 2009; Martin 2013 among others). Andreotti's framework is a tool for reflection, and although it presents two sides and encourages educators and students toward the critical side, it must not be understood as a prescription for what is right or wrong. Rather, the tool helps teachers and students to develop a reflexive ethic that engages with difference, complexity and systemic inequities. It pushes us to recognize when we are assuming a universal view of the world that is actually reflecting our experience and our culture. However, while it might make us uncomfortable when we realize that we have been engaged in "soft" approaches, soft GCE is everywhere as it has been the dominant paradigm, so the idea is to engage ourselves and our students more critically in questions of global importance.

Emanating from the good intentions of individuals to "make a difference," to help those experiencing global problems, a soft approach to GCE can represent a first step in some contexts. It may help to raise awareness of global issues, for example. However, those approaching GCE from a critical view are concerned that educators cannot stop at a soft approach that can reinforce the same assumptions and ways of relating to difference that caused global inequities to develop and continue. Rather, a critical approach to GCE centered on the idea of critical ethical reflection promotes interrogating the "good intentions" that drive action. Rather than inadvertently reproducing colonial systems of power (Abdi 2008; Willinsky 1998), a critical approach asserts that an action taken to promote global justice must first be considered situated, and understood within the context of the actor and of the site for action. This includes being aware and anticipating any implications locally and globally (Andreotti 2006; see also Abdi and Shultz 2008; Andreotti 2010a, b; Bryan and Bracken 2011; Lapayese 2003). Similarly Jorgenson and Shultz (2012) differentiate between "mainstream" and "critical" approaches to GCE where the former involves working within current structures and the latter prioritizes education and action that prioritizes challenging structural barriers to equity and social justice.

Although conceptions of and approaches to global citizenship education vary across the three countries discussed in this chapter, some common themes emerge. First, GCE in all three countries suffers from a lack of a clear curricular home. In Canada, most provincial and territorial jurisdictions affirm the desirability of educating students to be global citizens however there is little consistency across the country in terms of curricular expectations. In the USA, Rapaport (2009) found that only 15 states' Social Studies standards contained the world "globalization" and only two states' standards include the words "global citizen" (pp. 98–102). In Mexico, the civics curricula focus on intercultural understanding, democratic citizenship, and human rights although it is not clear the extent to which these goals are achieved in schools. Second, in all three jurisdictions, there are calls to move away from what Andreotti (2006) calls "soft" GCE to more critical engagement with global issues and concerns. The focus here is on better understanding one's own complicity in the emergence of global problems as well as one's interconnectedness with other global actors. Such understandings open up opportunities to broaden one's perspectives and join global initiatives to act for change. Lastly, it is clear that more empirical research with teachers and students is needed to assess the usefulness of the wide range of frameworks for GCE that currently exist in the literature. While these frameworks provide a strong theoretical base on which current and future GCE programs are and can be based, more needs to be known about how they shape teachers' and students' ideas about global issues.

References

Abdi, Ali A. (2008). De-subjecting subject populations: Historico-actual problems and educational possibilities. In A. Abdi & L. Shultz (Eds.), *Educating for human rights and global citizenship* (pp. 65–80). Albany, NY: State University of New York Press.

Abdi, A., & Shultz, L. (2008). Educating for human rights and global citizenship: An introduction. In A. Abdi & L. Shultz (Eds.), *Educating for human rights and global citizenship* (pp. 1–10). Albany, NY: State University of New York Press.

AE (Alberta Education). (2016). *Competencies: Descriptions, indicators and examples.* Edmonton, Alberta: The Crown in Right of Alberta. Retrieved from: https://education.alberta.ca/media/3272998/competency-indicators-september-30-2016.pdf.

Andreotti, V. (2006). Soft versus critical global citizenship education. *Policy and Practice: A Development Education Review, 3,* 40–51.

Andreotti, V. (2010a). Global education in the 21st century: Two different perspectives on the 'post-' of postmodernism. *International Journal of Development Education and Global Learning, 2*(2), 5–22.

Andreotti, V. (2010b). Postcolonial and post-critical global citizenship education. In G. Elliott, C. Fourali, & S. Issler (Eds.), *Education & social change* (pp. 233–245). London, England: Continuum.

Araujo-Olivera, S. S. & Gonçalves e Silva, P. B. (2009). The education of ethnic minority groups in Mexico. In J. A. Banks (Ed.), The Routledge International Companion to Multicultural Education (pp. 540–553). New York, NY: Routledge.

Bamber, P., & Hankin, L. (2011). Transformative learning through service-learning: No passport required. *Education and Training, 53*(2/3), 190–206.

Bryan, A. (with M. Bracken) (2011). Learning to read the world?: Teaching and Learning about global citizenship and international development in post-primary schools. Dublin: Identikit. Available online: http://www.spd.dcu.ie/site/chrce/Publications.shtml.

Bryan, A., Clarke, M. & Drudy, S. (2009). Social justice education in initial teacher education: A cross border perspective, A report for the standing conference on teacher education north and south (SCoTENS). Available online: http://scotens.org/docs/2009-Social%20Justice%20Education%20in%20Initial%20Teacher%20Education.pdf.

Bourn, D. (2009). Students as global citizens. In E. Jones (Ed.), *Internationalisation: The Student Voice* (pp. 18–29). London: Routledge.

Delanty, G. (2000). *Citizenship in a global age: Society, culture, politics.* Philadelphia, PA: Open University Press.

Delanty, G. (2006). Nationalism and cosmopolitanism: The paradox of modernity. In G. Delanty & K. Kumar (Eds.), *The sage handbook of nations and nationalism* (pp. 357–368). Thousand Oaks, CA: Sage.

Díaz Barriga, F., & Rigo, M. (2000). Formación docente y educación basada en competencias. In M. A. Valle (Ed.), *Formación en competencias y certificación profesional* (pp. 76–104). México: Universidad Nacional Autónoma de México.

Edge, K., & Khamsi, K. (2012). International school partnership as a vehicle for global education: Student perspectives. *Asia Pacific Journal of Education, 32*(4), 455–472.

Eidoo, S., Ingram, L., MacDonald, A., Nabavi, M., Pashby, K., & Stille, S. (2011). "Through the kaleidoscope": Intersections between theoretical perspectives and classroom implications in critical global citizenship education. *Canadian Journal of Education, 34*(4), 59–84.

Evans, M., Ingram, L. A., Macdonald, A., & Weber, N. (2009). Mapping the "global dimension" of citizenship education in Canada: The complex interplay of theory, practice and context. *Citizenship Teaching and Learning, 5*(2), 17–34.

Fitchett, P. G., Heafner, T., & VanFossen, P. (2014). An analysis of time prioritization for social studies in elementary school classrooms. *Journal of Curriculum and Instruction, 8*(2), 7–35.

Galczynski, M., Tsagkaraki, V., & Ghosh, R. (2011). Unpacking multiculturalism in the classroom: Using current events to explore the politics of difference. *Canadian Ethnic Studies, 43*(3), 145–164.

García, A. M. (2014). Pedagogical training and culture for global citizenship: Reflections for its creation. *BCES Conference Proceedings, 12,* 165.

GEFI (Global Education First Initiative). (n.d.). Priority #3: Foster global citizenship. Website of the UN Secretary General's Global Initiative on Education. Retrieved from http://www.globaleducationfirst.org/220.htm.

Hahn, C. (2016). Pedagogy in citizenship education research: A comparative perspective. *Citizenship Teaching and Learning, 11*(2), 121–137.

Harshman, J. (2015). Introduction: Research in global citizenship education. In J. Harshman, T. Augustine, & M. Merryfield (Eds.), *Research in Global Citizenship Education* (pp. 1–8). Charlotte, NC: IAP.

Humes, K. R., Jones, N. A., & Ramirez, R. R. (2011, March). *Overview of Race and Hispanic Origin: 2010.* Washington, DC: United States Census Bureau. Retrieved from: https://www.census.gov/prod/cen2010/briefs/c2010br-02.pdf

Jorgenson, S., & Shultz, L. (2012). Global citizenship education (GCE) in post-secondary institutions: What is protected and what is hidden under the umbrella of GCE? *Journal of Global Citizenship & Equity Education, 2*(1), 1–22. Retrieved from http://journals.sfu.ca/jgcee/index.php/jgcee/article/viewArticle/52.

Joshee, R. (2007). Opportunities for social justice work: The Ontario diversity policyweb. *The Journal of Educational Administration and Foundations, 18*(1/2), 171–199.

Kymlicka, W. (1998). *Finding our way: Rethinking ethnocultural relations in Canada.* New York: Oxford University Press.

Kymlicka, W. (2003). Multicultural states and intercultural citizens. *Theory and Research in Education, 1*(2), 147–169.

Lapayese, Y. V. (2003). Toward a critical global citizenship education. *Comparative Education Review, 47*(4), 493–501.

Levinson, B. (2005). Programs for democratic citizenship in Mexico's Ministry of Education: Local appropriations of global cultural flows. *Indiana Journal of Global Legal Studies, 12*(1), 251–284.

Levinson, B. (2010). The State and the citizen in Mexican civic education: An evolving story. In A. Reid, J. Gill, & A. Sears (Eds.), *Globalization, the nation-state, and the citizen: Dilemmas and directions for civic and citizenship education* (pp. 175–190). London: Routledge.

Marshall, H. (2009). Educating the European citizen in the global age: Engaging with the postnational and identifying a research agenda. *Journal of Curriculum Studies, 41*(2), 247–267.

Martin, F. (2013). Same old story: The problem of object-based thinking as a basis for teaching distant places. *Education 3–13 41*(4), 410–424.

Merryfield, M. M., Lo, J. T. Y., Po, S. C., & Kasai, M. (2008). Worldmindedness: Taking off the blinders. *Journal of Curriculum & Instruction, 2*(1), 6–20.

Mundy, K., & Manion, C. (2008). Global education in canadian elementary schools: An exploratory study. *Canadian Journal of Education, 31*(4), 941–974.

OECD. (2013). Education policy outlook: Mexico. http://www.oecd.org/mexico/EDUCATION%20POLICY%20OUTLOOK%20MEXICO_EN.pdf.

OECD. (2017). Country statistical profile: Mexico: Key tables from OECD. http://dx.doi.org/10.1787/csp-mex-table-2017-2-en.

Pashby, K. (2008). Demands on and of citizenship and schooling: 'Belonging and 'Diversity" in the global imperative. In M. O'Sullivan & K. Pashby (Eds.), *Citizenship Education in an Era of Globalization* (pp. 9–26). Rotterdam: Sense.

Pashby, K. (2011). Cultivating global citizens: Planting new seeds or pruning the perennials? Looking for the citizen-subject in global citizenship education theory. *Globalisation, Societies, and Education, 9*(3–4), 427–442.

Pashby, K. (2013). *Related and conflated: A theoretical and discursive framing of multiculturalism and global citizenship education in the Canadian context* (Unpublished doctoral dissertation). University of Toronto, Canada. Available online: http://hdl.handle.net/1807/35921.

Pashby, K., Ingram, L., & Joshee, R. (2014). Discovering, recovering, and covering-up Canada: Tracing historical citizenship discourses in K–12 and adult immigrant citizenship education. *Canadian Journal of Education/Revue canadienne de l'éducation, 37*(2), 1–26.

Pashby, K. (2016). Global, citizenship, and education as discursive fields: Towards disrupting reproduction of colonial systems of power. In I. Langran & T. Birk (Eds.), *Globalization and global citizenship: Interdisciplinary approaches* (pp. 69–86). New York: Routledge.

Pike, G. (2008). Reconstructing the legend: Educating for global citizenship. In A. Abdi & L. Shultz (Eds.), *Educating for human rights and global citizenship* (pp. 223–237). Albany, NY: State University of New York Press.

Previte, M. A., & Sheehan, J. A. (Eds.). (2002). *The NCSS presidential addresses, 1970–2000: Perspectives on the Social Studies.* ERIC Clearinghouse for Social Studies/Social Science Education. Washington, DC: Office of Educational Research and Improvement. Retrieved from: http://files.eric.ed.gov/fulltext/ED473229.pdf.

Rapaport, A. (2009). A forgotten concept: Global citizenship education and state social studies. *Journal of Social Studies Research, 33*(1), 91–112.

Rapoport, A. (2015). Global citizenship education: Classroom teachers' perspectives and approaches. In M. M. Merryfield, T. Augustine & J. Harshman (Eds.), *Research in global citizenship education* (pp. 119–135). Charlotte, NC: Information Age Publishing.

Richardson, G. (2008). Conflicting imaginaries: Global citizenship education in Canada as a site of contestation. In M. O'Sullivan & K. Pashby (Eds.), *Citizenship education in the era of globalization: Canadian perspectives* (pp. 53–70). Rotterdam, The Netherlands: Sense.

SACSC (The Society for Safe and Caring Schools & Communities). (n.d.a). *Grade 10 social studies, english language arts: Unit one: Global issues awareness: Lesson one: Issues, what issues?* [Lesson plan]. Retrieved from http://sacsc.ca/senior-high-lesson-plans-social-studies/.

SACSC (The Society for Safe and Caring Schools & Communities). (n.d.b). *Grade 10 social studies, english language arts: Unit one: Global issues awareness: Lesson three: A lived experience* [Lesson plan]. Retrieved from http://sacsc.ca/senior-high-lesson-plans-social-studies/.

Schattle, H. (2008). Education for global citizenship: Illustrations of ideological pluralism and adaptation. *Journal of Political Ideologies, 13*(1), 73–94.

Steinberg, M. W. (1999). The talk and back talk of collective action: A dialogic analysis of repertoires of discourse among nineteenth-century English cotton spinners. *The American Journal of Sociology, 105*(3), 736–780.

Tatto, M. T., Arellano, L. A., Uribe, M. T., Varela, A. L., & Rodriguez, M. (2001). Examining Mexico's values education in a globally dynamic context. *Journal of Moral Education, 30*(2), 173–198.

Taylor, L. (2012). Beyond paternalism: Global education with preservice teachers as a practice of implication. In V. Andreotti & M. Souza (Eds.), *Postcolonial perspectives on global citizenship education* (pp. 177–199). New York, NY: Routledge.

Todd, S. (2010). Living in a dissonant world: Toward an agonistic cosmopolitcs for education. *Studies in Philosophy of Education, 29*(2), 213–228.

Tully, J. (2000). The challenge of reimagining citizenship and belonging in multicultural and multinational societies. In C. McKinnon & I. Hampsher-Monk (Eds.), *The demands of citizenship* (pp. 212–234). London, England: Continuum.

Tully, J. (2008). Two meanings of global citizenship: Modern and diverse. In M. Peters, H. Blee, & A. Britton (Eds.), *Global citizenship education: Philosophy, theory and pedagogy* (pp. 15–39). Rotterdam, The Netherlands: Sense.

Tye, K. A. (2014). Global education: A worldwide movement. An update. *Policy Futures in Education, 12*(7), 855–871.

Urbina Garcia, M. A. (n.d.). Teaching values in Mexico. Unpublished paper, University of York, York.

Willinsky, J. (1998). *Learning to divide the world: Education at empire's end*. Minneapolis, MN: University of Minnesota Press.

AUTHORS' BIOGRAPHY

Carla L. Peck is Associate Professor of Social Studies Education in the Department of Elementary Education at the University of Alberta. Her research interests include students' understandings of democratic concepts, diversity, identity, citizenship and the relationship between students' ethnic identities and their understandings of history. In 2010, she was honoured with the Canadian Education Association's Pat Clifford Award for Early Career Research in Education and in the 2011 Publication Award from The History Education Network/Histoire et Education en Réseau. Dr. Peck has published widely on citizenship education and history education in prestigious journals including the *Canadian Journal of Education, Curriculum Inquiry, Theory & Research in Social Education,* and *Citizenship Teaching and Learning*. She is co-author of *Education, Globalization and the Nation* (Palgrave Macmillan, 2016).

Karen Pashby completed her Ph.D. at University of Toronto in 2013 where she also coordinated the Global Citizenship and Sustainable Development cohort of initial teacher education. She held a postdoctoral research position on the Ethical Internationalisation in Higher Education project at the University of Oulu (2013–2013) and a postdoctoral fellowship at the Centre for Global Citizenship Education and Research at University of Alberta (2014–2016). She recently joined the Faculty of Education at Manchester Metropolitan University where she lectures and does research in the area of global citizenship education, a field in which she has published widely.

CHAPTER 5

Global Citizenship Education in Latin America

Edda Sant and Gustavo González Valencia

INTRODUCTION

This chapter examines discourses on global citizenship encountered in education policies in Latin America. In line with the rest of the handbook, the chapter is informed by theories on global citizenship. In Latin America, nevertheless, the term 'global citizenship' coexists with alternative and competing approaches including planetary citizenship, Bolivarianism, and internationalism. We have decided to include all these approaches in our discussion about global citizenship and education.

The chapter focuses on the Central American, South American, and Caribbean states were Romance languages are predominant. The territory we examine is often named Latin America. But, in our analysis, we have excluded Mexico (considered in the North America chapter). The territory we cover includes 19 countries with different histories, languages, and political and economic systems and with different education policies. Considering the space limitations of this chapter, we have decided to focus our analysis on ten of these countries. The examined countries are Argentina, Brazil, Chile, Colombia, Costa Rica, Cuba, Ecuador, Nicaragua, Peru, and Venezuela. Our selection is based on the principle of obtaining a diversity of countries considering geographic and political/economic alliances (for a more precise description, see Table 5.1). We would like to acknowledge the diversity of this territory and the

E. Sant (✉)
Manchester Metropolitan University, 53 Bonsall Street, Manchester
M15 6GX, UK
e-mail: e.sant@mmu.ac.uk

G. González Valencia
Universidad de Medellin, Medellin, Colombia
e-mail: gustavoalonsogonzalez@yahoo.com

© The Author(s) 2018
I. Davies et al. (eds.), *The Palgrave Handbook of Global Citizenship and Education*, https://doi.org/10.1057/978-1-137-59733-5_5

67

difficulties of treating these countries as a 'group.' We also feel it is necessary to emphasize that this chapter is an in-between result of a constant conversation between two authors—one 'outside'[1] and one 'inside' the continent—who understand their analysis as being contextualized by their own experiences.

We have organized the chapter as follows. First, we provide an overview of the historical background and the political context of Latin American countries. Second, we describe the main discourses on global citizenship coexisting in the examined countries. Third, we analyze how global citizenship is constructed in core education policies and Citizenship and Social Studies Curricula in ten American countries. We conclude by examining desirable futures for global citizenship education in the Latin America.

HISTORICAL AND POLITICAL CONTEXT

In this section, we discuss key historical events that can shed some light on contemporary discussions on global citizenship in the examined countries. We do not analyze the history of any particular country, but rather we examine the continent as a 'whole.' We have decided to take the nineteenth century as the starting point of this historical background. This is not to say that previous historical events are not relevant, but to emphasize that most of the present Latin American states were created as such in this period.

An understanding of the processes of independence of the Latin American states is essential for the interpretation of global citizenship education on the continent. First, in Latin America, independence did not represent the beginning of a process of decolonization. Rather, social, economic, and cultural hierarchies derived from colonialism were integrated in the new Latin American order (Quijano 2000). Processes of independence from the European metropolis were always lead by 'criollos'—descendants of European natives (Díaz 2005). In certain ways, these 'criollos' were economically and ideologically dependent on other European countries. The processes of independence did not happen in isolation. Independence from the Portuguese and the Spanish Empire was supported by some European countries, mainly France and Britain (Uslar 1989). Ideologically, the 'criollos' had been highly influenced by the European Enlightenment. Francisco Miranda and Simon Bolivar, for instance, travelled to Europe to learn more about political, tax, and custom systems (Díaz 2005). Second, independence did not bring the end of colonial power but the transformation of a colonial power into others (Mignolo 1995). Soon after the independence of most Latin American states, the Monroe Doctrine (1823) was approved. The doctrine, a USA foreign policy, implicitly declared US control over the entire Americas (Selser 2001). Spain and Portugal were externally replaced by the USA.

Discussions on decolonization did not have a relevant impact on Latin American politics until the twentieth century, when forces supporting US imperialism and forces for anti-imperialism coming from both, inside and outside the continent, evidenced the socioeconomic division of American societies. In different territories of the Americas, revolutionary groups self-denominated socialist and anti-imperialist struggled against social and economic hierarchies supported by USA. After centuries of silence, indigenous movements' demands—essentially social and economic equality and the integration of indigenous group into the 'criollos' society—were mainly incorporated into these revolutionary groups (Bengoa 1995). Simultaneously, US governments were particularly suspicious about leftist ideologies on the continent considered to be a consequence of USRR's influence. The Cuban Revolution (1959) and the Missile crisis (1962) were followed by a surge of US intervention in Latin America with US political and military forces having a covert and uncovered presence on the continent and the islands. Coup d'états against democratically elected governments whose ideas were considered to be socialist were supported (e.g., Popular Unity Government in Chile) (Garcés 2013), and a campaign to stigmatize left wing political options was promoted (Magallón 2003). As a consequence of this, the area became explicitly divided between socialist Cuba, under the influence of Soviet Union, and the rest of the countries, under the US hegemony (Skisdmore and Smith 1996). Within many countries, those considered to be against the 'national will' (often defined by dictators or by civil governments under US control) were massacred, joined guerrilla and paramilitary movements or were forced into exile (Galeano 1997).

By the end of 1980s, the new liberal democracies were expected to create more cohesive societies. Economic crisis, abuse of power, constant human rights violations—particularly torture and forced disappearances—and social pressure forced the fall of most dictatorships (Magallón 2003). The new democratic constitutions,[2] nevertheless, brought a set of political and economic reforms limiting the real possibilities of reducing the socioeconomic and political gap. Economically, the Washington Consensus established the principles to be followed by the new Latin American market economies (Casilda 2004). The International Monetary Fund (IFM) and the World Bank introduced structural adjustment programs by with the purpose of developing a more market-orientated economy (Ocampo 2006). Simultaneously, free trade agreements were signed, including the Mercosur agreement (Calcagno 2001). The property of the land was concentrated in few hands supporting the USA's interests (Almeyra et al. 2014). Economic openness did not open the political sphere. Electoral modifications were introduced in an attempt to limit the possibilities of communist parties from gaining democratic access to power (Magallón 2003).

CONTEMPORARY SOCIAL AND POLITICAL CONTEXT

In the beginning of the twenty-first century, Latin America is ideologically and geopolitically divided. In Mercosur countries (i.e., Brazil, Argentina, and Venezuela), social, economic, and foreign affairs policies of the region shifted after the election of left-wing governments. Globalization and the role of international organizations were openly challenged, and the countries became Pan-American oriented while supporting protectionist economic policies (Bernal-Meza 2013). More radically, the ALBA (Bolivarian Alliance for the Peoples of Our America) organization was created (i.e., Cuba, Ecuador, Nicaragua, Venezuela) with the explicit aim of promoting anti-imperialism, a stronger state and a regional redistribution of the wealth. In opposition, a number of pro-globalization and market-orientated countries created the Pacific Alliance (PA) (e.g., Chile, Colombia, Peru). By the time of writing this chapter, two recent events have evidenced that the division also remains within the Latin American countries. In Brazil, an elected president belonging to the Workers' party was impeached in a process that evidenced the division of Brazilian society. In Colombia, the peace agreement referendum resulted in 50.2% of the population defending that the violent conflict between the Colombian Government and the Marxist Guerrilla FARC should not come to an end.

The division, we argue, is (at least) partially created by the existence of two main competing discourses, each of them holding a different worldview (traditional leftist/rightist division), a different analysis of historical colonial past and a different understanding of Latin America's desirable role in contemporary globalization processes (see Andreotti 2011). Following Mignolo (2002), we name these discourses Western civilization and World system discourse. We now examine these two discourses in more detail, and we discuss the links between these discourses and competing understandings of global citizenship.

The Western civilization discourse constructs modernity in relation to Europe—which is understood as the source of absolute rationality—and globalization as the process of expanding this rationality to other parts of the world (Andreotti 2011). Globalization is here considered a positive feature bringing the 'goodness' of Western civilization worldwide. Historically, the Western civilization discourse is in the basis of most Latin American states that, as we discussed, were created mirroring Enlightenment principles. More recently, the Western civilization discourse is present in the strategies defined by some international organizations including the promotion of Human Rights ('political civilization') and neoliberal principles ('economic civilization') (Grosfoguel 2011). In the twenty-first century, some Latin American countries have explicitly manifested their commitment to these strategies. PA countries believe in the need to foster Latin America's political relevance and economic competitiveness of in the world through the neoliberal strategies defined by the IFM, the World Bank and the Inter-American Development Bank (Bernal-Meza 2015) Within this discourse, education for global citizenship is desirable for two reasons. First, it provides students with the economic knowledge and civic instruction (Banco Mundial 1996) required "to make informed decisions" (World Bank 2011, p. 25). Second, global citizenship education is understood as necessary to ensure Latin American countries' participation in the global market (UNESCO 2014).

The World systems perspective understands globalization as the process of expansion of capitalism resulting in the exploitation and ideological control of some countries (including Latin American countries) by others (e.g. European). "From the discovery until our times" Galeano wrote, Latin America "has always been transmuted into European—or later United States—capital, and as such has accumulated in distant centers of power" (1997, p. 2). The World systems discourse is in the core of most historical anti-imperialist movements in Latin America. Today, anti-imperialist movements constitute a complex amalgam including (at least) indigenous movements defending greater autonomy, cultural recognition and land recovery, Marxist and social democratic parties—some of them often accused of being 'populist',[3] revolutionary guerrillas, Black power activists, and theology liberation movements (Azzellini 2007).

Some of these movements propose alternative forms of globalization. Rather than globalization from 'above'—this is, framed by neoliberal principles—they demand globalization from 'below'—framed by social justice and democratic principles (Torres 2015). These movements have proposed alternative forms of global citizenship education. For instance, Latin American Research Councils (mainly FLACSO and CLACSO[4]), have encouraged theory and research in areas related to social justice-oriented global citizenship, certain Christian institutions promote world, and planetary citizenship (see, e.g., Richard 2004) and the World Social Forum—with high impact in Latin America—defines in its objectives the need for an active planetary citizenship (WSF 2016).

Other movements, in contrast, openly define themselves as being anti-globalization. This is the case of most current governments of the members of the ALBA which "are highly skeptical of the 'goodness' of free market and globalization processes" (Bernal-Meza 2013, p. 10). In these countries, global citizenship—probably associated with the globalization process—is rarely discussed. Instead, the ALBA countries promote 'internationalism' and 'Boliviarism.' The concept of 'internationalism' has been particularly relevant in Cuba. Drawing upon traditional internationalist Marxist theory and the anti-imperialism of José Martí, Antonio Maceo, and Simón Bolívar (Risquet 2005), Latin American internationalism has supported national liberation struggles against imperialism and globalization, humanitarian assistance and "solidarity to progressive governments and a wide array of progressive international movements and organizations around the globe" (Harris 2009, p. 28). Internationalism, as understood in the region, seems to defend a horizontal collaboration in the globe rather than a vertical integration. The concept of 'Boliviaranism,' in contrast, focuses on the promotion of an integrated regional citizenship. Particularly fostered by recent Venezuelan governments, 'Bolivarianists' support a Pan-American socialist citizenry constructed in opposition to the USA, described as capitalist and imperialist.

In the following sections, we will use these discourses to shed some light on the curricular construction of global citizenship in Latin America. But before doing so, we provide a general overview of the examined education systems.

KEY FEATURES OF CURRENT EDUCATION SYSTEMS

Although some attempts have been made for educational integration (Muscará 2013), there is no common framework for the educational policies of the examined countries. There are, nevertheless, similar patterns in the evolution of the education systems in each of the three geopolitical regions we have considered (i.e., Mercosur, ALBA, PA). We explore the main characteristics of each region considering recent changes, curricular organization, and the role of citizenship education in each region.

Latin American countries' education policies have experienced profound changes in the last three decades. In PA countries, education systems have been reformed following the human capital principles as understood by the OECD and the World Bank (Bonal 2002). According to Gajardo (2011), recent modifications have tended to: (1) reorganize the schooling system, (2) emphasize the need for quality and equity in educational access and outcome, (3) establish evaluation and accountability mechanisms and (4) revise teacher education and teacher professional development. Mercosur and ALBA countries, in contrast, have increased considerably their education budgets to guarantee quality public schooling for everyone, reduce inequality and promote national cohesion (see various examples in Schwartzman 2015).

In all the examined countries, there is some sort of national curriculum or guidance to be followed by regional curriculums within the nation-state. In PA countries, following OECD's recommendations, the curriculum is often organized in relation to a set of "competences" students are expected to gain in order to have a "successful life and a well-functioning society" (DeSeCo 2005, p. 4). It is worth noting here that all countries organized through competences identify one or two competences named "social and civic competence." Instead, ALBA and Mercosur countries have not initially assumed the "competences" framework but rather have articulated the purposes of their education systems in alternative ways. In Ecuador, Venezuela, and Brazil, for instance, the curricula are organized in relation to cross-subject axes, and one of them is directly connected to the citizenry's education. Citizenship education, therefore, is always considered a key purpose of schooling.

Citizenship education is also a subject in the three regions (PA, Mercosur and ALBA). In some countries, citizenship education is defined as a subject area in itself. This is the case, for instance, of Costa Rica (2013), Cuba, and Nicaragua. In other countries, citizenship education is implicitly or explicitly included in social studies subjects. In Colombia, for example, one of the subjects is named "Social sciences, history, geography, political constitution and democracy" Colombia (1994).[5] In Venezuela, this is named "social sciences, citizenship and identity" (Venezuela 2007). In brief, the education of the citizenry seems to have an allocated time in the education of the Latin American students regardless of the region they live in.

STRATEGIES FOR EDUCATING ABOUT AND FOR GLOBAL CITIZENSHIP

In this section, we examine the Social Science and the Citizenship syllabuses for primary and secondary education (often 6–14/16 years old) in the ten mentioned Latin American countries (Argentina 2007; Brazil 2016; Chile n.d.; Colombia 2002; Costa Rica 2013; Cuba 2014: Ecuador n.d.; Nicaragua 2010; Peru 2005; Venezuela 2007). We organize our findings in relation to the ways in which citizenship, globalization and global citizenship are discursively constructed in the curricula. For each concept, we identify a set of emerging themes that we summarize in Table 5.1. Below, we discuss these findings in relation to the historical background, political, and social context and present discourses on globalization.

Table 5.1. Emerging themes in the discursive construction of 'citizenship,' 'globalization,' and 'global citizenship' in each country's programs of study.

CITIZENSHIP

In all the examined countries, citizenship education—as a purpose of education and as a subject in itself—is essentially constructed in relation to the nation-state. Curricula tend to emphasize the love for the homeland, its heroes, and symbols. For instance, Cuban primary school students are expected to "love and be proud" of their homeland. Students in Venezuela and Ecuador are taught about "patriotic symbols." Implicitly -and in some cases, explicitly—citizenship education focuses on the identity dimension, attempting to promote a national sense of belonging.

The nation is constructed simultaneously as diverse and without differences. On one hand, cultural and ethnic diversity, examining the contributions of indigenous, European and (sometimes) Africancommunities to present Latin American societies is a key feature of a number of curricula. Latin America is constructed as being 'mestiza' (see Mignolo 1995). In Brazil, for example, teachers are recommended to emphasize African and indigenous cultures' contribution to Brazil and to help students to deconstruct the concept of 'race.' Students are often expected to recognize and value the cultural and ethnic diversity of their local, national and global contexts. For instance, Peruvian students learn how to be respectful with diversity and how to cope with a culturally complex globalized world. On the other hand, gender, sexual, religious diversity, and socioeconomic differences are often omitted in the curricula. With minor exceptions, such as Brazil, where gender, religion, sexuality and age are considered aspects of diversity, and Argentina, where socioeconomic

Table 5.1 Global citizenship education in Latin American countries

	Characteristics of the country		Citizenship					Globalization	Global citizenship
	Geographic position	Alliance	Sustainability	Diversity	Differences	Rights	Peace	World systems/Western civilization	Key concepts
Colombia	South America	Pacific alliance	√	√		√	√	Western civilization	Global citizenship
Chile	South America	Pacific alliance	√	√		√	√	Western civilization	Global society
Peru	South America	Pacific alliance	√	√		√	√	Western civilization	Global community
Costa Rica	Central America	Pacific alliance (in process)	√	√		√	√	Western civilization/World systems	Global citizenship
Argentina	South America	Mercosur	√	√	√	√	√	World systems	Humanity, world society
Brazil	South America	Mercosur	√	√	√	√	√	Western civilization/World systems	Anti-imperialism, global society
Venezuela	South America	ALBA, Mercosur	√	√		√	√	Western civilization/World systems	Bolivarian, anti-imperialism
Cuba	Caribbean Islands	ALBA	√			√		World systems	Internationalism, anti-imperialism
Ecuador	South America	ALBA	√	√		√	√	World systems	Bolivarian, anti-imperialism, planetary, world citizenship
Nicaragua	Central America	ALBA	√	√		√	√	World systems	Anti-imperialism

differences are recognized, most Latin America curricula seem to avoid discussions regarding differences within the nation. For instance, in Venezuela, students celebrate the day of the indigenous and afro-descendant cultures, but no mention is made of the indigenous' land recovery demands.

The desirable nation is also understood as peaceful and ideologically homogenous. Discussions on ideological differences within the nation are often avoided and, when recognized, they are identified as the source of violent historical and contemporary conflicts (e.g., coup d'états, guerrilla movements). Within the nation, conflict is often discursively constructed in opposition to peace. In Latin America, peace education needs to be understood in a context of post-dictatorship regimes and/or in a context of structural and everyday violence. In some countries, such as Argentina and Chile, the recent history of coup d'états created a context in which consensus and democratic dialogue is understood in opposition to military actions. As a result of this, in Argentina and Colombia, for instance, social sciences aim to "use dialogue" as a way of solving conflicts. In Colombia but also in other American states, the conflict between Marxist guerrillas, Government armies and paramilitary groups have for long produced a situation in which peace education was relevant in the life of a large number of students. In this respect, peace is extremely important to the extreme of being identified as one of the purposes of education. In Colombia, schooling is explicitly aimed to "educate in the respect for life and other Human Rights, peace and democratic principles" (Colombia 1994, p. 2).

The concept of citizenship is often associated with notions of rights and responsibilities. The identification of 'national rights and duties' is a common feature in most curricula. In Colombia, for example, students specifically learn about their rights and duties as institutionally framed by the political constitution. In addition, in most countries, the Universal declaration of Human Rights seems to be the normative referent used to construct global but also national forms of citizenship. For instance, Costa Rican students specifically learn the history of Human Rights and their different legislations. In some cases, other frameworks replace (or are added to) Human Rights as global normative referent. Argentinean, Nicaraguan, and Venezuelan students learn about Children's Rights, and Venezuelan and Chilean students consider indigenous people's rights.

Education for sustainable development is often contextualized in relation to citizens' responsibilities. The curricula of the examined territories emphasize the need for students to work toward a more sustainable world. In this respect, Brazilian students are required to perceive themselves as agents of transformation of the environment. Environmental threats are not only considered from a global perspective (such as global warming), but also from a local one, in which the particular threats for each nation are emphasized (e.g. deforestation). In Argentina, students examine what are considered to be the most relevant environmental problems in their country.

GLOBALIZATION

Whereas the construction of citizenship is very similar in the different examined countries, globalization, in contrast, is constructed through (at least) two competing depictions. In PA countries (i.e., Colombia, Chile, Peru), the Western civilization discourse is assumed. The role of European and US imperialism in the recent history of the continent is minimized or perceived as unproblematic. Globalization is described as a finished process resulting in an integrated world under an economic system (global capitalism), certain global organizations (e.g. United Nations) and a set of universal values (Human Rights). Colombian, Peruvian, and Costa Rican students, for instance, are expected to learn the roles and functions of United Nations which is implicitly described as a democratic institution ruling the global order. The Chilean curriculum explicitly demands that students learn the "processes that cause the changes from a bipolar world to a globalized world" (Chile, n.d., p. 200).

On the other hand, ALBA countries and often Mercosur countries (i.e., Cuba, Ecuador, Nicaragua, Venezuela and Argentina), describe the globe as a conflictive terrain where economic, political and ideological power is unequally distributed. In the line of World systems analysis, modern colonialism and contemporary imperialism are emphasized as key features explaining the globalization process resulting in the world being divided between core (imperialist) and peripheral countries, whereas the capitalist block is defined as "wealthy" and neoliberalist, the socialist—Bolivarianist—block defines itself as "solidary." In Cuba, for instance, students are expected to demonstrate patriotism by rejecting "Yankee imperialism" which is defined as "our main enemy" (Cuba 2014, p. 45). Politically, students of these countries often learn the political alliances of their countries with other countries. Cuban students learn about internationalism and about how Cuba participates in the "internationalist aide" in different facets: education, health, defense, etc. Simultaneously, they learn that Cuba needs to be defended from other countries, particularly the USA.

Brazil requires a particular mention. Globalization is presented as having different interpretations—likely including the ones we described above. More precisely, teachers are advised to "compare different views examining the globalization phenomenon" (Brazil 2016, p. 455). Thus, students are expected to contrast these competing discourses rather than assume any of them.

GLOBAL (AND OTHER) CITIZENSHIPS

The concepts of 'global' and 'global citizenship' are only explicitly discussed in the educational policies of some PA countries. In Peru, the curriculum encourages the "sense of belonging" with the "family, school, local, regional, national and global community." More explicitly, Colombian and Costa Rican curricula mention directly the need to educate a global citizenry.

Global citizenship is presented here as the—unproblematic—citizenry of this integrated world. Similarly, to the national construction of citizenship, global citizenry is described as culturally and ethnically diverse but socioeconomic differences are easily dismissed. Latin American students are expected to acquire the necessary competences to participate in a globalized market that it is assumed to provide equal opportunities for all. In the Chilean curriculum, for instance, financial education is defined as being important to have an "educated citizenry in relation to the ways the market functions."

Most ALBA and Mercosur education policies do not mention "global citizenship" and "global society." Since the globe—as we have described—is presented in binary terms, the education of a global citizenry seems to be an impossible and undesirable outcome. Instead, they advocate for alternative forms of citizenship. Drawing on traditional Marxist analysis, Cuban curricula implicitly recognize a socialist citizenry opposed to a capitalist one. In other countries, a Latin American citizenship is privileged. These are the case of Nicaragua and Venezuela where the curricula implicitly aim to a "Bolivarian" citizenship or Argentina, where a Pan-American citizenship is promoted through Mercosur alliances. According to Torres (2015), these regional forms of global citizenship can be considered "as a step towards global citizenship" (p. 269).

In some countries, alternative forms of global citizenship are promoted. In Brazil, students are expected to be part of the global society but this global society is contextualized in relation to unequal relations of power, including colonialism and imperialism processes. In Ecuador, Boliviarism and anti-imperialism are key features of the program study, but the curricula also attempt to "create world identity." Ecuadorian curriculum seems to challenge neoliberal approaches to global citizenship while supporting alternative forms of global citizenship. Drawing upon alternative constructions of global citizenship (for instance, WSF, and Christian organizations' proposals), Ecuador encourages a form of planetary (social justice-oriented) citizenship radically opposed to neoliberal principles.

DESIRABLE FUTURES

In our analysis, we suggest that citizenship education in the examined Latin American countries is mainly constructed in relation to the nation. The nation is understood to be culturally and ethnically diverse, but discussions on socioeconomic and ideological differences and conflict are avoided or considered to be a problem to be solved. The concept of citizenship is essentially developed in terms of rights and duties, both having a national and a global dimension.

There are competing discourses in the way globalization is discussed. In PA countries, globalization is constructed in relation to the Western civilization discourse (Mignolo 2002) and global citizenship—often in its neoliberal form—is explicitly discussed as a curricular aim. In most ALBA countries, in contrast, World systems analysis (Mignolo 2002) is used to construct the globalization process and there is an attempt to work toward regional—rather than global—forms of citizenship. In Ecuador and particularly in Brazil, globalization is presented as a multifaceted concept involving power relations but also opportunities to construct alternative global societies.

Given this analysis, what are the desirable futures for global citizenship education in Latin America?

National and global citizenship education, in Latin American, needs to include discussions on difference. The history of the Americas is an example that illustrates that the world is far from being the unproblematic reality that the Pacific Alliance countries seem to suggest. The examined Alba countries, in this respect, might be right in using World systems analysis to encourage students to examine the unequal distribution of economic resources and political power in the world. But differences, we argue, are not only within the global society but also in the national one. Most examined states fail in considering that their national societies are not only ethnically and culturally diverse, but also different in terms of gender, sexuality, ideology, religious believes, socioeconomic status, and so on. Latin American policy (as it is the case of Brazilian and Argentinean curricula) and research have already begun to examine power relations within some countries (see, for example, Marolla 2016). We feel it is now time to expand this to other countries and illuminate education policy and practice on the entire continent.

In the core of this denial of difference, we argue, lies the difficulty of dealing with conflict. The history of the Americas is full of examples in which any form of conflict (including social conflict) has resulted in armed conflicts. Clear examples of these are the numerous coup d'états, covert civil wars, forced exile processes and more recently, the struggles for land recovery, and the result of the Peace referendum in Colombia. In this respect, the examined countries are arguably right in their emphasis on Peace education. However, their focus is up for debate. Peace education as an aspect of global citizenship education, we argue, might not always be about 'solving conflicts' as suggested in Colombian and Argentinean curricula. Conflict is a consequence of diversity of perspectives within and outside national contexts. Further, democracy requires different alternatives that may be in conflict. As Andreotti (2011) points out, there is a need for pedagogical emphasis on dissensus including helping students to develop their ability to live in situations of conflict and difference. We believe it is time for American teachers, teacher educators and researchers to consider how this time can be used not only to educate students to "solve" national and international conflicts, but also to accept (peaceful) conflicts as being necessary in any local, national and global democratic context.

Our emphasis on conflict and difference, however, should not be misread as supporting the fixed binarisms constructed in the educational policies of some ALBA and Mercosur countries. On the contrary, we understand the (national and global) realities to be far more complex and hybrid that any static frontier diving the 'we' and the 'other.' For instance, the same states which in their education policies highlight Western imperialism as the 'other,' can be accused of supporting a nationalistic and rights-orientated initially inherited from Europe. We believe global citizenship education, should allow students to reflect on the complex nature of most identities.

Education for global citizenship cannot be understood as the education of the Latin American students into what international organizations might define as 'global citizens.' Global citizenship education from above, we believe, will only lead to the reproduction of previous economic, political and cultural power relations. Instead, we argue for a global citizenship education framed by two principles. First, a geopolitical of knowledge (Andreotti 2011) in which concepts—including global citizenship—and identities—including global identities—can be broken down into more profound questions: "(1) Who is constructing what image? and (2) How does one construct a self-image in the face of one's definition or identification by others (whether by other people or by institutions)?" (Mignolo 1995, p. 176). Second, more democratic approaches to global citizenship education, in which alternative understandings of global citizenship (e.g., planetary citizenship) and/or competing anti-globalization views (e.g., Pan-American citizenship) are necessary. The role of educators and researchers here, we argue, is to create spaces were these competing discourses can be examined, contrasted and (perhaps) appropriated.

"What will the Latin America destiny be like?", Uruguayan writer, Ernesto Galeano once wondered: "Are we going to be a caricature of the North? Are we going to be like them? (…) Or are we going to create a different world? To offer the world a different world? This is our main challenge" (in Tendler 2006). We agree.

Notes

1. The authors are aware of (at least) some of the ethical implications of writing this chapter. Particularly, when one of the authors identifies as Catalan presently living in the UK and the other as Colombian who once lived in Catalonia. However, the discussion of these ethical implications is, unfortunately, outside the scope of this chapter. For a detailed discussion on this, see Mignolo (1995).
2. Colombia (1991), Argentina (1994), Perú (1993), Uruguay (1997).
3. For a more sophisticated discussion on populism, see Laclau (2007).
4. FLACSO is the Latin American Social Sciences Institute, CLACSO is the Latin American Social Science Council.
5. All names and quotes from the Latin American policies have been translated from Spanish or Portuguese to English by the authors.

REFERENCES

Almeyra, G., Bórquez, L., Mendes, J., & Porto, C. (2014). Capitalismo: tierra y poder en América Latina (1982–2012). Bolivia, Colombia, Ecuador, Perú, Venezuela (Vol. 2). México, D. F.: Consejo Latinoamericano de Ciencias Sociales.

Andreotti, V. (2011). *Actionable postcolonial theory in education*. New York: McMillan.

Argentina. Ministerio de educación, ciencia y tecnología. (2007). *Gestión curricular y formación docente*. http://www.me.gov.ar/curriform/edprimaria.html.

Azzellini, D. (2007). *La Revolución Bolivariana: "o inventamos o erramos"* (p. 36). Herramientas: Claves para leer el proceso de transformación social venezolano.

Banco Mundial. (1996). Prioridades y estrategias para la educación: Examen del Banco Mundial (No. 14948, pp. 1–218). Washington: The World Bank.

Bengoa, J. (1995). Los Indígenas y el Estado Nacional en América Latina. *Revista de Antropología, 38*(2), 151–186.

Bernal-Meza, R. (2013). Modelos o esquemas de integración y cooperación en curso en América Latina (UNASUR, Alianza del Pacífico, ALBA, CELAC): una mirada panorámica. Ibero-Amerikanisches Institut, Stiftung Preußischer Kulturbesitz.

Bernal-Meza, R. (2015). ALIANZA DEL PACÍFICO versus ALBA y MERCOSUR: Entre el desafío de la convergencia y el riesgo de la fragmentación de Sudamérica. Pesquisa & Debate. Revista do Programa de Estudos Pós-Graduados em Economia Política, (26(1/47), pp. 1–34).

Bonal, X. (2002). Plus ça change … The World Bank global education policy and the Post-Washington Consensus. *International studies in sociology of education, 12*(1), 3–22.

Brazil. (2016). Ministério da educação. Base nacional comum curricular. http://basenacionalcomum.mec.gov.br/documentos/bncc-2versao.revista.pdf.

Calcagno, A. (2001). Ajuste estructural, costo social y modalidades de desarrollo en América Latina. En El ajuste estructural en América Latina. Costos sociales y alternativas (pp. 75–98). Buenos Aires: CLACSO.

Casilda, R. (2004). América Latina y el Consenso de Washington. *Boletín económico de ICE, Información Comercial Española, 2803*, 19–38.

Chile. (n.d.). Ministerio de Educacion. Bases curriculares y programas de estudio. http://www.curriculumenlineamineduc.cl/605/w3-propertyvalue-49398.html.

Colombia. Congreso de la Republica (1994). Ley 115 de Febrero 8 de 1994.

Colombia. Ministerio de Education. (2002). Lineamientos curriculares. http://www.mineducacion.gov.co/1759/articles-339975_recurso_1.pdf.

Costa Rica. Ministerio de Education Publica. (2013). Programas de estudio. http://www.mep.go.cr/programa-estudio?term_node_tid_depth=9047.

Cuba. Ministerio de Educacion. (2014). Programas de studio. http://educaciones.cubaeduca.cu/index.php?option=com_content&view=article&id=12496:primaria-institucional-home&catid=99:institucional-home&Itemid=101.

DeSeCo. (2005). The definition and selection of key competencies. Executive summary.

Díaz, S. (2005). *La Ilustración en la Nueva Granada: su influencia en la educación y en el movimiento de emancipación. El caso de Mutis. En La América hispana en los albores de la emancipación* (pp. 167–178). Madrid: Marcial Pons.

Ecuador. Ministerio de educación (n.d.). Curriculo de EGB y BGU. https://educacion.gob.ec/wp-content/uploads/downloads/2016/08/CCSS-completo.pdf.

Galeano, E. (1997). *Open veins of Latin America: Five centuries of the pillage of a continent.* New York: NYU Press.

Gajardo, M. (2011). *La educación tras dos décadas de cambio. ¿Qué hemos aprendido? ¿Qué debemos transformar? En Calidad, equidad y reformas en la enseñanza* (pp. 59–76). Madrid: OEI—Fundación Santillana.

Garcés, J. E. (2013). *Allende y la experiencia chilena: Las armas de la política.* Madrid: Siglo XXI Editores.

Grosfoguel, R. (2011). Decolonizing post-colonial studies and paradigms of political-economy: Transmodernity, decolonial thinking, and global coloniality. *Transmodernity: Journal of Peripheral Cultural Production of the Luso-Hispanic World, 1*(1).

Harris, R. L. (2009). Cuban internationalism, Che Guevara, and the survival of Cuba's socialist regime. *Latin American Perspectives, 36*(3), 27–42.

Laclau, E. (2007). *On populist reason.* London: Verso.

Magallón, M. (2003). *La democracia en América Latina.* México: Plaza y Valdes.

Marolla, J. (2016). *Teaching and learning of women's history in Chile.* Unpublished PhD Dissertation.

Mignolo, W. D. (1995). Afterword: Human understanding and (Latin) American interests–The politics and sensibilities of geocultural locations. *Poetics Today,* 171–214.

Mignolo, W. (2002). The geopolitics of knowledge and the colonial difference. *The South Atlantic Quarterly, 101*(1), 57–96.

Muscará, F. (2013). Problems and challenges of educational policies in Latin America. The Argentina viewpoint. *Journal of New Approaches in Educational Research, 2*(2), 109.

Nicaragua. (2010). Curriculo Nacional. http://www.nicaraguaeduca.edu.ni/principal/articulos/628-ultimas/907-curriculonacionalnicaragua.

Ocampo, J. (2006). Más allá del Consenso de Washington. *Economía UNAM, 7,* 7–25.

Peru. Ministerio de Educacion. (2005). Diseno curricular nacional. http://www.minedu.gob.pe/normatividad/reglamentos/DisenoCurricularNacional.pdf.

Quijano, A. (2000). Coloniality of power and Eurocentrism in Latin America. *International Sociology, 15*(2), 215–232.

Risquet, J. (2005). *The deep roots of Cuba's internationalism. TRI continental,* 13. http://www.tricontinental.cubaweb.cu/REVISTA/texto22ingl.html.

Richard, P. (2004). *Fuerza ética y espiritual de la Teología de la Liberación: en el contexto actual de la globalización.* La Habana: Caminos.

Schwartzman, S. (2015). *Education in South America.* London: Bloomsbury.

Selser, G. (2001). *Cronología de las intervenciones extranjeras en América Latina: 1899–1945* (Centro de Investigaciones Interdisciplinarias en Ciencias y Humanidades, Universidad de Nacional Autónoma de México, Vol. III). México: UNAM.

Skisdmore, T., & Smith, P. (1996). *Historia Contemporánea de América Latina.* Barcelona: Critica.

Tendler, S. (2006). *Encontro com Milton Santos: O mundo global visto do lado de cá.* Documentary. http://www.videocamp.com/pt/movies/encontro-com-milton-santos-o-mundo-global-visto-do-lado-de-ca.

The World Bank. (2011). *Learning for all: Investing in people's knowledge and skills to promote development—World Bank Group education strategy 2020: executive summary* (No. 64487, pp. 1–16). The World Bank.

Torres, C. A. (2015). Global citizenship and global universities. The age of global interdependence and cosmopolitanism. *European Journal of Education, 50*(3), 262–279.

Uslar, J. (1989). *La Revolución Francesa y la independencia de Venezuela (Lagoven).* Venezuela: Lagoven.

Venezuela. Ministerio del poder popular para la educacion. (2007). Currículo del Subsistema de Educación Primaria Bolivariana. http://www.cerpe.org.ve/tl_files/ Cerpe/contenido/documentos/Actualidad%20Educativa/Curriculo%20Educacion%20Primaria%20Bolivariana.%202007.pdf.

WSF. (2016). About the world social forum. https://fsm2016.org/en/sinformer/ a-propos-du-forum-social-mondial/.

Authors' Biography

Edda Sant is a Senior Lecturer in the Department of Childhood, Youth and Education Studies at Manchester Metropolitan University. She has previously worked as a Teaching and Research Fellow at the Universitat Autònoma de Barcelona (Spain) and as Social science and Citizenship education teacher in different schools. Her research focuses on citizenship and history education, particularly on the topics of political participation and the education of national/global identities.

Gustavo González Valencia holds a Ph.D. in Social Science Education from the Universitat Autonoma de Barcelona (Spain) where he worked as training lecturer in the Faculty or Education. Presently, he lecturers at the Faculty of Humanities and Social Studies in the Universidad de Medellin (Colombia). His research interests are citizenship and democratic education, social studies education, initial teacher training and research methodology.

CHAPTER 6

Conceptions of Global Citizenship Education in East and Southeast Asia

Li-Ching Ho

INTRODUCTION

The definition, framing, and implementation of global citizenship education varies significantly across different national contexts in large part because of the considerable diversity in how nation-states experience and respond to the forces of globalization. While some nation-states react in ways that seem to emphasize the convergent effects of the economic, political, and cultural impact of globalization, others have adopted a more selective and exceptional approach. These disparate national responses to globalization greatly influence how the discourses of global citizenship are articulated by the state, and this in turn affects the nature and structure of the global citizenship education curriculum. Consequently, conceptions of global citizenship education can vary significantly, and these can include developing the capacity to participate in different local and global communities, learning about global issues, taking social and political action, becoming globally competitive, and emphasizing information technology and global connectivity (Gaudelli 2016).

While there have been a significant range of research studies highlighting various approaches to global citizenship education in Europe, Australasia, and North America, relatively little attention has been paid to how East and Southeast Asian countries conceptualize and define global citizenship education. In this chapter, East Asia is defined as including China, Japan, South Korea, Hong Kong, and Taiwan, while the region of Southeast Asia is defined

L.-C. Ho (✉)
University of Wisconsin-Madison, Madison, USA
e-mail: liching.ho@wisc.edu

© The Author(s) 2018
I. Davies et al. (eds.), *The Palgrave Handbook of Global Citizenship and Education*, https://doi.org/10.1057/978-1-137-59733-5_6

as the 10 ASEAN countries (Indonesia, Malaysia, Thailand, Singapore, Brunei, Vietnam, Cambodia, Laos, Myanmar, the Philippines, and East Timor). Given the number of countries in these two regions, I focus my attention on several case studies that represent a range of historical, political, economic, social, and religious contexts found in these two regions, namely China, Japan, South Korea, Hong Kong, Indonesia, Malaysia, and Singapore.

In this chapter, I highlight some of the significant exogenous and endogenous conditions that help shape East and Southeast Asian countries' responses to globalization, show how the different historical, cultural, religious, political, and economic contexts of these countries both frame and define global citizenship, and determine whether particular discourses of global citizenship education found in the curriculum are strong or marginalized.

HISTORICAL, POLITICAL, ECONOMIC, AND SOCIAL CONTEXTS

The diverse historical, economic, religious, and political circumstances of the countries in East and Southeast Asia pose a significant challenge to any scholar who seeks to make generalizations, draw parallels to, or identify trends for these two geographical regions. Indeed, the divergent experiences and historical settings of countries *within* each region further contribute to the complicated nature of the endeavor. For instance, South Korea, Japan, and Taiwan are East Asian states with advanced economies, shared Confucian heritage, relatively homogenous cultures, and moderately democratic systems. In contrast to Japan and Korea, however, Taiwan's and Hong Kong's national priorities are particularly affected by their political relationships with China. Southeast Asian countries such as Malaysia, Indonesia, the Philippines, and Thailand, on the other hand, are less economically developed, more religious, more ethnically diverse, and less democratic. A highly developed and ethnically diverse Southeast Asian country like Singapore, however, has political, economic, and historical characteristics that overlap with countries in both regions.

The countries within the East and Southeast Asian regions can be categorized using different ethno-cultural, geographical, political, and historical criteria. Politically, much of East and Southeast Asia (with the exception of Japan) has historically been shaped by what Diamond (2011) calls "developmental authoritarianism" (p. 301). Similarly, Thompson (2004) identified different types of "developmental dictatorships" in countries such as South Korea, Thailand, Indonesia, Malaysia, and the Philippines. The dominant political parties from these countries derived their political legitimacy from rapid and sustained economic development and generally, these political regimes prioritized economic efficiency above democratic goals. More recently, however, countries in the region such as Japan, South Korea, and Taiwan have established liberal democratic systems while other countries such as Singapore and Malaysia becoming "at least a mixed and progressing set of systems" (Diamond 2011, p. 301).

Economically, East Asian countries number among the most successful, technologically advanced, and industrialized nation-states in the world although in Southeast Asia, countries such as Myanmar, Cambodia, Laos, and East Timor still struggle economically. In terms of religious history, Malaysia, Brunei, and Indonesia have strong Islamic historical traditions, whereas the Catholic Church has historically dominated much of East Timor and the Philippines. Different variants of Buddhism, in addition, greatly influence two separate groups of countries: (1) Myanmar, Thailand, Laos, and Cambodia; and (2) Vietnam, Singapore, Japan, South Korea, Taiwan, Hong Kong, and China. Notably, the latter group of countries is also deeply influenced by Confucianism and various forms of Chinese folk religion.

In spite of the significant differences highlighted above, the countries in the two geographical regions appear to share two approaches to the emergent pressures of globalization: (1) the appropriation of globalization for nationalist and economic goals; and (2) the (re)definition of national identity.

APPROPRIATION OF GLOBALIZATION FOR NATIONALIST ECONOMIC GOALS

A significant proportion of East and Southeast Asian research studies and publications on global citizenship education emphasize the importance of the nation-state's ability to compete for and thrive amidst global competition for resources and technology. Because most of the countries in East and Southeast Asia have had historical experiences of authoritarianism and, in many cases, still maintain highly centralized political systems, these nation-states have sought to manage the impact of globalization by initiating top-down national strategic plans.

The use of national strategic plans and the resultant increase in focus on economic nationalism has manifested itself in distinctive ways in different countries. For instance, South Korea's *segyewha* globalization drive initiated by President Kim Young Sam in the mid-1990s was an attempt to fundamentally restructure the country's institutions in order to display "national pride to the globalized world" (Sung et al. 2013, p. 289). Notably, the policy of economic globalization, especially after the Asian financial crisis of 1997, also displaced previous national policies that emphasized national security issues and traditional Confucian values (Moon and Koo 2011), and focused more on achieving economic success while concurrently promoting Korean culture and values (Sun et al. 2013).

Likewise, the Malaysian government's attempt to transform and modernize the country has resulted in new education philosophies, including one that would "produce and provide the right mix of human capital to meet market needs at all levels" (Malakolunthu and Rengasamy 2012, p. 153). Notably, the goal of the National Vision (*Wawasan*) 2020 articulated by then Prime Minister Mahathir Mohamed in 1991 aimed to establish "a world-class education system that would be dedicated to producing a world-class workforce" (p. 154). More recently, the 2006 Ninth Malaysian Plan further emphasized the importance of human capital development for national dominance. The main purpose of the plan, according to Balakrishnan (2010), was to "stabilize the process of developing human capital comprehensively and continuously so that the output achieved is capable of fulfilling local and international needs as well as stabilizing Malaysia's position in the global arena" (p. 92).

Other states such as Japan, Taiwan, Hong Kong, and the Philippines have also attempted to gain advantages in the global market by focusing on economic nationalism (Sung et al. 2013). Taiwan and Hong Kong, for instance, sought to incorporate global dimensions of citizenship such as the acquisition of English language skills and information technology knowledge (Law 2004). Similarly, within China, scholars such as Lee and Ho (2005) pointed out that the rise the socialist market economy, accompanied by significant economic reform, political shifts, and social upheavals, have required the Chinese state to reconceptualize the role, responsibilities, and moral qualities of citizens. In a similar vein, Zhu and Camicia (2014) called attention to several dominant discourses within China, including nationalism, cosmopolitanism, and neoliberalism. They argued that the discourse of neoliberalism, defined as the "cultivation of competitive producers and consumers," has become a significant element of a conception of socialist citizenship (p. 48).

(RE)DEFINING NATIONAL IDENTITY: INCLUSION OR EXCLUSION

In this section, I explore how the pressures of globalization, especially global migration flows, have also compelled some of the East and Southeast Asian nation-states to redefine their national identities and to reconceptualize the fundamental nature of what it means to be a South Korean, Japanese, Singaporean, or Malaysian citizen. In general, countries with founding myths or constitutive stories that emphasize the fundamentally ethnically and culturally diverse origins of the nation-state respond in significantly different ways to the forces of globalization compared to countries with dominant historical narratives that highlight ethnic or cultural homogeneity.

South Korea and Japan, for instance, are examples of nation-states that face numerous tensions in terms of how they choose to define their national identities. For example, in South Korea, a pervasive founding myth articulated in social studies textbooks prior to 2007 stressed the homogeneity of the Korean peoples: "Korea consists of one ethnic group. We, Koreans, look similar and use the same language (Mo 2009, cited in Moon 2010, p. 4). The increasing number of transnational migrants workers and international marriages between Korean citizens and migrants especially from Southeast Asia, however, has compelled the South Korean government to move away from what Moon (2010) characterizes as "mono-ethnicism" and move towards incorporating ideas of cultural diversity and multiculturalism into the school curriculum. Similarly, Japan's society has been transformed by a significant increase in the number of new immigrants from the Philippines, Brazil, China, and other countries in large part because of a declining birth rate and an aging society. As a result, citizenship education has been changed to place less emphasis on nationalism and the idea of an ethnically homogenous nation (Fujiwara 2011).

Unlike Japan and South Korea, countries such as Malaysia, Indonesia, and Singapore emphasize cultural pluralism in their constitutive stories and founding myths. In Singapore and Malaysia, for example, successive governments have promoted a "mosaic model" through the development of what Hill and Lian (1995) call an ethnic-national identity (p. 95). This hyphenated national identity recognizes and accepts the cultural practices of diverse groups while concurrently instilling a common national identity premised on ethnic diversity (Hashim and Tan 2009). In order to develop a shared national identity premised on cultural pluralism, the governments of Indonesia, Malaysia, and Singapore established sets of national principles or values that define the nation-state called *Pancasila*, *Rukunegara*, and *Our Shared Values*, respectively. The ethnically inclusive nature of these national ideologies thus provides a significantly different political and social framework for countries such as Malaysia and Singapore to address the issues and tensions brought about by global cultural currents and transnational migration flows (Ho 2009).

EDUCATIONAL CONTEXTS AND GLOBAL CITIZENSHIP EDUCATION

In this section, I highlight several significant trends and discourses in global citizenship education, drawing particularly on examples from Singapore, Japan, South Korea, Taiwan, Hong Kong, China, Malaysia, and Indonesia. Taken together, these eight countries represent a range of historical, economic, religious, linguistic, social, geographical, educational, and political contexts that will help the reader better understand how countries have chosen to construct and enact global citizenship education.

Using frame and discourse analysis (Benford and Snow 2000; Wodak and Meyer 2001), I consider how particular discourses are especially dominant in different contexts and I examine how these discourses reinforce certain pedagogical or curricular practices while concurrently diminishing the impact of others. Benford and Snow (2000) define frames and collective action frames in the following manner: "Frames help to render events or occurrences meaningful and thereby function to organize experience and guide action... Collective action frames are action-oriented sets of beliefs and meanings that inspire and legitimate the activities and campaigns of a social movement organization" (p. 614). I employ these definitions to examine how political actors in each context articulate and utilize problem, solution, and motivational frames that resonate with certain audiences in order to advance their goals (Parker 2011).

For instance, within the USA, Parker (2011) identified particular discourses that dominated the International Education movement including strong discourses such as national security. Advocates of International Education positioned the movement as a solution for an important problem caused by globalization—the need to maintain the country's competitive edge in a globalized world. In this example, the maintenance of economic competitiveness was framed as a national security problem and a solution, International Education, was thus proposed. Concurrently, discourses such as global perspectives and cosmopolitanism were marginalized in the movement.

GENERAL TRENDS: INCREASING FOCUS ON GLOBAL CITIZENSHIP EDUCATION

In general, research studies seem to indicate an increasing interest in global citizenship education within school curricula in East and Southeast Asia. For instance, in Hong Kong, global citizenship education was first introduced in the 1998 secondary school curriculum guidelines and its aim was to promote consciousness of transnational issues such as global ecology, and to "help students think more globally… and produce citizens of the world" (Law 2004, p. 259). The education reforms of the 2000s also saw global citizenship themes included in subjects such as Integrated Humanities, the new Moral and Civic Education framework, and in Liberal Studies (Chong 2015). Similarly, the Taiwanese government has also sought to promote global citizenship within school curricula since 2001. Students are expected to develop values such as social interdependence and mutual trust, acquire knowledge of international issues, and see the world as a "global village" (Law 2004, p. 259). The government in China has also revised its citizenship curriculum in response to globalization. For instance, in the early 2000s, the primary and secondary curriculum shifted from its original focus on socialist collectivism to one that was multidimensional and comprised different domains including self, family, nation, and the world (Law 2014). Lee and Ho (2005) also highlighted a similar shift in focus within moral education and emphasized how the subject has gradually been oriented toward the development of a "global perspective" and preparing China to "become a more integrated member of the globalized world" (p. 428). This global perspective, according to the authors, consisted of several elements including global awareness (e.g., understanding interdependence, peaceful development), global knowledge (e.g., current international issues), global skills and values (e.g., human rights), and global behavior (participating in activities that to promote global justice).

Likewise, research suggests that citizenship education in South Korea, especially within the school subjects of social studies and ethics, has become significantly less nationalistic. Moon and Koo (2011), for instance, conducted an analysis of social studies and civics textbooks at all grade levels starting from the Fourth National Curriculum (1981–1986) to the Eighth National

Curriculum (2007–present). The researchers identified major national and global themes and counted the number of keywords mentioned. The researchers also classified themes as national or global depending on their context within the text. For instance, democracy was framed largely as a national value within South Korean civics texts in the 1980s because it was used to disparage the North Korean communist regime. In general, the researchers found that South Korean citizenship education has shifted from promoting loyal citizens of the nation-state towards a notion of a citizen that is "human rights-bearing, globally minded, (and) cosmopolitan... with a sense of collective responsibility as members of a common humanity" (Moon and Koo 2011, p. 394).

The same trends can also be observed in Southeast Asian countries such as Indonesia and Malaysia. In Indonesia, Kalidjenih (2005) observed that the *Kurikulum 2004: Mata Pelajaran Kewarganegaraan* (Curriculum 2004: Citizenship Education) launched in 2004 included new topics such as human rights, globalization, and regional autonomy. Similarly, in Malaysia, the revised Moral Education syllabus introduced in 2000 accorded more attention to the Vision 2020 goal of "global community building" and aimed to develop "responsible individuals of high moral standards who are able to contribute to the peace and harmony of the country and the global community" (Balakrishnan 2010, p. 98).

Human Rights Education as a Strong Discourse

Overall, human rights appears to be a strong discourse within global citizenship education in East and Southeast Asian countries, albeit with several notable exceptions particularly in countries with less democratic political systems. In South Korea, researchers observed that the use of global citizenship education themed words including human rights increased significantly from the 1990s and 2000s, potentially signifying a "fundamental change in the nature of civics education in Korea" (Moon and Koo 2011, p. 587). Even though social studies and ethics textbooks are still dominated by national citizenship themes, researchers found that global citizenship themes were accorded more attention in the later iterations of the textbooks, especially after the mid-1990s. Interestingly, the authors attributed the strong discourse of human rights within South Korean citizenship education to local developments such as the efforts of South Korean civil society groups to introduce human rights education especially after the presidential election of Kim Dae-jung. These non-governmental organizations, together with other international non-governmental organizations such as Amnesty International and the United Nations, sought to identify anti-human rights context in existing textbooks and advocated for the inclusion of more human rights content in the new curriculum standards (Moon and Koo 2011).

In Malaysia, of the seven learning areas in the 2000 Moral Education syllabus for secondary schools, one learning area is dedicated to human rights, including "protection of children's rights, respect for women's rights, protection of labor rights, respect for rights of the disabled, and protection of consumers' rights" (Balakrishnan 2010, p. 99). Likewise, in Indonesia, the *Curriculum 2004: Citizenship Education* for secondary students explicitly addresses the topic of human rights and students are expected to learn about international agreements such as the Universal Declaration of Human Rights and to learn how international institutions protect human rights. The 2004 curriculum document includes standards such as: "Explain the formulation of Universal Declaration of Human Rights, identify various international instruments of human rights, (and) mention international institutions of human rights protection and their roles" (Kalidjenih 2005, p. 327).

Finally, Hong Kong offers an interesting case study with regard to the inclusion and further development of human rights discourse within global citizenship education. Chong (2015) contends that the global citizenship education guidelines in the 2000s not only extend students' understandings of human rights issues around the world compared to the previous curricula but also provide numerous opportunities for critical discussion and taking action. Taken together, the different subjects that address human rights (*Moral and Civic Education*; *Personal, Social and Humanities Education*; *Integrated Humanities*; *History*; and *Liberal Studies*) emphasize how students should pay attention to issues of marginalization, discrimination, and inequality. Students are also taught that they have an obligation to all of humanity and that they have a duty to challenge injustice. For instance, the junior secondary Integrated Humanities curriculum guidelines require students to "inquire into the inequalities and discrimination that are associated with imperialism, colonization, and hegemony" (Chong 2015, p. 235). The curriculum also includes concepts such as interdependence, cosmopolitan society, decolonization, global ethics, global unity, and cultural imperialism. Notably, Hong Kong schools are also expected to provide civic and service learning experiences for students in order to encourage social activism. These experiences can include community involvement, participating in learning programs organized by different nongovernmental organizations such as Oxfam and learning about global poverty and injustice, and identification and investigation of opportunities for action.

GLOBAL COMPETITIVENESS AND NATIONAL PRIDE AS A STRONG DISCOURSE

Scholars in East and Southeast Asian countries such as Malaysia, Indonesia, Taiwan, China, South Korea, and Singapore have also identified another strong discourse—global competitiveness and national pride—within global citizenship education. For instance, under the Ninth Malaysia Plan, the Major

Plan for Education Development (2006–2010) focused explicitly on developing human capital in order to establish Malaysia's position in the global arena (Balakrishnan 2010). Likewise, in South Korea, Sung, Park and Choi (2013) observed that the national curriculum for the elite South Korean global high schools defined global citizenship education largely in terms of preparing students to be internationally competitive and they noted that the curriculum gave primacy to the goal of developing students to be more productive in the global labor market in order to enhance South Korea's status in the world. Similarly, Zhu and Camicia (2014) found that the discourses of neoliberalism and cosmopolitanism were gaining in importance in China's citizenship education discursive field. They argued that these discourses were intricately connected: "Cosmopolitanism adds a moral legitimacy to neoliberalism and Confucianism adds a moral legitimacy to nationalism" (p. 54). This neoliberal cosmopolitan discourse does not pay much attention to developing allegiance to a global community and but instead focuses on portraying Chinese citizens as productive workers and consumers in a global marketplace. For instance, the amendment to the junior high school's curriculum in 2007 emphasized the national strategy of prioritizing economic development for nation building (p. 54).

The discourse of global economic competitiveness is particularly dominant in Singapore albeit in a slightly different form. The Singapore state has consistently emphasized the importance of promoting economic development and being globally competitive *in order to* ensure national survival. More importantly, globalization is consistently perceived by the government as posing an existential threat to the survival of the nation-state. This survival narrative and discourse of vulnerability permeates the national social studies curriculum (Sim and Ho 2010) and unsurprisingly, teachers and students see the subject as a vehicle for the promotion of state-approved national history, values, and identity (Ho 2010). In spite of the curricular revisions made recently that aimed to develop more cosmopolitan citizens with broader worldviews, these economic goals remain foregrounded in the secondary social studies curricula (Ho 2013). For instance, the 2008 social studies syllabus included this guiding question: How do nations sustain their economic development in a globalized world?" (Singapore Ministry of Education 2008, p. 14). Notably, even topics like environmental management are framed in economic terms: "Students will be able to... understand how environmental management is necessary to ensure economic growth" (p. 14). Finally, the syllabus document reminds students that "the failure to respond to the changing global landscape" will have disastrous consequences for the country and "result in a nation fading into obscurity" (p. 15). The discourse of global economic competitiveness can also be found in the most recent secondary social studies textbook published in 2016. One of the three themes in the secondary social studies curriculum focuses on the topic: "Being part of a globalized world" and it includes inquiry questions such as "How do we respond to tensions arising from some economic impacts of globalization?" (Singapore Ministry of Education 2016, p. 250).

CONCLUSION AND FUTURE DIRECTIONS

This chapter provided an initial overview of how countries as diverse as South Korea, Japan, Taiwan, Singapore, Malaysia, and Indonesia respond to globalizing trends and it explained how these countries converged and diverged in their definitions of and approaches to global citizenship education. The previous sections also showed how global economic pressures have resulted in the governments utilizing the discourse of globalization to serve nationalistic economic goals and to define an inclusive or exclusive national identity. The section also described how another consequence of globalization—transnational migrant flows—differentially affected the construction of national identities of the countries in East and Southeast Asia. The chapter also highlighted a general trend of East and Southeast Asian countries giving greater attention to ideas and concepts related to global citizenship, albeit with a strong nationalistic focus. Finally, two strong discourses were also identified: (1) human rights education; and (2) global competitiveness and national pride.

Notably, in spite of an increase in attention paid to global citizenship themes, the discourses that appeared to dominate civics, citizenship, and social studies education in the East and Southeast Asian countries examined in this chapter were still very much focused on enhancing national economic productivity and maintaining the global status of the nation-state. The review of literature from this group of countries with strongly centralized governments and histories of developmental authoritarianism thus reminds us that the state plays a particularly central role in determining the inclusion and framing of strong discourses of global citizenship in citizenship education curricula. Drawing on his analysis of the changes in China's citizenship education curricula, Law (2006) writes: "In a globalizing world, the nation state is a principal selector and translator of global elements of citizenship and citizenship education in its jurisdiction… the nation state has the final power to prescribe what global elements will be introduced, emphasized, and materialized" (p. 620). Nevertheless, in spite of the power of the state to determine the scope and structure of national curricula, the case of human rights education in South Korea identified by Moon and Koo (2011) also demonstrates the influence of local and international non-governmental organizations on curriculum development.

The review of literature in this chapter, in addition, emphasizes how particular discourses of global citizenship have been sidelined in civic education and social studies curricula. In general, cosmopolitan and global social activism discourses are very much marginalized in the citizenship education curricula of countries in these two regions. For instance, as Sung et al. (2013) point out in their analysis of the South Korean Global High Schools (GHS) curriculum, not much attention has been paid to significant global issues such as social justice and global poverty. They write: "Little consideration is given to education's role in preparing students to be global citizens with responsibilities for global issues and problems" (p. 292). The case of Hong Kong described by Chong (2015), on the other hand provides educators with an indication of how these ideas and themes may be incorporated in citizenship education curricula.

Finally, it is important to remember that schools are important sites for both students and teachers as they negotiate the tensions between cultural, national, and global affiliations (El-Haj 2009). There is, however, a dearth of research studies on how these changes in citizenship education curricula are implemented, enacted and received in different national contexts, particularly in countries that are significantly less economically developed, such as Myanmar, Vietnam, Cambodia, and Laos. While this chapter focuses primarily on curricular development, readers also need to consider how the implementation of formal curricula varies significantly at the school and classroom level because teachers and students continuously try to navigate, negotiate, and resist the curricular scripts imposed on them by the state (Buras and Apple 2006).

REFERENCES

Balakrishnan, V. (2010). The development of moral education in Malaysia. *Asia Pacific Journal of Educators and Education, 25,* 89–101.

Benford, R. D., & Snow, D. A. (2000). Framing processes and social movements: An overview and assessment. *Annual Review Sociology, 26,* 611–639.

Buras, K. L., & Apple, M. W. (2006). Introduction. In M. W. Apple & K. L. Buras (Eds.), *The subaltern speak: Curriculum, power, and educational struggles* (pp. 1–39). New York, NY: Routledge.

Chong, E. K. M. (2015). Global citizenship education and Hong Kong's secondary school curriculum guidelines: From learning about rights and understanding responsibility to challenging inequality. *Asian Education and Development Studies, 4*(2), 221–247.

Diamond, L. (2011). Democracy's third wave today. *Current History, 110*(739), 299–307.

El-Haj, T. R. A. (2009). Becoming citizens in an era of globalization and transnational migration: Re-imagining citizenship as critical practice. *Theory Into Practice, 48,* 274–282.

Fujiwara, T. (2011). International, global and multicultural education as an issue in citizenship education. In N. Ikeno (Ed.), *Citizenship education in Japan* (pp. 107–115). New York, NY: Continuum International Publishing Group.

Gaudelli, W. (2016). *Global citizenship education: Everyday transcendence.* New York, NY: Routledge.

Hashim, R., & Tan, C. (2009). A hyphenated identity: Fostering national unity through education in Malaysia and Singapore. *Citizenship Teaching and Learning, 5*(1), 46–59.

Hill, M., & Lian, K. F. (1995). *The politics of nation building and citizenship in Singapore.* New York, NY: Routledge.

Ho, L. C. (2009). Global multicultural citizenship education: A Singapore experience. *The Social Studies, 100*(6), 285–293.

Ho, L. C. (2010). "Don't worry, I'm not going to report you": Education for citizenship in Singapore. *Theory and Research in Social Education, 38*(2), 298–316.

Ho, L. C. (2013). National and global citizenship education: Case studies from two Singapore social studies classrooms. In Z. Deng, S. Gopinathan & C. K.-E. Lee (Eds.), *Globalization and the Singapore curriculum: From policy to classroom* (pp. 169–185). Singapore: Springer.

Kalidjernih, F. K. (2005). *Post-colonial citizenship education: A critical study of the production and reproduction of the Indonesian civic idea.* Unpublished dissertation, University of Tasmania, Australia.

Law, W. W. (2004). Globalization and citizenship education in Hong Kong and Taiwan. *Comparative Education Review, 48*(3), 253–273.

Law, W. W. (2006). Citizenship, citizenship education, and the state in China in a global age. *Cambridge journal of education, 36*(4), 597–628.

Law, W. W. (2014). Globalisation, citizenship education, and international events: 2010 Shanghai world exposition education in China. In K. J. Kennedy, G. P. Fairbrother, & Z. Zhenzhou (Eds.), *Citizenship education in China: Preparing citizens for the "Chinese century"* (pp. 100–127). New York, NY: Routledge.

Lee, W. O., & Ho, C. H. (2005). Ideopolitical shifts and changes in moral education policy in China. *Journal of Moral Education, 34*(4), 413–431.

Malakolunthu, S., & Rengasamy, N. C. (2012). Education policies and practices to address cultural diversity in Malaysia: Issues and challenges. *Prospects, 42,* 147–159.

Mo, K. (2009). *Multicultural education in Korean social studies.* Paper presented at the KAME 2009. Seoul, S. Korea: International Conference, Hanyang University.

Moon, S. (2010). Multicultural and global citizenship in the transnational age: The case of South Korea. *International Journal of Multicultural Education, 12*(1), 1–15.

Moon, R. J., & Koo, J. W. (2011). Global citizenship and human rights: A longitudinal analysis of social studies and ethics textbooks in the Republic of Korea. *Comparative Education Review, 55*(4), 574–599.

Parker, W. C. (2011). 'International education' in US public schools. *Globalisation, Societies and Education, 9*(3–4), 487–501.

Sim, J. B. Y., & Ho, L. C. (2010). Transmitting social and national values through education in Singapore: Tensions in a globalized era. In T. Lovat, R. Toomey, & N. Clement (Eds.), *International research handbook on values education and student wellbeing* (pp. 897–917). Netherlands: Springer.

Singapore Ministry of Education. (2008). *Combined humanities ordinary level social studies syllabus.* Retrieved from http://www.seab.gov.sg/SEAB/oLevel/syllabus/2008_GCE_O_Level_Syllabuses/2192_2008.pdf.

Singapore Ministry of Education. (2016). *Upper secondary social studies.* Singapore: Ministry of Education, Government of Singapore.

Sung, Y. K., Park, M., & Choi, I. S. (2013). National construction of global education: A critical review of the national curriculum standards for South Korean global high schools. *Asia Pacific Education Review, 14*(3), 285–294.

Thompson, M. R. (2004). Pacific Asia after 'Asian values': Authoritarianism, democracy, and 'good governance'. *Third World Quarterly, 25*(6), 1079–1095.

Wodak, R., & Meyer, M. (Eds.). (2001). *Methods of critical discourse analysis.* Thousand Oaks, CA: Sage Publications.

Zhu, J., & Camicia, S. P. (2014). Citizenship education in China under discourses of nationalism, cosmopolitanism, neoliberalism, and confucianism. In J. E. Petrovic & A. M. Kuntz (Eds.), *Citizenship Education around the world: Local contexts and global possibilities* (pp. 43–65). New York, NY: Routledge.

AUTHOR BIOGRAPHY

Li-Ching Ho is a social studies professor at the University of Wisconsin-Madison. Her research focuses on three interrelated lines of inquiry: differentiated access to citizenship education, global issues of diversity in civic education, and environmental citizenship. She has published articles in journals such as the *Journal of Curriculum Studies*, *Teachers College Record*, and *Teaching and Teacher Education*. She is also a founding member and current President of the Singapore Association for Social Studies Education.

CHAPTER 7

Global Citizenship Education: A Southern African Perspective

Yusef Waghid

INTRODUCTION

An examination of the notion of global citizenship education in relation to southern Africa not only brings into reconsideration the advancement of people's rights, responsibilities, dignity and their sense of belonging on the continent, but also accentuates the significance of recognising southern Africa's response to political exclusion, violence and cosmopolitanism in and through higher education. To begin with, I firstly draw on a northern African example whereby, by far the majority of Africans euphorically supported the demise of the dictatorial Mubarak regime that has been responsible for more than four decades of political exclusion of many of Egypt's proponents of political democracy. The temporary ascendancy of the Muslim Brotherhood to political authority in the country was welcomed as a major advance towards political inclusion to the extent that the media referred to the changes in northern Africa as a product of the 'Arab Spring'. Momentarily, political life in northern Africa enjoyed some semblance of recognition for its adherence to tenets of democratic citizenship education in the sense that people's rights to franchise and their belonging to inclusive communities were respected. Despite the initial optimism in the democratic processes, the ugly face of despotism that so vehemently characterised political autocracy in northern Africa again surfaced, and the democratic aspirations

Y. Waghid (✉)
Department of Education Policy Studies, Stellenbosch
University in South Africa, Matieland, South Africa
e-mail: YW@sun.ac.za

© The Author(s) 2018
I. Davies et al. (eds.), *The Palgrave Handbook of Global Citizenship and Education*, https://doi.org/10.1057/978-1-137-59733-5_7

of many citizens were dealt a crushing blow. Higher educational institutions in several African states did not escape the wrath of political authoritarianism, as academic freedom was once again curtailed, and several academics, as well as students, who supported the 'Arab Spring' were either incarcerated or excommunicated from their nation-states. Like the African north, political uncertainty, so endemic to sub-Saharan Africa, continue to manifest, and it is not unusual to find that ethnic tensions and conflict ensue unabatedly. Often, university protestations and disruptions as extensions of political turmoil in countries such as Sudan, Nigeria, Ethiopia and Kenya happen as a corollary of political ambiguity and societal insecurity. More recently, in the African south, specifically South Africa (the focus of this contribution), student protestations against the increasing rise in university fees awakened in many the acute disparities between those who have economic access to university education and those students who do not enjoy equal access to higher education. In fact, due to student unrest in South Africa currently, some universities are either contemplating to cease academic programmes until the following year, or putting in place contingency plans so that students are able to graduate. Both scenarios hold serious implications for higher education and students alike. While a delayed graduation time frame might compromise and hamper employment opportunities, succumbing to student demands through the cessation of academic programmes sets a precarious precedent and controversy regarding the rights of students to an education—thereby raising profound questions about the role of the university as a community of thinking. To this end, southern African higher education remains challenged by ongoing political autocracy, negative (and often violent) disruptions, and unequal access to education.

This brings me to a discussion of some of the conceptual meanings that constitute global citizenship education in southern Africa

Conceptual Underpinnings and Some Theoretical and Practical Predicaments

From the plethora of literature in and about global citizenship education, I have identified at least three major strands: a participatory form of human attunement in relation to recognising people's rights and identities (Arthur, Davies and Hahn 2008); a human rights discourse that counteracts war crimes, crimes against humanity, and crimes against peace in an atmosphere of an openness to culture and democratic public life (Peters, Britton and Blee 2008); and, an equal moral respect to all humans discourse (Wallace Brown and Held 2010). Some aspects of the aforementioned strands of global citizenship education seemed to have manifested in southern Africa discourses, as most notably highlighted in post-apartheid South African educational policy changes. I shall now highlight some of the most pertinent policy changes in the advancement of democratic citizenship education in South Africa, which seems to resonate with aspects of the main ideas on global citizenship education as mentioned above.

Since the 1994 democratic constitutional changes, education has been aligned with values, education and democracy discourses that have culminated, firstly, in the promotion of six 'values' in all sectors of the education system—that is, general, further and higher education. These values include the cultivation of equity, tolerance, multilingualism, openness, accountability, and honour (DoE 2000: 22–50). Secondly, the cycles of post-apartheid educational reform culminated in the announcement of the 'Manifesto on Values, Education and Democracy' (MVE), comprising ten communitarian values, which call for the nurturing of democracy, social justice and equity, equality, non-racism and non-sexism, Ubuntu (human dignity and humaneness), an open society, accountability, the rule of law, respect and reconciliation at educational institutions (DoE 2001). The aforementioned six and subsequent ten 'values' seem to be commensurate with the main tenets of global citizenship education. For instance, recognising citizens' rights and responsibilities can be associated with the cultivation of accountability and equality, whereas human rights, democratic and universal moral respect discourses connect with the achievement of democracy, social justice and equity, non-racism and non-sexism, Ubuntu, an open society, the rule of law and respect and reconciliation.

To my mind, the 'values' of democratic citizenship education enumerated above do not only resonate with a global citizenship education agenda, but have also been advocated in post-apartheid policy texts with the aim to enhance both citizens' critical and intellectual capacities, in unison with a transformative socio-political and democratic (inclusive) mileau, as well as to promote their anti-racist, civic-minded and deliberative capacities in relation to pedagogical advancement (Waghid 2010: 122–126). Yet, the desire to implement the aforementioned 'values' of democratic citizenship education in South African educational institutions has not been without its predicaments. For purposes of this contribution, I focus on three blind spots that seemed to have troubled the implementation of the Manifesto thus far, namely blind patriotism, ambiguous safe expression, and a skewed notion of dialogue.

Firstly, through the following pledge of allegiance (as a manifestation of the value of social honour) it is wrongly assumed that South African citizens would express their patriotism towards the country and one another:

> I promise to be loyal to my country, South Africa, and do my best to promote the welfare and the well being of all its citizens. I promise to show self-respect in all that I do and to respect all of my fellow citizens and all of our various traditions. Let us work for peace, friendship and reconciliation and heal the scars left by past conflicts. And let us build a common destiny together (DoE 2001: 59).

It does appear as if the above pledge of allegiance is biased towards some kind of blind loyalty to one's country that seems to be somewhat removed from cultivating democracy and reconciliation after decades of political exclusion on the part of the majority black citizens. Any kind of blind loyalty expressed to one's country is often accompanied by a resistance towards opposition and criticism, as happened in the apartheid past with the white minority that unquestionably endorsed segregation and discrimination (Kahne and Middaugh 2006: 602). More recently, support for a corrupt ruling party leadership confirms the presence of blind and often dogmatic patriotism endemic to the country's existing political situation. And, pledging allegiance patriotically, as announced through the oath of allegiance, seems to be consistent with an aversion to criticism. Moreover, within a mounting climate of immigration, many southern African immigrant communities (especially from neighbouring states with volatile political climates) that have settled in South Africa could encounter deliberate exclusions on account of people adhering to such a pledge. Often members of such communities are subjected to xenophobic prejudice that results in cruelty and, at times, hatred and assassinations (Waghid 2010: 130). Thus, not being a citizen of the country—as misrecognised by the pledge of allegiance—potentially makes immigrants vulnerable to resentment, violent abuse and killings. It is in this regard that the pledge of allegiance seems to endanger democratic stability, reconciliation and the recognition of alterity. In this way, the pledge of allegiance lends itself to provoking blind patriotism that would make it unlikely for students (and teachers for that matter) to nurture their attentiveness to one another, and to act with a renewed responsibility.

Secondly, the Manifesto (2001: 40) summons students and teachers to nurture a culture of participation and communication in educational institutions attuned to 'space[s] of safe expression'. Of course, excluding people from conversations on the grounds of revolting speech and insults would not only undermine the potential contributions all people (students and teachers) can make towards building trust, democracy and co-existing together, therefore the urgency of 'safe expression' is intensified by educational authorities. Such disparaging speech acts would in any case undermine the continuation of speech and should at all cost be avoided. In this regard, I concur with Amy Gutmann (2003: 2000) who posits that free and unconstrained speech should be inhibited if people are discriminated against unjustly. But, the execution of 'safe' speech on the part of students and teachers can also be incriminating for pedagogical engagement on the basis that belligerence and distress that can evoke more deliberative encounters could be perceived as debilitating for the engagement itself. Such a situation would invariably inhibit students and teachers from taking risks under the false pretext of avoiding conflict and misrecognition of one another. The point is advocating 'safe expression' could potentially undermine pedagogical encounters on the basis that everything ought to be policed and controlled. If pedagogical encounters do not lead to participants taking risks, open and deliberative learning would in any case be stunted.

Thirdly, the extended Manifesto (as a bill of responsibilities for students) also advocates a limited conception of dialogue, often conflating the practice with notions of debate, negotiation and discussion. Quite interestingly, the quest for dialogue seems to be prejudiced towards reaching 'agreement' amongst teachers and students (DoBE 2008: 16). What is disconcerting about the notion of dialogue is the mechanical prompting advanced as if everything ought to be done for students beforehand without them engaging in the practice. Even more disturbing is the connection of dialogue with reaching agreement, after which dialogue is no longer required in pedagogical encounters amongst teachers and students. To couch dialogue as some technical exercise in which students have to engage is tantamount to reducing the practice to some policed activity of prompting and prodding on the part of teachers oblivious of the unexpected and unpredictable turns dialogue can assume. But perhaps the major concern is with the term 'dialogue' itself. It seems as if the practice is presented as some kind of technical exercise that would enable students and teachers to at least talk to one another. But this is the problem with considering dialogue as one person talking to another person as if the other person does not listen and should not engage with another's thoughts. In other words, dialogue seems to be presented as a unidirectional activity which teachers do to students instead of presenting dialogue as a pedagogical encounter whereby teachers and students engage collectively and deliberatively. To do things collectively is to do things with one another and not for one another. And, to engage deliberatively requires of participants to engage with listening to one another and taking one another's views into some kind of critical scrutiny. Such a form of dialogue seems to be distant from the mechanical, unidirectional dialogical perspective announced in the Manifesto. Instead, dialogue without deliberative aspirations would remain skewed as such a form of dialogue would be remiss of participants listening to one another and to talk back because agreement and disagreement could emanate from such a deliberative encounter.

Dialogue that is deliberative, says Seyla Benhabib (2011: 152), is so because it is concerned with iterations, and not with norms that are mechanically valid at all times and in all places. I concur with the notion that democratic iteration (as an expanded form of dialogue) is concerned with public self-reflection, argument, deliberation and democratic will formation where listening and talking back hold sway and both agreement and disagreement can emanate from people's judgments (Benhabib 2011: 129). As it stands, dialogue in the expanded Manifesto seems incongruent with conversational assent and dissent encouraged through democratic iteration.

Now that I have examined some of the predicaments that underscore democratic citizenship education initiatives in South Africa, I next turn to a discussion some of the implications of a value-based agenda of democratic citizenship education for global citizenship education.

Implications of a Value-Based Democratic Citizenship Education for Global Citizenship Education

Earlier, I identified six 'values' that the South African education system has mandated to promote, namely, equity, tolerance, multilingualism, openness, accountability and social honour. Subsequently, these 'values' have been extended to ten 'values' in the Manifesto that include, ideas of democracy, social justice, equality, non-racism and non-sexism, Ubuntu, an open society, accountability, the rule of law, respect and reconciliation (DoE 2001: 3). From my analysis of the Manifesto, it seems that the following aspects have been accentuated: cultivating civil spaces for students and teachers on the basis of mutual engagement with a recognition of human difference (attuned to a human rights discourse and democratic engagement); enlarging debate, discussion and critical thought in conjunction with upholding equal moral respect (attuned to a discourse of universal equal moral respect); and cultivating a culture of enacting one another's rights and being accountable to one another (commensurate with recognising one another's rights and responsibilities). By implication, a value-based democratic citizenship education agenda does not seem to be out of tune with enhancing an education for global citizenship. Instead a value-based democratic citizenship approach with its challenges highlighted previously offers opportunities for higher education to respond with dissonance to the challenges that it is confronted with. In other words, recognising one another's rights and responsibilities, enacting a human rights discourse and democracy, and enhancing universal, equal moral respect in educational encounters would more appropriately be cultivated if enacted within a discourse of dissonance. Through dissonance, people (students and teachers) potentially disrupt actions in which they [people] are/become situated. Here, dissonance implies that the taken-for-granted is brought into legitimate contestation, and previously unconsidered ways of thinking and being are brought to the fore. The point about dissonance is that it opens up students' and teachers' minds to unforeseen and unexpected possibilities—that is, referred to by David T. Hansen (2011: 113) as being reflectively open to what is known and what is yet to come. In a way, dissonance is a form of disruption that allows students and teachers to come to speech through sustained, critical reflection on that which they are confronted with and to think beyond the given, the taken-for-granted. Dissonance is a matter of thinking anew and being continuously open to the new and unexpected.

The question is: How can global citizenship education enhance dissonance in southern African higher education?

Firstly, southern African higher education is characterised by a lack of autonomy on the part of students and teachers that seem to be unresponsive to the challenges of democracy, development and self-determination in the region (Zeleza 2004: 66). The cultivation of global citizenship education with its overwhelming emphasis on dissonance could bring about higher educational contexts in which pedagogical rupturing can be realised. This implies that students and teachers would embark on what Jacques Rancière (1999) refers to as exercising their equal intelligence to disrupt pedagogical encounters—in the sense of producing learning contexts in which there is always the recognition that there is more to learn. That is, a matter of cultivating learning environments in which everything cannot be completely known and the possibility that there will always be more to learn would be enhanced. If the latter happens, not everything about global citizenship education ought to be considered as final and conclusive, as there is still more to encounter on the basis of continuous rupturing and re-ordering of ideas and events. One is reminded of the term 'glocal' that emanates on the basis of a ruptured sense of human engagement in which localness and globalness are asymmetrically foregrounded in educational experiences. In other words, at times local is more aptly situated than global and at other times global is more pronounced than local as long as the one (local or global) is not subsumed by the other.

Secondly, southern African higher education would become a seedbed through which more open and reflexive human encounters would be engendered. To become more open and reflexive through *Ubuntu* relations (considered in traditional African parlance as a communal form of human engagement and interdependence), educational encounters would create opportunities for people to engage humanely, caringly and with a readiness to enact just societal change (Gyekye 1992: 160). If the attainment of societal justice is considered as an a priori outcome of human engagement, then situating the local is not at variance with significant goals of global citizenship education in the sense that the latter accentuates the predominance of acts of societal justice such as equality, liberty, equitable change, and a desire to always see things anew. Werner Wintersteiner (2016) aptly reminds us of the importance of global citizenship education to cultivate educational experiences that undermine major dystopias such as colonialism, exclusion and human degradation. And, considering that local situatedness is commensurable with an enactment of global justice, harnessing global citizenship education might not be inappropriate for a southern African reconsideration of higher education.

Thirdly, inasmuch as global citizenship education involves interconnecting people to address societal injustices such as poverty, famine and hunger, inequality, and forms of human oppression and exclusion, it also urges people to enlarge their moral imaginations. The latter implies that people have to begin to imagine a southern African region where communities live under conditions of profound equality, freedom and human advancement. Only then the possibility for human flourishing would be enhanced on the basis that such a form of education would urge teachers and students to imagine alternative possibilities that people have not thought of before and offer ways of building more just human relations. Hence, to talk about a global citizenship education in the context of southern African higher education is aimed at cultivating a higher education in which 'the experience of reflective openness to the new [is] fused with reflective loyalty to the known' (Hansen 2011: 86). So, when students and teachers enact a global citizenship education in southern African higher education they show a conscious concern to conduct themselves imaginatively by being reflectively open themselves to what is familiar and strange to them, 'the surprising and the expected' (Hansen 2011: 86).

My contention is that global citizenship education can orientate people to 'the core value of reflective openness to the new and reflective loyalty to the known' (Hansen 2011: 113). For instance, when southern Africans reflect on their ways of seeing and living in the world they do not just abandon their own, say, traditional understandings of life in the communities. Rather, they bring their own understandings and practices into conversation with what is unfamiliar and other without necessarily abandoning their own cultural understandings. Their loyalty to what they know becomes subjected to their reflectiveness towards the unfamiliar. In this way, the possibility exists that people's ways of living might be influenced by what is still to come. When pedagogical encounters amongst students and teachers are provoked by a reflective loyalty to the known and concurrent openness to the new and unexpected, their willingness to engage deliberatively will not only be enhanced but also geared towards what is yet not there—that is, people's moral imaginations will be enlarged.

CONCLUSION AND RECOMMENDATIONS FOR FUTURE RESEARCH

Whether or not global citizenship education would ensue, depends on our innovative acts of situating our localness and encounters within globalness and vice versa. The point is, that global citizenship education cannot legitimately be construed as a practice worthy of consideration and enactment if it does not bring into contestation what is both of local and global significance, especially in light of cultivating just human encounters. Unless we show that our interconnectedness and responsibilities are to ourselves and the advancement of humanity, we would not have begun to take global citizenship education seriously enough. Hence, it does not seem to be such an irrelevant idea to reconsider global citizenship education as an *active* local-cum-global educational encounter as the current head of UNESCO in Hamburg, Werner Mauch (2016), so aptly reminds us of.

In the context of the aforementioned, I want to conclude this contribution in reference to my previous work on African philosophy of education in which I argued in defence of drawing on cultural reasonableness as a necessary good for situating the local (Waghid 2014) and, also to my most recent work through a massive open online course (MOOC) on 'Teaching for change: An African philosophical approach' through which I argue in defence of cultivating educational justice as an instance of an education for global citizenship. Firstly, it would not be inappropriate to again reiterate that cultural reasonableness—invoking local understandings in and about human encounters—is the first step towards enacting the metaphoric expression of global citizenship education. This is so, on the grounds that global citizenship education recognises all people's rights and responsibilities; creates conditions whereby all people can respect one another equally and morally; and engender opportunities for human rights discourses and democratic engagement to flourish.

Secondly, in reference to the MOOC on 'Teaching for change: An African philosophical approach' it can be argued that such a curriculum initiative has not only been directed at cultivating aspects of democratic citizenship education but also seem to have been geared towards engendering disruptive pedagogic encounters (more specifically educational encounters situated within dissonant practices) with the aim to establish just human relations. My reason for focusing on disruptive pedagogical encounters is corroborated by the argument that in any act of pursuing global citizenship education thoughts and practices ought to be framed differently, such as for teachers and students to rely on a pedagogical art of disruption in order to unsettle the taken-for-granted, established and often debilitating understandings of education.

At least three salient benefits can be identified in the quest to cultivate disruptive pedagogical encounters in higher education through MOOCs. Firstly, students' experiences with the 'Teaching for Change' MOOC enhanced their deliberative interaction with learning course material in association with online peers. Through this MOOC, students learned together and from one another especially 'by real access to other students around the world' (Ronaghi et al. 2015: 97). In other words, the potential of students to rethink taken-for-granted assumptions in their lives through the power of the social web has been amplified (Ranaghi et al. 2015: 97).

In addition, the high level of student engagement in the absence of the traditional incentive of a university degree is inspiring. The opportunity students' comments offered others and I to learn from their intellectual work is immense, especially considering how students uniquely created their own pathways to learning. Likewise, to have become a learner outside the physical classroom brought to the fore another aspect of learning, that is, a learning revolution that enabled these students to create connections and meanings that would invariably affect their own lives. For students to have created their own connections and meanings about the course content, which potentially affected their thoughts and practices, it can be argued that these MOOC students came to express what Jacques Rancière refers to as their 'equal intelligence'—that is, through the MOOC course material students were summoned to use their intelligence (Rancière 1991: 39) . In this way, the students demonstrated the capacity to learn for themselves without always having to be dependent on the university teacher. In other words, the university teacher did not assume that students lacked the capacity to speak and offer comments. Rather, in a subjectified or disruptive way, students autonomously appeared within the pedagogical activities and began to reconfigure their learning experiences (Rancière 1999: 35) . That is, students were able to come to their own speech as they interrogated the course material. My role as university teacher was to remind these students that they can see and think for themselves and that they (students) are not dependent on others for their learning, more specifically that they (students) can see and think without my teaching. As Rancière (1991: 12) puts it, these students learned without a 'master *explicator*'—that is, I (university teacher) engaged in teaching without explanation 'by summoning … [MOOC] students to use their intelligence' (Biesta 2011: 34). Furthermore, students learned without explanation by (de)constructing meanings in the course, thus having created their own paths to learning and having amplified the possibility for societal change. Students and I were intellectually equal in the very act of disrupting the MOOC pedagogical activities.

This MOOC on 'Teaching for Change' can be associated with the cultivation of democratic citizenship education—as an instance of global citizenship education—that remains in potentiality. Students and I recognised that, in the pedagogical activities of the MOOC, there is always the potentiality on our part to see things anew, and to think differently about our pedagogical experiences in relation to societal matters of concern and vis-à-vis our deliberative pedagogic encounters. In a way, the MOOC offered us (students and university teacher) an opportunity to engage in what Jacques Derrida refers to as a 'democracy to come'—that is, a radical possibility of deciding and making come about (Derrida 2004). The MOOC has the structure of a promise and not of orienting students towards pedagogical certainty for bringing about change tomorrow. When the students engaged with societal problems in an analytical fashion they came to the realisation that societal change has the potentiality 'to come about', thus linking their pedagogical encounters with (im)possible human experience (Friedrich, Jaastad and Pokewitz 2011: 70). It is not that change would ensue instantly. Rather, through disruptive pedagogic encounters, societal change becomes imminent—that is, there is always the possibility that change would be realised.

At the moment, I remain optimistic about the pedagogical advantages of MOOCs in the sense that students are included in pedagogical activities and are recognised for their coming to speech. In this way, learning though MOOCs is potentially liberating in the sense that students can act autonomously with pedagogical content and even contribute towards (re)shaping such content. MOOCs cannot be considered acritical pedagogical courses primarily because the potential is always there for students to act with openness to others' points of view without necessarily withholding and/or abandoning their own critical judgements. Such a form of learning then is associated not only with criticism in a Foucauldian sense but also with the cultivation of democratic experiences that are yet to come for the reason that what is yet to come is contrived and deliberated on collectively or democratically. Such democratic encounters would invariably motivate students and curriculum developers towards considering their work as always in potentiality as there is always more to be known because one cannot completely know at a given point in time. My MOOC experience has been guided by what is still to come, as ongoing critical student feedback on new pedagogical courses invariably influences the authenticity of curriculum (re)design and development.

Finally, global citizenship education in southern Africa, most notably South Africa, has the potential to gain more prominence through an enactment of the values-based approaches on democratic citizenship education that seemed to have emerged in response to political, social and cultural exclusion whether in the form of colonisation or apartheid. With the advent of constitutional democracies in the region, it became inevitable for democratic citizenship education—mostly values-based approaches—to have gained prominence in educational settings. My argument has been in defence of the implementation and enactment of democratic citizenship education 'values' with a glocal bias that could contribute towards the enhancement of recognising people's rights and responsibilities, cultivating human rights discourses in an atmosphere of democracy and openness, and exercising universal and equal moral respect to all individuals and groups. It is such an approach to global citizenship education that can contribute towards enlarging students' and teachers' moral and epistemological imaginations as they (students and teachers) endeavour to disrupt their encounters in dissonant fashion. Only then, by embracing global citizenship education critically and reflectively can southern African higher education plausibly lay claim to having been transformed.

Undoubtedly, southern African higher education discourses would increasingly be confronted with reimagined global citizenship education thoughts and practices primarily because of the unrelenting human interconnectedness facilitated by globalising educational discourses. My analytical account of a local/regional democratic citizenship education initiative underscored by 'values' of transformation is an instance of paving the way for local discourses to confront global ones. The resonance that was accentuated between a values-based democratic citizenship education initiative and global citizenship education accentuates the significant interconnectedness between the local and the global. It would be unwise to be oblivious of such a commensurability in the ongoing pursuit to cultivate more defensible notions of citizenship education. And, if only a disruptive dissonance would be cultivated in pedagogical encounters through such approaches to citizenship education, already a renewed hope in openness, transparency, and deliberative engagement would have been awakened.

REFERENCES

Arthur, J., Davies, I., & Hahn, C. (Eds.). (2008). *The SAGE handbook of education for citizenship and democracy*. Los Angeles: SAGE.

Benhabib, S. (2011). *Dignity in adversity: Human rights in troubled times*. Cambridge: Polity Press.

Biesta, G. (2011). Learner, student, speaker: Why it matters how we call those we teach. In M. Simons & J. Masschelein (Eds.), *Rancierè, public education and the taming of democracy* (pp. 31–42). London: Wiley.

Derrida, J. (2004). *Eyes of the university: Right to philosophy 2* (J. Plug, Trans.). Stanford: Stanford University Press.

DoBE (Department of Basic Education). (2008). *A bill of responsibilities for the youth of South Africa*. Pretoria: Government Printers.

DoE (Department of Education). (2000). *Values, education and democracy. Report of the working group on values in education*. Pretoria: Government Printers.

DoE (Department of Education). (2001). *Manifesto on values, education and democracy*. Cape Town: Cape Argus Teacher Fund.

Foucault, M. (1988). *Politics, philosophy, culture: Interviews and other writings 1977–1984*. New York: Routledge.

Friedrich, D., Jaastad, B., & Popkewitz, T. S. (2011). Democratic education: An (im)possibility that yet remains to come. In M. Simons & J. Masschelein (Eds.), *Rancierè, public education and the taming of democracy* (pp. 60–75). London: Wiley.

Gutmann, A. (2003). *Identity in democracy*. Princeton: Princeton University Press.

Gyekye, K. (1992). *Tradition and modernity: Philosophical reflections on the African experience*. Oxford: Oxford University Press.

Hansen, D. T. (2011). *The teacher and the world: A study of cosmopolitanism as education*. London: Routledge.

Kahne, J., & Middaugh, E. (2006). Patriotism and education: Is patriotism good for democracy—A study of high school seniors' patriotic commitments. *Phi Delta Kappan*, April, 600–607.

Mauch, W. (2016). *Active citizenship in the context of UNESCO's quest for global citizenship education*. Unpublished Paper delivered at the Summer School of Hamburg University's Faculty of Educational Sciences, 22 September. Hamburg: UNESCO.

Peters, M. A., Britton, A., & Blee, H. (Eds.). (2008). *Global citizenship education: Philosophy, theory and pedagogy*. Rotterdam/Boston/Tapei: Sense Publishers.

Rancière, J. (1991). *The ignorant school master: Five lessons in intellectual emancipation* (K. Ross, Trans.) London: Verso.

Rancière, J. (1999). *Disagreement, politics and philosophy*. Minneapolis: University of Minnesota Press.

Ronaghi, F., Saberi, A., & Trumbore, A. (2015). NovoEd, a social learning environment. In P. Kim (Ed.), *Massive open online courses: The MOOC revolution* (pp. 96–105). New York: Routledge.

Waghid, Y. (2010). *Education, democracy and citizenhsip revisited: Pedagogical encounters*. Stellenbosch: SUN Press.

Waghid, Y. (2014). *African philosophy of education reconsidered: On being human*. New York: Routledge.

Wallace Brown, G., & Held, D. (2010). *The cosmopolitan reader*. Cambridge: Polity Press.

Wintersteiner, W. (2016). *Global citizenship education reconsidered*. Unpublished Paper delivered at the Summer School of Hamburg University's Faculty of Educational Sciences, 21 September. Hamburg University: Faculty of Educational Sciences.

Zeleza, P. T. (2004). Neon-liberalism and academic freedom. In P. T. Zeleza & A. Olukoshi (Eds.) *African universities in the twenty-first century, volume 1 – Liberalisation and internationalisation* (pp. 42–68). Dakar: Codesria. Part 2 Ideologies.

AUTHOR BIOGRAPHY

Yusef Waghid is distinguished professor of philosophy of education at Stellenbosch University in South Africa. His most recent books include, *Education, assessment and dissonance* (Co-authored with Nuraan Davids, New York: Peter Lang, 2017), and *Philosophy of education as action: Implications for teacher education* (Co-authored with Nuraan Davids, Boulder & London: Lexington Books, 2017).

PART II

Ideologies

CHAPTER 8

Global Citizenship Education and Globalism

Silke Schreiber-Barsch

INTRODUCTION: THE IDEOLOGY OF SOCIAL INCLUSION

The ideology of social inclusion represents one of adult education's leading leitmotifs, claiming to provide *education for all—and especially for some* across adult education's more than 200-year-old history in the global North. The ideology serves to meet individual, collective and societal needs: stabilizing society's existing order of inclusion/exclusion by passing on its membership terms and conditions; legitimizing adult education's mandate to foster via learning and education, the social inclusion of adults and, in particular, of marginalized or vulnerable groups; and, moreover, promising the individual that, by taking part in lifelong learning, an adequate share of society's goods, opportunities and standards of living will be ensured. The ultimate *raison d'être* of the ideology is reiterated by public and polity rhetoric, affirming in modern liberal societies, a circular interdependency between democracy, social cohesion and citizenry: *democracy through social inclusion through (adult) education through democracy through social inclusion ....* Irrespective of its validness, it is the momentous intersection of social inclusion ideology and the issue of citizenship that is of particular interest in this chapter. As I will argue, it is the everyday practices and performances of subjects in the midst of social inclusion that allow insights into the ideology's powerful dimension as a tool for governing and controlling society, social groups and individuals. To tackle the issue of social inclusion means to cut right to the core of citizenship. Societal systems of inclusion/exclusion negotiate who's in and who's out, who is placed at the periphery and who is defined

S. Schreiber-Barsch (✉)
University of Hamburg, 20146 Hamburg, Germany
e-mail: silke.schreiber-barsch@uni-hamburg.de

© The Author(s) 2018   113
I. Davies et al. (eds.), *The Palgrave Handbook of Global Citizenship and Education*, https://doi.org/10.1057/978-1-137-59733-5_8

to be center, who is declared according to the existing order as a citizen or 'not-yet-being-a-citizen' (Biesta and Lawy 2006), a 'lesser citizen' (Kabeer 2005), and who is defined to be in need of *and* entitled to educational endeavors and, thus, varying kinds of (global) citizenship education.

Drawing on two aspects, the impact of globalism and neoliberalism and, furthermore, the issue of disability/ability, the chapter brings to the fore contested terrains of citizenship in contemporary social regimes and its embeddedness in knowledge and belief systems about 'the self, the other and the world' (Andreotti and Souza 2014) (see Section Conceptual Underpinnings: Deconstructing the Ideology of Social Inclusion). It helps to illustrate the profound shift from social inclusion as a public responsibility and achievement of modern nation states to a self-disciplinary governance instrument of globalized societies in the sense of 'self-inclusion' (Wrana 2006) as a citizen's obligation. This, furthermore, aggravates the terms of membership for those being labeled beyond the center of normalcy by means of, in this case, able-bodied norms, installing a 'regime of dis-citizenship' (Devlin and Pothier 2006) (see Section Key Issues and Debates). Ultimately, disruptions in the envisaged social order help to identify contemporary challenges and tasks for adult education with regard to their clientele: adult learners in global societies (see Sections Implications for Education for Global Citizenship and Conclusion and Recommendations Regarding Future Research).

CONCEPTUAL UNDERPINNINGS: DECONSTRUCTING THE IDEOLOGY OF SOCIAL INCLUSION

In outlining a conceptual framing of the issue under scrutiny, three threads are identified: (1) social inclusion in its polity dimension as an achievement of modern state societies, (2) as subject of social sciences discourse and, (3), its significance for launching adult education's public mandate. Approaching this from Isin and Nyers (2014) definition of citizenship as *an 'institution' mediating rights between the subjects of politics and the polity to which these subjects belong'* (ibid., 1; emphasis in original), requires putting aside over-simplistic assumptions such as that individuals or social groups would per se want to be included in those places, opportunities or citizens' labels that society is offering them. Deconstructing the ideology of social inclusion as a metaphor for democratic consensus and a warming sense of comfort, prepares the ground for its reconstruction as a useful and significant category for citizenship education.

Social Inclusion as Achievement of Modern State Societies

Historically seen, inclusion and exclusion are a constant parameter of societies, 'producing' insiders and outsiders and, like in European medieval times, literally excluding people such as vagabonds (Schroer 2010). The emerging nation states changed this landscape. It became a characteristic of a democratic nation state to award citizenship rights and responsibilities to—in principle—any man and woman, thus, offering a legal, territorially-bound instrument of social inclusion into a nation state (Schnapper 1996, 25; Peters, Blee and Britton 2008, 2). This illustrates that societal systems of inclusion/exclusion do not follow quasi-natural logics, but represent socially (re)produced entities that are constantly under negotiation between the dynamics of a global—local, public—private, collective—individual nature (Schreiber-Barsch 2017). Objects of negotiation are grounded in the parameters of a modern state-citizen-architecture, which is constituted, following Isin and Nyers (2014, 2), by a set of rights (civil, political, social) and a set of duties (conscription, taxation, participation). The modern welfare rationale proves the responsibility for the boundaries of inclusion/exclusion insofar as it specifies the limits of how much social inequality and marginalization is seen as acceptable before social state measures needs to come into force (Bartelheimer 2007). Arguments for minimizing risks of marginalization and exclusion are based on economic reasons (employability, lightening the burden of social security), democracy's requirements (stabilizing and legitimizing democratic society), social policy (welfare, social cohesion, national identity), and a subject-oriented perspective (development of one's personality, autonomy, participation). This argumentation has lastingly engraved a consensus on framing the justification for social inclusion with normative ideas of equality, social justice, human rights, and democracy (Young 2002; Wilson 2000; Kabeer 2005).

Concepts of welfare state typologies, on the other hand, demonstrate the possible range of translating the aforementioned consensus into societal systems of inclusion/exclusion (see e.g. Esping-Andersen (1990) for the European context). Furthermore, shifting to an individual's lens, opens up that experiences of being marginalized, socially isolated or excluded from the *demos*, materialize in quite different forms and public fabrics—and with quite different consequences for those involved (Gallie & Paugam 2000). Hence, referring to the idioms of social inclusion is of no use without a contextual reference (Wilson 2000).

Trajectories of the Social Sciences Discourse

Taking the conceptual dualism *inclusion/exclusion* as a category for analyzing socio-structural phenomena is moving beyond its common use as a policy buzzword, but refers to a long-standing, rich tradition in social sciences. Early empirical works at the heart of the great economic recession at the end of the 1920s, elicited the corrosive impact of longer-term unemployment on giving rise to poverty, social exclusion and a paralyzing climate of resignation, like the now-classic study on a small Austrian community called *Marienthal* by Lazarsfeld, Jahoda, and Zeisel (1933). Since the mid-1960s, the profound shifts in transforming to post-industrial societies manifested new forms of social divides, diagnosed by Myrdal (1963) as a new 'underclass' in the U.S.-American context. Similar to Luhmann's (1995, 239) systems-theory-inspired understanding, this diagnosis followed a binary approach to inclusion/exclusion, seeing the underclass literally outside of society. In contrast, works of the French discourse have contributed significantly in relocating marginalization and exclusion from the outer periphery or even the outside of societies to acknowledging the phenomena as genuinely *collective* in essence (see below). In 1974, in the midst of a tight labor market and social ruptures, the French social politician Lenoir (1974) published '*Les Exclus. Un Français sur dix*', rebutting quantitatively the view that social exclusion of individuals and groups is a mere bagatelle in modern societies. Thus, the rise of the term exclusion, as Paugam (1996) has analyzed, marked a disillusion with steady societal progress and the emergence of poverty and a new workers' precariat due to mass unemployment: the renewed social question of the nineteenth century.

Accordingly, Schnapper (1996) and Castel (1995) have clarified that inclusion/exclusion are dialectical processes that, furthermore, do not represent well-defined static groups or a stable societal condition. On the contrary, individuals or social groups are always gradually more or less included/excluded in and from the various spheres of society—and this not necessarily permanently: one might be included in the nation state via citizenship, but temporarily excluded from the labor market. To emphasize this fluidity, Castel (1995) speaks of three zones between which inclusion and exclusion happen in gradually varying degrees (*intégration—vulnérabilité—disaffiliation*). Yet, he emphasizes that in modern societies no one, not even the socially excluded one, exists beyond society; de-collectivization is in essence a collective situation (Castel 2005, 66). Like today's labeling of refugees or illegalized migrants as non-belonging, non-entitled outsiders clearly represents a collective procedure performed by local communities, nation states or transnational bodies (e.g., the European Union). However, in general terms, to be excluded is neither necessarily abnormal, nor necessarily negative. One might prefer to remain excluded, for instance, from the prison population. Likewise, to be included is not inherently positive without knowing in what (Wilson 2000; Edwards, Armstong and Miller 2001). In any case, social exclusion becomes problematic in the moment when to be excluded entails a solidified and biographically decisive loss of opportunities and margins to participate in society and of sharing a commonly agreed-upon standard of living (Bartelheimer 2007).

Summing up, inclusion/exclusion might refer to a normative idea of a desired societal *condition* (i.e., an 'inclusive society') and, at the same time, describe on-going social *processes* of including and excluding across the whole range of social features (be that gender, class, employment status or other) (Schreiber-Barsch 2017). Who's in the center and who's at the periphery, however, is defined and legitimized according to a *system* of inclusion/exclusion in a given society at a given time. Not least, this frames adult education's mandate in fostering via learning and education, the social inclusion of adult lifelong learners.

Adult Education's Mandate: Education for All—and Especially for Some

Approaching from the policy logics of social inclusion, one can argue that adult education regulates and guides, via learning and education, the ways adults navigate into and through society. As pointed out before (see Section Social Inclusion as Achievement of Modern State Societies), participation can be seen as one of the key *duties* that affects the state-citizen-relationship. Kronauer (2010), on the other hand, defines participation as an outcome of recognizing and realizing personal, social and civil *rights*, which, together with labor market integration and embeddedness in social networks, serve to ensure social inclusion of individuals and groups. However, both lines of argument crucially depend on political subjects (Isin and Nyers 2014) and their will, as well as their capacity, to perform citizenship (ibid.; Devlin and Pothier 2006)—irrespective of which kind of (non-/lesser/dis-)citizenship status society is granting them (see Section Introduction: The Ideology of Social Inclusion). Thus, through their performativity as citizens, political subjects negotiate a specific version of the interplay between the macro-political or also transnational level, belief systems and the surroundings of their everyday practices (Cele 2013). In this sense, the understanding of citizenship as 'practice of identification with public issues', as Biesta and Lawy (2006, 72) have put it, clarifies that citizenship is neither solely a to-be-reached end product of educational endeavors, nor a capability per se independent from any processes of education and learning.

Shifting the focus to adult education as a profession, it becomes apparent that, whereas the recognition of adults as having in fact the cognitive ability to be lifelong learners has been more of a recent success in the first half of the twentieth century in overcoming the traditional *adolescent-maximum-hypothesis* (Lehr 2000), the ideology of social inclusion served from the historical beginnings as a catalyst for establishing adult education's mandate to foster via learning and education, the social inclusion of adults and, in particular, of marginalized or vulnerable groups. Buoyed by the ideas of the Enlightenment, fostering social inclusion (of mainly men, though) represents a profound linkage to social struggles: in the sense of 'collective mediations' of citizenship (Isin and Nyers 2014, 1; see also Kabeer 2005). Be it in the nineteenth century the workers' movement or the reading societies of the emerging urban *bourgeoisie* as a learning setting for developing the bourgeois identity of citizens regardless of nobility (Zeuner 2009)—adult education's emancipatory agenda had been directed to enlighten and strengthen marginalized social groups towards the individual and collective enactment of political subjectivity, which means recognizing the right to claim rights, and, ultimately, learning the 'art of being with others' (Isin and Nyers 2014, 8; 4). Hence, adult education's agenda within the ideology of social inclusion continues to oscillate between fostering an adaptation to (global) society's requirements, on the one hand, and enabling to resistance just against these requirements and towards social transformation, on the other hand. In these struggles, supranational polities like the United Nations have served since the mid-twentieth century as a global driver in creating means for marginalized people or vulnerable groups in society to be recognized as indeed right-bearing subjects (see Section Disruptions: Adult Education, Disability/Ability and Citizenship).

However, identifying social struggles as 'collective mediations' of citizenship (see above) between and by social groups due to their specific needs and interests, points to the second part of adult education's mandate, to provide *education especially for some*. Hereby, social groups are defined as so-called target groups, composed through features like gender, employment status, biographical situation, ethnic origin, disability/ability and the like (Hippel and Tippelt 2009). Seen from the profession's perspective, members of target groups are declared both as capable of *and* vitally in need of learning and are addressed by specific target group-oriented offers. Gathering momentum again in the beginning of the 1970s, target group concepts have served as an important institutional planning category in order to ensure that the entire clientele of adult education, and, in particular, members of target groups, literally participate in its offers. This shall enhance social equality in access to education and learning, better address the (supposed) didactical–methodical requirements of learners and, finally, sharpen the profile of adult education providers for the overall benefit of raising attendance (Sork 2010; Hippel and Tippelt 2009). Yet, the comforting idea of fostering social struggles, social transformation and quality of education via lifelong learning opportunities *especially for some*, tends to disguise its underlying premises. Defining a range of (apparent) homogenous social groups by means of social, biographical, situational, or the like, criteria might be useful and reasonable seen through the lens of a professional provider. But assigning difference in this way not only entails the risk of codifying the center-periphery landscape of the overall societal system of inclusion/exclusion, but also gives evidence about who is seen *in need* of learning in order to be 'better' included in the given social order. Therefore, adult education's mandate within the wider ideology of social inclusion needs to be critically viewed whether it aims to reproduce professional allocations of deficiency just like it might install new tools of governance, as Stickley, Hitchcock and Bertram (2005) indicate in discussing mental health policy in the UK: 'The rhetoric of today's social inclusion agenda may well become the cover for tomorrow's social control' (ibid., 28).

KEY ISSUES AND DEBATES

The advent of globalism and neoliberal agendas in the 1990s and, even stronger, in today's times of austerity, provoked again fundamental shifts in societal systems of inclusion/exclusion and its framing for citizenship practices, its performativity and legality and the attached distribution of responsibilities, power relations, social goods and recognition (see, e.g., Merriam 2010;

Hyslop-Margison and Sears 2008). The ideologies of globalism and the widely visible and noticeable processes of globalization tend to confirm that it is now *global* political subjectivities who need to be educated and, in this sense, 'produced' (Andreotti and Souza 2014, 1). Liberal democracy continues to serve as dominant principle of the (global) social order, yet, criticized not only by Abdi and Shultz (2014, 162) as a 'dome' that works only one way in transmitting—first and foremost Western—societies' interests, demands and power issues to the citizens; not vice versa. Whereas supranational polities like the European Union or the United Nations by means of conventions or funding might indeed strengthen the voices and the recognition of marginalized people or vulnerable groups, at the same time, the paradigm of individualization bears far-reaching consequences for citizens in a globalized world, and especially for those who are blamed for social malfunctioning and/or abnormality.

'Technologies of the Self' (Foucault): Subjectivation as Self-governance of the Citizen

Neoliberal concepts claim the individual citizen as the responsible entrepreneur of his or her life, freely taking choices and autonomous decisions, mingling with other individual citizens and free-floating through society and the life course. However, this state-induced 'government of individualization' (Masschelein and Quaghebeur 2005, 54) leaves the citizen also with individualized problems and an individualized responsibility for qualifying for some 'good citizenship' (Biesta and Lawy 2006, 71–72). Wrana's (2006) work about landmark German policy frameworks on social inclusion from the 1960s until the beginning of the 2000s, using the *governmentality studies'* approach by Foucault (2006), help to understand the new quality in what is meant to be included or excluded in contemporary global societies. By means of the *governmentality* concept, Foucault identified so-called *technologies of the self* as a core principle of the modern nation state government at the end of the twentieth century. In brief, it is about the institutions and practices with which the state governs and disciplines its citizen—though, and this is the point, ultimately the individual governs him-/herself by, more or less consciously perceived *technologies of the self* in order to fulfill social requirements and expectations through processes of subjectivation.

As Wrana (2006) portrays, in the 1960s and at the beginning of the 1970s, Germany knew an overall societal climate of education euphoria, agreeing on lifelong learning as key to economic prosperity and raising human capital. Accordingly, policy documents brought forward a vision of full inclusion through education, promising the lifelong learner the chance to attain the pursued profession, position or life as such—as long as s/he takes part in learning and keeps to her/his allocated place in society. The transformation to post-industrial societies provoked in the 1980s a shift to an 'activating' welfare state. Publicly funded or subsidized adult education was now declared to concentrate on target groups at the outer periphery or, binary seen, at the outside of society, yet, without questioning the underlying social norms and labeling procedures (Castel 2005, 66). Need was interpreted in terms of employability—the inclusion of labor market excluded persons and for whom a quick return of (limited) investment could be expected. Thus, the risk of exclusion was seen at the outer periphery and not yet as an issue for substantial public action (Kronauer 2010, 14; see Section Trajectories of the Social Sciences Discourse). This changed fundamentally in the 1990s due to an emerging generation of neoliberal policies and an erosion of social security systems and standard employment structures. The risk of exclusion had arrived in society's core, manifested inter alia in mass and long-term unemployment. Public responsibility for providing education and lifelong learning opportunities was replaced by the regime of self-regulated lifelong learning, relocating social inclusion as an obligation of the individual, not of the public. Thus, responsibility for social inclusion via lifelong learning and, ultimately, for its inherent risks and potential failure, is handed to the individual, leaving adult education the task of giving instructions for 'self-inclusion' (Wrana 2006, 95): an act of governing and disciplining of the self.

Individualized failure of re/inclusion implies not only the risk of exclusion from societal resources and membership terms (or: being rejected first-time access to it), but, furthermore, the stigmatized labeling of, what Schroer (2010) has called, a 'deficient inclusion': In the precarious peripheries, polity measures prevent exclusion, though, with the cost for the political subjects of unquestionably accepting the inherent terms of condition. Therefore, the so-called *superflous* are indeed not superfluous, because qua their visible selves, they fulfill a disciplining function in reminding the included ones of their participation duties and obligations (ibid., 41). In keeping up this line of thought, Masschelein and Quaghebeur (2005) critically elaborate on the concept of participation under the auspices of neoliberal agendas and the government of individualization, referred to as a duty as well as a right in the state citizen relationship (see Section Trajectories of the Social Sciences Discourse). The regime of participation indeed offers opportunities for freedom and choice, yet, it governs and controls also its realization (ibid., 59). Within this 'hegemony of the individual' (ibid, 61), participation appears to be yet another governmental strategy to install the freedom for the citizen to govern him/herself.

Professional Rationalities for Meeting Needs of the Citizen

Thus, what is the role and what are the ultimate interests of pedagogical experts and the adult education profession as such in contemporary global societies? Armstrong, in an article published in 1982, challenges the idea of 'need' as representing a professional 'needs-meeting ideology'. His main argument is that the cloak of 'meeting needs' disguises the underlying conceptions and interests of adult education professionals themselves, legitimating their professional, institutional and disciplinary existence as experts rather than questioning automatisms, allegations and social embeddedness.

In this sense, adult education professionals do not facilitate the interests and desires of adult citizens, representing their clientele and their potential recipients, but act as a highly biased transmitter of dominant knowledge, norms and cultural expectations of normality: 'Definitions of 'acceptable needs,' and indeed the very idea that there are such things as 'needs' which can be defined or identified, expressed and met, are all part of the cultural hegemony of the ruling class, shared alike by state and professions' (ibid., 315). Adult education risks to turn to a 'disabling profession' (Illich 1977) that exercise social control and limits the variety of lifelong learning opportunities by defining needs and appropriate methods, contents and didactical settings.

Generally, whereas schools, with their compulsory education model, serve as smoothly running inclusion machinery via access to education and educational attainment, adult education is deeply grounded in the *voluntariness* of learners' participation. Thus, even though adult education providers or policies might prioritize participation of marginalized or vulnerable individuals or groups, it is still individual adults themselves who decide whether they would want to be included in what is on offer or not (Edwards, Armstrong and Miller 2001). But this only partly explains why decades of empirical studies have proven that the profession's efforts to reach learners and target groups labeled as being in need of learning, or as being in need of inclusion in democratic societies—via means of, for example literacy, language or citizenship tests—is not coherent with participation rates. Evidence has extensively come to shed light on the traditional, and yet still growing education-related gap in access to and participation in education, solidifying the terminology-wise bible-inspired *Matthew effect: To he who has* (employment, high educational background etc.), *will be given more* (learning opportunities in all varieties) (see, e.g., EUROSTAT 2015; Ginsberg and Wlodkowski 2010).

Apparently, the logic of the circular dynamic of: *democracy through social inclusion through (adult) education through democracy through social inclusion...* and its translation to target group-oriented measures in adult education, refers to limits and contradictions: The professional labeling of target groups in need of learning and inclusion generates neither the outcome of homogenous social groups to be taken care of, nor a clientele per se willing and inspired to learn. On the contrary, as for example Bolder and Hendrich (2000) demonstrated, it might provoke resistance to impositions of today's globalized knowledge society. Such resistance is not a display of lacking skills or capabilities, but can also be the result of an active, subjectively founded performance of an adult citizen, '*subculturally meaningful*' and '*individually reasonable*' (ibid., 32); in short: reasonable resistance. In summing up, adult education academia and profession must ask themselves critically whether they accept not only exclusion as a quasi-natural part of the lifelong learning arena, but also the idea of an adult citizen being in need of and willing to learn as the 'normal' condition and display of loyalty to the democratic state. Disruptions to this 'idyll' (Rancière 1999) Rancière, J of inclusion and exclusion provide the chance to re-examine its fundamental features.

Disruptions: Adult Education, Disability/Ability and Citizenship

The issue of disability/ability helps to concretize the topic under scrutiny: Firstly, who is declared in contemporary global societies, with their emphasis on specific forms of human productivity generating human capital, as a citizen? And, second, in what ways do global polities like the UN Convention on the Rights of Persons with Disabilities (2006) provoke disruptions in the lifelong learning system? Disruptions entail the potential to open up negotiations on citizenship and, through this performativity in everyday practices and spaces, opportunities for political subjectivation and a reordering of the state-citizen-architecture.

Adult education and the issue of disability/ability is not merely a question of inclusive learning settings, didactical tools or professional willingness, but cuts right to the core of democratic societies, of citizenship and polities (Schreiber-Barsch 2017). Historically, not even the status of a *potential* clientele, seen both as capable of and vitally in need of learning, had been granted to adults with impairments or learning difficulties in most countries. In the advent of introducing compulsory education in the seventeenth century in the emerging European nation states, the view became more widespread of recognizing that also children classified as non-abled in the common sense of normality, require education *and* also have a somewhat ability to learn (Bösl, Klein and Waldschmidt 2010). This went hand in hand with the establishment of spatially segregated learning institutions, like special schools for the deaf from the middle of the eighteenth century. Hence, for centuries, segregation was based on a deficit-oriented categorization of learners into 'normal' and 'special' learning institutions along the 'able/not-able divide' (Campbell 2009). This spread to adults in the nineteenth century by means of institutions that did not merely house non-abled adults, but started to educate them and engage them in activities (e.g., Evangelische Stiftung Alsterdorf 2016). Establishing such an *able/not-able divide* in education, with disability labeled as a 'diminished state of being human' (Campbell 2009, 5), has resulted in the on-going status quo that, in Germany, learning opportunities for adults with impairments or learning difficulties continue to be provided almost exclusively in sheltered workshops or in care institutions without any primary adult education mandate—hence not in public spaces such as public adult education centers (Lindmeier 2003; Heimlich and Behr 2009), but as part of a 'regime of dis-citizenship' (Devlin and Pothier 2006).

In this dynamic, the paradigm shift by the ratification of the UN Convention on the Rights of Persons with Disabilities (in Germany in 2009), serves to illustrate the influence of a global polity instrument on the mediating process between the 'subjects of politics and the polity to which these subjects belong' (Isin and Nyers 2014). In Germany (as elsewhere), the government's commitment to ensuring 'an inclusive education system at all levels and lifelong learning' (United Nations 2006, art. 24) claims to finally fully ensure the existing right to education. This agenda-setting not only shakes the very foundations of society's lifelong learning system, especially in countries like Germany with the traditionally highly segregated system (Richardson & Powell 2011), but also has strongly contributed to the now global terminology setting of 'inclusion' as linked first and foremost to the category of disability/ability; a segregated arena within the ideology of social inclusion.

The UN Convention argues disability in its linkage to participation, not as a nation-bound, but as a human right: 'Persons with disabilities include those who have long-term physical, mental, intellectual or sensory impairments which in interaction with various barriers may hinder their full and effective participation in society on an equal basis with others' (United Nations 2006, art. 1). Formulated the other way round, accessibility to life-long learning opportunities and society as a whole should enable all individuals to 'fully enjoy all human rights and fundamental freedoms' (ibid., preamble). However, it is not the issue of participation itself, which represents the crucial point. Franz and Beck (2007) argue convincingly that the excluding impact of disabilities/abilities are not the impairments, difficulties or whatever kinds of disabilities themselves, but their commonality in being labeled, perceived and internalized as barriers to participation—by others or by oneself. This brings to the fore that disability/ability does not represent an ontological category, but needs to be contextualized according to the *interrelatedness* of being in whatever sense individually impaired as well as living in disabling societal conditions (Rocco and Delgado 2011). A deconstruction is needed from a homogenous minority group approach towards a multifactorial account of disability/ability in its interrelatedness with biological, social, cultural *and* psychological aspects, attitudes and norms, as Shakespeare (2013), Snyder and Mitchell (2006) or also Riddell and Watson (2014) support. Whereas a critical discourse in adult education on disability/ability slowly gathers momentum, the lifelong learning terrain does not necessarily reorder any faster: Rare empirical data on participation of adults with impairments and/or disabilities in the (adult) education system, exemplified by German survey data, manifests the continuity of the traditional segregation order between learning opportunities for the abled and, on the other hand, for the non-abled (Koscheck, Weiland and Ditschek 2013; Autorengruppe Bildungsberichterstattung 2014).

Under the auspices of neoliberal concepts and increased dynamics of global knowledge economies, the state-citizen-relationship in the context of disability/ability continues to aggravate for citizens with disabilities. The financial crash at the end of the 2000s weakened the important thread of social inclusion via the labor market, as it led to a diminishment of less-skilled jobs, occupied frequently by people with disabilities (see, e.g., OECD 2013; Berthoud 2007). Furthermore, the *technologies of the self*, as Pfahl (2011) has elaborated, gained even stronger impact through engraining 'technologies of disability' (ibid.): The attribution, transmitted qua pedagogical experts and the (adult) education system, to be a disabled, not an abled learner, is being internalized to the figure of a 'needy and dependent' subject (ibid., 430).

This technology serves first and foremost the interests of the professionals, taking up Rule's and Modipa's (2012) objection, 'by naturalizing 'need' as the intrinsic state of people with disabilities' (ibid., 144). This highly influences the individual and collective anticipation of learning success, skills and competences and, overall, the ability to act autonomously in the arena of lifelong learning. The outcome is an institutionalized reproduction of inequality in an able-bodied social order and a 'regime of dis-citizenship' (Devlin and Pothier 2006). Yet, adults with disabilities/abilities are as well not *superflous* (Schroer 2010; see Section 'Technologies of the Self' (Foucault): Subjectivation as Self-Governance of the Citizen); they serve for perpetuating the existing power structures by being socially included as *marginalized* citizens, a hegemonic 'including exclusion' (Mecheril 2007).

IMPLICATIONS FOR EDUCATION FOR GLOBAL CITIZENSHIP

Against this backdrop of the contested terrain of social inclusion, adult education and citizenship, implications for (adult) education for global citizenship are brought together by four aspects.

Taking up the first issue, the impact of global polities like the UN Convention on the Rights of Persons with Disabilities (2006) emphasize the global potential of, basically, human rights (see Section Disruptions: Adult Education, Disability/ability and Citizenship). Huaman, Koenig and Shultz (2008) argue that this provides 'a global citizenship frame' by 'creating the means for marginalized people to claim those things that will allow them to live with dignity and with a full range of human possibilities' (ibid., 11). Fundamental to this potentiality of global instruments, however, is the understanding, as Dower (2008) further elaborates, that the status of *being* a global citizen is already given and needs not to be achieved by educational endeavors in *becoming* a global citizen; rather, education for global citizenship needs to foster the awareness of this status and to become capable in claiming its opportunities, rights and duties. It might be that due to, for example, physical, cognitive or other kinds of impairments or disabilities, a person is not capable of fully exercising the features of citizenship; however, this does not query having the status itself. In linking this to the professional rationales of adult education, Fraser's (1995) concept of recognition offers a fruitful perspective. Because in following Fraser, recognition as a regular client and prospective participant in adult education is grounded in terms of *individual* status (as a holder of human rights)—and not to membership of a minority group paternalistically labeled as abnormal, sick or deserving pity. This would mean establishing a parity of esteem for *all* adults interested in learning in being able to decide and to act in accordance with personal interests, needs and desires and, thus, as a political subject in the lifelong learning arena—whether this is *not* to participate or to participate. Non-participation, in this sense, might represent a deliberate and meaningful decision of the citizen in today's globalized knowledge society (see Section Professional Rationalities for Meeting Needs of the Citizen).

Secondly, establishing such a parity of esteem is not about participation itself or access to learning opportunities as such—these rationales are not context-free (Masschelein and Quaghebeur 2005). Young's work (2002) strongly points to acknowledging that formal rights may ensure pro forma social inclusion, but this does not yet reveal anything about its quality. Young's (2002) distinguishing between external and internal forms of exclusion helps to identify the inherent mechanisms: External exclusion refers to the a priori exclusion of individuals from the *demos* and deliberative democracy due to formal rights. But what is decisive is internal exclusion, happening a posteriori: 'Though formally included in a forum or process, people may find that their claims are not taken seriously and may believe that they are not treated with equal respect. The dominant mood may find their ideas or modes of expression silly or simple, and not worthy of consideration' (ibid., 55). Thus, even though formal access to deliberative democracy is provided, voices are not acknowledged and recognition is granted only pro forma. Young therefore argues for more inclusive political practice and participatory forms of democratic communication as a premise of political subjectivation. That's why educational endeavors that are targeted on a *taking part is what counts* might miss the crucial point; solely taking part in a territorial sense, as for example, a participant with disabilities in a public adult education center might fulfill formal rights, but does not necessarily mean a recognition of equal voices, interests and needs.

Thirdly, the current regimes of power strongly set the global as well as local frameworks of what *quality* of participation is aiming for and in what ways access is granted to political arenas as sites for learning, performing and communicating political subjectivities (Amin 2015; Cele 2013). Rancière (1999), in his work on *disagreement*, identified such mechanisms as rules set by the current regime of power in a deliberative democracy (called *police*), which 'is an order of the visible and the sayable that sees that a particular activity is visible and another is not, that this speech is understood as discourse and another as noise' (ibid., 29). This police order is a regime of *consensus*. In contrast, Rancière suggests that politics or democracy may be understood as a process of political subjectivation beginning at the moment of disagreement, when what he calls 'the part of those who have no part' (ibid.) in the given police order seeks to disrupt it—thus, rejecting their positioning as a non-citizen, lesser citizen or dis-citizen (see Section Introduction: The Ideology of Social Inclusion) and constituting themselves through their performativity as subjects of politics (Isin and Nyers 2014, 1). Whereas Young (2002) focuses on widening political practice and participatory forms of democratic communication as premises for political subjectivation, Rancière emphasizes the objective of such processes of subjectivation: not a (better) inclusion in the current regimes of power, but a revision of the regime itself by those who were previously not granted the right to be seen and to be heard. A note of caution: education for global citizenship might not necessarily produce the social regime's foreseen prototype of a 'good' citizen.

Lastly, this emphasizes the transformative force of being recognized as citizen in the public space and sharing lifelong learning's opportunities. Rule and Modipa's (2012) research on attitudes and experiences of adult learners with disabilities/abilities in South Africa derived the transformative force of virtually occupying places that were not meant for them before: 'This movement is a physical movement from the isolation of the home to a public space in which people with disabilities engage in public activities' (ibid., 154). Referring to the point made above concerning the quality of participation, this virtual change of place is not to be underestimated due to the fact that traditional places in the domain of disabled care are known rather for infantilizing procedures and restricted possibilities for autonomous decision-making regarding if, where and how to participate (see, e.g., Ackermann and Amelung 2009). Thus, acknowledging adult learners with disabilities/ abilities as regular clientele does, very visibly, reorder the terrain, the procedures and the pedagogical settings for adult learners of all kinds, for the teaching and administrative personnel and the physical premises, and, through this, the current order of public space. However, realizing such a 'counterculture of living together' (Amin 2015) crucially depends on persons actually participating and making use of access to such public space— performing as political subjects. On the other hand, this should not be confused with establishing a yet new regime of participation, expecting that every adult with disabilities/abilities now desires to take part in what is potentially on offer to him or her; subjective appropriation processes remain to include the option to reject offers and to choose the freedom not to be included

CONCLUSION AND RECOMMENDATIONS REGARDING FUTURE RESEARCH

In conclusion, it can be said that adult education should recollect its rich tradition in not only providing *education for all—and especially for some*, but also in fostering emancipatory agendas of social struggles and societal transformation in order to move beyond its neoliberal role as society's repair shop and agency for consolidating, not questioning the given ideology of social inclusion and citizenship order. Indeed, this might cause fundamental disruptions in the profession's 'idyll' (Rancière 1999) of declaring, not asking for learning needs and capabilities, of serving only the well-known clientele and of assigning the status of an expert in disability issues generally to those to be seen as outsiders from this issue. Keeping up idylls like the binary 'able/ not-able divide' (Campbell 2009) and comfortable differentiations between 'them' and 'us', between adult education and special needs education, certainly ensures the very existence of disciplinary responsibilities and specialized know-how for normalcy, respectively, abnormality. However, it violates global human rights and falls for the common platitudes of the social inclusion rhetoric, such as a socially inclusive system of lifelong learning is expensive, but exclusion and maintaining zones of welfare and care are for free, ignoring the economic 'price of exclusion' (Buckup 2009) and the empirically proven 'disability-poverty cycle' (Banks and Polack 2014). On the contrary, the far-reaching impacts of globalism and neoliberalism in global societies do not represent the answers, but the urgent demands of *and* for citizens to negotiate how to stake out the space of participation in society and lifelong learning. For this, research is needed that does not reproduce, but rather renders possible an, as unbiased as possible, discussion of the irreducible 'complexities of the construction of self and other' (Andreotti and Souza 2014, 2). In the case of disability/ability, this would mean research that is adapted to the respective research individual's situation, possibilities and preferences (see for example Riddell, Baron and Wilson 2001; Fordyce and Riddell 2015), and not to suggestions of ableist regimes of who is able to substantially communicate about what. Because, ultimately, experiences in the lifelong learning arena have, in every sense, a momentous quality for the individuals themselves, their life courses and learner's biographies and, not least, for their performativity as citizens in today's global societies.

References

Abdi, A. A., & Shultz, L. (2014). Recolonized citizenships, rhetorical postcolonialities. In V. d. O. Andreotti & L. M. T. M. d. Souza (Eds.), *Postcolonial perspectives on global citizenship education* (pp. 158–171). New York: Routledge.

Ackermann, K. E., & Amelung, M. (2009). *Gutachten zur Situation der Erwachsenenbildung von Menschen mit geistiger Behinderung in Berlin*. Berlin: Lebenshilfe.

Amin, A. (2015). Animated Space. *Public Culture, 2,* 239–258. doi:10.1215/08992363-2841844.

Andreotti, V. d. O., & Souza, L. M. T. M. (2014). Introduction Global Citizenship Education 'Otherwise'. In V. d. O. Andreotti & L. M. T. M. d. Souza (Eds.), *Postcolonial perspectives on global citizenship education* (pp. 1–6). New York: Routledge.

Armstrong, P. F. (1982). The 'Needs-Meeting' ideology in liberal adult education. *International Journal of Lifelong Education, 1,* 293–321. doi:10.1080/0260137820010402.

Autorengruppe Bildungsberichterstattung (2014) (Eds.), *Bildung in Deutschland 2014*. Bielefeld: W. Bertelsmann.

Banks, L. M., & Polack, S. (2014). *The economic costs of exclusion and gains of inclusion of people with disabilities: evidence from low and middle income countries*. London: International Centre for Evidence in Disability, London School of Hygiene & Tropical Medicine.

Bartelheimer, P. (2007). *Politik der Teilhabe*. Berlin: Friedrich Ebert Stiftung.

Berthoud, R. (2007). *Work-rich, work-poor: Three decades of change*. Bristol: Policy Press.

Biesta, G., & Lawy, R. (2006). From teaching citizenship to learning democracy: overcoming individualism in research, policy and practice. *Cambridge journal of education, 1,* 63–79. doi:10.1080/03057640500490981.

Bolder, A., & Hendrich, W. (2000). *Fremde Bildungswelten*. Opladen: Leske + Budrich.

Bösl, E., Klein, A., & Waldschmidt, A. (2010) (Eds.), *Disability History*. Bielefeld: transcript.

Buckup, S. (2009). *The price of exclusion: The economic consequences of excluding people with disabilities from the world of work.* International labour office employment working paper no. 43. http://www.ilo.org/wcmsp5/groups/public/—ed_emp/—ifp_skills/documents/publication/wcms_119305.pdf. Accessed Feb 23, 2016.

Campbell, F. K. (2009). *Contours of ableism.* New York: Palgrave Macmillan.

Castel, R. (1995). *Les métamorphoses de la question sociale. Une chronique du salariat.* Paris: Gallimard.

Castel, R. (2005). *Die Stärkung des Sozialen.* Hamburg: Hamburger Edition.

Cele, S. (2013). Performing the Political through public space: Teenage girls' everyday use of a city park. *Space and Polity, 1,* 74–87. doi:10.1080/13562576.2013.780714.

Devlin, R., & Pothier, D. (2006). Introduction: Toward a critical theory of dis-citizenship. In D. Pothier & R. Devlin (Eds.), *Critical disability theory* (pp. 1–22). Vancouver & Toronto: UBC.

Dower, N. (2008). Are we all global citizens or are only some of us global citizens? In A. A. Abdi & L. Shultz (Eds.), *Educating for Human Rights and Global Citizenship* (pp. 39–53). Albany: State University of New York Press.

Edwards, R., Armstrong, P., & Miller, N. (2001). Include me out: Critical readings of social exclusion, social inclusion and lifelong learning. *International Journal of Lifelong Education, 5,* 417–428. doi:10.1080/02601370120116.

Esping-Andersen, G. (1990). *Three worlds of welfare capitalism.* Princeton UP: Princeton.

EUROSTAT. (2015). *Lifelong learning statistics.* http://ec.europa.eu/eurostat/statistics-explained/index.php/Lifelong_learning_statistics. Accessed March 23, 2016.

Evangelische Stiftung Alsterdorf/Protestant Foundation Alsterdorf (2016). *Eine Bewegte Geschichte.* http://www.alsterdorf.de/ueber-uns/geschichte.html. Accessed Feb 22, 2016.

Fordyce, M., & Riddell, S. (2015). Employment experiences and outcomes people in Scotland who are deaf or hard of hearing: intersections of deafness and. In C. Grover & L. Piggott (Eds.), *Disabled people, work and welfare* (pp. 163–180). Bristol: Policy Press.

Foucault, M. (2006). *Geschichte der Gouvernementalität.* B. 1 & 2. Frankfurt a.M.: suhrkamp.

Franz, D., & Beck, I. (2007). Umfeld und Sozialraumorientierung in der Behindertenhilfe. *Geistige Behinderung, 4,* 284–294.

Fraser, N. (1995). From redistribution to recognition. *New Left Review, 212,* 68–92.

Gallie, D., & Paugam, S. (2000). *Welfare regimes and the experience of unemployment in europe.* Oxford: Oxford University Press.

Ginsberg, M. B., & Wlodkowski, R. J. (2010). Access and participation. In C. E. Kasworm, A. D. Rose, & J. M. Ross-Gordon (Eds.), *Handbook of adult and continuing education* (pp. 25–34). Los Angeles et al.: Sage.

Heimlich, U., & Behr, I. (2009). Inklusion von Menschen mit Behinderung in der Erwachsenenbildung/Weiterbildung. In R. Tippelt & A. V. Hippel (Eds.), *Handbuch Erwachsenenbildung/Weiterbildung* (3rd ed., pp. 813—826). Wiesbaden: VS Verl.

Hippel, A.v., & Tippelt, R. (2009). Adressaten-, Teilnehmer- und Zielgruppenforschung. In R. Tippelt & A.V. Hippel (eds.), *Handbuch Erwachsenenbildung/Weiterbildung* (3rd ed., pp. 801–812). Wiesbaden: VS Verl.

Huaman, S. H., Koenig, S., & Shultz, L. (2008). A call and response. Human rights as a tool of dignity and transformation. In In A. A. Abdi & L. Shultz (Eds.), *Educating for human rights and global citizenship* (pp. 11–23). Albany: State University of New York Press.

Hyslop-Margison, E. J., & Sears, A. M. (2008). Challenging the Dominant neo-liberal discourse. In M. A. Peters, A. Britton, & H. Blee (Eds.), *Global citizenship education: Philosophy, theory and pedagogy* (pp. 299–315). Sense: Rotterdam.

Illich, I., et al. (Eds.). (1977). *Disabling Professions*. London: Marion Boyars.

Isin, E. F., & Nyers, P. (2014). Introduction: Globalizing citizenship studies. In E. F. Isin & P. Nyers (Eds.), *Routledge Handbook of Global Citizenship Studies* (pp. 1–11) London: Routledge.

Kabeer, N. (2005). Introduction. The search for inclusive citizenship: Meanings and expressions in an interconnected world. In N. Kabeer (Ed.), *Inclusive Citizenship. Meanings and Expressions* (pp. 1–27). London: Zed Books.

Koscheck, S., Weiland, M., & Ditschek, E. J. (2013). *wbmonitor Umfrage 2012: Klima und Strukturen der Weiterbildungslandschaft*. BiBB & DIE. www.bibb.de/dokumente/pdf/wbmonitor_Ergebnisbericht_Umfrage_2012.pdf. Accessed Feb 22, 2016.

Kronauer, M. (2010). Einleitung – Oder warum Inklusion und Exklusion wichtige Themen für die Weiterbildung sind. In M. Kronauer (Ed.), *Inklusion und Weiterbildung* (pp. 9–23). WBV: Bielefeld.

Lazarsfeld, P., Jahoda, M., & Zeisel, H. (1933). *Marienthal: The sociology of an unemployed community*. London: Tavistock.

Lehr, U. (2000). *Psychologie des Alterns* (9th ed.). Wiebelsheim: Quelle & Meyer.

Lenoir, R. (1974). *Les exclus. Un français sur dix*. Paris: Le Seuil.

Lindmeier, C. (2003). *Integrative Erwachsenenbildung. DIE Zeitschrift für Erwachsenenbildung, 4,* 28–35.

Luhmann, N. (1995). Inklusion und Exklusion. In N. Luhmann (Eds.), *Soziologische Aufklärung* (pp. 237–264). Opladen: Westdt. Verlag.

Masschelein, J., & Quaghebeur, K. (2005). Participation for better or for worse? *Journal of Philosophy of Education, 1,* 51–65.

Mecheril, P. (2007). *Diversity. Die Macht des Einbezugs*. https://heimatkunde.boell.de/2007/01/18/diversity-die-macht-des-einbezugs Accessed May 10, 2016.

Merriam, S. B. (2010). Globalization and the role of adult and continuing education: Challenges and opportunities. In C. E. Kasworm, A. D. Rose, & J. M. Ross-Gordon (Eds.), *Handbook of Adult and Continuing Education* (pp. 401–409). Los Angeles et al.: Sage.

Myrdal, G. (1963). *Challenge to Affluence*. New York: Random House.

OECD. (2013). *Divided we stand: Why inequality keeps rising*. Paris: OECD.

Paugam, S. (Ed.). (1996). *L'exclusion, l'état des savoirs*. Paris: La Découverte.

Peters, M. A., Blee, H., & Britton, A. (2008). Introduction. Many faces of global civil society: Possible futures for global citizenship. In M. A. Peters, A. Britton, & H. Blee (Eds.), *Global citizenship education: philosophy, theory and pedagogy* (pp. 1–13). Rotterdam: Sense.

Pfahl, L. (2011). *Techniken der Behinderung*. Bielefeld: Transcript.

Rancière, J. (1999). *Disagreement: Politics and philosophy*. Minneapolis: University of Minnesota Press.

Richardson, J. G., & Powell, J. J. W. (2011). *Comparing special education*. Origins to Contemporary Paradoxes. Stanford: Stanford University Press.

Riddell, S., Baron, S., & Wilson, A. (2001). *The learning society and people with learning difficulties.* Bristol: Policy Press.

Riddell, S., & Watson, N. (2014). *Disability, culture and identity.* London: Routledge.

Rocco, T. S., & Delgado, A. (2011). Shifting Lenses: A Critical examination of disability in adult education. In T. S. Rocco (Ed.), *Challenging ableism, understand disability, including adults with disabilities in workplaces and learning spaces. New directions for adult and continuing education,* (vol. 132, pp. 3–12).

Rule, P., & Modipa, T. R. (2012). "We must believe in ourselves": Attitudes and experiences of adult learners with disabilities in KwaZulu-Natal, South Africa. *Adult Education Quarterly, 2,* 138–158. doi:10.1177/0741713611400303.

Schnapper, D. (1996). Intégration et exclusion dans les sociétés modernes. In S. Paugam (Ed.), *L'exclusion, l'état des savoirs* (pp. 23–41). Paris: La Découverte.

Schreiber-Barsch, S. (2017). Space is more than place: The urban context as contested terrain of inclusive learning settings for adults and arena of political subjectivation. In: H. Sacré & S. de Visscher (Eds.), *Learning the city. Cultural approaches to civic learning in urban spaces* (pp. 67–81). Cham: Springer Briefs in Education.

Schroer, M. (2010). Die im Dunkeln sieht man doch. Inklusion, Exklusion und die Entdeckung der Überflüssigen. *Mittelweg 36,* Okt/Nov, pp. 33–48.

Shakespeare, T. (2013). *Disability rights and wrongs revisited* (2nd ed.). London, New York: Routledge.

Snyder, S. L., & Mitchell, D. T. (2006). *Cultural locations of disability.* Chicago: University of Chicago Press.

Sork, T. J. (2010). Planning and delivering of programs. In C. E. Kasworm, A. D. Rose, & J. M. Ross-Gordon (Eds.), *Handbook of Adult and Continuing Education* (pp. 157–166). Los Angeles et al.: Sage.

Stickley, T., Hitchcock, R., & Bertram, G. (2005). Social inclusion or social control? Homelessness and mental health. *Mental Health Practice, 9,* 26–30.

United Nations (1948). *Universal Declaration of Human Rights.* http://www.ohchr.org/EN/UDHR/Documents/UDHR_Translations/eng.pdf. Accessed Feb, 22 2016.

United Nations (2006). *Convention on the rights of persons with disabilities.* www.un.org/disabilities/convention/conventionfull.shtml. Accessed Feb 22, 2016.

Wilson, J. (2000). Doing justice to inclusion. *European Journal of Special Needs Education, 3,* 297–304. doi:10.1080/088562500750017907.

Wrana, D. (2006). Die Differenz Exklusion/ Inklusion in der Theorie der Erwachsenenbildung. In H. J. Forneck, G. Wiesner, & C. Zeuner (Eds.), *Teilhabe an der Erwachsenenbildung und gesellschaftliche Modernisierung* (pp. 83–97). Schneider: Baltmannsweiler.

Young, I. M. (2002). *Inclusion and democracy.* Oxford: Oxford University Press.

Zeuner, C. (2009). Erwachsenenbildung: Begründungen und Dimensionen—ein Überblick aus historischer Perspektive. *Enzyklopädie Erziehungswissenschaft Online.* doi:10.3262/EEO16090019.

AUTHOR BIOGRAPHY

Silke Schreiber-Barsch is an Assistant Professor in Adult Education at the Faculty of Education, Unit of Lifelong Learning, University of Hamburg (Germany). Her main research areas are international and comparative adult education, theory and practices of lifelong learning, issues of participation and social inclusion/exclusion, and education and adults with dis/abilities through the analytical lens of relational spatial theory

CHAPTER 9

Living Together with National Border Lines and Nationalisms

Kanako Ide

INTRODUCTION

This article focuses on educational issues associated with nationalisms, using as a case study the national, transnational, and internationally controversial issue of the American military base in Okinawa, Japan. The case of Okinawa is an appropriate one for this topic because it contains multiple iterations of nationalism. At the same time, looking at the issues surrounding the Okinawa base through the framework of nationalism sheds new light in it. This article does not aim to solve the issue by taking a specific political position of being for or against the US base. Rather, it examines the kinds of educational approaches that are necessary for the context of the chaotic political tensions associated with nationalisms. Through the example of this case, the cultivation of specific attitudes is demonstrated as the foundational educational issue affecting the debate in Okinawa. In service of this argument, this paper firstly establishes the concept of nationalism, then describes details of the situation in Okinawa. Through an analysis of the social condition within the theoretical framework of nationalism, a blind spot within the discussion of nationalism is clarified at the theoretical level. The conclusion of this chapter is that the most important educational responsibility in Okinawa is to speak to people's conscience.

K. Ide (✉)
Soka University, 1-236 Tangi, Hachiouji, 1928577, Tokyo, Japan
e-mail: kide@soka.ac.jp

© The Author(s) 2018
I. Davies et al. (eds.), *The Palgrave Handbook of Global Citizenship and Education*, https://doi.org/10.1057/978-1-137-59733-5_9

133

CONFUSION AROUND NATIONALISM

Nationalism is a difficult term to define. Benedict Anderson explains that it is a complicated word because foundational assumptions about it are derived from a sense of nations as "Imagined Communities" (Anderson 2006). Since nations as well as nationalisms are imagined with the aid of cultural and historical factors, the meanings of the terms vary widely across social contexts and discussions. This indicates that the discussion of nationalism in this article should carefully be framed. There are two key points in this matter. First, that the term of nationalism is diverse. This article takes the following assumption that "Nationalism … can be liberal as well as conservative and democratic as well as authoritarian" (Feinberg 1997, p. 67). This implies that we should carefully examine the problems of nationalism without making the assumption that cosmopolitanism can solve them, because it functions in a larger social framework. Instead, this article presumes that the gap between nationalism and cosmopolitanism can be bridged in addressing questions of nationalism in Okinawa, which involve both international and domestic issues. Thus, the chapter does not assume that nationalism is the antithesis of cosmopolitanism. Rather, in order to focus on the analysis of different varieties of nationalisms in an international context, the antithesis of "… cosmopolitanism should be … xenophobia, intolerance, injustice, chauvinism, militarism, colonialism, etc. To be sure, some nationalists exhibit these vices, but being a nationalist is neither a necessary or sufficient condition for possessing them" (Kymlicka 2001, p. 220).

Second, this article is conscious about making a distinction in its use of nationalism as it applies to the nation versus the state. In particular, since the case of Okinawa is very complex in terms of state and national issues, these terms need to be clarified. The confusion of nation and state likely is a cause of the diversity of the definitions of nationalism. As David Miller points out:

> The first is the confusion of 'nation' and 'state'. In ordinary speech, 'nation' is sometimes used as a synonym for state: when someone refers to 'the newly emerging nations of the Third World', it is very likely that they are really talking about newly created *states*. This usage is not likely to be helpful if we are trying to clarify the principle of nationality, since one of the main issues we have to consider is precisely the relationship between nations and states, and in particular the question whether each nation has a right to its own state. (Miller 1995, pp. 18–19)

As Miller mentions, since nation, state, and nationalism are intricately connected to each other, the meanings of each term become complicated. Will Kymlicka says one cause of the confusion at the theoretical level is that "… contemporary liberal theorists implicitly assume that countries contain only one nation" (Kymlicka 1995, p. 128). In contemporary society, it is not reasonable to imagine that one state consists of one nation, because the actual structure of almost all countries is that one state consists of more than one nation.

However, the idea that one state equals one nation is a widespread and unquestioned paradigm, both in theory and in practice. As a result of this distortion, nationalism is on the rise. Thus, says Kymlicka, "By nationalism, we mean those political movements and public policies that attempt to ensure that states are indeed "nation-states" in which the state and nation coincide" (Kymlicka, 2001, p. 222). In this article, nationalism is divided into two categories: state nationalism and minority nationalism. State nationalism refers to the nationalist movements under which "… states have adopted various 'nation-building' policies aimed at giving citizens a common national language, identity and culture" (Kymlicka 2001, p. 222). On the other hand, minority nationalism is where "… ethnocultural minorities within a larger state have mobilized to demand a state of their own" (Kymlicka 2001, p. 222). This classification of nationalisms helps to understand the domestic conflicts in Okinawa, as will be discussed. In addition, the political movements and policies based on minority nationalism and state nationalism are divided again by Kymlicka into two further approaches: internal restrictions and external protections. Kymlicka explains these as follows:

> The first involves the claim of a group against its own members; the second involves the claim of a group against the larger society. Both kinds of claims can be seen as protecting the stability of national or ethnic communities, but they respond to different sources of instability. The first kind is intended to protect the group from the destabilizing impact of *internal dissent* (e.g., the decision of individual members not to follow traditional practices or customs), whereas the second is intended to protect the group from the impact of *external decisions* (e.g., the economic or political decisions of the larger society). (Kymlicka 1995, p. 35)

Both state nationalism and minority nationalism hold the dimensions of internal restrictions and external protections. In state nationalism, internal restrictions would involve standardizing members of the state, for instance through assimilation policies against minority groups in the state. External protections would involve discrimination against non-members of the state by members of the state, as well as against minority members by majority members. On the other hand, in minority nationalism, both internal restrictions and external protections are ways of expressing resistance to the power of the majority group. External protection defends the uniqueness of the group from standardization. Internal restrictions unify the members of the group. Internal restrictions, for example, may include demands that members of the minority group have to practice their own traditional customs without choice. Dividing nationalisms into these approaches will help us to organize the situation in Okinawa in terms of the aims of each nationalism and the policies associated with it.

I have described these usages of the term of nationalism to demonstrate how nationalisms can be understood as having multiple definitions at different levels of the community. Next, I will discuss the educational issues surrounding nationalisms, looking at political debates over the US military base in Okinawa.

NATIONALISMS IN MULTINATIONAL AND TRANSNATIONAL CONTEXTS

Okinawa: History and Debate

Okinawa is currently a prefecture of Japan, consisting of about 160 islands[1] located between South Japan and North Taiwan. Okinawa was called Ryukyu Kingdom from the fifteenth to the nineteenth century with dual subordination to Japan and China. In 1879, Ryukyu became a prefecture of Japan. Then, in 1945, Okinawa became a battleground for Japan and the US. Since then, US troops have been stationed in Okinawa. After World War II, Okinawa was ruled by the USA, but in 1972, Okinawa was reintegrated as a part of Japan. Due to an alliance between the Japanese and American governments, the US military has been stationed at the Okinawa islands until now. Statistically, about 20% of Okinawa's main-island is taken up by US military bases. This means that even though Okinawa geographically makes up 0.6% of Japan, 74% of American military related institutes are located in Okinawa (McCormack and Norimatsu 2013, p. 7). Also, it is estimated that about 50,000 American servicemen and associates are living in the Okinawa prefecture, comprising about 4% of its entire population (Okinawaken Soumubu Chijikousitsu Danjyo Kyodo Sangashitsu 1999, p. 1).

The stationing of the US military in Okinawa has been a controversial issue for over 70 years among three major political groups: the Japanese government, the American government, and the Okinawans. The Japanese and American governments take the pro-US base position, Okinawans take the anti-US base position. The most recent debate over stationing American military bases in Okinawa relates to the transformation of the Marine Corps Air Station in Futenma, Okinawa. Here is a brief history. In 1995, a 12-year-old Japanese girl was raped by three American service men in Okinawa. These three American servicemen were not immediately charged by Japanese police because of the status of the security treaty between the USA and Japan. This incident led to the biggest anti-US base movement in Okinawa. As a result, in 1996, US President Bill Clinton and Japanese Prime Minister Ryutaro Hashimoto made an agreement to close the Marine Corps Air Station in Futenma (McCormack and Norimatsu 2013, pp. 100–119). In 1998, the governor of Okinawa, Keiichi Inamine, agreed to use Henoko in the northeast of Okinawa as an alternative to Futenma for 15 years, but this alternative was not accepted by the US (McCormack and Norimatsu 2013, pp. 142–169). At that time, consensus-building between the Japanese, Okinawan, and American governments was proceeding with difficulty. In addition, in 2009, following a change of government in Japan, the new Prime Minister, Yukio Hatoyama, proposed not to build another US base in Okinawa, leading to the cancelation of the Henoko plan, but he withdrew his statement the following year, thereby reactivating it (McCormack and Norimatsu 2013, pp. 120–141). In 2012, Hirokazu Nakaima, the governor of Okinawa, accepted the proposal to use Henoko as an alternative to Futenma, and the plan was for the use of a base for the next 200 years. However, in 2014, an anti-US base candidate won the mayoral election in the Henoko area, the same year that Takeshi Onaga was elected as a new governor of Okinawa. In October 2015, Onaga refused to allow the construction at Henoko, and the following month, the Japanese government, under Shinzo Abe's cabinet, began legal proceedings against the Okinawa prefecture for subrogation of administrative acts to continue construction on the new Henoko US military base. This lawsuit was welcomed by the American government (Takamoto and Washington-Nishida 2015).

This ongoing controversial issue well expresses the confrontational nature of the relationship between Okinawa's local government and Japan's national government with regard to the question of US military bases, and contrastingly, the alliance between the Japanese and American governments. In order to understand the situation within the theoretical framework of nationalism, we will look at political tensions between these political groups.

Nationalisms at the Domestic Level: Japan and Okinawa

The first political contest between Japan's government and the Okinawa prefecture is a model of the notion that "… nationalist conflict is often due to attempts by civic nationalists to forcibly incorporate national minorities" (Kymlicka 2001, p. 247). Kymlicka says,

> The assumption that progress involves assimilating 'backward' minorities to 'energetic' majorities is still with us, although the labels have changed. Indeed, until very recently, most theorists of modernization argued that national identities would wither away, particularly in the case of smaller nations or national minorities. These smaller groups face strong economic and political pressures to assimilate into larger nations, and modernization theorists assumed that the members of these groups would accept this process, rather than fight to maintain themselves as culturally distinct societies at the price of economic well-being or social mobility. (Kymlicka 2001, p. 206)

In this case, state nationalism is represented by the Japanese government and minority nationalism is represented by the Okinawan government. Internal restrictions against Okinawa as a policy of state nationalism by Japan have been very powerful since the prefecture was established in 1879. Colonial assimilation policies were justified because Okinawans were identified at this time as "inferior" by main-island Japanese people, because of their unique culture. In order to meet the same standards as "Japanese citizens," Okinawa needed modernization and schools forced students in Okinawa to use standard Japanese language and to practice main-island Japanese culture, leading to the punishment of Okinawan students who spoke in local dialect at school.

According to Fujisawa, this discourse has been continuing in the contemporary debate about Okinawa (Fujisawa 2005). Instead of pressuring for modernization, state nationalism justifies the hosting of US military bases in Okinawa as beneficial to economic development. For instance, as a reward for the "severe burden" (McCormack and Norimatsu 2013), the Japanese government has given large-scale subsidies to Okinawa since 1972. Local property owners of US military bases in Okinawa also have been well-paid in rent (having been ordered out for the establishment of the bases). Thus, from the viewpoint of the Japanese government, continuous anti-US base movements by Okinawans look like anti-nationalist movements because their actions seem to be not only against the interests of Japan as a nation-state, but also against the interest of Okinawa as a local community. Here, it seems that Japan's understanding of state nationalism is as one nation for one state.

On the other hand, from the viewpoint of Okinawa, our anti-nationalist movement is justifiably a minority nationalist movement. As Kymlicka points out, "Such minority nationalisms often directly conflict with state nationalism, since the latter aims to promote a common national identity throughout the state. Indeed, such minority nationalisms are often the first target of state nationalism and of nation-building policies" (Kymlicka 2001, p. 230). For Okinawans, the issue of American military bases is one of the most important local issues, because it affects daily life and local peace in Okinawa significantly. Nevertheless, Okinawa has never been a decision maker in this matter. In search of this power, minority nationalisms have been on the rise in Okinawa. Thus, in the more detailed and specific understanding of nationalism proposed by Kymlicka, actions led by the Japanese government are identifiable as anti-nationalist because they serve Japan's interests in terms of state nationalism, but go against the interests of minority nationalism.

Nationalisms Between States: US and Japan

Political dynamics regarding US troops in Okinawa are divided between American and Japanese state nationalism. Even though it is questioned whether the power balance between the USA and Japan in the Security Treaty of 1951 is fair or not, the treaty is nonetheless an attempt to form an alliance at the state level. The treaty allows the presence of American military stations to defend Japan in case of emergency. Under this logic, the Japanese government provides land and materials to the USA, and the American government in turn sends human resources and armed forces to Japan. This is identified as a kind of peace cooperation, and it functions in an international context as a symbol of state nationalism for both countries.

Nationalisms at the International Level: America and Okinawa

In order to understand the political debate over the stationing of American military troops in Okinawa, it is important to understand the relationship between Okinawans and Americans in Okinawa. The theoretical limitations of nationalism, however, make this difficult, because the mobilization of Okinawa's minority nationalism against US state nationalism is not possible. In order to meet the illusion of nationalism as one nation for one state, state nationalism enforces assimilation on minority groups in the state. In turn, the minority nationalisms seek independence or at least a certain amount of autonomy. However, the political tension between Okinawans and Americans is outside of this framework, because while it does make sense for Okinawans to petition the Japanese government with minority nationalisms, Okinawa is disconnected from the US as a nation-state. As described above, the US–Japan treaty is a matter of foreign diplomacy which, as a rule, always simplifies both countries into single national identities. Thus, in the negotiation between the states, the local voice of Okinawa is forgotten and replaced by the state voice of the Japanese government. And yet, Okinawa's local government has been trying to have its own foreign diplomacy to the US on the issue of the military bases. Since being reintegrated into Japan, 6 out of 7 Okinawan governors have visited the USA to discuss this matter. However, again, since the issue is understood as a matter of foreign diplomacy at the state level, the negotiation between Okinawa local government and American federal government has been unsuccessful.

Anderson points out the vulnerable character of the term of nationalism. According to him, while the idea of nationalism can be linked with various political ideologies in the context of individual states, it cannot explain anything about the idea of nation in the global context (Umemori 2007). Nationalism can justify various political ideologies at the domestic level, but these political ideologies are limited by national border lines because internationally each state only represents one political position with sovereignty. This is how, theoretically, Okinawa's minority nationalism and American state nationalism are unable to meet. Since minority nationalism against US military bases in Okinawa is interpretable as a matter of nationalisms in Japan, it would be an act of intervention for the US government to step in. However, this is peculiar because regardless of the theoretical limitation, Okinawans and Americans in Okinawa have been literally living together in the same island for over 70 years. Geographically, Americans in Okinawa are immigrants, a minority group. However, politically, the group is not faced with the same pressure of assimilation, because of the powerful external protection promised by the security treaty. This is how American communities are sustained and realized in Okinawa. On the other hand, even though local Okinawans do not have access to the base and Americans are free to move to outside of it, it is impossible to separate them completely. For instance, there are shopping malls called American Villages and housing complexes for

Americans outside of the fenced base. Indeed, they know that they are sharing the island with each other.

NOT THAT SIMPLE

Amerasians in Okinawa

As described above, the relationship between different levels and kinds of nationalism is complicated, but at the same time, regardless of the confusing political contests, it is a fact that American soldiers and associates in Okinawa are geographically living together with local Okinawans. It indicates that the actual social situation provided by having the US military base in Okinawa over 70 years is much more complicated than the politics of being born Amerasian in Okinawa as an *unexpected* by-product of the treaty (Murphy-Shigematsu 2002). Amerasians in Okinawa are those who are born to Japanese mothers and American fathers, the latter being either current or former US military personnel in Okinawa Island in Japan. The Amerasian community in Asia spans various countries including Cambodia, Japan, Korea, Laos, Philippines, Thailand, and Vietnam, where US military stationing has led to the existence of offspring of US military fathers and local Asian mothers. Among these countries, Okinawa in Japan has the longer history. Since it has hosted US military stations since 1945, the oldest living Amerasians are around 70 years old.

Socially, Amerasians are a minority, but it is a challenge to identify them as a group because they cannot be framed as a racial minority group, ethnic minority group, first nation group, gender minority group, or sexual minority group. Since Amerasians have been born in various Asian countries, their mothers' ethnicities are diverse. Also, their fathers are racially diverse because American servicemen can be Caucasian, Latino, or African. They do not share the same language, either. Their mothers speak various Asian languages, but their fathers' mother tongue is the same, English. Unlike first nations peoples or immigrants, Amerasians do not share history or geographical origin. The only commonality among Amerasians is the origination of the birth, that their fathers came to their mothers' country for military-related missions, and they met each other in the mothers' homeland.

The social images of Amerasians are also divided along national border lines. For example, Amerasians in the USA are identified as a kind of new immigrant, and a reflection of the Vietnam war. The Amerasian Act of 1982 and the Amerasian Homecoming Act of 1987 allow Amerasians born in some Asian countries to easily emigrate to the USA with refugee status, as part of Cold War policy. The issues of Amerasians in the USA, thus, have been understood enough to allow them to be assimilated into American culture (Nwadiora and McAdoo 1996). On the other hand, in mainland Japan, Amerasians are not widely recognized as a minority. Historically, however, especially during the occupation period from 1945 to 1951, Amerasians were called GI-babies. 'GI-baby' carries the image of an abandoned child due to the social assumption that the mothers were either sexually assaulted by or performed sex work for American soldiers (Omodaka 2007).

It is estimated that there are about 250 newborn Amerasians every year, and about 3000–4000 Amerasians living in Okinawa (Hayata 2010, p. 266). According to research from 1998, 1 out of 100 children in Okinawa is identifiable as Amerasian (Okinawaken Soumubu Chijikoushitsu Danjyo Kyodo Sangashitsu 1999, p. 8). Another estimation released by an advocacy group for Amerasians is that Amerasian families are often fatherless (Hayata 2010, p. 267). Some official statistics might support these estimations. The number of marriages between American men and Japanese women in Okinawa is 15 times higher than the average in Japan, but the divorce rate between them in Okinawa is 14 times higher than the average.[2] Other supportive data, released from the women's center in Okinawa (service in Japanese only), says that 10% of counseling services each year is for "international issues".[3]

Nationalism and Amerasians

Nationalism in its various forms affects the lives of Amerasians. At the level of state nationalism, citizenship is a major issue for Amerasians, creating two main problems: non-citizenship (either of America or Japan), or choice of citizenship. Amerasians are sometimes at risk of sliding into a situation of having no citizenship in either country, especially if they were unexpected babies. There has not been a way to know details of these children except through estimations done by advocates, because they were not publically recognized at the time of birth. Some children have just one of the two citizenships. However, their status is fragile. For instance, if Amerasians' fathers met the status outlined in the agreement under Article VI of the 1960 US–Japan Status of Forces Agreement (SOFA), a newborn Amerasian would not be able to acquire Japanese citizenship. Then, if the child's parents got divorced and parental rights were granted to the mother (as it is estimated that they often are), the child would then be in danger of having Japanese social welfare withheld, because they do not have Japanese citizenship. Some Amerasian children have dual citizenship, but this privilege is still limited because Japan's Nationality Law allows dual citizenship to be held only until the age of 22.

Schooling is another important issue for Amerasians in Okinawa (Ide 2015). Since there is no consideration for the educational needs of school-age children who have dual citizenship, the choice of citizenship has to be mostly made through the choice of school (Uezato 1998). In Okinawa, the school options for Amerasians are either Japanese public schools, the Department of Defense Dependent's schools (DoDDs), private international schools, or nonprofit schools for Amerasians. There are curriculum mismatches in Japanese public school for Amerasians because, in order to maintain the heritage of their fathers, they want to learn American culture and English. However, Japanese public schools are formed and shaped for Japanese children. In addition, Amerasians are sometimes at risk of mistreatment in these schools. Apparent physical differences mean that they are easily recognized as Amerasians and are then at risk of becoming an object of the broader hatred against US forces in Okinawa, which may take the form of abusive speech ("Yankee Go Home" being one such insult), indicating that Amerasians do not belong to Okinawa or Japan. Another abusive phrase used is "dirty," associated with a stereotype of Amerasians as an outcome of the sex trade (Uezato 1998, p. 28).

Schooling in a DoDDs, which is identified as part of American public school in Okinawa, is a difficult choice because, in addition to limited quota, highly expensive tuition, and strict enrollment rules,[4] there are curriculum mismatches as well, because these children live in Okinawa. They need to learn Japanese culture and language in order to communicate with their mothers' side of family as well as the society they are placed in. Furthermore, DoDDs are not safe "homes" for Amerasians either. Within American society in Okinawa, hate speech against Amerasians takes the form of phrases such as "Japanese trash!" indicating that Amerasians are not considered to be American (Uezato 1998, p. 116). The hate speech from both sides shows the social situation Amerasians are faced with.

Another possibility is to attend a private international school, which seems to be the most favorable choice among Amerasians. There are various private international schools in Okinawa, some of which are following American curriculum, and others of which are following Japanese school laws. These schools are open to Japanese, American, and Amerasian students and have mores flexible curriculum. However, for Amerasians, the high tuition fees are an issue in attending these schools; most of the private international schools in Okinawa are for socially privileged families, and school environments are more likely to prepare for the entrance examinations to enter good high schools.

The AmerAsian School, a nonprofit alternative school in Okinawa since 1998, is another possibility (Uezato 1998). The school's principle is Double Education. Advocators of Amerasians' rights on education claim that Double Education is a process that "... develop[s] students who can be effective citizens of both the US and Japan and attempts to enable students to value and become part of both cultures/countries" (Noiri and Janes 2008, p. 172), while also being "... a model for thinking about international education in a time of globalization and increased diversity in the world's school system" (Noiri and Janes 2008, p. 175). The detailed educational approach of Double Education is to teach communication skills in both Japanese and English and to develop the students' identity as Amerasian. Acquisition of both English and Japanese is understood as a serious educational need for Amerasians. It facilitates family communication, develops identity, and provides some of the conditions of access to both American and Japanese society. On the other hand, the expectation after graduating from the AmerAsian School is to attend high school in Japan, which indicates an eventual marginalization into Japanese society after all.

As described above, the most urgent requirements for Amerasians are legal support and educational support. However, state nationalisms block the promotion of public liaison services between Japan and the United States that would support the lives of Amerasians. There has not yet been found a way to know the details of the situations and lives of Amerasians because their lives are in between public administrations of two states. Here, it is important to mark that, unlike any other children of mixed or international couples, the heritage of Amerasians is unique, and it is reasonable that the needs of these children receive certain public consideration from the USA and Japan. Amerasians are identifiable as one of outcomes of the international "peace" policy. And yet, there are discrepancies between the international "peace" policy and the lived experience of peace for Amerasians in society. In other words, their difficulties draw attention to the two fundamental problems of the security treaty. First, that current international peace diplomacy might well be in preparation for an emergency situation, but it does not adequately provide for times of peace; and second, that Okinawan minority nationalism includes Amerasians, despite potential incongruences in political positions and the fact that Amerasian national identity exists in a grey area between Japan and the USA.

EDUCATION FOR CONNECTING PEOPLE

Samuel Huntington discusses that Japan and the US are very different in terms of civilizations (Huntington 1996). He predicts that the clash between different civilizations (Huntington 1996) will be one of the most concerning political issues in the globalized future society because differentiations of civilizations fundamentally separate people. In his argument, contracting states of the alliance between USA and Japan is interpretable as an effective way to avoid conflicts caused by differentiations of civilizations. In the case of Okinawa, however, the problem is that the alliance between USA and Japan is powerless to support Amerasians' life. Rather, Huntington's assumption does not take intimate interracial partnerships into account, nor the fact that conflicting political ideologies do not prevent the existence of mixed race offspring. In other words, Huntington's argument proves that it is necessary to invent a way to cultivate a sense of connection among people as another kind of peace diplomacy.

Martha Nussbaum criticizes the framework of the country from the viewpoint of cosmopolitanism. She pursues a cosmopolitan community. "We should give our first allegiance to no mere form of government, no temporal power, but to the moral community made up by the humanity of all human beings" (Nussbaum 1996, p. 7). She says that the moral community is larger than any national community. For Nussbaum, any nationalism "… is not and should not be taken to be a determinant of moral worth" (Nussbaum 1996, p. 133). because "the accident of where one is born is just that, an accident; any human being might have been born in any nation" (Nussbaum 1996, p. 7). According to this analysis, moral values and geographical communities are different because moral values are shared with anyone in the cosmopolitan world.

Nussbaum's view is insightful but it does not quite match the situation of Okinawa. Nussbaum understands that local communities should be merely provisional to develop the cosmopolitan view because she assumes that it is important for cosmopolitans to imagine those who are geographically far from them. But, this is not the case for Amerasians. The cause of the problem for Amerasians is that Okinawans and Americans are actually living together on the same island, but the official position that they are separated blocks the development of the moral community in the island. As a result, even though they are not geographically located at a distance from each other, people are not feeling each other.

David Miller argues that even though a sort of shared morality in global society exists and is becoming more and more important to discuss, it will not be gained simply by replacing the theoretical argument with a notion of cosmopolitanism (Miller 2003). Kymlicka also pursues a "Cosmopolitan Alternative" (Kymlicka 2001, p. 210) without giving up national frameworks as a country. For those nationalist thinkers, it seems to be more important to have careful discussions to bridge the distance between nationalisms and cosmopolitanisms, rather than simply to switch the argument from nationalism to cosmopolitanism. Nationalist thinkers try to explore "the idea of a *shared identity*" (Kymlicka 1995, p. 188) with the consideration of the contemporary social framework. Kymlicka argues:

> But what sorts of shared identity? If we examine different existing democracies to see what sort of commonalities have proved necessary for deliberative democracy, I think we would find that deliberative democracy does *not* require a common religion…; a common political ideology…; or a common racial or ethnic descent. We can find genuinely participatory democratic forums and procedures that cut across these religious/ideological/racial cleavages. (Kymlicka 2001 p. 212)

He points out that the ideal community for fostering shared identity should pursue a formation of deliberative democracy. In order to form the deliberative democratic community, the educational responsibility is to cultivate "the qualities and attitudes of its citizens" (Kymlicka 1995, p. 175). Then the foundational assumption of deliberative democracy can be the basic attitude of its citizens. It is important to note here that the current school system cannot meet the request. It is impossible for schooling to do so because fostering a sense of shared moral worth across the states is against the school system which is established, controlled, and sustained by state nationalism. It, however, does not mean that it is impossible to teach a sense of shared identity. Rather, it opens the discussion to reclaim the meaning of education as well as promoting the discussion to renew the structure of schooling. It also teaches that the development of a sense of connection should be taken as a lifelong educational task for all of us.

What can be then the idea of a shared identity as a cosmopolitan alternative in the context of Okinawa? This article concludes that it is necessary to become conscious of the fact that American servicemen and associates, as well as local Okinawans and Amerasians, are actually living together on the same island. This may seem like an obvious fact, but it has been misunderstood as if it can be seen indifferently through the misconception that people are separated by nationalisms. Realization of this fact requires courage, because it troubles the current political dynamics which sustain the individual nationalisms of the American government, the Japanese government, and local Okinawans. Even though these different aspects of nationalism have created various tensions in Okinawa, they have nonetheless shaped the society for over 70 years, meaning that any significant shift in perspective could lead to social anxiety. In order to overcome this anxiety about reforming the ways of perceiving Okinawan society, and seeing it through the lens of connection rather than separation, educational responsibility needs to speak to people's conscience.

NOTES

1. Man living islands are about 40. 2275 km² about 1/7 size of Hawaii.
2. See Year 2013s Statistics by Ministry of Health, Labour and Welfare in Japan. http://www.mhlw.go.jp/toukei/saikin/hw/jinkou/geppo/nengai13/.
3. See Okinawa Women Foundation's Tyruru Soudanshitsu Soudan Kensuu Shukeihyo from 1998–2012.
4. Some of American children whose parents working at US base in Okinawa even cannot attend DoDDs as long as their parents status do not have sufficient status in military. These children have to pay tuition to attend DoDDs or are required to attend private schools located outside of bases.

This work was supported by JSPS KAKENHI Grant Number JP26780456 and JP17K04583.

REFERENCES

Anderson, B. (2006). *Imagined communities: Reflections on the origin and spread of nationalism Brooklyn*. NY: Verso.

Feinberg, W. (1997). Nationalism in a comparative mode: A response to Chalrs Taylor. In R. McKim & J. McMahan (Eds.), *The morality of nationalism* (pp. 66–73). New York: Oxford University Press.

Fujisawa, K. (2005). *Okinawa/Kyouiku Kenryoku no Gendaishi [Contemporary history of authority of education and Okinawa]*. Shakai Hyoron Sha: Tokyo.

Hayata, M. (2010). "Doube no Kyouiku wo Mezasu Amerasian School. In Okinawa Kodomo Hakusho: Chiiki to Kodomo no "Ima" wo Kangaeru [White paper on children in Okinawa: Thinking of "current" community and children] In Okinawa Kodomo Hakusho (Ed.), *Henshuu Iinkai* (pp. 266–272). Okinawa: Border Inku.

Huntington, S. P. (1996). *The clash of civilizations and the remaking of world order.* New York: Simon and Schuster.

Ide, K. (2015). For the sake of peace: Maintaining the resonance of peace and education. *Ethics and Education, 10*(1), 73–83.

Kymlicka, W. (1995). *Multicultural citizenship: A liberal theory of minority rights.* New York: Oxford University Press.

Kymlicka, W. (2001). *Politics in the Vernacular: Nationalism, multiculturalism, and citizenship.* New York: Oxford University Press.

McCormack, G., & Norimatsu, S. O. (2013). *Okinawa no Ikari: Nitibei heno Teiko* [Anger of Okinawa: Protest to US and Japan]. Kyoto: Houritsubunkasha.

Miller, D. (1995). *On nationality.* New York: Oxford University Press.

Miller, D. (2003). *Political philosophy: A very short introduction.* Oxford: Oxford University Press.

Murphy-Shigematsu, S. (2002). *Amerasian no Kodomotachi: Shirarezaru Minority Mondai* [Amerasian Childen: Unknown Minority Issue] (J. Sakai, Trans.). Tokyo: Shueishashinsho.

Noiri, N., & Janes, D. (2008). Preparing for double citizenship: Educational innovation at the AmerAsian school in Okinawa. In *The 10th Anniversary of the AmerAsian School in Okinawa.* Okinawa.

Nussbaum, M. (1996). Patriotism and cosmopolitanism. In J. Cohen. (Ed.), *For love of country? For Boston review* (pp. 3–20). Boston: Beason Press.

Nwadiora, E., & McAdoo, H. (1996). Acculturative stress among Amerasian refugees: Gender and racial differences. *Adolescence, 31*(122), 477–488.

Okinawaken Soumubu Chijikousitsu Danjyo Kyodo Sangashitsu. (1999). *Heisei 11nendo Beigun Kichi kara Haseisuru Jyosei no Shomondai Chousa Jitsugyo Hokokusho* [The reports about the research on women's issues associated with American military base]. Okinawaken. (document provided from local government).https:// dbs.g-search.or.jp/aps/WSKR/main.jsp?ssid=20151211082515403gsh-ap03.

Omodaka, N. (2007). *Yoshiaki wa Sensou de Umare Sensou de Shinda [Yoshiaki was born and dead by wars].* Kodansha Bunko: Tokyo.

Takamoto, K., & Washington-Nishida, S. (2015, December 3). Close up 2015: Henoko Daishikkou Soshou Houteide Yoron Kanki Nerau Okinawa Tsugi Tsugi Soshou no Kamae." *Mainichi News Paper.* Accessed December 10, 2010.

Uezato, K. (1998). *AmerAsian: Mouhitotsu no Okinawa [Amerasian childen: Another Okinawa].* Kamogawa Shuppan: Kyoto.

Umemori, N. (Ed.). (2007). *Benedict anderson globalization wo Kataru [Benedict anderson talks about globalization].* Kobunsha: Tokyo.

Author Biography

Kanako Ide is Associate Professor of the Faculty of Education at the Soka University in Tokyo, Japan. Her main research interests are in democratic education, peace education, and patriotic education from a situated philosophical perspective. Her current research project, based in Japan, examines educational issues faced by children of Amerasian who are born in between local Japanese mothers and U.S. military fathers in Okinawa. She has also been working with French/American artist Fabrice Lemire, an artistic director for the Touring Show Division of Cirque du Soleil, to explore the embodiment of democracy in dance and contemporary performing arts. Her recent works are "Rethinking the Concept of Sustainability: Hiroshima as a subject of peace education," in *the Journal of Educational Philosophy and Theory* (2016), "For the Sake of Peace: Maintaining the resonance of peace and education," in *the Journal of Ethics and Education* (2015), and "Lost in Citizenship Education: Questions Faced by Amerasians in Japan", in *Citizenship Education: Global Perspective, Local Practices* (Routledge, 2014).

CHAPTER 10

Internationalism in Global Citizenship and Education

Tracey I. Isaacs

INTRODUCTION

Rizvi's thesis on teaching global interconnectivity begins by contextualising globalisation as a historical phenomenon (Rizvi 2008). He argues that the macro and micro dimensions of global interconnectivity may historically be seen from the perspective of colonial expansion (Rizvi 2008). In this context, the global movement of money, people and information also surreptitiously channelled the ideologies, cultural tastes and aspirations of the colonisers into the colonies (Rizvi 2008). Thus it may be considered that the successful economic features of globalisation were responsible for legitimising colonial political control and colonial cultural hegemony in the minds of the colonised. Furthermore, the concept of globalisation opens up debate on Wallerstein's (1976) world-systems theory which identifies how the universal (colonial power for example) influences the particular (colonies for example), thereby creating (colonial) subjectivities (Wallerstein 1976). However, more worrying, Rizvi (2008) alludes to globalisation's 'invisible' footprint by suggesting that "contemporary global interconnectivity does not assume a political centre to coordinate political and economic activity across the world" (Rizvi 2008: 2). In what appears as an appraisal of contemporary global interconnectivity, Rizvi (2008) celebrates the organic nature that networks occur through the continuous progression and exchange of goods, ideas, money, people and media (Rizvi 2008: 3). To Rizvi (2008), global interconnectivity

T.I. Isaacs (✉)
English Department, Alasala University, Dammam, Kingdom of Saudi Arabia
e-mail: tracey.isaacs@alasala.edu.sa

© The Author(s) 2018
I. Davies et al. (eds.), *The Palgrave Handbook of Global Citizenship and Education*, https://doi.org/10.1057/978-1-137-59733-5_10

(which is a feature of globalisation) facilitates the exercise of a more expansive social imagination by providing subjectivity through greater personal choice, and admission into a club of global citizens. Yet, Rizvi (2008), admittedly re-evaluates global interconnectivity more objectively by indicating that it is interpreted and experienced differently based on the continuously varying subjectivities of people (Rizvi 2008: 3). Simply stated, this means that people with strong economic agency may leverage political and cultural hegemony over those people who do not possess economic agency and capital. But what Rizvi's (2008), view presents is a rather benign characterisation of globalisation, without the attendant problematics it renders in terms of unequal distribution of capital and consequently unequal access to markets, resources, information technology and ecology. In addition, by and neutralising globalisation as 'some inherent good', disengages it from the problems of economic, political and cultural hegemony it appears to create. For example, some critical education theorists assume that the global economic power of the privileged classes subverts state power to be used in the interest of capitalist expansion. The significance of the global transfer of capital therefore impacts political and cultural configurations, since categories such as national sovereignty, and by implication national citizenship becomes issues for debate. In this light, globalisation is recast as state power working in the interest of transnational corporations to maintain economic, political and cultural domination and continued exploitation of the labouring classes (McLaren 2001). Ultimately, globalisation under these terms appears as the corporate domination of society, the absence of self-determining governments and people, and the lack of democratic accountability (McLaren 2001). These unflattering features of globalisation confront individuals and nations via unequal power configurations (dependence, the drive for independence, and sustained interdependence) that should deliberately be made visible in global citizenship education. Understood differently, the power asymmetries in economics, culture and politics suggest that the flow of social interaction might flow unidirectionally, to benefit one group over another. Therefore, one of the aims of global citizenship education should be to ameliorate situations of global economic, political and cultural inequality. Consequently, as we shall discover in the upcoming section, Byram (2011) presents an alternative interpretation of global citizenship education (Byram 2011). Briefly, Byram's (2011) account of intercultural citizenship redirects the focus towards heightened interdependence between equal social agents or groups, rather than the undemocratic, capitalist ideologies that govern globalisation.

Conceptual Underpinnings of the Theme of the Chapter

An Internationalist Perspective on Intercultural Citizenship

Building upon the previous section that grappled with the changing nature of social relations under globalisation, concepts such as national sovereignty, democratic accountability and national citizenship were problematised as contested ideas. To overcome the problems created by globalisation in terms of global citizenship education, Byram (2011) suggests an education based on intercultural citizenship (Byram 2011). In this model, the aim is to foster dialogue among groups with different languages and cultures within, and across nation-state boundaries (Byram 2011). Furthermore, Byram (2011) proposes that an internationalist perspective on intercultural citizenship combines objectives of foreign language education with citizenship education. Consequently, a more culturally sensitive approach to citizenship education is imagined that provides opportunity for young people to engage in internationalism through international dialogue and action (Byram 2011). In this conceptualisation of citizenship education, the global society is seen to be made up of mankind as a whole and is not regarded exclusively within the context of smaller social groups such as nations (Byram 2011: 11). Thus, the ideology of internationalism in global citizenship education is considered as the "international bonding of a worldwide society that overrides individual states, nations and groups of people" (Byram 2011: 12). This suggests that the nation-state does not become obsolete, but that at the very least nationhood becomes the starting point of a membership that joins nations with people in other countries (Byram 2011: 12). Ultimately, Byram (2011) argues that internationalism in global citizenship education overcomes the limits of the nation- state as it eliminates a desire in young people towards selfish, nationalist prejudice and attachment (Byram 2011: 12). So, avoiding blind allegiance to a single nation state, young people are given mental preparation through global citizenship education of living in an international community and globalised economy (Byram 2011: 12). In order for the global citizenship education model to succeed, Byram (2011) advances the idea of building political and social institutions that are multilingual and multi-ethnic (Byram 2011: 12). By showing sensitivity to cultural diversity, it is supposed that full respect for the values and cultural identities of other nations is observed (Byram 2011: 13). The practical dimensions of the language learning proposal is understood to facilitate inter-lingual and intra-lingual comprehension with the view to stimulate democratic consensus through dialogue (Byram 2011: 12). In so doing, the traditional elements of citizenship education are infused with foreign language education in order to develop communicative competence, political competence, as well as the attitudes and behaviours to live successfully in a global society (Byram 2011: 14).

While Byram (2011) and Kuehl (2009) consider the field of internationalism in global citizenship education to be under-researched, Noddings (2005) seems to have already elaborated similar notions of global interconnectivity (Noddings 2005). Noddings' constructivist view of global citizenship education is centred on economic and social justice (Noddings 2005). This view takes seriously the issues of social and cultural diversity, while it simultaneously treats the earth as a unified place. And while Byram (2011) places foreign language education at the nucleus of global citizenship education; Noddings (2005) advances peace education as the focus in her model of internationalising citizenship education. Yet, both these models continue to satisfy the basic conceptions of a traditional global citizenship education in that the emphasis still remains on social and moral responsibility; community involvement, and political literacy (Byram 2011). Conversely, the skill-based paradigm adopted by Gardiner (2006), follows a behaviourist model of global citizenship education (Gardiner 2006). The framework of the behaviourist model of education appears to be premised on positivistic rationality and the ability to analyse issues; and the ability to solve problems from multiple perspectives (Gardiner 2006). So, while both the constructivist and behaviourist models of citizenship education appraise cognitive flexibility and cultural sophistication highly; they differentiate between competence and skill. Constructivist interpretations of cognitive competence; competence in citizenship and foreign language education; and competence in interaction and mutual influence of democratic process, is based on the adaptability and sensitivity of citizens. In contrast, behaviourist models of citizenship education are based on skills (knowledge and training) to work collaboratively in diverse groups (diversity in intelligence and background). However, constructivist views regarding global citizenship run into massive difficulty as it is hard to overcome and immobilise the powerful discourse of globalisation within a concept of internationalism. Simply, the hegemonic tendencies within globalisation support ideologies rooted in unequal economic power, unequal political control and cultural dominance (English language hegemony, priority given to Western tastes, attitudes and behaviours). In this light, it becomes hard to reconcile an ideology of internationalism premised on intercultural bonding and peace with the ideology of globalisation which operates foremost on financial competitiveness (markets and product innovation). Now, having tried to grapple with the problematics of global interconnectivity and the implications thereof on conceptions of internationalism and intercultural citizenship; the upcoming section deals with a critical theoretical conception of internationalism.

Key Issues/Debates

Critical Theory and Critical Rationality in Global Citizenship

The various interpretations of globalisation discussed above present the contested elements of homogenisation and diversity, and thereby raise questions about how (global/universal) plurality and (local/particular) distinctiveness can be maintained. Further, it calls for the re-examination of categories such as national sovereignty, national citizenship and democratic accountability within the context of global citizenship. For example, if transnational corporations hold the highest degree of economic agency in a nation, how is this reflected in the nation-state's political, economic and social institutions?

More, importantly, following an assumption that the state is founded on liberal democratic principles, how would homogenisation brought about by globalisation affect democratic processes such as political literacy, civic engagement, and citizen participation? To relate these concerns more specifically to schooling, Giroux (1980) considers it debatable that significant elements of liberal democratic theory survive in the daily practices of school classrooms (Giroux 1980: 329). Following its Greek origins, education was seen as political: not to train citizens, but rather to develop a virtuous character in the ongoing pursuit for freedom (Giroux 1980: 329). Thus the creation and fight for freedom required and depended on an intelligent and active political community (Giroux 1980: 329). Yet, under the rubric of globalisation that operates on aggressive capitalist expansion, the rights of transnational corporations seem to take precedence over the rights of working-class citizens (McLaren 2001). Given this understanding, political, economic and social institutions such as schools are seen to reproduce the rationality of economic elitism, social control and cultural dominance (Giroux 1980: 329). In keeping with the school's socialisation function, under globalised capital, schools are thought to develop students through conformity and obedience to authority (Giroux 1980: 329). Further, another feature of globalisation is the effective management and control of society through technical rationality, where it is assumed that the elite classes exclusively hold the requisite economic, social and political skills to decide and organise society (Giroux 1980: 329). Thus, the problematic that technical rationality through globalisation and schooling raises for democratic theory is one of exclusion, where the laity are assumed not to be intelligent enough to actively participate in the political community. In contrast, critical theory upholds the ideals of liberal democratic theory (voluntary belonging, rights, responsibilities and action) and supports emancipatory knowledge premised on interpretive paradigms (Giroux 1980: 334). And whereas the technical management of society is seen as socialising students into passive, uncritical and apathetic citizens; critical theory proposes critical character development through reflective inquiry, challenging assumptions, and studying the contradictions in economic, social and political life (Giroux 1980: 339). Yet criticalists such as Giroux (1980) and Johnson and Morris (2011) refuse to accept that schools serve only a social reproductive function (Giroux 1980: 335; Johnson and Morris 2011: 1). These critical theorists believe that critical actors (students, parents, community organisations) react to the social reproductive function of schools through the kind of resistance that challenges what is not made explicit under schooling and globalisation. For example, critical actors might question why (their) education is aligned more closely to the economy than to other forms of social interaction (Johnson and Morris 2011: 2)? In this light, a critical and constructivist view of citizenship education at the school level gives students access to increased political engagement and more active forms of citizenship (Johnson and Morris 2011: 2). Driven by the imperatives of critical pedagogy as an ethical instructional approach, critical teachers are thought to stimulate students towards dialogue for critical consciousness; reflective action, and a concern for social justice (Johnson and Morris 2011: 2). Consequently, a critical approach to citizenship education at schools is thought to advance the democratic citizenship discourse away from the symbolic (as seen in abstract legal and political rights). Instead, it requires students to actively practice their democratic rights and responsibilities in the interest of self and social equality, justice and freedom. Thus far the discussion has focused on some of the complexities within the global citizenship education discourse. It has been argued that globalisation presents threats and opportunities for inter-cultural citizenship. Further, the concept of internationalism was examined in the context of the universal (global) and particular (local), where the local distinctiveness and national sovereignty is challenged by the homogenisation of globalisation. In the upcoming section, the discussion will continue with an examination of the particular (local) by looking more closely at critical citizenship education at the national and school level.

Critical Citizenship Education Before Global Citizenship Education

Any notion of global citizenship education must ostensibly first rest upon a foundation of (national/democratic) citizenship education. This is so because student citizens need to have a starting point to be inducted into a system of essential education in local state formation; and to help them develop a common (national/democratic) identity (Johnson and Morris 2011: 2). Though even at the national and individual level, citizen nations and citizens form supranational associations that identify with international organisations such as the United Nations (UN), European Union (EU) and African Unity (AU). Yet, this should not detract from the responsibility towards self-determination and independence (Johnson and Morris 2011: 2). As a way to defining national citizenship at the school level, critical theorists recommend particular knowledge and dispositions be developed in citizen students. First, students need to inquire into their national histories, society and institutional systems to evaluate how issues such as injustice and oppression have been navigated in social relationships. This pedagogic approach is imagined to promote critical democratic dispositions in citizen students such as active questioning, and the desire to act against injustice and oppression (Johnson and Morris 2011: 5). Second, critical students ideally should develop a social and collective imagination that makes connections between culture, power and transformation. Thus a pedagogy turned towards non-mainstream writings and ideas, in addition to dominant social discourse, is thought to encourage citizen students to become socially aware, cooperative, and to be socially responsible to themselves and others (Johnson and Morris 2011: 5). Third, citizen students should gain knowledge about their own subjectivity. In other words, students should develop their own sense of self-identity through an understanding of their social position, culture and historical context. Critical theorists believe that this kind of knowledge is intended to inspire an autonomous and critical perspective on individual and social reality (Johnson and Morris 2011: 5). And lastly, critical theorists see social engagement as a key knowledge domain in democratic citizenship education. Thus, critical education introduces students to concepts such as knowledge itself is power, even while critical education teaches students how to collectively effect systemic change through knowledge, behaviour and action. Ultimately, knowledge for effective social engagement is intended to inspire civic courage, civic responsibility and a commitment to social transformation in students (Johnson and Morris 2011: 2). Taken together, positions adopted in critical education, constructivist and intercultural citizenship theory share particular ideologies that help to better define how internationalism within global citizenship education might be viewed outside of the terms of an overpowering globalisation. This is not to mean that the theorising thus far has reconciled the threats of globalisation to global citizenship education, but it at least provides a framework where different educational and social alternatives may be imagined. While the above section dealt with an account of critical citizenship education as a prerequisite for global citizenship education, it still did not resolve some theoretical tensions such as whether any concept of internationalism and global citizenship education may be fully free of the unequal economic, social and political rights that the globalisation discourse produces. Thus, in the upcoming section, I reconsider globalisation, internationalism and critical citizenship education from Arendt's view of citizenship to understand how these positions inform an account of global citizenship education.

Collective Identity, Political Agency and the Public Sphere

Two specific trends dominate theories on globalisation. On the one hand, globalisation is seen as homogenising (through domination and exploitation) economic, political and cultural life through global interconnectivity. On the other hand, international and intercultural networks are seen to provide a platform for the exchange of goods, money, ideas, media and people. However, what remains ambiguous and obscured within both these notions is the fact that economic, political and cultural inequality characterise globalisation more as a threat than an opportunity for global social and economic cohesion. Further, related to a democratic theory of citizenship, terms such as 'public sphere, political agency and collective identity' become contaminated by elitist and bureaucratised forms of politics through globalisation. Yet, in defence of citizens' rights, Arendt theorises that plural political agency under conditions of equality continually present new political spaces where freedom may appear (Passerin d'Entreves 2006). But Arendt also cautions that political action only survives so long as citizens are free to act, and when the actions serve public interests (Passerin d'Entreves 2006). Arendt's theorising thus problematises global citizenship education when seen in the macro framing of globalisation as bureaucratised and elitist forms of politics, rather than public and participatory democracy (Passerin d'Entreves 2006). In addition, globalisation complicates the discourse on global citizenship education because of its spatial quality. In this sense, it becomes difficult to establish a collective identity because issues such as 'we', 'the collective', and 'consensus' are spatially difficult to determine or imprecise outside of the framework of the nation-state (Passerin d'Entreves 2006). Consequently, 'democratic debate', 'disagreement', 'common deliberation', 'direct involvement' and 'civic engagement' become hard to navigate within a discourse on globalisation (Passerin d'Entreves 2006).

And while Byram (2011) provides some convincing thoughts on infusing global citizenship education with foreign language learning to promote internationalism, it is still questionable whether these propositions overcome the economic and cultural hegemony wrought by globalisation (Byram 2011). If globalisation is accepted as the integration and control of financial markets; possession of natural resources; the production of knowledge through information technology; and a reason for ecological degradation, one is inclined to ask how effective intercultural bonding and dialogue alone might be in overcoming these challenges. In as much as international dialogue and action between citizen students is seen as indispensable to global citizenship education, it might be of even greater benefit if students worked significantly harder at the local and national levels to deliberate and address complex social, economic and, cultural issues that entrench domination and exploitation.

Regarding critical theorists' conceptions of citizenship education, the emphasis was foremost on helping citizen students develop knowledge and dispositions at the local and national level. Critical theorists therefore specified the knowledge citizen students would need to exercise plural political agency. Further, the emancipatory and participatory ideologies that support this type of citizenship education was different from the passive and obedient dispositions brought about by the scientifically managed society under globalisation. Under these terms it might be understood that critical citizen students are initially focused on transforming themselves, their institutions, and their communities locally, then their society (nationally) before they engage fully in internationalism and intercultural citizenship. While the intention is not to slavishly advance the critical approach to global citizenship education, the critical approach holds much promise in breaking with traditional citizenship education as it avoids naïve and romanticised engagement with social reality. In sum, the focus thus far was on trying to understand what a collective global identity really looks like within the context of a global 'public sphere', and how political agency might be exercised therein. This thinking exposed some problems, like the power dynamics evident in theories of global systems and structures, which become unavoidable to ignore when the aim of global citizenship education is global social cohesion. These understandings also pointed to the shortfalls in a theory of foreign language learning, that while persuasive in its aims, it does not go far enough as an intensive approach to overcome the deficits in global citizenship education that is threatened by aggressive globalisation. Lastly, the critical approach to citizenship education that begins with the cognitive, social, and emotional development of school students seems to present a practical way of grooming students to first master their own environments, and then later to engage in global-scale citizenship education and activism. In the upcoming section, the discussion will centre on how the above-considered theoretical and conceptual frameworks impact education for global citizenship.

IMPLICATIONS FOR EDUCATION FOR GLOBAL CITIZENSHIP

Policy Implications

To observe globalisation as a self-evident good, is to avoid confronting that globalisation affects individuals, groups and nations differently. In this regard contexts such as geographical positioning (the global North versus the global South) and, historical legacy (slavery, colonialism) situate people and nations contextually different in terms of national culture, political organisation and economic activity. Thus, from an education policy perspective, it would seem that particular (national) citizenship education policies must assign priority to their local needs and aspirations before any thought is given to intercultural or global citizenship education. Further, policy directives will need to be dictated by the political ideology of the nation-state, since it cannot simply be assumed that all governments follow a liberal democratic tradition. However, realistically, the nation-state will most likely develop citizenship education policies based primarily on its engagement with corporate society and multinational corporations and institutions. In this case, it may be fair to say that (based on the structure of the economy), nation-states might rely on global citizenship principles first to align national citizenship education policies so as to integrate into the global economy easier. What then emerges is that national sovereignty (from a policy perspective) seems to be in a precarious position, because by succumbing to global economic imperatives in national citizenship education policies, governments also invite foreign-based values and ideologies into local policy. Yet operationally, most governments cannot afford global economic exclusion. Consequently, a policy response might then be to jealousy guard against the social and cultural domination of other nations so that the nation-state may have time to establish its own national identity. This is precisely why strong national citizenship education policies are necessary in the age of globalisation because the national interests can very easily be subsumed into global interests. Lastly, in appraising citizenry as intelligent and critical, governments should make citizenship education policies very transparent by elaborating its choices and the policy dimensions it holds in the national economic, social and political interests. In this way, the nation-state is able to work within the limits of a 'self-defined globalisation' by formulating policy that seeks first to establish local and national social and collective agency; critical agency; and political engagement. In sum, the policy implications that need to be reflected in a theory of global citizenship education are

- citizenship education that seeks to maintain political and cultural independence at the national level,
- (at the global level) global citizenship education aimed at achieving interdependence through global interconnectivity
- the visibility of ideologies that minimise domination and exploitation
- the appraisal of the nation-state and its citizens as the political centre
- the commitment to minimise cultural and capitalist hegemony
- the commitment to eradicate social, economic and political inequality
- leveraging the 'good' from economic activity to benefit all
- the commitment to peace and social cohesion.

While it has been argued the concept of internationalism in global citizenship education extends the boundaries of the nation-state, conceptions of internationalism should guard against overshadowing national priorities. Thus the driving ideology of internationalism in global citizenship education, which is thought to promote intercultural bonding and membership into a globalised economy, must be carefully observed. Also, internationalism in global citizenship education is imagined to open pathways to new and diverse economic, political and social institutions built on dialogue and democratic consensus. Therefore the policy directives for internationalism in global citizenship education must reflect an inclusive ideology based on social and moral responsibility, community involvement and political literacy. Now that the implications of global citizenship education have been discussed from an internationalist perspective, what follows is an attempt to derive the curriculum implications that accompany such thinking.

Curriculum Implications

Following critical education theorists, critical citizenship education must be differentiated from citizenship education because the former attempts to give greater clarity to citizenship as a practice, while the latter is still preoccupied with the symbolic nature of citizenship. And as stated before, citizenship education may be differentiated from internationalism in global citizenship education since the latter specifies a programme of intercultural citizenship and global connectivity. What remains an unresolved tension within conceptions of internationalism in global citizenship education

Table 10.1 Competence

Competence	Dialogue for critical consciousness	Reflective action	Concern for social justice
Knowledge	• Develop the political orientation to understand societies, systems and their histories • Power and structures and their social relations • Oppression and injustice	• Understand the interaction between power, culture and transformation • Study diverse discourses: dominant and non-dominant ideas and texts	• Study and practice how to collectively effect systemic change • Use knowledge as social and cognitive power • How social resistance influences society and (in)justice
Disposition	• Ability to question critically • Ability to act against oppression and injustice	• Commitment to social awareness, cooperation • Responsibility to self and to others • Ability to learn with others	• Commitment to social transformation • Show civic courage • Be responsible for your decisions and actions

is macropower asymmetries in social relations such as politics, culture and economics. Thus, a curriculum that is serious about global social transformation must first prioritise how it will work within the limits of global political, cultural and economic inequality. Such a curriculum should therefore avoid neutral and unambiguous phrases in its conceptualisations, even while it confronts the problematic nature of society and schooling. Guided by the policy recommendations made above, curriculum development in this section will be formulated against critical theoretical impulses that demand for active forms of citizenship to be made explicit in the curriculum. Practically, this means that policy imperatives such as political literacy, community involvement and social and moral responsibility will be aligned (respectively) to critical concepts such as dialogue for critical consciousness, reflective action, and concern for social justice. The areas that will be the focus in this section are essential knowledge, and the dispositions that the curriculum should help develop in critical citizen students as shown in the table below (Table 10.1).

Of course, all curriculum propositions are premised firstly on student self-identification and the ability of citizen students to recognise their own subjectivity; to adopt a critical perspective; and to have knowledge of their social class, culture and context. Under this framework, the cognitive, affective, social and political domains of citizen student development is addressed, and its import is seen to challenge the social reproductive functions of schooling. Further, the implications of critical global citizenship education means that citizen students reject homogenisation, conformity, obedience and passivity. Instead, critical global citizenship education creates opportunity in citizen students for the types of dispositions that imagine new economic, political and social systems and institutions. Ultimately, the critical theoretical positions help clarify the active political roles citizen students play when they are able to transform social reality in concrete terms by altering negative subjectivities; affecting positive local change; influencing national politics, and impacting global structures and systems. Thus far the curriculum implications of internationalism in global citizenship education have been considered from a critical, constructivist and emancipatory perspective. What follows in the next section is a discussion on the teaching and learning implications of internationalism in global citizenship education.

Teaching and Learning Implications

Maintaining Giroux's (1980) critical theoretical conceptions of schooling, teaching may be seen as reproducing the rationality of social control and class domination (Giroux 1980: 329). By extending the policing function of schools, teachers develop habits in students to respect authority, punctuality, silence and industry (Giroux 1980: 329). Consequently, students act out of obedience and conformity, even while they do not understand the hidden function of teaching. Students therefore misrecognise the complex interaction between schooling, politics and citizenship (Giroux 1980: 329). More importantly, the transmission of facts through teaching circumvents the development of the critical intellectual habits that problematise complex relations between knowledge, power, ideology, class and economics (Giroux 1980: 329). Resultantly, students understand their social reality through abstract theoretical models and not lived experience. This means that teaching mediates the knowledge, beliefs, expectations and biases of the dominant classes, while acritical students may not actively oppose these terms (Giroux 1980: 331). Ultimately, this view of schooling and teaching is not coincident with notions of democratic citizenship education, and completely incongruent with notions of critical democratic citizenship education. In contrast to transmission pedagogy, a critical conception of citizenship education is based on modes of social inquiry that focus on emancipatory knowledge and interests (Giroux 1980: 334). The student roles in emancipatory pedagogy are therefore seen as active, critical, dialogical and participatory. And the student dispositions in emancipatory pedagogy are inclined to challenge assumptions, study contradictions (inequality, discrimination, injustice, and suffering) and engage in social activism (Giroux 1980: 339). Therefore a plausible model of global citizenship education must begin with teaching student self-identification through self-knowledge, local knowledge and national knowledge, and lastly its global relevance. In this way, students may be able to critically determine the uses and application of knowledge in local and global social relations. Further, a distinction should be made between internationalisation and internationalism in global citizenship education. Byram (2011) considers internationalisation as the activities university staff and students engage in such as the exercise of spatial mobility; the delivery of education to other countries; and the international content and material of the curriculum

(Byram 2011). While the skill-based paradigm of citizenship education favours the latter model; this model runs in opposition to the critical, competence, constructivist model of citizenship education based on political literacy, social and moral responsibility, and community involvement. This further reinforces the importance of a critical pedagogy at school and local levels of social engagement to introduce and mentor citizen students into civil democratic practices that are connected with global citizenship education. Finally, Byram (2011) suggests that teaching focused on a respect for pluralism, the valuing of indigenous knowledge, cooperation, equality, anti-discrimination (racism and prejudice) should constitute the pedagogy to advance internationalism in global citizenship education (Byram 2011).

The implications for studying intercultural citizenship and global connectivity places onus on citizen students to critically understand their lives as individuals versus their lives as citizens. Therefore, following Arendt (in Passerin d'Entreves 2006) citizen students have a national and global responsibility to learn

- Civic and global friendship and solidarity
- To engage in democratic debate and search for collective solutions to local and global social problems
- That deliberation involves continuous renegotiation and struggle
- To focus on a shared public where students go beyond self-interest and national interest
- To engage in direct and active political participation locally and globally (Passerin d'Entreves 2006).

Bearing local and national priorities as the primary reference point, global citizen students might deliberate on these (see Table 10.2) complex social issues as a form of collective agency.

Therefore, learning that induces citizen students to submit social problems to democratic debate indicates a commitment to struggle for meaningful social change. Critical global citizen students then create promise for the reformation of economic, political and social systems and institutions. Now that the teaching and learning implications of internationalism in global citizenship education have been considered, the next section will summarise the prevailing ideologies and perspectives that were presented thus far.

CONCLUSION AND RECOMMENDATIONS REGARDING FUTURE RESEARCH

The discourse on globalisation which is intertwined in a discourse on global citizenship education presents globalisation as (1) an intrusive process of hegemonic economic, political and social control and (2) as benign global intercultural connectivity. Since the harmful consequences of globalisation

Table 10.2 Interconnectivity

Interconnectivity: the relationship between local, national and global issues	• Availability of resources, employment, food scarcity, water scarcity • Rights and responsibilities • Good governance • Atrocities, asylum seekers, child labour, child soldiers • Disease (HIV/AIDS, Ebola) • Conflict, genocide, violence, war • Economic disparities, global poverty • Civil society, corporate society, religious society, NGOs, multi-national corporations, youth, the state • Biodiversity, climate change, disaster and risk management, environmental emergencies • Critical geography, critical history, critical literacy, critical media literacy, legacy of slavery, legacy of colonialism

cannot simply be ignored, it creates a challenge for creating a socially cohesive international community and equitable globalised economy. What has been suggested in this chapter is the consideration of a critical global citizenship education to augment what might already exist as the internationalism of global citizenship education. While internationalism in global citizenship education promotes an ideology of intercultural citizenship; an expansive global social imagination; and the extension of the boundaries of the nation-state, its propositions still rest on a high degree of abstraction. For example, an ideology of internationalism does not minimise the technical management or the school effectiveness theories supported by globalised education. The result is that schools are seen to perpetuate social reproduction and social exclusion; as well as to develop passive, uncritical and apathetic citizen students. In contrast, a critical approach to education and citizenship seeks to promote emancipatory pedagogy in the interests of self- and social freedom and transformation. Further, a critical global citizenship education specifies how it aims to affect teaching and learning through the knowledge and dispositions it seeks to develop in citizen students. Thus a critical approach to citizenship education helps citizen students problematise issues such as domination, exploitation and alienation, through the mastery of political literacy. Consequently, by developing critical consciousness of social reality, it is imagined that citizen students show concern for social justice and are motivated towards active community involvement. However, critical theory in educational practice is marginally understood and rarely practised. Therefore consideration should be given to infuse education policy and pedagogy with critical social theory. And following policy and pedagogy adjustments, education research should focus global citizenship education on building durable public sector organisations and highlighting the role and importance of student participation at the school level. By considering global citizenship education from a school perspective it is hoped to stimulate intellectual sensitivity to political participation and the early induction of youth in a tradition of democratic practice.

REFERENCES

Byram, M. (2011). Intercultural citizenship from an internationalist perspective. *Journal of the NUS Teaching Academy, 1*(1), 10–20.

Gardiner, H. (2006). How education changes: Considerations of history, science and values. In M. M. Suarez-Orozco & D. B. Qin-Hiliard (Eds.), *Globalization: Culture and education in the new millennium* (pp. 235–258). Berkeley, CA: University of California Press.

Giroux, H. A. (1980). Critical theory and rationality in citizenship education. *Curriculum Inquiry, 10*(4), 329–366.

Johnson, L., & Morris, P. (2011). Towards a framework for critical citizenship education. *Curriculum Journal, 21*(1), 77–96.

Kuehl, W. F. (2009). Concepts of internationalism in history. *Peace and Change, 11*(2), 1–10.

McLaren, P. (2001). The role of critical pedagogy in the globalisation era and aftermath of September 11. Interview with Peter McLaren. *Revista Electronica de Investigacion, 3*(2), 2–16.

Noddings, N. (Ed.). (2005). *Educating the global citizen.* New York, NY: Teachers College Press.

Passerin d'Entreves, M. (2006). Hannah Arendt 1906–1975. In H. N. Zatta (Ed.), *The Stanford encyclopaedia of philosophy.* Stanford, CA: Metaphysics Research Lab Centre for the Study of Language and Information Stanford University.

Rizvi, F. (2008, 11 November). *Teaching global interconnectivity.* Champaign, IL: University of Illinois at Urbana-Champaign.

Wallerstein, I. (1976). *The modern world-system: Capitalist agriculture and the origins of the European world-economy in the sixteenth century* (pp. 229–233) New York: Academic Press.

AUTHOR BIOGRAPHY

Tracey I. Isaacs completed her Ph.D. entitled *Critical Student Agency in Educational Practice: A South African Perspective,* at Stellenbosch University. This research was inspired by her professional work with culturally and economically marginal students who had struggles with literacy and numeracy development. And while she thought she had established sufficient pedagogical skill to help students comply with standardized testing mandates, there was a nagging and reluctant admission that this technical requirement could never suffice in truly helping students to learn. Inspired by a need to act ethically and pedagogically, the author began to study the political dimensions of education through critical pedagogy. Critical pedagogy has subsequently provided a conceptual bridge where the author may connect her pedagogy more closely to the lived experience of students' private lives in order to help raise a critical consciousness and develop critical literacy ability that empowers students to intervene in their own lives and transform situations of injustice and un-freedom.

CHAPTER 11

Transnationalism in Education: Theoretical Discussions and the Implications for Teaching Global Citizenship Education

Hannah Soong

INTRODUCTION

The need to attend to global citizenship education is essential for our young regardless of where they come from or where they live. In discussing citizenship education, it is important to locate civic responsibility to common humanity, as grounded in global citizenship education (Peterson 2011, 2013). Yet, to be a global citizen can mean different things to different people which can lead to lack of clarity regarding the aims, content and enactment of global citizenship (Peterson 2012). Global citizenship education notably provides students with opportunities to explore, imagine, understand and act as global citizens: at local, national and transnational levels (Reid et al. 2010).

However, driven mainly by policy regimes and a neo-conservative cultural politics, citizenship education in a number of contexts is said to have been slanted towards a weak version of citizenship (see, for example, Tudball and Henderson 2014). The challenge is particularly acute because we live in fast changing, information-rich and increasingly diversified societies. The globalisation of economic, social and cultural goods has not only paradoxically increased human aspirations but also contributed to a loss of identity and sense of belonging because of ongoing migration and increased cross-border connections (Chu 2010; Guarnizo 2012; Soong 2016).

H. Soong (✉)
University of South Australia, North Adelaide, Australia
e-mail: Hannah.soong@unisa.edu.au

© The Author(s) 2018
I. Davies et al. (eds.), *The Palgrave Handbook of Global Citizenship and Education*, https://doi.org/10.1057/978-1-137-59733-5_11

How immigrants adjust to and are integrated into new countries has been a long-term interest of social scientists engaged in migration studies (e.g. Castles 2015). A new trend in migration is that a large portion of migrants today retain lasting ties with their home country through social networks that transcend national borders (n 2011). Such increased cross-border interactions and activities indeed challenge the basic assumptions that the processes of acculturation for migrants to their new society are identical (Portes and Rumbaut 2001). Thus, the emergence of a transnational perspective has changed the study of immigration (Boccagni et al. 2016). Transnationalism also can reformulate the concept of citizenship so that it is no longer confined by the boundaries of national identity or political affiliation.

The goal in this chapter is twofold. First, I propose the need to study global citizenship by attending to the concept of transnationalism from the approach of social field theory. Second, I argue that the growing interest in global citizenship and its nexus with education cannot be adequately understood without the use of a transnational lens, broadly linked to the shifting imaginaries of people and the processes of globalisation. Given the limited space, this chapter is not a comprehensive review of transnational migration scholarship, but rather it explores a formulation of the concept of global citizenship education through the use of a transnational lens to rethink the boundaries of social life and nation-state. It also explores the basic assumptions about social institutions such as citizenship, to re-examine the tenets of educating for global citizenship.

CONCEPTUAL UNDERPINNINGS OF TRANSNATIONALISM

Transnationalism is a construct that places the experiences of migrants at the core of global mobility (Castles et al. 2014). Increasing attention has been paid to the complexities of focusing on migrants' mutual adaptations to both home and host societies to capture the notion of 'transnationalism'. By linking them with the varying levels of occurrences and intensities of maintaining ongoing relationships back home, the concept of '*trans*' has preceded the term 'nation'. However, like the discourse on global citizenship, the notion 'transnationalism' has also been variously debated. Transnationalism was initially conceptualised out of economic theory formed within a modern socioeconomic context to be discussed in social and political arenas (Castles 1999). The core of globalisation, in reality, happens 'on the ground' where smaller communities, individual families or individuals directly respond to the growing globalisation and take on a transnational role (Vertovec 2009: 2). While Vertovec (2009) asserts the distinct lack of consensus surrounding 'transnationalism', the term, nonetheless, currently frames various kinds of global or cross-border connections and the concerns of migrants becoming global citizens.

To date, several waves of transnational migration scholarship have fine-tuned concepts and analysed transnational relations in a nuanced manner. In earlier reformulations, the term 'transnationalism' was distinguished by the way activities are conducted and by whom. For instance, Basch et al. (1994) conceptualised 'transnationalism from above' to refer to differentiating between cross-border activities conducted by the multinational corporate sector, governments, and elite-controlled macrostructural processes. By contrast, 'transnationalism from below' refers to the experiences of people living across borders (Basch et al. 1994). More recently, another form known as 'middling transnationalism' reveals a particular group of highly skilled and mobile individuals who have been treated as vulnerable and exploitable labour migrants in the receiving country (e.g. Yeoh et al. 2000). Thus, with the growing flow of globalisation, the analysis of these forms of transnational activities and groups has rendered transnational migration processes more varied, layered, complex and nuanced.

Although the notion 'transnationalism' inherently highlights the social practices and processes of migration transcending national and social boundaries, it too suggests some form of common identity of cross-border individuals or groups. In this sense, researchers adopting this framework question the nation-state as a unit of social analysis or a 'container model' of society (Wimmer and Schiller 2003). The use of transnationalism can also be understood as a 'new analytical work' to provide insights into the nature of transnational flows (Vertovec 2004). A number of contributors of transnational migration have attempted to decipher transnational theory and methodology in greater detail, and examine how the core of human international mobility sits at a more complex interconnectivity than the operational scale of globalisation (Guarnizo et al. 2003; Levitt and Schiller 2004; Sassen 2008). In order to understand how transnationalism is shaped by forces of globalisation, as elaborated from Levitt and Schiller's (2004) work, three distinct categories of transnationalism have been identified: 1) transnationalism from a socio-constructionist perspective, referring to how class gender and race relations have changed social life and sense of belonging, 2) transnationalism from a social field theory perspective suggests the changing boundaries of cultural and social belonging and 3) using the concept of 'minor transnationalism' (Lionnet and Shih 2005) to reformulate the concept of social.

Transnationalism as a Socio-Constructionist Perspective

Within migration scholarship, there has been a long-standing debate between social constructionist and positivist approaches to transnationalism (Portes 2001). The use of a social constructionist perspective on transnationalism highlights the agency of transnational individuals and one's variety of strategies to respond to the practices of 'contemporary neo-liberal restructuring of space, self and modes of legitimation' (Schiller and Faist 2010: 111).

By paying more attention to the complexities of how migrants engaged in maintaining cross-border practices and social ties, some transnational migration studies have drawn a nuanced parallelism between migration and globalisation studies. Using mainly ethnographic research on migrant communities, transnational scholars—such as Glick Schiller et al. (1995)—have observed how the intensified processes of globalisation, transnational processes can be viewed as a product of late-capitalism. The outflow of transnationals from non-industrialised sending countries (e.g. Latin America, Nepal or India) is said to have reduced the countries' capacities for economic autonomy. Instead, the effect of transnationalism has given more space to individual agency (e.g. Itzigsohn 2000; Levitt and Schiller 2004).

Such a transnational framework has given way to a new insight about the immigrant experience and acculturation, challenging the proponents of classic migration approaches. The old frame of migration analysis has been said to give reason to believe that children of the foreign-born, or so-called the second-generation immigrants, will acculturate better than their parents did and that they will, as a result, be more successful educationally and economically (Rumbaut 2002). Yet, such assimilationist perspectives have ignored important aspects of immigrant experiences. The rise of the transnational framework demonstrates how migration practices cannot be conceived of as a well-defined move from one bounded space to another. Rather, migration practices are embedded in networks stretching across multiple states, leading to production of multiple identities and cultural inventions. It also means that migrations are impermanent and they can be in the form of 'back migration', 'circular migration', 'return migration' and 'transient migration' (Faist 2000).

One key feature of 'citizenship' is depicted as a complex category embedded with the logics of the state (Sassen 2001), involving a sense of belonging and contributions made by individuals as well as groups to their society. Transnationalism, as a socio-constructionist perspective, can thus highlight how the access to citizenship can be fragmented along different social fault lines. For instance, in one transnational study, Goldring (2003) has observed how gender can shape transnational citizenship. Goldring reports on how men who lost social status in the migration process had developed a stronger orientation towards their community of origin. By contrast, as a result of migration, some women who might have experienced status gain instead of loss, were more interested in improving their livelihood in the receiving county. The use of a transnational lens to understand such experiences does not recognise class, race or gender as discrete entities. Instead, a transnational perspective can promote an understanding of certain social processes and explain why individuals—who occupy different gender, racial and class positions within different states at the same time – redefine their identities and practices (Soong et al. forthcoming). Consequently, transnationalism can impact on ones' sense of belonging and the value of 'citizenship' in both home and host societies which also can be differentiated by one's gender.

Transnationalism as a Social Field Theory

Rather than seeing the social identities and practices enacted across states boundaries as out of ordinary, Levitt and Schiller (2004) have regarded developments in social theory being challenged by both the boundedness of nation-state and the social life or networks operating across borders. Building on Bourdieu's (1990) original view of a concept of social field, Levitt and Schiller (2004) call for attention to building a transnational social field theory of society. Transnational social fields are not only multidimensional, they connect actors through direct and indirect relations across borders which are often unequally exchanged, organised and transformed because of power relations. By recognising that individuals can be embedded in a transnational social field, Levitt and Schiller further argue that it calls into question the neat divisions of connections and society into local, national, transnational and global. In doing so, they have distinguished the everyday relationships and relationships of individuals by their ways of being and ways of belonging.

According to Schiller (2004), ways of being refers to the actual social relations and practices that individuals engage in rather than to the identities associated with their actions. This means that individuals who are embedded within a social field, such as an organisation or institution, can choose to act or identify with any cultural politics or label that are associated with that field. By contrast, ways of belonging refers to practices that enact an identity which shows an intentional connection to a particular group. Such ways of belonging mark the kind of identity that combine visible action, such as wearing a Jewish star or Hijab, an awareness of what that action signifies. Despite the differentiation, studies have shown that individuals within transnational social fields combine both ways of being and ways of belonging in specific contexts, at a non-sequential way and at sporadic points of time. In this sense, the work of becoming global citizens can involve a meaningful understanding of the knowledge of ways of being and ways of belonging. This is closely related to the next category of minor transnationalism.

REFORMULATION OF THE CONCEPT OF SOCIAL IN MINOR TRANSNATIONALISM

Minor transnationalism is derived from the broader concept of transnationalism (Vertovec 2009; Khagram and Levitt 2004). Developed by Francoise Lionnet and Shu-Mei Shih (2005), minor transnationalism interprets the interactions between different groups of transnational themselves, rather than between transnationals and the larger host society they moved into. They define minor transnationalism as approaching 'transnational movement and discourse through the lens of minority populations; or more specifically, the interaction of "minor" peoples cross-culturally but within the same space and as agents of cultural interaction' (2005: 5). In this space, the concept of the social provides a concrete tracing of the movement and interactions of transnationals, visualised as 'space of exchange and participation wherever processes of hybridization occur (p. 5).

Although the model of minor transnationalism has been mainly used in reference to contemporary and recent historical narratives, it can also invoke ways about thinking of 'being' and 'becoming', that is implicated between 'an embodied self-coupled to concrete others and to the world of objects' (Venn 2000: 11), framed within the context of 'minor' transnationalism. In other words, the actual elements of transnationalism can exist in many contexts at many time periods because it pays close attention to the agents themselves. Such 'minor transnationalism' problematises the prevalent notions of globalisation as a homogenising force. Although political, social and cultural borders are increasingly permeable, they do not challenge territorial influence (Ong 1999; Sassen 2008); nevertheless, a growing overlap of 'minor' transnationals are straddling the complex, multiple and interactive transnational spaces.

In summary, understanding the lived realities of transnationals within different contexts has, I argue, brought a cluster of related questions: how have their worlds as 'minor' transnationals been constituted—patterns of complex affiliations and social formations (Levitt and Schiller 2004) or increasing 'portability of national identity' (Sassen 1999)? Building on Sassen (2008), given the possibilities of transnational flows and networks, will the notion of 'border' be challenged in today's global world? Will there be different types of citizenships emerging given such form of portability which has been referred by Ong (1999) as kinds of 'flexibility' or as a form of 'negotiated transnationality' (Robertson 2008)?

KEY ISSUES: RECONSIDERING GLOBAL CITIZENSHIP

Transnationalism allows for new ways of thinking about the nexus between global citizenship and migration which, I argue, will help interpret the consequential implications for global citizenship education. The reasons are in twofold. First, transnational social field reminds us that we are living in a global era. Given that at the heart of globalisation is the effect of living in 'overlapping communities of fate' (Held 2005: 1) which requires citizens to think and act globally, transnational social field can show how this is done in greater detail.

In one of the most developed empirical study of how transnational migration processes can change the hierarchies of social relations and authority structures to empower but also disempower, Levitt and Schiller (2004) has usefully categorised the process of cultural transformation that takes place as a result of individual's periodic social encounters with a new society. Levitt conceptualised this as 'social remittances'. Social remittances refer to 'ideas, behaviours, identities, and social capital that flow from host to sending-country communities' (p. 54). Social remittances, in Levitt and Schiller (2004) view, create a process of micro-cultural change between transnational members who live in host and home countries. This process, according to Levitt's work, is how transnational communities are built where parts of the new cultural repertoires are transmitted to families and relatives in the country of origin. As such, despite the connection, these transnational members are, engaging transnational ways of being, but not expressing a transnational way of belonging (Schiller 2004). Even though globalisation has expanded, so has the simultaneity of transnational movement and connection.

A second implication is that transnationalism can address and contribute to the nuanced nexus of globalisation and citizenship: transnationalism, in opposition to globalisation, does not require massive movements of people or constant communications between the transnationals and home/host countries. The real emphasis of minor transnationalism is the individuals, one's actions or reactions that occur because of the 'border-crossing' practices. Yet, not all globally dispersed migrants from the same homeland, relate to one another as equals (e.g. Goldring 2003). The approach of minor transnationalism under acknowledges cross-border practices of transnational mobile communities, who are weakly embedded either in the host society or country of origin, to the fore. For instance, studies that explore the deprivation of individual agency—such as with refugees, stateless or undocumented people, where cross-border practices and circulations are not an option—can shine light on the tensions and contradictions inside the entity of globalisation. By contrast, as shown in Soong (2016), some transnational individuals are able to preserve their freedom of circulation and choose to retain and nurture the duality of their identity and sense of continued belonging between the host and source countries.

Transnationalism, on one hand, presents distinct mutations of migration and citizenship. The extent, directions and forms of interactions and partnerships between transnational individuals and families back home challenge the established notions of global citizenship that involve rights and responsibilities, as an informal process, in preparing our young for their roles as global citizens. Instead, because people's lives span borders, we need concepts and theorists that make sense of those lives and, at the same time, account for the very real differences that exist between different locations of the transnational community (Levitt and Schiller 2004).

On the other hand, transnationalism is also favoured by the growing multiplication of citizenship statuses at the local, national and international levels, which are linked to the political strategies of state and civil society actors of both host and source countries (Itzigsohn 2000). If globalisation is referred to as an ongoing process towards worldwide integration and interdependence in various areas such as economics, politics, culture, finance, technology and environment, how will transnationalism be seen as a window onto the dynamics and contradictions of increasing insecurities rooted in globalised neo-liberal economies impacting on the terms 'globalisation' and 'citizenship'? In particular, how will transnationals without residence permits, be given the capacity to think and act globally, when they are in constant fear of deportation from host countries? These are possible questions and issues that transnationalism, as an analytical construct, can address in relation to global citizenship education.

Implications for Education for Global Citizenship

Citizenship education is assumed to have taken a commitment to fulfill common humanity and equal ends for all. For instance, according to studies on the needs of refugee students (e.g. Taylor and Sidhu 2012), countries accepting refugees and asylum seekers for settlement, encounter serious implications for institutions concerned with human rights and citizenship. In order to foreground citizenship education, educators should take note of the border work in the form of transnational social interconnectedness, cross-border mobility and differentiated lived experiences of transnationals today.

Paradoxically, although transnationalism as a concept places the experiences of migrants at the core, it has importantly placed citizenship as a key site for constituting the nation. In one small study (Soong and Comber (forthcoming), refugee families and children who were resettling in a local community, were found to navigate and negotiate the Australian cultural and socio-political conditions in order to reimagine themselves as becoming Australian citizens. Yet, because they were economically and socially marginalised, they were caught living in a transnational state of limbo, of not knowing whether their previous nationality, religion, ethnicity and culture would be recognised as legitimate forms of citizenship. Their liminal state of transnational experience can raise critical questions about the purpose of citizenship education and its benefits for members, as well as non-members, of host society.

Reconfiguring the concept of a changing society through the transnational lens can, therefore, help to make sense of what is happening to citizenship and how our everyday transnational social relations and social contexts can be a useful conceptual lens to understanding global citizenship education. For this to happen, Beck (2000) argues for a new paradigm of 'reflexive cosmopolitanization' (p. 1) which examines the inner quality of the social and political itself, rather than the relations between national states and societies. Such a notion of cosmopolitanism implies a culture of openness and acceptance of difference in a globalising world.

Yet, we should also remember that such a broad formulation can be problematic. For instance, recent scholarship on educational migration has framed the educational experiences of an emerging group of transnational student-migrants, as a form of middle-class reproduction (Waters and Leung 2014). In this framing, educational credentials obtained from 'western' societies are seen as an esteemed form of cosmopolitan cultural capital which can be converted into economic gains in the future (Soong 2016). Such cultural interaction and exchange positioned within the logic of consumption impedes the possibilities of authentic interaction among different groups of people from various transnational groups and cultural traditions. It appears counterintuitive to the core idea of cosmopolitanism where a shared sense of humanity and respect for one another can occur amongst different people, regardless of their class, race, gender and beliefs. Through the lens of transnationalism, the inclusion of 'reflexive cosmopolitanisation' in a global citizenship education not only requires one to be critical of its own positioning, it also foregrounds the need to refocus attention away from narrow discourses that confine cosmopolitan sensibilities to a rarefied capital of the social elite.

In advocating the recognition for complexity, global citizenship education must take into account an understanding of internal transnational diversity, mediated by, for example, country of origin, age, class and gender. In particular, citizenship education needs to address more theoretical work on the relevance of different transnational social worlds for individual and social actions. As mentioned in the concept of minor transnationalism, unequal transnational experiences of migrants exists between those who are either forced to uproot or those who perceived themselves to be forced to uproot because of discrimination, repression or civil wars. For either of these minor transnationals, their ties with country of origin are not desired or hard to sustain. Such diversity can influence how transnationals respond to host society adaptation, homeland engagement and relations with co-ethnics members, thereby influencing their way of being and way of belonging to a community of humanity.

To capture global citizenship as a variable, the transnational lens needs to be developed as a new analytic. Increasing attention should be paid to the complexities needed to promote global competencies and consciousness (Oxley and Morris 2013), and not just by way of performing community work or having a shallow understanding of the knowledge, skills and attributes necessary for acting as global citizens (Peterson 2012). By using a transnational social field framework, not only is the constitution of nation-state as a container theory of society being challenged, it can also be used for mobilising new social movements, such as environmental activism or anti-racism, as forms of contemporary global citizenship education. In so doing, the purpose of citizenship education is not to introduce young people into an already existing democracy. Instead, it is to enable them to conceptualise the global dimension of citizenship in all individual subject disciplines, as well as through wider school values, ethos and practices.

CONCLUSION AND RECOMMENDATIONS

The chapter has taken up the question of how transnationalism can usefully inform our understanding of global citizenship by re-invigorating citizenship education as post-nationalism. Rather than a study of economic and demographic flows and movement, transnationalism and in its various conceptualisations are used to increase the capacity of education to imagine new forms of identity, nationhood and citizenship. The study of transnationalism in the social sciences is a new area of research and, as such, is under-theorised, even though it is not a new phenomenon among immigrants.

A key concern must be the promotion of quality global citizenship education to foster the development of values of peace, tolerance, mutual understanding, and developing capacities for resolving conflicts in a non-violent way. This chapter responds to Sassen's (2007) call to unsettle the current conceptualisations of global citizenship education. This unsettling comes from an awareness of the messiness and instability that is inherently present in the world of transnationalism. For this to happen, it calls for an awareness of the messiness and instability to unsettle the meaning of 'globalisation' (Sassen 2007) that is inherently present in the world of transnationalism. Rather than focusing on the integration of migrants into the new host society or how migrants maintain shared identity despite their dispersion: transnationalism is a concept that focuses on practices and networks across borders. Although the word 'transnationalism' includes the term 'nation', its relevance to education should not be discounted because the 'nation' in the modern sense of the term is still slippery and problematic.

In this context, transnationalism is not used to address issues of bounded nation-states but for 'its openness as an historical concept' that goes beyond than 'the confines of a nation (Clavin 2005: 438). Such transnational space can be used to assist in understanding how the world of 'minor' transnationals is constituted by cross-border relationships (Faist 2000), cultural interconnectedness (Ong 1999) and patterns of complex affiliations and social formations (Levitt and Schiller 2004). These multi-layered, multi-sited transnational fields are pointing to the importance of considering globalisation as *trans*-centric rather than nation-centric. In this sense, global citizenship education may well benefit from paying close attention to border work that integrates subject disciplines at an intermediary level situated between the global and the local. This approach can be viewed as a mode of consciousness to understand how structures and power reformulate one's ways of being and ways of belonging, which emerge from linkages, networks and institutions forged by migrants across borders: as a new social field in contemporary global citizenship education.

Transnationalism can present important insights into the fluid nature of social process. This in turn will provide opportunities for teaching about global issues, and increase the capacities of learners to learn about the complex contemporary social, cultural and political issues, particularly about human displacement, war, conflict and forced migration. By introducing the transnational lens implies a change of valuation of global citizenship education.

REFERENCES

Basch, L. G., Schiller, N. G., & Blanc-Szanton, C. (1994). *Nations unbound: Transnational projects, post-colonial predicaments, and de-terriorialized nation-states.* Langhorne: Gordon and Breach.

Beck, U. (2000). The cosmopolitan perspective: Sociology in the second age of modernity. *British Journal of Sociology, 5*(1), 79–107.

Boccagni, P., Lafleur, J.-M., & Levitt, P. (2016). Transnational politics as cultureal circulation: Toward a conceptual understanding of migrant politcal participation on the move. *Mobilities, 11*(3), 444–463.

TODO

Bourdieu, P. (1990). *The logic of practice*. London: Polity Press.

Castles, S. (1999). Thirty years of research on migration and multicultural societies. In S. Castles (Ed.), *From migrant worker to transnational citizen*. London: Sage.

Castles, S. (2015). International human mobility: Key issues and challenges to social theory. In S. Castles, D. Ozkul, & M. A. Cubas (Eds.), *Social transformation and migration: National and local experiences in South Korea, Turkey, Mexico and Australia*. Basingstoke: Palgrave Macmillan.

Castles, S., De Haas, H., & Miller, M. (2014). *The age of migration: International population movements in the modern world*. New York: Guilford Press.

Chu, J. (2010). *Cosmologies of credit: Transnational mobility and the politics of destination in China*. United States: Duke University Press.

Clavin, P. (2005). Defining transnationalism. *Contemporary European History, 14*(4), 421–439.

Faist, T. (2000). *The volume and dynamics of international migration and transnational social spaces*. Oxford: Oxford Univesrsity Press.

Goldring, L. (2003). Gender status and the state in transnational spaces: The gendering of political participation in Mexican hometown association. In P. Hondagneu-Sotelo (Ed.), *Gender and U.S. immigration*. Berkeley: University of California Press.

Guarnizo, L. E. (2012). "Going home": Class, gender, and household transformation among Dominican return migration. *Special issue: Caribbean circuit new directions in the study of Caribbean migration, 16*(4), 13–60.

Guarnizo, L. E., Portes, A., & Haller, W. (2003). Assimilation and transnationalism: Determinants of transnational political action among contemporary migrants. *American Journal of Sociology, 108*(6), 1211–1248.

Held, D. (2005). Globalization: The dangers and the answers. In D. Held (Ed.), *Debating globalization*. Cambridge: Polity Press.

International Organization for Migration. (2011). *Protection of migrants*. Accessed on 16 September 2014. http://www.un.org/ga/search/view_doc.asp?symbol=%20A/RES/66/172.

Itzigsohn, J. (2000). Immigration and the boundaries of citizenship: The institution of immigrants' political transnationalism. *International Migration Review, 34*, 1126–1154.

Khagram, S., & Levitt, P. (2004). *Conceptualising transnational studies*. Retrieved from Harvard University.

Levitt, P., & Schiller, G. (2004). Conceptualizing simultaneity: A transnational social field perspective on society. *International migration review, 38*, 1002–1039.

Lionnet, F., & Shih, S.-M. (2005). *Minor transnationalism*. Durham: Duke University Press.

Ong, A. (1999). *Flexible citizenship: The cultural logistics of transnationality*. Durham: Duke University Press.

Oxley, L., & Morris, P. (2013). Global citizenship: A typology for distinguishing its multiple conception. *British Journal of Educational Studies, 61*(3), 301–325.

Peterson, A. (2011). The common good and citzenship education in England: A moral enterprise? *Journal of Moral Education, 40*(1), 19–35.

Peterson, A. (2012). The educational limits of ethical cosmopolitanism: Toward a virtue theory of political and cultural cosmopolitan communities. *British Journal of Educational Studies, 60*(3), 227–242.

Peterson, A. (2013). An introduction to education and values. In J. Artur & T. Lovat (Eds.), *The Routledge international handbook of Education* (pp. 108–113). United Kingdom: Sage.

Portes, A. (2001). Introduction: The debates and significance of immigration transnationalism. *Global Networks, 1*(3), 181–193.

Portes, A., & Rumbaut, R. (2001). *Legacies: The story of the immigrant second generation.* Berkeley: University of California Press.

Reid, A., Gill, J., & Sears, A. (2010). *Globalization, the nation-state and the citizen.* London: Routledge.

Robertson, S. (2008). *Negotiated transnationality: Memberships, mobilities and the student-turned-migrant experience.* Melbourne: RMIT University.

Rumbaut, R. (2002). "Severed and sustained attachments? Language, identity, and imagined communities in the post-immigrant generation. In L. Peggy, S. Glick, L. G. Basch, & C. Blanc-Szanton (Eds.), *Towards a transnational perspective on migration: Race, class ethnicity and nationalism reconsidered.* New York: SAGE.

Sassen, S. (1999). *Globalization and its discontents.* New York: The Free Press.

Sassen, S. (2001). *The global city: New York, London, Tokyo.* Princeton: Princeton University Press.

Sassen, S. (2007). *Deciphering the global: Its spaces, scale and subjects.* London: Routledge.

Sassen, S. (2008). *Territory, authority, rights: From medieval to global assemblages.* Princeton: Princeton University Press.

Schiller, G. (2004). Transnational theory and beyond. In D. Nugent & J. Vincent (Eds.), *A Companion to the Anthropology of Politics.* Malden, MA: Blackwell.

Schiller, G., Basch, L. G., & Szanton, B. C. (1995). From immigrant to transmigrant: Theorizing transnational migration. *Anthropological Quarterly, 68*(1), 48–63.

Schiller, G., & Faist, T. (Eds.). (2010). *Migration, development and transnationalization: A critical stance.*

Soong, H. (2016). *Transnational students and mobilities: Lived experiences of migration.* Milton Park and New York: Routledge.

Soong, H. & Comber, B. (forthcoming). 'An imagined 'haven' for refugee Muslim families: Slowly re-making the school'. *International Journal of Innovation in Education* (accepted for publication on 5th September 2016).

Soong, H., Stalh, G., & Shan, H. (forthcoming). Transnational mobility through education: A Bourdieusian insight on life as middle transnationals in Australia and Canada. *Globalisation, education and societies.*

Taylor, S., & Sidhu, K. (2012). Supporting refugee students in schools: What constitutes inclusive education? *International Journal of Inclusive Education, 16*(1), 39–56.

Tudball, L., & Henderson, D. (2014). Contested notions of civics and citizenship education as national education in the Australia curriculum.

Venn, C. (2000). *Occidentalism, modernity and subjectivity.* London: SAGE.

Veretovec, S. (2004). Migrant transnationalism and modes of transformation. *International Migration Review, 38*(2), 970–1001.

Veretovec, S. (2009). *Transnationalism.* London: Routledge.

Waters, J., & Leung, M. (2014). "These are not the best students": Continuing education, transnationalisation and Hong Kong's young adult "educational non-elite". *Children's Geographies, 12*(2), 56–69.

Wimmer, A., & Schiller, G. N. (2003). Methodological nationalism, the social sciences, and the study of migration: An essay in historical epistemology. *International Migration Review, 37,* 576–610.

Yeoh, B., Huang, S., & Willis, K. (2000). Global cities, transnational flows and gender dimensions: The view from Singapore. *Journal of Economic and Social Geography, 2,* 147–158.

AUTHOR BIOGRAPHY

Hannah Soong is lecturer and a sociologist in education at the University of South Australia. Her research interests include intercultural experiences in educational contexts, the education-migration nexus, and transnationalism and identity shifts. In recognition of her research, Hannah was named as a 2015 Hawke Research Social Sciences Fellow as well as being awarded an Endeavour Cheung Kong Fellowship. In 2016, Hannah published her first sole-authored book by published Routledge entitled *Transnational Students and Mobilities: Lived Experiences of Migration.*

CHAPTER 12

Why Cosmopolitanism Needs Rethinking

Marianna Papastephanou

INTRODUCTION

The concept of cosmopolitanism has infiltrated educational discourses. It comes up in various educational disciplines as: a keyword in research questions; an identity or virtue to be cultivated in schools; a curricular provision for shaping future citizens and for guiding their thoughts and actions; an ideal for a future society in whose advent educational policy has a preparatory role; and an ideology that largely frames the self-understanding and goal-setting of current political-educational scope.

Let us be more precise. What has passed through the filter of educational ideality is not quite *a* concept of cosmopolitanism but, rather, a rich and sometimes incongruent variety of conceptions of cosmopolitanism, some of which become hegemonic. This variety reflects the long conceptual history of the term 'cosmopolitanism'. It also reflects the diverse theorizations of cosmopolitanism that often emerge through dynamics and polemics of thought (e.g., the 'modern versus postmodern' divide) or through reactive responses to new global realities, challenges, potentialities, and risks. Among those conceptions, manifest in many writings, two stand out as hegemonic: a conception of cosmopolitanism as a rootlessness that enables people to live and work across borders; and a conception of cosmopolitanism as the political ideology of a well-ordered and conflict-free world respectful of human rights. The education that corresponds to the former conception prepares global citizens as mobile subjects who feel strangers nowhere and everywhere. The education

M. Papastephanou (✉)
University of Cyprus, Nicosia, Cyprus
e-mail: edmari@ucy.ac.cy

M. Papastephanou
Faculty of Educational Sciences, University of Oslo, Oslo, Norway

© The Author(s) 2018
I. Davies et al. (eds.), *The Palgrave Handbook of Global Citizenship and Education*, https://doi.org/10.1057/978-1-137-59733-5_12

that corresponds to the latter conception serves a political socialization suitable to the advent of a borderless order of free movement, hospitality, tolerance and citizenship rights.

Below, the section on the conceptual underpinnings of cosmopolitanism unpacks operations of cosmopolitan semantic contents more fully. This will be the first step of the present chapter, which requires such a conceptual mapping prior to arguing that cosmopolitanism invites further conceptual work. Then, connections between cosmopolitan semantics and current debates will indicate how our definition and understanding of cosmopolitanism affects and, indeed, has strong implications for what we consider a key cosmopolitan issue and a relevant educational task. Education for global citizenship is such a task; the rethinking that, as this chapter argues, cosmopolitanism requires directs political educational thought toward under-theorized normative territories. Hence, the concluding section contains recommendations for future research which emanate from conceptual challenges.

CONCEPTUAL UNDERPINNINGS

Most conceptual accounts of cosmopolitanism disseminated and popularized in and through education map the history of cosmopolitan semantic contents as a largely standardized narrative. Regardless of such accounts operating within a modern or postmodern framework, the favored narrative is the modern, uniform one, which begins with a specific moment in ancient Greek cosmopolitanism. Hegemonic accounts trace cosmopolitanism back to the Cynic Diogenes' declaration: 'I am a cosmou polites' (citizen of the world). As such, this theoretical decision 'to begin with' a specific localization and historicization already demarcates a scope of definition and conceptualization of cosmopolitanism and, further, a scope of interest and relevance to current politics and education. Let me indicate some failures of this operation.

Narratives that single out Diogenes' cosmopolitan self-declaration establish a beginning of the notion in opposition to belonging in the city-state and define it as an I-centered ideal of rootless identification, self-description and self-prescription. This 'territorialization' of cosmopolitanism (its grounding in late fifth-early fourth century Athens) is then followed by a 'de-territorializing' operation by which cosmopolitanism (in its minimal definitions that make it workable as a conceptual tool) is generalized as just any identification of just any self with just any sense of global citizenship. Such narratives de-contextualize Diogenes' own, well-founded reasons for, and performativities of, his self-declaration. They place the opposition 'rootedness versus rootlessness' squarely within the definition of cosmopolitanism, which then becomes understood as rupture with locality for a higher and more abstract allegiance. In other words, they give conceptual 'citizenship' to this opposition. And the rest of Diogenes' worldview, which made higher demands on the self than merely identifying with cosmos and involved a break with treating profit as one's 'patria,' is also silenced.

Such definitions/conceptions involve various undesirable operations. They block the possibility of cosmopolitanism being compatible with, rather than oppositional to, a kind of rootedness. Or, they declare the rooted/rootless opposition a 'paradox' of cosmopolitanism. They commit a genetic fallacy by which a certain spatiotemporal thematization of a notion is elevated to *the* proper conceptualization of it, hindering alternative conceptualizations. Ironically 'uncosmopolitan,' they limit the territorialization of cosmopolitanism to a specific ancient locality and fail to investigate in other spatiotemporalities: neither the Upanishads nor the African philosophical oral traditions (Papastephanou 2012) are sufficiently explored regarding notions that can shed new light on cosmopolitanism.

Such operations of narrativity fall into the Eurocentric habit of seeking the origins of a positive idea within a tradition (typically, the Greek) that they appropriate as modernity's proper precursor. In an uncosmopolitan way, the appropriated elements of the Greek cultural-philosophical tradition are filtered through the lens of what matters in the (post)modern context. Cosmopolitan ideas prior to the Diogenic self-declaration, as encountered in Hesiod or, say, in Democritus—ideas that do not set the declarative 'I' center stage (Papastephanou 2012)—are bypassed. Material that reveals cosmopolitan concerns [see, Eikeland (2016)] within ancient Greek thought often found in the writings of the now usual suspects of Ur-Eurocentrism such as Plato or Aristotle is ignored. It is assumed that whatever preceded Hellenistic and Roman expansion must have been exclusively inward and city-centered and, thus, of no interest to the researcher. This matches the prior and often implicit assumption that cosmopolitanism was an adaptive reaction to imperial empirical realities instead of a self-standing vision nourished by relationality as such. Apart from failing to retrieve older material of cosmopolitan significance, this move is also Eurocentric and uncosmopolitan because it reflects the currently popular operation of making cosmopolitanism dependent upon globalization. Failing to distinguish between the global and the cosmopolitan many thinkers today turn to the past with an eye for the digestible that is easily associated with the modern conception of cosmopolitanism as rootless and unattached movement in a world of compressed time and space. This conception, which certainly does not exhaust the modern conceptualization of cosmopolitanism but has nevertheless acquired a lasting popularity, is thus further enforced by being projected onto antiquity. In turn, ancient cosmopolitanism reconstructed in such a truncated and non-historicized way comes to underpin the very modern assumptions that framed its reconstruction in the first place.

The smooth narrative that proceeds from the Diogenic self-declaration to Roman Stoic conceptions of cosmopolitanism [particularly that of Marcus Aurelius which, according to Martha Nussbaum (2008) denies particular attachments] produces a specific conceptual history of cosmopolitanism. Within it, cosmopolitanism is deployed as a Western preoccupation with: the relationship of the self with the world; the I and the common human nature (understood as universal in modern terms); and nature set anthro-pocentrically as 'home' and object of ethico-political obligation only to the extent that such obligation saves us from destroying 'our home'. The selec-tively constructed cosmopolitan history contributes to further constructions of a suitable selfhood: the liberal 'I' is interpellated to think and act as a mobile, rootless, 'progressive' and unattached subject rather than as a static, rooted, regressive subject immersed in a locality. However, in the effort to avoid chauvinism, Eurocentrism and other pathologies typically associated with risky particularist attachments, this move only secures a normativity that sweepingly rejects any attachment, incriminates or overlooks any rootedness, and under-theorizes non-regressive local allegiance. Ironically, it performs Eurocentric operations of rigidifying the rooted/rootless division, attribut-ing universal normativity to a rootless mode of being and glorifying lifestyles closer to, and typically favored by, the Western affluent footloose élites.

There also comes a neglect of any subjective or collective accountability for the impact of actions on others. For, even in more 'up-to-date' concep-tions that add nuances related to hospitality, cosmopolitanism becomes depo-liticized. Cosmo-political questions—for instance, questions dealing with how exercise of power by some has generated (or, at least, contributed to) new realities for others who are now forced to flee from their localities—are not posed. Instead, political issues take a humanitarian gloss (e.g., citizenship rights discourse confined to universal humanness). 'Cosmopolitanism recog-nizes the rights of others to "universal hospitality." Simply put, others have the right to be treated hospitably' (Waghid 2009, 88). The demarcated and recommended obligation is that the I recognize the right to hospitality of the *arrivant*. Two issues here: first, the (subjective and collective) I often owes to some arrivants more than just hospitable treatment; second, the framework of hospitality obfuscates what might be owed to those who, by remaining rooted, are never encountered as arrivants. Sometimes, either due to inability to flee or due to a decision to stay in her locality, the other does not become a visitor and does not test the I's acknowledgment of obligation to offer hospi-tality. Does the I (individual and collective) have no further or deeper cosmo-politan obligations than acknowledging the right to hospitality, if, and when, the other decides to reach our shores? Cosmopolitan conceptual underpin-nings revolving around hospitality fail to instigate searching questions that challenge the Western I's (self-described or self-prescribed as nomadic) narcis-sist empathic identifications with the moving other and homogenizations of all movement.

More on this conceptual and normative failure follows in other sections along with educational examples that make this complex point less obscure. Suffice it here to note that the cosmopolitan is monologically typecast as the identity and practice of the unattached, mobile self rather than as a relational, critical engagement with other people and nature that should decenter the I. As Spector (2015, 423) remarks, 'in the educational strand of cosmopolitanism, much attention has been placed on theorizing and describing who is cosmo-politan'. In my opinion, this evokes a Cartesian anxiety, a solipsistic concern with self-image and a neglect of how otherness is treated when the stake is not hospitality. Surprisingly, given an intellectual climate so hostile to mod-ern Cartesianism understood solely through Descartes declarative 'cogito, ergo sum', and so fascinated with the postmodern rhetoric of effacing the subject, hegemonic conceptions of cosmopolitanism focus on the self and on how (or whether) she embodies a cosmopolitan way of life. The related cos-mopolitan imaginary involves: the Ego-ideal of enriched existential choice and fortified subjectivity through knowledge of other cultures, languages and 'curi-osities'; the Ego-ideal of the benevolent, charitable and entrepreneurial Western burgher who is everywhere welcome and, by being unrestricted by particularist allegiances, is able to adapt anywhere; the Ego-ideal of the tolerant, progres-sive, wet liberal prepared to include and respect any otherness (so long as this otherness is not dangerous); and the Ego-ideal of the progressive educator who agrees with his country's extending citizenship rights to those crossing the bor-ders (yet, this educator says next to nothing about those who, unable to flee and escape war, do not constitute a refugee crisis for his country).

If there had not been strict length limits, it would have been interesting to review some such conceptualizations of cosmopolitanism that underpin political educational research. For lack of space, let me just indicatively map related cosmopolitan conceptual underpinnings. In much citizenship edu-cation, cosmopolitanism is thought as openness of the self to other cultures and lifestyles, preparedness to contact others and to learn about or from them, and caution regarding how the self speaks about the other. This cosmopolitanism primarily has a cognitive, cultural and existential touch. Sometimes, in more demanding versions, cosmopolitanism is thought through: a cluster of positive moral concepts such as tolerance and inclusion of others; virtue-ethical notions or political emotions; and legal terms such as cosmopolitan right, human rights and citizenship rights. Such cosmopolitan-isms primarily have a moral-ethical, affective (or, worse, sentimental), politi-cal, and legal touch. As for an educational humanist cosmopolitanism likewise stands accused of merely reforming rather than transforming and dethroning the self (especially the hegemonic and empowered self of the affluent, edu-cated, footloose global benefactor) (Papastephanou 2012).

Cosmopolitanism is also associated with a curriculum of refuge, hospitality, granting asylum to others and forgiveness. Yusef Waghid (2010, 104) perti-nently warns that, despite its value, this conception of cosmopolitanism runs the risk of reifying 'encounters with otherness as some romanticized dream.' He adds that it fails to discuss 'the nature of cosmopolitan encounters with others and otherness' and to theorize the relevance of democratic dialogue and of 'deliberative iterations as a cosmopolitan imaginary'. This conception of cosmopolitanism fails to take into account 'an epistemological and psycho-logical endeavour (that is, iterations) to talk back or to learn to talk back' as the cosmopolitan encounter unfolds (ibid., 105).

Yet, in my view, even the cosmopolitan ethic of deliberative iterations, such as Seyla Benhabib's (2006), has its own failures. For, it relies on a communicative utopian imaginary. The term 'utopia' is not meant disparagingly; my objection concerns the communicative and its confines. I object to the reduction of cosmopolitanism to merely deliberative demands and the resulting failure to consider more material cosmopolitan measures (e.g., settlement of damages on grounds of pending historical ethico-political debts, global redistribution of wealth on grounds of justice beyond self-congratulatory framings of charity and aid). Also, a non-anthropocentric concern for nature equally escapes the scope of cosmopolitanisms that emphasize encounter and deliberation. Deliberative cosmopolitanisms do not challenge the self enough regarding historical, economic and ecological matters. Or, they seem to expect such demands just to be raised by the other, thus making them dependent upon the other's attainment of a communicative ability or potentiality to make a case that the Western burgher would find convincing and compelling. Therefore, I see historical, economic and ecological cosmopolitanisms as indispensable dimensions of a stereoscopically conceived cosmopolitanism (that is, one which has many faces, all necessary and synergizing for rethinking cosmopolitanism more boldly).

Key Issues/Debates

Based on the above-sketched cosmopolitan conceptual underpinnings many debates within citizenship education and outside revolve around questions about rootedness and rootlessness. Jeremy Waldron defines the adjective 'cosmopolitan' as indicating 'a way of constructing an identity for oneself that is different from, and arguably opposed to, the idea of belonging to or devotion to or immersion in a particular culture' (2000, 227). This is most revealing of the nodal point of liberal and communitarian debates: liberals such as Waldron connect the cosmopolitan with a fluid and mixed-up identity constructed by the cosmopolitan himself rather than by an 'always already' of society. Communitarians, by contrast, favor conceptions of identity based on belonging to, immersion in, and devotion to a particular culture. When they make room for cosmopolitanism [e.g., Taylor (1996)], they accommodate it as solidarity for the world, a solidarity that protects local attachment from sliding into self-immurement and chauvinism. Unlike communitarians, liberals define the cosmopolitan precisely as the identity that undoes rootedness: cosmopolitan is someone who does 'not associate his identity with any secure sense of place' (Waldron 2000, 228).

The above set the premises of further debates: cosmopolitanism is often endorsed not quite as an abstract regulative '-ism' but rather as an embodied identity typified by the mobile, mixed-up self who, in turn, takes identity as nothing definitive, homogenous or 'pure.' Thus, many debates direct the scholar's energies and the researcher's investigations toward issues of identity and its relativization and toward drastic choices between oppositions such as 'authenticity versus hybridity', 'homogeneity versus heterogeneity' and 'particularity versus universality'. The focal point is the encounter of the I as 'citizen of the world' with alterity, and the ability of the I to incorporate the habits, languages, manners and customs of cities throughout the world (ibid, 227).

When the 'liberalism versus communitarianism' debate turns to less cultural and more political, moral and legal key issues the focus shifts to the scope of obligations. Theorists voicing communitarian concerns accept cosmopolitan solidarity[1] but limit the scope of citizens' regular obligations toward compatriots alone, granting them political, moral, and legal priority. Liberals differ in their positioning: some approach issues of obligations along lines of social justice within the state; others, mainly egalitarian cosmopolitans, extend obligations to the whole world and promote global justice and redistribution of wealth (Beitz 1999). In such debates too, the focus is on the I who ponders upon what might be feasible or advisable to grant to the other and seems, once again, to be pressed to make drastic choices between locally and globally determined duties.

However, new 'either/or's' of the 'modern versus postmodern' divide have shifted debates of cosmopolitanism and added new stakes. Poststructuralist and postcolonial criticisms of universalism initially produced unfavourable, even downright damning stances toward cosmopolitanism. Though 'popular debates have made hay about the theoretical oppositions between post-structural and approaches to ethics like cosmopolitanism', there have also been pleas for engagement rather than opposition (Brassett 2008, 322). Indeed, often due to postcolonial and poststructuralist influence, cosmopolitanism is not discarded but rather qualified through adjectives such as 'vernacular' (Bhabha 1995) and 'rhizomatic' (Connolly 2000), which are tasked with keeping away risks of 'liberalization', 'modernization' and 'universalization'. Against the concentric circles illustration of cosmopolitanism, more polycentric structures and metaphors are recruited to hold old cosmopolitanism in check and to infuse discourses with sensibilities absent in liberal and communitarian settings.

And yet another opposition has come to frame cosmopolitan debates, that between 'classic' and 'new' cosmopolitanism. Classic cosmopolitanism, its revivals, and related educational initiatives appeal to universal humanity, rights and/or world citizenship (Todd 2009, 25). New cosmopolitanism, dependent as it is, in my view, upon accomplished realities for resourcing its ideality, responds, in Sharon Todd's words (ibid), to the 'mounting pluralism in societies around the globe'. Reflecting postcolonial and poststructuralist critiques of abstract universalism, new cosmopolitanism emphasizes diversity and endorses 'bottom-up practices for human rights and global justice' (Spector 2015, 424).

Cosmopolitanism—old and new efforts to sanitize it notwithstanding—is debatable and ambiguous, especially as regards its political operations. Cosmopolitan theorists 'seem to leave the world of power politics roughly as they find it—merely painting over its cracks with a bright cosmopolitan gloss' (Fine 2003, 466). The question about 'the extent to which cosmopolitanism replicates in its own normative proposals the defects of that which it criticizes' (ibid, 451) is also pertinent. From an environmental perspective, it is noted with a rightly critical tone that, 'whether in its classic or new strand, educational cosmopolitanism is devoted, by and large, to the world of human beings and/or human emergencies' (Spector 2015, 423).

Many educational engagements with cosmopolitanism not only fail critically to respond to such challenges but even perform their theories as if such challenges have never been aired. Let me add here another weakness: within hegemonic cosmopolitanism, acts of border-crossing are invested with ethico-political value. Such theoretical operations rely on processes of political homogenization of acts of border-crossing and hasty politicization of locations hosting such acts. The nuance that resists these processes is often ignored. For, in reality, acts of border-crossing vary from being politically significant, subtly or overtly subversive, unavoidable and heart-rending, to being optional, individualistic, profit-seeking or, in some cases, mainly recreational. Bypassing the polymorphous character of movement, contemporary political thought attaches uniformly idealized implications to acts of mobility and their hospitable reception and considers them promising of a better political future beyond cultural purism, isolationism, and xenophobia.

An accurate and powerful criticism concerns the following two hegemonic and concurrent articulations: the one formulates cosmopolitanism as negotiating and/or embodying 'such paradoxes as rootedness and rootlessness, local and global concerns, private and public identities'; the other formulates cosmopolitanism 'as a globally-minded project for and ethico-political responsibility to human rights and global justice'. Both 'underscore cosmopolitanism in anthropocentric terms' (Spector 2015, 423). However, as much as this criticism succeeds in introducing important environmental sensibilities, it operates as if the attacked cosmopolitanisms fare well concerning human issues, and their only failure is the neglect of nature. It thus makes common cause with the attacked cosmopolitanisms at a deeper level by enforcing the wrong (though hegemonic) impression that the attacked cosmopolitanisms suffice to articulate the human-centered issues and need solely to be supplemented with ecological issues that will mitigate or even stave off the anthropocentric undertones.

Hence, I disagree with such ecological alternatives when they miss: the extent to which anthropocentric cosmopolitan sensibilities fail to deal adequately with the human-centered issues; and the deep synergy of assumptions about the cosmopolitan self that glorify it as mobile, potentially hospitable to, and respectful of, otherness and assumptions that cosmopolitanism exclusively concerns human relations. Thus, cosmopolitanism needs to be rethought for environmental sensibilities that decenter the I but also for ethico-political sensibilities that decenter the I even more.

IMPLICATIONS FOR EDUCATION FOR GLOBAL CITIZENSHIP

I have indicated that the western 'I', self-declared as cosmopolitan or aspiring to cosmopolitanism, is more prepared to identify with the rootless—narcissistically projecting onto them a valued Western nomadism—than with the rooted subjects and their rights. In this section, I illustrate my point by referring to a very recent philosophical-educational mobilization for global citizenship. The oft-repeated operation of framing global citizenship and manifesting cosmopolitanism as response to an emergency, thus perpetuating the assumption that cosmopolitanism is crisis-dependent and global-reality-dependent, is also evident in otherwise well-meant educational initiatives to 'do something about' the current 'refugee crisis' in Europe.

Among such initiatives, there has been a theoretical one that is all the more challenging precisely because it is more sophisticated than similar ones, more cautious and modest in its claims and more difficult to deconstruct through established tools—which, let me add, often obfuscate global problems instead of radicalizing our outlooks. The December 2015 issue of *Educational Philosophy and Theory* (henceforth EPAT) hosts, in a special section, an editorial on 'the refugee crisis and the right to political asylum' and five responses to it. This timely intervention energizes education for global citizenship toward responsiveness to current realities and promotes practiced rather than merely theorized cosmopolitanism. Simultaneously, it takes vigilant distance from unsubstantiated cosmopolitan declarations. However, despite its importance, the EPAT special section performatively reproduces the hegemonic cosmopolitanism that focuses on hospitality. Before discussing it, let me indicate implications of a specific framing of hospitality.

Benhabib contrasts hospitality as virtue and hospitality as right. To her (2006, 22), hospitality should not 'be understood as a virtue of sociability, as the kindness and generosity one may show to strangers who come to one's land or who become dependent on one's act of kindness through circumstances of nature or history'. Instead, 'hospitality is a right that belongs to all human beings as far as we view them as potential participants in a world republic'. By implication, 'such a right to hospitality imposes an obligation on democratic states and their citizens not to deny refuge and asylum to those whose intentions are peaceful, particularly if refusing them would result in harming them' (Waghid 2009, 89). This chimes with a reference in the EPAT editorial to cosmopolitanism having 'its philosophical roots in Ancient Greece and its juridical notion of a single community based on a shared morality and cosmopolitan law or right anchored in an extended hospitality' (Peters and Besley 2015, 1372).The rightly non-differentiated, universal right to hospitality informs most responses to the recent 'refugee crisis'. But, unfortunately, it seems to exhaust the scope of Western citizens' responsibilities and potentialities. It puts a full stop after hospitality, as if no other obligations or mobilizations are required beyond acknowledging universal rights of asylum and citizenship and providing education to immigrant children. This is evident throughout the EPAT special section and has implications for its underlying normativity.

The editorial and the responses to the 'European migrant crisis' hosted in EPAT register important educational and political tasks of hospitality but miss equally important thought-provocations. Iraq, which is not mentioned in the listing of the numerous migration corridors from war-torn states, and the Iraqi refugees also missing in the provided statistics of the EPAT special section, challenge the assumption that all we owe is granting asylum and citizenship. Beyond human rights discourses and their poststructuralist reshufflings and renewals, Iraq is a counter-memory in the sense of bringing to mind that which escapes the Western hegemonic time consciousness. Iraq reminds us the promise of 'peace' of the Western supra-national invasion and its gruesome twist into an accomplished reality of a cemetery-like perpetual peace. It poses the question: through what genealogies have some people become refugees? What surplus of responsibility beyond mere hospitality do such genealogies indicate? Iraq is not the only case of a 'created wilderness called peace' but it also generates questions that constitute 'un-timely interruptions' of smooth humanitarian narratives, for such questions escape the time consciousness underneath timely interventions in the refugee crisis.

Though one response acknowledges that some refugees suffer the 'consequences of "our" policies and discourses' (EERJ INITIATIVE GROUP 2015, 1379), its initiative to 'amplify the voices of the refugees' offers no indication that the voiced claim is for creating conditions of true choice between the right to receive hospitality and the right to return. The description of the initiative makes refugees sound too univocal. Have some refugees been asked whether they would have fled, if they had had a viable choice to stay? That the localities of some became constructed wastelands through coordinated global actions beyond (the much disparaged) nation-state divisions or through plundering or blundering external interventions remains unexplored as to how it diversifies responsibilities and their perception.

This is neither useless nor spiteful genealogy inappropriate and misdirecting of theory in a context of urgent need for hospitable actions. It is crucial to action itself, because, harkening to diverse voices of refugees, paying attention to diverse reasons for movement facilitates awareness of diversified obligations and responsibilities, ranging from easy ones of granting citizenship and hospitable, empowering education to more difficult ones of pressing a global public sphere toward creating more enabling conditions for whoever wishes to exercise the right of return and have a true choice of residency. 'A European destiny, identity, residency and security, is the dream that drives the current wave of refugees' (Arndt 2015, 1377). I do not know whether this statement is based on empirical research that 'amplifies' the voice of refugees, but, to me, it runs the risk of being read in ways that enforce a globally dispersed half-truth that eutopianizes Europe, uni-vocalizes refugees and homogenizes motivation to movement. Though this is certainly not the intended meaning of the statement, still, that the other half of the truth is not thought through to its implications is a risky textual operation. To stave it off, I spell out another truth, which is that some people flee not because they find our EU/eutopianized 'dreamworld' as appealing as we imagine but because they have no other choice. Undifferentiated accounts of movement block outlooks beyond the narcissist assumption that all we owe to others is just to make them room and let them enjoy our idealized locality. Believing to inhabit *the* advanced space of promise and possibility, many Europeans eutopianize their locality as an appealing Promised Land and fail to realize that, to some immigrants, coming to Europe is a necessity, not an option. If those immigrants could stay home, some of them may have preferred to do so rather than flee. Hence, instead of expecting from Europeans just to open Europe as a Land *promised* to the 'other', many non-Europeans would expect those measures that would enhance their capability of free choice of residency.

The EPAT special section provides statistics with numbers of immigrants arriving, but not of people remaining, suffering and dying. They are nowhere mentioned as a parallel and non-circumventible humanitarian or political issue—the other side of the coin of this 'crisis'. Crisis should be thought as decision point for judgment rather than as a situation of chaos and disorder (Biesta 2015, 1381), but this normativity remains an empty letter so long as 'our' thought and judgment fails to reach the imaginative 'shores' of responsibilities other than citizenship and to explore the rootedness that complicates the facile concentration of thought on rootlessness.

We are urged to 'instil some courage in our politicians' so as 'to work faster to reintroduce education' for migrant children (Devine 2015, 1376). Though admirable (and, sadly, as yet unmet), is this urge exhaustive of Western responsibility? As too minimal a demand on the West, it deep-down responds Eurocentrically to migration. It silences how some migrants feel about having no other choice but to move westward and of why their choice is so limited in the first place. This and other pleas throughout the EPAT special section are important, but they all involve the moving subject. They concern the subject who moves westward and, in so doing, the subject who manages to move the West. For, an implication of the hegemonic cosmopolitanism that has nurtured education for global citizenship is that the Western self, valuing mobility as she does, rooted as she is in her self-description as rootless and declaring herself constantly on the move, finds it much easier to identify and sympathize with the mobile subject than with any rooted self. The latter may not require the West's cosmopolitan attention by coming ashore (and thus by problematizing Western comfort zones of citizenship). But she may nevertheless complicate facile cosmopolitanisms by making demands on the West based on pending ethico-political debts.

The positioning of the Western self, as much as this designation seems homogenous and problematic, becomes plain through operations of Nesta Devine's response. After an introductory plea similar to that of other responses, Devine moves to a biographical and declarative point: 'I have to make my own position plain here; I am myself a migrant' with a migrant family history (ibid). She admits 'a vested interest in the education of migrants', as she is 'a boat person' and her history is typical 'of the citizens of New Zealand, Australia and the United States'. Devine pertinently remarks: 'how such immigration-formed countries can so piously deny access to the new wave of immigrant/refugees is beyond me' (ibid). But she overlooks (in a *mise-en-âbime* denial) that these 'immigration-formed countries' are also implicated in making the localities of some refugees uninhabitable.

We indulge in the psychic discharge of the morally convenient self-image of the subject who grants citizenship to non-European arrivants. Simultaneously, we ignore a higher sense of justice owed to those entangled in Western politics and still suffering concrete damage. We especially ignore material measures (compensations, radical political redirection as concerns decision-making). Limiting responsibility to welcoming mobile arrivants—narcissistically misrecognized by the European mobile burgher as reflections of himself—proves not only self-exculpations and self-congratulatory attachments to political generalities but also EU/eutopianizations of 'our' space.

We 'should be reminding ourselves, each other, and our governments that as human beings we all have a responsibility to these people who have been moved, by war, famine, potential or actual poverty, to venture into the unknown to seek a decent life' (Devine 2015, 1375). By introducing counter-memories, I have indicated varying responsibilities in plural. We should also remind ourselves, each other and related governments of overlooked diversified movement and of rootedness (as necessity or choice) that invites acts beyond the singular responsibility of hospitality. Measures (especially those beyond charity and aid) that increase life choice for non-Europeans presuppose, in some cases, the heightened political consciousness that acknowledges responsibility to concrete others who need real choices rather than mere citizenship rights.

Conclusion and Recommendations Regarding Future Research

The cosmopolitanism that is significant for future research for and beyond global citizenship is certainly not that which Biesta (2015, 1380) rightly charges with sentimentalism and obsession with cosmos as an ordered, all-encompassing whole with no cracks. True, that was the meaning that modernity projected onto cosmos and its politics. Yet, the feeling one has from reading the special section (Biesta's response included) is that the verbal negation of hegemonic cosmopolitanism does not fare much better than cosmopolitan affirmations. More, it does not stand up to searching cosmopolitan questions. This is why cosmopolitanism needs to be rethought along lines of esthetic (rather than orderly) connotations of cosmos (Papastephanou 2012) and of the ethico-political surplus involved in cosmo-politics that exposes (post)modern global politics as so wanting.

I indicated that rethinking cosmopolitanism should begin with awareness of how hegemonic conceptions of cosmopolitanism infiltrate (educational) normativity and perform uncritical cosmetic operations on ugly global realities. Regrettably, the ultimate judge of what is owed to the other remains the self. Ironically for a world otherwise fascinated by movement, and despite the glorification of literal crossing of borders, the self remains the immovable center and simultaneously the *primum movens* from which emanates all reflection on responsibility. Unmoved by the other so long as the other is not a recognizably similar Ego also self-defined as rootless, the narcissist 'cosmopolitan' imagines that he has escaped identity by merely indicating identity. No wonder that so much lip service is paid to the responsibilities to the immigrant, the refugee, the asylum seeker, with no concern for those who are unable to travel or too rooted to stop fighting for their country against regressive forces in whose strengthening significant role has been played by imperial legacies and by recent military–'humanitarian' interventions.

Deconstruction should precede the required reconstruction of an alternative cosmopolitanism and simultaneously enact it. Cosmopolitanism can then be reconstructed as critical only when its interrelated strands (cognitive, affective, ethical, ecological, historical, economic, etc.) are set to work together in mutually directive and corrective operations. These require an eccentric view (Papastephanou 2012) that, instead of expecting us to shrink our distances from others or to undo identities, invites us to take more distances from our own selves and to revisit identities critically.

Note

1. One wonders, can global action be theorized with terms such as cosmopolitan solidarity, which echo a symmetrical relation with no prior engagement or responsibility for the condition in which some others are found today?

References

Arndt, S. (2015). Young children's education and identity: A response to the European refugee crisis. *Educational Philosophy and Theory, 47*(13–14), 1377–1378.

Beitz, C. R. (1999). Social and cosmopolitan liberalism. *International Affairs, 75*(3), 515–529.

Benhabib, S. (2006). The philosophical foundations of cosmopolitan norms. In R. Post (Ed.), *Another cosmopolitanism* (pp. 13–44). Oxford: Oxford University Press.

Bhabha, H. (1995). Unpacking my library again. *The Journal of the Midwest Modern Language Association, 28*(1), 5–18.

Biesta, G. (2015). So much for Cosmopolitanism? Refugees, asylum and world politics. *Educational Philosophy and Theory, 47*(13–14), 1381–1382.

Brassett, J. (2008). Cosmopolitanism vs. Terrorism? Discourses of ethical possibility before, and after 7/7. *Millennium: Journal of International Studies, 36*(2), 311–337.

Connolly, W. E. (2000). Speed, concentric cultures, and cosmopolitanism. *Political Theory, 28*(5), 596–618.

Devine, N. (2015). The refugee crisis and education: How should educators respond? *Educational Philosophy and Theory, 47*(13–14), 1375–1376.

EERJ Initiative Group. (2015). We need to talk about Europe! Amplifying the voices of refugees. *Educational Philosophy and Theory, 47*(13–14), 1379–1380.

Eikeland, O. (2016). Cosmópolis or Koinópolis? In P. Marianna (Ed.), *Cosmopolitanism: Educational, philosophical and historical perspectives* (pp. 21–46). Springer International Publishing.

Fine, R. (2003). Taking the 'Ism' out of cosmopolitanism: An essay in reconstruction. *European Journal of Social Theory, 6*(4), 451–470.

Nussbaum, M. (2008). Toward a globally sensitive patriotism. *Daedalus, 137*(3), 78–93.

Papastephanou, M. (2012). *Thinking differently about cosmopolitanism*. Paradigm: Boulder.

Peters, M., & Besley, T. (2015). Editorial: the refugee crisis and the right to political asylum. *Educational Philosophy and Theory, 47*(13–14), 1367–1374.

Spector, H. (2015). The who and the what of educational cosmopolitanism. *Studies in Philosophy and Education, 34*(4), 423–440.

Taylor, C. (1996). Why democracy needs patriotism. In J. Cohen & M. Nussbaum (Eds.), *For love of country: Debating the limits of patriotism*. Boston: Beacon.

Todd, S. (2009). *Toward an imperfect education: Facing humanity, rethinking cosmopolitanism*. Boulder: Paradigm Publishers.

Waghid, Y. (2009). Education for responsible citizenship. *Perspectives in Education, 27*(1), 85–90.

Waghid, Y. (2010). On the limits of cosmopolitanism and a 'curriculum of refuge'—A response to Molly Quinn. *Transnational Curriculum Inquiry 7*(1), http://nitinat.library.ubc.ca/ojs/index.php/tci. Accessed February 2016.

Waldron, J. (2000). What is cosmopolitan? *The Journal of Political Philosophy, 8*(2), 227–243.

AUTHOR BIOGRAPHY

Marianna Papastephanou teaches philosophy of education in the Department of Education at the University of Cyprus. She studied and taught at the University of Cardiff and also studied and did research in Berlin. Her research interests include political philosophy, the modern-versus-postmodern divide, utopia, and the Frankfurt School. Among her recent publications are *Thinking Differently About Cosmopolitanism: Theory, Eccentricity and a Globalized World* (Paradigm, 2012) and, as editor, *Cosmopolitanism: Educational, Philosophical and Historical Perspectives* (Springer, 2016).

CHAPTER 13

Global Citizenship Education, Postcolonial Identities, and a Moral Imagination

Nuraan Davids

INTRODUCTION

The incredulous preoccupied politicisation of hair in American society has seen black` women desperately trying to straighten their hair, ironically, since the abolishment of slavery in 1865. In apartheid South Africa, the texture of hair took on even more grotesque importance as people were subjected to the 'pencil test' to determine whether they were white, black or coloured. Perhaps, even more grotesque, was the willingness of people to undergo the test in the hope of 'upgrading' their racial status. At once diabolical and absurd, the Population Registration Act of 1950—under the ministry of Hendrik Verwoerd, the architect of perverse apartheid—allowed people to undergo a 'verblankingsproses' or a 'whitening process'; also known as 'blanqueamiento', or 'racial whitening' The sheer parody of this process is perhaps most vividly captured by Joseph Lelyveld, who writes:

> In my first year back in South Africa, 558 coloureds became whites, 15 whites became coloureds, eight Chinese became whites, seven whites became Chinese, 40 Indians became coloured, 20 coloureds became Indians, 79 Africans became coloureds, and eight coloureds became Africans (1986: 85).

Two decades later, in post-apartheid South African, hair continues to irk the dress codes of schools, as they struggle to keep all hairstyles streamlined and aligned. Recent student protests, which first erupted at a prominent girls

N. Davids (✉)
Stellenbosch University, Stellenbosch, South Africa
e-mail: nur@sun.ac.za

© The Author(s) 2018
I. Davies et al. (eds.), *The Palgrave Handbook of Global Citizenship and Education*, https://doi.org/10.1057/978-1-137-59733-5_13

school, saw black students accusing the principal and teachers of forcing girls to chemically straighten their hair so as to tame their 'untidy afros'. The girls reported that their 'unfixed' hair' was described as a 'bird's nest', and distracting to other students, who wished to learn (Pather 2016).

> A student detailed how a teacher had told her to tie her dreadlocks in a way that would fit into the school's view of tidiness. The student says she tried to explain that her dreadlocks were too heavy and cut into different lengths so a hairband would not work. Her teacher put her in front of a mirror after class and told her to fix it, the student said (Pather 2016).

In terms of the code of conduct of one of the schools:

> If hair is long enough to be tied back, it must be tied in a neat a ponytail... Cornrows, natural dreadlocks and singles/braids (with or without extensions) are allowed, provided they are a maximum of 10 mm in diameter...Braids shorter than collar length must be kept off the face with a plain navy or tortoise shell alice band...Cornrows must run parallel from each other from the forehead to the nape of the neck. No patterned cornrows. All styles should be conservative, neat and in keeping with a school uniform (Pretoria Girls' High, Code of Conduct, 2015/2016).

In similar regulatory attempts, students are forbidden from speaking local African languages, and are issued with demerits or fined R10 when caught 'making those noises' (Nicholson 2016). At another girls-only school, students are expected to carry a yellow merit book at all times. Transgressions, such as speaking Xhosa—even during break-time—are recorded as a demerit in the book (Isaacs 2016). Black students at the school compare the yellow book to the 'dompas'. During apartheid all blacks were required to carry a 'dompas', or 'internal passport', designed to segregate the population, and allocate migrant labour. The schools in question justify the prohibition of local African languages on the basis of promoting English. They maintain that if the girls speak English during all their engagements and conversations, they will not only improve their language skills, but have a better chance of academic success. In the opinion of the schools, the prohibition of African languages is not an indictment on those languages, but rather a means to academic achievement. It is not hard to understand why students, however, might consider the prohibition of indigenous African languages as an affront to their identity and human dignity—described by one student as: 'You are not allowed to have braids, and we can't speak our mother tongue. It is understandable during class hours, but during breaks, we sit in fear that we must look for a teacher, that a teacher may come while we are speaking our language' (Isaacs 2016).

How certain historically advantaged (white schools) perceive indigenous African languages is, perhaps, captured in their preference of referring to these languages as 'black languages'. The language is assigned to a particular race, and as such, it is denigrated to 'blackness', with the implication that it is less than, and hence undesirable. In this regard, the languages which black students bring are as undesirable at their hairstyles. Black students, therefore, are not considered as bringing any worth to historically whites only school. Instead, black learners are expected to adapt not only to pre-existing norms and traditions, but also to pre-existing languages and accents. Seemingly, the logic applied to black students entering historically whites only spaces is that they have nothing to offer these spaces. These spaces are pre-defined in relation to particular constructions of what is right, and acceptable; of what holds power, and what does not. Black students, with their black hair styles and black languages are considered as an intrusion that need to be (re)-shaped in line with what is right and fixed.

In recalling his punishment and humiliation for speaking his mother tongue of Gikuyu at an English medium school, renowned Kenyan author, Ngũgĩ wa Thiong'o describes language as 'the most important vehicle through which that [colonial] power fascinated and held the soul prisoner...Language was the means of the spiritual subjugation' (1981: 286). Following on the above discussion, it becomes apparent that the regulation of language, as with hair, dress code, or way of acting, has little to do with what it is actually seen or encountered. It has to do with the meanings that an afro hairstyle or an African language might hold; it has to do with the deliberate misrecognition of that hairstyle or language, so that the subject expressing it, is not afforded any power. As such, the regulations, fines, demerits and prohibitions applied by a good number of historically advantaged schools in South Africa, are enactments of a much deeper judgement. This judgement, seemingly drawn from an Anglo-normativity, is based on a logic that is at odds with other forms of being and speaking. In turn, the judgements, as lived by students, are not simply experienced as a prohibition of this or that action. Because issues of appearance, as found in particular dress codes, or hairstyles, and language are intricately tied to constructions of identity, the experience of students is that of humiliation, exclusion, discrimination and racism. Consequently, in considering whether global citizenship education might offer an adequate and worthwhile response to postcolonial constructions and expressions of identity, there are at least two other agitations, which this chapter seeks to address. Firstly, are postcolonial societies, such as post-apartheid South Africa, really in need of a global citizenship education? Secondly, to which extent, if any, are ideas of global citizenship education actually reconcilable with constructions of postcolonial societies? And, then, in taking into account the specific challenges mentioned previously, how, and if it can, might a global citizenship education allay the types of discrimination, exclusion and humiliation, encountered in postcolonial societies?

UNDERSTANDING GLOBAL CITIZENSHIP EDUCATION

The construction of global citizenship education not only implies the amalgamation of three broad and deeply contentious terms, but also implies that it is indeed possible to integrate these three terms into a cohesive endeavour, and outcome. Moreover, in its fusion, global citizenship education implies that it is possible, perhaps, even desirable, to educate an individual to be a global citizen, or, at least, be prepared for some sort of global citizenship. Among the multiple and complex questions that now arise, is, what type of education would prepare an individual to be a global citizen? Who or what decides what a global citizenship is? Is such a form of citizenship realisable, let alone desirable? And then, in light of living in a world where stateless migrants seek refuge on a daily basis, does either global citizenship or citizenship, for that matter, hold any value, at all? Davies (2006: 5) suggests that perhaps the notion of 'global citizenship' is 'simply a metaphor, a linguistic fancy which deliberately transposes a national political reality to a wider world order'.

To scholars, like Griffiths (1998: 40), a global citizen is 'not merely aware of her rights but able and desirous to act upon them; of an autonomous and inquiring critical disposition; but her decisions and actions tempered by an ethical concern for social justice and the dignity of humankind...' In turn, Davies (2006: 6) asserts that 'global citizenship education is a confirmation of the direct concern with social justice and not just the more minimalist interpretations of global education which are about 'international awareness' or being a more rounded person'. Davies (2006: 6) continues that while citizenship has implications both of rights and responsibilities, of duties and entitlements, these concepts, however, are not necessarily explicit in global education. The construction of a global citizenship education, therefore, holds the expectation of a more active role. This active role sees global citizenship as one that privileges 'reciprocal and transformative encounters with strangers' beyond geographical, ideological, linguistic, or other representational boundaries, (Andreotti 2010: 234). These encounters, according to Andreotti (2010: 234), are 'framed around radical appeals to openness, to difference and to the negotiation of meaning, rather than around normative appeals to notions of impartial reasoning or ideas of democracy, freedom, rights and justice that are presented as universal'. To this end, Andreotti's (2010: 234) understanding of global citizenship *education* is that it should equip people to live together in collaborative, but uncoercive ways, in contemporary societies. In order for people to live together collaboratively, she continues, requires an acknowledgement that contemporary societies are complex, diverse, changing, uncertain and deeply unequal. Andreotti (2010: 234) considers the role of global citizenship education as one of decolonization—that is, 'to provide analyses of how these inequalities came to exist, and tools to negotiate a future that could be 'otherwise''. Similarly, Pike (2008: 45–46) maintains that global citizenship education challenges educators to acknowledge the ever-changing patterns of relationships among human communities, as well as their opportunities for meaningful participation' (10)

Munck (2010) explains that if global citizenship education is to be meaningful, then it has to be fostered in relation to having a sense of responsibility to the world and those who live in them. So, if one were to become aware of students deliberately being prevented from speaking their mother tongue, one might be more inclined to speak out against it. Or, if one were to be privy to hate speech, one might be likely to counter it, so that any form of injustice is not simply overlooked. In other words, someone who has been educated to be a global citizen must be willing and prepared to speak out against forms of social injustice. Such willingness to action is made explicit in the UK Oxfam Curriculum for Global Citizenship (1997), which considers a global citizen as not only having a sense of his or her role as a world citizen, and valuing diversity, but as a citizen who is also 'outraged' by social injustice. Al-Maamari (2014: 109) concurs that global citizenship education is an umbrella term, comprising overlapping themes, which include education for tolerance and appreciation of diversity, conflict resolution and peace, human rights education and education for sustainable development.

In Andreotti's (2010: 233) opinion, the relatively recent rise in the popularity of global citizenship education can, on the one hand, be interpreted as a response to a major social crisis and the perceived failures of education to address the complexities of globalisation and to fulfil the project of human rights, freedom, democracy and global justice that could be a response to the crisis itself. On the other hand, says Andreotti (2010: 233), if global citizenship education is shaped by the forces and ways of thinking that have framed traditional accounts of education in the first place, we are bound to have more of the same kind of failures.

Following on the afore-mentioned explications, one becomes aware of the multi-layered complexities attached to global citizenship education. What, for instance, does it mean to be a global citizen? How does a displaced refugee find entry, let alone participation in this idea of a global citizen? Are notions of global citizenship at all reconcilable with ideas of indigeneity? Who determines the outrage that a global citizen is expected to express? In returning to the South African example in the introduction to this chapter, when the students expressed outrage at being told to straighten their hair, and to refrain from speaking 'black languages', their outrage was, similarly, met by outrage: the students were told by teachers that because they 'focus on race and politics', there has been 'no black student among the top 10 achievers'. In turn, reports on social media condemned these students for not 'being appreciative enough of their good education, and should return to their black schools' (Pather 2016). Many students reported that when they voiced their outrage at what they perceived as institutionalised racism, their outrage was met by a threat from teachers: 'If you don't want to come to the school you can find another school' (Nicholson 2016).

Furthermore, how does global citizenship education account for the deep linguistic, traditional, religious, and cultural identities that constitute a globalised world? Of course, it might be important to expect a global citizen to have 'an understanding of how the world works economically, politically, socially, culturally, technologically and environmentally', and 'willing to act to make the world a more equitable and sustainable place' (Oxfam 1997). But, what does it mean to live and participate in a world of difference so that all identities are not only taken into account, but receive equal respect? Consequently, argues Roman (2003: 270), attention has to be given to the serious normative considerations, such as race, culture, language, and gender, which inform global citizenship education, but are often overlooked. To this end, the particular norms, and hence, interests which inform global citizenship education cannot be undermined. And more to the focus of this chapter, one has to consider, whether it is, firstly, possible, and secondly, desirable, to tie these norms to the particular racial, social, cultural, and political identities of a postcolonial context.

POSTCOLONIAL CONTEXTS AND IDENTITIES

Robert Young (2003: 1) asks:

> 'Do you ever feel that whenever you speak, you have already in some sense been spoken for? Or that when you hear others speaking, that you are only ever going to be the object of their speech? Do you sense that those speaking would never think of trying to find out how things seem to you, from where you are? That you live in a world of others, a world that exists for others?

To Young (2003), the first question that postcolonialism seeks to answer is how we can talk about these questions. Young (2003: 2) is of the opinion that making sense of, and addressing these questions, requires a preparedness to engage from another perspective, what he describes as 'turning the world upside down'. Postcolonialism, explains Young (2003: 3), offers you a way of seeing things differently, 'a language and a politics in which you come first, not last'. The main preoccupation of postcolonialism, explains Andreotti (2010: 238), is 'the epistemic violence of colonialism and the interrogation of European cultural supremacy in the subjugation of different peoples and knowledges in colonial and neocolonial contexts'. She continues that:

> It borrows the poststructuralist tool of deconstruction to destabilize Western/European/White supremacy and it appropriates tools from Marxism and critical theory to make explicit the connection between assumptions of cultural supremacy and the unequal distribution of wealth and labour in the world. It highlights the flow of capital and resources from the 'Third' to the 'First' worlds, while the flow of expert knowledge, interventions packages and rights-dispensing initiatives (based on the interests of the donor countries) take the opposite

direction. One strand of postcolonial theory proposes hyper-self- reflexivity as a strategy that acknowledges everyone's complicities and investments in coercive and repressive belief systems. It does so in order to imagine a way of relating to each other that can be 'otherwise'. Other strands focus on reviving and protecting voices that have historically been subjugated by colonial violence' (Andreotti 2010: 238).

Yet, inasmuch as postcolonialism might invite us to look at things differently and placing ourselves first, postcolonial discourses, as Giroux (1992a: 22) reminds us, have made clear that the old legacies of the political left, centre, and right can no longer be so easily defined. Indeed, continues Giroux (1992b: 18), postcolonial critics have gone further and challenged 'the authority and discourses of those practices wedded to the legacy of a colonialism that either directly constructs or is implicated in social relations that keep privilege and oppression alive as active constituting forces of daily life within the centres and margins of power'.

According to Giroux (1992b: 19), postcolonial critics have made it clear that the history and politics of difference are often informed by a legacy of colonialism that warrants analysing the exclusions and repressions that allow specific forms of privilege to remain unacknowledged in the language of Western educators and cultural workers. At stake here, says Giroux (1992b: 19), are deconstructing forms of privilege that benefit males, whiteness, and property as well as those conditions that have disabled others to speak in places where those who are privileged by virtue of the legacy of colonial power assume authority and the conditions for human agency. Secondly, states Giroux (1992b: 19–20), postcolonial discourse rewrites the relationship between the margin and the centre by deconstructing the colonialist and imperialist ideologies that structure Western knowledge, texts, and social practices. In a similar fashion McLaren (1995: 6) contends that:

> When we situate the discourses of postcolonialism and its reactionary response geopolitically, such as within the dominant discourse communities in the United States, we see that they are well equipped to deal with the situation *by privileging the discourses of the metropolitan center and undermining forms of moral or epistemic authority that are attempting to make the often perilous intellectual journey from the hybrid cultural margins inhabited by the Other to the center of Western discursive traditions.*

In attempting to situate the term geographically, historically and institutionally, Shohat (1992: 100), in an equally critical manner, questions which perspectives, and what purposes are actually being advanced by a 'postcolonial'. He argues that since the 'post' in the term 'postcolonial' suggests 'after' the demise of colonialism, it is imbued, quite apart from its users' intentions, with an ambiguous spatio-temporality (Shohat 1992: 102). To this end, Shohat (1992: 102–103) maintains that the 'critical differences between Europe's genocidal oppression of Aboriginals in Australia, indigenous peoples of the Americas and Afro-diasporic communities, and Europe's domination of European elites in the colonies are levelled with an easy stroke of the 'post''. Moreover, and perhaps, of greater concern, the term 'postcolonial', argues Shohat (1992: 105), implies that colonialism is now a matter of the past, thereby 'undermining colonialism's economic, political, and cultural deformative traces in the present'. In grappling with similar concerns to Shohat, De Oliveira Andreotti and De Souza (2012: 2) believe that postcolonial theory itself is 'not immune from the complexity and heterogeneity of the contexts in which it arises, and when imagining education otherwise, different strands of postcolonial theory propose different frameworks for what 'education otherwise' should look like or do'. They conceptualise the prefix 'post-' in post-colonialism as a constant interrogation, 'a possibility that is 'not yet' but that may announce the prospect of something new'. In acknowledging the situatedness and partiality of postcolonial theories, De Oliveira Andreotti and De Souza (2012: 2) define these postcolonial theories as tools-for-thinking rather than theories-of-truth.

Clearly, from the South African examples, the push of colonialist language and dress code is embedded in how these particular schools understand a schooling space, and how they construe an 'educated' person to look and sound. In this instance, the girls feel coerced into looking, being and acting a certain way. Yet, the colonialist push is not always an overtly imposed one. Sometimes, it is a desired one—consciously or unconsciously. In South Africa, it is common practice for young Xhosa men (generally while they are still at school) to participate in *Ulwaluko*. *Ulwaluko* involves young men spending time in at traditional initiation schools where they are circumcised and initiated into manhood. Until Xhosa boys undergo this ritual, they are referred to as an *inkwenkwe* (a boy), regardless of their age, and as such, will not be allowed to participate in particular tribal and cultural practices. In signifying their transition to manhood, the new Xhosa initiates or *Amakrwala*, adhere to a strict dress code after initiation for a period of 6 months. Traditionally, animal skins and animal skin sandals formed an important part of this dress code. Over time, the animal skin became a cloak or a blanket. Today, it is common to see Xhosa initiates wearing a hat, a tailored jacket (suede, or tweed), including a silk handkerchief in the top pocket, smart trousers, and a shirt with the top button tied. The image which one encounters is no different from that of a typical English gentleman.

In continuing, and in drawing on the South African example, the rest of this chapter will consider whether the ideas of global citizenship education are reconcilable with postcolonial identities, and hence, potentially allay practices of discrimination, exclusion and humiliation.

GLOBAL CITIZENSHIP EDUCATION AND POSTCOLONIAL
IDENTITIES: ON FINDING A COMMON LANGUAGE?

Seemingly, one of the commonalities between global citizenship education and postcolonialism is that both are hankering towards that which might not be tangible. Global citizenship education locates its concerns in social justice, tolerance, appreciation of diversity, and dignity of humankind, and equipping people to live together colloboratively (Al-Maamari 2014; Davies 2006; Andreotti 2010). In turn, postcolonialism invites us to turn the world upside down, to consider the world from different perspectives, and to revive and protect the voices that have historically been subjugated by colonial violence' (Young 2003; Andreotti 2010). In both conceptions is the desire for a world that might be otherwise. Secondly, in acknowledging the broad inequalities among societies, both global citizenship education and postcolonialism endeavour to make sense of these inequalities so that the ultimate objective of decolonisation might be reached. What seems to be equally missing, however, from both conceptions and agendas is what is understood by a decolonised society, or way of life. Indeed, there are clearly articulated ideas about the promotion of peaceful co-existence, about being open to otherwise unconsidered ways of being and thinking, and about re-centring the centre, so that the marginalised might no longer be on outside of privilege. But, what does this decolonised state actually look like? And, perhaps, more importantly, what tools and language do one use to make sense of the epistemic violence that has been inflicted upon colonised societies and communities so that this decolonised state might be attained? Can the same tools and language that were used for colonisation be used to (re)construct a postcolonised society and communities? And if not the same tools and language, then what does one use, and how does one turn the world upside down so that colonialism's deformaties are (re)formed?

The only tools and language that apartheid South Africans have to make sense of their pain, the disconnectedness from the other, and the untold stories of unlived lives are the very tools and language which have subjugated and dehumanised them in the first place. This means that when Young (2003: 1) states that the first question that postcolonialism seeks to answer is how we can talk about these questions—referring to questions, such as 'Do you sense that those speaking would never think of trying to find out how things seem to you, from where you are? That you live in a world of others, a world that exists for others?'—these questions have already been enframed in a particular language. Something or some action would have already unfolded, which have led to these questions being asked in the first place. In the case of colonialist South Africa, certain courses of action and discourses have taken root, which continues to construct schools in relation to colonialist pasts, not only in terms of their architectural imagery, but in terms of their dress codes, their language, and their customs. How else does one explain the distinct English look of young Xhosa initiates?

When schools in a post-apartheid society insist on particular codes of hairstyling, and the favouring of English at the expense of students' mother tongues, then what we witness is not only the sustained marriage between a post- and a colonised society, but also the embedded social and cultural practices, that persist in maintaining the divide between privilege and marginalisation. Of deeper concern, however, is not only the persistence of institutionalised discriminatory practices, but the realisation that these particular exclusions and repressions remain unacknowledged, and hence uncontested. To this end, postcolonialist discourse might have to rethink its consideration of rewriting the relationship between the margin and the centre. If the dismantling of apartheid has dismantled the centre of white, racial dominance and privilege, then that centre has simply been re-centred in white cultural, social and economic privilege.

Therefore, while the signal of a post-apartheid or postcolonialist South Africa might invite gestures and actions of reconciliation, collaboration and forgiveness, the language being used remains embedded in violence, and detachment. And thus far, the outcomes have not turned South Africa upside down; people do not look at things differently, and those who previously and historically came last, are still unseen and unheard—meaning, that they have still not entered the centre of their decolonised state. And while institutional and structural colonisation has indeed been destabilised, the ideological imperatives of racism, humiliation, and misrecognition live undisturbed, and redefined in other forms of institutional practices. Such is the epistemic violence inflicted on the psyche of people, that they find it hard to establish the tools and language necessary for the severing from their past. This is true not only for those who were colonised and repressed, but also for those who propagated these forms of humiliation.

On Re-Imagining Postcolonialist Identities

What, then, is necessary for colonised societies to shift from the periphery to the centre of what it means to be human, and to therefore be treated with dignity? In drawing on De Oliveira Andreotti and De Souza's (2012) argument that postcolonial theory itself is 'not immune from the complexity and heterogeneity of the contexts in which it arises', what tools can be used to think differently about the decolonisation of people? What is necessary to dispel postcolonialist identities from the complexity of their own situatedness?

In his essay, 'Marvelous Realism: The Way out of Negritude', Michael Dash (1974: 66) states that:

> [C]olonisation and slavery did not make things of men, but in their own way, the enslaved people might have in their own imagination so reordered their reality as to reach beyond the tangible and concrete and to acquire a new re-creative sensibility which could aid in the harsh battle for survival. The only thing

they could possess (and which could not be tampered with) was their imagination and this became the source of their struggle against the cruelty of their condition.

Most appealing from Dash is his evocation of imagination, as the only immune and preserved space to colonisation. Equally appealing is De Oliveira Andreotti and De Souza's (2012: 2) conceptualisation of not only constantly subjecting postcolonialism to interrogation, but to understand postcolonialism as a possibility that is 'not yet'. In this sense, postcolonialism resides in a perpetual state of possibly being and becoming, but has not yet become. There are at least two implications for a 'not yet' postcolonialist society. The first is that although Young's (2003) upside down world might be desired, it might not be realised. Secondly, while postcolonialism, according to Young (2003: 3), might offer 'a language and a politics in which you come first, not last', perhaps, this should not be the desire outcome of any politics, since the implications of such placements are that someone else has to be last. And this why questions have to be asked about the types of language being embarked upon as societies navigate themselves towards postcolonial forms of thinking, being, and identities.

If global citizenship education is to fulfil its objective of privileging 'reciprocal and transformative encounters with strangers' beyond geographical, ideological, linguistic, or other representational boundaries, (Andreotti 2010: 234), then the mere appeal to be open to difference, tolerant of others, and to express outrage, might not be enough. Instead, what is needed is an imaginary shift towards that which is 'not yet'. Desiring global social justice for all human beings, requires what Rizvi (2003: 39) refers to as a 'moral imagination to view the world through the other's eye, and a commitment to build cultural bridges across regimes of fear and suspicion of others'. The conception of a 'moral imagination' was first used by Edmund Burke, in his *Reflections on the Revolution in France* (1790):

> All the pleasing illusions, which made power gentle, and obedience liberal, which harmonized the different shades of life, and which, by a bland assimilation, incorporated into politics the sentiments which beautify and soften private society, are to be dissolved by this new conquering empire of light and reason. All the decent drapery of life is to be rudely torn off. All the superadded ideas, furnished from the wardrobe of a moral imagination, which the heart owns, and the understanding ratifies, as necessary to cover the defects of our naked shivering nature, and to raise it to dignity in our own estimation, are to be exploded as a ridiculous, absurd, and antiquated fashion.

Kirk (1996) explains that to Burke, the civilised being is distinguished from the savage by his possession of this moral imagination. Mackenzie and Scully (2007: 338–339) explain that the suggestion to 'Put yourself in x's place' is a commonly used method of enjoining ourselves, or others, to expand our moral horizons. They continue that it 'urges us to try to see things from the point of view of another whose situation and perspective may be very different from our own or whose actions, responses or judgements we may find bewildering, or disagree with, or have trouble comprehending'. The problem, however, according to Mackenzie and Scully (2007: 345), with imaginatively putting oneself in another's place is that what we are most likely to do is to simply to imagine ourselves differently situated. They argue:

> But imagining oneself differently situated, or even imagining oneself in the other's shoes, is not morally engaging with the other; rather, it is projecting one's own perspective onto the other. When the other person is very different from ourselves, the danger of this kind of projection is that we simply project onto the other our own beliefs and attitudes, fears and hopes, and desires and aversions.

In moral imagination, state Mackenzie and Scully (2007: 347), 'one does not try to imagine *being* the other from the inside'. Rather, one recognises that the other is different from oneself, and one imaginatively engages with his or her perceptions and experiences, as she represents them. In recognising that the other is indeed different, that the other indeed has different experiences of the world in which we live, we begin to realise how we choose to engage with the other resides in our imagination, and not in pre-existing norms and ways of doing. Inasmuch as postcolonial identities are 'not yet', our capacities to deal with others, and the different perceptions of others are similarly 'not yet'. What a moral imagination allows us to do is to embark upon a language which is as uncontaminated as our imagination allows. To this end, how we choose to engage with those who are different to us, does not depend on the extent to which we might imagine ourselves as differently situated. Most of us cannot imagine what it is like being instructed to chemically straighten our hair, any more than we can imagine not being allowed to speak in our mother tongue. But, through our moral imagination, we can engage with the pain and perceptions of humiliation without projecting our own perspectives onto those who live these experiences.

Finally, it is the contention of this chapter that what postcolonial societies, such as South Africa need is to find their own way towards a moral imagination of recognition of the other, and their differences, and a preparedness to engage with those differences, rather than trying to establish sameness. When one morally imagines oneself in relation to others and otherness, the possibility of two (inter-related) realisations exist. Firstly, that the other is only the other in relation to someone else, and that as an individual by him or herself the notion of the other ceases to exist. In this sense, the otherness that one might experience in relation to another is only such insofar as one does not know the other. Moreover, whatever otherness one might experience in relation to another might be equally true for the other in relation to one. Secondly, to imagine oneself morally in relation to others and otherness, necessarily implies a willingness to engage with the experiences, perceptions, and pain of what it means to be othered. An individual, therefore, who is able to morally imagine him or herself in relation to others, would find greater resonance and reconcilability with the differences of others, rather than perpetually trying to establish sameness. Most significantly, when one is morally willing to imagine oneself in relation to others and their otherness, one might be better placed, and more inclined to witness, and hence express outrage against any form of social injustice. In this regard, one might imagine the humiliation of being instructed to straighten one's hair so that it becomes less offensive. And, as a moral response, one might recognise that such undignified treatment of another human being is in itself immoral, and in contradiction to any meaningful engagement or reconcilability.

Indeed, notions of global citizenship education are reconcilable with constructions of postcolonial identities when the reconcilability extends beyond mere enactments of tolerance and regard for the other. While tolerance might hold some implications of forbearance and patience, it also holds some association with 'putting up with the other', rather than engaging with the otherness of the other. But, when one is prepared to engage with that which makes the other different, then such enactments hold the potentiality of a more meaningful encounter and reconcilability. Meaningful reconcilability resides in our willingness to see the other as other, and not as in relation to ourselves. It also means having a willingness to put aside commonly held perceptions and ideas of the other, so that the other might present him or herself as she really is, without being filtered through predetermined constructions or ideas, or who we would like him or her to be. In this sense, all of us are 'not yet', and postcolonial societies have the privilege of yet becoming who they imagine to be.

References

Al-Maamari, S. (2014). Education for developing a global Omani citizen: Current practices and challenges. *Journal of Education and Training Studies, 2*(3), 108–117.

Andreotti, V. (2010). Postcolonial and post- critical 'global citizenship education'. In G. Elliot, C. Fourali & S. Issler (Eds.), *Education and social change: Connecting local and global perspectives* (pp. 233–245). London: Continuum International Publishing Group.

Burke, E. (1790). Reflections on the revolution in France, and on the proceedings in certain societies in London relative to that event. In a letter Intended to Have Been Sent to a Gentleman in Paris (1st edition.). London: J.Dodsley in Pall Mall.

Dash, M. (1974). Marvelous realism: The Way out of negritude. *Caribbean Studies, 13*(4), 57–70.

Davies, L. (2006). Global citizenship: Abstraction or framework for action? *Educational Review, 58*(1), 5–25.

De Oliveira Andreotti, V. & De Souza, L.M.T.M. (2012). 'Introduction: (Towards) global citizenship education 'otherwise'. In V. De Oliveira Andreotti & L.M.T.M. De Souza (Eds.), *(2012) Postcolonial perspectives on global citizenship education* (pp. 1–8). New York: Routledge.

Giroux, H. (1992a). Paulo Freire and the politics of postcolonialism. *Journal of Advanced Composition, 12*(1), 15–26.

Giroux, H. (1992b). Postcolonial ruptures and democratic possibilities: Multiculturalism as anti-racist pedagogy. *Cultural Critique, 21,* 5–39.

Griffiths, R. (1998). *Educational citizenship and independent learning.* London, UK: Jessica Kingsley.

Isaacs, L. (2016). San Souci girls protest racist language rules. www.iol.co.za/cape-times/sans-souci-girls-protest-racist-language-rules-2063682. Accessed September 12, 2016.

Kirk, R. (1996). *Redeeming the Time.* Wilmington, Del.: Intercollegiate Studies Institute.

Lelyveld, J. (1986). *Move your shadow: South Africa, black and white.* New York: Times Books.

Mackenzie, C., & Scully, J. L. (2007). Moral imagination. *Disability and Embodiment Journal of Applied Philosophy, 24*(4), 335–351.

McLaren, P. (Ed.). (1995). *Postmodernism, postcolonialism and pedagogy.* Australia: James Nicholas Publishers.

Munck, R. (2010). Civic Mackenzie engagement and global citizenship in a university context: Core business or desirable add-on? *Arts and Humanities in Higher Education: An International Journal of Theory, Research and Practice, 9*(1), 31–41.

Nicholson, G. (2016). Pretoria girls high: A protest against sacrificed cultures and identities. www.dailymaverick.co.za/%85/2016-08-30-pretoria-girls-high-a-protest-against-sacrific%85. Accessed September 10, 2016.

Oxfam. (1997). *A curriculum for global citizenship.* Oxford: Oxfam.

Pather, R. (2016). Pretoria girls high school pupil: I was instructed to fix myself as if I was broken. mg.co.za/%85/2016-08-29-pretoria-girls-high-school-pupil-i-was-instructed-to-fix-myse%85. Accessed September 10, 2016.

Pike, G. (2008). Citizenship education in global context. *Brock Education Journal, 17,* 38–49.

Pretoria Girls' High Code of Conduct. (2015/2016). www.phsg.org.za/uploads/cms/files/code_of_conduct_leaners.pdf. Accessed September 12, 2016.

Rizvi, F. (2003). Democracy and education after september 11. *Globalisation, Societies and Education, 1*(1), 25–40.

Roman, L. G. (2003). Education and the contested meanings of 'global citizenship'. *Journal of Educational Change, 4,* 269–293.

Shohat, E. (1992). Notes on the 'Postcolonial'. *Social Text (Third World and Postcolonial Issues), 31*(32), 99–113.

Wa Thiong'o, N. (1981) *Decolonising the mind: The politics of language in African literature.* London: James Currey.

Young, R. (2003). *Postcolonialism: A very short introduction.* Oxford: Oxford University Press.

AUTHOR BIOGRAPHY

Nuraan Davids is an Associate Professor in the Department of Education Policy Studies at Stellenbosch University. Her research interests include philosophy of education, democratic citizenship education, and Islamic education. She has previously published: *Women, cosmopolitanism, and Islamic education: On the virtues of education and belonging* (2013) New York & London: Peter Lang; *Citizenship education and violence in schools: On disrupted potentialities and becoming* (2013) (with Y. Waghid) Rotterdam/Boston/Taipei: Sense Publishers; *Ethical dimensions of Muslim education* (2016) (with Y. Waghid) New York & London: Palgrave Macmillan; *Educational leadership-in-becoming: On the potential of leadership in action* (2017) (with Y. Waghid) New York & London: Routledge; and *Education, assessment and the desire for dissonance* (2017) (with Y. Waghid) New York & London: Peter Lang.

CHAPTER 14

Indigeneity and Global Citizenship Education: A Critical Epistemological Reflection

Philip Higgs

INTRODUCTION

The process of globalisation in the twenty-first century has affected and altered all aspects of human life including education, and especially citizenship education (see, Arnove et al. 2013; Zahabioun et al. 2013; Nicoll et al. 2013; Sefa Dei 2014; Pashby 2015). Globalisation is a complex and multifaceted concept. Held (1999: 9), for example, defines globalisation as 'the intensification of worldwide social relations which link distant localities in such a way that local happenings are shaped by events occurring many miles away and vice versa'. Another view sees globalisation as 'a feature of late capitalism, or the condition of postmodernity, and, more importantly, the emergence of a world system driven in large part by a global capitalist economy' (see, Luke and Luke 2000: 287). And still others see it as an assault on traditional notions of society and nation-state, whereby the very nature of citizenship and social change are dramatically altered (see, Castells 1996, 1997).

But globalisation can also take on different forms. One of these forms is referred to by Torres (2009a, b) as 'globalisation from above'. This form of globalisation is framed by an ideology of neo-liberalism and calls for an opening of borders, the creation of multiple regional markets, the proliferation of fast-paced economic and financial exchanges, and governing systems other than nation-states. A second form of globalisation Torres (2009a, b) claims

P. Higgs (✉)
University of South Africa, Pretoria, South Africa
e-mail: higgsp1@unisa.ac.za

can be described as 'globalisation from below' or anti-globalisation. It manifests itself in individuals, institutions, and social movements that are actively opposed to what is perceived as corporate globalisation. For these individuals and groups, their motto is 'no globalisation without representation'. Another form of globalisation is identified by Rhoads and Szelényi (2011) and in this instance refers to rights rather than to markets, namely, the *globalisation of human rights*. With the growing ideology of human rights taking hold in the international system and in international law, many traditional practices that are endemic to the fabric of particular societies or cultures are now being called into question, challenged, forbidden, or even outlawed. The advancement of cosmopolitan democracies and plural democratic multicultural global citizenship is the theme of this form of globalisation.

It, therefore, goes without say that the multiple faces of globalisation and globalisation agendas as evidenced in the world play a major role in defining the role and purposes of education today and more so when one confronts the dialectics of the global and the local, especially in regard to indigenous forms of knowledge and global citizenship education.

Debates in the past few years on the question of knowledge production have revealed a growing interest in indigenous forms of knowledge and the contribution that they can make to civil society. The interest in indigenous forms of knowledge stems in part from the reaction to the hegemony of Western forms of knowledge production. This hegemony has been interrogated, even as it is evidenced in the phenomenon of global citizenship education (see, for example, Agrawal 1995; Banks 2013; Hunt 2014; Mason 2005; Shizha 2010).

The epistemic theory behind indigenous forms of knowledge understands the production of knowledge as being initiated by the local as opposed to the universal. This emphasis, however, on knowledge production as being concerned with local knowledge immediately raises the question of how we should understand the local? What, to put it differently, makes certain knowledge local, as opposed to knowledge which can be considered to be universal? And perhaps of greater import, what is the relationship between local knowledge, and knowledge that is considered to be universal? Can both forms of knowledge be considered to be valid? These questions are of import, not only for determining the significance of indigenous forms of knowledge in knowledge production, but also, need to be considered in framing the epistemological and curriculum concerns of citizenship education.

In proceeding I will argue for a (global) citizenship education agenda that is 'relevant' and culturally responsible by first presenting two responses that have been given to these questions in the context of epistemological theory. The first is the response that argues for the universal construction of knowledge. The second is the response that argues for the social construction of knowledge in which the universal is understood as a social construction. I will discuss the strengths and weaknesses of both these positions and argue that in relation to the universal and social construction of knowledge the 'local' might well be under threat. Against this background I will then present a third response that legitimates local knowledge, and which is taken from Bruno Latour and his work on the extension of local practices. In conclusion, I will consider the import of Latour's work for indigenous forms of knowledge in the production of knowledge, and what this means for a 'relevant' and responsible a (global) citizenship education agenda.

The Universal and Local Construction of Knowledge, and Indigeneity

Traditionally, knowledge is considered to be universal if it is valid and can be applied everywhere and at any time. In this instance, the universal validity and applicability of knowledge is taken as proof of the fact that this knowledge represents reality 'as it is'. The universal construction of knowledge is based on two assumptions: the idea that reality itself is universal (which means that ultimately there exists only *one* reality), and the idea that knowledge represents (this) reality. Taken together, these two assumptions guarantee that universal knowledge is objective knowledge, or, to put it the other way around, that objective knowledge is universal knowledge.

There are, however, limitations in the discourse which argues for the universal construction of knowledge. First, the universal construction of knowledge holds to a naïve view of knowledge in arguing that knowledge simply 'is' and that truth simply 'is'. Secondly, the universal construction of knowledge ignores human involvement in the production of knowledge.

In an indigenous context, the argument for the universal construction of knowledge can be traced to the apologetic for an indigenous epistemic that has universal validity. In other words, what is argued for in this instance is for a political and cultural resolute which universalises indigenous knowledge systems as the epistemic order of the day. In this instance, the hegemony of indigenous knowledge systems is projected in a way which is meant to counteract the hegemony of Western systems of knowledge production. Given this view, some proponents of indigenous knowledge systems would argue that such systems should be credited with the universal construction of knowledge. In other words, indigenous knowledge systems would then be seen to represent reality itself and as such can be applied everywhere and at any time. Claiming such universal validity for indigenous knowledge systems makes them vulnerable to the same limitations, as already mentioned, for arguments which promote the universal construction of knowledge.

Whilst the universal construction of knowledge perceives the universal as an *intrinsic* quality of knowledge, the social construction of knowledge claims that the social is *extrinsic* to knowledge. Sociologists of knowledge argue that all knowledge is historically and socially determined. Unlike proponents of the universal construction of knowledge who assume that knowledge reveals reality as it really is, undisturbed by human intervention, proponents of the social construction of knowledge acknowledge the role that human beings play in knowledge production. Human beings do so, by embedding knowledge in socio-economic, sociocultural and political contexts. This means that knowledge is ideological in that it only exists in the context of those who claim to produce it.

The social construction of knowledge suggests, in sum, that the universal is a social construction. It suggests, in other words, that what is universal (or what is taken to be universal) are an expression and a product of social relationships, and hence an expression and a reinforcement of a certain way in which power in a society are distributed. This argument suggests that knowledge is an ideology constructed by power relations in society, and in this sense, the social construction of knowledge is problematic. If the social construction of knowledge is correct in claiming that knowledge is historically and socially determined, then this raises serious problems for the idea and even the possibility of universal knowledge. Its claim is that the universal is nothing but a social construction, nothing, that is, but an expression of the way in which power is distributed at a certain moment in time (and hence, that the universal is in fact a specific manifestation of the local). If universal knowledge follows from a relationship with what is general and enduring, a relationship, in other words, with what lies beyond the local, then the social construction of knowledge implies that universal knowledge is no longer possible. Universal knowledge in other words, itself becomes an ideology. Consequently, the social construction of knowledge makes it possible to free ourselves from the naivety of that view that argues for the universal construction of knowledge. It makes it possible to free ourselves from the idea that knowledge simply 'is', that truth simply 'is'.

Biesta (2007, 2013), however, finds the social construction of knowledge problematic on two counts. He argues that the first problem is a theoretical, but also a practical and political problem. It concerns the status of the social construction of knowledge itself and is known as the problem of reflexivity. We have seen that the central claim of the view arguing for the social construction of knowledge is that all knowledge is an expression of social relations, which are understood as power relations. The problem is, however, that if the social construction of knowledge wants to offer an insight into these power relations, it can only do so, first, if its own knowledge about power relations stands outside of the realm determined by these relationships, and, second, if it can assume that the social construction of knowledge itself provides a correct representation of the social and historical situation upon which our knowledge is said to depend. If attempts at the social construction of knowledge can claim such an extrinsic position, then this means that the sociology of knowledge eventually falls back upon the same epistemological structures of thought for which it sought to provide a (critical) alternative. The critical impetus of the sociology of knowledge can only exist, in other words, if it is possible to provide knowledge about social reality.

The second problem alluded to by Biesta (2013) is that; it is difficult for the social construction of knowledge to provide an adequate explanation for the success of modern technology. If knowledge is 'only' a social construction, if knowledge is essentially an expression of social relations of power, how then can we explain the fact that knowledge is instrumentally effective? And how can the social construction of knowledge explain that some knowledge seems to work and seems to be true everywhere, irrespective of particular social, cultural or political configurations? The problem here is, in other words, that the social construction of knowledge is not able to provide an adequate account for explaining the advances of modern technology in knowledge production.

To sum up, the social construction of knowledge is problematic for the following reasons. As an ideology, such knowledge is based on power relations and claims universal validity. Lastly, such knowledge is unable to explain why some knowledge seems to work and seems to be true everywhere, irrespective of particular social, cultural or political configurations.

But despite these shortcomings, what can be said about the implications for indigenous knowledge systems, of an epistemological position which advocates the social construction of knowledge. Such an epistemological position recognises that all knowledge (scientific or indigenous) is inherently local, and that, as Turnbull (1994) notes, because of its sense of locality, different knowledge systems may differ in their epistemologies, methodologies, logics, cognitive structures and socio-economic contexts. As such indigenous knowledge systems are freed from the 'universality' constraint that was projected by western knowledge systems as a legitimising factor. In this regard, indigenous knowledge systems can, therefore, assert their 'rightful' place as legitimate knowledge production systems. The danger for indigenous knowledge systems, however, of an epistemological position that advocates the social construction of knowledge, is that these systems may then become an ideologically corrupted, the same consequences, problems and implications that hold for epistemological positions that advocate the universal construction of knowledge.

Does this than mean, that the universal construction of knowledge with its claim to objective knowledge is the only feasible epistemological alternative, even when it comes to considering the epistemological nature of indigenous knowledge systems? Such a conclusion would, however, bring the notion of the local under threat.

Within an era of a New Knowledge Society, assumptions abound regarding the 'goodness' and justice of global interconnections and distributions of knowledge through international educational organisations and structures worldwide. In this instance, little understanding is given to issues of recontextualisation (Bernstein 2000) in local contexts of the take up of 'progressive' educational discourse. Neither is preponderance given to local communities as to whether 'new ways' necessarily serve their interests. In this sense, the dissemination and universalisation of these discourses as a 'common sense' pragmatic enacts a symbolic violence (Bourdieu and Wacquant 1992) on local communities or situated contexts in constituting toxic understandings of the new settled order of things.

Through symbolic control (Bernstein 2000), the recontextualisation of knowledge and meanings from the perspective of the dominant gaze reconfigures the playing field with often naïvely unintended, if not unnoticed, consequences for those made vulnerable by such effects. As a result, the marginalisation of local and indigenous knowledge is reproduced in favour of global universal (ized/izing) forms of knowledge production. In commenting on this state of affairs, Swanson (2007, 2010) claims that the, "... dependency on modes of global knowledge has been verticularised over local, indigenous or situated ways of knowing and being."

Consequently, what is a needed is a critical approach to (global) citizenship education that engages with what Pashby (2015: 345) refers to as, '... the tensions inherent in issues of diversity rather than reducing them to theoretically and conceptually vague ideas of universalism.' In this regard, I want to present another epistemological position that takes as its point of departure reliance on the universal construction of knowledge in legitimating local knowledge. This epistemological position is taken up in the work of the French philosopher and 'anthropologist of science', Bruno Latour.

BRUNO LATOUR AND THE EXTENSION OF LOCAL PRACTICES

Latour, a trained philosopher and anthropologist, has done work in philosophy, history, sociology, anthropology of science and collaborative work in science policy and research management. Some of his seminal works include the following books. *Laboratory life, the construction of scientific facts; Science in action: how to follow scientists and engineers through society; the pasteurization of France; we have never been modern; Pandora's hope: essays in the reality of science studies; Aramis or the love of technology.* He has also published a number of books in French, monographs, journal articles, exhibitions and photographic essays (Latour 2004).

Latour observes that the success of what he calls 'techno-science' is attributed to the fact that techno-scientists construct facts and machines that are then distributed to the world outside of the laboratory in which they were constructed. The successful distribution of facts and machines, or to be more precise: the fact that, facts and machines appear to be able to survive outside the laboratory, is taken as a sign of the special (intrinsic) quality of these facts and of the knowledge that lies at the basis of these machines.

Latour sees no reason for doubting that techno-scientists are indeed able to create facts and machines in their laboratories. He also sees no reason to doubt the fact that at a certain moment in time facts and machines show up at other places than where they were originally produced. But what Latour does challenge is the claim that what has happened in the meantime is a displacement of these facts and machines from the 'safe' environment of the laboratory to the 'real' world outside.

Latour (1993: 166) argues that, what in fact has happened is a displacement of the laboratory, that is, a displacement of the only conditions under which the facts and machines can exist and operate successfully. It is not the facts and machines that have moved into a world outside of the laboratory. The outside world has been transformed into the laboratory: 'No one has ever seen a laboratory fact move outside unless the lab is first brought to bear on an "outside" situation and that situation is transformed so that it fits laboratory prescriptions'.

Latour's work provides many fascinating examples of this process. In his book on the work of Louis Pasteur, Latour (1988) shows that the success of Pasteur's approach was not the result of the distribution of a robust technique from Pasteur's laboratory to the farms in the French countryside. It could only happen because significant dimensions of French farms were transformed into Pasteur's laboratory. It is, as Latour (1993: 152) argues, 'only on the conditions that you respect a limited set of laboratory practices [that] you can extend to every French farm a laboratory practice made at Pasteur's lab'. What took place, therefore, was, as Latour (1988) describes, a *Pasteurisation of France*.

Latour (1987: 251) refers to 'this gigantic enterprise to make of the outside a world inside of which facts and machines can survive' as *metrology*. Metrology can be conceived, according to Latour (1987: 253) as a process of creating 'landing strips' for facts and machines. Metrology is a transformation of society, an incorporation of society into the network of techno-science, so that, as a result, facts and machines can spread out comfortably and *apparently* as a result of some inner, intrinsic force. There is, as Latour (1993: 167) puts it, 'no outside of science but there are long, narrow networks that make possible the circulation of scientific facts'.

The idea of metrology provides an answer to the question as to how technology and knowledge can become universal, that is both different from the view that sees knowledge as a universal construction, and the view that sees knowledge as a social construction. In contrast to the latter, metrology does not need to question that we have technology and that we have knowledge. It only questions the idea that technology and knowledge contain an intrinsic force or quality that makes their easy displacement through space and time possible.

Latour does not doubt the fact that we can make mobile phones. He only points to the fact that these phones only work everywhere, only become universal after a network of transmitters and receivers that provides 100% coverage has been set up. Similarly, Latour sees no reason to doubt the fact that medical techno-science has developed effective therapies and treatments (which is not say that all of them are good or desirable and that there are no alternatives). The only point that he wants to make is that the apparent universal applicability of products of medical techno-science is the result of a transformation of society so that it fits the conditions under which the products of medical techno-science can work. One 'landing strip' for medical techno-science to which it can retreat if it turns out that it cannot prove its truth and effectiveness 'out on the street' is, of course, the modern hospital.

Latour's contribution to our exploration of the idea of the universal first of all shows that the apparent universality of modern techno-science should not be accounted for in terms of some inner or intrinsic quality of facts and machines. It is important to see, however, that Latour does not so much provide a different *explanation* for the universal presence of techno-science. He rather argues that we are dealing with a different phenomenon: *not* the displacement of facts and machines to a world outside of the laboratory, but an incorporation of the outside world into the order of the laboratory.

Latour is thus critical of the view of knowledge as a universal construction, which is that it is the special quality of the knowledge invested in facts and machines that makes their universal displacement possible. But, this is crucial as well as Latour does not simply reverse the argument. He does not say that the spreading of facts and machines *causes* the knowledge invested in them to become universal. (This is what the view that argues for the social construction of knowledge would assert, claiming that interest groups try to gain power by spreading 'their' facts and machines as widely as possible). The crux of Latour's analysis is that there is no displacement of facts and machines at all. They just stay where they are. It is only because more and more 'points' (places, locations, people) become incorporated into a network that gives rise to the illusion of movement and the illusion of universality. But in fact it is not that facts and machines move from the centre to the periphery. It is rather that the margins are moved towards the centre.

This, then, provides a different way to understand the relationship between the universal and the local. With Latour, we can see the world as a plurality of local practices. Some of these practices have been more successful in incorporating and transforming the world 'outside' than others. Latour (1993) refers to this situation as *asymmetry*. It is important to see that this asymmetry is *not* to the expression of qualitative, intrinsic or epistemological differences. There is no doubt that there *are* qualitative differences between these practices, depending, among other things, upon the criteria we use to evaluate them. But these differences in quality do not *cause* asymmetry. Asymmetry denotes only that some networks are bigger, longer and stronger than others.

What appears to be universal is, from this point of view, nothing more (and nothing less) than an extension of a particular local practice. This does not say anything about the quality or value of such a practice, although, as Latour argues, scientists (and others) often try to define asymmetry in qualitative terms (for example, in terms of the rational *versus* the irrational). But apart from the rhetorical gain, there is no real point in doing this. But what is the significance of Latour's different way of understanding the relationship between the universal and the local for addressing the tension inherent in subjecting the local to a dominant universal discourse when it comes to indigenous forms of knowledge?

LATOUR AND THE DEMYSTIFICATION OF UNIVERSAL AND LOCAL FORMS OF KNOWLEDGE

It is my contention that Latour's different way of understanding the relationship between the universal and the local demystifies the relationship between Western forms of knowledge and indigenous forms of knowledge. But in order to appreciate Latour's epistemic contribution in this regard, I will provide glimpses into what I refer to as *conflicting epistemic theories* that have come to characterise the process of knowledge production.

The significance of indigenous knowledge systems, for example, is taken up in the words of President Mbeki when he stated that: '... the generation of new knowledge needs to be preceded by an opening of the African door to the world of knowledge, to elevate Africa's place within the universe of research, the formation of new knowledge, education and information'. The call for the inclusion of an indigenous African knowledge systems stems from, as Gough (2002) observes, the exclusionist stance that so-called Western knowledge systems has portrayed to other knowledge systems, labelling and classifying them as non-formal, uninformed, non-contemporary, traditional, and so on.

Gough (2002: 1224), whilst engaging the notion of 'thinking globally and acting locally', cites a contribution by Yencken et al. (2000), which he regards as sincere in its respect for indigenous forms of knowledge but that, inadvertently also, '... maintain(s) a culturally imperialistic view of science through the use of rhetorical strategies that privilege Western scientists' representations of 'reality' and go on to reproduce the conceit that the knowledge Western science produces is universal'. Gough proceeds to show how Yencken et al. privileges Western science in terms of referring to it as 'unique', 'formal' and 'dependable'. Given these insinuations, Gough asks: Does Yencken et al. suggest that non-Western knowledge traditions *ignore* 'the formal analysis of the physical world' or are they saying that non-Western analyses of the physical world and environmental change are 'informal'? If so, then in what sense is Western science an 'informed source'? 'Informed' by what and/or by whom?

The foregoing indicates that even authors purportedly taking a stand for the authenticity of indigenous forms of knowledge may fall into the trap of accepting Western science and its knowledge systems as universal. Some indigenous knowledge systems researchers have even accepted descriptions of indigenous knowledge systems from Western authors who regard indigenous forms of knowledge as irrational and even regard some systems of knowledge production as superior to others. In this regard, Rouse (1999) maintains that, practices based on beliefs, religion and spirituality are difficult to document, as they are seemingly based on 'irrationality', and cannot be captured in the logic that is required for conventional journals or scientific writing.

In responding to such critical sentiments regarding what I refer to as, the so-called *scientific limitations of indigenous forms of knowledge*, Gough (2002) presents Peat's (1997) discussion of Blackfoot knowledge traditions that seeks to demonstrate that Western forms of knowledge have no monopoly over forms of knowledge production that have the qualities that are said to be attributed to 'science'. According to Peat (1997: 566–567), 'the nature of Blackfoot reality' is 'far wider than our own, yet firmly based within the natural world of vibrant, living things … a reality of rocks, trees, animals and energies'. He goes on to observe that:

> Once our European world saw nature in a similar way, a vision still present in poets like Blake, Wordsworth and Gerard Manley Hopkins who perceived the immanence and inscape of the world. Nevertheless our consciousness has narrowed to the extent that matter is separated from spirit and we seek our reality in an imagined elsewhere of abstractions, Platonic realms, mathematical elegance, and physical laws. The Blackfoot know of no such fragmentation. Not only do they speak with rocks and trees, they are also able to converse with that which remains invisible to us, a world of what could be variously called spirits, or powers, or simply energies. However, these forces are not the occupants of a mystical or abstract domain; they remain an essential aspect of the natural, material world.

In a discussion with an African philosopher, Higgs (personal communication) tells of a story where a colleague had to bring his son from a developed Western European country, with all its intricate and advanced medical technologies, to a rural underdeveloped South African healer and find healing for his son. A similar account is given by Hountondji (2002: 23) who tells of medical doctors, in 'modern hospitals', who refers patients to African indigenous healer's, and of renowned physicists and chemists who consult indigenous practitioners for solving their social problems.

I am not suggesting that the Blackfoot views of reality, nor the Inyanga healing powers, are in any way superior (or inferior) to Western environmental and medical science. Rather the argument I put forward is that the Blackfoot people and the South African *Inyanga*, to use Gough's words, 'rely on their knowledge tradition' for dealing with environmental and medical issues and that knowledge systems other than Western knowledge systems also have and need their space. This argument, therefore, seeks to question the dominant and exclusionary stance that Western knowledge systems have projected over other knowledge systems. It also seeks to question the varied ways in which Western science is projected as superior to other knowledge systems. For example, Gough (2002) refers to Hawthorne's 'unmarked category' to demonstrate how Western scientists designate themselves and Western science into positions of power and privilege, thereby keeping other people and knowledge systems on the periphery.

Until recently, *indigenous* forms of *knowledge* were regarded as belonging to the domain of anthropology and were often associated with superstition. Today, the study of *indigenous* forms of *knowledge* is no longer regarded as belonging to the domain of anthropology, and has become as Warren, Slikkerveer and Brokensha (1995: xvi) observe, a field of study for various disciplines in the natural, social and cultural sciences. Ombe (2003) notes that the growing interest in indigenous knowledge and development today is due to the participation of local people in decision-making about development projects, and because reliance on *local knowledge is seen to* significantly enhance the success rate of such projects. This together with other factors has certainly prompted research into indigenous forms of knowledge systems and has also shown that local knowledge is important in various spheres of the functioning of civil society.

The significance of indigenous forms of knowledge has also brought with it a projection of indigenous knowledge systems as not only essential, but superior to other knowledge systems. This projection of the superiority of indigenous knowledge systems on the one hand, and the exclusionist tendencies of Western knowledge systems on the other hand, have resulted in what I have called, *conflicting epistemic theories*. And what I have attempted thus far, in referring to the seminal work of Latour, is to provide a response to these conflicting epistemic theories by referring to his work on the extension of local practices that takes into account the significance and contribution of all knowledge production systems.

As soon as Western practices were extended to Africa, through colonisation, they were used by the West to subjugate local forms of knowledge and practices. The former were regarded as traditional, superstitious, and of no relevance. What this meant is that, Western knowledge systems, in their imperialistic advances, claimed for themselves, the right to universal knowledge. Universality was regarded as the major cultural filter for participation in 'Western science'. On the basis of this claim, only forms of knowledge and practices that were extended rapidly through space and time were legitimised as 'scientific' and used to exclude other forms of knowledge and practices. Local forms of knowledge and practices were not even spared their cultural identity. In this regard, Gough (2002: 1220) observes that even the English word 'science' signified knowledge 'uniquely co-produced with industrial capitalism in seventeenth-century north-western Europe and that the internationalisation of what we now call 'modern Western science' was enabled by the colonisation of other places in which the conditions of its formation (including its symbiotic relationship with industrialisation) were reproduced'.

However, what we are seeing now in the impetus given to indigenous knowledge is the re-assertion of local practice, a voice that says local knowledge and practice is, after all, not inferior but rather, a way of knowing. Bearing in mind Latour's reference to *metreology* in his argument for the extension of local practices we can, therefore, perceive all forms of knowledge as systems of local knowledge in a plurality of global local knowledge systems, without having to justify to the West anything about the quality of indigenous forms of knowledge. In the same instance, Western knowledge systems do not have to justify their knowledge systems to any indigenous form of knowledge. Moreover, the challenge for indigenous knowledge systems, therefore, given Latour's notion of the *asymmetric extension of local knowledge*, is the readiness to transform not only local societies, but also other societies in the interchange and interaction of epistemic networks in a global context.

We have seen the danger inherent in the universal and social construction of knowledge when it comes to indigenous forms of knowledge. And in this regard, Latour's notion of the asymmetrical expansion of local knowledge promotes a more reasonable way forward and can possibly help us in avoiding the political rhetoric associated with endeavours which view indigenous forms of knowledge as either a universal or social construction of knowledge. This possibility is suggested in Latour's reference to the *asymmetrical expansion of knowledge* which explains the interdependence of a global network of indigenous knowledge systems in confronting the ever present dialectic of so-called universal and local knowledge.

CONCLUSION

In setting out to argue for a (global) citizenship education agenda that is 'relevant' and culturally responsible this chapter was concerned with an epistemological reflection on the relationship between universal and local knowledge. In critically discussing the strengths and weaknesses of both these forms of knowledge it was concluded that local knowledge might well be under threat. Against this background, I then presented a third epistemological response that legitimates local knowledge, and which takes its cue from Bruno Latour and his work on the extension of local practices.

In conclusion, what might be said in considering the import of Latour's work on the extension of local practices and what it means for a 'relevant' and responsible a (global) citizenship education agenda?

Firstly, a 'relevant' and responsible (global) citizenship education agenda will recognise the legitimacy of a global network of local knowledge systems.

Secondly, a 'relevant' and responsible (global) citizenship education agenda will recognise the interdependence of a global network of local knowledge systems in confronting the ever present dialectic of so-called universal and local knowledge.

Thirdly, a 'relevant' and responsible (global) citizenship education agenda will reveal a readiness to transform not only local societies, but also other societies in the interchange and interaction of epistemic networks in a global context when it comes to citizenship education.

From the above it is evident that Latour's work on the extension of local practices opens the discourse on indigeneity and a 'relevant' and responsible (global) citizenship education agenda, to other ways of thinking. Working with the idea of opening up this discourse might be more helpful than the normalisation of the discourse which, I believe, tends towards a narrow discourse and closure. In doing so, we will be able to construct a way of providing citizenship discourses which have been marginalised with just as much attention as that given to others that appear to have more significance and authority. But of greater import will be the acknowledgement that citizenship is constituted in and through a complex, heterogeneous, fragmented and what I call, a *discursive regime* governed by what people in different locations say they are, may do, achieve, hold or receive as citizens in the specific situation that they identify.

REFERENCES

Agrawal, A. (1995). Dismantling the divide between indigenous and scientific knowledge. *Development and Change, 26*(3), 413–439.

Arnove, R., Torrres, C. A., & Franz, S. (2013). *Comparative education: The dialects of the global and the local.* London: Lanham, Rowman and Littlefield.

Banks, J. A. (2013). Group identity and citizenship education in global times. *Kappa Delta Pi Record, 49*(3), 108–112.

Biesta, G. (2007). Towards the knowledge democracy? Knowledge production and the civic role of the university. *Studies in Philosophy and Education, 26*(5), 467–479.

Biesta, G. (2013). "Knowledge democracy and higher education". *Learning democracy in school and society: Education, lifelong learning and the politics of citizenship.* Rotterdam: Sense Publishers.

Bernstein, B. (2000). *Pedagogy, symbolic control and identity: Theory, research and critique.* NY: Rowman & Littlefield.

Bourdieu, P., & Wacquant, J. D. (1992). *An invitation to reflexive sociology.* Chicago, USA: University of Chicago Press.

Castells, M. (1996). *The rise of the network society.* Oxford: Blackwell.

Castells, M. (1997). *The information age: Economy, society and culture: The power of identity.* Oxford: Blackwell.

Gough, N. (2002). Thinking/acting locally/globally: Western science and environmental education in a global knowledge economy. *International Journal of science Education, 24*(11), 1217–1237.

Held, D. (1999). *Political theory today.* Stanford: Stanford University Press.

Hountondji, P. J. (2002). "Knowledge appropriation in a post-colonial context". In C. A. Odora-Hoppers (Ed.), *Indigenous knowledge and the integration of knowledge systems, towards a philosophy of articulation* (pp. 23–38). Claremont: New Africa Books.

Hunt, S. (2014). Ontologies of indigeneity: The politics of embodying a concept. *Cultural Geographies, 21*(1), 27–32.

Latour, B. (1987). *Science in action: How to follow scientists and engineers through society.* Cambridge: Harvard University Press.

Latour, B. (1988). *The pasteurization of France.* Cambridge: Harvard University Press.

Latour, Bruno. (1993). *We have never been modern.* Cambridge: Harvard University Press.

Latour, B. (2004). *Bruno Latour's Website.* Accessed August 4, 2015, http://www.ensmp.fr/~latour/biography.html.

Luke, A., & Luke, C. (2000). A situated perspective on cultural globalization. In N. Burbules & C. A. Torres (Eds.), *Globalization and education: Critical perspectives.* New York: Routledge.

Mason, D. (2005). Indigenous knowledge within a global knowledge system. *Higher Education Policy, 18*(3), 301–312.

Nicoll, K., Fejes, A., Olsen, M., Dahlstedt, M., & Biesta, G. (2013). Opening discourses of citizenship education: A theorization. *Journal of Education Policy, 28*(6), 828–846.

Ombe, Z. A. (2003). Indigenous land use management in lower Changane Chibuto: Sacred and profane desacralisation and recovery. *Indilinga: Journal for African Indigenous Knowledge Systems, 2*(1), 1–9.

Pashby, K. (2015). Conflations, possibilities and foreclosures: Global citizenship education in a multicultural context. *Curriculum Inquiry, 45*(4), 345–366.

Peat, F. D. (1997). Blackfoot physics and European minds. *Futures, 29,* 563–573.

Rhoads, R., & Szelenyi, K. (2011). *Global citizenship and the university: Advancing social life and relations in an interdependent world.* Stanford CA: Stanford University Press.

Rouse, J. (1999). Global dissemination of indigenous knowledge: Contradictions, or the way forward? Accessed May 26, 2015, http://www.worldbank.org/afr/ik/global/ik990615.htm.

Sefa Dei, G. J. (2014). Global education from an 'indigenist' anti-colonial perspective. *Journal of Contemporary Issues in Education, 9*(2), 4–23.

Shizha, E. (2010). The interface of neo-liberal globalisation science education and indigenous African knowledge. *Journal of Alternative Perspectives in the Social Sciences, 2*(1), 27–58.

Swanson, D. M. (2007). Ubuntu: An African contribution to (re)search for/with a "humble togetherness". *The Journal of Contemporary Issues in Education, 2*(2), 53–67.

Swanson, D. M. (2010, July). Value in shadows: A critical contribution to values education in our times. In T. Lovat & R. Toomey (Eds.), *International Research Handbook on Values Education and Student Wellbeing.* NY: Springer Press.

Torres, C. A. (2009a). *Education and neoliberal globalization.* New York: Routledge.

Torres, C. A. (2009b). Globalizations and education. *Collected essays on class, race, gender, and the state.* New York: Teachers College Press, Columbia University.

Turnbull, D. (1994). Local knowledge and comparative scientific traditions. *Knowledge and Policy, 6,* 29–54.

Warren, D. M., Slikkerveer, L. J., & Brokensha (Eds.). (1995). The cultural dimension of development: Indigenous knowledge systems. London: Intermediate Technology Publications.

Yencken, D. (2000). Attitudes to nature in the East and West. In D. Yencken, J. Fien & H. Sykes (Eds.), *Environment, Education and Society in the Asia-Pacific: Local Traditions and Global discourses.* London: Routledge.

Zahabioun, S., Yousefe, A., Yarmohammadian, M. H., & Keshtiarav. (2013). Global citizenship education and its implications for curriculum goals in the age of globalisation. *International Education Studies, 6*(1),195–206.

Author Biography

Philip Higgs is Emeritus Professor and Research Fellow in the College of Education at the University of South Africa. His most recent book publications include, *Rethinking Truth* 2nd edition (2012), *Rethinking our World* 4th edition (2015), *Philosophy of Education Today: An Introduction* (2016) and, *A Reader in Philosophy of Education* (2017).

PART III

Key Concepts

CHAPTER 15

Justice and Global Citizenship Education

Edda Sant, Sue Lewis, Sandra Delgado and E Wayne Ross

In 1795 Kant published his 'Perpetual Peace: A Philosophical Sketch' in which he wrote,

> The social relations between the various Peoples of the world have now advanced everywhere so far that a violation of Right in one place of the earth, is felt all over it. (...) A Cosmo-political Right of the whole Human Race, (...) is a necessary completion of the unwritten Code which carries national and international Right to a consummation in the Public Right of Mankind. Thus the whole system leads to the conclusion of a Perpetual Peace among the Nations (2010/1795, p. 24).

Since then, humanity has seen two world wars (and a cold war), hundreds of other wars, multiple genocides, processes of colonization and decolonization, the growth of a new Empire including the consequences of this growth, multiple violent revolutions, numerous coup d'états supported by countries

E. Sant (✉)
Manchester Metropolitan University, 53 Bonsall Street, Manchester
M15 6GX, UK
e-mail: e.sant@mmu.ac.uk

S. Lewis
Independent consultant, St. George, Grenada
e-mail: suelewis06@talktalk.net

S. Delgado · E.W. Ross
Department of Curriculum and Pedagogy, University of British Columbia, 2125 Main Mall, Vancouver BC V6T 1Z4, Canada
e-mail: sandra.delgado@alumni.ubc.ca

E.W. Ross
e-mail: wayne.ross@ubc.ca

I. Davies et al. (eds.), *The Palgrave Handbook of Global Citizenship and Education*, https://doi.org/10.1057/978-1-137-59733-5_15

declaring themselves liberal democracies, and increasing numbers of poverty pools following the expansion of capitalism worldwide. Some of these events have taken place after the United Nations General Assembly adopted the Universal Declaration of Human Rights in 1948. The failure of the enlightenment promise of a peaceful and fair future has left many humans with the feeling that justice is an impossibility (see, e.g., Biesta 1998). The hypothesis that globalization and interdependence will bring, as Kant suggests, something like empathy, mutual understanding, and global compassion is, for some of us, implausible. And yet here we are discussing the links between universal justice and a (at least a priori) re-vitalized form of Kant's cosmopolitanism named global citizenship. The questions we face in this chapter are, does globalization shed some additional light on discussions about universal justice, including the identification of possible situations of injustice? Can discussions on justice inform more democratic approaches to global citizenship and education?

A discussion on justice and global citizenship can be considered an 'updated' and 'globalized' version of the traditional philosophical debates on the links between ethics and politics. In these debates, questions on the possibility, meaning and desirability of any universality are essential. Two philosophical grounds are often used to frame these questions. For the universalists, a global notion of justice is necessary and possible. Within the liberal tradition, Nussbaum (2002), revisiting Kant's notion of cosmopolitanism, highlights the urgency of defining a global ethics that, in her understanding, should be grounded in liberal principles, compassion and respect. McLaren (2005), instead, defends a totalizing social justice project based on Marxist social theory. Within a spiritual framework, Ikeda (2001) proposes a form of inner universalism based on the principals of human dignity and interconnectedness. Although defending competing views, Nussbaum, McLaren and Ikeda construct their views based on a superior positivity in which global politics is understood as plausible practices of human ethics. For particularists, in contrast, any notion of justice is historically and geographically constructed and any definition of global justice is an attempt to universalise and impose some situated views (MacIntyre 1988). "Saying", Biesta writes, "that something is just, or that one is just, is a betrayal of the very idea of justice to the extent to which it forecloses the possibility for the other to decide whether justice has indeed been rendered" (1998, p. 406). Universal justice, in this respect, can be considered un-democratic.

The authors of this chapter hold different views in relation to these debates and yet we all hold a firm commitment toward democratic and social-justice-orientated educational practices, theories and research. We take as a starting point of the discussion in this chapter the (non-shared) assumption that there is no pre-determined universal justice in itself but yet multiple and contingent discourses on justice competing to gain hegemonic primacy (Laclau and Mouffe 2001). Simultaneously, we understand justice, as Derrida (2004) does, as a "a call, a promise of an independent future for what is to come" that "we must seek, very carefully, to give force and form" to. In this chapter, we discuss three different discourses on justice competing for hegemony, trying to give form to this promise of "justice to come". These discourses—economic, recognition and democratic justice—draw upon our interpretations of Fraser's framework on "justice in a globalized world" (2005).[1] For each discourse, we outline the conceptual underpinnings, key issues and implications for education for global citizenship. We conclude the chapter by highlighting some possibilities for justice-orientated practices and research on the field of global citizenship education.

ECONOMIC JUSTICE

Economic justice is often described in relation to distributive theories of justice. As Fanon wrote, "what counts today, the question which is looming on the horizon, is the need for a redistribution of wealth. Humanity must reply to this question, or be shaken to pieces by it" (1963, p. 98). The meaning of "redistribution of wealth" is, nevertheless, controversial. Redistribution is often understood through the lends of liberal theory (e.g., Fraser 2003). Here, the capitalist mode of production is assumed and so they are the consequent socioeconomic injustices (Biesta 1998). To weaken these injustices, liberal theorists propose to redistribute the accumulated wealth in the sense of what Rawls calls a "duty of assistance". 'Certain provisions', Rawls exposes, "will be included for mutual assistance among peoples in times of famine and drought, and insofar as it is possible, provisions for ensuring that in all reasonably developed liberal (and decent) societies people's basic needs are met" (2002, p. 38).[2]

Economic justice, nevertheless, can also relate to the notion of exploitation, one of the central ideas in Marxian theory. Exploitation is the modus operandi and the foundational basis of the capitalist mode of production. Under capitalism, it is the exploitation of labor and resources that makes profit possible. Therefore, exploitation is one of the main sources of business growth, wealth accumulation and further, the origin of class struggle. The ultimate source of profit and the force behind capitalist production is the unpaid labor of workers or the new value created by workers in excess of their own labor-cost, which is appropriated by capitalists as profit when products are sold. In this sense, the capitalists' appropriation of productive labor permits the accumulation of wealth, since profits are the result of the surplus value that is not reflected in the worker's wage. Class struggle emerges from the capitalists' attempts to extract more profit from labor and maximize their appropriation of surplus value, and the workers' resistance to such exploitation. From a Marxist perspective, labor exploitation is an inherent injustice deeply embedded in a capitalist mode of production.

Exploitation has reached a global scale in the neoliberal phase of capitalism. In the neoliberal age, the idea of economic justice not only includes the traditional understandings of labor exploitation, but is also part of a wider struggle joined by people who are marginalized, excluded, underprivileged, oppressed, and segregated by capitalism. Global capitalism has forced "poorer regions and countries into a subordinate economic and political position where they can (at best) have some dependent standing as a provider of basic goods (be it natural resources or labor) for which they are scarcely compensated" (Forst 2001, p. 61). For some, rich countries try to legitimize their capitalist power by using educational aid agencies to teach students of the Global South their 'proper' roles in the capitalist society (see Wallerstein 2004).

Within countries, economic injustices have intensified because neoliberal reforms advance the idea that governments have to withdraw from their social welfare function and instead focus on expanding private markets and creating conditions for entrepreneurship, competition and new private investments (Rizvi and Lingard 2010; Robertson and Verger 2012). Therefore, economic inequality and disfranchisement rises as neoliberalism advances a series of reforms that support an aggressive privatization of public services, grow international private markets, and advance economic austerity policies that lead to decreases in state funding for health, education, housing and other public services (Kumar 2014; Ross and Gibson 2007). In a globalized neoliberal world, the accumulation of capital is not only the result of capitalists' exploitation, but, as Harvey (2005) argues, accumulation under neoliberal capitalism is the result of dispossessing the most vulnerable people in society of their wealth, opportunities, land and means of survival.

Education is one of the areas where neoliberal reforms have been advanced during the last decades. This movement is composed of a series of market-based reforms best conceptualized as a coordinated effort by an entwined and complex global network of governments, international governmental organizations, private corporations, think tanks, nonprofits, and venture philanthropists who influence and steer national education policies in countries across the world (Anderson and Herr 2015; Ball 2012). There are several examples of how neoliberal-based reforms spread and influence educational policies, global standardized testing and their impact in test-based accountability policies is one of the most salient examples (Mathison and Ross 2008). One of the most recent examples of the influence of Neoliberal Capitalism is Teach for All (TFA), a global network of organizations including Teach for America and Teach First among others, which advances a corporate and an entrepreneurial approach to solving educational inequity and strives to forge a global vision of quality in education (Friedrich 2014). As the TFA network expands throughout the world, it has become an example of a global effort to reform teacher education by affecting teacher identity and the public perception of good teaching. TFA is pushing schools toward corporate management models and has become a platform that exemplifies precariousness of employment use of the private sector. Lastly, TFA rests on notion that educational inequality can be reduced by placing graduates from elite universities, without professional preparation, into marginalized schools (Gautreaux and Delgado 2016; Vellanki 2014).

Some researchers have examined the functioning of the education systems and schooling in capitalist contexts.[3] For instance, in the USA, Malott and Ford (2015) expose attacks on critical thinking and social studies and illustrate processes that lead to working-class students experiencing standardized curriculum that serves the interest of capital, while bourgeois students are taught critical thinking and creativity. Their analysis poses a major challenge to notions of social justice education within capitalism, which suggests exploitation is the result of greed, prejudice, and bias. Similar results have been found by researchers investigating other subject areas and other institutions. In Germany, Straehler-Pohl and Pais (2014) have examined capitalist ideology at work in current mathematics educational classes where working-class students "can only postpone the materialization of an already-determined exclusion" (p. 91) from further education. In the UK, researchers have examined how even some 'successful' higher education working-class students are forced to choose between their working-class and their student identities (Reay et al. 2010). Radical thinkers have concluded that the influence of social class characteristics is so powerful that schools cannot overcome them (Marsh 2011).

There are also some examples of what we understand as global-citizenship-oriented practices framed by Marxist understandings of justice. In the USA, Greg Queen, a social studies teacher in Detroit, engages in what we understand to be one of the most elaborated examples of contemporary classroom practice focusing on economic justice (Ross and Queen 2013). Queen has for years used economic justice, social class, and class struggle as the organizing principles for his American Studies course, which interweaves five themes (inequality, capitalism, racism, globalization, and war) and fits within National Council for Social Studies curriculum standards and campaign for teaching global citizenship. Similarly, Malott and Ford (2015) propose a Marxist social studies course that begins with the insight that to capital and capitalists all people are equal, differences among people's living conditions, or race, gender, abilities, and so on, do not exist. In capitalism the most important economic goal is to accumulate as much surplus value as possible, without any respect for workers' lives or their rights. In this context, the capitalist state relies on intensified ideological management to devalue producers and justify exploitation, which also suppresses social unrest of laborers. Malott and Ford are conceptualizing a social studies education that bends toward communism, while responding to its capitalist context.

Economic justice and class exploitation, nevertheless, are virtually absent from school curriculum and the research literature in social studies and global education, the key areas for teaching and research global citizenship. This absence contributes to the poverty of both curriculum and research on global citizenship education and leaves little or no room for consideration of class-based identity as a social, cultural, or economic subjectivity—an irony in an age of hegemonic identity politics. And because economic justice and class issues intersect and interact with cultural and psychological processes (e.g., identity) as well as relations of power (e.g., subjectivities) our understandings and explorations of the full range of human experience are impoverished. The failure to think and learn about citizenship issues without reference to economic justice and social class weakens efforts to understand the nature of social problems and distorts our conceptions of and inquiry into possible responses and solutions.

RECOGNITION JUSTICE

The cultural politics of difference are often seen as alternatives to theories of economic justice. The roots of the controversy can be found in two different debates. First, against Marxist views, the so-called identity politics theorists argue against the primacy of economic injustices above other injustices. The redistribution of material goods is in itself no longer considered to be sufficient to bring about social justice. As Fraser (2003) points out, what really matters, is not the injustice itself but the experience of injustice. Only through a reorganization of institutions and practices, structural and cultural changes, will these experiences of injustice be called into question (Young 1990). Second, liberals often defend the need for inspecting justice at an individual level (see Kymlicka and Norman 1994). For identity politics theorists, "the community is the source of any right; and strong communitarian allegiances, the origin of any identity" (Laclau 1999, p. 104). By operating as difference-blind politics, economic justice theories can reinforce injustice by falsely universalizing dominant group norms, requiring subordinate groups to assimilate to them (Honneth 1995). The denial of the role of identity in politics can also lead to a denial of the cultural and social practices that make us individual. To quote a young activist in the 'Black Lives Matter' campaign following the shootings in Ferguson (USA),[4] "if you don't see that I am black, you don't see all of me!".

Identity politics arguments have widely been used to discuss the relation between social justice and education. Recognition theories have informed more socially just micro practices in social structures such as education whereas misrecognition is a matter of externally manifest and publicly verifiable impediments to some people's standing as full members of society (Gewirtz 1998). Recognition theorists have also cut across all social movements (including economic) and required a new evaluation of identities that have become devalued and disrespected (Young 1990). In this respect, identity politics have arguably helped to denounce processes of marginalization and misrecognition in education contexts including those caused by reason of gender, ethnicity, and religion (Gewirtz 1998).

There is, however, a key question that identity politics have not yet solved. "How a politics", Hall wondered, "can be constructed which works with and through difference, which is able to build those forms of solidarity and identification which make common struggle and resistance possible but without suppressing the real heterogeneity of interests and identities?" (2006, p. 445).

The acceleration of the globalization process, with increasing overlaps within most communities, has fostered the need of debating this question. Indeed, recognition approaches have been seen by some as responses to the ethical paradox of post modernity (Bauman 1998). By the time of writing this text, the four authors of this chapter are living in a country different of the one of their birth. In a less privileged situation, refugees, asylum-seekers and economic migrants have become increasingly visible in the past few years, among them, 'the most vulnerable people on earth-children on the edge' (Unicef 2016). The 'vagabonds', in Bauman's term (1998), face major barriers to participate in the societies they live in, including barriers to participate in their education institutions and practices (Pinson et al. 2010).

Previous experiences of migration and nomadic lifestyle have not left a lot of scope for optimism. Attitudes toward peoples such as the Gypsy, Roma and Traveller communities, have remained remarkably consistent across countries and throughout history (Wilding 2008). Gypsies have been present in large numbers in Europe alone since the fifteenth century, yet "in many ways the discrimination GRT groups face throughout Europe and internationally is distinct and distinguishable from other immigrant groups" (Bhopal and Myers 2009, p. 420). While progress has been made with documented accounts of more inclusive practices, (Levinson 2007; O'Hanlon and Holmes 2004), for most societies, the figure of the Gypsy is still 'an exaggerated stranger' (Bhopal and Meyer 2009). They are simultaneously perceived as a threat to the values and social norms of the majority, while remaining invisible and unrecognised in relation to access to mainstream services. Sir Trevor Phillips[5] famously described attitudes to GRT communities as "the last respectable form of racism" (Foster and Norton 2012, p. 87). The transnational nature of discrimination reflects, in some respects, the failure of Gypsy groups to be recognised internationally. There are strong cultural and social links among the different GRT communities in different countries, and it could be argued that they are truly European, or even, global citizens. Yet, ironically, as Hancock (1987, in Bhopal and Myers 2009) hints they have never become a single nation, with the rights this status would command and this, perhaps, contributes to a perception of relative political powerlessness.

Traditional communities (including the nation itself), nevertheless, might have been called into question by the globalization process. Some claim that the world is slowly integrating into a single global culture that gathers the best of all cultures (see, e.g., Baker and LeTendre 2005). Post-colonialists authors, instead, have long argued against this 'global culture'. For them, global culture is not understood as 'the best of all cultures' but as an attempt to impose certain forms of (Western) knowledge—including Western-style schools—onto others (Spring 2008). Global citizenship framed by world culture perspectives, tend to fail in "educational practices that unintentionally reproduce ethnocentric, ahistorical, depoliticized, paternalistic, salvationist and triumphalist approaches" (Andreotti and Sousa 2012, p. 1). Simultaneously, globalization is also perceived as a threat by some (Western and non-Western) nations (Brown 2014). Whereas in the local/national scale, nationalism is often understood as being related to the imposition of dominant values, in the global scale, "the claim to nationhood affirmed the dignity of the people and legitimated the demand for independence and equality" (Hardt and Negri 2000, p. 106). What is misrecognized here is not a particular community within the nation, but a particular nation within the globe.

All these issues are particularly relevant in educational theory, policy and research. Education—including but not limited to schools—is often perceived as being essential for the survival of any community (Durkheim 1956). The questions here are, which community? And at what cost? Schools have often been criticized for educating (or indoctrinating) children into the dominant national values, principles and traditions (e.g., Sant et al. 2015). Indeed, assimilationist approaches are antagonistic to most understandings of social justice, including but not limited to the one we propose in this section (e.g., McLaren 2005). But there is also a question of whether these national values, principles and traditions can be a 'weapon' against the homogenization character of the globalization process (e.g., Sant 2017). And within these debates, the education of the 'stateless' (to use Arendt's term) cannot be forgotten. The history of Gypsies, including the failure of education systems in recognizing their diversity, alerts us of some of the risks that education faces in post-modern times in which states are fixed but people decide or are forced to move. Negative feelings toward groups of people who have become stateless and, therefore, dehumanized are open to exploitation by politicians.

DEMOCRATIC JUSTICE

Most of the issues highlighted in the two previous sections could be framed by a discussion on democratic justice. According to Fraser, justice "requires social arrangements that permit all (adult) members of society to interact with one another as peers" (2003, p. 5). Two conditions need to be satisfied: "First, the distribution of material resources must be such as to ensure participants" independence and "voice" [distributive justice]. Second, the institutionalized cultural patterns of interpretation and evaluation express equal respect for all participants and ensure equal opportunity for achieving social esteem' [recognition justice] (Fraser 2003, p. 5). But simultaneously, both economic and recognition justice can only be granted if the conditions are met for democratic interactions. Indeed, liberal, marxist, and communitarian authors argue for democracy and democratic practices as a way of giving form to 'justice'. What differs is the way in which they define democracy.

Democracy is often associated with liberal institutions and practices such as parliament, the participation in elections and the division of power. For some, living in a democracy in which elections are periodically held can be understood as a symptom of democratic justice (e.g., Friedrich 2007). However, according to Fraser (2003), national liberal democracies suffer from a lack of democratic justice themselves. The existence of transnational private powers, international organizations of governance, and power relations between states challenge any notion of national popular sovereignty (Habermas 2005). In the line of Marxian theory, it is the global market and not the nation-state who is, indeed, sovereign (e.g., Brown 2014). In addition, liberal democracies privilege certain forms of participation over others. Although there is a wide range of participatory activities from voting, to rioting, to radical forms of non-participation, education for participation in liberal democracies seems to be reduced to an electoral participation (e.g., Farthing 2010) from which certain citizens feel (or perhaps are) excluded (e.g., Hughes 2011). For instance, concerns have been raised in relation to the lack of possibilities for children and young people to contribute in democratic societies and the tokenistic character of the few opportunities of participation directly addressed to them (e.g., Wall 2011).

In addition, in the post-Westphalian era, new questions arise about the real possibilities of liberal institutions to be globally democratic. Liberals often place their expectations for a more democratic globe in the constitution of a 'world government.' Drawing upon the work of Kant, Held (2005) argues that the acceleration of globalization processes requires a common framework for global political action to take place. The assumption here is that an ethical framework (global values) can be agreed—through a process of deliberation—and transformed into a political one (universal rights) (McGrew 2005). The 'world government,' in this respect, would be responsible that universal rights are granted to all global citizens in the same way national governments are expected to guarantee the rights of national citizens. For some, cosmopolitan demands can be understood as overarching regional, national, and local 'sovereignties' (Held 2005). If this was the case, and all citizens of the world were granted the same rights, issues such as the right of residence would likely arise. As Žižek argues, "under present conditions, such a step would trigger an invasion of cheap labor from India, China and Africa into the USA and Western Europe, which would result in a populist revolt against immigrants" (2001, p. 3). Alternatively, universal rights could rely on treaties between countries as Kant himself suggested (see Derrida 2001). Article 21 of the Universal Declaration of Human Rights (UNESCO 1948) states that "Everyone has the right to take part in the government of his country, directly or through freely chosen representatives." But in the line of what we have discussed in the previous section, this would mean that those defined by Arendt as 'stateless' would lack any framework in which their universal rights, including any possibility of challenging these rights, are or can be guaranteed

(Arendt 1962). The lack of national citizenship, in the case of stateless children and adults, seems to evolve into an exclusion from other forms of citizenry including the global. To an extreme, the education of the 'stateless' results in a paradox. There is an attempt at socializing migrant, asylum-seekers and refugees children into national forms of good citizenship, although it is not clear how non-citizen children can fit into these principles (Boyden 2009). For instance, Palestinian and Syrian children in Lebanon follow a Lebanese civic education curriculum but who themselves as curtailed rights with no foreseeable route to citizenship (Fincham 2013).

Democratic justice has, nevertheless, alternative meanings. Communitarians understand citizenship not as "a status given by the institutions of the modern constitutional state and international law, but negotiated practices in which one becomes a citizen through participation" (Tully 2014, p. 9). Here, if democratic justice is possible, it is, precisely, because it is always situated and contextualized. This implies raising "'women's issues' or 'black issues' or 'gay issues' rather than as raising questions of equality, fairness or justice" (Laden 2014, p. 120). Citizenship education for democratic justice should be about examining the actual conditions of young people's participation and interrogating the meaning of different concepts such as citizenship, democracy or justice (Biesta and Lawy 2006).

Communitarians' particularism has also been challenged. By failing to raise questions on universality (such us questions on universal justice), communitarians might privilege hegemonic conceptions (Laclau 2007b). For instance, if only liberals (or perhaps neoliberals) attempt to define 'justice', it is more than likely that their understanding will prevail. Democratic justice—including discussions on the meaning of universal justice and global citizenship themselves—requires different possibilities for each of us to examine. Further, if no attempt to reach universality is undertaken, the possibilities of "solidarity in a common struggle" (Žižek 2000, p. 220) are lost. Paradoxically, by defending the particularities of each individual community and rejecting any projection toward universality, communitarians might commit themselves to work against a global community.

Some contemporary conflict theorists argue for antagonistic forms of democratic justice. They understand conflict and antagonism as the driving force of politics (Mouffe 1999) and liberal institutions—only—as one of the multiple public spaces where democratic culture is created (Laclau 2007b). Commitments to 'Black issues' and 'class struggle', for instance, can compete in this chapter to define the causes of injustices with some arguing that the source of all injustice is the capitalist system in itself and others arguing that injustices are caused by institutionalized racism. In other occasions, for instance in a parliamentary context, they might work as allies against neoliberal understandings of justice as meritocracy. The global context brings additional demands—for example, 'nation issues' and 'stateless issues'—and additional spaces—international organizations, internet, world forums, etc.—where these demands can be discussed. The role of education here is essential. As suggested by Ruitenberg (2009), students need to develop an understanding of possible democratic spaces including but not limited to liberal spaces. Further, students need to understand that a political adversary is different from a moral enemy and from a competitor. In other words, "students may learn that engaging a political adversary is not a game, but an expression of a serious commitment to democracy" (Ruitenberg 2009, p. 278).

Radical democrats also assume—as we did in the beginning of this chapter—that concepts such as justice and global citizenship function as nodal points of different discourses (e.g., liberalism, communitarism, marxism) attempting to reach hegemonic primacy (Laclau 2007b). If democracy is possible, it is because the meaning of justice is not (and should not be) fixed but will be (provisionally) defined by antagonistic political actors who will (contingently) result in more convincing. Discussions on global citizenship can be here understood as permanent (and impossible) political attempts to define universal justice. In this respect, global citizenship education might offer opportunities for students to learn "to read the social order in political terms, that is, in terms of disputes about the interpretation of liberty and equality [and justice] and the hegemonic social relations that should shape them" (Ruitenberg 2009, p. 278).

Conclusions: Common Struggles and the Promise of Justice

In this chapter, we have deployed different discourses attempting to define justice in a context in which the promise of justice has become more than ever a universal (global) one. Global justice has here been examined through the lens of marxian, identity politics and radical democracy theories. We contrast these different interpretations to illuminate some of the key issues and challenges that a present-day justice-orientated education for global citizenship might need to consider.

First, capitalism cannot be left out of discussions on global citizenship and education. Not only because some scholars understand capitalism to be the root of all injustices, but also because there is nothing democratic in considering capitalism as the only alternative. There are numerous examples in which class struggle has moved societies toward more justice-orientated practices and nothing stops us thinking that this is also a possibility in the future. Researchers and educators, we believe, should continue considering how discussions on class struggle can be articulated in the curriculum and how capitalism can be examined in both, its local and global scale, as one among multiple possibilities.

Second, globalization has shaken traditional balances of majorities and minorities. Whilst nationalism has often been considered by social-justice-orientated authors as a weapon to impose dominant ideologies upon minorities, some contemporary authors suggest that the nation (or some nations) can be in the side of those claiming justice, asking not to disappear under globalized homogeneity. The traditional understanding of the working class as a majority can also be challenged if one considers that identity and community-based politics seem to be the basis of most contemporary claims on justice and, perhaps consequently, most social-justice-orientated educational practice and research. Researchers and educators might need to tackle the role of the 'other' as fluid, probably now more than even. There is also a need for researchers to keep on examining how different minorities can build alliances to construct new understandings of justice that might challenge present situations of injustice. Race issues and gender issues, among others, have been extremely helpful in educational practice, policy, and research to denounce situations of discrimination. But if a real attempt has to be made to challenge hegemonic notions of justice (e.g., meritocracy), researchers and educators might have to consider also people's issues (see Laclau 2007b).

Third, globalization has generated a new form of *lumpen proletariat* (in Marx's term) or 'people without history' (in Hegel's term). The 'stateless' seem to lack any form of justice including economic and recognition. Further, there is lack of spaces for them to claim democratic justice. Educational research and policy must take their situation seriously. Asylum seekers, refugees, migrants, etc., cannot be educated to follow the rules of a liberal game in which they cannot participate. Instead, alternative spaces of participation in which they can demand economic and recognition justice must be explored, investigated, and ideally, financially supported.

We would not like to finish this chapter without leaving the door open to all possible interpretations of global citizenship. A few months before his death, Derrida defined alter-globalization movements, those gathering "the weak of the earth, all those who feel themselves crushed by the economic hegemonies, by the liberal market, by sovereignism, etc." (2004) as one of the main political actors trying to give shape to the justice to come. Universal justice—in the way the authors of this chapter understand—does not necessarily lead to the integration of humanity in a global community in which we are all educated as global citizens. There might be times in which universal justice will be mostly interpreted as a return to the local or as a challenge to certain forms of globalization. If a justice-orientated global citizenship is to have a space on national and global educational policies, this space needs to be open to competing understandings of globalization, citizenship, and education. Global citizenship, in this understanding, cannot be an outcome to be learnt or achieved. The best contribution of global citizenship education toward the justice to come is not, we argue, the promise of a perpetual peace in Kant's terms, but the creation of a space in which we all can debate about the promise of universal justice.

NOTES

1. Fraser (2005) understands justice as recognition, redistribution and participation.
2. For a more in depth account of the relation between liberal distributive justice and global ethics, see Forst (2001).
3. For a more detailed discussion on research in social class, see the chapter on social class in this handbook.
4. In August 2014, Michael Brown, an 18-year-old black man, was shot by Darren Wilson, 28, a white Ferguson police officer in Ferguson (USA). The shooting evolved into a chain of civil protests against systematic racism.
5. Chair of the Equality and Human Rights Commission in UK from 2007.

REFERENCES

Anderson, G., & Herr, K. (2015). New public management and the new professional educator: Framing the issue. *Education Policy Analysis Archives, 23*(84).

Andreotti, V., & Sousa, L. (Eds.). (2012). *Postcolonial perspectives on global citizenship education*. New York: Routledge.

Arendt, H. (1962). *The origins of totalitarianism*. New York, NY: Houghton Mifflin Harcourt.

Ball, S. J. (2012). *Global education inc.: New policy networks and the neo-liberal imaginary*. New York, NY: Routledge.

Banks, J. A. (2008). Diversity, group identity, and citizenship education in a global age. *Educational Researcher, 37*(3), 129–139.

Baker, D., & LeTendre, G. (2005). *National differences, global similarities: World culture and the future of schooling*. Palo Alto, CA: Stanford University Press.

Bauman, Z. (1998). *Globalization: The human consequences*. New York, NY: Columbia University Press.

Biesta, G. (1998). Deconstruction, justice and the question of education. *Zeitschrift Für Erziehungswissenschaft, 1*, 395–411.

Biesta, G., & Lawy, R. (2006). From teaching citizenship to learning democracy: Overcoming individualism in research, policy and practice. *Cambridge Journal of Education, 36*(1), 63–79.

Bhopal, K., & Myers, M. (2009). Gypsy, Roma and Traveller pupils in schools in the UK: Inclusion and 'good practice'. *International Journal of Inclusive Education, 13*(3), 299–314.

Boyden, J. (2009). What place the politics of compassion in education surrounding non-citizen children? *Educational Review, 61*(3), 265–276.

Brown, W. (2014). *Walled states, waning sovereignty*. New York: Zone Books.

Derrida, J. (2001). *On cosmopolitanism and forgiveness: Thinking in action*. London: Routledge.

Derrida, J. (2004). *For a justice to come: an interview with Jacques Derrida. The Brussells Tribunal*. Retrieved from http://archive.indymedia.be/news/2004/04/83123.html.

Durkheim, E. (1956). *Education and sociology*. Glencoe: Free Press.

Fanon, F. (1963). *The wretched of the earth*. New York: Grove Press.

Farthing, R. (2010). The politics of youthful antipolitics: Representing the "issue" of youth participation in politics. *Journal of Youth Studies, 13*(2), 181–195.

Fincham, K. (2013). Shifting youth identities and notion of citizenship in the Palestinian diaspora. In D. Kiwan (Ed.), *Naturalisation policies, education and citizenship: Multicultural and multi-nation societies in international perspective* (pp. 150–177). Basingstoke: Palgrave Macmillan.

Forst, R. (2001). Towards a critical theory of transitional justice. *Metapilosophy, 32*(1/2), 160–179.

Foster, B., & Norton, P. (2012). Educational equality for Gypsy, Roma and Traveller children and young people in the UK. *The Equal Rights Review, 8,* 85–111.

Fraser, N. (2005). Reinventar la justicia en un mundo globalizado. *New Left Review, 36,* 31–50.

Fraser, N. (2003). Social justice in the age of identity politics. In G. Henderson & M. Waterstone (Eds.), *Geographic thought: A Praxis perspective* (pp. 72–89). New York, NY: Routledge.

Friedrich, D. (2007). Old wine in new bottles? The actual and potential contribution of civil society organisations to democratic governance in Europe. Recon Online Working Paper. Retrieved from https://www.researchgate.net/publication/5015748_Old_wine_in_new_bottles_The_actual_and_potential_contribution_of_civil_society_organisations_to_democratic_governance_in_Europe.

Friedrich, D. S. (2014). Global microlending in education reform: Ensenar por Argentina and the neoliberalization of the grassroots. *Comparative Education Review, 58*(2), 296–321. doi:10.1086/675412.

Gautreaux, M., & Delagdo, S. (2016). Portrait of a Teach for All (TFA) teacher: Media narratives of the universal TFA teacher in 12 countries. *Education Policy Analysis Archives, 24*(110). doi: 10.14507/epaa.24.2149.

Gewirtz, S. (1998). Conceptualizing Social Justice in Education: mapping the territory. *Journal of Educational Policy, 13*(4), 469–484.

Habermas, J. (2005). The post national constellation. In D. Held & A. McGrew (Eds.), *The global transformations reader* (pp. 542–547). Cambridge: Polity Press.

Hall, S. (Ed.). (2006). *Stuart Hall: Critical dialogues in cultural studies.* London: Routledge.

Hardt, M., & Negri, A. (2000). *Empire.* Cambridge, MA: Harvard University Press.

Harvey, D. (2005). *A brief history of neoliberalism.* London: Oxford University Press.

Held, D. (2005). Cosmopolitanism: Taming globalization. In D. Held, & A. McGrew (Ed.), *The Global Transformations Reader,* (pp. 514–529). Cambridge: Polity Press.

Honneth, A. (1995). *The struggle for recognition: The moral grammar of social conflicts.* Cambridge: Polity Press.

Hughes, M. M. (2011). Intersectionality, quotas, and minority women's political representation worldwide. *American Political Science Review, 105*(3), 604–620.

Ikeda, D. (2001). *For the sake of peace: Seven paths to Global Harmony.* Santa Monica: California: Middleway Press.

Kant, I. (2010). Perpetual peace: A philosophical sketch. Philadelphia, PA: Slought Foundation and Syracuse University Humanities Center. Retrieved from https://slought.org/resources/perpetual_peace (Original work published 1975).

Kumar, R. (Ed.). (2014). *Neoliberalism and education.* Delhi, India: Aakar.

Kymlicka, W., & Norman, W. (1994). Return of the citizen: A survey of recent work on citizenship theory. *Ethics, 104*(2), 352–381.

Laclau, E. (1999). Politics, polemics and academics: An interview by Paul Bowman. *Parallax, 5*(2), 93–107.

Laclau, E. (2007a). *On populist reason.* London: Verso.

Laclau, E. (2007b). *Emancipation.* London: Verso.

Laclau, E., & Mouffe, C. (2001). *Hegemony and socialist strategy: Towards a radical democratic politics.* London: Verso.

Laden, A. S. (2014). The authority of civic citizens. In J. Tully (Ed.), *On global citizenship: James Tully in dialogue* (pp. 103–130). London: Bloomsbury.

Levinson, M. P. (2007). Literacy in English Gypsy communities: Cultural capital manifested as negative assets. *American Educational Research Journal, 44*(1), 5–39.

McGrew, A. (2005). Models of transitional democracy. In D. Held & A. McGrew (Eds.), *The global transformations reader* (pp. 500–513). Cambridge: Polity Press.

MacIntyre, A. (1988). *Whose justice? Which rationality?.* Notre Dame, Indiana: University of Notre Dame Press.

Malott, C., & Ford, D. R. (2015). *Marx, capital, and education: Towards a critical pedagogy of becoming.* New York: Peter Lang.

Marsh, J. (2011). *Class dismissed: Why we cannot teach or learn our way out of inequality.* New York, NY: Monthly Review Press.

Mathison, S., & Ross, E. W. (Eds.). (2008). *The nature and limits of standards-based reform and assessment.* New York: Teachers College Press.

McLaren, P. (2005). *Capitalists and conquerors: A critical pedagogy against empire.* Lanham, MD: Rowman & Littlefield.

Mouffe, B. Y. C. (1999). Deliberative democracy or agonistic. *Social Research, 66*(3), 745–758.

Nussbaum, M. (2002). Education for citizenship in an era of global connection. *Studies in Philosophy and Education, 21,* 289–303.

O'Hanlon, C., & Holmes, P. (2004). *The Education of Gypsy and Traveller children.* Stoke on Trent, UK: Trentham Books.

Pinson, H., Arnot, M., & Candappa, M. (2010). *Education, asylum and the 'non-citizen' child: The politics of compassion and belonging.* Basinstoke, UK: Palgrave Macmillan.

Rawls, J. (2002). *The law of peoples.* London: Harvard University Press.

Reay, D., Crozier, G., & Clayton, J. (2010). "Fitting in" or "standing out": Working-class students in UK higher education. *British Educational Research Journal, 36*(1), 107–124.

Rizvi, F., & Lingard, B. (2010). *Globalizing education policy.* New York, NY: Routledge.

Robertson, S. L., & Verger, A. (2012). Governing education through public private partnerships. Centre for Globalisation, Education and Societies. Retrieved from http://susanleerobertson.com/publications/.

Ross, E. W., & Gibson, R. (2007). *Neoliberalism and education reform.* Cresskill: Hampton Press.

Ross, E. W., & Queen, G. (2013). "Shut up. He might hear you!" Teaching Marx in social studies education. In C. S. Malott, & M. Cole (Eds.). *Teaching Marx across the curriculum: The socialist challenge* (pp. 203–228). Charlotte, NC: Information Age Publishing.

Ruitenberg, C. (2009). Educating political adversaries: Chantal Mouffe and radical democratic citizenship education. *Studies in Philosophy and Education, 28*(3), 269–281.

Sant, E. (2017). Can the subaltern nation speak by herself in the history curriculum? *Educational Studies, 53*(2), 105–121.

Sant, E., Pages, J., Santisteban, A., & Boixader, A. (2015). ¿Quién y cómo se construye el 'nosotros'? La construcción narrativa del 'nosotros catalán' a partir de los acontecimientos del 1714. *Ensenanza de Las Ciencias Sociales, 14,* 3–17.

Spring, J. (2008). Research on globalization and education. *Review of Educational Research, 78*(2), 330–363.

Straehler-Pohl, H., & Pais, A. (2014). Learning to fail and learning from failure–ideology at work in a mathematics classroom. *Pedagogy, Culture & Society, 22*(1), 79–96.

Tully, J. (2014). *On global citizenship.* London: Bloomsbury.

Unicef. (2016) Children on Move. Retrieved from http://www.unicef.org/emergencies/childrenonthemove/.

UNESCO. (1948). The Universal Declaration of Human Rights. Retrieved from http://www.unesco.org/education/information/50y/nfsunesco/doc/humrights.htm.

Vellanki, V. (2014). Teach for India and education reforms: Some preliminary reflections. *Contemporary Education Dialogues, 11*(1), 137–147.

Wall, J. (2011). Can democracy represent children? Toward a politics of difference. *Childhood, 19*(1), 86–100.

Wallerstein, I. (2004). *World-systems analysis: An introduction.* Durham, NC: Duke University Press.

Wilding, D. (2008). The educational experience of Gypsy Travellers: The impact of cultural dissonance and reinvention. *Reinvention: An International Journal of Undergraduate Research, 1*(1). Retrieved from http://www2.warwick.ac.uk/fac/cross_fac/iatl/reinvention/issues/volume1issue1/wilding/.

Young, I. M. (1990). *Justice and the politics of difference.* Princeton, NJ: Princeton University Press.

Žižek, S. (2000). *The ticklish subject: The absent centre of political ontology.* London: Verso.

Žižek, S. (2001). Have Michael Hardt and Antonio Negri rewritten the Communist Manifesto for the Twenty-First Century? Rethinking Marxism, 3/4. Retrieved from http://www.lacan.com/zizek-empire.htm.

Authors' Biography

Edda Sant is a Senior Lecturer in the Department of Childhood, Youth and Education Studies at Manchester Metropolitan University. She has previously worked as a Teaching and Research Fellow at the Universitat Autònoma de Barcelona (Spain) and as Social science and Citizenship education teacher in different schools. Her research focuses on citizenship and history education, particularly on the topics of political participation and the education of national/global identities.

Sue Lewis is currently working as an independent consultant in the Caribbean after retiring from leading and developing a range of Education Studies programmes. She had previously worked in Sweden, London and North Wales in a teaching and advisory capacity in the fields of English, English for Speakers of Other Languages, Traveller Education and Equality. She represented Wales in the European Women's Lobby in Brussels and was a founding member of the British Education Studies Association. Her research interests include social justice in education, identity, mentoring and collaborative action research and she has worked on research projects funded by the European Social Fund, the HEA and charities such as Timebank and The Big Lottery Fund.

Sandra Delgado is a PhD student in the Department of Curriculum and Pedagogy. She holds a Bachelor's degree in management and a MSc. in Economics from Universidad Nacional of Colombia. As researcher, her interests include social movements, activism, critical pedagogy, curriculum studies, academic capitalism and academic freedom. Some of her articles have been published in Education and Policy Analysis Archives, Workplace: A Journal for Academic Labor and in Revista Íber: Didáctica de las Ciencias Sociales, Geografía e Historia.

E. Wayne Ross is Professor in the Department of Curriculum and Pedagogy and co-director of the Institute for Critical Education Studies at The University of British Columbia in Vancouver, Canada. His research focuses on the role of curriculum and teaching in building democratic communities that are positioned to challenge the priorities and interests of neoliberal capitalism as manifest in educational and social policies that shape both formal and informal education experiences. His most recent books are Rethinking Social Studies (Information Age Publishing, 2017), Working for Social Justice Inside and Outside the Classroom (Peter Lang, 2016), and The Social Studies Curriculum: Purposes, Problems, and Possibilities (State University of New York Press, 2014).

CHAPTER 16

Global Citizenship and Equity: Cracking the Code and Finding Decolonial Possibility

Lynette Shultz

INTRODUCTION AND CONTEXT FOR GLOBAL CITIZENSHIP EDUCATION

This chapter explores how global citizenship and global citizenship education interlock with equity in both theory and practice. The array of ideas and education approaches claimed to be part of global citizenship has been widely discussed and reveal a tremendous range and difference in definition, aspiration, and intention for what *global citizenship* and *global citizenship education* might contribute in the world. In this chapter, I will narrow the focus to equity issues, and I will discuss the underlying tensions and possibilities that exist when global citizenship becomes a project of education for equity by addressing two questions: (1) How can global citizenship, conceptually and practically, address the conditions of injustice? (2) Can global citizenship education contribute to alleviating inequity in the world? The perspective and position from which I approach this topic and these questions come from my worldview and experience as a Canadian citizen whose ancestors were settlers in North America where indigenous communities had been living for centuries. I declare this because our worldview matters in an analysis of global citizenship, and throughout this chapter I critique the idea that a global citizen might have a "view from no-where," and I make links to how this can perpetuate colonial relations in the world. I further argue that the legacy of European colonialism is visible when we take a global view of equity issues.

L. Shultz (✉)
University of Alberta, 7-104 Education North, Edmonton T6G2G5, Canada
e-mail: lshultz@ualberta.ca

© The Author(s) 2018
I. Davies et al. (eds.), *The Palgrave Handbook of Global Citizenship and Education*, https://doi.org/10.1057/978-1-137-59733-5_16

Equity concerns often emerge when discussing global citizenship as this combination of scale (local to global) and citizenship engagement in relation to complex international, transnational, and planetary issues and events surfaces patterns in how disenfranchised people and their issues become invisible at all levels of society. When we add an analysis of the context and history of exclusion, what might look like equality often turns out to be inequality. We need an equity analysis. Struggles for justice around the world have demonstrated that it is not only equality of distribution that is required but also much better action to ensure equity where the contexts, histories, and relations of exclusion are considered as the way to create even the possibility for equality to exist. An equity analysis helps us see how categories of exclusion, for example race, sex, gender, class ability, geography, age or ability, create impassable and often interlocking barriers for some people to access both their "equal" share of the benefits of being part of their community, country, or the world, or their responsibility to assume their "equal" share of the burdens.

Global citizenship as a concept emerged in the late 1990s mainly from the area of development education and concerns of inequality. This was a time when the rosy ideals of "development" as a way of eliminating poverty were critiqued in every part of the world (see for example, Rahnema and Bawtree 1997). It was clear that national and international development agendas were key in a global project of integration into a global economy that many viewed and experienced as creating more misery than it alleviated (Abdi and Cleghorn 2005; Escobar 1995; Kapoor 2002, 2008; Rodney 1981). In response, anti-globalization movements developed and linked people around the world. Global citizenship was used to describe the movement and the people connected through their protests and, for a short period, *global citizenship* worked as a transformational platform for 'the people' to engage across borders in their solidarity struggles (see Shultz 2007). It was soon taken up by other actors as a signifier for a myriad of engagements that were brought about by the intensification of globalization in the twenty-first century such as traveling for work or recreation or, for many people in wealthy countries, to carry out charity work that was aimed at ameliorating some of the devastating consequences of the global economy (See Andreotti 2006; Jefferess 2008). Therefore, we saw global citizenship being used to describe activities as disparate as global corporate social responsibility activities by mining companies and participation in the G8 anti-globalization street protests or volunteering to build schools in rural communities in poor countries (Shultz 2007). At this point, many people abandoned the idea of global citizenship because of the great tension between global citizenship as a category to challenge inequity and one that described, if not promoted, the liberalism of transnational corporate entities and an elite enclave of mobile people able to transcend challenges and inequality at so many social, political, and economic borders (Shultz 2007). Despite this, by the second decade of this century, global citizenship had demonstrated a surprising durability. It remained a conceptual pillar in social and education policies, in international engagement by development organizations and agencies, in local communities, and for research, although mainly limited to the United Kingdom, Canada, Australia, and New Zealand. As UNESCO began its evaluation of the 1990–2015 *Education for All* policy goals, "global citizenship" began to appear in documents that bridged new policy arenas, new policy demands, and old concepts such as sustainable development and peace education (See, for example, UNESCO 2015). By naming global citizenship as its key organizing concept for Post-2015 education agenda (UNESCO 2015), we can expect the terrain of GCE to shift significantly again. Already, we see that new actors, for example, the governments of South Korea and Taiwan, have taken up the reframing of what global citizenship might contribute to education and equity around the world (Shultz 2015). The question of how this might contribute to global equity remains unanswered. Generally, the UNESCO approach to global citizenship education remains under-theorized and therefore, continues to be used in ways that cannot address the main equity issues of our times (Shultz 2015).

A Global Equity and Justice Framework for GCE

To begin a discussion of global citizenship and equity requires a theoretical framework of justice that addresses the scales and spaces that we encounter in both the "global" and the "citizenship" considerations of equity and inequity. Global social justice is a frame used to bring in both contextual and historical relations of injustice (see, for example, Shultz 2013, 2015). In relation to global citizenship education, global social justice provides not only a conceptual and communicative framework to understand the political, social, environmental, and economic conditions needed for even discussing global equity, but a way to understand struggles for justice and citizenship rights that span across sites and scales in a world linked through globalization and globalism. As T.H.Marshall outlined in 1950, citizenship rights have evolved or thickened to include civil rights, political rights, and social rights. From a global equity perspective, we should explore citizenship issues from the perspective of those who are excluded or have diminished civil, political or social rights. In a globalized world, these conditions require a global or multi-scalar consideration. What are our rights and responsibilities on a planet that must face the impact of climate change? Do refugees, whether escaping war or climate catastrophe have a right to asylum? If so, who is responsible for them? Can a global financial system be created to ensure more equitable distribution of wealth? How can we address these global issues in a socially or relationally just way?

Theories of social justice and equity focus on the fairness of conditions of distribution of both benefits and burdens within a society as citizens struggle for their rights. Nancy Fraser (1996, 2009) and Fraser and Nash (2014) provide an analytic frame that nests together the conditions of (re)distribution, recognition, and representation or participative parity, as a way to frame situations of injustice. Here, we understand that "social justice has been central to the evolution and expansion of citizenship rights, providing the language for the 'systemically disadvantaged to talk back to the state, to make claims as citizens who had been actively denied this promise of social justice' (Brodie 2007, p. 99). Global social justice conditions should also be understood through these nested processes whereby the relational status of actors is acknowledged including historical social, economic and political positions within global histories and systems (see for example, Abdi 2008; Mignolo 2011). Social justice theorists identify the importance of understanding how reciprocity in these relations of recognition works (Coulthard 2014; Fraser 1996, 2009; Honneth 1995; Odora Hoppers 2009, 2015; Simpson 2008) in an attempt to understand relations of colonialism and/or solidarity. Both the global scale and citizenship struggles are important here.

Global Citizenship and Poverty

The Global Wealth Report 2015 by Swiss bank Credit Suisse (Ocotber 2015) finds that global wealth inequality continues to worsen and has reached a new milestone, with the top 1% owning more of the world's assets than the bottom 99% combined.

Data from Oxfam (January, 2016) report "An Economy for the 1%," the following statistics paint a grave picture of global economic equity:

- In 2015, just 62 individuals had the same wealth as 3.6 billion people—the bottom half of humanity. This figure is down from 388 individuals as recently as 2010.
- The wealth of the richest 62 people has risen by 45% in the five years since 2010—that's an increase of more than half a trillion dollars ($542bn), to $1.76 trillion.
- Meanwhile, the wealth of the bottom half fell by just over a trillion dollars in the same period—a drop of 38%.
- Since the turn of the century, the poorest half of the world's population has received just 1% of the total increase in global wealth, while half of that increase has gone to the top 1%.
- The average annual income of the poorest 10% of people in the world has risen by less than $3 each year in almost a quarter of a century. Their daily income has risen by less than a single cent every year. (Oxfam, January, 2016, p. 2).

As Pogge (2002) in Dobson 2006, points out, "we are familiar through charity appeals, with the assertion that it lies in our hands to save the lives of many or, by doing nothing, to let these people die. We are less familiar with the assertion examined here of a weightier responsibility: that most of us not merely let people starve but also participate in starving them" (Pogge 2002 in Dobson 2006, p. 182). In studies of global citizenship within education policy, being a global citizen is promoted differently based on position within the global economic system. The elitism of the global citizen as a person who has unlimited mobility is promoted in wealthy countries as the way to access the resources of the world (see for example, Shultz 2011) and what Zemach-Bersin describes as "entitled to the world" (2012). Beside this, global citizenship is also promoted to these students as a responsibility for their success and to valorize charity work, mostly in the "global south."[1] Here students are offered opportunities to travel to poor communities and contribute their labor or funds toward a development project (see Shultz 2012, Zemach-Bersin 2012). If a global social justice frame is used to view these conditions of poverty, global citizenship might be more readily used to describe the need and process for poor people to make claims against this system of inequality and to critique the position of wealthy students in perpetuating the inequity through misrecognition of people and the histories and legacies of the systems of exclusion. However, the perpetuation of an imaginary of a global citizen who has a sanctioned ignorance of how colonialism has and continues to work, along with no awareness of his or her own complicity in the global system, stands to reproduce the very conditions they might imagine alleviating. Global citizenship education that challenges and transcends this ignorance will demand that a "global citizen" not speak from "nowhere" but declare and understand their own position within the historical and current colonial matrix of relations.

Global Citizenship, Misrecognition, and the Abyssal Line of Colonialism

The many legacies of European colonialism are revealed in a global social justice analysis, making visible how these legacies continue to shape most aspects of citizenship struggles for political, civic, and social rights particularly in territories that were colonized. We can look to theories of post-colonial and anti-colonial relations, and anti-oppression activists who provide evidence on how justice must also overcome the historical, social and material legacies of colonial relations based on imperialism, patriarchy, and racism that continue to exert organizing strength in the lives and relations of people around the world (Abdi 2008; Andreotti and de Sousa 2012; Colthard 2014; Dussel 2013; Fanon Fanon 1959; Mignolo 2011; Monga 1996; Shultz and Abdi 2017; Visvanathan 1997). Global citizenship can play a role both conceptually and as an education goal in both highlighting and ameliorating these. To begin with, however, we must wrestle with the issues of recognition in colonial relations. Global citizenship education that engages this way stands a chance of becoming an important contribution to a decolonized future.

Greg Coulthard (2014) provides an important contribution to understanding the links between conditions of justice, recognition, and colonial power. He argues for a decolonial recognition that reconfigures colonialist, racist, and patriarchal state power in relation to indigenous/colonized peoples (see for example pages 3–6). Enrique Dussel (2013) echoes this demand in his description of "the dawning of a pluriversal, trans-modern age" (pp. 16–18) where the global system is decentered revealing global relations that are a system that is beyond modernity, capitalism, eurocentrism, colonialism (p. 18) and its "univocal universalism" (p. 19) that is limited to a single culture on the planet" (p. 19). This call to pluriversalism addresses what scholars describe as the "abyssal line of colonialism" (de Sousa Santos 2007, 2014) where systems were put in place that misrecognized the knowledge contributions of the majority of the world's people. Europeans were considered to have knowledge and the rest of the world viewed as a vast space devoid of thinking people (see, for example, Abdi 2013; Amin 2011; Harding 2008; Mignolo 2000; Odora Hoppers 2009; Visvanathan 1997). The construction of "the savage" or the "child" waiting to be taught or developed by thoughtful Europeans was at the base of the devastating colonial education system that continues today (see for example Battiste and Youngblood Henderson 2001; Shiza 2008; Odora Hoppers 2009). The result is what de Sousa Santos described as a vast abyss separating Europeans and the rest of the world and essentially creating a global and un-crossable "abyssal line" of colonialism. If there is any doubt about the legacies, one needs only to look at the Canadian example and the "Truth and Reconciliation Commission" work to address the damage of colonial residential schools (Truth and Reconciliation Commission 2015) or the earlier process in South Africa (Mack 2014) where collective spaces held of untold horrors of colonialism and an underlying dehumanization of non-European people in all aspects of colonial–colonizer contact.

In relation to global citizenship education, the abyssal line of colonialism continues as a key problem with ongoing exclusion of indigenous knowledges (or any non-western knowledge) from any educational canon in the world. In fact, with the globalization of comparisons and ranking of children's school achievement and higher education institutions, we see an even more rigourous move to harmonize knowledge with what is legitimized in North American and European education systems (Shahjahan 2011).

In recent study of "world knowledge" by Graham et al. (2011), the authors described the extent of the North American and European dominance of academic publications (86%) with "the USA and UK publishing more than the rest of the world rest of the world combined" (p. 14). The authors point out that "[t]he non-western world is not only underrepresented in these rankings, but also ranks poorly on average citation score measures" (p. 14). Their research also highlighted that the relatively small country of Switzerland published more than three times the number of scientific articles than the whole continent of Africa (p. 14). Graham et al. (2011) also found this trend outside of the academy where, in a study of 1.5 million Wikipedia articles, European articles were heavily dominant with North America being a distant but clear second, with the two as the most represented geographies in this knowledge-sharing site (p. 22). In addition, to highlight further the exclusion of non-western knowledge, they state "there are remarkably more Wikipedia articles (7800) written about Antarctica than any country in Africa or South America" (p. 22). Another finding of this study was that "the USA, and to a lesser extent Europe and Japan, are home to the bulk of the world's user-generated content on Google" (p. 26). (see also, Shultz and Abdi 2017).

When what Célestin Monga (1996) calls "brain trusts" (p. 33) refuse to acknowledge or include knowledge from outside the UK/USA, we see the abyssal line of colonialism continue working to marginalize and exploit those people "on the other side of the line" (de Sousa Santos 2015). This exclusion, treated as a local justice issue, cannot be addressed through the politics of recognition alone even if addressing issues of identity and difference belong to efforts to understand injustice. Coulthard argues that colonialism's continued power requires a "resurgence" (2014, pp. 153–159) and "self-recognition" (pp. 153–159) as the foundation of redoing settler colonial politics and finally, the full inclusion as citizens with knowledge, experience, interests, and contributions to the world. Adding a global scale to this resurgence brings us to the possibility of what Walter Mignolo (2011) and Boaventura de Sousa Santos (2007, 2014) call "cognitive justice," a resurgence against the continued global colonization of knowledge.

Cognitive Justice as a Response to the Abyssal Line of Colonialism

Of course, none of this is new information and we are really past time for arguing whether colonized people have a knowledge history or philosophy but now a valid question is whether there is a right for different forms of knowledge to survive (see for example Odora Hoppers 2009, 2015; Odora Hoppers and Richards 2012; de Sousa Santos 2007, 2014; Visvanathan 1997). Odora Hoppers argues that to democratize knowledge is to "survive creatively and sustainably, turning the toxic hierarchy left behind by colonialism into a circle, in which the inner cry for self-determination meets the outer voice of co-determination" (2015, p. 96). This concept of cognitive justice is based on a reciprocal recognition of the plurality of knowledge and is a statement of the rights of different forms of knowledge to co-exist. It is an idea first described by Shiv Visvanathan in his 1997 book "*A Carnival for Science: Essays on science, technology, and development*" (1997). The concept of cognitive justice is based on the recognition of the plurality of knowledge and expresses the right of the different forms of knowledge to coexist.

The idea of cognitive justice has been further developed by Boaventura de Sousa Santos (2014); Walter Mignolo (2011); and Catherine Odora Hoppers (2009, 2015). Odora Hoppers argues that given the equity condition of

cognitive justice, indigenous knowledges must be included in the global dialogues of knowledge without having to fit in the structures and standards of
Western knowledge. She highlights that this must happen "without duress"
(2015) referring to how knowledge inclusion must be without the non-
western knowledge holder having to suffer the burden of knowledge exchange
and with fewer benefits as the difficult work of pushing against the hegemony
of Western epistemologies and Western education norms and Western systems
of exchange. This is a radical approach in that it is "a democratization that
rejects the idea that the majority of the world's population that have sustained
their livelihoods on "other" formulas elliptical to the Western model are now
"disposable" as far as the modern project is concerned" (2009, p. 94).

GLOBAL SOCIAL JUSTICE AND COGNITIVE JUSTICE AS THE FOUNDATION OF GLOBAL CITIZENSHIP EDUCATION

This chapter began with questions about how global citizenship might
address the conditions of injustice and how global citizenship education
might contribute to alleviating inequity in the world. Bringing together theories of global social justice and equity with colonial and decolonial thought,
we can see the need for a concept of multi-scalar citizenship to describe and
understand the uneven working and impact of global systems and relations
on people in the world. Global citizenship makes a conceptually rich contribution to education that seeks to create good relations today by engaging
with the histories and legacies of colonialism as well as addressing how current forms of globalization reproduce and/or reflect patterns of exclusion set
in place during the era of European colonization of much of the world. A
global social justice and equity framing of global citizenship lead us to the
condition of participative parity as a requirement of justice. From a global
perspective, this reveals the problems of the misrecognition and exclusion of
most of the world's non-European people through violence that includes the
genocide of communities but also a wide project of epistemicide (de Sousa
Santos 2015). There can be some movement toward reconciliation through
processes of reciprocal recognition of the legitimacy of non-western epistemologies by engaging in education based cognitive justice. This idea speaks
to the urgent need to decenter Eurocentrism in language and knowledge
exchanges to allow for the flourishing of non-western knowledge and the
contribution to global knowledge from these many parts of the world. This
radical democratization of knowledge spaces is a foundational condition of
equity from all locations in a multi-scalar system of relations. In a time when
any of the global systems—political, environmental, social, economic—keeps
us teetering on the edge of collapse, we can welcome the diversity of knowledges, some that kept societies healthy and strong for millennia, to contribute
to our well-being on our planet. Global citizenship as a decolonial contribution to "the creation of the world" (Nancy 2007) does make global equity
more understandable.

It must, of course, be acknowledged that global citizenship education has many faces. If we are to employ it to address issues of equity, there are some approaches to global citizenship that must be named for what they actually produce, in some cases, a neoliberal citizen attempting to live without connection to place or people or system. A global citizen or global citizenship education that works to increase the privilege for a global elite is not conceptually or practically about relations of citizenship and cannot contribute to any project of equity. We can get rid of global citizenship education that positions a global elite as not only more wealthy and therefore more deserving, but also endowed with superior knowledge, worldview, and responsibility to "improve" the lives of others as an affirmation of their own goodness. Instead, global citizenship education becomes a platform that demands decolonial relations to repair systems of inequality and inequity, recognizing that whether these exist in local contexts or beyond, they reflect global patterns and histories of exclusion and decitizenization of particular people.

The Classroom as a Fractal of the World

To more clearly understand the relationship between classrooms and their global contexts, we can employ the mathematical idea of a fractal, a seemingly irregular or random relationship or event that, with closer study, shows itself to be a detailed copy of a wider and regularly occurring pattern (Mandelbot 2004). Our classrooms, whether in higher education or basic education, are fractals of the world, places where "the local" and "the global" cease to be understandable as separate and dichotomous locations. The complexity of global economic, environmental, political, and cultural relations becomes visible in the daily interactions of the classroom. This happens through engagement among the diverse people present but also through the media, curriculum, community issues, and global problems that become the text and substance of thought and action in daily teaching and learning. Some of these relations become visible through exchanges and deliberation and others are kept silenced through the normalization of dominant relations. Everyday, fractals of the world are created and recreated in classrooms and sites of learning. When teachers can see the patterns that include injustice, they can transform what is possible through global citizenship education founded on equity and global justice. This foundation demands more than a global citizenship education that is an activity tucked into an overloaded schedule (it is surprising how many teachers claim their global citizenship education activities all happen outside regular education programming). Participative parity and cognitive justice can be made powerful influences on how we organize the daily events and activities of education. As we address equity claims at all levels, including how to provide safe and inclusive classrooms for children who have faced exclusion based on sexual orientation, racism, sexism, classism, geographical origin, religion, or ability, understanding how these claims are legacies and extensions of global patterns of injustice can open powerful possibilities for transformation. Cognitive justice demands we educate by drawing on the rich knowledges too often ignored in western/ized curriculums and materials, again transforming who it is we understand as "educated." In turn, each student, each relationship that is transformed at the local level, reflects back to the wider context as part of the global project of justice. A focus on transformed relations and imaginations based on global equity and justice can be a critically important part of today's education. Teachers who bring a strong conceptualization of global histories and issues that create and maintain patterns and hierarchies of inclusion and exclusion and how to disrupt these, will be prepared to create classrooms that are fractals of global justice and equity.

NOTE

1. I acknowledge the term "global south" is a term that is a problem because of its contribution to "the abyssal line" of colonialism that I am trying to highlight. I have used it because it is a term used within the development field and in global citizenship education to describe the "Third World" (another development category) without naming the colonialism from which the conditions of poverty and racism permeate.

REFERENCES

Abdi, A. A. (2008). Europe and African thought systems and philosophies of education: 'Reculturing' the trans-temporal discourses. *Cultural Studies, 22*(2), 309–327.

Abdi, A. A. (2013). Decolonizing educational and social development platforms in Africa. *African and Asian Studies, 12,* 64–82.

Abdi, Ali A., & Cleghorn, Ailie (Eds.). (2005). *Issues in African education: sociological perspectives*. New York: Palgrave Macmillan.

Amin, S. (2011). *Global history: A view from the South*. Daker: CODESRIA & Pambazuka Press.

Andreotti, V. (2006). Soft vs critical global citizenship education. *Policy & Practice: A Development Review*. Autumn, 2006, 3, 40–51.

Andreotti, V., & de Souza, L. M. (Eds.). (2012). *Postcolonial perspectives on global citizenship education*. London: Routledge.

Battiste, M., & Youngblood Henderson, J. S. (2001). *Protecting indigenous knowledge and heritage: A global challenge*. Saskatoon, CAN: Purich Publishers.

Brodie, J. (2007). The social in social citizenship. In E. Isin (Ed.), *Recasting the social in citizenship* (pp. 20–43). Toronto: University of Toronto Press.

Coulthard, G. (2014). *Red skin, white masks: Rejecting the colonial politics of recognition*. Minneapolis: University of Minnesota Press.

Credit Suisse. (October, 2015). *Global Wealth Report 2015*. https://publications.credit-suisse.com/tasks/render/file/?fileID=F2425415-DCA7-80B8-EAD989AF9341D47E.

Dei, G. S., & Simons, M. (Ed). *Fanon & education: Thinking through pedagogical possibilities*. New York: Peter Lang.

de Sousa Santos, B. (2007). *Cognitive justice in a global world: Prudent knowledges for a decent life*. Lanham, MD: Lexington Books.

de Sousa Santos, B. (2014). *Epistemologies of the South: Justice against epistemicide.* London: Routledge.

de Sousa Santos, B. (2015). *Epistemologies of the South: Justice against epistemicide.* London: Routledge.

Dobson, A. (2006). Thick cosmopolitanism. *Political Studies, 54*(1), 165–184.

Dussel, E. (2013). Agenda for a South-South philosophical dialogue. *Human Architecture. Journal of Self-Knowledge, 11*(1), 3–18.

Escobar, A. (1995). *Encountering development: The making and unmaking of the Third World.* Princeton: Princeton University Press.

Fanon, F. (1959). *A dying colonialism.* New York: Grove Press.

Fraser, N. (1996). *Justice interruptus: Critical reflections on the "Post-socialist" condition.* London: Routledge.

Fraser, N. (2009). *Scales of justice: Reimaging political space in a globalizing world.* New York: Columbia University Press.

Fraser, N., & Nash, K. (2014). *Transnationalizing the public sphere.* Cambridge, UK: Polity Press.

Graham, M., Hale, S. A., & Stephen, M. (2011). Geographies of the Worlds' Knowledge [PDF]. Retrieved from http://www.oii.ox.ac.uk/publications/convoco_geographies_en.pdf.

Harding, S. (2008). *Science from below: feminisms, postcolonialities and modernities.* Durham, NC: Duke University Press.

Honneth, A. (1995). *The struggle for recognition.* Cambridge, MA: MIT Press.

Jefferess, D. (2008). Global citizenship and the cultural politics of benevolence. *Critical Literacy: Theories and Practices, 2*(1), 27–36.

Kapoor, I. (2002). Capitalism, culture, agency: Dependency versus postcolonial theory. *Third World Quarterly, 23*(4), 647–664.

Kapoor, I. (2008). *The postcolonial politics of development.* London: Routledge.

Mack, K. E. (2014). *From apartheid to democracy: Deliberating truth and reconciliation in South Africa University Park.* PA: Penn State Press.

Mandelbrot, B. B. (2004). *Fractals and chaos.* Berlin: Spinger.

Marshall, T. M. (1950). *Citizenship and social class.* Cambridge: Cambridge University Press.

Mignolo, W. (2000). *Local histories/global designs: Coloniality, subaltern knowledges, and border thinking.* New Jersey: Princeton University Press.

Mignolo, W. (2011). *The darker side of western modernity: Global futures.* Decolonial Options. Durham & London: Duke University Press.

Monga, C. (1996). *Anthropology of anger: Civil society and democracyin Africa.* Lynn Boulder, CO/ London: Reinner Publishers.

Nancy, J. L. (2007). *The creation of the world or globalization.* Translated and with Introduction by Francois Raffoul and David Pettigrew. New York: SUNY Press.

Odora Hoppers, C. (2009). From bandit colonialism to the modern triage society: Towards a moral and cognitive reconstruction of knowledge and citizenship. *International Journal of African Renaissance Studies, 4*(2), 168–180.

Odora Hoppers, C. (2015). Cognitive justice and integration without duress. *International Journal of Development Education and Global Learning, 7*(2).

Odora Hoppers, C., & Richards, H. (2012). *Rethinking thinking: Modrenity's other and the transformation of the University.* Pretoria, SA: University of South AfricaPress.

Pogge, T. (2002). World poverty and Human Rights. Cambridge: Polity Press.

Rahnema, M., & Bawtree, V. (1997). *The post-development reader.* London: Zed Books.

Rodney, W. (1981). *How Europe underdeveloped Africa*. Washington, DC: Howard University Press.

Shahjahan, R. A. (2011). Decolonizing the evidence-based education and policy movement: revealing the colonial vestiges in educational policy, research, and neoliberal reform. *Journal of Education Policy, 26*(2), 181–206.

Shizha, E. (2008). Globalization and indigenous knowledge: An African postcolonial theoretical analysis. In S. Guo & A. A. Abdi (Eds.), *Education and social development: Global issues and analysis*. Rotterdam Holland: Sense Publishers.

Shultz, L. (2007). Educating for global citizenship: Conflicting agendas and understandings. *Alberta Journal of Educational Research, 53*(3), 248–258.

Shultz, L. (2011). What do we ask of global citizenship education? A study of global citizenship education in a Canadian University. *International Journal of Development Education and Global Learning, 3*(1), 5–22.

Shultz, L. (2012). Youth study tour to Africa. In L. M. de Souza & V. Andreotti (Eds.), *Postcolonial perspectives on global citizenship education* (pp. 172–173). London: Routledge.

Shultz, L. (2013). Decolonizing social justice education: From policy knowledge to citizenship action. In A. A. Abdi (Ed.), *Decolonizing philosophies of education* (pp. 29–42). Rotterdam: Sense Publications.

Shultz, L. (2015). Decolonizing UNESCO's post-2015 agenda: Global social justice and a view from UNDRIP. *4*(2), 96–115.

Shultz, L., & Abdi, A. (2017). Decolonizing information ethics for the liberation of knowledge. In T. Samek & L. Shultz (Eds.), *Essays on information ethics, globalization, and citizenship: Ideas to praxis*. New York: McFarlane.

Simpson, L. (2008). *Lighting the eighth fire: The liberation, resurgence, and protection of indigenous nation*. Winnipeg, CAN: Arbeiter Ring Publisher.

Truth and Reconciliation Commission (2015). *Truth and Reconciliation Commission of Canada: calls to action*. Winnipeg, Manitoba: Commission of Canada.

UNESCO. (2015). UNESCO's *"Concept note on the post-2015 education agenda."* http://en.unesco.org/post2015/sites/post2015/files/UNESCOConceptNote-Post2015_ENG.pdf (Post-2015 EA).

Visvanathan, S. (1997). *Carnival for science. Essays on science technology and development*. Oxford, UK: Oxford University Press.

Wa Thiong'o, N. (2009). *Re-membering Africa*. Nairobi: East African Publishers.

Zemach-Bersin, T. (2012). Entitled to the world. In V. Andreotti & L. M. de Souza (Eds.), *Postcolonial perspectives on global citizenship education* (pp. 87–104). London: Routledge.

AUTHOR BIOGRAPHY

Lynette Shultz Ph.D., is Associate Dean, International, and Director of the Centre for Global Citizenship Education and Research in the Faculty of Education at the University of Alberta. She has published widely on the topics of social justice and global citizenship education. Her most recent book publications are co-edited book, *Decolonizing Global Citizenship Education* and *Assembling and Governing the Higher Education Institution: Democracy, Social Justice and Leadership of Global Higher Education*.

CHAPTER 17

Diversity, Global Citizenship and the Culturally Responsive School

INTRODUCTION

This extract from the website of the Australian *Federal Department of Immigration and Border Protection* typifies a common sense about cultural diversity that circulates in the Australian public sphere.

> Since the department [of Immigration] was established on 13 July 1945, seven million people have been granted a visa for permanent migration. As a result, Australia is among the world's most culturally diverse nations. About 45 per cent of all Australians were born overseas, or have at least one parent who was born overseas.
>
> Australia has derived substantial economic benefits from the skilled migration and temporary entry programs during the past 65 years. Skilled migrants are filling positions that remain in chronic shortage despite the effects of the

A version of this background statement was first developed for a *Hawke EU Centre for Mobilities, Migrations and Cultural Transformations* funded workshop titled: *Learning to Live in Culturally Diverse Societies* and used in subsequent publications. (http://www.unisa.edu.au/Education-Arts-and-Social-Sciences/school-of-education/News-and-Events/Events1/Learning-to-live-together-in-culturally-diverse-societies-/)

R. Hattam (✉)
School of Education, Magill Campus, University of South Australia, C1-77, St. Bernard's Road, Magill 5072, Australia
e-mail: robert.hattam@unisa.edu.au

© The Author(s) 2018
I. Davies et al. (eds.), *The Palgrave Handbook of Global Citizenship and Education*, https://doi.org/10.1057/978-1-137-59733-5_17

257

global economic crisis. International students and visitors to Australia contribute to our foreign exchange revenue. Social benefits have been reaped through the high levels of community harmony and cohesion which draw Australia's diverse society together—Australians are regarded internationally as a friendly, respectful and welcoming people. (Department of Immigration and Border Protection 2014)

This common sense asserts that Australia is an increasingly culturally diverse country, one which can demonstrate that cultural diversity *does* contribute substantially to its economy and society, and also claims high levels of community *harmony and cohesion*. Put simply, Australia should be considered as a hopeful global example for building an economically successful and socially cohesive nation *that is* culturally diverse.

But then internationally, nations such as Australia are dealing with significant tensions related to increasing cultural diversity. We need only reflect on Brexit, the recent election of Trump as President of the USA, and the increasing popularity of all manner of right-wing political parties in most nations[1] for three potent exemplars. In which case, all nations now grapple with 'ungovernability' (Offe 1987) demands from within and outside of the nation. Contemporary times are characterised by increasing global flows of money, technology, and people (migration), and a compression of space and time, that contribute increasing pressure on governments (Robertson 1992). From outside of the nation, transnational corporations avoid paying their fair share of tax to host countries, and 'the state now has a very limited role in mediating between capital and workers as key decisions are made at a global level to which states have little connection and over which they have even less power' (Bates 2012, p. 60). Most significantly for Australia, manufacturing moves off-shore, resulting in growing income inequality (Whitford 2013) as traditional working class jobs disappear.

Inside of the nation, historical modes of sociality and community are breaking down, such as family, church, and local community as understood in Tönnies famous book, *Community and Society*, as the 'little community' characterised in terms of 'an understanding shared by all its members' (Bauman 2001, p. 10). Such a breakdown of traditional community, Bauman (2001) argues is significant because it intensifies a key malaise of our times: our need for both freedom and security. But freedom and security are 'simultaneously, complementary and incompatible', and hence 'equally indispensable' yet 'hard to reconcile without friction' (p. 19). But then new formations of sociality and community are evident, such as trends towards various kinds hyper-nationalism and religious fundamentalism: 'Hyper-nationalism is often associated with ethnicity and celebrated through mythologies rooted in particular interpretations of the past, especially in interpretations that celebrate victories and/or humiliations and call for the exercise of domination or revenge' (Bates 2012, p. 60). And fundamentalism provides stability for identity and community through adherence to narrow and authoritarian readings of religious texts, often against scientific reason and commitments to universal human rights (e.g. towards women and children). Borrowing from Offe (1987), these ungovernability pressures have forced nations to off-load demands onto the market, and increase steering capacity through expanding horizons for conceptualising and acting. As well, nations have intensified their border work, for example, increased attention to border protection and tightly up on definitions and processes for legal citizenship.

While Australians might be proud of their version of multiculturalism, cultural diversity is still highly contested on the street, in the workplace, and in media culture. Cultural diversity is still one of the divisive sites for Australian realpolitic. As examples, on the street, we witnessed the Cronulla riots, (Poynting 2006), violence against Indian students in 2009 (Mason 2012), racist incidents on public transport that go viral on social media, and the daily experiences of hate speech that many non-Anglo Australians experience (Australian Human Rights Commission 2003; Gelber and McNamara 2015). In the workplace, there are policies for skilled migration, yet often we hear the refrain that 'they are stealing our jobs'. In the media, there is a culture war being played around a politics of representation and examples include: the stolen generations being represented as myth (Manne 2001), and contesting how recent migrant groups such as Sudanese refugees get represented (Nunn 2010). In politics in Australia in the last decade or so, we have witnessed the rise and fall and rise again of right-wing, nationalist politician Pauline Hanson (Manne 2004; Ack 2016; Lueck et al. 2015), the Tampa Affair (McNevin 2011), and the development of 'dog whistle politics' (Haney-Lopez 2014) around issues connected to cultural difference. In thinking about cultural difference in Australia there are many attempts to theorise the contemporary Australian condition such as: or *'settler colonialism'* (Moran 2005); *'internal colonialism'* (Short 2005); the possibility of a *colonial paranoia* (Carter 1996, p. 11); *'the unhappy country'* (Beilharz 2005); *'a politics of bad feeling'* (Ahmed 2004); *'paranoid nationalism'* (Hage 2003). Papastergiadis (2004) pushes this further and argues for an *'invasion complex'* that is 'deeply embedded within the national imaginary'.

However, as Noble (2011) rightly argues, too much theory, policy and practice in this area:

- misunderstands the nature of cultural diversity. 'Cultural complexity is much more than the sum of nationally defined 'cultures', and it goes well beyond an awareness of the degree of differentiation within and across those nationally defined cultures; it must also be seen in the multiple forms of adaption and mixing that mark the process of settlement, intermarriage, intergenerational change and the plural social contexts in which difference is negotiated' (p. 827);

- asserts outmoded stereotypes of 'multiculturalism' based on reified notions of culture rather than understanding cultures as always in translation, and hence hybridisation;
- sets up unhelpful binaries that claim a high moral ground for complexity against any attempt as theorising reduction or simplification;
- assumes 'an easy invocation of cultural harmony' that itself 'entails dangers' (p. 838); and
- focuses too much on macro-policy analyses for problematisation and pays too little attention to grounded studies that examine 'the capacities humans employ in their daily lives to navigate the complexities of their world. We do not need more elaborate theorisation but 'grounded analysis using middle-order conceptual tools to make sense of the ways people manage the complex milieu in which they move' (p. 838).

My brief analysis of the challenges of cultural diversity for Australia into the future, mean that Australian 'schools are currently sandwiched between demands of the economy on one side and increasingly fundamentalist communities on the other' (Bates 2012, p. 60). Importantly though schools are affected by these global pressures, they also provide spaces for hopeful interventions. Educational researchers could examine the effects of increasing cultural diversity on life in schools but I prefer to focus instead on how schools teach *for* cultural diversity. While the focus here is on the Australian context, the findings and arguments presented resonate in other nations and—crucially—provoke important reflections about both educating for global citizenship and educating in a globally diverse contexts.

Importantly also for an introduction to this chapter, I need to provide some clarity around my use of the concept of cultural diversity. In reviewing the field of education studies on this theme, there is a confused and highly contested plethora of ideas; Educational researchers across many countries use multiple conceptual frameworks to research cultural diversity in their schools. In the Australian case, there has been no proper review of the research in this field but the following examples of research inform my study:

- Examples of school-based studies into cultural diversity and schools (Burridge, and Chodkiewicz 2008);
- Examination into Australian multiculturalism and schooling and especially policy studies that have involved researching policy effects, that is, how policies are being interpreted by teachers (Watkins et al. 2013);
- Research into refugee schooling in Australia. Whilst there is a paucity of research in this area there has been some recent research that provides insights in how specific case studies of cultural diversity (i.e. refugee communities) and schooling. Some of this research has been policy studies with some ethnographic type research in schools (Christie and Sidhu 2016; Matthews 2008; Hattam and Every 2010);

- Anti-racism pedagogy is also a focus for important research in Australia that contributes significant understandings (Arber 2012); and from Indigenous Studies (Aveling 2012);
- Indigenous perspectives on curriculum and pedagogy, including culturally responsive pedagogy (Bishop et al. 2007; Villegas and Lucas 2007) and Indigenous pedagogies (Grande 2004);
- New studies into the intersections of space, schooling and racism (Gulson and Webb 2012).

In this chapter, I have decided to work with the transnational work on developing culturally responsive approaches to schools and pedagogy. Some important examples that inform my framework are the following approaches:

a. Gloria Ladson-Billings (1995) provides an alternative versions of culturally responsive pedagogy for improving learning outcomes for **African–American children**. Her version of culturally responsive pedagogy'rests on three criteria or propositions: (a) Students must experience academic success; (b) students must develop and/or maintain cultural competence; and (c) students must develop a critical consciousness through which they challenge the status quo of the current social order' (p. 160).

b. For Villegas and Lucas (2002) the key issue is the **increasing cultural and linguistic diversity of classrooms** that requires attention and they argue for a culturally responsive teacher that has these six characteristics: (a) is socioculturally conscious, (b) has affirming views of students from diverse backgrounds, (c) is capable of bringing about educational change that will make schools more responsive to all students; (d) is capable of promoting learners' knowledge construction; (e) knows about the lives of his or her students; and (f) uses his or her knowledge about students' lives to design instruction that builds on what they already know while stretching them beyond the familiar (Villegas and Lucas 2002).

c. The **Eight Alaskan Culturally Responsive Teacher Standards** define culturally responsive pedagogies in these terms: (1) teaching philosophy encompassing multiple worldviews; (2) learning, theory and practice knowing how students learn; (3) teaching for diversity; (4) content related to local community; (5) instruction and assessment building on student's cultures; (6) learning environment utilising local sites; (7) family and community involvement as partners; and (8) professional development' (Assembly of Alaska Native Educators 1999).

Across this research, diversity is understood in terms of linguistic and cultural diversity and the emergent concept of super-diversity. Linguistic diversity views 'literacy as critically important, [whereby] schools are not simply literacy delivering machines but as places of settlement, safety and security, where they facilitate the creation of learning environments and spaces for participation, communication, relationships, friendships, belonging and learning about oneself and others' (Matthews 2008, p. 42). As a consequence of various policies on migration and refugee resettlement, Australian society is now defined by an increasing number of people from different cultural backgrounds. In which case, many schools in Australia cater for thirty, forty or even more, cultural backgrounds. Cultural diversity quite literally walks into the classroom. More recently, Vertovec (2007) has coined the term 'super-diversity' to refer to a social:

> condition distinguished by dynamic interplay of variables among an increased number of new, small and scattered, multiple-origin, transnationally connected, socio-economically differentiated and legally stratified immigrants who have arrived over the last decade (p. 1024).

This chapter reports on research which adopted a case study approach informed by ethnographic methods (Marcus 1998; Troman et al. 2006) and that brings into one study an examination of school structures, cultures and pedagogy at *Diversity Secondary College*. This research examines: How do schools respond to the challenge of teaching future Australian global citizens how to live together in communities of increasing cultural diversity? How do schools improve understanding between Muslims and non-Muslims students, with the intention of developing more engaged and positive attitudes among young people and building resilience? The specific focus for the ethnographic investigations is to develop an explanatory account of teaching for cultural diversity as an innovative school-based response to the question of teaching future Australian citizens how to live together in communities of increasing cultural diversity. The research used ethnographic methods, such as 'purposeful conversations' (Burgess 1988), observations, analysis of artefacts, and various texts, including policies. This study is significant because it contributes to the urgent (inter) national need to understand how schools teach for cultural diversity and citizenship/global citizenship.

INTRODUCING *DIVERSITY SECONDARY COLLEGE*

> I live in the real world, and my real world has a thousand students with 70% of them from other countries and other cultures, and my job as a leader is to ensure that the school is safe and harmonious and peaceful, and that there are opportunities for everyone to feel included. Now how do you want that to happen? (Principal of Diversity Secondary College)

Diversity Secondary College is public school situated in the suburbs of Adelaide and now focuses on providing educational provision for young people over 16 years of age and adult re-entry students. The school is a *United Nations Global Peace School* and provides curriculum on peace-building, community responsibility, celebration of diversity, and human rights. Many of the students have come to Australia under the humanitarian/refugee programme and they undertake an intensive English as a Second Language (ESL) course in preparation for future study alternatives.

What follows is an edited version of interview transcripts with the school leaders including the Principal, which was judiciously edited into two short portraits. These portraits offer a glimpse into 'a 'scheme of interpretation' (Garfinkel 1967, p. 36) through which school life can and is made recognizable and intelligible. School practices—and specifically citizenship/global citizenship education—arise out of a school-based and local problematisation and in response to locally diagnosed problems and are sustained as an 'ongoing practical accomplishment' (Freebody and Freiberg 2012, p. 80), constituted out of the 'practical reasoning' or 'practical theorising' (p. 80) at the local school level.

On drafting portraits as a textual strategy in academic writing, I draw on Marcus's (1998) argument for innovation in the poetic dimension of research practice. 'Poetics' here refers to a site for innovation and critique about ethnographic writing itself and getting past the paralysis of grappling with the 'crisis of representation' (Clifford and Marcus 1986). On this theme, Marcus (1998) argues for '*messy texts*' (p. 198). Simply put, a messy text is an experiment with our representations that grapples with these postmodern challenges of giving an account. One way of writing messy texts, is producing polyvocal or polyphonic texts, or put simply, 'saying more by letting "others" say it' (Marcus 1998, p. 36) and one of the experiments in messy polyvocal texts is the use of portraits (Santaro et al. 2001; Smyth et al. 2004; Smyth and McInerney 2013).

> Against the 'normal' textual strategy of the educational sociologist—one that splices small bits of 'others' voice from our interview 'data' into our authorial monologue as evidence of the 'reality' of our argument and then to tell the reader how to interpret that bit of text—the portrait provides much longer narrative fragments from our informants that are too extensive to limit inside of an authorial monologue. (Smyth et al. 2014, p. 70)

The two portraits focus on providing a rich account of the school context, and the schools citizenship programmes. At the end of portraits, I offer some short commentary as a final concluding section. The portraits begin now.

THE SCHOOL CONTEXT AND PHILOSOPHY

The school has doubled in size in the last ten years. It was a senior secondary college with the new Arrivals Program in it, it was a Registered Training Organisation, but it had a total of enrolment of about 600 students when I first got here, and what we have seen is a huge increase in numbers across all programmes. Many of the students come through the government's

Humanitarian Refugee Program,[2] and in the past there was a significant cohort who had came as 'Unauthorised Maritime Arrivals'. There were 318 young asylum seekers that we had to tell that they could not continue to study because they were on Bridging Visas and there was a government decision made that they were not allowed to study in school when they were over 18.[3] Our students come from one side of Adelaide to the other. Some of our students are catching three buses to get here, and they come because there's a particular level of support that's available here, and structures in place, and a particular culture within the college, that is really inclusive and great for learning for students who have been disengaged or experienced some form of disadvantage. The school has had to respond to significant cohort changes during the past decade. For instance, in one year there might be a flood of Bhutanese students, and their needs are quite different across a range of levels, to the Afghan students, for instance. Even though some of their settlement needs are similar, there are cultural differences, and you have to work with that. You cannot make assumptions that everyone that everyone is the same. The school provides teachers with basic the information, such as: *Okay, over the holidays there's been a flood of this group of students. Here's what you need to know about what's going on in their country at the moment. These are the visas that they've come on,* and that means our teachers are not coming in cold. Our teachers are very good at building the relationships though, and finding out very quickly what's happening for their students.

In part these changes have come about as a consequence of the *Adult Education Policy* that was implemented about five years ago. This policy was designed to ensure that any adult enrolled in public schools needed to be studying South Australian Certificate of Education[4] (SACE) and on a SACE Completion path. Whilst that presented some challenges, we had always had students in accredited courses. We were not a school that had anything that was really unaccredited because our students are very much of the belief if it's not accredited it's not worth doing, and so changes to that policy did not affect us in quite the same way as it affected other schools who were running non-accredited courses as engagement courses.

In the 1980s we established a New Arrivals Program and from that time the school has focused its school improvement plan on the broad aim to have all students, working together and integrated, and a respectful school environment. We did a great deal of work on our college values. The school has always operated from a relationships-based approach in terms of the teaching, learning, and leadership.

The leaders here are much more about service to others, and bringing everybody along the journey with them, rather than, *I'm going to tell you what to do and how to do it, and what it is,* and these things did not happen overnight. They have been developing since 1989 at least, and each leader who's come to the school subsequently, has added to that and promoted it further, and included it in other ways. There are teachers who have been at this school for 25 or 30 years, and so you cannot just blow in and tell a person who's been here all that time what to do. There has to be a vision that everyone is committed to, and there have to be values that underpin what that vision is, and then there has to be a collegiate approach to actually make that all happen, because in the end we are talking about over 110 teachers and 50 support staff alone, let alone the 1200-odd students. At present, the school cohort is at least 40% Muslim students that are mostly from Afghani and African backgrounds. The teaching staff is stable and committed. It's a big machine that you are trying to have running all in the same direction, and all behaving in a particular way with a particular belief system.

The teachers who come here mostly commit to the school's philosophy which entails embracing everybody's prior knowledge, as well as what you might have to offer them. As well, if teachers do not have an humanitarian and compassionate point of view, they find it very difficult to teach here, and so this school attracts a particular type of teacher, as well as a particular type of leader, and people are very committed to what is a very, the difficult process of getting our students who might come with all sorts of issues, including often very little English, through to the end of year 12 usually three years later. So this is not an easy task.

The school runs an in-depth induction programme that helps new people settle in and encompasses all of the following: student learning needs, their well-being needs, the cultural norms of being in a senior secondary site, and expectations of adult learners, so there's a lot of hours that goes into nurturing student success. If the students are not succeeding and they are not meeting their goals, their goals not yours, then you are getting nowhere, you are doing nothing for them.

There does need to be understanding that we are a service organisation, and our service is to our students. We try and encourage the students to then have service mentality towards each other and towards organisations, clubs and things within the school as well, but we have to understand that first and foremost is understanding our students, what is it that they are in need of, what are their goals, what are their timelines. Their timelines are usually different to ours because we have an understanding of what it takes to get to university, many of them do not, but it is about building their capacity towards reaching their goals; their settlement needs, very strong settlement needs. For every student in the college, there are very strong well-being and emotional and psychological well-being needs, every student. So those are the priorities. If you have not got your eye on those and you are thinking that you are teaching Algebra, then you are wrong. The content has to be there for the student's satisfaction of those academic goals, it has to be there, but it has to be taught in a way that is supportive of the students; their sense of success is so important without it being fake.

Citizenship/Global Citizenship Education

So our school values are *respect, excellence, innovation,* and *sustainability*. We have had those values in place now for the better part of 10 years, with *sustainability* added just a few years ago. We have got this induction programme that we do with students in the first four weeks of the year. We call it the *First Five Lessons*, and every teacher with every class discusses with their class: *What does respect look like and what does it sound like, and what does it feel like?* The same with *excellence, innovation,* and *sustainability*. We focus on *sustainability* as a link to peace building later on. Importantly, these lessons help our students understand how those four values drive the decisions that are made in the school, and how that might impact on them, but it also helps them understand their responsibilities.

What we have to do and what we need to accept in our situation, is the students have not been together for 5 years—like in a 'normal' secondary school—they are coming from all over, and what we are trying to develop is a secure community of learners who feel supported. If they do not connect with each other in those first four or five lessons, they walk, they do not stay. Secondly, the teachers also do some work around what it means to be a student in a *United Nations Global Peace School*, because you have to work out very quickly whether we have got students who are going to cope, or not, with that. We try to emphasise what the students bring as a citizen to this learning environment as a Peace School, and how they might contribute, because it is really important that they understand the need to serve others as part of their personal growth. The third arm of these discussions is explaining the restorative practices used at this school. We get a lot of students here who have been in other high schools and they have not experienced fair process necessarily, or they do not think they have experienced fair process. *When things go wrong here this is how we're going to deal with it, and this is why we're going to deal with it,* and this is why it is important for them to understand the underlying principles of restorative practices. We use the traditional restorative practices (Lohmeyer 2016), which comes from the youth justice system, and it takes a non-blame, non-adversarial approach. Part of the importance of that is that often, young people, but I would say most people, do not really know why they do what they do in a volatile situation. So what happens in our situation, when we have got lots of students who are traumatised, have got abuse-related trauma, or some other issue going on, there is no point asking why. So we work through the narrative instead, which helps build a path between what happened and what the outcome was. We work through the questions: *What happened? What were you thinking? What have you thought about since? Who's been harmed, and what did you need to do to put that right?*

The school does not have Pastoral Care, and so this induction happens in every subject with all teachers spending some time looking at school values, what it means to be in a Peace School, and the restorative practices.

You know for us it comes from that perspective of we see our responsibility as partly helping young people understand who they can be, and what their power can be, in a community, and so that's where the citizenship comes from. Getting them to start thinking about what they can give back, and, if you have rights you also have responsibilities, and what those responsibilities are, and partly it's because we have young people who come to us who have not really considered about their broader responsibilities, both within a school setting and in the local community, and also on a national or international scale. The students contribute to a whole range of things here. They have an opportunity to be leaders through the *Rotaract Club for Global Peace*, where they contribute both in the community and at school. We have students who are part of the School Council, and represent the student body. I think what's different in our school, is we do not have that same construction of power that you have in a mainstream secondary school. By way of some examples, the students do not call us *Mr.* or *Mrs.*, they call us by our first names. The students are also empowered to email or visit anyone at any level of leadership, to talk about anything. So a student can come and see me without an appointment, so from that point of view, they know that they are very powerful in the school, and they know that if they talk to us about something that they'll see some change. What that means is that the relationships are not based on power, but based on respect. We are respecting each other as equals, and that we might learn as much from the student as the student learns from us.

A class can have 20 different cultures in it, and so they are all bringing their cultural perspective to that discussion, and there is an aspiration that everyone is treated equally, so that's a really hard one ... So for instance when the Paris terrorism[5] event unfolded recently, I sent an email out to the staff saying: *We're going to have a whole lot of students here who are upset for all sorts of different reasons*—I this on the Monday morning—*It's important that we allow the discussion to happen in the classes, but we need to be careful of this, this, this.* I had a kind of a style guide of what would be appropriate and what would not be appropriate in this sort of situation for unpacking it in the classroom, because they are watching the news unfold on *Facebook*, on their iPhones, as it happens, and they are thinking about it, and they have not had an opportunity to separate from it, between leaving home and coming to school, because they are attached to their phones, as young people are, and so what we have to do is never shy away from the discussion of those really big issues. That is the opportunity for young people to really find some connection to each other about what they value. I knew that our students would be affected, and teachers were asked to be mindful. You can talk about protective interruption all you like, but sometimes the discussion is going to happen whether you want it or not, so at least have some tools in order to be able to deal with that discussion. By having the discussion we know who's travelling well and who is not, and you can actually then put in place some kind of either counselling support or trauma support, or whatever it is that the student needs, to accommodate that situation. And what was interesting; many classes requested a minute's silence to consider and to reflect on the people who had died as a result, or people who are dying in conflict anywhere, and that was not a directive from me, that just sprung from the students as a way of giving them a moment to come and meditate and think.

On citizenship; students need to understand what are the recognised *human rights*, and we study the *Universal Declaration of Human Rights* (United Nations 1948). They need to be able to articulate them, they need to know how they relate to them. They need to be able to unpack for themselves so it helps them better understand their experiences if they understand the Rights. They need to know what *human rights* are so that they can better understand and critically reflect on all the garbage that they watch on *YouTube*, and provide them with the appropriate language and underpinning knowledge, so they become much more critical about what they are viewing and thinking. This is so important for our English-speaking background students and or our New Arrivals to have that language, and so we look for every opportunity to embed it in the curriculum. It is really easy to do it in English, it is really easy to do it in SOSE, and we are actually finding it quite easy to do in Science these days because water as a Human Right, you know, resources and sustainability, all that kind of stuff, yeah, I think I said in English, teachers can bring articles in from the paper and then they deconstruct it by looking at what Human Rights are being abused.

We have been a UN Peace School since 2007, and many of our students have come in through the UNHCR process. The UN flag is a comforting symbol to them at the school as they recognise the flag and they know what it means, and so they understand straightaway when they come here that this is a place of peace. It's valuable to us because as a UN Global Peace School, we commit to the teaching of *human rights* to students, which is so important when you have got students who have had their rights taken away from them, or just they lived in a situation where their rights just were not available to them, be that their language or their culture, or the right to go to school. That learning starts in New Arrivals Program (South Australian Government 2016) with particular emphasis on various key focus days. For example, in the first part of the year, we have *Harmony Day* (Australian Government 2016), and that's our first opportunity to teach new students about the importance of cultures living harmoniously together, and what that means in an Australian context.

Sometimes such multiculturalism days come under some fire, probably rightly because too often the educational work is just a bit superficial. As another example, tomorrow, is *White Ribbon Day* (White Ribbon Australia 2014), against domestic violence, and so there's been an undertaking about getting young men from different cultures to talk about domestic violence. The men in the college have made a film, and this is important because this is a different type of peace. Men will be standing at the gates handing out white ribbons. One of the teachers and his class will be doing white ribbon chalk paintings on all of the walls in the morning. They are running like a cinema activity, followed by a reflective activity. We also do activities for *International Day of Peace*, *World Environment Day*, and *World Refugee Day*. We try not to look at that as *World Refugee Day* because it's really a little bit of a deficit model and our students do not really need to be taught about what it's like to be a refugee. We run a celebration of languages, and we have an annual *Languages Festival* where students teach each other their language.

COMMENTARY: TOWARDS A THEORY OF THE CULTURALLY RESPONSIVE SCHOOL

One of the key words in education studies that frames some of the important debates in this area is *culturally responsive* schooling (Castagno and Brayboy 2008; Dick et al. 1994; Bishop et al. 2007; Smith 2003). Most often the term used is *culturally responsive pedagogy*. By way of a definition, culturally responsive pedagogy 'emphasises and respects students identities and backgrounds as meaningful sources for optimal learning' (Klump and McNair 2005: 3). It also demands 'high expectations of students and ensuring that these expectations are realized' (p. 3). Additionally, Castagno and Brayboy (2008) argue that culturally responsive pedagogy is realized when teachers redesign: teaching pedagogy; methods; curricular materials; teacher dispositions; and school–community relations' (p. 941).

Unfortunately, the theory and practice of culturally responsive pedagogies in Australia is weakly developed and has no significant peer evaluated reviews (e.g. Perso 2012; Krakouer 2015), with a few advocates (e.g. Sarra 2007; Yunkaporta and McGinty 2009; Nakata 2011; Rahman 2013). This work has yet to significantly inform the curriculum and pedagogical reform projects of the state and federal educational departments. There is presently no significant Australian version of culturally responsive pedagogy available to Australian teachers. There is certainly no attempt to bend this concept to account for the work of schools attempting to cater for increasing culturally diverse student cohorts, and for this paper, that means including Indigenous students but also refugee students now attending Australian schools. And there are no attempts to develop a theory of the culturally responsive school in Australia. [The only serious attempt I could find has been developed by the Assembly of Alaska Native Educators (1999)].

By way of a small beginning to that urgent work, this single school case study can be analysed to suggest these characteristics for a culturally responsive school, characteristics which provide an important frame for educating for global citizenship:

1. Working with cultural diversity as an asset, not only for enriching life at school, but most importantly, as an opportunity for enhancing learning rather than as challenges and/or deficits of the student or particular community.
   - Committing to a school philosophy that entails embracing everyone's prior knowledge
   - Cultural diversity seen as a key theme for developing curriculum across the curriculum.
2. Working to ensure that students experience academic success that leads to credible accredited qualifications that provide the where-with-all to be successful in future educational endeavours such as training or university.
   - the curriculum offering provides pathways into success in credentialed programmes
   - high levels of support for learning school literacies, including intensive English language support
   - working on assessment tasks to ensure students can achieve their best
   - multiple levels of student support including counselling, homework support, library, holiday workshops
   - supporting academic success sometimes requires support for social and well-being needs of students (e.g. re-settlements needs of refugee students)
   - sustaining high expectations for academic learning across the curriculum
   - making major decisions on the basis of reliable data such a literacy levels and classroom assessments of various kinds to inform timely and specific interventions.
3. Learning at school ensures that students develop and/or maintain cultural competence and especially a positive sense of their own cultural identities.
   - students have opportunities to learn about each others' cultures and to explore the Australian multicultural context
   - multiple opportunities to engage with the cultural resources that students bring to schools, including in the mainstream curriculum but also in well-organised events that celebrate and/or acknowledge the school values.
4. Working on ensuring the school is safe, harmonious and peaceful and that there are opportunities for everyone to feel included.
   - there is a whole school narrative that is widely enacted by leaders and teachers
   - works on enacting a school vision that encapsulates the school values in relationships, curriculum and leadership practices
   - engagement with other agencies through the school such as hospitals, psychologists, youth workers, and Women's organisations
   - there is coherence between the school vision, curriculum development and professional learning for staff

- providing an in-depth induction programme for staff and students.
5. Working on developing and sustaining productive and respectful educative relationships between students, teachers and leadership.
  - distributive and democratic forms of educational leadership
  - restorative justice approaches to conflict resolution (focused on sustaining relationships rather that being punitive).
6. Sustains a 'strong' version of student voice.

- focusing on building student capacity towards reaching their educational goals
- supporting a school culture that encourages personal responsibility and the need to serve others as a part of their personal growth
- opportunities to study human rights, being able to articulate them and to know how they relate to their lives
- opportunities for students to experience active citizenship as part of the way the school functions, and to learn about citizenship in their communities and globally.

By way of a concluding comment, my one school case study brings into focus the imperative for researchers to conduct more ethnographic studies on schools who demonstrate they are teaching *for* cultural diversity in contexts shaped and complicated by the global. This chapter provides some criteria for selection of such schools. Unfortunately, educational policy studies pay too little attention to the autonomy of the local school and often fails to understand that policy enactment actually happens at the local school level. As well, this case, takes as a starting point for a discussion, that citizenship/global citizenship is not some abstract curriculum idea, but can be experienced in schools as an integral part of school life. In those schools that are fortunate enough to have culturally diverse student populations, citizenship/global citizenship can be learned in ways that cultural diversity is understood as an asset for learning to live with others.

NOTES

1. On Brexit there are special issues in *Political Insight*, 2016, 7(2): *Political Studies Review*, 2016, 14(3). Specific papers include: Vreese and Boomgaarden (2016) Projecting EU Referendums: Fear of Immigration and Support for European Integration, *European Union Politics*, 6(1): 59–82: Cowden and Singh (2017) Community cohesion, communitarianism and neoliberalism, *Critical Social Policy*, DOI:10.1177/0261018316670252 csp.sagepub.com; Davidson and Saul (2016) Neoliberalism and the Far-Right: A Contradictory Embrace, Critical Sociology, DOI:10.1177/0896920516671180. On Trump: Henry A. Giroux| Fascism in Donald Trump's United States, http://www.truth-out.org/news/item/33951-fascism-in-donald-trump-s-united-states; Sperber, The Concept of the Wall, http://www.truth-out.org/news/item/39140-the-concept-of-the-wall; Henry Giroux: "Donald Trump and the

Plague of Atomization in a Neoliberal Age, http://monthlyreview.org/press/
henry-giroux-donald-trump-and-the-plague-of-atomization-in-a-neoliberal-age/.
2. http://www.border.gov.au/Trav/Refu/What.
3. http://www.internationalstudents.sa.edu.au.
4. The SACE is the local credential for finishing secondary school.
5. On the evening of 13 November 2015, a series of coordinated terrorist attacks
occurred in Paris and its northern suburb, Saint-Denis.

Acknowledgements This paper was developed through research that was funded
by the *International Centre for Muslim and non-Muslim Understanding* (MnM),
University of South Australia.

REFERENCES

Ack, T. (2016). How we stopped pauline hanson last time. *Marxist Left Review*.
http://marxistleftreview.org/index.php/no-12-winter-2016/137-how-we-
stopped-pauline-hanson-last-time.
Ahmed, S. (2004). *The cultural politics of emotion*. New York: Routledge.
Arber, R. (2012). Encountering an-other: The culture of curriculum and inclusive
pedagogies. In Z. Bekerman & T. Geisen (Eds.), *International handbook of migration, minorities and education: Understanding cultural and social differences in pro-
cesses of learning* (pp. 461–477). Dordrecht, Netherlands: Springer.
Aveling, N. (2012). Indigenous studies: A matter of social justice. *A Matter of
Urgency, Diaspora, Indigenous, and Minority Education, 6*(2), 99–114.
Assembly of Alaska Native Educators. (1999). *Guidelines for Preparing Culturally
Responsive Teachers for Alaska's Schools*. Accessed March 12, 2016, http://ankn.
uaf.edu/Publications/teacher.pdf. Anchorage, Alaska.
Australian Human Rights Commission. (2003). *HREOC website: Isma—listen: National
consultations on eliminating prejudice against Arab and muslim Australians*.
Accessed March 12, 2014, https://www.humanrights.gov.au/publications/hreoc-
website-isma-listen-national-consultations-eliminating-prejudice-against-arab–22.
Australian Government. (2016). *Harmony day*. http://www.harmony.gov.au.
Bates, R. (2012). An anarchy of cultures: Aesthetics and changing school. *Critical
Studies in Education, 53*(1), 59–70.
Bauman, Z. (2001). *Community: Seeking security in an unsafe world*. Cambridge:
Polity Press.
Beilharz, P. (2005). Australia: The unhappy country, or, a tale of two nations. *Thesis
Eleven, 82*, 73–87.
Bishop, R., Berryman, M., Cavanagh, T., & Teddy, L. (2007). *Te Kōtahitanga Phase 3
Whānaungatanga: Establishing a culturally responsive pedagogy of relations in main-
stream secondary school classrooms*. New Zealand: Ministry of Education.
Burgess, R. (1988). Conversations with a purpose: The ethnographic interview in
educational research. In R. Burgess (Ed.), *Studies in qualitative methodology: Con-
ducting qualitative research* (pp. 137–155). Greenich, CT: JAI Press.
Burridge, N., & Chodkiewicz, A. (2008). *Representations of cultural diversity in school
and community settings*. Sydney: UTS.
Carter, P. (1996). *The lie of the land*. Faber and Faber: London & Boston.

Castagno, A., & Brayboy, B. (2008). Culturally responsive schooling for indigenous youth: A review of the literature. *Review of Educational Research, 78*(4), 941–993.

Christie, P., & Sidhu, R. (2016). Governmentality and 'fearless speech': Framing the education of asylum seeker and refugee children in Australia. *Oxford Review of Education, 32*(4), 449–465.

Clifford, J., & Marcus, G. (1986). *Writing culture: The poetics and politics of ethnography.* Berkeley: University of California Press.

Cowden, & Singh. (2017). Community cohesion, communitarianism and neoliberalism. *Critical Social Policy, 37*(2), 268–286.

Davidson, & Saul. (2016). Neoliberalism and the far-right: A contradictory embrace. *Critical Sociology,* doi:10.1177/0896920516671180.

Department of Immigration and Border Protection. (2014). *Immigration history 2006 to today.* http://www.immi.gov.au/about/reports/annual/2009-10/html/65-years-of-nation-building/Immigration-history-2006-to-today.htm.

Dick, G., Estell, D., & McCarty, T. (1994). Saad Kaakih Bee'enootiilji Na'alkaa: Restructuring the teaching of language and literacy in a Navajo community school. *Journal of American Indian Education, 33*(3), 31–46.

Freebody, P., & Freiberg, J. (2012). Ethnomethodological research in education and the social sciences: Studying 'the business, identities and cultures' of classrooms. In L. Markauskaite, P. Freebody & J. Irwin (Eds.), *Methodological Choice and Design: Scholarship, Policy and Practice in Social and Educational Research.* Heidelberg: Springer.

Garfinkel, H. (1967). *Studies in ethnomethodology.* Cambridge: Polity Press.

Gelber, K., & McNamara, L. J. (2015). The effects of civil hate speech laws: Lessons from Australia. *Law and Society Review, 49*(3), 631–664.

Grande, S. (2004). *Red pedagogy: Native American social and political thought.* Lanham: Rowman & Littlefield.

Gulson, K., & Webb, P. (2012). Education policy racialisations: Afrocentric schools. *Islamic schools, and the new enunciations of equity, Journal of Education Policy, 27*(6), 697–709.

Hage, G. (2003). *Against paranoid nationalism: Searching for hope in a shrinking society.* Annandale, NSW: Pluto Press.

Haney-Lopez, H. (2014). *Dog whistle politics: How coded racial appeals have wrecked the middle class.* New York: Oxford University Press.

Hattam, R., & Every, D. (2010). Teaching in fractured classrooms: refugee education, public culture, community and ethics. *Race Ethnicity and Education, 13*(4), 409–424.

Klump, J., & McNeir, G. (2005). *Culturally responsive practices for student success: A regional sampler.* Retrieved October 17, 2006, from www.nwrel.org/request/2005june/textonly.html.

Krakouer, J. (2015). *Literature review relating to the current context and discourse on Indigenous cultural awareness in the teaching space: Critical pedagogies and improving Indigenous learning outcomes through cultural responsiveness.* Melbourne: ACER.

Ladson-Billings, G. (1995). Toward a theory of culturally relevant pedagogy. *American Educational Research Journal, 32*(3), 465–491.

Lohmeyer, B. (2016). Restorative practices and youth work: Theorizing professional power relationships with young people. *Young*, https://doi.org/10.1177/1103308816640080.

Lueck, K., Due, C., & Augoustinos, M. (2015). Neoliberalism and nationalism: Representations of asylum seekers in the Australian mainstream news media. *Discourse and Society, 26*(5), 608–629.

Manne, R. (2001). *In denial: The stolen generations and the right*. Melbourne: Black Ink.

Manne, R. (2004). *Left right left: Political essays, 1977–2005*. Melbourne: Black Ink.

Marcus, G. (1998). *Ethnography through thick and thin*. Princeton, NJ: Princeton University Press.

Mason, G. (2012). 'I am tomorrow': Violence against Indian students in Australia and political denial. *Australian & New Zealand Journal of Criminology, 45*(1), 4–25.

Matthews, J. (2008). Schooling and settlement: Refugee education in Australia. *International Studies in Sociology of Education, 18*(1), 31–45.

McNevin, A. (2011). *Contesting citizenship: Irregular migrants and new frontiers of the political*. New York: Columbia University Press.

Moran, A. (2005). White Australia, settler nationalism and aboriginal assimilation. *Australian Journal of Politics and History, 51*(2), 168–193.

Nakata, M. (2011). Pathways for indigenous education in the Australian curriculum framework. *Indigenous Education, 40*, 1–8.

Noble, G. (2011). 'Bumping into alterity': Transacting cultural complexities. *Continuum, 25*(6), 827–840.

Nunn, C. (2010). Spaces to speak: Challenging representations of Sudanese–Australians. *Journal of Intercultural Studies, 31*(2), 183–198.

Offe, C. (1987). Ungovernability: On the renaissance of conservative theories of crisis. In J. Habermas (Ed.), *Observation of the "Spiritual Situation of the Age"*. Cambridge, MA: MIT Press.

Papastergiadis, N. (2004). The invasion complex in Australian political culture. *Thesis Eleven, 78*, 8–27.

Perso, T. F. (2012). Cultural responsiveness and school education: With particular focus on Australia's first peoples. *A Review & Synthesis of the Literature*. Darwin: Menzies School of Health Research, Centre for Child Development and Education.

Poynting, S. (2006). What caused the cronulla riot? *Commentary, Race and Class, 48*(1), 85–92.

Rahman, K. (2013). Belonging and learning to belong in school: the implications of the hidden curriculum for Indigenous students. *Discourse: Studies in the Cultural Politics of Education, 34*(5), 660–672.

Robertson, R. (1992). *Globalization: Social theory and global culture*. London: Sage.

Santoro, N., Kamler, B., & Reid, J.-A. (2001). Teachers talking difference: Teacher education and the poetics of anti-racism. *Teaching Education, 12*(2), 191–212.

Sarra, C. (2007). Young, black and deadly: Strategies for improving outcomes for Indigenous students. In M. Keeffe & S. Carrington (Eds.), *Schools and diversity* (2nd ed., pp. 74–89). Pearson Education Australia: Frenchs Forest, NSW.

Short, D. (2005). Reconciliation and the problem of internal colonialism. *Journal of Intercultural Studies, 26*(3), 267–282.

Smith, L. T. (2003). *Decolonizing methodologies: Research and indigenous peoples*. London: Zed Books.

Smyth, J., Hattam, R., with Cannon, J., Edwards, J., Wilson, N., & Wurst, S. (2004). *Dropping out, drifting off, being excluded: Becoming somebody without school.* NY: Peter Lang Publishing.

Smyth, J., & McInerney, P. (2013). Whose side are you on? Advocacy ethnography: Some methodological aspects of narrative portraits of disadvantaged young people, in socially critical research. *International Journal of Qualitative Studies in Education, 26*(1), 1–20.

Smyth, J., Down, B., Hattam, R., & McInerney, P. (2014). *Doing Critical Educational Research.* New York: Peter Lang.

Troman, G., Gordon, T., Jeffrey, B., & Walford, G. (2006). Editorial. *Ethnography and Education, 1*(1), 1–2.

United Nations. (1948). *Universal declaration of human rights.* http://www.ohchr.org/EN/UDHR/Documents/UDHR_Translations/eng.pdf.

Vertovec, S. (2007). Super-diversity and its implications. *Ethnic and Racial Studies, 30*(6), 1024–1054.

Villegas, A. M., & Lucas, T. (2002). *Educating culturally responsive teachers: A coherent approach.* Albany: SUNY Press.

Villegas, A., & Lucas, T. (2007). The culturally responsive teacher. *Educational Leadership, 64*(6), 28–33.

Vreese, & Boomgaarden. (2016). Projecting EU referendums: Fear of immigration and support for European integration. *European Union Politics, 6*(1), 59–82.

Watkins, M., Len, G., Noble, G., & Dunn, K. (2013). *Rethinking multiculturalism reassessing multicultural education: Project report number 1 surveying new south wales public school teachers.* Penrith: University of Western Sydney.

Whiteford. (2013). *Australia: Inequality and prosperity and their impacts in a radical welfare state.* Accessed March 12, 2014, https://Crawford.Anu.Edu.Au/Public_Policy_Community/Content/Doc/Australia_Inequality-And-Prosperity_Final-15-March-13.Pdf.

White Ribbon Australia. (2014). *White ribbon day.* http://www.whiteribbon.org.au.

Yunkaporta, T., & McGinty, S. (2009). Reclaiming aboriginal knowledge at the cultural interface. *Australian Educational Researcher, 36*(2), 55–72.

AUTHOR BIOGRAPHY

Robert Hattam is Associate Professor in the School of Education, at the University of South Australia. He has been involved in numerous book projects with others including: Schooling for a Fair Go, Connecting Lives and Learning, Literacy, Leading and Learning: Beyond Pedagogies of Poverty, and Pedagogies for Reconciliation. He also has published a book entitled Awakening-Struggle: Towards a Buddhist Critical Theory.

CHAPTER 18

Identity, Belonging and Diversity in Education for Global Citizenship: Multiplying, Intersecting, Transforming, and Engaging Lived Realities

Karen Pashby

INTRODUCTION

Global citizenship refers to a sense of belonging to a broader community and common humanity. It emphasizes political, economic, social, and cultural interdependency and interconnectedness between the local, the national and the global. (UNESCO 2015, p. 14)

[Through global citizenship education] learners learn about their identities and how they are situated within multiple relationships (for example, family, friends, school, local community, country), as a basis for understanding the global dimension of citizenship. (UNESCO 2015, p. 23)

UNESCO's (2015) guidance on global citizenship education connects two key ideas: Everyone belongs to a human community, and identities are multiple and extend from local to national to global. The emphasis on multiple identities and relationships reflects ongoing discussions and debates in recent scholarship related to education for global citizenship (EfGC). This chapter will aim to articulate some key conceptual framings of these discussions,

K. Pashby (✉)
Manchester Metropolitan University, 1.43 Brooks Building, 53 Bonsall St, Manchester M15 6GX, UK
e-mail: k.pashby@mmu.ac.uk

© The Author(s) 2018
I. Davies et al. (eds.), *The Palgrave Handbook of Global Citizenship and Education*, https://doi.org/10.1057/978-1-137-59733-5_18

identify some key issues and debates, and consider implications for research and practice.

Since the turn of the twenty-first century, the concept of global citizenship has responded to the idea that human lives are increasingly interdependent in a fast changing and increasingly interconnected world. Freer and increasing movements of people, ideas, goods, and resources are occurring alongside perpetuating inequalities within and between societies. In the field of education, scholarly conversations about global citizenship reflect what Agbaria (2011) terms a "double crisis" in formal education and globalization (p. 63). Schooling has become responsible both for developing capacities in students that enable competitive workers for the global economy and for responding to increasingly diverse and unequal student populations. There are overlapping and competing agendas under the umbrella of educating for global citizenship (Marshall 2009). There is also a growing field of critical global citizenship scholarship pointing to the often unintentional ways that EfGC can serve to reinforce rather than redress colonial systems of power (e.g., Andreotti 2006; Eidoo et al. 2011). The imperative to respond to diverse student demographics and engage critically with globalization has raised key issues within the scholarship on citizenship education regarding identity and belonging, particularly in relation to an ideal of a global community (Pashby 2008). Yet, it is important to note that although EfGC has received international attention recently, the bulk of the scholarly writing is from countries of the Global North (Parmenter 2011). Consequently, and as a key limitation, this chapter focuses largely on how belonging and citizenship are taken up in discussions in multicultural, English-speaking democracies.

Conceptual Underpinnings

Discourse and discursive fields: EfGC and Critical Scholarship

To understand the possibilities and risks of rooting EfGC in ideas of diversity, identity, and belonging, it is important to first map out the conceptual and theoretical trends in scholarship that frame scholarly discussions on this topic. The popularity of EfGC at the turn of the twenty-first century corresponded with a turn in social science research toward recognizing the discursive nature of social and political concepts. This involves emphasizing the ideological nature of language and the social and historical construction of social identities and realities (Andreotti 2010). A rise in educational scholarship informed by the post-traditions (e.g., post-modernism, post-structuralism, post-colonialism) has led to a critical unpacking and interrogation of taken for granted ideals and concepts such as identity, belonging, and diversity.

The idea of social constructivism is tied to scholarship operating within the discursive turn. Ross (2007) describes social constructivism as "the idea that we can only develop our sense of self-identity through social processes: all of our identities are socially determined as we define ourselves in relationship to others, whether as in a direct relationship or as the same as or different to the other" (p. 288). This is a dialectical process, for as we define ourselves to ourselves, others define our identity based on assumptions that may or may not correspond with the identities we hope to assume (Ross 2007, p. 288). The shift to discourse studies and social constructivism has opened up for study and theorizing the complex and dynamic ways that identities are neither natural nor neutral but intersect with social processes and power dynamics.

Within this wider context of critical scholarship on identities, the rising prominence of the ideals of EfGC has been both promoted and criticized within the field of education. As Abowitz and Harnish (2006) point out, "critical discourses raise issues of membership, identity, and engagement in creative, productive ways" (p. 666). Their study of citizenship education discourses in the USA found that in scholarship and social movements, the critical discourses aim to expand and/or deepen what are often taken for granted ideals of individual freedom by recognizing exclusions based on gender, culture, ethnicity, nationality, race, sexuality, and socioeconomic class. Abowitz and Harnish (2006) also point out that the relative silence of critical language, values, and practices in curricula and taught texts of citizenship education demonstrate that while educational scholarship on citizenship education and globalization have increasingly taken-up critical theory, it is less evident in practices of EfGC in formal education (see also Rapoport 2009).[1]

Intersecting Discourses: Identity, Belonging, Global Citizenship and Intersectionality

Identity and belonging are complex and fundamental social concepts. Ghosh, Abdi and Naseem (2008) highlight the predominance of culture in how identities and belonging are constructed socially:

> As cultural identities are not absolute, they are the points of identification that continue to change with the discourses of history and culture. In addition, there is a dialectical relationship between social identity and personal identity....Personal identity is different from social identity because the former defines the characteristics of an individual while the latter defines the features shared by an individual with other members of a particular group. (pp. 57–58)

Gillborn and Youdell (2009) contribute a call for more attention to how culture intersects with other identity categories, insisting that not one single marker of identity or axis of inequality be foregrounded (see also James 2008). The concept of intersectionality highlights both the complexity of social identities and the intersecting relations of power ascribed to social identities.

Importantly, identity-based social movements have influenced political as well as academic arenas. Mohanty (2010) refers to a contemporary geopolitical landscape within which various movements are mobilized including "anti-war, anti-globalization, prison abolitionist, labor, national liberation, women's and LGBT rights, indigenous, disability, and civil rights, environmental justice, and pro-democracy movements continue to mobilize complex formulations of identity in confronting power" (p. 538). The concept of identity is both unpacked discursively and used strategically politically in a variety of ways. The combination of new social movements and theoretical frameworks of the discursive turn highlight subjectivities that have not fit easily the culturally and historically normalized citizen (Arnot and Dillabough 2004; Delanty 2000, 2006; Rosaldo 1999). These dynamics are played out, taken up, and resisted in scholarship on global citizenship.

Key issues/debates

Several key issues and debates proceed from the contributions of critical scholarship in the areas of citizenship, globalization and global community, identity, and belonging.

CITIZENSHIP AND IDENTITY: BELONGING TO THE IMAGINED NATION

Critical theory presents a matrix of analytical and conceptual frameworks within which citizenship is critiqued and contested as well as put forward as a site of social struggle and justice (Pashby 2008). On a basic level, citizenship is a set of relationships: rights, duties, participation, and identity (Delanty 2000, p. 9). These central aspects are mutually reinforcing so that critiquing or changing one can impact how the others are conceptualized and practiced (Scott and Lawson 2002; see also Patten Patten 2001). It is fundamental to this matrix of citizenship that an individual identify and be recognized legally and socially as a citizen in order to participate and enjoy the benefits of being a citizen (Pashby 2008). As citizenship is socially constructed and adapted through economic, political, and social changes (Abowitz & Harnish 2006), individuals and groups experience citizenship differently. Multicultural policies in many countries have sought to specify the right of individuals to certain collective rights seen as necessary for them to access the societal culture of the nation without having to face discrimination based on ethnicity, and indigenous populations also fight for recognition of self-governance as another example (Kymlicka 1998; see also Kiwan 2007). Thus, citizenship must be theorized as non-static and always contested (Balibar 2006). The conceptualization of global citizenship is implicated in the dynamic critical approaches that deconstruct identity and challenge a neutral conceptualization of citizenship and national identity.

NATIONAL IDENTITY AS CONTESTED

A central debate related to the role of the concepts of identity and belonging in theorizing and practicing EfGC is the contestation of national identity as a neutral basis of citizenship. Richardson (2002) points out that Enlightenment tenets presented citizenship as a contract between state and citizen that was both a rational relationship of protection by the state based on the rights of autonomous individuals and an emotional relationship of loyalty and fraternity based on a strong sense of national culture. Ross (2007) points out that despite a consolidation of the idea of a shared national identity as a rooted political organizing principle (see also Anderson 2006), citizenship has always been contested. Rights have been unequally distributed, and borders have been imposed onto, and thus have separated, cultural groups. Furthermore, while citizenship has organized around nation-states, ties with local identities (e.g. of a city or region) and "supranational identities (e.g., European, Muslim, globalized youth culture" have had great significance for individuals (Ross 2007, p. 293).

As scholars have challenged the dominance and neutrality of national identity as the basis of citizenship, a key debate has been the degree to which expanding citizenship to include excluded groups has served to promote social justice. The seminal sociologist T.H. Marshall (1950) determined a typology tying citizenship to evolving rights—civil then political then social. However, his typology was critiqued for an assumed linear progress and for failing to account for the social struggles accompanying changing notions of who counts as a citizen subject (Faulks 2006). Marshall's work nonetheless served as an important impetus for further critiques of citizenship and for raising key questions such as: "How does citizenship contribute to or ameliorate sexual, gender, national, ethnic and regional identities?" (Isin and Wood 1999, p. 30). Critical interpretations of Marshall's typology highlight the citizenship narrative as one of exclusion and struggle on the part of marginalized groups for recognition (McCollum 2002, p. 169). In relation to multiculturalism, Tully (2000) argues that such critical interrogations of the concept of citizenship have opened discursive spaces for contestations over recognition and accommodation.

Other scholars point out that simply including marginalized groups by recognizing and expanding citizenship rights without addressing the roots of the exclusions may neither serve to transform power relations nor to redistribute power in a more just way (see Arnot and Dillabough 2004; Jiwani 2006; Goldberg 1993 among others). Here, intersectionality becomes a critical frame for contesting an expansion model of citizenship. As Tupper (2008) argues,

> [Citizenship] status and practice are often not understood as separate realities; rather, as long as individuals are citizens (status) they are able to fully engage as citizens (practice). But this is exactly where the meta-narrative falls apart. The practices or lived-experiences of citizenship are very much dependent upon

factors such as gender, race, class, culture, ethnicity, religion, and sexual orientation. (p. 70)

There is a strong line of tension in the scholarship between the importance of expanding liberal citizenship through collective rights and the importance of recognizing how the nation itself has been complicit in the exclusion of various groups and of reproducing colonial systems of power (Pashby 2011, 2013).

In the current context of critical theory and experiences of various phenomena of globalization, important issues emerge around the concepts of identity, belonging, and diversity as related to citizenship. In contemporary globalization, changing ideas of subjectivities and critical understandings of positionalities within local, national, and global communities give rise to new ideas and criteria for belonging (Painter 2002). The individual citizen subject is constructed and reconstructed in this context given that "our notions of citizenship rest upon our notions of subjectivity" (McAfee 2000, 13).

The concept of cosmopolitan citizenship has a long history and saw a resurgence at the turn of the twenty-first century (Beck 2011). Strand refers (2010a) to "the cosmopolitan turn" in social and political sciences, including education (p. 229). He defines cosmopolitanism as generally the idea that all humans belong to the same community and that an idea of a global community should be cultivated (Strand 2010a). Rizvi (2009) adds that "the notion of cosmopolitanism has the potential to bring together both the facts and the values associated with complex connectivity" (p. 259). This literature has included ideas of extending national citizenship to encompass rights and responsibilities beyond the nation-state (e.g., Appiah 2005; Nussbaum 2002). On the one hand, normative theories of cosmopolitanism reflect an ideal of global connectedness naturally extending beyond national, religious, and political borders while on the other hand "long-established ideas and ideals of cosmopolitanism are now being contested by a developing worldwide and extremely complex social reality" (Strand 2010b, p. 233). For example, Glick Schiller, Darieva, and Gruner-Domic (2011) note how "ordinary individuals and social groups" are making a "new cosmopolitan order by transcending symbolic and social boundaries" (p. 407).

Another strong discourse, multiple citizenship, has emerged that both challenges and reinforces the expansion model. While there is continued debate as to how a global citizen identity is possible given that nation-states remain the main political apparatus, critical scholarship has contributed ideas of hybrid and multiple citizenships. Pike (2008) points out that "each of us is a 'multiple citizen' (Heater 2004), a person with 'plural and parallel' (Selby 1994) allegiances and responsibilities to community, city, region, continent and planet as well as to a nation" (p. 80).

Yet, the ideas of multiple, cosmopolitan, and global citizenship raise a key debate within the context of schooling, given its basis in state structures. Banks (2009) speaks to identity as "multiple, changing, overlapping, and contextual" and asserts that a "major problem facing nation-states throughout the world is how to recognize and legitimize difference and yet construct an overarching national identity that incorporates the voices, experiences, and hopes of the diverse groups that compose it" (p. 310). Indeed, Marshall (2009) points to a proliferation of citizenships that educators must consider including

'multiple', 'multi-levelled', 'flexible', 'shifting', 'manufactured', and 'imagined' citizenships accompany those geographically specified concepts such as 'local', 'community', 'national', 'European', 'South-American', and 'global' citizenships, or those indicating levels of involvement such as 'maximal', 'minimal', 'active', 'thick', 'thin', 'participatory', and 'passive'. These types of citizenships, in turn, may be situated among more traditional divisions among social, political, civil, republican, liberal, communitarian, and cosmopolitan citizenships. Notions of other 'new' citizenships can also be identified. (p. 247)

Thus, the critical conversations in scholarship on citizenship and identity in the context of the global imperative in education point to a) a need for a flexible conception of citizenship that includes multiple and overlapping identities, b) a recognition and addressing of the roots of exclusion inherent to the concept of citizenship itself, and c) a promotion of a complex sense of common humanity and solidarity across difference. Citizenship identity involves a negotiation of diverse identities within groups and between groups categorized socially and culturally. While some scholars promote a continued expansion of the idea of national citizenship, others suggest that the modern, liberal categories are no longer sufficient to capture these complexities.

Balarin (2011) sums up the debate. She describes a shift "from 'modern' or 'enlightened' forms of citizenship to the 'multiple' or 'diverse citizenship'" which is meant to account for a perceived growing heterogeneity of demographics (pp. 356–357). Key to adapting this approach to citizenship education is to focus on questions of identity while also highlighting epistemological exclusions that limit a more inclusive understanding of knowledge and identity (Balarin 2011, p. 357). Interestingly, Balarin (2011) indicates that within the debates about multiple and global citizenship in education, there is an almost exclusive concern with normative, national aspects of citizenship. The focus is on defining new and better models that can address those political and social issues that preoccupy the social imaginary at any given moment. She points out that many practices based on more inclusive models of citizenship education end up emphasizing changing individual attitudes with little attention to or impact power relations. Another important implication is the increased recognition of diverse citizenship experiences. Engaging and reflecting the lived realities of today's students is an important aspect of the connection of multiple citizenship theorizing to EfGC. Arnot and Swartz (2012) point out the diverse civic experiences and identities of youth around the world today; for many "global change has not necessarily brought social, economic or political rights" (p. 4). Citizenship education in a global context must address various experiences of citizenship and the distinct ways identities are being asserted and constructed.

A related issue emerging from critical approaches to multiple citizenship is who gets to define global citizenship and for whom is EfGC intended (Pashby 2011). Gundara (2011) points out that dominant social groups adopt various individual or group identities while subordinated groups are generally ascribed one identity which is most often "ethnic" (p. 306). This raises the question of who is the dominant group in global citizenship:

> The aim of developing a global form of citizenship stands in a rather tense relation with the realities of vast numbers of marginalised citizens across the globe, to the extent that marginality appears to be the hidden other of global citizenship. (Balarin 2011, p. 355)

She notes that literature on EfGC often fails to take into full account the ways in which the harsh material realities of marginalized citizens can be in direct contradictions to the ideals inherent to the concept of global citizenship. Further, a focus on changing individuals' attitudes toward global others or on helping those 'poor others' who are 'less fortunate' can avoid and even reinforce unequal power relations.

A key point of contention in regards to how EfGC can serve to reinforce rather than redress colonial power relations within and between societies is the deconstruction of how EfGC often inherently assumes an 'Us' and a 'Them'. Global citizenship can suggest a unifying identity, but critics point out that very often when it comes to an ethic of action, "the global citizen is defined as one who helps an unfortunate Other" (Jefferess 2008, p. 28; see also Zembylas 2010).[2] And, it is important to note research indicates that young people of all backgrounds and positionalities demonstrate interest and seek ways to be actively involved in civic life (El Haj 2009).

To summarize, the concept of EfGC is contested at the same time that much is desired of it. Some common rationales include a sense of the world being more interdependent and the idea that young people require knowledge, skills and dispositions to be more globally minded, to relate ethically with diverse global others, and to promote social cohesion and tolerance at local, national and international levels. Across rationales and agendas is a shared notion that global citizenship education can open spaces for multiple and multi-leveled identities of young people (Marshall 2009; Willinsky 2008).

For the most part, in the context of formal education, EfGC draws heavily on an expansion model from national to global rather than a complex and multifaceted understanding of citizenship. Nussbaum (2002) has expressed a strong argument for cosmopolitan citizenship education based on an ideal of belonging to a human community above all else whereby identity reaches out from local to global through concentric circles representing spatial attachments, e.g., family, local community, region, nation, global community. Mitchell and Parker (2008) draw on a case study of teenager's views of patriotism in relation to the post-9/11 context in the USA. They challenge the idea of expanding one's identity and sense of belonging with and responsibility to others in community through normative spatial categories as in Nussbaum's cosmopolitan citizenship, arguing it "constrains the social imaginary" by assuming these exist independently of economic, political and cultural production of identity categories (p. 777). It is possible that many students identify more strongly with communities and spatial categories that belong to the wider circles than with those in the smaller circles (e.g., El Haj 2009). The expansion model fails to account for the distinct ways marginalized communities face barriers to inclusion at various spatial scales. As Andreotti (2011) articulates, "the different meanings attributed to 'global citizenship education' depend on contextually situated assumptions about globalization, citizenship, and education that prompt questions about boundaries, flows, power relations, belonging, rights, responsibilities, otherness, interdependence, and social reproduction and/or contestation" (p. 307).

Implications for Education for Global Citizenship: Research and Practice

EfGC necessarily involves engaging with complex notions of identity and belonging. In considering the role of formal school curriculum in relaying strong messages regarding what it means to identify and participate as citizens, citizenship education is implicated in "a political economy of social, cultural and economic relations related to sometimes competing visions of community" (Camicia and Franklin 2011, p. 312). The various social changes tied to contemporary globalization and inherited from the legacy of modern formal schooling presents a set of quandaries regarding how educators can implement policies to contribute to social cohesion when it is acknowledged that both citizens and non-citizens identify and are identified with a range of hybrid, multiple, and singular social identities (Gundara 2011, p. 294).

Banks (2009) highlights the importance of EfGC engaging directly with the lived realities and "the complicated, contextual, and overlapping identities of immigrant students" (pp. 311–312). He points to research showing "the cultural and national identities of immigrant youth are contextual, evolving, and continually reconstructed" (Banks 2009, p. 312). Arnot and Swartz (2012) take this idea further, arguing that much of the research on how schooling promotes particular civic ideals, identities, and participatory habits tends to focus on normative democratic values and not on how civic virtues and values are framed by "unequal power relations and social inequalities in relation to education" (p. 2). This is confirmed by research about civic education in the Canadian context. Tupper (2008) found normative and universalized citizenship goals render invisible the realities of differences between students in regards to "race, culture, gender, class, sexual orientation, etc." (p. 72).

Some scholars suggest that framing citizenship education through a global understanding can open up critical spaces by considering multiple identities, loyalties, and beliefs representing the diverse experiences of students in the classroom (Myers 2016, p. 10). Such an approach would not be a "one-size-fits-all approach" but rather would enable students to construct their own sense of "self-in-the-world" (Myers 2016, p. 10). However, Arnot and Swartz (2012) point out that research on loyalties and political identities in the lived experience of youth is rare.

At the same time, other scholars point out dangers and risks of constructing and relaying notions of global citizenship through schooling (Koyama 2016). For example, Zembylas (2010) points out that learning about others and their cultures without experiencing democracy in the life of schools is a mistake. He promotes "developing a social outlook geared toward examining taken-for-granted realities and power relations" (p. 242). Jefferess (2012) adds that EfGE can reinforce Western humanitarian discourses of learning about global "others" who need "our" help. In this sense EfGC can step over the key ways in which individuals and groups are both interconnected and interdependent. Research with school children in Ireland by Niens and Reilly (2012) confirms a general consensus in the critical EfGC scholarship that in the right context and with appropriate pedagogy, EfGC can potentially reduce prejudice (p. 114). However, in accordance with critiques of EfGC, they found a tendency for students to speak to injustices in other parts of the world or as a global phenomenon and to step over local prejudices.

A critical and reflexive approach to EfGC focuses on the dynamic construction of one's identity in relation to learning about others. Andreotti (2006) and Rizvi (2009) promote the importance of reflecting on the situatedness of one's own context and how this shapes understanding of selves as global citizens. Thus, critical EfGC scholarship pushes against a universalizing approach that focuses simply on becoming aware of global interconnections and promoting critical attention to social privilege (see also Wang and Hoffman 2016).

Myers' (2010) research on how American secondary students understand global citizenship found that they use a "flexible identification with multiple elements":

> it seems…appropriate in light of these findings to focus on the diverse ways that adolescents combine different scales of citizenship and to consider their thinking about specific elements of citizenship. In short, global citizenship is not a monolithic or natural affiliation that can be easily classified. (p. 499)

EfGC opens up a discursive space for imagining identity and belonging beyond a national citizenship framework. As Banks (2009) notes, there is a transformative potential when citizenship education promotes students to develop reflexive cultural, national, and global identifications. Scholars promoting this transformative approach link such an approach to promotion of social justice in local, national and global communities. Transformation will require more than new identifications, however. Andreotti (2010) promotes EfGE that equips "people to live together in collaborative, but uncoercive ways, in contemporary society" (p. 234). This requires a pedagogy that engages with the complexity of ways that contemporary societies are "diverse, changing, uncertain and deeply unequal" (Andreotti 2010, p. 234). She contributes a decolonizing approach to transformational EfGE, one that both analyzes how inequalities between identity groups have been created historically and promotes a negotiation of future relations between groups and individuals that can be dramatically different, or "otherwise" (p. 234). She insists that this is different from provision of normative and universal views of a more just role for students and teachers. Educators can enable "the emergence of ethical, responsible and responsive ways of seeing, knowing and relating to others 'in context', as an ongoing project of agonistic co-authorship and co-ownership" (Andreotti 2010, p. 234). Overall, research on EfGC raises both possibilities and tensions of working with a concept of global citizenship to open up a critically reflexive approach to citizenship.

Conclusions and Recommendations for Future Research

Much of the debates and points of contestation in the scholarship on EfCE consider how global citizenship can be a signifier for a critically reflexive approach to citizenship education. Scholars point out that students experience multiplicitiy in their experiences of citizenship and engagement with the world, and this is an area for further research. In addition, more research and innovations in curriculum and pedagogy could contribute to developing some language through which students can articulate nuanced and complex experiences of being interconnected and interdependent with local and global others (Myers 2010). An emphasis in EfGC on engaging with diverse lived realities complicates a paradigm of an expanded notion of citizenship neutrally extending from national to global and refocuses the connection between the students in classrooms and those about whom they are learning. Rather than simply seeking to bring the world into the classroom, it recognizes that "our classrooms are always already in this world" (Taylor 2012, p. 177).

UNESCO's (2015) stated guidance for learning objectives in global citizenship education raises the complexities of identity and belonging debated in scholarship on EfGC. It emphasises multiple identities and belonging to a shared humanity while respecting differences. This represents a space around which research and practice in EfGC can work with curriculum and pedagogy that takes up the possibilities while remaining vigilantly aware of the risks. There is some very important work to be done in curriculum and pedagogy to mobilize the critical possibility in the current momentum around EfGE. Global citizenship education is included with education for sustainable development in the United Nations' Sustainable Development Goals. And, as the *[Canadian] National Youth White Paper on Global Citizenship* (2015), written by 15-17 year olds from across diverse contexts in Canada, indicates, youth are prepared for a critical approach to EfGC. They are demanding an approach that directly and explicitly tackles inequalities and that revises a Westerncentric dominant view (p. 3). Their recommendations serve to direct future research and practice in this area:

- Adding to and revising elementary and high school curricula to create a focus on changing the dominant narrative on global issues.
- Intergenerational discussions to inform and challenge adults while magnifying the youth voice.
- Understanding other cultures and minorities to diversify perspective, build solidarity, challenge injustices, and promote equity. (p. 7)

Engaging explicitly with a critical approach to understanding identity and belonging in relation to global citizenship and promoting further research in this area will head the call of scholars and of youth.

NOTES

1. While this finding is focused on formal education, it is important to note that these debates and conversations are also occurring in regards to informal education. For example, several key publications emerged from discussions of critical approaches to development education and EfGE through the DEEEP 4 project initiated by the Development Awareness Raising and Education Forum through the European NGO confederation for relief and development (e.g., Troll and Skinner 2013 and Skinner and Bailie Smith 2015).

2. The discussions around the extent to which EfGC reinforces and/or transforms colonial positions of power and potentially reinscribes an 'us' and 'them' mentality is a source of much critical work and practice in informal as well as formal education. For a further break-down of these discussions in regards informal education see for example Shutt (2009) and Skinner and Bailie Smith (2015).

REFERENCES

Abowitz, K., & Harnish, J. (2006). Contemporary discourses of citizenship. *Review of Educational Research, 76*(4), 653–690.

Agbaria, A. K. (2011). The social studies education discourse community on globalization: Exploring the agenda of preparing citizens for the global age. *Journal of Studies in International Education, 15*(1), 57–74.

Anderson, B. (2006). *Imagined communities*. New York, NY: Verso.

Andreotti, V. (2006). Soft vs. critical global citizenship education. *Policy and Practice: A Development Education Review, 3,* 40–51.

Andreotti, V. (2010). Postcolonial and post-critical global citizenship education. In G. Elliott, C. Fourali, & S. Issler (Eds.), *Education & social change* (pp. 233–245). London, England: Continuum.

Andreotti, V. (2011). The political economy of global citizenship education. *Globalisation, Societies and Education, 9*(3–4), 307–310.

Arnot, M., & Dillabough, J. (2004). A magnified image of female citizenship in education: Illusions of democracy or liberal challenges to symbolic domination? In J. Demaine (Ed.), *Citizenship and political education today* (pp. 158–180). New York, NY: Palgrave Macmillan.

Arnot, M., & Swartz, S. (2012). Youth citizenship and the politics of belonging: introducing contexts, voices, imaginaries. *Comparative Education, 48*(1), 1–10.

Appiah, K. A. (2005). *The ethics of identity*. Princeton, NJ: Princeton University Press.

Balibar, E. (2006). *Strangers as enemies: Further reflections on the aporias of transnational citizenship. Talk delivered as part of the globalization working paper series at McMaster University May 2006*. Available online http://www.socialsciences.mcmaster.ca/institute-on-globalization-and-the-human-condition/documents/IGHC-WPS_06-4_Balibar.pdf. Accessed 06/22/12.

Balarin, M. (2011). Global citizenship and marginalisation: contributions towards a political economy of global citizenship. *Globalisation, Societies and Education, 9*3–4, 355–366.

Banks, J. A. (2009). Diversity, group identity, and citizenship education in a global age. In J. A. Banks (Ed.), *The routledge international companion to multicultural education* (pp. 303–322). New York, NY: Routledge.

Beck, U. (2009, September). Imagined Communities of Global Risk. In *Lecture for the Risk Conference in Shanghai. First Draft: Uncorrected Version*. Available online: http://www.worldeconomyandfinance.org/PDFs/ulrich_beck_global_risk.pdf.

Beck, U. (2011). Cosmopolitanism as imagined communities of global risk. *American Behavioral Scientist, 55*(10), 1346–1361.

Burns, K. (2008). (re)Imagining the global, rethinking gender in education. *Discourse: Studies in the Cultural Politics of Education, 29*(3), 343–357.

Camicia, S. P., & Franklin, B. M. (2011). What type of global community and citizenship? Tangled discourses of neoliberalism and critical democracy in curriculum and its reform. *Globalisation, Societies and Education, 9*(3–4), 311–322.

Delanty, G. (2000). *Citizenship in a global age: Society, culture, politics*. Philadelphia, PA: Open University Press.

Delanty, G. (2006). Nationalism and cosmopolitanism: The paradox of modernity. In G. Delanty & K. Kumar (Eds.), *The sage handbook of nations and nationalism* (pp. 357–368). Thousand Oaks, CA: Sage.

Eidoo, S., Ingram, L., MacDonald, A., Nabavi, M., Pashby, K., & Stille, S. (2011). Through the kaleidoscope: Intersections between theoretical perspectives and classroom implications in critical global citizenship education. *Canadian Journal of Education, 34*(4), 59–84.

El-Haj, T. R. A. (2009). Becoming citizens in an era of globalization and transnational migration: Re-imagining citizenship as critical practice. *Theory into Practice, 48*(4), 274–282.

Faulks, K. (2006). Rethinking citizenship education in England Some lessons from contemporary social and political theory. *Education, citizenship and social justice, 1*(2), 123–140.

Ghosh, R., Abdi, A., & Naseem, M. A. (2008). Identity in colonial and postcolonial contexts. In A. Abdi & G. Richardson (Eds.), *Decolonizing democratic education* (pp. 57–66). Rotterdam, The Netherlands: Sense.

Gillborn, D., & Youdell, D. (2009). Critical perspectives on race and schooling. In J. A. Banks (Ed.), *The Routledge international companion to multicultural education* (pp. 173–185). New York, NY: Routledge.

Goldberg, D. T. (1993). Modernity, race, and morality. *Cultural Critique, 24,* 193–227.

Glick Schiller, N., Darieva, T., & Gruner-Domic, S. (2011). Defining cosmopolitan sociability in a transnational age: An introduction. *Ethnic and Racial Studies, 34*(3), 399–418.

Gundara, J. S. (2011). Citizenship and Intercultural Education in an International and Comparative Context. In C. A. Grant & A. Portera (Eds.), *Intercultural and Multicultural Education: Enhancing global interconnectedness* (pp. 294–314). New York, NY: Routledge.

Heater, D. (2004). *Citizenship: The civic ideal in world history, politics and education.* Manchester: Manchester University Press.

Isin, E. F., & Wood, P. K. (1999). *Citizenship and identity.* London, England: Sage.

James, C. E. (2008). Re/presentation of race and racism in the multicultural discourse of Canada. In A. Abdi & L. Shultz (Eds.), *Educating for human rights and global citizenship* (pp. 97–112). Albany, NY: State University of New York Press.

Jefferess, D. (2008). Global citizenship and the cultural politics of benevolence. *Critical Literacy: Theories and Practices, 2*(1), 27–36.

Jefferess, D. (2012). Unsettling cosmopolitanism: Global citizenship and the cultural politics of benevolence. In V. Andreotti & M. Souza (Eds.), *Postcolonial perspectives on global citizenship education* (pp. 27–46). New York, NY: Routledge.

Jiwani, Y. (2006). *Discourses of Denial: Mediations of Race, Gender, and Violence.* Vancouver: UBC Press.

Kymlicka, W. (1998). *Finding our way: Rethinking ethnocultural relations in Canada.* Don Mills, Canada: Oxford University Press.

Kiwan, D. (2007). Developing a model of inclusive citizenship: 'Institutional multiculturalism' and the citizen-state relationship. *Theory and Research in Education, 5*(2), 225–240.

Koyama, J. (2016). The elusive and exclusive Global Citizen. Report. Retrieved from http://mgiep.unesco.org/the-working-paper-series-the-elusive-and-exclusive-global-citizen/.

McCollum, A. (2002). Endpiece: Citizenship education and the challenges of cultural diversity. In D. Scott & H. Lawson (Eds.), *Citizenship education and the curriculum* (pp. 167–182). Westport, CT: Ablex.

Marshall, H. (2009). Educating the European citizen in the global age: Engaging with the postnational and identifying a research agenda. *Journal of Curriculum Studies, 41*(2), 247–267.

Marshall, T. H. (1950). *Citizenship and social class: And other essays.* Cambridge, England: University Press.

McAfee, N. (2000). *Habermas, Kristeva, and citizenship.* Ithaca, NY: Cornell University.

Mitchell, K., & Parker, W. (2008). I pledge allegiance to: Flexible citizenship and shifting scales of belonging. *Teachers College Record, 110*(4), 775–804.

Mohanty, C. T. (2010). Social justice and the politics of identity. In M. Wetherell & C. T. Mohanty (Eds.), *The SAGE handbook of identities* (pp. 529–540). London: Sage Publications Ltd.

Myers, J. (2006). Rethinking the social studies curriculum in the context of globalization: Education for global citizenship in the U.S. *Theory and Research Social Education, 34*(3), 370–394.

Myers, J. (2010). 'To benefit the world by whatever means possible': Adolescents' constructed meanings for global citizenship. *British Educational Research Journal, 36*(3), 483–502.

Myers, J. P. (2016). Charting a democratic course for global citizenship education: Research directions and current challenges. Education Policy Analysis Archives/ Archivos Analíticos de Políticas Educativas, 24. Retrieved from http://www.redalyc.org/jatsRepo/2750/275043450043/html/index.html.

National Youth White Paper on Global Citizenship. (2015). Report. Retrieved from http://www.cgcer.ualberta.ca/en/NewsCollection/2015/July/~/media/cgcer/ Documents/National_Youth_White_Paper/National_Youth_White_Paper.pdf.

Niens, U., & Reilly, J. (2012). Education for global citizenship in a divided society? Young people's views and experiences. *Comparative Education, 48*(1), 103–118.

Nussbaum, M. (2002). Education for citizenship in an era of global connection. *Studies in Philosophy and Education, 21*, 289–303.

Painter, J. (2002). Multi-level citizenship, identity and regions in contemporary Europe. In J. Anderson (Ed.), *Transnational democracy: Political spaces and border crossings* (pp. 93–110). New York, NY: Routledge.

Parmenter, L. (2011). Power and place in the discourse of global citizenship education. *Globalisation, Societies and Education, 9*(3–4), 367–380.

Pashby, K. (2008). Demands on and of citizenship and schooling: 'Belonging' and 'diversity' in the global imperative. *Brock Education, 17*, 1–21.

Pashby, K. (2011). Cultivating global citizens: Planting new seeds or pruning the perennials? Looking for the citizen-subject in global citizenship education theory. *Globalisation, Societies, and Education, 9*(3/4), 427–442.

Pashby, K. (2013). *Related and conflated: A theoretical and discursive framing of multiculturalism and global citizenship education in the Canadian context.* Unpublished doctoral dissertation. University of Toronto, Canada. Available online: http://hdl.handle.net/1807/35921.

Patten, A. (2001). Liberal citizenship in multinational societies. In A.-G. Gagnon & J. Tully (Eds.), *Multinational democracies* (pp. 279–298). Cambridge: Cambridge University Press.

Pike, G. (2008). Peddling 'humbug and false piety': Reflections on the road to educating global citizens. In A. Abdi & G. Richardson (Eds.), *Decolonizing democratic education* (pp. 79–85). Rotterdam, The Netherlands: Sense.

Rapoport, A. (2009). Lonely business or mutual concern: The role of comparative education in the cosmopolitan citizenship debates. *Current issues in comparative education, 12*(1), 23–32.

Richardson, G. H. (2002). *The death of the good Canadian: Teachers, national identities and the social studies curriculum*. New York, NY: Peter Lang.

Rizvi, F. (2009). Towards cosmopolitan learning. *Discourse: Studies in the Cultural Politics of Education, 30*(3), 253–268. doi:10.1080/01596300903036863.

Rosaldo, R. (1999). Cultural citizenship, inequality and multiculturalism. In R. D. Torres, L. F. Mirón, & J. X. Inda (Eds.), *Race, identity, and citizenship: A reader* (pp. 253–261). Oxford, England: Blackwell.

Ross, A. (2007). Multiple identities and education for active citizenship. *British Journal of Educational Studies, 55*(3), 286–303.

Scott, D., & Lawson, H. (Eds.). (2002). Introduction. In *Citizenship Education and the Curriculum* (pp. 1–6). Westport, CT: Ablex.

Selby, D. (1994). Kaleidoscopic mindset: New meanings within citizenship education.*Global Education, 2,* 20–31.

Shutt, C (2009) *Changing the world by changing ourselves: reflections from a bunch of BINGOs*, Institute of Development Studies, Practice Paper No.3. Available online: http://www.ids.ac.uk/files/dmfile/RSPP3.pdf.

Skinner A. & Baillie Smith M. (2015). Reconceptualising global education from the grassroots: the lived experiences of practitioners. Brussels: DEEEP. Retrieved from http://deeep.org/wp-content/uploads/2015/12/DEEEP4_QualityImpact_Report_2015_web.pdf?x99724.

Strand, T. (2010a). Cosmopolitanism in the making. *Studies in Philosophy of Education, 29,* 103–109.

Strand, T. (2010b). The Making of a new Cosmopolitanism. *Studies in Philosophy of Education, 29,* 229–242.

Taylor, L. (2012). Beyond paternalism: Global education with preservice teachers as a practice of implication. In V. Andreotti & M. Souza (Eds.), *Postcolonial perspectives on global citizenship education* (pp. 177–199). New York, NY: Routledge.

Troll, T., & Skinner, A. (2013). Catalysing the 'Shadow Spaces': Challenging development discourse from within the DEEEP Project. *Policy & Practice-A Development Education Review, 17,* 90–102.

Tupper, J. (2008). Feminism confronts democracy. In A. Abdi & G. Richardson (Eds.), *Decolonizing democratic education* (pp. 67–76). Rotterdam, The Netherlands: Sense.

United Nations Educational, Scientific and Cultural Organization (UNESCO). (2015). *Global Citizenship Education: Topics and Learning Objectives*. Retrieved from http://unesdoc.unesco.org/images/0023/002329/232993e.pdf.

Wang, C., & Hoffman, D. M. (2016). Are WE the World?Are WE the World? *Education Policy Analysis Archives, 24*(56), 1–19.

Weatherall, A. (2002). *Gender, language and discourse*. New York: Routledge.

Willinsky, J. (2008). Preface. In A. Abdi & G. Richardson (Eds.), *Decolonizing democratic education* (pp. vii–x). Rotterdam, The Netherlands: Sense.

Zembylas, M. (2010). The ethic of care in globalized societies: Implications for citizenship education. *Ethics and Education, 5*(3), 233–245.

AUTHOR BIOGRAPHY

Karen Pashby Completed her Ph.D. at University of Toronto in 2013 where she also coordinated the Global Citizenship and Sustainable Development cohort of initial teacher education. She held a postdoctoral research position on the Ethical Internationalisation in Higher Education project at the University of Oulu (2013–2013) and a postdoctoral fellowship at the Centre for Global Citizenship Education and Research at University of Alberta (2014–2016). She recently joined the Faculty of Education at Manchester Metropolitan University where she lectures and does research in the area of global citizenship education, a field in which she has published widely.

CHAPTER 19

Sustainable Development and Global Citizenship Education: Challenging Imperatives

Annette Gough

INTRODUCTION

The concept of sustainable development is not new. The need for sustainable forest management practices was recognised in Europe in the eighteenth century, if not earlier (Blewitt 2015), the notion of 'maximum sustainable yield' has long been used by fisheries managers to denote the maximum fish catch per year in order to maintain a stable fish population (Sachs 2015), and sustainable development "existed in the conservation philosophy of the Theodore Roosevelt administration in the USA (1901–1909) and its concern for the rational uses of natural resources" (McCormick 1986, p. 178). More recently, the United Nations has endorsed the Sustainable Development Goals for transforming the world by 2030, which cover economic development, social development and environmental protection (United Nations 2016). This chapter unpacks the concepts, debates and challenges associated with sustainable development, argues for its core role in world transformation, and relates sustainable development to the global citizenship education agenda and future research needs.

A. Gough (✉)
RMIT University, Melbourne, VIC, Australia
e-mail: annette.gough@rmit.edu.au

© The Author(s) 2018   295
I. Davies et al. (eds.), *The Palgrave Handbook of Global Citizenship and Education*, https://doi.org/10.1057/978-1-137-59733-5_19

Early Uses

'Sustainable development' received its first major international recognition in 1972 at the UN Conference on the Human Environment held in Stockholm (United Nations 1972). Although not referred to explicitly as 'sustainable development', there was agreement to the idea, now seen as fundamental to sustainable development, that development and the environment, which had previously been addressed as separate issues, were not incompatible, and that they could be managed to their mutual benefit in order to create a sustainable society: "[e]conomic growth was no longer to be distrusted; in fact it was seen as essential, provided that it was sustainable" (McCormick 1986, p. 177). However, these concerns about the use of natural resources and limiting economic growth were only a preoccupation of environmentalists in the industrial societies of Western Europe and North America (often called the Global North), which had been responsible for overdevelopment and reckless exploitation and consumption of natural resources. Developing countries (often called the Global South) had differing priorities in that they were still seeking to develop their economies and fulfil basic human needs through a fairer distribution of resources. In the 1970s these countries started to convince environmentalists in the Global North of the need to acknowledge, accommodate, and understand the differing priorities of the emerging economies. As Blewitt (2015) summarises,

> Sustainable development has emerged through political and environmental struggles, through a business, citizen and governmental engagement with the complexity of contemporary ecological and other problems, and a vast array of perspectives, values and interests that have been applied in seeking to understand and deal with them. (p. 6)

Although initially resistant, conservationists came to support the development of environmentally sound technologies, advocating for the equitable sharing of limited resources, and recommending sustainable uses for renewable resources in the decade after the Stockholm conference. This change of emphasis is reflected in the argument of the *World Conservation Strategy* (IUCN 1980) that the conservation of living resources is essential to sustainable development. This document was developed by the International Union for the Conservation of Nature and Natural Resources (IUCN) with advice from the World Wildlife Fund (WWF) and the United Nations Environment Programme (UNEP), incorporating a focus that was consistent with IUCN's interest in reconciling conservation and development since its inception in 1948 (McCormick 1986). The introduction to the document notes that

> Conservation must therefore be combined with measures to meet short term economic needs. The vicious circle by which poverty causes ecological degradation which in turn leads to more poverty can be broken only by development. But if it is not to be self-defeating, it must be development that is sustainable – and conservation helps to make it so. (IUCN 1980, Introduction, paragraph 11)

The *Strategy* saw conservation and development as interdependent, stressing that long-term development will not happen without living resources being conserved and conservation will not happen without minimal standards of development being met (that is, basic needs of food, shelter and clean water). However, the Strategy provided no single clear definition of 'sustainable development', though it was implied in the statement: "For development to be sustainable it must take account of social and ecological factors, as well as economic ones; of the living and non-living resource base; and of the long term as well as the short term advantages and disadvantages of alternative actions." (IUCN 1980, Introduction, paragraph 3). These three 'pillars' of sustainable development—economic development, social development and environmental protection—continue to underpin the concept today, albeit in a much-expanded understanding from that envisaged in the *World Conservation Strategy*. Indeed, the social pillar (which can be understood in terms of public awareness of sustainability, equity, participation, and social cohesion (Murphy 2012) together with adequate provision of social services such as health and education and political accountability (Harris 2003), and social inclusion (Sachs 2012), as discussed below) only came to prominence as a significant component in sustainable development discussions after the 1992 United Nations World Conference on Environment and Development as its report, *Agenda 21* (United Nations 1993), was implemented in various contexts (Colantonio 2007).

Worldwide Attention

The term 'sustainable development' came to worldwide attention through the report of the World Commission on Environment and Development (1987), also known as *Our Common Future* or the Brundtland Report, which included what is now frequently quoted as the standard definition of sustainable development: "Sustainable development is development that meets the needs of the present without compromising the ability of future generations to meet their own needs." (World Commission on Environment and Development 1987, p. 43).However, it was not until the 1992 United Nations World Conference on Environment and Development, also known as the Rio Summit, that sustainable development was recognised as a major challenge by world leaders who agreed to *Agenda 21* (United Nations 1993) as a multilevel action plan on sustainable development. This plan was seen as the beginning of a new global partnership for sustainable development, with the concept expanded through discussions of its social and economic dimensions as well as conservation and management of resources for development. For example, *Agenda 21* argues that "integration of environment and development concerns and greater attention to them will lead to the fulfilment of basic needs, improved living standards for all, better protected and managed ecosystems and a safer, more prosperous future." (United Nations 1993, paragraph 1.1).

A decade later, the United Nations World Summit on Sustainable Development was held in Johannesburg in 2002, to assess progress since the Earth Summit. The Declaration from this Summit included reference to the three pillars of sustainable development (paragraph 5) and expanded conceptions of sustainable development:

> We recognize that poverty eradication, changing consumption and production patterns and protecting and managing the natural resource base for economic and social development are overarching objectives of and essential requirements for sustainable development (United Nations 2002, paragraph 11).

Another decade on, in 2012, the United Nations World Conference on Sustainable Development, also known as Rio + 20, agreed on *The Future We Want* (United Nations 2012), as the outcomes document and framework for action. Here, the Common Vision (p. 1, paragraph 4) repeated the above sentence and added a further explication of sustainable development:

> We also reaffirm the need to achieve sustainable development by promoting sustained, inclusive and equitable economic growth, creating greater opportunities for all, reducing inequalities, raising basic standards of living, fostering equitable social development and inclusion, and promoting the integrated and sustainable management of natural resources and ecosystems that supports, inter alia, economic, social and human development while facilitating ecosystem conservation, regeneration and restoration and resilience in the face of new and emerging challenges.

More recently, as an outcome of Rio + 20, the United Nations adopted the 2030 Agenda for Sustainable Development (United Nations 2015a) with 17 Sustainable Development Goals (SDGs), which replaced the eight Millennium Development Goals (MDGs) from 2016. Launched in 2000 and focused on developing countries, "The Millennium Development Goals set time bound targets, by which progress in reducing income poverty, hunger, disease, lack of adequate shelter and exclusion—while promoting gender equality, health, education and environmental sustainability—can be measured" (Ban Ki-Moon 2008, p. 2). Although the MDGs took on many aspects of what is understood as 'sustainable development', the focus was strongly on poverty eradication, halting the spread of HIV/AIDS and achieving universal primary education (none of which were achieved by 2015).

The successor SDGs are applicable to all countries (rather than just developing countries), and they include goals related to poverty eradication (Goal 1), zero hunger (Goal 2), good health and well-being (Goal 3), education (Goal 4), and gender equality (Goal 5), together with a greater emphasis on environment and development related issues including climate action (Goal 13), life below water and on land (Goals 14 and 15) as well as affordable and clean energy, water, economic development, food security, and responsible consumption, among others (United Nations 2016). The view of sustainable development encapsulated in these goals expands considerably on the *World Conservation Strategy* (IUCN 1980) which focused only on "living resource conservation for sustainable development".

As discussed below, there is no consensus on the meaning of sustainable development, however, with different groups arguing for various approaches to transform society towards sustainability.

Conceptual Underpinnings of Sustainable Development

Starting from the concept of "living resource conservation for sustainable development" in the *World Conservation Strategy* (IUCN 1980), and the recognition that there cannot be development without taking account of social and ecological as well as economic factors, sustainable development as a concept has expanded in both scope and depth in the intervening years. At the same time, there has also been much academic discussion of how to achieve sustainable development. This includes discussions around the relationships between economic growth and global inequality (Piketty 2014; Sen 2009; Stiglitz 2012) with little attention being given to environmental protection (Anand and Sen 2000 are an exception), while others, such as Hopwood et al. (2005) have argued for the need to combine environmental and socio-economic concerns. As Hopwood et al. (2005, p. 47) conclude: "All proponents of sustainable development agree that society needs to change, though there are major debates as to the nature of sustainable development, the changes necessary and the tools and actors for these changes."

The *World Conservation Strategy* (IUCN 1980) defined conservation as "the management of human use of the biosphere so that it may yield the greatest sustainable benefit to present generations while maintaining its potential to meet the needs and aspirations of future generations" with "living resource conservation [being] specifically concerned with plants, animals and microorganisms, and with those non-living elements of the environment on which they depend" (Introduction, paragraph 4). Within this context, the objectives of living resource conservation are: "to maintain essential ecological processes and life-support systems, to preserve genetic diversity, and to ensure the sustainable utilization of species and ecosystems" (Introduction, paragraph 7). The *Strategy* (IUCN 1980) defined development as "the modification of the biosphere and the application of human, financial, living and non-living resources to satisfy human needs and improve the quality of human life" (Introduction, paragraph 3). As already noted, the Strategy did not define sustainable development but introduced the notion that social, ecological and economic factors together with the living and non-living resource base needed to be taken into account if development is to be sustainable. It also introduced many potential complications to the original understandings of what constituted economic development by adding the need to consider the environmental and social impacts of any development.

The previously mentioned (and frequently referenced) definition of sustainable development as "development that meets the needs of the present without compromising the ability of future generations to meet their own needs" (World Commission on Environment and Development (WCED) 1987, p. 43) is in many ways quite imprecise, and has been a source of contestation as people try to understand sustainability. The WCED report expands on this definition by stating that "it contains within it two key concepts:

- the concept of 'needs', in particular, the essential needs of the world's poor, to which over-riding priority should be given; and
- the idea of limitations imposed by the state of technology and social organisation on the environment's ability to meet present and future needs." (WCED 1987, p. 43)

Doughnut economics

Through this expansion, the WCED "tacitly recognise the internal contradictions within the concept" (Blewitt 2015, p. 9). The expansion of the definition prioritized poverty reduction and emphasised social development as the third 'pillar' of sustainable development. Although the environment and the economy were still the dominant pillars at the 1992 UN Conference on Environment and Development (the Earth Summit), as reflected in documents such as the Rio Declaration on Environment and Development, the Framework Convention on Climate Change and the Convention on Biological Diversity, the importance of social development was included in the Conference's action plan for sustainable development, *Agenda 21* (United Nations 1993).

Three Pillars

The three pillars of sustainable development have increasingly been recognised since *Agenda 21* although, as discussed in the next section, the balance between the three has changed over time. The three pillars can be distinguished as follows (Harris 2003, p. 1):

- Economic: An economically sustainable system must be able to produce goods and services on a continuing basis, to maintain manageable levels of government and external debt, and to avoid extreme sectoral imbalances which damage agricultural or industrial production.
- Environmental: An environmentally sustainable system must maintain a stable resource base, avoiding over-exploitation of renewable resource systems or environmental sink functions, and depleting non-renewable resources only to the extent that investment is made in adequate substitutes. This includes maintenance of biodiversity, atmospheric stability, and other ecosystem functions not ordinarily classed as economic resources.

- Social: A socially sustainable system must achieve fairness in distribution and opportunity, adequate provision of social services including health and education, gender equity, and political accountability and participation.

Rather than seeing these as pillars, Griggs et al. (2013, p. 306) recommend that sustainable development should be seen as a nested concept: "The global economy services society, which lies within Earth's life-support system". They then suggest that the WCED definition of sustainable development should be re-phrased as "development that meets the needs of the present while safeguarding Earth's life-support system, on which the welfare of current and future generations depends" (p. 306). Another approach comes from Haughton (1999, in Hopwood et al. 2005, p. 40) who developed five principles for sustainable development based on equity. These help clarify the ideas of sustainable development, link human equity to the environment and challenge the more bland and meaningless interpretations of the term: futurity—inter-generational equity; social justice—intra-generational equity; transfrontier responsibility—geographical equity; procedural equity—people treated openly and fairly; interspecies equity—importance of biodiversity.

Another way of referring to sustainable development—as "triple bottom line" (Elkington 1998)—comes from the corporate world, but it is also used elsewhere. It means that businesses need to satisfy meeting the usual bottom line of economic goals (profits) together with the need "to meet environmental and social goals (or bottom lines) in carrying out business" (Harding 2006, p. 234). However, according to Hopwood et al. (2005, p. 43), "it is assumed that governmental and commercial systems can be nudged towards improvements with the use of management techniques", but there is a need for more government action and political reform, and Gray and Milne (2014, np) conclude that "after nearly 25 years of voluntary initiatives, cajolery and claims that business can get its own house in order, the triple bottom line remains a most attractive but unfulfilled notion".

Up until the Rio + 20 conference, no single assessment matrix for sustainable development had been devised and accepted. Thus, a recommendation from the conference was for a set of sustainable development goals (SDGs) to be developed, which would supersede the Millennium Development Goals (MDGs) from 2016: "These goals would be action orientated, concise, easy to communicate, limited in number, aspirational, global in nature and universally applicable to all countries" (Blewitt 2015, p. 14). Rather than providing general statements about sustainable development, the 17 Sustainable Development Goals (United Nations 2016) provide targets for transforming the world by 2030, and can be grouped under the three pillars (see Table 19.1). These 17 goals and their targets are not new. Their origins can be traced back to *Agenda 21*, which integrated environmental, social and economic concerns, and articulated "a participatory, community-based approach

Table 19.1 The 17 sustainable development goals and the three pillars of sustainable development

Economic development	Environmental protection	Social development
1. No poverty	2. End hunger	1. No poverty
2. End hunger	6. Clean water and sanitation	2. End hunger
4. Quality education	7. Affordable and clean energy	3. Good health and well-being
7. Affordable and clean energy	12. Responsible consumption and production	4. Quality education
8. Decent work and economic growth	13. Climate action	5. Gender equality
9. Industry, innovation and infrastructure	14. Life below water	6. Clean water and sanitation
11. Sustainable cities and communities	15. Life on land	7. Affordable and clean energy
12. Responsible consumption and production		8. Decent work and economic growth
13. Climate action		9. Industry, innovation and infrastructure
17. Partnerships for the goals		10. Reduce inequalities
		11. Sustainable cities and communities
		12. Responsible consumption and production
		16. Peace, justice and strong institutions
		17. Partnerships for the goals

to a variety of issues, including population control, transparency, partnership working, equity and justice, and placing market principles within a regulatory framework" (Blewitt 2015, p. 12).

Each of these goals is an essential concept for sustainable development, but it is important to note that some of the goals are potentially in conflict—such as energy provision and climate change prevention.

Key Issues/Debates

There are a number of issues and/or debates around sustainable development. These include, but are not limited to: confusion and contestation around the meanings and interpretations of the term; the distinction between sustainable development and sustainability; the changing balance between the three pillars of sustainable development over the years; and other challenges and barriers to implementing and achieving sustainable development, including those discussed below.

Contested Meaning

Although "sustainable development" has been around for nearly 40 years, there is still confusion and lack of agreement about its meaning and interpretation. 'Sustainable development' is frequently confused and/or conflated with 'sustainability', and the terms are used interchangeably, but they can be distinguished because 'sustainability' is a goal or destination—such as the desire to live sustainably—and 'sustainable development' is a process or pathway followed to achieve sustainability (Anand and Sen 2000; Blewitt 2015; Colantonio 2007; Harding 2006; Harris 2003; Hopwood et al. 2005; Scott and Gough 2003; Sutton 2004). Over time, sustainability has come to mean "the balancing of environmental, social and economic issues", rather than "the ability to maintain or sustain something of value" (Sutton 2004, p. 9). However, "[e]xactly what defines the state of being, of what *is* sustainable (whether it be a society, logging, fishing etc.), is informed by science but ultimately depends on personal values and world views" (Harding 2006, p. 233). As a result, "[s]ustainable development is eluding the whole planet" (Sachs 2012, p. 2208).

The previously quoted and often-cited WCED (1987) definition has been criticised for suggesting that economic growth, industrial modernisation and market imperatives should be key drivers and goals for all nations. According to Blewitt (2015, p. 9),

> Whereas the industrialized North seemed to be, and in many ways still is, concerned with environmental impacts, the issues confronting the majority South included poverty, health, v, agricultural sustainability, food security, educational opportunity and achievement, shelter, sanitation, desertification and armed conflict.

These issues confronting the Global South are now being reflected in the Sustainable Development Goals (SDGs) (see Table 19.1), much more than they had been included on previous sustainable development agenda, although many of them had been included in the Millennium Development Goals (2000–2015).

Balancing Priorities

Achieving sustainable development requires balancing the three pillars, but this has been difficult to achieve because the different dimensions of sustainable development have not been equally prioritised by policy makers within the sustainability discourse due to shifts in stakeholder concerns (Brent and Labuschagne 2006; Colantino 2007; Colantonio and Potter 2006; Drakakis-Smith 1995; Mebratu 1998). As already discussed, environmental issues dominated sustainable development debates in the 1980s and into the mid-1990s, although economic concerns were increasingly included in the discussions during this period. This was "mainly because sustainable development was born out of the synergy between the emerging environmental movement of the 1960s and the 'basic need' advocates of the 1970s" (Colantino 2007, pp. 3–4).

Economic concerns became equally (or more) prioritised compared with environmental concerns in the period after the 1992 Rio Earth Summit (United Nations Conference on Environment and Development) (United

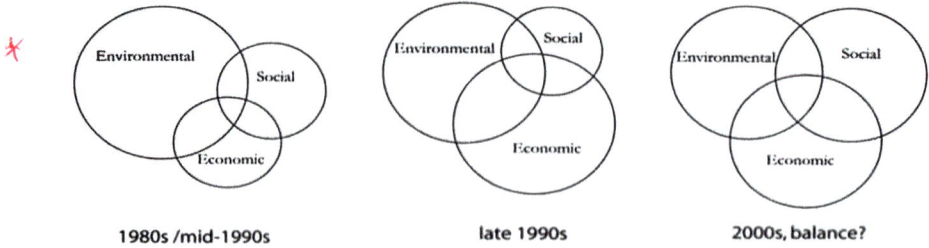

Fig. 19.1 Different dimensions of sustainable development and their relative importance. *Source* Marghescu (2005)

Nations 1993), and social issues became a stronger voice in the discussions after the 2002 Johannesburg World Summit on Sustainable Development (United Nations 2002) and through the Millennium Development Goals (United Nations 2000). The changing balance between the 'pillars' is illustrated in Fig. 19.1. Marghescu (2005) promulgated this diagram over a decade ago, and in the light of the SDGs it may well be that the 'balance' between the three pillars has shifted to a greater dominance by social and economic development and a diminished environmental protection emphasis (Gough and Gough 2016; Griggs et al. 2013; Marghescu 2009). This is of major concern to scientists who argue that "the stable functioning of Earth systems—including the atmosphere, oceans, forests, waterways, biodiversity and biogeochemical cycles—is a prerequisite for a thriving global society" but "human pressure risks causing widespread, abrupt and possibly irreversible changes to basic Earth-system processes", which needs coordinated international action, such as the SDGs (Griggs et al. 2013, p. 305, 306).

Commitment

A major issue in achieving any sustainable development goals is the lack of international consensus on how to balance economic, social and environmental goals:

> Almost all the world's societies acknowledge that they aim for a combination of economic development, environmental sustainability, and social inclusion, but the specific objectives differ globally, between and within societies. Certainly, as yet, no consensus regarding the tradeoffs and synergies across the economic, environmental, and social objectives has been agreed. (Sachs 2012, p. 2206)

And even when consensus is reached, such as with the United Nations Framework Convention on Climate Change's (UNFCCC) 2015 Paris Agreement on Climate Change (United Nations 2015b), the targets can be set too low to actually achieve the desired outcome (Rogelj et al. 2016) . For example, "The pledges made by countries at the historic Paris agreement on climate change would lead to 'completely catastrophic' global warming, scientists have warned." (Johnston 2016, np).

The absence of broad international commitment to sustainable development has been related to government processes favouring short-term thinking and actions over "the longer-term thinking, planning and investment required for sustainability" (Harding 2006, p. 234), which is consistent with the overall weaknesses of the institutional frameworks of society in many countries. The SDGs require longer-term thinking, to 2030, and while the goals do have targets (United Nations 2016), these are not easily measurable, a requirement that is seen as essential for their achievement (Griggs et al. 2013).

Implications for Education for Global Citizenship

Since its earliest formulations, environmental education has had a focus on educating for global citizenship—as reflected in "Think globally, act locally", the mantra that came from the first Earth Day, 22 April 1970. Both global citizenship and sustainable development were integral to the Belgrade Charter Framework for Environmental Education (UNESCO 1975, pp. 1–2) where it states:

> It is absolutely vital that the world's citizens insist upon measures that will support the kind of economic growth which will not have harmful repercussions on people – that will not in any way diminish their environment and their living conditions...

> Millions of individuals will themselves need to adjust their own priorities and assume a 'personal and individualised global ethic' – and reflect in all of their behaviour a commitment to the improvement of the quality of the environment and of life for all the world's people...

> The reform of educational processes and systems is central to the building of this new development ethic and world economic order...

> This new environmental education must be broad based and strongly related to the basic principles outlined in the United Nations Declaration on the *New Economic Order*.

The Belgrade Charter was written over 30 years ago, but the above sentences could have been written as part of the framing of the SDGs. In both, there is a concern with reforming educational processes and with balancing quality of human life, environmental protection and economic growth.

Education was also seen as important for achieving sustainable development in the succession of United Nations reports on environment and development. Although this was not framed in terms of education for global citizenship, it is implicit in the focus of educating citizens for informed participation in sustainable development, as for example, in the WCED report: "the world's teachers... have a crucial role to play" in helping to bring

Our Common Future

"the extensive social changes" (1987, p. xix) needed for sustainable development to be achieved. In *Agenda 21*, the Education chapter has as its first priority "reorienting education towards sustainable development" which is described in the following terms (United Nations 1993, para 36.3):

> Education is critical for promoting sustainable development and improving the capacity of the people to address environment and development issues... It is also critical for achieving environmental and ethical awareness, values and attitudes, skills and behaviour consistent with sustainable development and for effective public participation in decision-making.

ESD and Global Citizenship

In 2002 the United Nations World Summit on Sustainable Development declared education as critical for promoting sustainable development, but global citizenship was not yet directly mentioned as part of the education agenda, although it was implied within paragraph 2 of the Johannesburg Declaration on Sustainable Development (United Nations 2002, p. 1), which states "[w]e commit ourselves to building a humane, equitable and caring global society, cognizant of the need for human dignity for all". Another outcome from this Summit was a recommendation from the United Nations General Assembly that "it consider adopting a decade of education for sustainable development, starting in 2005" (p. 62), which was accepted. The UNESCO international implementation scheme for the *Decade of Education for Sustainable Development 2005–2014* (UNESCO 2004) brought together the Millennium Development Goals (MDG) process, the Education for All (EFA) movement, and the United Nations Literacy Decade (UNLD) with education for sustainable development (ESD):

> All of them aim to achieve comparable impacts: an improvement in the quality of life, particularly for the most deprived and marginalised, fulfilment of human rights including gender equality, poverty reduction, democracy and active citizenship. (UNESCO 2004, p. 9)

Thus education for sustainability is increasingly being interwoven with other international education priorities as part of what was being seen as a global roadmap (UNESCO 2014). In reviewing the Decade, Wals and Nolan (2012, p. 65) concluded that

> given the world's increasing concern with SD issues, ESD appears well positioned to play a synergizing role among a wide variety of sub-fields of education. These include environmental education, global citizenship education and, more recently, consumer education, climate change education and disaster risk reduction.

The close association between education for sustainable development and global citizenship education has developed rapidly in the past few years. The UN Secretary General's Global Education First Initiative that was launched in 2012 sees global citizenship education as drawing on learning from education for sustainable development in order to achieve its goal (UNESCO 2013, p. 3):

> Global citizenship education aims to empower learners to engage and assume active roles both locally and globally to face and resolve global challenges and ultimately to become proactive contributors to a more just, peaceful, tolerant, inclusive, secure and sustainable world.

The Global Action Programme on Education for Sustainable Development (UNESCO 2014) that is the successor program to the Decade of Education for Sustainable Development post 2014, acknowledges the need to promote global citizenship and builds on the outcome document of the United Nations Conference on Sustainable Development (Rio + 20) (United Nations 2012), where member states agreed "to promote education for sustainable development and to integrate sustainable development more actively into education beyond the United Nations Decade of Education for Sustainable Development" (UNESCO 2014, p. 3). Specifically, this programme recognises that "sustainable development challenges have acquired even more urgency since the beginning of the Decade and new concerns have come to the fore, such as the need to promote global citizenship" (UNESCO 2014, p. 33).

Education continues to be an overarching requirement for achieving sustainable development in the SDGs, as the preamble to Goal 4 states: "Obtaining a quality education is the foundation to improving people's lives and sustainable development" (United Nations 2016, np). In particular, with respect to global citizenship, Target 4.7 of the SDG 4 on Education calls on countries to

> ensure that all learners are provided with the knowledge and skills to promote sustainable development, including, among others, through education for sustainable development and sustainable lifestyles, human rights, gender equality, promotion of a culture of peace and non-violence, global citizenship and appreciation of cultural diversity and of culture's contribution to sustainable development (United Nations 2016, np).

Challenges

The challenge for both sustainable development and global citizenship education is finding a place in the curriculum of schools, which is seen by some as already overcrowded (see, for example, Donnelly and Wiltshire 2014). Unfortunately, the history of environmental education and education for sustainable development in schools is one of marginalisation within the curriculum. For example, Australia and England both commenced the development of national curricula in the late 1980s (Chatzifotiou 2006; Education Council 2014; Gough 1997), but while the English national curriculum was introduced in 1990, Australia only implemented its national curriculum in all states and territories from 2014. In both curricula, environmental education (later called sustainability) was originally included as a cross-curriculum theme, but this status is now being diminished in both countries (Donnelly and Wiltshire 2014; Hickman 2013). For example, a Department of Education (2013) press release spelt out how the new National Curriculum would provide pupils with better understanding of climate change, but the new curriculum no longer refers to sustainable development, and it "has removed any notion of environmental stewardship at just the age when children are most curious about—and in awe of—the natural world they see around them" (Hickman 2013, np). According to the UK National Commission for UNESCO (2013), the "reduced government focus on sustainable development has resulted in increased uncertainties amongst educational institutions and practitioners about how much emphasis to place on sustainability within teaching and learning" (p. 17). There is also a recent reduction of a focus on sustainability in the Australian curriculum, as reflected in Recommendation 17 of the Donnelly and Wiltshire review report (2014): "ACARA reconceptualise the cross-curriculum priorities and instead embed teaching and learning about … sustainability explicitly, and only where educationally relevant, in the mandatory content of the curriculum" (p. 247).

In an Australian context, The *Melbourne Declaration on Educational Goals for Young Australians* was released in 2008, and it includes as Goal 2, "All young Australians become successful learners, confident and creative individuals, and active and informed citizens… work for the common good, in particular sustaining and improving natural and social environments" (MCEETYA 2008, pp. 8–9). This goal is best presented in the Year 6 Humanities and Social Sciences Civics and Citizenship curriculum content statement (Australian Curriculum 2015, np)—"The obligations citizens may consider they have beyond their own national borders as active and informed global citizens"—and the two associated elaborations:

- identifying the obligations people may consider they have as global citizens (for example, an awareness of human rights issues, concern for the environment and sustainability, being active and informed about global issues).
- using a current global issue (for example, immigration across borders or clearing native forests to establish palm oil plantations) to discuss the concept of global citizenship.

Sadly, while the current English National Curriculum (Department of Education 2013) does include citizenship, there is no mention of global citizenship or sustainability in the study description.

CONCLUSION AND RECOMMENDATIONS
REGARDING FUTURE RESEARCH

Sustainable development means approaching development by balancing "different, and often competing, needs against an awareness of the environmental, social and economic limitations we face as a society" (Sustainable Development Commission 2011, np). It has increasingly been linked with global citizenship education in recent years, and this relationship should become closer as countries pursue achievement of the SDGs. There is a need for more research to demonstrate how these two areas, combined, can be included in school curricula and in public education programs, particularly given the ongoing resistances.

Achieving sustainable development is just as challenging. Analyses of the increasing global inequalities have led a number of researchers (including Hopwood et al. 2005; Piketty 2014; Sachs 2012; Stiglitz 2012) to suggest that there is a need for governments to take a stronger role "to protect the interests of future generations from the short-sighted despoliation caused by the present generation" (Sachs 2012, p. 2209). Others, such as Anand and Sen (2000), Hopwood et al. (2005), Murphy (2012) and Sen (2009) have argued for a more social justice and equity based approach "concentrating on sustainable livelihoods and well-being rather than well-having, and long-term environmental sustainability, which requires a strong basis in principles that link the social and environmental to human equity" (Hopwood et al. p. 38). The SDGs are a beginning, but there is a need for global-scale problem-solving research and development of "new technologies and new ways to organise human activity to combine improving living standards and ecological imperatives" (Sachs 2012, p. 2211) to achieve the necessary social transformations around energy, food, urbanisation, climate resilience and the other goals. This will require the engagement of governments, universities, corporations, non-government organisations as well as formal and informal networks.

REFERENCES

Anand, S., & Sen, A. (2000). Human development and economic sustainability. *World Development, 28*(12), 2029–2049.

Australian and Assessment and Reporting Authority (ACARA). (2015). *The Australian Curriculum 8.2.* Retrieved from www.australiancurriculum.edu.au/.

Ban Ki-Moon. (2008). *Committing to action: Achieving the Millennium Development Goals. Background note by the Secretary-General to the United Nations high-level event on the Millennium Development Goals,* 25 September 2008. Retrieved from http://www.un.org/millenniumgoals/2008highlevel/pdf/commiting.pdf.

Blewitt, J. (2015). *Understanding sustainable development* (2nd ed.). Abingdon, Oxon: Routledge.

Brent, A., & Labuschagne, C. (2006). Social indicators for sustainable project and technology life cycle management in the process industry. *The International Journal of Life Cycle Assessment, 11*(1), 3–15.

Chatzifotiou, A. (2006). Environmental education, national curriculum and school teachers: Findings of a research study in England and possible implications upon education for sustainable development. *The Curriculum Journal, 17*(4), 367–381.

Colantonio, A. (2007). *Social sustainability: An exploratory analysis of its definition, assessment methods metrics and tools. EIBURS Working Paper Series, 2007/01.* Oxford: Oxford Brooks University, Oxford Institute for Sustainable Development (OISD)—International Land Markets Group. Retrieved from http://oisd.brookes.ac.uk/sustainable_communities/resources/SocialSustainability_Metrics_and_Tools.pdf.

Colantonio, A., & Potter, R. B. (2006). *Urban tourism and development in the socialist state: Havana during the special period.* Aldershot: Ashgate.

Department of Education. (2013). *Citizenship programmes of study: Key stages 3 and 4.* Retrieved from www.gov.uk/government/uploads/system/uploads/attachment_data/file/239060/SECONDARY_national__-_Citizenship.pdf.

Donnelly, K., & Wiltshire, K. (2014). *Review of the Australian curriculum: Final report.* Canberra: Australian Government Department of Education.

Drakakis-Smith, D. (1995). Third world cities: Sustainable urban development, 1. *Urban Studies, 32*(4–5), 659–677.

Education Council. (2014). *The Hobart Declaration on schooling (1989).* Retrieved from http://www.educationcouncil.edu.au/EC-Publications/EC-Publications-archive/EC-The-Hobart-Declaration-on-Schooling-1989.aspx.

Elkington, J. (1998). *Cannibals with forks: The triple bottom line of 21st century business.* Stony Creek, CT: New Society Publishers.

Gough, A. (1997). *Education and the environment: Policy, trends and the problems of marginalisation.* Melbourne: Australian Council for Educational Research.

Gough, A., & Gough, N. (2016). The denaturation of environmental education: Exploring the role of ecotechnologies. *Australian Journal of Environmental Education, 32*(1), 30–41. doi:10.1017/aee.2015.34.

Griggs, D., Stafford-Smith, M., Gaffney, O., Rockström, J., Öhman, M. C., Shyamsundar, P., et al. (2013). Policy: Sustainable development goals for people and planet. *Nature, 495,* 305–307.

Gray, R. & Milne, M. J. (2014, February 6). *Explainer: what is the triple bottom line? The Conversation.* Retrieved from https://theconversation.com/explainer-what-is-the-triple-bottom-line-22798.

Harding, R. (2006). Ecologically sustainable development: Origins, implementation and challenges. *Desalination, 187*(1), 229–239.

Harris, J. M. (2003). *Sustainability and sustainable development. International Society for Ecological Economics Internet Encyclopaedia of Ecological Economics.* Retrieved from http://isecoeco.org/pdf/susdev.pdf.

Hickman, L. (2013, July 9). *Climate change will still not be taught in English primary schools. The Guardian.* Retrieved from www.theguardian.com/environment/blog/2013/jul/08/climate-change-geography-national-curriculum.

Hopwood, B., Mellor, M., & O'Brien, G. (2005). Sustainable development: Mapping different approaches. *Sustainable Development, 13*(1), 38–52.

International Union for the Conservation of Nature and Natural Resources (IUCN). (1980). *Gland.* Switzerland: IUCN.

Johnston, I. (2016, June 30). *Paris climate summit put planet on course for 'catastrophic' warming despite being seen as success, study finds. The Independent.* Retrieved from www.independent.co.uk/environment/paris-climate-summit-deal-climate-warning-catastrophic-impact-on-planet-global-warming-emissions-a7109231.html.

Marghescu, T. (2005). Greening the Lisbon agenda? = Greenwashing? In *Presentations at the Greening of The Lisbon Agenda Conference, EPSD*. 23 February, unpublished. Strasbourg: European Parliament.

Marghescu, T. (2009). Price for Nature—More Value to Land Property. In C. Otero (Ed.), *Creating the future of the countryside: The European estate* (pp. 24–26). Madrid, Spain: Instituto Ibérico para el Medio Ambiente (IIMA).

McCormick, J. (1986). The origins of the world conservation strategy. *Environmental Review, 10*(3), 177–187.

Mebratu, D. (1998). Sustainability and sustainable development: Historical and conceptual review. *Environmental Impact Assessment Review, 18*, 493–520.

Ministerial Council on Education Employment Training and Youth Affairs (MCEETYA). (2008). *Melbourne declaration on educational goals for young australians*. Retrieved from http://www.curriculum.edu.au/verve/_resources/National_Declaration_on_the_Educational_Goals_for_Yung_Australians.pdf.

Murphy, K. (2012). The social pillar of sustainable development: A literature review and framework for policy analysis. *Sustainability: Science, Practice, & Policy, 8*(1), 15–29.

Piketty, T. (2014). *Capital in the Twenty-First Century*. Translated by Arthur Goldhammer. Cambridge, MA: Belknap Press of Harvard University Press.

Rogelj, J., den Elzen, M., Höhne, N., Fransen, T., Fekete, H., Winkler, H., et al. (2016). Paris Agreement climate proposals need a boost to keep warming well below 2 C. *Nature, 534*, 631–639.

Sachs, J. D. (2012). From millennium development goals to sustainable development goals. *Lancet, 379*, 2011–2206.

Sachs, J. D. (2015). *The age of sustainable development*. New York: Columbia University Press.

Scott, W., & Gough, S. (2003). *Sustainable development and learning: Framing the issues*. London: RoutledgeFalmer.

Sen, A. (2009). *The idea of justice*. Cambridge, MA: Belknap Press of Harvard University Press.

Stiglitz, J. (2012). *The price of inequality*. New York and London: W. W. Norton & Company.

Sustainable Development Commission. (2011). *What is sustainable development*. Retrieved from www.sd-commission.org.uk/pages/what-is-sustainable-development.html.

Sutton, P. (2004). What is sustainability? *Eingana: The Journal of the Victorian Association for Environmental Education, 27*(1), 4–9.

UNESCO. (1975). *The Belgrade charter: A global framework for environmental education*. Retrieved from http://portal.unesco.org/education/en/files/33037/10935069533The_Belgrade_Charter.pdf/The+Belgrade+Charter.pdf.

UNESCO. (2004). *United Nations Decade of Education for Sustainable Development 2005–2014. Draft international implementation scheme*. October 2004. Retrieved from portal.unesco.org/education/en/file_download.php/03f375b07798a2a55dcdc39db7aa8211Final+IIS.pdf.

UNESCO. (2013). *Global citizenship education: An emerging perspective. Outcome document of the technical consultation on global citizenship education*. Retrieved from unesdoc.unesco.org/images/0022/002241/224115E.pdf.

UNESCO. (2014). *Roadmap for implementing the global action programme on education for sustainable development*. Retrieved from unesdoc.unesco.org/images/0023/002305/230514e.pdf.

United Kingdom National Commission for UNESCO. (2013). *Education for sustainable development (ESD) in the UK—Current status, best practice and opportunities for the future*. London: United Kingdom National Commission for UNESCO Secretariat.

United Nations. (1972). *Declaration of the United Nations conference on the human environment*. Retrieved from www.unep.org/Documents.Multilingual/Default.asp?documentid=97&articleid=1503.

United Nations. (1993). *Agenda 21: Earth summit: The United Nations programme of action from Rio*. Retrieved from sustainabledevelopment.un.org/content/documents/Agenda21.pdf.

United Nations. (2000). *United Nations millennium declaration*. Retrieved from www.un.org/millennium/declaration/ares552e.pdf.

United Nations. (2002). *Report of the World summit on sustainable development: Johannesburg, South Africa, 26 August–4 September 2002*. Retrieved from www.un.org/jsummit/html/documents/summit_docs/131302_wssd_report_reissued.pdf.

United Nations. (2012). *The future we want: Outcomes document adopted at Rio + 20*. Retrieved from https://sustainabledevelopment.un.org/content/documents/733 FutureWeWant.pdf.

United Nations. (2015a). *Transforming our world: The 2030 agenda for sustainable development. Resolution adopted by the General Assembly on 25 September 2015*. Retrieved from www.un.org/ga/search/view_doc.asp?symbol=A/RES/70/1&Lang=E.

United Nations. (2015b). *Paris agreement*. Retrieved from http://unfccc.int/files/essential_background/convention/application/pdf/english_paris_agreement.pdf.

United Nations. (2016). *Sustainable development goals*. Retrieved from https://sustainabledevelopment.un.org/sdgs.

Wals, A., & Nolan, C. (2012). *Shaping the education of tomorrow: 2012 Report on the UN decade of education for sustainable development, Abridged*. Paris: UNESCO. Retrieved from http://unesdoc.unesco.org/images/0021/002166/216606e.pdf.

World Commission on Environment and Development. (WCED). (1987). *Our common future*. Oxford: Oxford University Press.

AUTHOR BIOGRAPHY

Annette Gough is Emeritus Professor of Science and Environmental Education in the School of Education at RMIT University. She has held senior appointments at RMIT and Deakin University and has been a visiting professor at universities in Canada, South Africa and Hong Kong, as well being life fellow of the Australian Association for Environmental Education and the Victorian Association for Environmental Education. Her research interests span environmental, sustainability and science education, research methodologies, posthuman and gender studies and she has completed research projects for national and state governments as well as working with UNESCO, UNEP and UNESCO-UNEVOC on several research and development projects.

PART IV

Principal Perspectives and Contexts

CHAPTER 20

Economy and Economics

Reinhold Hedtke

INTRODUCTION

Globalisation is often narrowed to its economic dimension only. Hence, economics' explanations of globalisation and proposals for globalisation policies enjoy a great deal of attention. Economics has sustainable political impact and contributes to shaping beliefs, blueprints, behaviours and institutions and, thereby, co-creates global economic reality. Global citizenship education, therefore, should make citizens aware of economics' ways of thinking, its capacity, controversies and consequences for public policy, institutions and wellbeing of social groups, industries, nations and regions.

First of all, we briefly discuss the ambiguity of the term globalisation and its economic meanings and outline some key empirics revealing a chequered picture of economic globalisation. The second part of the chapter presents basics of economics' understanding of globalisation, trade and the role of governments, and mentions some characteristics of financial globalisation. Moreover, it sketches the impact of economics on the economy and relates globalisation to political debates. The final part considers consequences for global citizenship and future research.

R. Hedtke (✉)
Chair of Social Science Education and Economic Sociology, Faculty of Sociology, Bielefeld University, Postfach 100 131, 33501 Bielefeld, Germany
e-mail: reinhold.hedtke@uni-bielefeld.de

© The Author(s) 2018
I. Davies et al. (eds.), *The Palgrave Handbook of Global Citizenship and Education*, https://doi.org/10.1057/978-1-137-59733-5_20

Conceptual Underpinnings

Multi-perspective Approach

Economic globalisation is an issue of multidisciplinary and often even trans-disciplinary social science research. As a 'typical' social science discipline, economics is characterised by pluralism in schools of thought and methodology. Hence, there is no such thing as *the* economics' perspective or *the* economics of globalisation. Rather, economics can be seen "as a collection of models, along with a system of navigation among models" (Rodrik 2015, p. 208), accompanied by continuous controversy on economic policies. Neoclassical, Radical or Marxist, Post-Keynesian, Institutionalist, Evolutionist, Feminist and Socio-Economics are prominent paradigmatic approaches.

Meanings of Globalisation

Globalisation is understood as a multidimensional and heterogeneous complex of real-world processes connecting local, regional, national, supranational-regional actors, networks, organisations, institutions or policies on a worldwide scale. It goes without saying that globalisation has economic, political, cultural, spatial, historical, technical, legal, personal, mythical etc. dimensions (Steger 2015, p. 26).

In everyday life, the most important domains of economic globalisation or supranational regionalisation are consumption, travel, labour mobility and, more rarely, money investment. In many nations, the vast majority of consumers, tourists, viewers and readers behave like "globalists" while small groups of consumers strive for economic nationalism or localism with slogans like "Be American—buy American!" People experience many effects of globalisation mainly on the *local* level (Dicken 2015, p. 305).

Generally, the term economic globalisation may be used in three basic understandings (cf. Dicken 2015, pp. 4–8). First, it serves as an *empirical* concept of describing processes of advancing structural integration of the world economy. Main globalisation indicators, then, are global trade growth outpacing production and growth of foreign direct investment overrunning trade. Further important indicators are global technologies, transnational corporations, transnational production networks, and foreign ownership of capital and land. Financial globalisation may be measured by the extent of foreign banking, interest rate parity as an indicator of a unitary global capital market or the ratio of total capital flows or assets to gross domestic product (GDP).

Second, globalisation is a *theoretical* notion used by different strands of explaining the processes, structures and outcomes of a worldwide integration.

Third, globalisation is an *ideological* narrative, referring to global integration as a discursive and political project, based on beliefs like free market optimism and state pessimism, political-economic constructs like neo-liberalism and aiming at public and political hegemony.

Some scholars add a fourth, *political* understanding of economic globalisation, including Marxist approaches (cf. Jessop 2014). They observe class-conscious political strategies like weakening the bargaining and political power of labour force, unions and related political parties, or deregulation strategies enabling an externalisation of production costs to society, the environment or future generations (cf. Genschel and Seelkopf 2015; Jessop 2014).

Controversy on Globalisation

Generally speaking, economic globalisation and financial globalisation are contested concepts, competing stories of globalisation are told. Controversy revolves around theories and evidence, key actors and policies, governance and evaluation (cf. Arestis and Singh 2010, p. 233). Contentious positions encompass hyper-globalist pictures of a "borderless world" breeding a new type of economic system, sceptical accounts of an international or regional-supranational economy, euphoric notions of globalisation-as-solution and anti-globalist stances assessing globalisation as the main culprit of economic and societal problems (Hirst et al. 2009, pp. 13–18; Dicken 2015, pp. 380–383).

Many see economic globalisation as a unique and recent process. Others, however, take a historical perspective and find globalisation already in the colonial trade of the seventeenth and eighteenth centuries, the manufacturing multinationals of the Industrial Revolution, the high level of mass migration in the nineteenth century or the very high degree of international trade in the decades before World War I (Hirst et al. 2009, pp. 24–67).

This sceptical assessment of the uniqueness of current globalisation has been criticised for narrowing globalisation to the *volume* of trade, for failing to grasp the *qualitative* property of production through "deep integration" which characterises today's world economy "organized primarily within and between geographically extensive and complex *global production networks*" (Dicken 2015, p. 6).

In addition, a trade-focussed approach, according to its critics, masks the international integration of financial markets and their real-time operation all over the globe, thus missing the current key feature of global finance. This evidence points to worldwide integrated markets and the first of two ideal types: the economy as a *globalised economy* (Hirst et al. 2009, pp. 20–21). Key actors in this picture of globalisation are transnational corporations searching for profit via access to capital, markets, knowledge and labour around the world, as well as states, believed to be global competitors in striving for foreign investment from corporations and finance, promising growth and jobs (Dicken 2015, pp. 118–123, 173–225).

Empirical Evidence of Globalisation

Some key features characterize the global economy (cf. Dicken 2015, pp. 14–46). Among them are strong cyclical volatility of economic key figures like aggregate growth and trade, increasing interconnectedness as measured by the growth of trade outplaying growth of output, growth of foreign direct investment (FDI) overhauling growth of trade, strong imbalances of the world economy in terms of trade surpluses and deficits in manufacturing, services and agriculture. The structure of the global economy has changed towards multi-polarity in terms of division of labour and production centres, relatively higher growth rates in developing countries, and increasing international importance of East Asian economies. The global economic predominance of the triad Europe, North America and East Asia persists, however. Moreover, many countries or regions remain disconnected from economic prosperity. Post-Soviet economies also provide a telling example of an extreme diversity of economic evolution by international integration.

Today, a mixed picture of globalisation emerges from empirical evidence (Arestis et al. 2012, p. 490; Beckfield 2010): Increasing globalism, especially in capital and finance, coexists with resilient regionalism. An example in this vein is trade taking place in a general structure of supra-national networks persistent over decades, keeping internationalisation of production and trade "extremely unequally distributed" among countries instead of somewhat equally spreading over the world (Hirst et al. 2009, pp. 98–100). The past two decades witnessed a significant increase of supranational *regional* trade agreements, albeit with limited liberalisation effects. By contrast, unilateral liberalisation boomed and deeply depreciated multilateral negotiation, e.g. within the institutional frame of the WTO, pointing to the picture of an increasingly fragmented world market (Bureau et al. 2016, pp. 30–31). Thus, empirics seemingly support the second of the two ideal types: an international economy, not a globalised one (Hirst et al. 2009, pp. 18–19).

Over time, however, the dynamics of economic globalisation have outpaced regionalism since the 1990s, then experienced a backlash after the financial crisis of 2007/2008 and show today some signs of de-globalisation (Arestis et al. 2012, pp. 490–492). In the end, neither extreme viewpoint on globalisation is completely right. Rather, we are confronted with a multifaceted world and, above all, an open future of globalisation (Hirst et al. 2009, p. 17).

Moreover, recent research reveals very different degrees of globalisation of a single country or a supra-national region along dimensions such as goods, service, capital or labour markets. As a rule, international mobility on labour markets remains rather restricted (Rodrik 2007, p. 197). The level of societal and economic integration between the national and the global, especially in terms of transnational human mobility, seems to be comparatively high in Latin America, the Caribbean and Europe (Deutschmann 2015). Yet regional openness of nations may coincide with external closure against the rest of the world (Delhey et al. 2014). Globalisation, therefore, should be empirically distinguished from regionalisation.

Accounting for country-level mediation of globalisation effects is relevant, especially with respect to developing economies (McMillan et al. 2014).

Principally, pressure from foreign competition forces domestic industries to enhance their productivity and become more efficient (ibid.). National productivity, however, also depends on domestic structural change in form of the reallocation of resources, mainly labour force, *across* traditional and modern sectors. In this regard, past globalisation ended up with "a highly uneven result", declining growth in Latin America and Africa and increasing it in Asia.

Taking these pieces of evidence into account, vague but popular terms like "the global economy" or "economic globalisation" should be avoided. Scholars from the social sciences emphasise that national institutions and policies still make a difference (e.g. Acemoglu and Robinson 2012; Bell and Hindmoor 2015). Therefore, national differences and national policies are of persistent relevance for the national as well as for the supranational level of globalisation and global governance.

In sum, (economic) globalisation should be considered as a very complex and contested "*syndrome* of processes and activities", driven by a plurality of causes and entangled with domestic and local processes (Dicken 2015, pp. 6–7). Economic globalisation turns out to be a complex of heterogeneous, inconsistent and even reversible processes.

KEY ISSUES AND DEBATES OF ECONOMIC GLOBALISATION

Despite its multidimensionality, globalisation is principally perceived and mostly measured in terms of *economic* exchange and integration between *nations*. Thus, the term globalisation denotes the interpenetration of national economies' markets by foreign actors, preferably expressed in figures of international *trade*.

Basic Models of International Trade

The focus on international trade stems from the origin of economics as *national* political economy—epitomised in Adam Smith's *An Inquiry into the Nature and the Causes of the Wealth of Nations* (1776) —and its preoccupation with analysis and praise of free trade on all kinds of markets—represented in David Ricardo's classical trade model of *comparative* advantage (1817). Accordingly, in comparison to another country, a country benefits from importing goods it produces *relatively* less well while exporting those produced domestically *relatively* less badly. Opening markets will therefore increase trade (trade creation effect). Properly understood, the effect that a country collectively gains does not implicate that every group will benefit as well. On the contrary, some groups will lose through trade (Rodrik 2015, pp. 52–56). Moreover, if some countries allow free trade among each other, like in the European Union, but still restrict trade with other countries, the latter will be worse off (trade diversion effect).

From the alternative strand of protectionist thinking of international trade in the tradition of the German Friedrich List (1841), a country not faced with level playing field but with catch-up development would do better to postpone liberalisation, impose protective tariffs and subsidise domestic industries until they are competitive abroad. The strategy of partial protectionism including heavy regulation of capital flow was rather successfully applied by East Asian countries like South Korea, Taiwan, China or India (cf. Rodrik 2015, pp. 160–164). In the last decades of the nineteenth century, U.S. protective tariffs were higher than in most developing countries today (Rodrik 2007, p. 240). Obviously, economics' trade theories and policy advice did and do not evolve in a vacuum but were and are embedded in specific economic, historical and political circumstances (contextual embeddedness of theories; cf. Fourcade 2009).

Different theoretical approaches entail different notions of economic globalisation. To illustrate, we roughly sketch the starting points of neoclassical and institutionalist thinking on globalisation.

The basic idea of a neoclassical perspective on globalisation assumes that single world markets emerge through self-supporting microeconomic processes—driven by individual entrepreneurs, investors, managers, employees searching for better opportunities—which result in the integration of national markets in supranational markets, provided that the states abstain from intervention in the markets and that capital and labour are free to move. Competition as human nature is taken for granted (Palermo 2016).

Unsurprisingly, a neoclassical approach which understands the world economy as the outcome of open national economies—international merchandise, labour and capital markets, international trade and international trade policies—can do without the term globalisation. Interestingly, such a subsumption of globalisation under universal economic laws neatly corresponds to Marxian approaches which conceive globalisation as an intrinsic tendency of capitalism, an outward movement of capital competing for the appropriation of further profit sources and monopolistic rents (cf. Palermo 2016, p. 264). Marx and Engels argued in *The Manifesto of the Communist Party* (1848) that the "logic of capitalism points to the formation of a single world market", a process, however, which is "inherently unstable" (Jessop 1999, p. 26).

To simplify, for neoclassics, unified international markets are a kind of natural state, created by the natural force of individual voluntary behaviour based on economic interest, hampered only by political regulation (cf. Steger 2015, p. 30). For neoclassic economics, globalisation is brought about by the nature of man, for Marxist economics by the nature of capital. By contrast, a social science perspective perceives economic globalisation as a complex of *contingent* economic, social and political processes which also include the use of power, repression and coercion.

Institutionalist thinking paints another picture and draws on at least two principally different, but not incompatible institutionalist approaches of economic behaviour (cf. Bell and Hindmoor 2015, pp. 332–340).

First, institutions create concrete incentives (constraints) which steer the behaviour of instrumentally rational agents whose preferences are exogenously predefined (institutionalist rational choice approach). Second, agents' ideas, beliefs, mental models and collective cultures shape their behaviour within institutions, along with actors who have agency within institutions and are continuously interpreting them and their own interests, and with institutions which may even generate actors' preferences (interpretative institutionalist approach). From this understanding, it may be—above all—the *idea* of globalisation which generates and fosters globalisation and globalisation policies.

How can economic globalisation be principally assessed? Mainstream economics appreciates increasing international interconnectedness via trade and investment in open markets. Liberalisation of trade and capital movements, internationalisation of production, consumption and finance will increase competition and competitiveness, hence productivity and economic efficiency of open economies, economic growth and the overall level of economic wealth of participating nations, regions or industries.

As a rule, the internationalisation of a market increases the number of competing companies and reinforces competition. But on the level of stakeholder groups, different outcomes are to be expected: customers may benefit from better products or price cuts, prosperous companies' shareholders from higher returns on investment, employees, perhaps, from higher earnings. On the other hand, less competitive enterprises will suffer from falling yields and their employees from wage reduction or losses of jobs. In general, employees in globalised sectors may be affected by increasing intensity of labour, subsequent decline of the performance/pay-relation and job insecurity.

For the system level, however, mainstream economics' market models predict a higher degree of overall economic efficiency when the internationalisation of a market increases economic competition. Although the general empirical assessment of economic globalisation remains a contested issue, some evidence seems to rather support a mainly positive evaluation (Potrafke 2015). Based on its models, mainstream economics generally advocates free international markets whereas it usually remains silent on consequences for inequalities and distribution policies and (un)sustainability. Thus, the unequal impact of globalisation in various dimensions may be underestimated.

Narrow national approaches to the impact of economic globalisation are problematic. They blank the manifold forms of transnational and subnational economic interconnectedness like corporate economies with global regimes of rights and duties, global commodity chains, border-crossing economic regions or transnational migrant workers' networks, global care chains or migrants' money transmittances. Even financial markets, an epitomisation of the global homogenous market of mainstream economics, have turned out to be shaped by national markets, institutions and economic policies, different key agents' beliefs, preferences and patterns of behaviour, different corporate cultures within the same institutional setting (Bell and Hindmoor 2015).

Financial Markets and Globalisation

Notwithstanding, financial markets are deemed to be the incarnation of an integrated, borderless economy. Mainstream economics' modelling, in principle, equals the impact of free flows of goods with free capital movement. Provided that they are liberalised, capital markets would secure savings to allocate more efficiently around the world, and free foreign finance would fuel domestic investment and growth. The famous "market efficiency hypothesis" has transferred this merchandise market model and the assumption of a frictionless functioning of its unbiased, self-adjusting mechanisms to financial markets (Arestis and Singh 2010).

Criticism, however, challenges this analogy and stresses specificities of capital markets like information asymmetry, agency problems or moral hazard because of which the theory of welfare gains through free trade in goods cannot be simply transferred to free capital markets (Arestis and Singh 2010). For Keynesians, the often failing self-coordination of financial markets tends to create suboptimal low level equilibria. In a post-Keynesian view, unsurmountable uncertainty, wide-spread speculation, and, in consequence, intrinsic instability of financial markets are the main causes of financial crises.

Empirically, structural financial imbalances characterise a world economy with liberalised capital markets. They comprise, for instance, current account deficits and surpluses, a general shift to risky, finance-led speculative international investment or the flow of capital from poor to rich economies. The upsurge of globalised, de-regulated finance has boosted the income of capital owners, executives and employees of this sector, thus exacerbating income inequality (Philippon and Reshef 2012).

The model mechanism that more market pressure, principally, fosters the intensity of competition may be empirically backed by banking markets showing that executives' propensity of taking risk to not fall behind "the market" increases significantly (Bell and Hindmoor 2015, pp. 156–164). On the downside, such a rise of competition fosters risky investments entailing a higher degree of systemic uncertainty. Policies creating and enforcing rules for competition, merger and takeover may provide for some risk limitation, but such policies may be more feasible on the national level and difficult to attain in international settings with very different national interests in an industry (cf. for banking in Australia and Canada Bell and Hindmoor 2015, pp. 259–288).

Most importantly, globalisation policies drive economic and financial integration of national economies and markets and thus enable crises to spread quickly around the globe (Stiglitz 2016, p. 6), especially in the global finance industries. Whereas the globalisation of finance like internationalisation of banking, investment banking, pension funds, private equity firms, rating agencies and benchmarking may improve competition, company performance and industry efficiency, it extends risk taking on the system level of finance (Stiglitz 2016, p. 29).

Economics Shapes the Economy

Until recently, mainstream economics' models proving the efficiency of markets built strongly upon an atomistic view of the economic world, conceived as populated by rational independent individuals and aggregate outcomes of independent individual behaviour at the system level. This basic assumption neglected the diverse institutional embedding of economies and markets, for example, industry standards, commercial customs or international trade law, and the impact of economic organisation and organisations, think of international supply chains, multinational corporations or the World Trade Organisation (WTO). Today, institutionalist strands of economics and socio-economics emphasise the relevance of institutions and organisations for economic analysis.

The interdependency of economics 'theory and economies' reality has to be taken into account (performativity of economics; MacKenzie et al. 2007). Mainstream economics' theories and instruments strongly shaped beliefs and policies, at least in North America and Western Europe (Hirschman and Berman 2014, p. 801). International economic institutions and regimes, for instance, have been constructed following economics' theories, and economists fill many of its positions and endorse economics' based policies (Chwieroth 2010; Stiglitz 2002, pp. 34–37). Thus, economics has become performative in terms of contributing to create the reality its models have—so far counterfactually—assumed.

More generally, economics can have effects via four sources of power of economists: professional authority, institutional positions in policymaking and cognitive models present in policymaking infrastructure as patterns of thinking or sociotechnical devices (Fourcade 2009, pp. 247–250; Hirschman and Berman 2014, p. 790). Examples are the influence of economists and their economics on policies of key players like the World Bank, International Monetary Fund, World Trade Organisation or European Commission.

National Economies and Governments in Times of Globalisation

Dimensions and levels of globalisation differ from nation to nation, from region to region, from industry to industry, and so do effects of globalisation, e.g. their repercussions on socioeconomic inequality across countries or within a country. However, empirical evidence for the distribution of income is ambiguous (Dicken 2015, pp. 308–328). In developed economies, for example, the openness to international trade tends to favour high-skilled labour at the expense of low-skilled workers because of foreign low-wage competition. Although globalisation seems to operate as the driver of economic inequality, other mechanisms like offshoring, foreign investment or information and communication technologies also foster inequality (cf. Rodrik 2015, pp. 138–145). Economic inequality may rise in terms of wage differentials, capital assets and income, political inequality in form of political power of capital. At the same time, empirical evidence shows that the *over-all* prosperity level of many countries has improved whereas the gap between the rich and the poorest seems to have widened (Dicken 2015, pp. 308–313; Potrafke 2015).

Obviously, most national governments cannot escape economic pressure from globalisation. Quite the contrary, external economic constraints matter, the "impossibility of complete national economic autonomy" seems to be hard facts (Hirst et al. 2009, p. 67). The example of international *corporate* tax competition illustrates that global economic change may trigger national policy change (Genschel and Seelkopf 2015, p. 250).

But governments still do matter because they evidently have a considerable choice of different domestic policies. Economic trade theory, for instance, holds that the winners of globalisation could be made to compensate the losers, but in reality compensatory policies are very rare (Stiglitz 2013, p. 79). As a complex of economic processes, globalisation neither enforces welfare cuts nor tax relief for higher income earners or income from capital. Accordingly, there is no evidence of a general decline of the welfare state driven by economic globalisation. Rather, policies and effects strongly differ depending on country size (Genschel and Seelkopf 2015, pp. 249–250). In addition, whether and which groups pursuing compensation for or insurance against losses from economic globalisation are successful or not depends on national power relationships and policies. The political outcome, again, "is contingent on configurations of national democratic institutions" (Swank 2001, p. 139).

Moreover, and most importantly, it is national institutions such as the employment system, education system and welfare regime "which channel the rising uncertainty in times of globalization in specific ways" (Buchholz et al. 2009, p. 55). Although, for instance, national policies like labour market flexibilisation are generally justified by pressure from economic *globalisation*, they are designed and decided on the *national* level in different ways with varied outcomes, e.g. for the uncertainty of life courses and patterns of social inequality (Buchholz et al. 2009, p. 67).

Remarkably, uncertainty and inequality in the context of domestic effects of globalisation-related policies affect rather *specific* groups than the labour force or the economy as a whole. In most European countries, for example, qualified men in mid-career enjoyed protection from economic globalisation pressure whereas young adults were the main losers (Buchholz et al. 2009, p. 67). Socioeconomic inequality is often home-grown and not so much caused by globalisation. Some empirical backing for this interpretation is provided by research showing "that globalization triggers a strengthening of existing social inequality structures" of present-day class societies (Buchholz et al. 2009, p. 67). Further evidence is widespread tax relief for big corporations and higher-income earners but not for small business and employees (opportunity of tax evasion).

States and governments, however, not only matter on their domestic level. Nation states still have agency to cooperate in designing and enforcing *international* governance to re-regulate key issues of economic globalisation (Hirst et al. 2009, pp. 232–239). On the international level, governments still play a crucial role in the collective institutional design of global economic regimes, in which entities like the WTO or IMF function as "powerful capabilities for the making of a new order" (Sassen 2008, p. 420).

In the long run of such polycentric governance of economic globalisation, some scholars envisage "a world of global federalism" (Rodrik 2007, pp. 211–212). It may emerge from integrative global technologies, people's experience of the benefits of an increasingly efficient world market, claims of citizens for securing the current accountability of politicians to a definite electorate, and the insight of self-perceived loser and winner groups into the advantages of efficacious supranational rules and standards.

However, at the national level and, above all, from a global perspective, a severe tension between efficiency, equity, and legitimacy remains and awaits a solution which can only be political by nature (cf. Dicken 2015, pp. 354–380; Rodrik 2007). A widespread institutionalist argument holds that a globally integrated world with free global markets requires global institutions, global coordination and global economic governance (cf. Ocampo and Stiglitz 2012; Rodrik 2011).

Yet the emergence of a world polity seems to be even more remote than the integrated world economy. As evidence from network analysis of international governmental and non-governmental organisations shows, the world polity is institutionalised, above all, at various regional levels and much less on a global scale (Beckfield 2010, p. 1026). In this regard, nation states may "assert and transform sovereignty through the construction of regional polities"; a paramount example is provided by the European Union (Beckfield 2010, p. 1055).

Political Debate and Globalisation Policies

In many countries, globalisation policies of national governments and supranational bodies like the European Commission are highly controversial. Key controversies centre on questions such as which groups will be exposed to global market forces, which will benefit, which will lose, which will be protected or compensated, and according to which rules are the uncertainties and risks, gains and losses from economic globalisation distributed in the national economy.

Negotiations on free trade agreements like CETA or TTIP, for instance, spark heated debates. Prosperity is more than growth of GDP. Therefore, against all evidence of *general* gains in economic growth through open economies, de-internationalisation and de-globalisation are legitimate options of economic policy. Then, however, the trade-offs of such policies in terms of lost *economic* wealth—as well as possibly informational, cultural and political openness—have to be taken into account (Rodrik 2011, pp. 240–242).

One outcome of economic globalisation policies in general is the big divide between rather free moving goods and capital and sharply restricted labour force. This asymmetry discriminates poor countries in preventing them to selling their competitive manpower abroad, thus hindering their economic development (Rodrik 2007, 9, 237–242).

Migration belongs to the most contentious issues of globalisation and gives rise to political protest from those parts of domestic labour force which feel threatened by employment competition from foreigners and unprotected from their government. Even migration within the European Union fuels fierce political conflicts with far-reaching outcomes like leaving the EU (Brexit).

The broad notion of economic globalisation obscures the big divide of globalisation in terms of rights and protection of business—corporations, capital, trade and professionals—on the one hand, and citizens, labour and migrants, on the other. Corporate actors and trade interests enjoy better international regimes of protection than citizens and migrants. The WTO regime, for example, is much stronger than that of human rights (Sassen 2008, p. 417).

It is important, of course, to differentiate carefully *within* the very broad categories of labour and capital because of the rather diverging impact of globalisation on different types of employees, industries, investors and owners in different economies. Moreover, a very relevant differentiation concerns gender-specific impacts of economic globalisation on labour force, household or care which, again, varies by country, industry and occupation (Benería et al. 2016). Evidence of globalisation's impact on gender justice in terms of employment is mixed, but women tend to be disproportionately among the losers (Dicken 2015, pp. 321–322; Scholte 2007, pp. 334–338).

Some Implications for Education for Global Citizenship

As an issue of global citizenship education, economic globalisation is first and foremost a domestic matter. It concerns vested interests, power relationships and alternative policies of *international* cooperation and global governance as well as alternative policies of dealing *domestically* with challenges and options of globalisation. The design of rules and the distribution of assets and drawbacks are nearly always subject to national political decisions.

As a matter of course, debates on economic globalisation and economic globalisation policies have to take *global* perspectives into account, but they remain strongly anchored in the national polity. Therefore, students should preferably start a critical analysis of—actual or seemingly—globalisation effects in domestic contexts with questioning the *domestic* economic structure, institutions, interests, values, key actors and policies which, intentionally or accidentally, mediate the impact of globalisation in national contexts (McMillan et al. 2014).

Critical global citizenship education, however, teaches students to ask a more fundamental question. They should learn to analyse whether economic pressure from capitalist globalisation is used to transform democracy towards post-democracy (cf. Jessop 2014, p. 102). They should become aware that (economic) theories are contextually embedded and often related to vested interests. This key insight allows deconstructing the legitimisation of current globalisation policies as being without any alternative. Students recognise that invoking globalisation as an absolute necessity for a specific policy may be a convenient political opportunity or a well-considered strategy to legitimise policies, interests and politics by means of shifting the responsibility to anonymous external pressure from "natural" economic processes. In consequence, participatory global citizenship education empowers students to address first and foremost national governments and their political responsibility for national and global globalisation issues.

Against this backdrop, global citizenship education is, above all, a special case of citizenship education applied to global issues. Then, it is about analysing *classical* key issues and asking the social sciences, politicians and stakeholders *standard* questions applied to the case of globalisation and policies.

Relevant key questions are: What are the beliefs behind a model or theory of economic globalisation? Do its assumptions and mechanisms meet a *satisficing* degree of realism? Do they consider real world economic *and* political mechanisms and practices? Are they substantiated by real world data? Which alternative models, theories and policies do exist? Why not choose them? Are the recommended policies feasible? How long does it take until they will work? What are the distributional effects of proposed measures and institutions? Who will be among the winners, who among the losers in economic, social, cultural and political terms? Are the winners legally compelled to compensate the losses of others? Are recommended institutions, policies and practices expected to be reversible or irreversible?

Conclusion

Economic globalisation is a contested issue, and the key debate should focus "on matters of policies and priorities" (Rodrik 2007, p. 222). Moreover, the political debate on globalisation is performed as part of the general conflict about income, power and institutions, "a constant in all societies" and entailing contingent results (Acemoglu and Robinson 2012, p. 431). Globalisation and its policies are contingent and pluralistic processes, considerably shaped by rather persistent country-specific institutional, social and political structures (Buchholz et al. 2009, p. 67).

Today, economic globalisation is an important fact but far from creating a flat world and depriving governments from power and constituencies from political influence. Future research, therefore, should analyse whether citizenship education should frame economic globalisation as a *standard* issue or as a unique topic requesting *specific* approaches. Against much of the empirical evidence, economic globalisation may be treated as a topic among others located in fields of public policy such as international relations, foreign trade policy, macroeconomic policy or income, asset and distribution policy and related to issues of government, governance and the governed. Such a sober approach of global citizenship education, however, is itself up to debate.

Acknowledgement I am very grateful for proposals from Thorsten Hippe which helped very much to conceptualise the chapter.

REFERENCES

Acemoglu, D., & Robinson, J. A. (2012). *Why nations fail: The origins of power, prosperity and poverty.* New York: Crown Publishers.

Arestis, P., Chortareas, G., Desli, E., & Pelagidis, T. (2012). Trade flows revisited: Further evidence on globalisation. *Cambridge Journal of Economics, 36*(2), 481–493.

Arestis, P., & Singh, A. (2010). Financial globalisation and crisis, institutional transformation and equity. *Cambridge Journal of Economics, 34*(2), 225–238.

Beckfield, J. (2010). The social structure of the world polity. *American Journal of Sociology, 115*(4), 1018–1068.

Bell, S., & Hindmoor, A. (2015). *Masters of the universe, slaves of the market.* Cambridge, Massachusetts: Harvard University Press.

Benería, L., Berik, G., & Floro, M. S. (2016). *Gender, development, and globalization: Economics as if all people mattered* (2nd ed.). New York, London: Routledge.

Buchholz, S., Hofäcker, D., Mills, M., Blossfeld, H.-P., Kurz, K., & Hofmeister, H. (2009). Life courses in the globalization process: The development of social inequalities in modern societies. *European Sociological Review, 25*(1), 53–71.

Bureau, J.-C., Guimbard, H., & Jean, S. (2016). *Competing liberalizations: Tariffs and trade in the 21st century* (CEPII Working Paper No. 2016-12). Paris.

Chwieroth, J. M. (2010). *Capital ideas: The IMF and the rise of financial liberalization.* Princeton, NJ: Princeton University Press.

Delhey, J., Deutschmann, E., Graf, T., & Richter, K. (2014). Measuring the Europeanization of everyday life: Three new indices and an empirical application. *European Societies, 16*(3), 355–377.

Deutschmann, E. (2015). Regionalization and globalization in networks of transnational human mobility, 2000–2010. *SSRN Electronic Journal.*

Dicken, P. (2015). *Global shift: Mapping the changing contours of the world economy* (7th ed.). Los Angeles, California: Sage.

Fourcade, M. (2009). *Economists and societies: Discipline and profession in the United States, Britain, and France, 1890s to 1990s.* Princeton: Princeton University Press.

Genschel, P., & Seelkopf, L. (2015). The competition state: The modern state in a global economy. In S. Leibfried, E. Huber, M. Lange, J. D. Levy, F. Nullmeier, & J. D. Stephens (Eds.), *The Oxford handbook of transformations of the state* (pp. 237–252). Oxford: Oxford University Press.

Hirschman, D., & Berman, E. P. (2014). Do economists make policies? On the political effects of economics. *Socio-Economic Review, 12*(4), 779–811.

Hirst, P. Q., Thompson, G., & Bromley, S. (2009). *Globalization in question* (3rd ed.). Cambridge, UK: Polity.

Jessop, B. (1999). Reflections on globalisation and its (il)logic(s). In P. Dicken, P. F. Kelly, L. Krong, K. Olds, & H. W.-C. Yeung (Eds.), *Globalisation and the Asia Pacific. Contested territories* (pp. 19–38). London: Routledge.

Jessop, B. (2014). Finance-dominated accumulation and post-democratic capitalism. In S. Fadda & P. Tridico (Eds.), *Institutions and development after the financial crisis* (pp. 83–105). London: Routledge.

MacKenzie, D. A., Muniesa, F., & Siu, L. (Eds.). (2007). *Do economists make markets? On the performativity of economics.* Princeton: Princeton University Press.

McMillan, M., Rodrik, D., & Verduzco-Gallo, Í. (2014). Globalization, structural change, and productivity growth, with an update on Africa. *World Development, 63,* 11–32.

Ocampo, J. A., & Stiglitz, J. E. (2012). From the G-20 to a Global economic coordination council. *Journal of Globalization and Development, 2*(2), Article 9.

Palermo, G. (2016). Power, competition and the free trader vulgaris. *Cambridge Journal of Economics, 40*(1), 259–281.

Philippon, T., & Reshef, A. (2012). Wages and Human capital in the U.S. Finance: 1909–2006. *The Quarterly Journal of Economics, 127*(4), 1551–1609.

Potrafke, N. (2015). The evidence on globalisation. *The World Economy, 38*(3), 509–552.

Rodrik, D. (2007). *One economics, many recipes: Globalization, institutions, and economic growth.* Princeton: Princeton University Press.

Rodrik, D. (2011). *The globalization paradox: Democracy and the future of the world economy.* New York, London: Norton.

Rodrik, D. (2015). *Economics rules: The rights and wrongs of the dismal science.* New York: Norton.

Sassen, S. (2008). *Territory, authority, rights: From medieval to global assemblages.* Princeton, Oxford: Princeton University Press.

Scholte, J. A. (2007). *Globalization: A critical introduction* (2nd rev. ed.). Basingstoke: Palgrave Macmillan.

Steger, M. (2015). Market globalism. In M. B. Steger, P. Battersby, & J. M. Siracusa (Eds.), *The Sage handbook of globalization* (pp. 23–38). London: Sage.

Stiglitz, J. E. (2002). *Globalization and its discontents.* New York, NY: Norton.

Stiglitz, J. E. (2013). *The price of inequality.* New York, London: Norton.

Stiglitz, J. E. (2016). *Towards a general theory of deep downturns: Presidential address from the 17th World congress of the international economic association.* Houndmills, Basingstoke, New York: Palgrave Macmillan.

Swank, D. (2001). Mobile capital, democratic institutions, and the public economy in advanced industrial societies. *Journal of Comparative Policy Analysis, 3*(2), 133–162.

AUTHOR BIOGRAPHY

Reinhold Hedtke holds the Chair of Social Science Education and Economic Sociology at the Faculty of Sociology at Bielefeld University, Germany. Before moving to Bielefeld University in 2002, he was a Professor of Economics and Economic Education at the University of Education Weingarten. His main research areas are concepts of civic and economic education, approaches and practices of socioeconomic education, participatory citizenship education, theory of socioeconomics and economics of convention. He is editor-in-chief of the Journal of Social Science Education.

CHAPTER 21

Politics, Global Citizenship and Implications for Education

Lynne Parmenter

INTRODUCTION

The aim of this chapter is to examine politics as a perspective and context that has implications for global citizenship education. The Oxford English dictionary definition of politics as "activities associated with the governance of a country or area" is used for the purposes of this chapter, alongside politics defined as the academic study of these activities. The area of focus throughout the chapter is the global level.

The main argument of this chapter is that the field of politics recognizes the emergence of global citizenship in a world of plural citizenships, but that political theory on global citizenship is constrained by (a) the reality of a world politically structured in nation-state form and (b) the pervasiveness of Western discourses and ideologies on global citizenship, bolstered by a strengthening academic dissemination arena that favors these discourses and ideologies. Moving forward from this situation raises debates over whose global citizenship should carry authority and why. This is connected to the issue of global hegemony and global leadership. Further, while the need for change of the modern nation-state system is widely recognized, and evident in such developments as the European Union, there are debates in the politics literature over whether change should be incremental or whether it requires radical restructuring. Finally, there is the issue of how education as a

L. Parmenter (✉)
Centre for Tertiary Teaching and Learning, University of Waikato,
Hamilton, New Zealand
e-mail: lynne.parmenter@waikato.ac.nz

© The Author(s) 2018
I. Davies et al. (eds.), *The Palgrave Handbook of Global Citizenship and Education*, https://doi.org/10.1057/978-1-137-59733-5_21

focus of study is viewed by politics specialists. These issues regarding how to move politics forward in relation to globalization and education have implications for education for global citizenship.

In line with this argument, the chapter is structured into four main sections. The first section examines some of the ways politics specialists conceptualize ideas related to global citizenship. The second section focuses on key issues in politics literature relevant to global citizenship education. This is followed by a section directly discussing implications for global citizenship education. The final section concludes the chapter and suggests recommendations for future research in this area.

CONCEPTUALIZING GLOBAL CITIZENSHIP IN THE POLITICS LITERATURE

The starting point for conceptualizing global citizenship in the politics literature is debate over the changing interwoven concepts of state, globalization, politics, and citizenship. As Carter (2001) points out, citizenship is traditionally defined as membership of a specific political unit that excludes other people and this essential feature of exclusivity "might well suggest that global citizenship is an oxymoron" (p. 7). At the same time, the nature of statehood and states is debated in a globalized world, as Cerny (2013) notes:

> ...the future of statehood itself... is increasingly uncertain and contested at a number of levels in a world characterized by increasing transnational and global problems, cross-cutting political alliances and the emergence of more complex forms of awareness and expectations that new kinds of political action and policy-making are necessary. (p. 33)

One outcome of this increasing uncertainty and blurredness has been a shift of spotlight in the relationship between individual and polity from the traditional focus on "the political unit" to a sharper focus on the "membership" aspect, the people who cause and resolve global problems, engage in political alliances at all levels, and participate in various forms of political action, in other words, citizens. This can also be seen as a shift in focus from citizenship as a legal status to citizenship as activity, in the sense defined by Seubert (2014):

> Citizenship as legal status defines spheres of action without prescribing how one makes use of them; citizenship as activity is related to a political form of life, the flourishing of which one deliberately strives to foster. (p. 548)

As this shift has occurred, definitions of citizenship have gradually widened beyond the narrow legal definition of membership of a specific political unit to incorporate social and cultural aspects. This widened definition of citizenship reflects a widening definition of politics itself, described vividly by Minogue (1995) in the following way:

...politics has broken out from its familiar haunts in legislatures, ministries, and hustings and roams the streets and invades the remotest corners of kitchen and bedroom. (p. 107)

Expanded in this way, global citizenship becomes theoretically possible. Within the literature, important areas of conceptualization exploring these changes include deterritorialized and denationalized citizenship (Benhabib 2004; Sassen 2006, 2007); multicultural citizenship (Kymlicka 1995, 2001) and cosmopolitan citizenship (Linklater 2007).

While the scope of politics in general and citizenship, in particular, have both expanded, Western perspectives on politics and Greek-/Roman-rooted notions of citizenship (Heater 1999) continue to dominate textbooks and academic literature in the field, even in comprehensive textbooks on global politics. To give just one example, by no means isolated, the reference list for a chapter on competing theories, methods and intellectual debates in one college textbook on global politics (Jackson 2013) includes 22 authors, of whom 19 are/were affiliated to US universities. While this is no criticism of the quality of content of the chapter or the book, it illustrates the point that "global politics" tends to be conceptualized in terms of how Western theories are extended to apply to global level rather than in terms of how alternative theories from other parts of the world can be used to address political issues, even in a chapter on competing theories and debates.

Accordingly, discussions of citizenship in the politics literature tend to center on rights and responsibilities. In terms of rights, debates over political and legal rights are framed in terms of human rights at global level, although discussions of human rights at a global governance level always have to go through or consciously bypass the state level (Pegram 2015). Furthermore, although human rights are universally applicable, interpretations of human rights are not universally meaningful in the same way. As Vincent (2010) argues, "rights—including human rights [are] not so much legal facts as a series of socially recognised and accredited reasons for action or inaction" (p. 14). This suggests that more research about conceptualizations of human rights from perspectives of different "socially recognised and accredited reasons for action or inaction" would enrich the discussion. In the area of social rights, discussion at the global level centers on the SDGs, but research on how global governance is/could be organized to facilitate these rights is still in its infancy (Marshall 2014). In terms of responsibilities, the area in which global responsibility has been most thoroughly addressed in the politics literature, as in other fields, is the environment (e.g., Harris 2014).

While Western conceptualisations of citizenship as rights and responsibilities are dominant in the literature, and it has been argued that politics has been slower than other academic fields in decolonizing the discipline (Mills 2015), other conceptualizations of (global) citizenship grounded in other views of politics exist, of course. They include perspectives from specific countries with various political systems. For example, China (Guo 2013), where confident nation-building and expansion of political and economic interests to Africa (Zhao 2015) and other parts of the world, exemplified by the "one belt, one road" initiative (Xinhua 2015), combined with a historical consciousness of Chinese civilization, Communist history and socialist politics, provides fertile ground for conceptualizations that may offer new insights into citizenship. Many views of citizenship from such perspectives are not represented in English-medium global debates, as key researchers may not have the motivation or the ability to publish in a foreign language (English) for an international audience, and leading researchers publishing in the global English-language academic discourse may not be able to read research disseminated in other languages.

Other conceptualizations from different cultural and religious backgrounds are another perspective. For example, (global) citizenship can be conceptualized from the perspective of the Islamic concept of the ummah, or "universal community based on a shared faith" (Hassan 2006, p. 311), which encompasses almost a quarter of the world's population and overwhelmingly advocates much more moderate views of citizenship, governance and self and polity than the extremist views widely publicized in the media. Research exploring conceptualizations grounded in such perspectives would be informative.

As far as other ways of seeing the political world are concerned, feminist perspectives on globalization-related issues are evident in the politics literature (Rai 2002; Shepherd 2015), but it is still relatively difficult to find perspectives from other non-dominant (especially non-Western) research backgrounds. Mirroring the point made earlier about the chapter on competing theories and debates in a college textbook, plenty is written in the politics literature about non-Western places and people, but little of the dominant research literature comes from non-Western places and people. There are exceptions, of course, but it is important to note in this chapter that discusses politics as a perspective and context with implications for global citizenship education that the academic field of politics, like most other fields, is constructed in such a way that Western views predominate and other perspectives often remain unheard. As Shilliam (2011) points out, "the attribution of who can 'think' and produce valid knowledge of human existence has always been political" (p. 2). In the contemporary world, this is played out in access to and management of global academic discourse. While the inequity, assumptions and bias of this global academic discourse have been challenged by some researchers (e.g. Appadurai 2006), they remain entrenched in most fields, including politics (Young 2014), strengthened by the growing pressure on academics in many countries to conform to the global rules of publishing in a particular academic style in international impact factor journals to meet local requirements for obtaining a post, promotion or a Ph.D. Add to this the hegemony of English language in global academic discourse (Flowerdew

2001), and the global balance of power in favour of English-fluent, Western-trained researchers becomes clear. This is not a level playing field.

Returning from academic discourse to the reality of the world, conceptualizations of global citizenship are also influenced by the fact that the economic and social reality of the world has outpaced the political structure of the world. While politics in terms of "activities associated with the governance of a country or area" is still bound largely to state-bound territory, economics and social links cross boundaries much more easily in the age of globalization. Where politics becomes detached from territorial boundaries and defined membership (e.g., through migration, displacement, global media), it can cause strain, as political structures have not yet caught up with the impact of globalization. This is the arena in which the nature and central concepts of global citizenship come into the spotlight. For example, global citizenship is often framed in terms of shared fate and interdependence (Arneil 2007). The principle, however, still rests politically on the requirement that people stay in their own places. Shared fate and interdependence do not count as valid grounds to allow a Syrian refugee to enter and remain in the UK, for example, as recent events have shown. Although migration is an indivisible aspect of globalization, it is much easier if you have a passport from the right country and are choosing to migrate rather than being forced to do so. In this respect, regardless of normative conceptualization, the balance of power in this shared fate and interdependence still lies with certain nation-states and their citizens.

Similarly, there is unlikely to be global equity for as long as the current nation-state system continues to function as it is, simply because there is little incentive for currently powerful nation-states to engage in the restructuring of the world system that would be necessary to make global equity a reality, or even to develop effective ways of working toward this aim. As Held (2006) argues, "the collective issues we must grapple with are of growing extensity and intensity and, yet, the means for addressing these are weak and incomplete" (p. 157). The implications for global citizenship are clear.

In this way, individual states and groups of states still control the politics of global citizenship, and it is not necessarily in their interests to make major changes, just as it is not in the interests of those who control global academic discourse to fundamentally restructure it. While it is recognized that the current global political system does not fully reflect the realities and needs of a globalized world, it is difficult to fundamentally change the political world system when it is under the control of a few nation-states that do not necessarily trust each other and would not necessarily benefit from the changes. At the same time, modifications and challenges to nation-state dominance are appearing in many parts of the world, for example, through multi-layered sub-state and state citizenship such as Hong Kong and China, or Scotland and the United Kingdom, or through state and supra-state multiple citizenship, such as Germany or Malta and the European Union. While such trends do not threaten the existence of nation-states per se, they do blur the edges and raise important questions about the relationship of individuals and polities.

KEY ISSUES AND DEBATES

Having examined some of the main areas of conceptualization around global citizenship in the politics literature, this section turns to some of the key issues in the area. Four key issues are raised here for discussion as being most relevant to education for global citizenship. They are (1) global hegemony and global leadership, (2) whose global citizenship and for what purpose? (3) incremental or radical change, and (4) education as a focus of politics research.

The first issue is global hegemony and global leadership. At present, global hegemony tends to overshadow global leadership, insofar as the leaders of the most powerful states tend to dominate global political action rather than leaders of trans-state institutions such as the United Nations. This, however, raises questions of authority—in the most basic terms, the leaders of the most powerful states are often obliged and more motivated to put their own state ahead of a global perspective when it comes to making decisions, yet the wellbeing of the world's population is dependent to some extent on these decisions. In such cases, leaders are exerting national leadership globally, rather than global leadership. Of course, political leaders do collaborate for global good, as is evident in environmental agreements, for example, but in their exercise of power, their authority usually derives from the state, not from any global status or body. In this respect, as Mendenhall and Bird (2013, p. 167) emphasize, global leadership remains a huge challenge, and this is particularly true of global political leadership, an area that is remarkably under-researched. In an analysis of global political leadership in contrast to leadership in other fields or in domestic spheres, Helms (2014) provides the following definition:

> global political leadership... refers to the actions of actors that pursue particular goals and seek to mobilize support in favour of these goals among potential followers. Typically, these goals relate to the solution of collective problems and the accomplishment of these goals would mark a change of the status quo. (p. 266)

As Helms goes on to emphasize, legitimacy of the leader plays a major role here, as the goals will only be achieved to the extent that "potential followers perceive [the leader's] actions and goals as legitimate" (p. 266). This is a point of tension between global hegemony and global leadership, as authority derived through the state does not necessarily provide global legitimacy, and it may not be in the interests of national leaders to accomplish "change of the status quo" in global terms.

Turning from global leaders to global "followers," the second related issue arising from the politics literature on global citizenship is "Whose global citizenship?" and "For what purpose?" The bias of academic discourse at one level and the reality of a world of unequal states at another level, as discussed in the previous section, raise more questions than answers about issues of global citizenship from a politics perspective. Who is conceptualizing global citizenship in the politics field? On what grounds? Representing whom? In whose interests? For what purposes? These debates are still not fully addressed in the politics literature. The most rigorously developed area of research connecting global leadership (or the lack of it) and global citizenship in the politics literature is research on global governance. Weiss (2013) defines global governance as "collective efforts to identify, understand, or address worldwide problems that go beyond the capacities of individual states to solve.... the capacity within the international system at any moment to provide government-like services and public goods in the absence of a world government" (p. 32). Highlighting a key distinction between national and global governance, he points out that governance at the national level goes hand in hand with government, while governance at global level is "governance minus government," making it much more difficult to exercise control and compliance (p. 32), which suggests that governance is much more dependent on the will and motivations of people involved, the global citizens. Weiss (2013) goes on to outline five gaps that act as barriers to effective global governance, namely, knowledge gaps, gaps in norms, policy gaps, institutional gaps and compliance gaps. While all areas are relevant to global citizenship, the one most pertinent to the questions outlined at the beginning of this paragraph is the norms gap. As Weiss states, "there is no agreement about who can legitimately claim to articulate or pinpoint "global" norms" (p. 49). Neither is there agreement about the extent to which global norms are necessary. However, the argument that greater attention needs to be paid to discussion of global norms and of ethics underpinning those norms is important in debates about global citizenship. As Widdows (2011) emphasizes:

> How we resolve (or fail to resolve) the dilemmas of global ethics will determine the framework of future global governance. This will shape and limit the possible relationships and opportunities of all global actors... (p. 1)

Addressing the questions at the beginning of this paragraph from the viewpoint of norms and ethics through a political lens would potentially open up fruitful insights and discussion on global leadership, global governance, global citizenship, and the connection of the three areas.

At present, the dominant view in discussions of global governance—implicitly or explicitly—tends to be that global governance is or should be an expansion of Western democratic political structures, principles and practices to a global level. Ecker-Ehrhardt (2016) provides an example:

> The idea of democratizing global governance ultimately requires a significant level of global public consensus on the basic rationale of a cosmopolitan order... (p. 111)

Once again, this underlying approach to thinking globally represents the phenomenon discussed earlier of expanding Western ideas to global level, rather than widening the political debate to global level by integrating other perspectives. There are exceptions, for example, Sinclair (2012) provides an interesting analysis of global governance from a range of alternative perspectives, including rejectionism, but there is still potential for research from alternative perspectives in this area, as well as research on the interface between global governance and global citizenship. Exploratory studies on topics such as citizen participation in the UN SDGs consultation process (Fox and Stoett 2016) have been conducted, but research on the political motivations, roles, and impact of global citizens in global governance, particularly from under-represented perspectives, is still lacking.

As the effects of globalization permeate the political as well as economic and social structures of the world, the third issue arising from politics literature in relation to global citizenship is the debate over incremental versus radical change of the state system. From a global citizenship perspective, the starting point for this debate is the idea proposed by Kivisto and Faist (2007) that "people increasingly feel that their ability to possess a genuine voice in decision making is constricted... [because] the decisions with the greatest impact on their lives can no longer be addressed satisfactorily simply at the level of the nation-state" (p. 140). This leads to debates about systems of representation, and who should have a voice in decision-making. The basic argument here is the "all-affected principle," which states that all those affected by a decision should have a say in the making of the decision. Broadly speaking, this argument is developed in two ways: the first is incremental change of the existing state system, and the second is fundamental restructuring of the same system. Following the incremental approach, the argument is that those people affected by the policy decision of a particular government or governing body should have rights to voice an opinion on this decision through proportional or reciprocal citizenship rights, labeled by Koenig-Archibugi (2012) as "fuzzy citizenship." For Koenig-Archibugi, the proposed solution is to widen citizenship rights flexibly, on a case-by-case basis, so that "participatory entitlements with regard to the decision-making process of those jurisdictions are accorded to all those who are likely to be causally affected by any possible decision under any possible agenda, rather than only to individuals with a privileged legal relationship to the jurisdiction (nationals) or those formally bound to comply with policy decisions because of their presence in the territory (residents)" (p. 457). In this view, the scope of state and citizenship is adjusted, but basic notions of state and citizenship are left intact. In contrast, the radical restructuring argument is based on fundamental scrutiny of the notions of state and citizenship. At the level of academic discourse, the point is made by Arneil (2007):

...liberal theory in its classical form used citizenship to assimilate "others" into a certain set of supposedly "universal" norms that in reality reflected Euro/Anglo-centrism and fraternalism, respectively. Thus, what emerges in late twentieth century citizenship theory, under the auspices of feminism, multiculturalism and post-colonial theories is not so much a call for universal inclusion under an existing set of political principles, but a rearticulation of the principles themselves..." (p. 311)

Extending this idea, the argument is that liberal theory, as "the metacategory of Western political discourse" (Bell 2014, p. 683), has been extremely powerful in shaping ideas about citizenship and associated concepts such as rights and democracy, but that continued assumptions that the theory is correct and just needs to be expanded further and/or adjusted to fit different contexts may need to be questioned. That is, there may be a need to go back and rethink core principles, including basic notions about the individual, society, the citizen, the state, and the world, and the relationships between them. Taking political theory to this level means going against the grain, and the challenges of doing this are explained by Sterling-Folker (2015), in her discussion of how international relations theory operates within acceptable boundaries, allowing limited analytical diversity that actually serves to perpetuate dominant liberal discourse:

Like the larger global political project it reflects, I suspect that the landscape of IR theory enjoys a kind of circumscribed analytical diversity in which multiple voices may speak but power does not listen. (p. 42)

As Sterling-Folker suggests here, political academic discourse is reflecting rather than challenging the global system. The lack of will to engage in fundamental restructuring of political conceptualization, even at theoretical level, must be even greater at the level of reality, where vested interests and power are magnified many times over.

Finally, the fourth issue, which is directly relevant to education for global citizenship, is education as a focus of interest for politics specialists. It would be difficult to find a government that does not pay attention to education, whether this is through education policy, curriculum standards, control of textbooks, teacher education, assessment or other means. Yet, unlike other areas of state/regional policy, education has not been a major field of study in its own right among politics specialists. Jakobi Martens and Wolf (2010) point out "the stunning discrepancy between the important position of education on the current political agenda and the reluctant attitude of political scientists towards this phenomenon" (p. 3), emphasizing that "education policy as a field of political science has been under-researched despite its growing significance on the political agendas worldwide" (p. 218). While education specialists have built up a substantial body of knowledge and research on the politics of education and education policy, politics specialists seem to have shown little interest in the field of education, especially school-level education. A brief perusal of three comprehensive college textbooks on global politics (Heywood 2011; Jackson 2013; Mansbach and Rafferty 2008) supports this argument. While all three textbooks cover environment, economics, development, terrorism, human rights, international organizations and identity, none have any section on education, and none even include "education" in the index. Enders (2010) calls this a "neglected relationship," but argues that:

> ...recent developments in the field of education have created new windows of opportunity for the study of this societal sub-system from the perspective of political science. The relationship between the nation-state and education is continuously changing and education has become a field of major social transformations and political experimentation. (p. 214)

Given that education has not been a major focus for politics specialists, it is hardly surprising that research on global citizenship education within the politics field is yet to be developed.

These four issues—global hegemony and global leadership, the political questions of whose global citizenship and what for, raising questions about links between global citizenship and global governancev, the debate over incremental or radical change, and the issue of education as a focus of study in the politics literature—demonstrate from different angles some of the actual and possible contributions politics research makes and could make to discussions of global citizenship education.

IMPLICATIONS FOR EDUCATION FOR GLOBAL CITIZENSHIP

On the basis of the conceptualizations and issues outlined in the previous two sections, this section focuses on five specific implications of the views of politics specialists and gaps in the politics literature for education for global citizenship.

The first implication relates to historical understanding of the current political world order of states. Alongside education about international organizations and the position and role of one's own state and other states in the world, it is important that young people learn about the way in which the current world system and balance of power in the world has come about. It is only by understanding this that they can question the current political world system and see issues from alternative perspectives. For example, learning about the United Nations Security Council and its role is important, but so is consideration of why the five permanent members of the Security Council are China, France, Russia, the UK and the USA, why 60 United Nations member states have never been members of the UN Security Council, and what the implications are for decisions made about the world. In this respect, politics literature, including international relations and global politics textbooks, provides a valuable resource for education for informed global citizenship.

The second implication concerns awareness and development of multiple perspectives on global inequity and global citizenship. This means building on the historical understanding mentioned above, but moving beyond knowledge and understanding to be able to comprehend and engage with global inequity and global citizenship from unfamiliar perspectives. This requires intercultural competence combined with political understanding, but can be approached at many different levels. In concrete terms, for example, a project exploring how global citizenship differs from the perspective of an international business executive and his family in the USA and a refugee and her family in Lebanon would develop students' political knowledge and understanding as well as their intercultural competence. The ability to see multiple perspectives in this way, although largely lacking in the politics literature as discussed above, is considered to be a core skill for living in a globalized world (Greenstein 2012).

Connected to this is the third implication of rethinking political relations in terms of global governance. Education for global citizenship still sits firmly within the purview of national governments. Although this does not preclude the possibility of teachers and students developing a global view of the world, including of their own state and government, it requires development of the ability to switch channels of vision from state-global to global-state. In other words, as well as seeing a global issue through the lens of the state, for example, the Paris Agreement (within the United Nations Framework Convention on Climate Change) through their own country's engagement with it, students also develop the ability to take a global view and see the impact and implications of the Paris Agreement on a number of countries, including their own, from a global governance perspective.

The fourth implication relates to the issue of global political leadership. While this is still a developing field of research in the politics literature, there are important issues to be addressed here in regard to education for global citizenship. At local and national levels, citizens generally know who their leaders are, and have a more or less clear idea of what they are supposed to be doing. At the global level, it is difficult to claim that this is the case (Sell 2014). Who are the global political leaders? What can global political leaders actually do? Whose agendas do they follow? What can they achieve and not achieve in the current world system, and why? How do they collaborate and what happens when they disagree? Even if there are no clear answers to these questions at present, they are questions that need to be addressed in education for global citizenship.

Finally, the fifth implication is the need to encourage creativity, imagination and ideas in education for global citizenship. As referred to above, there are gaps in the politics literature, and substantial areas of innovative research to be done as politics catches up with rapid global change. These gaps can also provide a stimulus for education for global citizenship by providing a discursive space of possibilities rather than established set answers.

Children growing up in a globalized world, where the existing world political system is showing cracks but no alternative is yet apparent, have the capacity to imagine otherwise.

There are many other possible implications emerging from perspectives from politics literature, of course, but these seem to be important points to consider for researchers and teachers in the area of education for global citizenship.

CONCLUSION AND RECOMMENDATIONS REGARDING FUTURE RESEARCH

The aim of this chapter was to examine politics literature as a perspective and context with implications for global citizenship education. As discussed in this chapter, politics literature provides useful insights into global citizenship (education) in terms of conceptualizations of citizenship, the state and the world, relationships between individuals and polities, and discussions around leadership, governance and change, through lenses including authority, legitimacy and participation. Having said that, education per se has not been a major focus of politics education in recent years, and there is potential for much more research in this area from politics perspectives. The following three areas, for example, would provide a valuable foundation for global citizenship education teaching and research.

1. Political research examining non-Western conceptualizations, perceptions, and experiences of the changing relationships between individuals and polities, and of citizenship at all levels.
2. More political research on education in general and areas related to global citizenship education in particular, including the politics of global citizenship in global agendas, e.g., UN and OECD, and in diverse contexts.
3. More applied research conducted collaboratively by politics and education specialists to explore ways of effectively using politics research and concepts to inform education for global citizenship.

With global citizenship now officially part of the Sustainable Development Goals, politics has an important part to play in contributing to the conceptualization of education that, in the words of UN Secretary General Ban Ki-Moon (UN News Centre 2016), "empowers people to contribute to our common future."

REFERENCES

Appadurai, A. (2006). The right to research. *Globalisation, Societies and Education,* *4*(2), 167–177.

Arneil, B. (2007). Global citizenship and empire. *Citizenship Studies, 11*(3), 301–328.

Bell, D. (2014). What is liberalism? *Political Theory, 42*(6), 682–715.

Benhabib, S. (2004). *The rights of others. Aliens, residents and citizens.* Cambridge: Cambridge University Press.

Carter, A. (2001). *The political theory of global citizenship.* Abingdon: Routledge.

Cerny, P. (2013). Globalization and statehood. In M. Beeson & N. Bisley (Eds.), *Issues in 21st century world politics* (pp. 30–46). Basingstoke: Palgrave Macmillan.

Enders, J. (2010). Political science and educational research: Windows of opportunity for a neglected relationship. In A. Jakobi, K. Martens, & K. D. Wolf (Eds.), *Education in political science: Discovering a neglected field* (pp. 205–217). Abingdon: Routledge.

Ecker-Ehrhardt, M. (2016). Why do citizens want the UN to decide? Cosmopolitan ideas, particularism and global authority. *International Political Science Review, 37*(1), 99–114.

Flowerdew, J. (2001). Attitudes of journal editors to nonnative speaker contributions. *TESOL Quarterly, 35*(1), 121–150.

Fox, O., & Stoett, P. (2016). Citizen participation in the UN sustainable development goals consultation process: Toward global democratic governance? *Global Governance, 22*(4), 555–573.

Greenstein, L. (2012). *Assessing 21st century skills: A guide to evaluating mastery and authentic learning.* Thousand Oaks: Corwin.

Guo, S. (2013). *Chinese politics and government: Power, ideology, and organization.* Abingdon: Routledge.

Harris, Paul (Ed.). (2014). *Routledge handbook of global environmental politics.* Abingdon: Routledge.

Hassan, R. (2006). Globalisation's challenge to the Islamic *ummah. Asian Journal of Social Science, 34*(2), 311–323.

Heater, D. (1999). *What is citizenship?.* Cambridge: Polity Press.

Held, D. (2006). Reframing global governance: Apocalypse soon or reform! *New Political Economy, 11*(2), 157–176.

Helms, L. (2014). Global political leadership in the twenty-first century: Problems and prospects. *Contemporary Politics, 20*(3), 261–277.

Heywood, A. (2011). *Global politics.* Basingstoke: Palgrave Macmillan.

Jackson, R. (2013). *Global politics in the 21st century.* Cambridge: Cambridge University Press.

Jakobi, A., Martens, K., & Wolf, K. D. (2010). Introduction. In A. Jakobi, K. Martens, & K. D. Wolf (Eds.), *Education in political science: Discovering a neglected field* (pp. 1–20). Abingdon: Routledge.

Kivisto, P., & Faist, T. (2007). *Citizenship: Discourse, theory, and transnational prospects.* Oxford: Blackwell.

Koenig-Archibugi, M. (2012). Fuzzy citizenship in global society. *The Journal of Political Philosophy, 20*(4), 456–480.

Kymlicka, W. (1995). *Multicultural citizenship: A liberal theory of minority rights.* Oxford: Oxford University Press.

Kymlicka, W. (2001). *Politics in the vernacular: Nationalism, multiculturalism and citizenship.* Oxford: Oxford University Press.

Linklater, A. (2007). *Critical theory and world politics: Sovereignty, citizenship and humanity.* Abingdon: Routledge.

Mansbach, R., & Rafferty, K. (2008). *Introduction to global politics*. Abingdon: Routledge.

Marshall, K. (2014). Global development governance. In T. Weiss & R. Wilkinson (Eds.), *International organization and global governance* (pp. 564–579). Abingdon: Routledge.

Mendenhall, M., & Bird, A. (2013). In search of global leadership. *Organizational Dynamics, 42,* 167–174.

Mills, C. (2015). Decolonizing Western political philosophy. *New Political Science, 37*(1), 1–24.

Minogue, K. (1995). *Politics: A very short introduction*. Oxford: Oxford University Press.

Pegram, T. (2015). Global human rights governance and orchestration: National human rights institutions as intermediaries. *European Journal of International Relations., 21*(3), 595–620.

Rai, S. (2002). *Gender and the political economy of development: From nationalism to globalization*. Cambridge: Polity.

Sassen, S. (2006). *Territory, authority, rights: From medieval to global assemblages*. Princeton: Princeton University Press.

Sassen, S. (2007). Response. *European Journal of Political Thought, 6*(4), 431–444.

Sell, S. (2014). Who governs the globe? In T. Weiss & R. Wilkinson (Eds.), *International organization and global governance* (pp. 73–85). Abingdon: Routledge.

Seubert, S. (2014). Dynamics of modern citizenship democracy and peopleness in a global era. *Constellations: An International Journal of Critical & Democratic Theory, 21*(4), 547–559.

Shepherd, L. (Ed.). (2015). *Gender matters in global politics: A feminist introduction to international relations* (2nd ed.). Abingdon: Routledge.

Shilliam, R. (2011). Non-Western thought and international relations. In R. Shilliam (Ed.), *International relations and non-Western thought*. Abingdon: Routledge.

Sinclair, T. (2012). *Global governance*. Cambridge: Polity.

Sterling-Folker, J. (2015). All hail to the chief: Liberal IR theory in the new world order. *International Studies Perspectives, 16,* 40–49.

UN News Centre. (2016). DPI/NGO: Let us work together to foster education for global citizenship. Ban tells UN conference. Retrieved from http://www.un.org/apps/news/story.asp?NewsID=54086#.WDqk0_mLSUk.

Vincent, A. (2010). *The politics of human rights*. Oxford: Oxford University Press.

Weiss, T. (2013). *Global governance: Why? What? Whither?* Cambridge: Polity.

Widdows, H. (2011). *Global ethics: An introduction*. London: Routledge.

Xinhua. (2015, March 28). China unveils action plan on Belt and Road Initiative. Retrieved from http://english.gov.cn/news/top_news/2015/03/28/content_281475079055789.htm.

Young, A. (2014). Western theory, global world: Western bias in international theory. *Harvard International Review, 36*(1), 29–31.

Zhao, S. (Ed.). (2015). *China in Africa: Strategic motives and economic interests*. London: Routledge.

AUTHOR BIOGRAPHY

Lynne Parmenter After earning a Ph.D. in education from Durham University (UK) in 1997, Lynne Parmenter held academic posts at Fukushima University and Waseda University in Japan, then moved to Manchester Metropolitan University (UK) as international lead of the Faculty of Education. After this, she spent 4 years in Kazakhstan, helping to set up a new Graduate School of Education in the role of Vice-Dean. Since February 2017, she has been working at University of Waikato in New Zealand. Her research interests cover global citizenship education, intercultural education and language education at all levels from school through university.

CHAPTER 22

Culture and Citizenship

Theresa Alviar-Martin

INTRODUCTION

Culture and citizenship are inextricably linked (Ladson-Billings 2004). Historically, the political legitimacy of nation-states was built upon the conjoining of the political entity of a state with the cultural identity of a nation (Couldry 2006). Culture was mobilized as a means of strengthening citizens' national identities by emphasizing shared values, territories, histories, and beliefs (Kymlicka 1995). Conditions of globalization, however, raise questions regarding the ways nationalistic constructions of culture and citizenship reflect dominant groups' agendas while diminishing the entitlement of cultural minorities to attain the full spectrum of social and political rights. Transnational flows of ideas and capital, furthermore, have compelled examination of how individuals' affiliations based on class, gender, race, religion, or language complicate notions of cultural identity and inform emerging conceptions of citizenship unanchored from the nation-state (Banks 2008).

The fluidity of culture and citizenship in the era of globalization implicates the historical role of schools as sites of institutionalized learning where policies, curriculum, and pedagogies are strongly associated with nations' cultural and political traditions (Hahn and Alviar-Martin 2008). Thus, schools today face questions regarding how to welcome students from diverse cultural backgrounds, acknowledge and develop their multilayered identities, and cultivate national values while recognizing young citizens' potential to build affinities to the shared human community of common argument and aspiration (Nussbaum 2002).

T. Alviar-Martin (✉)
Education University of Hong Kong, Hong Kong, People's Republic of China
e-mail: tpbalviar@ied.edu.hk

© The Author(s) 2018
I. Davies et al. (eds.), *The Palgrave Handbook of Global Citizenship and Education*, https://doi.org/10.1057/978-1-137-59733-5_22

The following chapter explores the intersections of culture and citizenship. I begin by discussing conceptions of culture and citizenship within the nation-state, then highlight issues in the global context. I consider implications for global citizenship and education and conclude by recommending future research directions in light of emerging global cultures and questions regarding policies and practice of civic education.

CULTURE, CITIZENSHIP, AND THE NATION-STATE

Scholarship in various disciplines has brought attention to the intersections of culture and citizenship. This section outlines key principles surrounding culture as shared identity. I then discuss theories of citizenship within the nation-state to illustrate conceptions of identity, cultural diversity, and equality.

Culture and Shared Identities

Culture is a system of shared meanings that allows people to communicate, maintain, and develop an approach and understanding of life (Sorrells 2013). Anthropologists emphasize how shared symbolic systems—embodied in words, images, action, and ideas—construct a framework of reality within a social group. Through communication, groups are able to "transmit patterns of meaning" across generations, and "perpetuate and develop their knowledge and attitudes about life" (Geertz 1973, p. 89). Although culture is ever changing, common histories, geographic location, language, or social class create values, symbols, and interpretations that shape groups' identities. These may manifest overtly, through artifacts and technology; or less tangibly, such as through orientations toward time, gender role assignations, or outlook regarding individualism and collectivism (Spring 2008).

Culture as shared meaning focuses on local constructions of identity that develop within micro-cultures organized along commonalities such as ethnicity, religion, or language. Historically, common identities and values became the basis of governance among tribal groups and early civilizations. Aspects of culture such as religion framed societal structures and hierarchies, as evidenced by the Egyptian and early Roman empires where rulers functioned as both religious and political figureheads. These models presaged the divine right of kings in European monarchies, and resonate in the West African Ashanti kingdom's leadership system and the "mandate of heaven" that bestowed conditional legitimacy over rulers in East Asian societies (Beasley 1999).

History likewise points to the ways shared identities extended to the community of human beings, which is captured in the idea of cosmopolitanism (Appiah 2008). Cosmopolitanism's origins are often traced to the Stoics; however, cosmopolitan principles are evident in cultural traditions across societies. Buddhism speaks of the essential equality of all humanity.

Early Confucian scholars exhorted harmony among citizens and between people and nature (Sen 2010). Aljunied (in press) writes of deep cosmopolitan foundations embedded within societies across Muslim Southeast Asia.

Spring (2008) contrasts two cultural traditions to illustrate how shared meanings shape people's worldviews and fundamental understandings of knowledge. Many aboriginal cultures develop "indigenous knowledge" that reflects a systems view of the world (Ishemo 2004). It is an empirically based body of information and beliefs gained through careful observation about relationships between living things and their environment. Indigenous knowledge is conveyed through narratives or metaphorical language, passed on from one generation to the next through oral traditions, and includes a system of organization that governs resource use. In contrast, "scientific knowledge" that is based on rational worldviews rooted in the European Enlightenment categorically organizes ideas and emphasizes discrete ways of seeing and knowing the world. It separates intellectual activity from the emotional domain and amplifies the fragmentation of the individual and the world, because it reifies human beings' dominion over other species rather than interconnectedness with nature (Houde 2007).

Culture as shared identity further underlines the role of power, particularly, the ability of dominant groups to establish systems by which minority cultures are included in society. Early cultural studies scholarship—informed by Marxist and critical theories—illustrates how culture operates as a form of hegemony, or domination through consent (Gramsci 1971); where the goals, ideas, and interests of the ruling group or class are normalized and institutionalized so that people consent to their own subordination (Sorrells 2013). Viewed from the lens of hegemony, the dominance of certain cultures and worldviews—such as scientific knowledge, patriarchal social systems, and heteronomativity—are the result of colonization, political and educational systems imposed by Western colonizing powers, normalization through constant use, and the exoticizing of alternative ways of thinking (Willinsky 1999).

Citizenship, Diversity, and Equality

The rise of nation-states in the modern era brought attention to national identities based on citizenship. Conventional political thought argues that building a shared national culture is "an essential lubricant of the wheels of citizenship and politics" (Almond and Verba 1989; Couldry 2006, p. 322). Nations, thus, seek to strengthen common cultures and experiences. Yet, democratic theories forward a concept of citizenship premised upon citizens' equal status, and therefore, democratic societies must pursue the inclusion of different cultural groups under the protection of political frameworks. Marshall's (1964) explication of cultural citizenship extended these arguments to cover civic rights such as freedom of speech and political rights such as voting, but also social rights that provided citizens with the health and education needed to participate fully in their cultural communities and the national civic culture.

Dominant groups, however, are likely to define national culture by continuing the hegemony of colonialism and patriarchal systems (Mohanty 2003). Governments and elites wield the power to normalize culture and delineate parameters of inclusion through social policies, schooling, and media; enabling dominant groups to forward assimilationist agendas while maintaining institutional barriers that perpetuate social inequalities. In the USA, Whites "have the luxury of substituting their cultural identities for an 'American' identity" (Ladson-Billings 2004, p. 113). Their interests are usually equated as the "public" interest, whereas "those of people of color...are regarded as 'special' interests that undermine the polity" (Banks 2008, p.132). Such arguments are evident in criticisms of affirmative action policies in the United States and in French municipalities' recent attempts to ban Muslim women's use of *burkini* on public beaches (Fishwick 2016).

Three narratives of citizenship illustrate approaches toward cultural diversity within democratic societies. Each offers different visions of individual and group identities, citizens' rights and participation in the public sphere, and equality for cultural minorities. The *liberal* view emphasizes citizens' rights to construct their own identities while escaping the confines of traditional roles and fixed identities. Although liberalism promotes visions of citizenship as possibility, it posits group rights as inimical to individual rights, and assumes that strong attachments to ethnic, religious, and other identity groups lead to harmful divisions within societies (Osler and Starkey 2005). Thus, proponents of liberalism have often extolled the primacy of individual rights to rationalize cultural minorities' assimilation into the dominant national culture (Banks 2008).

Communitarianism acknowledges the importance of a sense of identity conferred by a cultural group; however, it limits individuals to predetermined identities within which they may not feel at ease. Meanwhile, *civic republicanism* underlines political institutions' capacities to resolve societal conflicts. It recognizes cultural groups' rights and emphasizes responsibilities to the community as a public sphere regulated by the state; but restricts identities of class, religion, or culture to the private sphere (Osler and Starkey 2005). For Kymlicka (1995), communitarian and civic republican approaches fail to take into account the historical and structural discrimination faced by minority groups. In his arguments for multiculturalism, he calls for group rights to help marginalized groups—specifically those excluded on the basis of language and ethnicity—to attain civic equality. Similarly, Young (1997) decries nationalistic conceptions of universal citizenship where principles of equal treatment are strictly applied, but result in cultural minorities becoming second-class citizens, especially within stratified societies. Instead, she proposes a differentiated citizenship that considers the history of how the group became a cultural minority and the degree to which the group has been welcomed into the economic and political life of society.

CULTURE, CITIZENSHIP, AND GLOBALIZATION

Since the end of World War II, the nation-state has emerged as the most visible political entity, and the nation remains as the primary basis of citizenship. Migration, transnational exchanges of ideas, and increasing cultural diversity of nation-states, however, disrupt the premise of national citizenship founded on a static shared identity and amplify challenges to entrenched social order (Ladson-Billings 2004). In this section, I focus on three issues to explore culture and citizenship under conditions of globalization.

Individual Identities and the Limits of Diversity

Multiculturalism is a theoretical and political framework that argues against static notions of national identity. It draws upon the democratic idea that, although cultural groups may hold differing values, discussion and deliberation in the public realm allow exchanges of ideas that help to construct new meanings about citizenship, identity, and belonging (Kymlicka 1995). In Australia, Canada, South Africa, the United States, and other countries, non-White citizens challenged exclusionary policies through individual protest, collective action, and judicial rulings. These actions brought attention to systemic discrimination faced by minority groups, while questioning long-standing conceptions of what it means to be citizens of those nations (Banks 2008).

Despite increasing visibility in policy agendas, multiculturalism faces criticism from differing quarters. The influx of refugees fleeing wars in the Middle East re-energized conservative European and Australian politicians' contentions that multicultural policies destabilize national solidarity. Donald Trump's election in the USA and the Brexit campaign highlighted allegations of the ways immigration policies favor cultural minorities while undermining White, working-class citizens' economic prospects (Greenwald 2016). From a contrasting perspective, scholars question how multicultural approaches to diversity tend to homogenize identities across the composition of a cultural group; and contend that cultural groups narratively construct meanings within "interlocking, fluid, and often competing strands of signification" (Benhabib 2006, p. 385).

Other critics argue against nation-centric frameworks of diversity that overlook how citizenship is evolving from a legal status, to a feeling and practice that considers citizens' abilities to develop multiple identities based on simultaneous affiliations to collectivities based on gender, race, or class (Osler and Starkey 2005). The limits of diversity are encapsulated in Singapore's communitarian policies that designate citizens' ethnicities within four groups: Chinese, Malay, Indian, and Other. These narrow assignations fail to capture the experiences of citizens of mixed racial heritage or who practice religions that differ from their assigned ethnic category (Alviar-Martin and Ho 2011).

Static constructions of national identity and the recognition of multiple identities underline several issues regarding culture and citizenship. For one, they compel shifting analyses from shared group identities to individuals' constructions of identity. Such a shift implicates the ways minority groups have historically fought exclusion under principles of social rights (Marshall, 1964). Barry (2010) contends that group-based analyses tend to minimize "traditional arrangements" that may be "oppressive and exploitative when looked at up close" (p. 109). Unlike proponents of liberalism who draw on individual rights as a rationale for assimilation, he cites principles of "moral cosmopolitanism" in judging institutions by their impact on individuals as human beings, rather than "appeals to the shared destiny of a class, race, or nation" (p. 109).

Cosmopolitanism and Global Cultures

Barry (2010) reiterates how constructions of citizenship are no longer anchored solely to the nation-state, but encompass feelings of attachment to multiple groups, including the human community. Today, globalization has made available resources for citizens to cultivate affinities on global dimensions and mobilized transnational efforts calling attention to policies that perpetuate inequalities based on gender, ethnicity, language, or social class. Such efforts have often drawn on cosmopolitan principles, particularly, the idea of human rights as a moral aspiration and motivator of civic and political action (Sen 2010). A second cosmopolitan principle argues that although an individual is charged with ultimate responsibility for his or her own life, each person must reflect on how they are "doing their fair share" to "ensure everyone has the chance at a dignified human existence" (Appiah 2008, p. 95). A third principle aligns with the democratic tenet that people have much to gain from conversation with one another across differences (Appiah 2008).

Renewed interest in cosmopolitanism points to emerging global cultures that are reviving notions of shared civic identities across the human community and within the natural world. Global connectivity and exchanges of ideas are awakening shared values in a global civil society (Strijbos 2002). The United Nations' campaigns for human rights have paralleled transnational feminist movements and scholarship that have illuminated the complexity of power in women's historical and lived realities. As Mohanty (2003) observed, "First World" feminist studies tended to view "Third World" women's struggles from lenses that restated colonial hierarchies. Today, there is increased recognition that visions of equality among communities of women and other minority groups necessitate attention to specific power differences that are situated in intersections of social class and economic structures both within and across nations. Organizations such as the World Wildlife Fund have made visible ecological issues and the custodial role of human beings with regards the planet's resources. International and regional agencies such as the Southern

African Research and Documentation Centre are revitalizing forms of indigenous knowledge that emphasize human beings' interconnectedness to nature
by promoting sustainable development practices and fair trade (Ishemo 2004).

Studies of popular culture show how a sense of solidarity can form across
national borders by drawing on shared struggles. For example, hip-hop—
which originated in African-American communities but has taken root in
youth subcultures worldwide—highlights the legacy of civic exclusion faced
by Black and other cultural minorities (Chang 2014). Scholars surmise that
although popular culture presents possibilities in building cosmopolitan civic
spaces, entrenched social biases pose barriers to its transformative potential. The term "high culture" is commonly used to refer to cultural products
found in museums whose value is defined by elite tastes, whereas popular
culture is regarded as "low culture" due to its originating from the masses
(Erickson 2007). Yet, popular culture's transnational and political influence became apparent in the Black Lives Matters movement, where hip hop
music, fashion, and social media spurred efforts to protest anti-Black violence
around the world (Khan 2015).

New Global Hegemonies

Despite gaining visibility in scholarly circles and civil society, cosmopolitanism remains at the periphery of global cultural movements. Rather, powerful
sectors that control resources that are able to influence culture at a global
scale—such as entertainment media, news outlets, and advertising—promote
a growing culture of consumerism and economic success within conditions of
widening social inequalities (Herman and Chomsky 2002).

Critical theorists link the global culture of consumerism to the ideology
of neoliberalism, wherein governments and institutions reinvent themselves
"as global entities in order to survive in a global economy" (Gaudelli 2009,
p. 71). Students are educated to become conversant in the homogenization
and hybridity brought by globalization, but their participation as citizens is
defined primarily through their capacities to produce and consume. Attendant to neoliberalism is the influence of transnational corporations. The 2008
economic crisis illustrated how powerful financial institutions could threaten
global economic stability while relegating millions of people to poverty
(Barofsky 2012). The influence of corporations extends to monopolies on
news and entertainment media; and the power to shape information, cultural
trends, consumer habits, and political discourse in the public sphere.

Scholars theorize how corporate media forward an ideological hegemony
that tightens economically rich and powerful political forces' control through
the propagandizing of certain views, silencing of dissenting voices, distrac-
tion, and the dilution of knowledge (Herman and Chomsky 2002). They
contend that since the terrorist attacks of September 11, 2001, an alliance of
media and corporate-military interests has pushed to understand the world in

ways that support American imperial ambitions (DiLeo, Giroux, Saltman, and McClennan 2016). The discourse of the war on terror—coupled with neoliberal education reforms that emphasize standardized curricula—"obliterate the democratic values of equality, public debate of political problems, and respect for diversity" while validating violence as a social value (p. 138).

Television news has devolved into a form of entertainment programming featuring theme music, visual images, and shallow exploration of political topics (Postman 2005). This was evident during the 2016 U.S. presidential campaign, where a "horserace mentality" resulted in news coverage dominated by the candidates' "struggle to get out on top," with little attention paid to policy positions (Shorenstein Center 2016, n.p.). Advertising further compromises news media's impartiality and citizens' ability to consider issues critically (Herman and Chomsky 2002). On the one hand, media revenues are dependent upon funding through advertising; and on the other, viewers are bombarded with messages of product consumption. In all, these create scenarios where citizens' rights are exchanged for consumers' entertainment (Postman 2005).

Digital and social media offer new spaces to challenge entrenched social disparities, the ideological hegemony wrought by neoliberalism, and the global consumer culture (Van Dijck 2013). The Arab Spring (Khondker 2011), the global reach of Black Lives Matter (Khan 2015), worldwide Occupy protests in 2011, and Hong Kong's 2014 Occupy Central protests (Alviar-Martin and Baildon 2016a) attest to the potential of social media to embolden previously ignored voices and spur horizontal civic action against the political and economic status quo. The corporate-sponsored media, however, wield power to diminish such movements, as evidenced by the frivolous framing of Occupy Wall Street. *The New York Times* portrayed the protesters as "deviant and unruly disturbers of the established order" while obscuring "the obvious issue that (the protesters) were raising: income inequality" (DeLuca et al. 2012, p. 491).

IMPLICATIONS FOR GLOBAL CITIZENSHIP AND EDUCATION

Recent educational reforms across nations have attempted to grapple with the demands of an increasingly culturally diverse, economically disparate, and interconnected global community. Yet, schools are traditionally structured to replicate nations' hierarchies of power and established identities. In this section, I revisit issues of culture and citizenship to discuss implications for civic education policy, curriculum, and practice.

Individualizing and Integrating Cultural Citizenship

Benhabib (2006) and Young (1997) underline how citizens are able to form cultural attachments that do not necessarily reflect the shared identities of their cultural group. The focus on individuals' cultural identities presents several implications on the education of citizens. For one, it necessitates teachers' abilities to build awareness of their own preconceptions about students' cultures. As illustrated in Singapore's Chinese, Malay, Indian and Other framework, schools may operate within predetermined constructions of culture that may not reflect the ways that citizens define their identities (Alviar-Martin and Ho 2011). The case of Muslim students who were banned from donning *hijab* in French public schools presents another example. Rather than giving voice to the students' personal motivations for wearing *hijab*, the incident highlighted debates between politicians, school officials, and activists regarding France's republican-secularist traditions, while depriving the students of the "capacity for self-definition" (Benhabib 2006, p. 387).

Shifting the focus of civic identity from shared culture to individualized cultural citizenship not only necessitates detaching subjectivities from exclusively national concerns but also integrating the personal with the political. Myers (2016) calls for global citizenship education that builds on citizens' intersecting local, national, and global experiences in order to become aware of the ways "political issues and actors shape the local, familiar world around them" (p. 4). This type of schooling compels an integrated and post-structural curriculum, enabling the exploration of issues that bridge the ideological gap between the needs of the individual and the wider community. Heilman (2009) reiterates, however, that existing forms of education are based on modernist conceptions of knowledge that separate the individual from society while reflecting binary rational choices within predetermined linguistic, psychological, political, and cultural structures.

Sustaining Culture Through Pedagogy and Curriculum

Aside from recognizing the complexity of cultural citizenship, schools today face the challenge of honoring students' community cultures while gaining access to dominant cultural practices (Ladson-Billings 2004). In many countries, the culture of consumerism intertwines with the culture of economic success, creating a dominant culture comprised of the power elite: business and government leaders who can impact the lives of most citizens (Spring 2008). While the power elite in the USA may include Whites, African-Americans, Latino/a Americans, and Asian Americans, they are not a culturally diverse group, but share an upper-class, White, Christian culture that is learned from school and family. Thus, students who do not have access to elite schools and the cultures in these settings are less likely to become economically and socially mobile. Spring (2008) argues instead for developing a type of biculturalism, or the ability to function in White elite culture and the culture of the home.

Biculturalism mirrors *difference approaches* to diversity that posit minority students' literacies and cultural ways of being as equal to, but different from, the ways demanded in school teaching and learning (Paris 2012). For example, formulations of *funds of knowledge* (Moll and Gonzales 1994) and *culturally relevant pedagogy* (Ladson-Billings 2004) argue that teachers and students can successfully use cultural minority home languages and literacy practices to achieve academic and cultural competence while developing explicitly critical and praxis-oriented stances to challenge the entrenched societal order. Paris (2012), however, argues that the term, "culturally relevant" overlooks young people's linguistic dexterity and cultural plurality that are shaped by local and global popular cultural exchanges. Instead, he argues for a *culturally sustaining pedagogy* that fosters and perpetuates linguistic, literate, and cultural pluralism as a fundamental function of democratic schooling.

Parmenter's (2010) study of national curricula in Japan and New Zealand illustrate that culturally relevant and sustaining pedagogies cannot be divorced from contexts that frame the ways that the "cultural" and "global" are constructed in schools. For example, New Zealand's curriculum foregrounds its multicultural identity and Maori heritage in noting how European values "tend to saturate curricula" (p. 191). It frames the need to honor the nation's multicultural society through human rights, makes clear that assumptions and values are open to negotiation, and encourages acceptance of cultural change while recognizing multiple cultural traditions. In contrast, Japan's curriculum couches the role of schools within the premise of national citizenship and cultural persistence. Curriculum reform initiatives cite Japanese cultural traditions and homogeneity as a means of inoculation against global ills, including the threat of terrorism and social disconnection (Alviar-Martin and Baildon 2016b). Although in both nations, there is growing consciousness of the need to recognize young citizens' identities and interests, relative to Japan, New Zealand's stance toward cultural change has encouraged more school-based efforts to give voice to immigrant and indigenous students (Parmenter 2010).

Critiquing Culture and Citizenship

Interrogating static shared identities and creating culturally sustaining pedagogies requires both teachers and students to cultivate critical thinking. The term, 'critical thinking' has been co-opted by neoliberal and standards-based educational reform geared toward global economic competition (Myers 2016). Scholars, however, clarify that what is needed is criticality built on democratic and cosmopolitan principles of analysis, dialogue, and deliberation over public issues regarding culture and citizenship (Appiah 2008).

The rise of global popular cultures and transnational civil society opens new possibilities of citizenship identity and involvement, but also neoliberal influences that stimulate forms of individualization promoted by the market (Stevenson 2003). Stevenson (2003) argues for criticality that fosters "cosmopolitan individualization" where individuals are able to reconcile principles of justice and difference, develop complex understandings of culture and various kinds of normalization, and an emotional capacity to be able to live with the "Other." Toward this end, schools must expose young citizens to intercultural questions, a broad appreciation of political institutions, and recognition of the power of mass communications. Given the influence of social media, information technology, and advertising, this necessitates fostering in young citizens information literacy "enriched with analytical skills and critical judgment" so that they are aware of power structures and "intelligent systems in which networks define the production and distribution of social and scientific knowledge" (Van Dijck 2013, p. 176).

For DiLeo and his colleagues (2016), the ubiquity of a culture of consumerism, discourses of the war on terror, and the influence of neoliberalism in education, bring about the erosion of political activity and demise of dissent. Therefore, they call not only for the cultivation of criticality among citizens, but for scholars and educators to push back against education that is commodified, commercialized, and quantified, and that diminishes opportunities for democratic dialogue and debate.

DIRECTIONS FOR FUTURE RESEARCH

The evolving links between culture and citizenship under conditions of globalization raise questions and point to new paths of inquiry. To conclude, I suggest several ways that research can broaden understandings of culture and citizenship and the role of schools in building societies founded upon democratic and cosmopolitan principles.

The first direction of inquiry builds on the fluidity of culture and citizenship. Given the ascendance of global popular cultures and civil society, and increasing recognition of citizens' potential to form cultural identities through local and global affinities, studies can portray these processes of signification, especially among citizens who have been historically marginalized. There is a need, particularly, to expose the ways that citizens draw on global discourses to build a sense of agency and empowerment (Myers and Zaman 2009). Such inquiries necessitate grounded, interpretivist, or narrative approaches where the subject to be interrogated is the process of meaning-making, rather than how objective definitions are evident in individuals' understandings. Beyond giving voice to participants' stories and experiences, such research demands exploration of the contexts of power by which culture and citizenship "relationally, as well as narratively, gain significance" (Dhamoon 2006, p. 365).

Transnational settings raise further research possibilities. Sassen (2005) has brought attention to contradictions in global cities, where cross-border dynamics result in political, cultural, and social expansion and economic opportunity, but where residents without the necessary credentials are savagely sorted, expelled, and marginalized. Other studies have explored international schools that cater to globally mobile families and subscribe to internationally recognized curricula (Alviar-Martin 2010/2011).

Within transnational contexts, researchers can illuminate the narratives, ideologies, and power structures that inform people's civic and cultural identities. For example, Ong (2004) surmises that elite transnationals develop a type of flexible citizenship "based on amassing individual knowledge capital" rather than sharing basic values of democratic citizenship (p. 65). Similarly, "third culture kids" are globally-mobile children who have spent a significant part of their developmental years in cultures other than their parents', and who develop a sense of belonging in relationship to others with comparable transnational experiences (Pollock and Van Recken 2009). Research in international schools reveals how teachers and students can develop civic perceptions that simultaneously draw from principles of human rights and affinities to their localities, cultural groups, and nations (Alviar-Martin 2010/2011).

Beyond probing individuals' perceptions, research can illuminate the ways schools and societies create cultures of citizenship. Dahlgren (2003), for example, builds on Almond and Verba's (1989) framework of *civic culture* to examine features of the sociocultural world that constitute pre-conditions for people's actual participation in civil and political society. Several studies have examined the role of school and classroom climates in preparing young citizens to participate in democratic processes (Hahn and Alviar-Martin 2008). Dahlgren's model of civic culture, however, attends to several dimensions: values, affinity, knowledge, practices, identities, and discussion that bring together meaning-making, dialogue, and deliberation necessary to determine how schools encourage students to make sense of their cultural identities and consider actions as citizens in response to social problems.

As culture and citizenship continue to intersect and evolve under conditions of globalization, a challenge for educators, scholars, and policymakers is to reimagine how societies are able to honor citizens' complex identities and aspirations. In many ways, then, the shift from static cultural identities to fluid and multiple individual identities; calls for critiquing new global hegemonies; pedagogies geared toward fostering and sustaining pluralism; and creating empowering civic cultures pose imperatives to view schools as spaces in which policies and entrenched conceptions regarding cultural diversity, power, and equality are interrogated, rather than as structures that perpetuate the status quo. Instead of preparing young citizens to learn "to live up to what our democracies have become," schools in our globalized world can help create democratic societies that "live up to what we have become" (Heilman 2009, p. 45).

References

Aljunied, K. (in press). *Muslim cosmopolitanism: Southeast Asian Islam in comparative perspective*. Edinburgh: Edinburgh University Press.

Almond, G., & Verba, S. (1989). *The civic culture*. Thousand Oaks, CA: Sage.

Alviar-Martin, T. (2010/2011). Reconciling multiple conceptions of citizenship: International school teachers' beliefs and practice. *Journal of Education, 19*(3), 49–59.

Alviar-Martin, T. & Baildon, M. (2016a). Context and curriculum in two global cities: A study of discourses of citizenship in Hong Kong and Singapore. *Education Policy Analysis Archives, 24*(56), na.–n.a.

Alviar-Martin, T., & Baildon, M. (2016b). Issues-centered global citizenship education in Asia: Curricular challenges and possibilities in nation-centric and neoliberal times. *Curriculum Perspectives, 36*(2), 65–75.

Alviar-Martin, T., & Ho, L. C. (2011). "So where do they fit in?" Teachers' perspectives of multicultural education and diversity in Singapore. *Teaching and Teacher Education, 27,* 127–135.

Appiah, K. A. (2008). Education for global citizenship. In D. Coulter, G. Fenstermacher, & J. R. Wiens (Eds.), *Yearbook of the national society for the study of education, 107,* 83–89.

Banks, J. A. (2008). Diversity, group identity, and citizenship education in a global age. *Educational Researcher, 37*(3), 129–139.

Barofsky, N. (2012). *Bailout: An inside account of how Washington abandoned main street while rescuing wall street.* New York: Free Press.

Barry, B. (2010). International society from a cosmopolitan perspective. In G. W. Brown & D. Held (Eds.), *The cosmopolitan reader* (pp. 100–113). Cambridge: Polity Press.

Beasley, W. (1999). *The Japanese experience: A short history of Japan.* Berkley: University of California Press.

Benhabib, S. (2006). The "Claims" of culture properly interpreted: Response to Nikolas Kompridis. *Political Theory, 34*(3), 383–388.

Chang, B. (2014). Upset the set-up: A path towards self-determination rooted in conscious hip-hop, Pilipina/o, and panethnic communities. In R. Labrador, K. Kandi, & M. Villegas (Eds.), *Empire of funk: Hip-Hop and representation in Filipina/o America* (pp. 55–62). San Diego: Cognella.

Couldry, N. (2006). Culture and citizenship: The missing link? *European Journal of Cultural Studies, 9*(3), 321–339.

Dahlgren, P. (2003). Reconfiguring civic culture in the new media Milieu. In J. Corner & D. Pels (Eds.), *Media and the restyling of politics* (pp. 151–170). London: Sage.

DeLuca, K., Lawson, S., & Sun, Y. (2012). Occupy wall street on the public screens of social media. *Communication, Culture & Critique, 5,* 483–509.

Dhamoon, R. (2006). Shifting from 'culture' to 'the cultural': Critical theorizing of identity/difference politics. *Constellations, 13*(3), 354–373.

DiLeo, J., Giroux, H., Saltman, K., & McClennan, S. (2016). *Neoliberalism, education, and terrorism: Contemporary dialogues.* New York: Routledge.

Erickson, F. (2007). Culture in society and in educational practices. In J. A. Banks. & C. A. McGee Banks (Eds.), *Multicultural education: Issues and perspectives* (pp. 33–57). Danvers, MA: Wiley.

Fishwick, C. (2016, August 31). Why we wear the burkini: Five women on dressing modestly at the beach. *The Guardian.* Retrieved from: https://www.theguardian.com/world/2016/aug/31/why-we-wear-the-burkini-five-women-on-dressing-modestly-at-the-beach.

Gaudelli, W. (2009). Heuristics of global citizenship discourses towards curriculum enhancement. *Journal of Curriculum Theorizing, 25*(1), 68–85.

Geertz, C. (1973). *The interpretation of culture: Selected essays.* New York: Basic Books.

Gramsci, A. (1971). *Selections from the prison notebooks.* New York: International Publishers. ISBN 0-7178-0397-X.

Greenwald, G. (2016, November 9). Democrats, Trump, and the ongoing, dangerous refusal to learn the lesson of Brexit. *The Intercept.* Retrieved from: https://theintercept.com/2016/11/09/democrats-trump-and-the-ongoing-dangerous-refusal-to-learn-the-lesson-of-brexit/.

Hahn, C. L., & Alviar-Martin, T. (2008). International political socialization research. In L. Levstik & C. Tyson (Eds.), *Handbook of Social Studies Research* (pp. 81–108). New York: Routledge.

Heilman, E. (2009). Terrains in global and multicultural education: What is distinctive, contested, and shared? In T. Fuss Kirkwood-Tucker (Ed.), *Visions in global education* (pp. 25–46). New York: Peter Lang.

Herman, E. S., & Chomsky, N. (2002). *Manufacturing consent: The political economy of the mass media.* New York: Pantheon.

Houde, N. (2007). The six faces of traditional ecological knowledge: challenges and opportunities for Canadian co-management arrangements. *Ecology and Society, 12*(2), 34.

Ishemo, S. (2004). Culture & historical knowledge in Africa: A Cabralian approach. *Review of African Political Economy, 99,* 65–82.

Khan, J. (2015, August 9). Black lives matter has become a global movement. *Common dreams.* Retrieved from: http://www.commondreams.org/views/2015/08/09/black-lives-matter-has-become-global-movement.

Khondker, H. (2011). Role of the new media in the Arab Spring. *Globalizations, 8*(5), 675–679.

Kymlicka, W. (1995). *Multicultural citizenship.* Oxford: Clarendon.

Ladson-Billings, G. (2004). Culture versus citizenship. In J. A. Banks (Ed.), *Diversity and citizenship education* (pp. 99–126). San Francisco CA: Jossey-Bass.

Marshall, T. H. (1964). *Class, citizenship, and social development: Essays of T. H. Marshall.* Westport, CT: Greenwood.

Mohanty, C. T. (2003). Under western eyes revisited: Feminist solidarity through anticapitalist struggles. *Signs, 28*(2), 499–535.

Moll, L., & Gonzalez, N. (1994). Lessons from research with language minority children. *Journal of Reading Behavior, 26*(4), 23–41.

Myers, J. P. (2016). Charting a democratic course for global citizenship education: Research directions and current challenges. *Education Policy Analysis Archives, 24*(55), 1–16.

Myers, J. P., & Zaman, H. A. (2009). Negotiating the global and national: Immigrant and dominant culture adolescents' vocabularies of citizenship in a transnational world. *Teachers College Record, 111*(11), 2589–2625.

Nussbaum, M. (2002). Patriotism and cosmopolitanism. In J. Cohen (Ed.), *For love of country* (pp. 2–17). Boston: Beacon.

Ong, A. (2004). Higher learning: Educational availability and flexible citizenship in global space. In J. A. Banks (Ed.), *Diversity and citizenship education* (pp. 49–70). San Francisco, CA: Jossey-Bass.

Osler, A., & Starkey, H. (2005). *Changing citizenship: Democracy and inclusion in education.* Maidenhead, UK: Open University.

Paris, D. (2012). Culturally sustaining pedagogy: A needed change in stance, terminology, and practice. *Educational Researcher, 41*(3), 93–97.

Parmenter, L. (2010). Global citizenship, cultural change, and education policy in Japan and New Zealand. In W. Ascher & J. M. Heffron (Eds.), *Cultural change and persistence* (pp. 183–201). New York: Springer.

Pollock, D., & Van Reken, R. (2009). *Third culture kids: The experience of growing up between worlds*. Yarmouth, ME: Intercultural Press.

Postman, N. (2005). *Amusing ourselves to death: Public discourse in the age of show business*. New York: Penguin.

Sassen, S. (2005). The repositioning of citizenship and alienage: Emergent subjects and spaces for politics. *Globalizations, 2*(1), 79–94.

Sen, A. (2010). *The idea of justice*. Cambridge, MA: Harvard University Press.

Shorenstein Center. (2016). News coverage of the 2016 presidential primaries. *Harvard Kennedy school*. Retrieved from http://shorensteincenter.org/news-coverage-2016-presidential-primaries/.

Sorrels, K. (2013). *Intercultural communication: Globalization and social justice*. Los Angeles: Sage.

Spring, J. (2008). *The intersection of cultures*. New York: Lawrence Erlbaum.

Stevenson, N. (2003). *Cultural citizenship, cosmopolitan questions*. Maidenhead, UK: Open University.

Strijbos, S. (2002). Citizenship in our globalising world of technology. In N. Dower & J. Williams (Eds.), *Global citizenship* (pp. 222–230). New York: Routledge.

Van Dijck, J. (2013). *The culture of connectivity*. Oxford, UK: Oxford University Press.

Willinsky, J. (1999). *Learning to divide the world*. Minneapolis: University of Minnesota Press.

Young, I. M. (1997). A multicultural continuum: a critique of will Kymlicka's ethnic-nation dichotomy. *Constellations, 4*(1), 48–53.

AUTHOR BIOGRAPHY

Theresa Alviar-Martin is an Assistant Professor in the Department of Curriculum and Instruction and Co-Director of the Center for Governance and Citizenship at the Education University of Hong Kong. Previously, she worked as an ESOL teacher in a refugee camp in the Philippines, and as a primary teacher in international schools in Manila, Bangkok, and Hong Kong. She received a BSc in Family Life and Child Development from the University of the Philippines, an MA in Curriculum and Teaching from Teachers College, Columbia University, and a Ph.D. from Emory University. Her research examines citizenship education in culturally diverse democracies from global and comparative perspectives. Theresa's writing has been published in several academic books and peer-reviewed journals, including *Teaching and Teacher Education, Journal of Educational Research, Teachers College Record*, and *Theory and Research in Social Education*.

CHAPTER 23

Morality

Thomas Misco

INTRODUCTION

"Globalization" entered the English language in the 1960s to describe a "process in which the constraints of geography on social and cultural arrangements receded and [as a consequence] people become increasingly aware that [such constraints] are receding" (Waters 1995, p. 3). Since that time, the implications of globalization for citizenship education have only accelerated. First, globalization changed our reality and our perceptions of reality. Second, those changes translate into qualitatively different social relations. Third, as a result of the changes in human relations, the way in which we consider choices that influence others, domestically and internationally, demands re-examination given the close moral proximity that we inhabit.

A global morality needs to confront numerous questions. For example, to whom are we obligated, including those to whom we have no special relationship, and what defines the moral minimum? Who has moral standing and what are our duties and obligations to nonpersons and persons (Arneson 2015; Chadwick and Connor 2015)? Because enabling all to achieve basic human capacities is a prerequisite for justice to occur (Nussbaum 2006), what beliefs and values are consistent with this aim? The salience of these questions in a globalized world points to a clear ethical imperative for educators to provide a moral education that helps students engage in just and fair relationships with other people and the environment as global citizens (Apel 2000; Runte 2001; Ruiz and Minguez 2001). To accomplish this, students must

T. Misco (✉)
College of Education, Health, and Society, Miami University, 301G McGuffey Hall, Oxford, OH 45056, USA
e-mail: miscotj@miamioh.edu

© The Author(s) 2018   363
I. Davies et al. (eds.), *The Palgrave Handbook of Global Citizenship and Education*, https://doi.org/10.1057/978-1-137-59733-5_23

have abundant opportunities to complicate their epistemological orientations with cross-cultural understanding (Hanvey 1976) and perspective recognition (Barton and Levstik 2004), and to reconsider their own moral positions in light of deep understandings of multiple cultures and perspectives (Commeyras and Mazile 2001).

Global citizenship is a form of citizenship whereby the processes of globalization intersect with human rights, and it can include an ultimate obligation of responsibility for the world, which is primarily (2012) a moral undertaking (Dill 2012; Veugelers 2011). Global citizens understand how the world works, are willing to take participatory action to meet global challenges, and are "outraged by injustice" (Andreotti 2010; Davies 2006, p. 7). Global citizenship education contains a moral vision that involves "commitment and empathy beyond the individual and his/her own interests" (Dill 2012, p. 541). It concerns rights, responsibilities, and actions that unfold in collaborative and non-coercive ways, resting on the assumption that contemporary societies are complicated, diverse, dynamic, and unequal (Andreotti 2010; Veugelers 2011). As such, morality for global citizenship education intersects with social justice and intercultural relations. It also recognizes the commonality of humans, independent of borders, while attending to the proliferation of normative problems and issues the world faces (Dhillon 2014; Zhao 2013).

Within the context of global citizenship and education, morality has a central role, to be sure, but also a complicated one involving a series of perennial tensions that lack a sense of convergence. Given the infinite permutations of multiple and overlapping identities, realities, and contexts, we could well imagine our world as beset with "incommensurable ideologies" involving morality (Torcello 2014, p. 3). Reconciling morality as it exists within particular cultures, for example, with the idea of a cosmopolitan global citizen who holds universalized commitments, would appear to be an impossible task (Saito 2006). Yet, there are persistent calls for a global moral theory (Apel 2000; Dhillon 2014; Runte 2001) that is not overly simplified, nor lacking relevance for real life (Koh 2012). Because schools too often rely upon group approbation as sources of knowledge for behavior which are largely ineffective (Berkowitz and Bustamante 2013; Misco and Hamot 2007; Misco 2011), a global moral theory needs to be engaging, meaningful, and substantive.

CONCEPTUAL UNDERPINNINGS

In a general sense, we can think of morality as the normative decisions, actions, duties, and obligations that involve others. Morality involves "mutual awareness and consideration" (Waks 2007, p. 30) insofar as *what* is done or intended, as well as *why* and *how* the act is accomplished (Dewey and Tufts 1910). All societies locate themselves somewhere along a continuum of two distinct social approaches to moral questions, those of closed societies, which subscribe to "naïve monism," and those of open societies, which engage moral questions with "critical dualism" (Popper 1962a, p. 59).

In closed societies, groups and institutions act as moral purveyors with the intent to train a closed mind which accepts *preferred* ideas that hold special status as "sacrosanct-taboo" (Popper 1962a, p. 174), immune from rational critique. Within a critical dualism paradigm, a moral responsibility to observe and alter normative laws and ideas exists as these "standards are of our making in the sense that our decision in favour of them is our own decision . . . we alone carry the responsibility for adopting them" (Popper 1962a, p. 61). When people are asked to accept a prescribed morality based on naïve monism, or authority, or any other false idol of knowledge (Dewey 1933), they, by definition, abdicate legitimacy to judge them. Religion, authority, tradition, impulse, and personal experience should not undermine humankind's faith in reason (Dewey 1933; Popper 1962b) and they should also not act as adversaries to rational claims about the normative world.

One of the central problems of global moral theory is the need to balance uniformity while also honoring multiple and overlapping cultural contexts (Myers 2006) and especially the tensions between the universal versus the particular, the global versus the local, and individual autonomy versus group harmony. Epistemology is therefore critical for arriving at a morality for global citizenship, especially one that is anti-colonial, global, and inclusive of a transnational form of community (Roman 2003). Because strong attachments to ethnic, racial, religious, or other identities can lead to conflict and division that is harmful (Banks 2008), a global morality needs to reject ideas that are purveyed or assigned through authority and instead invite intellectualization of its own position, whereby nothing is so sacrosanct as to be timeless or eternal (Griffin 1942; LePage et al. 2011). Through the use of reflection, a global morality enables citizens to explore *how* values come into being and critically examine established habits and beliefs (Griffin 1942).

In this way, morality for global citizenship can be decolonizing to the extent that it provides the room for analysis of how inequalities have come into existence and the tools to "negotiate a future that could be 'otherwise'" (Andreotti 2010, p. 234). Post-colonial theory and other "post" theories ask us to "raise our professional game" by increasing the levels of intellectual engagement and autonomy in the profession" (Andreotti 2010, p. 233), which permit more informed choices within diverse contexts. Post-positivism and post-colonialism invite us to imagine what can be, while reviving and securing the voices that have historically been marginalized (Andreotti 2010) and avoiding any sense of the "outsider knows better" (Jackson 2014, p. 1073). Colonization is not only physical, as there are psychological renderings of colonization and "unresolved feelings of inferiority" (Urrieta 2004, p. 436). Education is where the legacies of colonialism and globalization intersect (Lavia and Mahlomaholo 2012) and a decolonizing approach to morality within curriculum seeks to "uncover, deconstruct, and interrogate the insidiousness of colonial discourses in the perpetuation of relationships of domination and subjugation" (Camicia and Bayon 2012, p. 74).

Critical pragmatism is another useful epistemological heuristic for a global morality as it takes local understandings seriously and aims for inclusive and educationally meaningful experiences (Feinberg 2015). The main task of critical pragmatism is to "bring competing norms to the surface" (Feinberg 2015, p. 151) so that they might be addressed as we live across and navigate "different competing systems of meaning and value" Feinberg 2015, p. 154). Prefatory to "what is going on here?" is the question of "what should be going on here?" and "what productive alternatives might now be blocked from consideration?" (Feinberg 2015, p. 156). Because inquiry is always informed by social commitments and values (Popkewitz 1980), the process of making globally moral choices requires student evaluation of antecedent values, beliefs, and consequent choices. Within post-colonial and critical pragmatism lenses, we might therefore abandon the idea of a "single legitimate moral register" (Feinberg 2015, p. 152) for global morality.

Although both post-colonialism and critical pragmatism serve to caution us against moral universalism, they do not imply a strict moral relativism, as moral positions that contradict the basic assumptions of global human equality and mutual obligation are inherently anathema to a global morality. The concept of a global morality presumes that global citizenship must contain a moral obligation to the material conditions of those in other parts of the world (Blades and Richardson 2006). Simply put, humans are bound to all other humans and we have a responsibility to one another (Arendt 1968/1974).

If every person ultimately has standing and is "entitled to equal consideration" (Brock 2015, p. 62), then global morality would reposition all others as neighbors and not strangers (Ruiz and Minguez 2001; Saito 2006). This ontological compression necessitates a widening of our moral ken (Chadwick and Connor 2015) and an expansion of our "universe of obligation" (Strom 1994, p. 56), beyond individual interest and ends and toward a "system of ends for all" (Dhillon 2014, p. 46). This kind of global morality expands our obligations, thereby widening and emancipating ourselves from the parochial (Waks 2007) since intrahuman moral obligations supersede local attachments (Banks 2008). If we regard others as "autonomous sources of normative claims within a justificatory practice" (Forst 2015, p. 78) and take on a global consciousness that "transcends geographic, economic, political, and (2012) religious boundaries" (Dill 2012, p. 542), we can move closer to bridging any schism of unity and diversity. In this way, global morality is transcendental in terms of borders, yet honors other perspectives through the lens of a "common humanity" and "global community" (Dill 2012, p. 542).

The culmination of this inherent obligation is action. Global citizenship education needs to prepare students to participate in active ways to "improve the world for those less fortunate" and engage distant others as world citizens empowered to deal with injustices (Jackson 2014, p. 1079). If we accept the mandate for a larger universe of obligation with ends for all, then issues of human dignity and justice become central to global citizenship education for morality. Poverty and exploitation are problems of human dignity, and are thus moral problems involving the victims, perpetrators, and global bystanders. The primary imperative for a global morality is therefore affronting human suffering through moral education, whereby the liberation of oppression recovers lost dignity, which is an inviolable right (Ruiz and Minguez 2001).

Global morality intersects with global justice (Chadwick and Connor 2015), and securing dignity for all through restitution is one heuristic for social justice as a moral imperative (Swartz 2011). Given asymmetrical power relations and the imposition of private interests, the ideal conditions are those in which engagement is impartial, equal, open, and free from compulsion or unanimity (Ruiz and Minguez 2001). To get there, moral education for global citizenship can position students to participate in the Rawlsian (1971) notions of "justice as reversibility," "ideal reciprocity," and "moral musical chairs" (Parker 2003, p. 65). This sort of rational empathy builds upon the expanded universe of obligation and positions students to learn how to stand up for justice and against injustice (LePage et al. 2011).

In particular, global morality is informed by social justice education, which is "the pedagogical practice of guiding students toward critically discussing, examining, and actively exploring the reasons behind social inequalities and how unjust institutional practices maintain and reproduce power and privilege that have a direct impact on students' lives" (King and Kasun 2013, p. 1). The end goal of social justice is the "full and equal participation of all groups in a society that is mutually shaped to meet their needs" (Bell 2013, p. 21). It is process oriented, with a goal of undermining the systems that create exploitation, marginalization, powerlessness, cultural imperialism, and violence, all of which constitute oppression (Young 2013). Todd (2003) cogently encapsulated this idea, suggesting that morality is central to social justice and is concerned with "those who have been 'Othered' and marginalized through discriminatory relations that are seen as violent, both in symbolic and material forms" (p. 1).

KEY ISSUES AND DEBATES

Perhaps the most basic and perennial schism in moral theory concerns the nature of the individual *qua* other individuals. In short, is morality rooted in culture and understood within the domains of relativism and communitarianism, or is it best understood as containing universal truths and responsibilities? These are the tensions of universality and difference, and of human rights and cultural determination (Jones and Long 2015). Central to this question is the role of moral agency, or moral autonomy, which appears prima facie as conflicting with a communitarian ethos. For example, cultural relativism holds that as societies and cultures evolve, so too do their moral systems.

Cultural relativism, furthermore, suggests that culture and morality are inextricably linked (Dei 2013; Jones and Long 2015). Indeed, people of unique cultural contexts have legitimately different and logical ways of understanding and therefore educators need to enable the "emergence of ethical, responsible, and responsive ways of seeking, knowing, and relating to others 'in context'" (Andreotti 2010, p. 234). Given the multiple identities informing epistemologies of morality, a key determinant for engaging issues of injustice within a larger universe of obligation is the extent to which students are positioned to understand culture deeply.

One result of such positioning is a realization that within cultural contexts are varying degrees of expected and realized moral autonomy, which is a Kantian construct that, in its purest form, rejects "anything other than one's practical reason as the source of morality" (Chan 2002, p. 281). This does not imply an individual *sui generis* who does not make reference to others within their moral calculus. Rather, it is an ideal to make decisions about one's life without "undue interference by others" and with the capacity to make these decisions with "due reflection and independence of mind" (Hill 2013, p. 24). A morally autonomous agent also needs to have the "power to deliberate about and to change her values and motivations to alter significant relations in her life if she so chooses" (Oshana 2005, p. 198). More than simply having freedom and free will, autonomy within moral decision-making has to guarantee that the moral agent has "de facto authority over her will and her circumstances" (Oshana 2005, p. 199).

Whereas autonomous moral agents need to grapple with the deontological evidence, reasons, and motives for a particular course of action, those without moral autonomy largely have teleological conclusions and ends formulated for their acceptance *a priori*. The autonomous and deontological moral agent focuses on the method of determining the legitimacy of moral beliefs and behaviors while the moral agent lacking autonomy experiences established and codified directives for consumption without reflection. Therefore, moral autonomy is fundamentally deontological whereby all moral beliefs and values are open for debate, circumspection, and reconsideration in light of current conditions, beliefs, values, and experiences.

Reflective Morality

This Kantian foundation is compatible with Dewey's (1908/1960) notion of moral autonomy as reflective morality. Reflective morality, unlike morality of custom, places emphasis on appeals to "conscience, reason, or to some other principle which includes thought" (Dewey 1932/1960, p. 3). Most critically, this demands that all morally consequential conclusions be held tentatively and arrived at through reflection. Dewey suggested that within a system of customary morality, parents, teachers, and the state ultimately compel adherence to accepted moral codes. But the essence of morality, suggested

Dewey, is "to know the reason for these customary instructions,"(p. 4) for we cannot blindly accept seemingly arbitrary rules and regulations. True moral decision-making, by its very nature, involves *doubt* and the need for reflection. Rules, regulations, and virtues that teachers and parents put forth are quite often rationalized through superior position rather than ethical or moral principle. Instead, reflective morality is a *struggle* with seemingly incompatible belief systems within or between the domains of the individual, family, religion, school, or community. It exists "between values each of which is an undoubted good in its place but which now get in each other's way,"(p. 6) which includes an accommodation of new moral beliefs.

In short, Dewey called for each generation to recognize their "responsibility of overhauling its inherited stock of moral principles and reconsidering them in relation to contemporary conditions and needs"(p. 145). Reflective morality is not moral relativism because the obligation for us is to discover which principles are relevant and salient for our current time and place through dialogue, evidence, and reasoned reflection. There is nothing fixed or finished within reflective morality. All beliefs and values should exist only insofar as they promote a satisfactory experience and are consistent with a global morality grounded in liberty, equality, dignity, and justice. Reflective morality is very much an intellectual endeavor. As such, customary morals naturally "make it hot" for those question or criticize custom or tradition (Dewey 1932/1960, p. 112). Customary or traditional moral beliefs that flow from false "idols" of knowledge found in tradition, authority, and custom (Dewey 1933, p. 25) are therefore not sufficient for informing a morally autonomous agent's determinations.

An authoritarian state which seeks to influence the ways in which citizens think, or a communitarian Confucian paradigm that focuses on harmony, would seem to be epistemologically incompatible with moral autonomy. Yet, voluntary endorsement and reflective engagement, the first two of Kant's four stages of moral autonomy, are compatible with a communitarian paradigm (Chan 2002). In particular, voluntary endorsement suggests a minimal sense of moral autonomy since moral agents cannot live a moral life if they are coerced to act or if actions are based on fear of punishment. Voluntary endorsement is not necessarily reflective or deliberative, but it does denote a sense of agency. The second level, reflective engagement, describes an agent who is able to lead a moral life "according to *my own* understanding of what morality requires of me" (Chan 2002, p. 285). This kind of autonomy includes reflection as well as deliberation and judgment. Chan (2002) suggested that Confucianism does not ask for people to "blindly follow the rites as endorsed by society or the majority" (p. 288). Rather, it calls for reflection and appropriateness of application based on circumstances, which are dynamic and contextual.

Ethics of Care

The ethics and morality of care emphasize caring and emotional relations of any context beyond those we care most strongly for and extends into the realm of the universe of obligation (Held 2015). The ethics and morality of care transcends either/or schisms, which advances a caveat for moral universality by noting that traditional liberalism emphasizing freedom, autonomy, and individual rights may not be universally desired and therefore present a risk of evangelism (Noddings 2010). A morality or ethics of care offers an approach to moral education within the context of globalization by ontologically positioning humans as born "from and into relation" (Noddings 2010, p. 390). As such, care "appreciates the moral value of emotions such as empathy and concern for others in enabling us to understand what we ought to do" (Held 2015, p. 51). A care approach eschews universalization of any particular version or any attempt to coerce or convert others to a particular view. Rather, persistent dialogue in order to continuously explain why some practices are unjust dovetails with an education aimed at developing people who will "engage successfully in caring relations" (Noddings 2010, p. 394). Care is neither egoistic self-interest nor altruistic sublimation of self—rather, it is the "cooperative pursuit of the mutual good of, and carrying relation between, care recipients and care providers" (Held 2015, p. 53).

Yet, emotional education has "grave risks" and can lead to an inappropriate "*sentimental* reaction" stemming from a "deficiency imaginary" where some are taught to be missing something that others can provide (Jackson 2014, p. 1072). Once empathy is achieved, there is a "naïve assumption" that "problems of a structural nature can be easily solved" (Jackson 2014, p. 1072). If we think of compassion as meeting the dispossessed in the totality of their reality and the universality of complicity, perhaps we can view compassion and care not as an alternative per se, but as the beginning step of understanding justice as a generalizable moral requirement (Jackson 2014; Ruiz and Minguez 2001). Feelings only become moral after the intervention of reason, thus making reason a necessary condition for morality (Jackson 2014; Ruiz and Minguez 2001). As scale increases and the rights and obligations of individuals become universal (Waks 2007), this philosophical positioning of complicity suggests "a solidarity among men [and women] as human beings that makes each co-responsible for every wrong and every injustice in the world, especially for crimes committed in his presence or with his knowledge" (Jaspers 1947).

Cosmopolitanism

Cosmopolitanism addresses the conflict between relativism and universalism by first recognizing the immutable ontological connection and interaction of contexts and peoples while being open to and being willing to learn from others. The Stoics developed the idea of *kosmopolitēs*, or world citizen, as inhabiting a nexus of local and humanity writ large (Wahlström 2015). It also suggests that we do have some clear obligations and responsibilities to others and that while some values should be local, others are universal. Cosmopolitanism embraces the notion that every person has "global stature as the ultimate unit of moral concern, and is therefore entitled to equal respect and consideration" (Brock 2015, p. 61). Cosmopolitanism identifies with diverse cultures and people from throughout the world and views social justice and equality in global ways (Banks 2008). It is inclusive of all identities, ranging from local to global, yet underscores obligations to all and to whom we are bound independent of context (Brock 2015; Jones and Long 2015).

Most salient of these obligatory rights are human rights, which logically flow from an expanded universe of obligation and recognition of universal dignity. If every individual is an "equal authority in the space of reasons where reciprocally valid judgments are being sought," then human rights are sought to ensure no human is treated in a way that is not justified to them as a "person equal to others" (Forst 2015, p. 78). Although some critics submit that the notion of human rights are fundamentally informed by western values (Myers 2006), we can also think of human rights as occupying a space within a "region of bedrock beyond which we cannot go" (Rawls 1993, p. 79). Human rights, as central to global morality, invites divergence in terms of contextual institutions (Forst 2015), to be sure, and just because human rights are not universally recognized and respected does not mean they ought not be (Jones and Long 2015).

A global morality inclusive of human rights and social justice ultimately requires a "commitment to inquiry" which is in itself, ethical (Torcello 2014, p. 8). Inquiry is not antithetical to care or harmony but rather the rational mechanism that allows for the maximization of dignity, human rights, and justice through defensible practices informed by care and empathy. Inquiry must also be shared, given "*the* problem of the public," which calls for the improvement of the "methods of debate, discussion, and persuasion" (Dewey 1927/1954, p. 208). The vibrancy of global citizens in terms of their decision-making and efforts toward improving the common good is predicated on the ability to improve discussion and debate, which is based on "freeing and perfecting the process of inquiry" (Dewey 1927/1954, p. 208).

CONCLUSION: RECOMMENDATIONS AND IMPLICATIONS FOR GLOBAL CITIZENSHIP

Given the broad range of moral ideas addressed within this chapter, I submit five implications related to morality for global citizenship and education: diverse dialogue, an ongoing dialectic of unity and diversity, commitment to fallibility, attending to controversial issues, and disrupting normativity through reflective morality. First, dialogue and communication create meaning through the interaction and transaction of ideas (Wahlström 2015).

Ongoing dialogue about the common good is a prerequisite for global morality (Blades and Richardson 2006; Chadwick and Connor 2015) and encounters with diversity and difference increase moral capacity (Fry and Souillac 2013). The more viewpoints that are present in the mind when contemplating an issue, the better one can "imagine how I would feel and think if I were in their place, the stronger will be my capacity for representative thinking and the more valid my final conclusions" (Arendt 1968, p. 241). The dialogue, modeling, practice, and confirmation asked of the ethics of care are coterminous with the dialogue of reflective morality.

Second, an ongoing dialectic of universal and local obligations (Jones and Long 2015) need not be subjected to a hard dialecticism. Rather, both locally unique and globally universal obligations can and do coexist, and providing a framework to negotiate conflicts between them is a central purpose of a global morality. Moral pluralism and diversity demand that we reason and engage in dialogue together in order to avoid "violent ideological disputes" (Torcello 2014, p. 7).

Third, open-mindedness and the recognition of fallibility permits conceptions of the good that are alternatives to those in parochial contexts in the form of "evolving moral commitments" (Bull 2006, p. 25). This ongoing dialectic is predicated on open-mindedness, an epistemological construct based on realizing our imperfect understanding and the acceptance of epistemological limitations that make us fallible (Soros 2006; Torcello 2014). Knowledge and truth are not only difficult to find, but they are also subject to continuous revision (Walhström 2015). Accepting and embracing fallibility implies that no group or institution should be able to impose its views on others, which is inconsistent with the morality found in closed societies and minds (Soros 2006).

Fourth, moral issues requiring "immediate public attention" (Blades and Richardson 2006, p. 116) are typically controversial issues (e.g., global warming, water resources, human-induced extinction). Although teachers are reluctant to engage controversial issues, including those of race, gender, and human rights, they are "crucial in preparing young people to be citizens" (Davies 2006, p. 15) and constitute the most pressing moral concerns by virtue of vehement disagreement. Their discussion leads to understanding and decision-making concerning how the world works as a system, how changes ramify, how the effects of change are helpful or hurtful to others, and how questions bring "subterranean assumptions to the surface" (Hanvey 1976, p. 102). Raising questions concerning the *meaning* of progress, what constitutes *desirable* change, the cascading effects resulting from consumption, and the complexity of seemingly insignificant decisions, can help students grapple with the world as a system in which they play a major role. Students who engage in discussions involving controversial issues are well-positioned to become agents of change; recognize, celebrate, and embrace diversity among and within groups; expand content knowledge though the consideration of other perspectives; and develop understandings of justice and the common good (Crossa 2005; King 2009; Misco and DeGroof 2014; Young 1996).

Fifth, all ideas and conclusions should therefore be held *tentatively* within an assumption of falsifiability, which embodies a sense of uncertainty and ambiguity. In a similar way, Dewey's distinction of customary and reflective morality directs our attention to the reality of parents, teachers, and the government ultimately compelling adherence to accepted or customary ideas. We should not blindly accept arbitrariness but rather "know the reason for these customary instructions" (Dewey 1932/1960, p. 4). The existence of seemingly *a priori* normative beliefs contradicts reflective morality and reflective thinking, to be sure, but they also introduce the toxicity associated with taboo topics, closed areas, and silenced discourses. An open mind rests upon individual freedom of thought, expression, and inquiry precisely for this reason (Soros 2006). When operationalized in this way, morality within education changes from saccharine, banal, hortatory, and moribund to meaningful, relevant, applied, pragmatic, controversial, and justice-oriented. Finally, given the pressing need for cross-cultural interaction for a global morality, teacher training and resources are critical. Without these, we might maintain habits and prescribed customs while maintaining complicit roles in ongoing injustice and suffering.

References

Andreotti, V. (2010). Postcolonial and post-critical "global citizenship education." In G. Elliott, C. Fourali & S. Issler (Eds.), *Education and social change: Connecting local and global perspectives* (pp. 238–250). New York, NY: Continuum.

Apel, K. (2000). Globalization and the need for universal ethics. *European Journal of Social Theory, 3*(2), 137–155.

Arendt, H. (1968/1974). *Between past and future: Eight exercises in political thought.* New York, NY: Viking.

Arneson, R. (2015). Theories, types, and bounds of justice. In D. Moellendorf & H. Widdows (Eds.), *The Routledge handbook of global ethics* (pp. 35–48). New York, NY: Routledge.

Banks, J. (2008). Diversity, group identity, and citizenship education in a global age. *Educational Researcher, 37*(3), 129–139.

Barton, K. C., & Levstik, L. S. (2004). *Teaching history for the common good.* Mahwah, NJ: Lawrence Erlbaum.

Bell, L. A. (2013). Theoretical foundations. In M. Adams, W. Blumenfeld, C. Castañeda, H. W. Hackman, M. L. Peters, & X. Zúñiga (Eds.), *Readings for diversity and social justice* (pp. 21–26). New York, NY: Routledge.

Berkowitz, M., & Bustamante, A. (2013). Using research to set priorities for character education in schools: A global perspective. *KEDI Journal of Educational Policy (KJEP Special Issue)*, 7–20.

Blades, D. W., & Richardson, G. H. (2006). Restarting the interrupted discourse of the public good: Global citizenship education as moral imperative. In G. H. Richardson & D. W. Blades (Eds.), *Troubling the canon of citizenship education* (pp. 115–123). New York, NY: Peter Lang.

Brock, G. (2015). Cosmopolitanism and its critics. In D. Moellendorf & H. Widdows (Eds.), *The Routledge handbook of global ethics* (pp. 61–71). New York, NY: Routledge.

Bull, B. (2006). Can civic and moral education be distinguished? In D. Warren & J. J. Patrick (Eds.), *Civic and moral learning in America* (pp. 21–32). New York, NY: Palgrave Macmillan.

Camicia, S., & Bayon, A. (2012). Curriculum development collaboration between colonizer and colonized. In T. C. Mason & R. J. Helfenbein (Eds.), *Ethics and international curriculum work: The challenges of culture and context* (pp. 75–93). Charlotte, NC: Information Age Press.

Chadwick, R., & Connor, A. O. (2015). Ethical theory and global challenges. In D. Moellendorf & H. Widdows (Eds.), *The Routledge handbook of global ethics* (pp. 24–34). New York, NY: Routledge.

Chan, J. (2002). Moral autonomy, civil liberties, and Confucianism. *Philosophy of East and West, 52*(3), 281–310.

Commeyras, M., & Mazile, B. (2001). Imagine life in another country on another continent: Teaching in the age of globalization. The Social Studies *92*(5), 198–204.

Crossa, V. (2005). Converting the "small stories" into "big" ones: A response to Susan Smith's "States, markets and an ethic of care." *Political Geography, 24*, 29–34.

Davies, L. (2006). Global citizenship: Abstraction or framework for action? *Educational Review 58*(1), 5–25.

Dei, G. J. S. (2013). African Indigenous proverbs and the institutional and pedagogic relevance for youth education: Lessons from Kiembu of Kenya and Igbo of Nigeria. *Journal of Education and Training 59*(3), 344–362.

Dewey, J., & Tufts, J. H. (1910). *Ethics.* New York, NY: Henry Holt and Company. (Original work published 1908).

Dewey, J. (1908/1932/1960). *The theory of the moral life.* New York, NY: Holt, Rinehart, & Winston.

Dewey, J. (1927/1954). *The public and its problems.* New York, NY: H. Holt.

Dewey, J. (1933). *How we think.* Lexington, MA: D.C. Health & Company.

Dhillon, P. A. (2014). Examples of moral perfectionism from a global perspective. *The Journal of Aesthetic Education, 48*(3), 41–57.

Dill, J. S. (2012). The moral education of global citizens. *Society 49*(6), 541–546.

Feinberg, W. (2015). Critical pragmatism and the appropriation of ethnography by philosophy of education. *Studies in Philosophy and Education, 34*(2), 149–157.

Forst, R. (2015). Human rights. In D. Moellendorf & H. Widdows (Eds.), *The Routledge handbook of global ethics* (pp. 72–81). New York, NY: Routledge.

Fry, D. P., & Souillac, G. (2013). The relevance of nomadic forager studies to moral foundations theory: Moral education and global ethics in the twenty-first century. *Journal of Moral Education, 42*(3), 346–359.

Griffin, A. F. (1942). Teaching in authoritarian and democratic states. In W. C. Parker (Ed.), (1996). *Educating the democratic mind* (pp. 79–94). Albany: State University of New York Press.

Hanvey, R. G. (1976). An attainable global perspective. In Willard M. Kniep (Ed.), *Next steps in global education: A handbook for curriculum development.* New York, NY: The American Forum.

Held, V. (2015). Gender, care and global values. In D. Moellendorf & H. Widdows (Eds.), *The Routledge handbook of global ethics* (pp. 49–60). New York, NY: Routledge.

Hill, T. E. (2013). Kantian autonomy and contemporary ideas of autonomy. In O. Sensen (Ed.), *Kant on moral autonomy.* New York, NY: Cambridge University Press.

Jackson, L. (2014). "Won't somebody think of the children?" Emotions, child poverty, and post-humanitarian possibilities for social justice education. *Educational Philosophy and Theory, 46*(9), 1069–1081.

Jaspers, K. (1947). *The question of German guilt*. New York, NY: Capricorn Books.

Jones, P., & Long, G. (2015). Universalism, relativism, and difference. In D. Moellendorf & H. Widdows (Eds.), *The Routledge handbook of global ethics* (pp. 82–94). New York, NY: Routledge.

King, L., & Kasun, G. S. (2013). Food for thought: A framework for social justice in social studies education. *Focus on Middle Schools, 25*(3), 1–4.

Koh, C. (2012). Moral development and student motivation in moral education: A Singapore study. *Australian Journal of Education, 56*(1), 83–101.

Lavia, J., & Mahlomaholo, S. (2012). Imagining the postcolonial. In J. Lavia & S. Mahlomaholo (Eds.), *Culture, education, and community: Expressions of the postcolonial imagination*. New York, NY: Palgrave Macmillan.

LePage, P., Akar, H., Temli, Y., Şen, D., Hasser, N., & Ivins, I. (2011). Comparing teachers' views on morality and moral education, a comparative study in Turkey and the United States. *Teaching and Teacher Education, 27*(2), 366–375.

Misco, T., & Hamot, G. E. (2007). Post-Soviet moral education: The case of Kyrgyzstan. *International Education, 36*(2), 48–69.

Misco, T. (2011). Deontological reconceptualization: A study of moral education in Beijing. *Theory and Research in Social Education, 39*(4), 298–316.

Misco, T., & DeGroof, J. (Eds.). (2014). *Case studies in controversial issues*. Oisterwijk, The Netherlands: Wolf Legal Publishers.

Myers, J. P. (2006). Rethinking the social studies curriculum in the context of globalization: Education for global citizenship in the US. *Theory and Research in Social Education, 34*(3), 370–394.

Noddings, N. (2010). Moral education in an age of globalization. *Educational Philosophy and Theory, 42*(4), 390–396.

Nussbaum, M. (2006). *Frontiers of justice: Disability, nationality, and species membership*. Cambridge, MA: Harvard University Press.

Oshana, M. A. L. (2005). Autonomy and free agency. In J. C. Taylor (Ed.), *Personal autonomy*. New York, NY: Cambridge University Press.

Parker, W. C. (2003). *Teaching democracy: Unity and diversity in public life*. New York, NY: Teachers College Press.

Popkewitz, T. S. (1980). Global education as a slogan system. *Curriculum Inquiry, 10*(3), 303–316.

Popper, K. R. (1962a). *The open society and its enemies*. New York, NY: Harper & Row.

Popper, K. R. (1962b). *The open society and its enemies*, Volume II. Princeton, NJ: Princeton University Press.

Rawls, J. (1971). *A theory of justice*. Cambridge, MA: Harvard University Press.

Rawls, J. (1993). The law of peoples. In S. Shute & S. Hurley (Eds.), *On human rights*. New York, NY: Basic Books.

Roman, L. G. (2003). Education and the contested meanings of "global citizenship". *Journal of Educational Change, 4*, 269–293.

Ruiz, P. O., & Mínguez, R. (2001). Global inequality and the need for compassion: Issues in moral and political education. *Journal of Moral Education, 30*(2), 155–172.

Runte, R. (2001). Re-educating humankind: Globalizing the curriculum and teaching international ethics for the new century. *Higher Education in Europe, 26*(1), 39–46.

Saito, N. (2006). Reawakening global awareness: Deweyan religious democracy reconsidered in the age of globalization. *Studies in Philosophy and Education, 25*(1), 129–144.

Soros, G. (2006). *The age of fallibility: The consequences of the war on terror*. New York, NY: Public Affairs.

Strom, M. S. (1994). *Facing history and ourselves: Holocaust and human behavior resource book*. Brookline, MA: Facing History and Ourselves National Foundation.

Swartz, S. (2011). Being turned inside out: Researching youth, morality and restitution from the global South. *Journal of Moral Education, 40*(3), 407–415.

Todd, S. (2003). *Learning from the other*. Albany, NY: State University of New York Press.

Torcello, L. (2014). Moral agnosticism: An ethics of inquiry and public discourse. *Teaching Ethics, 14*(2), 3–16.

Urrieta, L. (2004). Dis-connections in "American" citizenship and the post/neo-colonial: People of Mexican descent in whitestream pedagogy and curriculum. *Theory and Research in Social Education, 32*(4), 433–458.

Veugelers, W. (2011). The moral and the political in global citizenship: Appreciating differences in education. *Globalization, Societies and Education, 9*(3–4), 473–485.

Wahlström, N. (2015). Cosmopolitanism as communication? On conditions for educational conversations in a globalized society. *Scandinavian Journal of Educational Research, 60*(1), 32–47.

Waks, L. J. (2007). Rereading "Democracy and Education" today: John Dewey on globalization, multiculturalism, and democratic education. *Education and Culture, 23*(1), 27–37.

Waters, M. (1995). *Globalization*. London: Routledge.

Young, I. M. (1996). Communication and the other: Beyond deliberative democracy. In S. Benhabib (Ed.), *Democracy and difference: Contesting the boundaries of the political* (pp. 120–137). Princeton, NJ: Princeton University Press.

Young, I. M. (2013). Five faces of oppression. In M. Adams, W. Blumenfeld, C. Castañeda, H. W. Hackman, M. L. Peters, & X. Zúñiga (Eds.), *Readings for diversity and social justice* (pp. 35–45). New York: Routledge.

Zhao, Z. (2013). The shaping of citizenship education in a Chinese context. *Frontiers of Education in China, 8*(1), 105–122.

Author Biography

Thomas Misco is a professor of social studies education and Naus Family Endowed Faculty Scholar at Miami University. He earned his B.A. in history and geography at the University of Wisconsin-Madison and his M.A. and Ph.D. degrees at the University of Iowa. He has conducted a wide variety of research studies on controversial issue education throughout Asia, North America, and Europe and his current work focuses on postcolonial citizenship education in historically colonized US territories. Misco is a past recipient of the Miami University Distinguished Scholar Award and a Fulbright Senior Specialist Fellowship.

CHAPTER 24

Transformative Spirituality and Citizenship

Binaya Subedi and Jeong-eun Rhee

INTRODUCTION

Nation-states have always been imagined (Anderson 1983) through particular racial, gendered, heterosexual, and religious articulations. In other words, the boundaries of citizenship that determine what constitutes a nation-state have been always marked by its own Others/outsiders. Therefore, what counts as legitimate citizenship education reveals how race, social, class, ethnicity, sexuality, gender, religion, etc., are (always) used to imagine a nation-state as a political and cultural entity. How we speak about citizenship matters and who speaks for/about citizenship is always contested since discussions of citizenship can be both inclusionary and exclusionary. Marginalized people in a given nation-state have existed outside of the official boundaries of citizenship education in schools and in society and contest the official narratives of citizenship produced by the state (Banks 2004).

In the USA,[1] educating students about what constitutes citizenship has operated via two interconnected domains. First, the USA has historically used schools as an official space to inculcate students into citizenship ideals and

---

Portions of this chapter was published in Rhee and Subedi (2014).

B. Subedi (✉)
The Ohio State University at Newark, 1179 University Drive,
Newark, OH 43055, USA
e-mail: subedi.1@osu.edu

J. Rhee
College of Education, Information, & Technology, Brookville,
NY 11548-1300, USA
e-mail: jeong-eun.rhee@liu.edu

© The Author(s) 2018   377
I. Davies et al. (eds.), *The Palgrave Handbook of Global Citizenship and Education*, https://doi.org/10.1057/978-1-137-59733-5_24

practices. This includes teaching about "good" values, "good" behaviors and the rituals of patriotism in all aspects of school culture: in classrooms, in athletic contexts and various school activities (plays, school clubs, etc.). In other words, students are being schooled, if not required, to learn, identify with and perform dominant social norms and citizenship values. Thus learning and teaching about citizenship promotes a mainstream binary thinking of us vs. them, fosters an acceptance of capitalism as the norm, and reinforces a hierarchy of gender, race, disability, etc. (Banks 2004; Olser and Starkey 2003).

Secondly, education for citizenship has also been interconnected with ways students are socialized into US society. This includes ways students learn about what constitutes as "American" cultural norms through exposures to media, social media, and popular culture and affiliations with community organizations (church, etc.). Through these interactions, students are socialized into mainstream notions of citizenships that reinforce whiteness, heterosexuality, and patriarchal values as norms and ways of performing US citizenship. Moreover, education for citizenship often operates within a nation-state framework and makes a sharp (binary) distinction between (narrow/monolithic) national citizenship and global citizenship. The larger conversation about human rights has been largely absent in relation to research in citizenship education (Guadelli 2016).

Since formal and informal ways of educating students about citizenship reinforces and are bound by dominant forms of knowledge/power (Foucault 1980), it promotes obedience to and conformity with authority and socializes students to not question power relations in society. For example, Ladson-Billings (2004) writes how mainstream ways of theorizing citizenship has historically silenced discussions of race despite that racial policies and politics have always been an integral part of constructing US citizenship. Thus, within the official project of citizenship education, students rarely are encouraged to learn critical thinking skills to question power and authority, to examine the racial and capitalist structure that disciplines their minds and bodies, and to speak out against injustices. With this discussion as a pretext, the chapter, using the USA as our focal case, traces the problematic relationship between religion and citizenship and the educational politics that the religion/citizen matrix has generated to socialize students into mainstream narratives of citizenship.

In this chapter, our use of the term religion is to highlight more formal ways religion enters the overall school culture. We invoke the term religion to speak about the political ways conversations about religion enters schools and, in particular, its ideological manifestations. We do not make claims about whether religion or spirituality is a more useful term to speak about the relationship between religion/spirituality and citizenship. Clearly, dominant subjects who use religion in ideological ways also invoke the spirit or spirituality to claim how the *real* spirit is on their side (missionaries, etc.). Our use of the term spirituality calls upon to look at how we may critically look at the conversation on religion and spirituality. We use spirituality to signify the alternative ways people may negotiate religion or even secular aspect of spirit-ness. In fact, more often, many scholars have discussed spirituality as an analytic category that can be used to trace the sustaining energy for decolonizing, anti-oppressive endeavors and social justice commitments (Dillard 2006; hooks 1994; Kumashiro 2009). Although religion is a term that is often used in schooling contexts to speak about the separation of church and state, etc., in recent years, the concept of spirituality has become more visible in both mainstream cultural and academic discourses. Many schools have started using yoga or various mindfulness practices (as secular practices) to help student explore mind and body relationships. Yet, these practices (of spirituality) even when they are presented as secular (such as mediation, contemplative mind, and yoga) they generate different political and cultural implications.

Paying attention to these complex dynamics around spirituality and religion, we offer (1) a postcolonial reading (Subedi & Daza 2008) of how religion and spirituality has entered the sphere of citizenship in the USA; (2) how critical spirituality can be a site of decolonizing citizenship projects; and (3) how to rethink the relationship between religion/spirituality and citizenship education. By problematizing how we think about religion and politics in US context, we work to disrupt taken-for-granted assumptions about religion and citizenship so that our discussion can enable readers to imagine a radically different global world and citizenship.

CONCEPTUAL THEMES: THE UNEASY ALLIANCE BETWEEN RELIGION AND CITIZENSHIP

Religion, similar to race and gender, has played an integral role in how citizenship is being taught and learned. Although most modern nation-states may claim religious neutrality or secular politics, religious ideology has been often inherent part of the (un)official marker of citizenship. Similar to racial, gender or economic privilege, religious privilege plays out in social context by rewarding those from dominant religious backgrounds with more cultural, political and economic power/legitimacy. For example, despite its official claim of separation of religion (read: Church) and State, expansion of the USA as a nation-state towards the western geographies was undoubtedly fueled by religious dogmatism that equated civilizational progress with territorial and (Christian) religious expansion. The belief was that God was on the "right" side and those who came in between (e.g., American Indians) ought to be civilized or eliminated. It is not too difficult to trace how the formation of USA as a nation-state (and its citizenship politics) has religious roots, whether it has been openly religious or hidden by its claiming on separation of Church and State (yet privileging mainstream/white Christianity in virtually every facet of life).

While our discussion is directed toward the case of the USA, we want readers to consider that nations-states in the Global South, under the ideology of nationalism, have similarly used religion as a tool to write a particular national story that suppressed communities that were not part of the official story or those who resisted the cultural/religious narratives of nationhood that excluded them (Fanon 1963; Prashad 2000). For example, in India, one's Hindu religious affiliation, compared to Muslims, can give a person more power and privilege. Although India claims itself as a secular nation-state, it (un)officially grants more citizenship rights to the Hindu population. Or consider how one's Jewish identity can give one more power in the state of Israel compared to Palestinians subjects or Ethiopian immigrants who continue to seek equal rights and social justice. The State ideology, whether openly pronounced or not, shapes how religious discourse overlaps with citizenship narratives.

Thus, naming legitimacy or illegitimacy of religions or spiritual practices is always political since States strategically mobilize religious symbols and language to discipline citizen subjects. We argue that all forms of religious orthodoxy and its citizenship requirements ought to be challenged. Official and unofficial State sanctioning of religion discriminates the rights of marginalized religious communities who do not fit within official narratives of citizenship. However, this can be done in quite complex ways. Consider how the population of Europe and North America has shifted over the years and the demographic changes have created renewed fear over how the Other has become a threat to dominant ways of being. While race and ethnicity shape how different immigrant or refugee communities are being discriminated against, discussion on religion also needs to be examined in relation to questions of gender, race, etc. For instance, the Islamophobia is part of the "racialization of religion" (Rizvi 2004) in which Muslim claims of citizenship in Europe and North America are continually been denied and contested. Consequently, we argue that the neutrality claims of State/Church (religion) equation needs to be critiqued since the very idea that there is or was a clear separation of State/religion silences those who have not been part of the religion/citizenship narrative.

RELIGION AND SPIRITUALITY AS ORIENTALISM

If religion has never been separable from political (and thus social and economic) structures and relations, then where does our assumption emanate that they are separate? This constructed and normalized idea that politics (e.g., citizenship) and religion are separated or separable is largely derived from European Enlightenment projects and the subsequent establishment of

Western nations that purported to be rational, modern, and secular (Urban 2005). Thus, this very idea that there is a neat separation between religion and politics/citizenship is a myth since religious politics has always shaped the governing of subjects or "souls." While there are many different ways of conceptualizing what religion and spirituality mean, we treat them here representing diverse ways of being and knowing that are materialized and practiced through rituals, activities, and relationships. This framing allows a (postcolonial) historical understanding on how the Enlightenment episteme provided a particular logic for European colonial power to triumph their ways of knowing (rational, scientific, etc.) over other ways of knowing that were constructed as being illegitimate, primitive or intellectually inferior. It is this categorization of the inferiority of the Other people's beliefs (including religious/spiritual beliefs) that justified the violence wrought by colonialism and its civilization missions. Colonial and neo-colonial projects have always created a hierarchy between acceptable and unacceptable citizenships or spiritualities and forced the need to replace the "demonic" spirituality with a more "progressive" spirituality (Germain 2011). Even in contemporary USA, evangelical Christians often call for restoring faith/spirituality as an expression of their desire to save the soul of those who are marked as having no (appropriate) faith. These speaking subjects who claim spirituality as the only way to read the world are relying on a particular epistemological stance that reinforces colonial relations about the Other.

Once conversations about religion and spirituality are contextualized in the history of colonial discourse, it becomes clear how they stem from larger narratives of Orientalism. Said (1978) defines Orientalism as a form of knowledge that constructs, catalogues and codes the Other. According to Said, a key idea within the Orientalism or the colonial representation of the Other was, in fact, its emphasis on spirituality: the belief that the Other was spiritual or was connected to exotic spirits rather than embodying religion which was seen as a more legitimate relationship to higher powers and evidence of higher civilization. Therefore, western representation of the Other tended to place emphasis on how the Other was spiritual, not religious. For example, the representation of India often included its mystical characteristics, which implied and also openly stated that India's spirituality was inferior to Western (Christian) cultural and religious formations (Prashad 2000). In other words, spirituality signified a lesser or less legitimate form of citizenship and knowledge system—civilizations—as it was relegated more keen to (super) natural and thus was interpreted as being primitive and embodying savage instincts.

Saving narratives are only possible through this hierarchical frame of religious belief systems and often through converting the Other since the Other is read as being inferior and in need to saving (Abu-Lughod 2002). What cannot be missed here is how the logics of racist colonial relations have been deeply interwoven with these cultural constructions and interpretations of spirituality, religion, and civilization superiority. Simultaneously, this Othering relation was a fundamental ground for whiteness to gain "in strength and identity by setting itself off against the Orient as a sort of surrogate and even underground self" (Said 1978, p. 3). This subtext has been integral part of how white Christian "American" citizen has been historically imagined in relation to indigenous spiritual Others in the spectrum of progress, development, and civilization. Inscribed is the colonial violence in the construction of US citizenship. Consequently, the narrative of normalizing Christianity as part of the "good" citizenship has always been part of citizenship education in schools whether mainstream Christianity is openly endorsed or subliminally filtered as a normal practice of citizenship.

CRITICAL DEBATES: NEOLIBERAL TURNS ON CITIZENSHIP, RELIGION, AND SPIRITUALITY

An emerging neoliberal discourse on religion versus spirituality has added another layer of complications to how Orientalist logic works in the construction of national and global citizenship vis-a-vis religion and spirituality. In this section, we provide a brief analysis on how the contemporary use of the terms, religion, and spirituality, have been affected by a shift of global ideologies and economic structures, which is neoliberalism. This shift also reflects messier boundary of nation-state vis-à-vis imagining global citizenship. While there have been some debates among scholars who work with post-coloniality, anti-colonial relations, new imperialism, and decolonizing theories, neoliberalism as a global force must be analyzed in our continuing history and the neo-colonial present.

In order to explicate the current popular use of spirituality, it is important to note how the development of psychology as a discipline has invented the science of the self in Western societies (Carrette and King 2005; Shahjahan 2010; see also Rose 1990, 1998). Carrette and King (2005) elaborate how a psychologized neoliberal self that is private, autonomous, and free (Rose 1990, 1998) has provided a foundation for the (new) concept of spirituality that can be interiorized, individualized, and psychologized by moving away from the institutionalized, social, and collective forms of relations and expressions (read: religion). Along with the psychologized self, which serves the logics of neoliberalism, spirituality now takes part in the pursuit of individual wealth and happiness without any concerns and actions for community building and collective well-being. Consequently, there is a serious conflation between how people conceptualize spirituality and self-help. Spiritual (western neoliberal) self who devours and consumes any and every element of ancient, indigenous, Asian, African traditions and knowledge systems for one's needs and happiness is now considered to be liberated from religious institutions and is represented as a more enlightened or worldly member of a nation-state and globe.

This aligns with how globally (consuming) citizens are imagined, in fact, along with a neoliberal nation-state building project. This decontextualized spiritual (global) self uses their citizenship (or consumer) rights to consume the Other and this consumption becomes a basis of imagining global citizenship within the global economy. This is precisely what is taking place in US curriculum in which global citizenship is often equated with learning skills/knowledge on how to economically succeed in society (see Myers 2010). Thus, global citizenship becomes an economic–cultural–spiritual consumption project. Similar to seventeenth and eighteenth-century colonial Orientalist narratives, the contemporary turn of (neoliberal and neocolonial) spirituality appropriates the Other through neoliberal subjects' exploitations of the Other and commodification of spirituality through market ideology without engaging with questions of oppression and injustice. In search of various spiritual practice and knowledge, these global consumers/citizens seek to affiliate with the spiritualities of the Other as they desire to escape the conditions of life governed by capitalist nation-state and enter the space of nature/spirit. Unfortunately, such a framework locates the Other (whether it is people or culture) in one-dimensional framework (nature-only, etc.) and perpetuates stereotypes about the Other. Then, spirituality of the Other is appropriated and placed in educational markets to be consumed by the neoliberal/neocolonial citizen subjects within the context of global learning and re/creation.

Indigenous scholars have criticized how consuming the Other is directly connected to producing neoliberal citizenship ideals through their analysis on the New Age Movement that appropriates indigenous ways of being. For instance, Aldred (2000) argues that the commercialization of American Indian spirituality is connected to the large disaffections among middle-class white Americans from consumer capitalism who "feel uprooted from cultural traditions, community belonging and spiritual meaning" (p. 329). To be saved from the capitalistic structure of nation-state, many white Americans come to "romanticize an 'authentic' and 'traditional' Native American culture whose spirituality can save them from their worn sense of malaise" (p. 329). What is ironic about the attachment to American Indian spirituality is that while claiming to critique capitalist practices, they reinforce capitalistic citizenship ideals by being part of the commercialization of American Indian spirituality. The fetishization of indigenous spirituality not only masks the social oppression of indigenous people and the failure of capitalist nation-state but also perpetuates the neoliberal regime of neo/colonization without resolving the fundamental tensions between the USA as a nation-state and indigenous population. This, in fact, raises serious questions on how inclusion is conflated with consumption, often in the name of learning about national and global citizenship.

US schools often appropriate indigenous themes mascots to claim school spirit and citizenship values. These practices are claimed to promote ideas of courage and honor as the citizenship ideals of the school. Yet, such practices appropriate Indigenous histories and experiences in the name of teaching "good" citizen values. As Fryberg and Stephens (2010) argue, the appropriation and commodification of American Indian histories and experiences harm ways in which American Indian youth come to identify themselves. Whites benefit psychologically from stereotypes since the misrepresentations of indigenous communities "enhance the self-worth of European Americans" (p. 117). Fryberg and Stephens maintain that too often the uses of American Indian mascots are spoken of as a "positive" form of citizenship and as a token of inclusion. However, such portrayals, "which are largely created by majority group members (e.g., Whites), depress feelings of self-worth (i.e., self-esteem), community efficacy (i.e., the confidence that one's community can improve itself), and achievement-related possible selves (i.e., future achievement goals) for American Indians" (Fryberg and Stephens 2010, p. 117). Pewewardy (2004) also writes that the use of indigenous people as mascots has particular ramifications for American Indian communities as "mascots give life to racial stereotypes, as well as revivify historical patterns of appropriation and oppression" (p. 180). Pewewardy criticizes mascot supporters' failure to recognize how the "symbols used by cheerleaders and cheering fans—war chants, peace pipes, eagle feathers, war bonnets, and dances—are highly revered and even sacred in many American Indian tribal communities" (p. 80).

This neoliberal desire can be observed at a global level through the spiritual tourism industry that markets travel to locations that are historically seen as being spiritual sites. This is often sold as an adventure on global citizenship and often marketed to high school and college students. This may include travels in locations in India or Japan or in indigenous spaces that are often seen as places where the (neoliberal) self can be rejuvenated thus gaining global citizenship and "culture" in the process. Mehta (1994) documents how, beginning in the late 1960s, westerners' renewed fascinations with Indian spiritualism, which have their roots in Orientalism, have (re)brought European and American "pilgrims" to India in search of their true selves and spiritual freedom and how their travels to rural India have devastated the local communities, traditions, and lives. Consider the popularity of Gilbert (2006)'s book *Eat, Pray, Love* in the USA that uses a similar spiritual journey that Mehta's (1994) Western pilgrims had taken in order to escape their capitalistic and neoliberal cultural constraints. As colonizers felt entitled to travel all over the world and claimed to discover the new land, natural resources, and labor for their own wealth, the contemporary self-discovery citizenship journey assumes their passport and economic privilege and entitlement to travel anywhere and consume everything they wish in the name of spiritual pursuit.

Amidst the popularity of desiring and taking in Other's spiritual systems, we must ask: why are then certain people of color whose identities, life styles, and communities built through faith-based spirituality such as Islam still considered backward, oppressed, and irrational? While this liberating self-recovery citizenship spirituality renders other religious traditions as unintelligible and thus denies their significance and values within this (post)modern neoliberal world, how does it still allow the USA and other western governments' "avid mobilization of faith-based initiatives in the service of renewing American imperialism [e.g., war in Iraq]" (Alexander 2005, p. 296)? How, in the USA, do the exotic trends of spirituality coexist with norms associated with oppressive mainstream Christianity?

Asking these questions illuminate that, within the interlocked domains of religion and citizenship as politics of nation-state, the hierarchy still conflates spirituality and "Christianity with good tradition while consigning 'others' to the realm of bad tradition and thus to serve as evidence of the need for good Christian tradition" (Alexander 2005, p. 296). At the same time, the shifting binary between religion and spirituality in neoliberal logics conveniently serves the neo/colonial mode of self-other hierarchy and continuously reproduces the logics of Orientalism both in nation-state and in the context of global society.

CRITICAL SPIRITUALITY

Writers who work with historical or contemporary coloniality have argued how the projects of demonizing the spiritual beliefs of the Other and converting the Other is a political and cultural project of western/white citizenship (Achebe 1989; Kaomea 2000). Postcolonial critiques of how spirituality has been appropriated for the (re)colonizing project of citizenship allows us to confront its governing logics and technologies within dominant imaginations. However, it is important to take a step that is more than an oppositional stance. Therefore, in this section, we introduce a concept of transformative spirituality to examine how spirituality has been a space of possibility for radical ways of articulating citizenships for more democratic futures (Alexander 2005; Smith 1999). This move has implications to rethinking citizenship education, particularly in relation to the intersection between religion and citizenship.

Transformative aspect of spirituality critiques ways in which religious entities have oppressed marginalized communities (both within and outside nation-state) to claim dominant (read: white) narrative of citizenship. Critiquing settler colonialism, Trask (1999) writes how churches and religious institutions have historically been complicit in the oppression of Hawaii people and their spiritual ways of being/knowing. Trask argues that "churches must examine their history of involvement in Hawaii's past and recognize their role in the loss Native Hawaiian control over their land and destiny and in the overthrow of the Hawaiian monarchy" (p. 247). Trask notes that for reconciliation and reparations to take place churches need to "return those church lands that justly belong to the Native Hawaiian people" and that religious institutions must "refuse to participate in the public blessing of those projects that adversely impact Native Hawaiians or the environment" (pp. 248–249). The transformative aspect of spirituality that Trask advocates raises questions on indigenous rights over ancestral places and foregrounds how spirituality has always been part of indigenous culture(s). Trask argues that churches and religious institutions need to recognize how there are multiple ways of being spiritual and that indigenous people have the right to "utilize and access religious symbols for traditional ceremonies and rituals" (p. 20). To advocate social justice and citizen rights for indigenous communities, Trask argues that religious leaders unlearn their association with US government, religious entities and tourist industries that have appropriated indigenous spirituality, labor and culture. For Trask, the question of indigenous Hawaii sovereignty is intimately connected to the indigenous communities' having "access to and protection of sacred sites and burial grounds and publics lands for ceremonial purposes" (p. 250).

Locating the discussion of spirituality within discourses of epistemology, black feminist scholar Dillard (2006) similarly argues that the discourse of spirituality has historically been a (required) space for African American communities. In this space, spirituality becomes a critical consciousness that provides a legitimate way to "participate in the social and political struggles of the world, including those we engage [as educators]" (p. 41). Consequently, "any effort we make to bring about peace and justice are indeed forms of spiritual practice" (p. 40). When spirituality is approached as a site of cultural citizenship, anti-racist practices and political mobilization (West 1993; hooks 1992), it challenges educators to rethink the category of spirituality (and its relationship to citizenship). It can also enable educator to recognize how spirituality cannot be a monolithic category of analysis that elides questions of racism, colonialism and white supremacy.

These critiques enable alternative ways of imagining spiritual/citizenship nexus in school and societal context. In school, curriculums often exoticize (and racialize) local and global cultures including religions in the name of learning about global citizenship. What we argue here is that educators can approach spirituality as a way of knowing and being: a topic that has been subjugated in learning about themes on imperialism and external and internal colonialism of nation-state. This approach carries a strong possibility of decolonizing move since spirituality as epistemology and ontology (and a critical practice of citizenship) opens up a space beyond Eurocentric-modern-colonial-scientific discourse and knowledge system. Invoking spirituality as a site of possibility regarding citizenship situates how the notion of spirituality has been a dynamic and inherent part of a community's ways of making sense of history and experiences in various oppressive conditions of life. Consequently, spirituality is engaged to serve political, cultural, epistemological, and ontological emancipatory goals. This engagement allows alternative ways of articulating citizenship that is attentive to questions of oppression, racism, etc. In this interconnected, embedded nature of transformative spiritual knowledge, spirituality does not purport to be dogmatic or become a proselytizing endeavor (see Shahjahan 2010, 483). Transformative spirituality demands rewriting of citizenship paradigms that limit experiences within the simple binary of citizens and non-citizens as well as the materiality as tangible and the spirituality as invisible or non-existent (Alexander 2005; Shahjahan 2005; Zine 2004).

Our purpose here is not simply overturning a hierarchy of various epistemological and ontological frameworks so that transformative spirituality/citizenship triumphs all other ways of knowing and being. Rather we agree with scholarships that anticolonial and decolonizing work requires centering indigenous and colonized communities' knowledge construction as alternative knowledge systems in our pursuit of criticality, justice, and decolonizing for different citizenship education. Educators ought to read carefully how and who speaks about spirituality. Rather than trying to interpret spirituality within existing neocolonial and neoliberal scientific discourse, we agree with Zine (2004) that spirituality and faith-based knowledge can be read as "contextualized and historicized paradigms of thought that are referenced in metaphysical realities" (p. 183).

Implications for Education for Global Citizenship

How can educators apply what we have discussed so far in their practice of national-global citizenship education? We reiterate that religion has always been part of the citizenship discourse in schools, particularly ways in which students are socialized into learning about what constitutes citizenship, including what are legitimate and illegitimate forms and performances of citizenship (legal/illegal, etc.). Therefore, students' religious or secular identities matter. Too often, in US school, students who negotiate non-mainstream religions or those who embrace secular orientations are seen as being less of citizens. For example, consider how the politically charged climate of Islamophobia in schools makes any faith claims made by Muslim students (or in general non-white students) suspicious and illegitimate. Being a Muslim in US school means one's faith being affiliated with fundamentalism or terrorism and associated with being anti-US state. The racism and constant surveillance of one's behaviors and speech make any claims to citizenship an impossible act. A critical practice of citizenship education needs to take all discriminations faced by students seriously, especially as religiously motivated discriminations are often overlooked in schools based on the assumption that such discriminations are acceptable or that they are not significant enough to be scrutinized. It is useful to examine how religious discriminations interconnect with racial, language and gender identities.

Educating students for critical global citizenship means questioning the culture of the school that privileges one religion over others. This means, in the US context, questioning ways in which other religions and spiritual prac-tices are seen as foreign, different, or even deviant. The tendency to treat mainstream (white) Christianity as the un(official) national religion insidi-ously marks the boundary of what is acceptable and not acceptable religion to affiliate in schooling and societal contexts. This discourse, then, relegates religions such as Islam and Hinduism as being illegitimate and even funda-mentalist so that these other religions become threats to the US mainstream culture. Similarly, the discourse does not question the fact that fundamental-ism is not isolated to one religion or secular orientation and that Christianity has always included violent fundamentalism. In other words, fundamentalism has been part of every religion and secular politics.

A critical approach to citizenship examines how religion enters various seg-ments of school cultures. Consider the case of athletics in schools and how athletics is often seen as a way to instill discipline and citizenship. It is worth asking: do schools openly or less overtly promote religions in the everyday athletic events? For example, do coaches use religious texts (Bible, etc.) or religious prayers in athletic related events? The very idea of using prayer to motivate or to instill a sense of community/citizenship within a group of stu-dents is problematic since it imposes beliefs on those students who may not desire to be part of the prayer or religiously oriented community. In fact, con-tinuing controversies in US schools include whether or not students should be forced to recite the Pledge of Alliance. The use of voluntary or non-volun-tary prayer reinforces the legitimacy of some religions while discounting the value of others, and it silences those who do not fit within the religious norms of the school context.

A critical approach to global citizenship also questions how religions are represented in textbooks and discussed in classrooms. Clearly, what is noted in textbooks or school curriculum is political and curricular knowledge is deeply implicated in politics (Apple 1997). Too often, US textbooks tend to focus on the glories of Christianity and deemphasize knowledge concerning other religions considered to be peripheral or small. In everyday classroom contexts, educators need to critically examine the politics (of knowledge) around when (and why) parents may seek to opt-out children from lessons on which reli-gion and how such choice affects ways in which we practice citizenship.

Critical citizenship education also critiques how threats (especially terrorist threats) vs. (national) security/safety are being spoken about in the school-ing contexts. Students can question how a binary of us-them and security threats deploy religious rationales (threats as being Islam-oriented or the Muslim world(s) as being against the USA, etc.). Media outlets also tend to sensationalize the binary of us–them to reinforce the boundary of legitimate citizenship. Who are causing these threats to whom? If they are politically produced by racial minorities, non-dominant religious affiliates, or interna-tional/foreign origins, the causes are framed as "their Othered/different identity." However, this reductionist tendency to view threats, for example, as being religiously oriented, see conflicts only in religious terms without examining other economic, geopolitical, and historical variables. Similarly, threats triggered by European Americans rarely receive religious scrutiny and (international) conflicts (particularly which impact the USA) are viewed as a simple effect of "their" religious dogmatism and not because of the violence of USA imperialism and neo/colonialism.

We encourage educators to initiate discussions on spirituality/citizenship as a transformative category of analysis and as a way of being and knowing that do not avoid everyday material questions of neo/colonial historical and social structures and conditions of life such as modernity, capitalism, post-coloniality, civilization, race, gender, etc. Some may doubt the possibilities created by transformative spirituality since it may appear remaining at the level of epistemology and ontology. However, as Mignolo (2011) argues, this discussion is fundamental to the decolonization of economy and politics, since both—political theory and political economy—have become imperial tools in the formation of the subjectivity of consumers and voters that nourish and support imperial actors and institutions in the state and corporations. (p. 62). Because of the link between materiality and epistemology that allows/enables particular citizenship narratives, it is absolutely necessary to ask if educators are consuming spirituality that is a historical or a kind of spirituality that is based on narrow interpretations of religious texts to invoke one's individual well-being.

CONCLUSION AND RECOMMENDATIONS REGARDING FUTURE RESEARCH

Spirituality as an analytical category of discussion is often missing within educational research, particularly how spirituality is connected to discussions on citizenship. Future research may benefit by examining how marginalized subjects, in a particular nation-state, may negotiate citizenship discourses (Osler and Starkey 2003). Research is particularly needed on how youth subjects negotiate spirituality in relation to prevailing citizenship discourses. Research is also needed on how spirituality may be an alternative site of individual and collective transformation. There is also limited research on how citizenship education programs in schools may include or exclude students who negotiate non-mainstream ways of being spiritual.

Considering that citizenship discussions often entail negotiating legal framework that often limit or constrain the rights of marginalized people, the analytical category of "cultural citizenship" (Ong 2003) can be an alternative site to reconsider the meaning of citizenship and how citizenship can be a more inclusive practice. Research on cultural citizenship can be linked to transformative spiritual practices of marginalized communities and way in which marginalized youth may negotiate spirituality within the sphere of cultural citizenship. Similarly, research is also needed on how communities may conceptualize citizenship beyond human needs or experiences and how citizenship may entail animal rights, ecological and environmental concerns.

New research possibilities of citizenship can be actualized within the context of local knowledge, particularly when we approach the concept of spirituality being connected to the politics of knowledge. Such an approach speaks about how we politically come to understand citizenship - our conditions of life and relations with each other. For example, Dei (2000) argues how indigenous forms of knowledge are often placed on the margins and how the inclusion of indigenous knowledge challenges traditional teaching and learning. Dei also writes that the question of indigenous knowledge cannot be understood outside of spirituality and that spirituality "is grounded in people, a place and a history" (p. 115, emphasis is added). Such grounding provides transformative possibilities for spirituality in relation to citizenship ideals and offers ways to reconnect and rebuild relationships with marginalized communities as people, places, and histories both in national and global contexts. Rather than mindlessly participating in neoliberal use of spirituality only to benefit "us" at the expense of them/the Other, transformative spirituality/citizenship can ask: What decolonizing contributions are we as global/national citizens making to the (Other) communities through our newly learned spirit/identity/ways of knowing?

NOTE

1. In this chapter, we use the U.S. as our particular case to contextualize our discussion so that concepts and analytic approaches can be historicized and localized. Rather than claiming a universal analysis, we emphasize that theorizing and decolonizing citizenship education needs to be contextualized vis-à-vis its own global-local history, politics, and dynamics (see Rhee and Subreenduth 2006).

REFERENCES

Abu-Lughod, L. (2002). Do Muslim women really need saving? Anthropological reflections on cultural relativism and its others. *American Anthropologist, 104*(39), 783–790.

Aldred, L. (2000). Plastic shamans and astro turf sun dances: New age commercialization of Native American spirituality. *The American Indian Quarterly, 24*, 329–352.

Achebe, C. (1989). *Hopes and impediments: Selected essays.* New York: Doubleday.

Alexander, J. M. (2005). *Pedagogies of crossing: Meditations on feminism, sexual politics, memory and the sacred.* Durham: Duke University Press.

Anderson, B. (1983). *Imagined communities: Reflections on the origin and spread of nationalism.* New York: Verso Books.

Apple, M. (1997). *Cultural politics & education.* New York: Teachers College Press.

Banks, J. A. (Ed.). (2004). *Diversity and citizenship education: Global perspectives.* New York: Jossey-Bass.

Carrette, J., & King, R. (2005). *Selling spirituality: The silent takeover of religion.* London: Routledge.

Dei, G. J. S. (2000). Rethinking the role of indigenous knowledge in the academy. *International Journal of Inclusive Education, 4*, 111–132.

Dillard, C. B. (2006). *On spiritual strivings: Transforming an African American woman's academic life*. Albany, NY: SUNY Press.

Fanon, F. (1963). *The wretched of the earth*. New York: Grove Press.

Foucault, M. (1980). *Power/knowledge: Selected interviews and other writings 1972–1977*. New York: Pantheon Books.

Fryberg, S. A., & Stephens, N. M. (2010). When the world is colorblind, American Indians are invisible: A diversity science approach. *Psychological Inquiry, 21*, 115–119.

Gaudelli, B. (2016). *Global citizenship education: Everyday transcendence*. New York: Routledge.

Germain, F. (2011). The earthquake, the missionaries, and the future of vodou. *Journal of Black Studies, 42*, 247–263.

Hooks, B. (1994). *Teaching to transgress*. New York: Routledge.

Hooks, B. (1992). *Black looks: Race and representation*. New York: Routledge.

Kaomea, J. (2000). Curriculum of aloha? Colonialism and tourism in Hawai'i's elementary textbooks. *Curriculum Inquiry, 30*, 319–344.

Kumashiro, K. (2009). *Against common sense: Teaching and learning toward social justice*. New York: Routledge.

Ladson-Billings, G. (2004). Culture versus citizenship: The challenge of racialized citizenship in the United States. In J. A. Banks (Ed.), *Diversity and citizenship education* (pp. 99–126). New York: Jossey-Bass.

Mehta, G. (1994). *Karma cola: Marketing the mystic east*. New York: Vintage.

Mignolo, W. (2011). *The darker side of western modernity: Global futures, decolonial options*. Durham, NC: Duke University Press.

Ong, A. (2003). *Buddha is hiding: Refugees, citizenship, the new America*. Berkeley, CA: University of California Press.

Osler, A., & Starkey, H. (2003). Learning for cosmopolitan citizenship: Theoretical debates and young people's experiences. *Educational Review, 55*(3), 243–254.

Pewewardy, C. D. (2004). Playing Indian at halftime: The controversy over American Indian mascots, logos, and nicknames in school-related events. *The Clearing House, 7*, 180–185.

Prashad, V. (2000). *The karma of brown folk*. Minneapolis, MN: U of Minnesota Press.

Rhee, J., & Subreenduth, S. (2006). De/colonizing education: Examining transnational localities [Special issue]. *International Journal of Qualitative Studies in Education, 19*, 545–672.

Rhee, J. A., & Subedi, B. (2014). Colonizing and decolonizing projects of re/covering spirituality. *Educational Studies, 50*(4), 339–356.

Rizvi, F. (2004). Debating globalization and education after September 11. *Comparative Education, 40*(2), 157–171.

Rose, N. (1990). *Governing the soul: The shaping of the private self*. London: Taylor & Frances.

Rose, N. (1998). *Inventing our selves: Psychology, power, and personhood*. Cambridge: Cambridge University Press.

Said, E. W. (1978). *Orientalism*. New York: Vintage.

Shahjahan, R. A. (2005). Spirituality in the academy: Reclaiming from the margins and evoking a transformative way of knowing the world. *International Journal of Qualitative Studies in Education, 18*, 685–711.

Shahjahan, R. A. (2010). Toward a spiritual praxis: The role of spirituality among faculty of color teaching for social justice. *The Review of Higher Education, 33,* 473–512.

Smith, L. T. (1999). *Decolonizing methodologies: Research and indigenous peoples.* London; New York: Zed Books.

Subedi, S., & Daza, S. L. (Eds.). (2008). Postcolonial Perspectives on Education: A Special Issue. *Race Ethnicity and Education,* 11(1).

Trask, H. (1999). *From a native daughter: Colonialism and sovereignty in Hawai'i.* Honolulu: University of Hawaii.

Urban, H. B. (2005). Politics and religion: An overview. In L. Jones (Ed. 2nd ed.), *Encyclopedia of religion* (pp. 7248–7260). Detroit: Macmillan Reference USA. Retrieved from http://ic.galegroup.com/ic/whic/ReferenceDetailsPage/Documen tToolsPortletWindow?displayGroupName=Reference&action=2&catId=&docume ntId=GALE%7CCX3424502465&zid=d1010e23b21fa15fcc5d3c53b2966b46&so urce=Bookmark&u=fl_marionlibserv&jsid=8e6084c975f6ca677f78bcfad5f9198d.

West, C. (1993). *Prophetic fragments: Illuminations of the crisis in American religion and culture.* Trenton, NJ: World African Press.

Zine, J. (2004). Creating a critical faith-centered space for antiracist feminism: Reflections of a Muslim scholar-activist. *Journal of Feminist Studies in Religion, 20,* 167–187.

Author's Biography

Binaya Subedi teaches classes on diversity and equity, global education, race, poverty and immigration at the Ohio State University. He has published articles in a number of journals and is editor of the journal *Educational Studies.* Professor Subedi has conducted community work in Nepal and in urban areas of the Midwest. His current research examines the identities and experiences of refugee/immigrant youth in midwestern U.S. cities.

Jeong-eun Rhee is a professor of education at Long Island University, New York. Her scholarship focuses on anti-oppressive education through the lens of race, class, gender, immigration and other socially constructed differences; qualitative research methodology; and international education, empire, and politics of knowledge. Her commitment has been to opening up a space for the unsayable, silenced, and marginalized in the production of knowledge to delineate historical, material, and spiritual interdependence. Professor Rhee is editor of *Educational Studies.*

CHAPTER 25

Race, National Exclusion, and the Implications for Global Citizenship Education

Jennifer M. Bondy and Aaron Johnson

INTRODUCTION

Race and citizenship is a very controversial subject in the world today. Debates circulate around the globe about whether or not immigrants—subjects who reside in a country, but who are not citizens of that country—should have access to equitable education, placement in the labor market, language rights, and religious freedom. Questions arise about, for example, who is a "normal"[1] American, German, Irish, British, or French citizen. Although these questions are not new, we continue to quarrel over the rights that citizens should be entitled to; where the boundary is drawn between citizen and other; and, who is included in the category of "citizen." In the context of globalization and shifting demographics, these debates have taken on rather violent tones, stirring emotions and provoking worrisome reactions when it comes to the question of race and citizenship.

Explorations of race, therefore, hold vast potential for furthering our understanding of citizenship in the context of global migration. Race is often bypassed, circumvented, or omitted in classroom conversations and lessons on citizenship (Banks 2004; Marshal 2015). This omission often occurs even though youth of color, including immigrant youth, indicate that race is salient

J.M. Bondy (✉)
Virginia Tech, Blacksburg, USA
e-mail: jmbondy@vt.edu

A. Johnson
University of Nebraska Lincoln, Lincoln, USA
e-mail: ajohnson147@unl.edu

© The Author(s) 2018
I. Davies et al. (eds.), *The Palgrave Handbook of Global Citizenship and Education*, https://doi.org/10.1057/978-1-137-59733-5_25

to their experiences with citizenship, belonging, and exclusion (e.g., Abu El-Haj 2009; Bondy 2015; Brown et al. 2011; Maira 2009). This suggests that it is important to explore how race is mobilized to potentially fortify dichotomies between "us/them," "citizen/immigrant," and "belonging/not-belonging" (Lukose 2007; Sánchez and Kasun 2012). This also suggests that immigrant youth experiences are an appropriate lens through which to examine race and its relationship to citizenship.

In this chapter, we present transnationalism and cultural citizenship as frameworks for a more critical approach to notions of race and citizenship among immigrant youth of color. Transnationalism and cultural citizenship allow educators to grasp the complexity of immigrant youths' lives, particularly as this complexity expands due to globalization and intersects with race-based societal inequities (Sánchez & Kasun 2012; Maira 2009). We draw upon one of the author's research with Latina youth and their experiences with race and citizenship in a US context of anti-Latina/o immigration (Bondy 2014, 2015, 2016). We also draw upon follow-up interviews conducted with the Latina youth four years after the original study. Although we focus on how Latina youth in the USA navigate broader structural processes of citizen–subject formation with the nation-state, their perspectives might provide insight into how they and, by extension, other marginalized state subjects around the world negotiate various aspects of citizenship and belonging. We argue that young people's experiences with race are central to debates on education for global citizenship. This chapter highlights the importance of thinking about nationalism, globalization, and citizenship for different groups of youth. While some youth cross national borders and may think of themselves as global citizens, borders around the world are being reinvested with xenophobic and political strategies designed to restore fictions of the nation as uniform, timeless, pure, and White (Pérez Huber et al. 2008).

After discussing transnationalism and cultural citizenship, we explore some of the key issues arising in the research with Latina youth and their experiences with race and citizenship in a US context. We then offer some implications of this research for education for global citizenship and conclude with recommendations on future lines of inquiry.

Conceptual Framework: Transnationalism and Cultural Citizenship

Many who participate in cross-border migrations often form identities and a sense of belonging between two different countries, or transnationally, via economic, political, religious, or familial affiliations (Sánchez and Kasun 2012; Villenas 2007). Even if physical travel between countries is not possible, these lived experiences, frames of reference, and belonging are often influenced by nation-state discourses and practices on immigration. For Latina/o youth migrating between Latin America and the USA, US policies and practices around immigration and citizenship play an important role in youths' identity formations. As Kearney (1995) noted, transnationalism underscores the cultural and political work of nation-states as they compete for predominance over citizens and "aliens." Within the Latina/o diaspora, many Latina/o immigrants have the ability and desire to preserve political, economic, and social connections across nation-states (Sánchez and Kasun 2012; Villenas 2007).

In her exploration of how nation-states produce ideas of citizenship, Lukose (2007) argued that transnational approaches to educational research utilize the nation-state as an object of analysis rather than as a unit of analysis. This contrasts much of the research on immigration and education in which immigrant youth of color are regarded as engaging in unilinear, processes of incorporation and assimilation into the receiving country (e.g., Peguero and Bondy 2015; Rong and Preissle 2009). However, some scholars broaden the incorporation approach to transnationalism. For example, in her research with Latina youth, Sánchez (2007) contended that transnationalism and assimilation were not necessarily mutually exclusive processes. She offered that transnationalism helps to buffer racial discrimination experienced by immigrant youth of color and to facilitate positive incorporation into the USA. Transnationalism is therefore salient for immigrant youth in contending with and resisting racist nativist practices embedded in incorporation processes. Lukose (2007) argued, however, that such studies are "still situated within an assimilationist framework that seeks to assess the impact of transnationalism on processes of national assimilation" (p. 408). Transnational studies must broaden and deepen their analytic lens by revisiting basic assumptions about the nation-state, its borders, race, and citizenship (DeJaeghere and McCleary 2010; Lukose 2007; Ong 1996).

Ong (1996) provided a useful analytic for exploring immigrant youths' citizenship identities within a transnational framework. She argued that citizenship, rather than being solely a formal legal status, is a socioculturally embedded process that entails dual dimensions of "being made" and "self-making" (1996, p. 738). Ong drew on Foucault's concept of governmentality to understand how state institutions recruit civil society and social groups to create and discipline constructions of the citizen. The second dimension entails "self-making," or the everyday practices immigrants engage to negotiate the contested relations of belonging. Ong proposed that immigrants' of color desire for inclusion in the social body may not be convincing claims for larger society and the state. Research on youth and citizenship is sparse and tends to come out of developmental perspectives and adult-centric views of what constitutes politics; yet, there is a growing body of literature that centers youth understanding of citizenship and politics as they negotiate racialized relations of power in their everyday lives (e.g., Abu El-Haj 2009; Bondy 2016, 2015; Maira 2009).

LATINA YOUTH AND CULTURAL CITIZENSHIP

In the context of shifting demographics and anti-Latina/o immigration, questions about citizenship and racialization take on new meanings for Latina youth. Many Latinas/os, both immigrants and citizens, have been victims of racial profiling, verbal assaults, and physical attacks. Our analysis focuses on 7 first- and second-generation[2] Latina youth who lived in Palmetto City,[3] which is located in Broward County, Florida. More specifically, our analysis draws from (i) an interview study conducted with the youth Latina in autumn 2010, and (ii) follow-up interviews with 6 focal participants in autumn 2014. Both the original and follow-up studies explored how adolescent Latinas formed their citizenship identities within broader structural processes of the nation-state, and how these identities were shaped by daily lived experiences with racialized exclusion. More specifically, data collected from the original study in 2010 included three, progressively layered, semi-structured interviews (Seidman 2006) that were designed to: (a) establish trust and rapport between the participants and Bondy as the researcher; (b) to provide the participants an opportunity to explain what citizenship meant to them; and (c) to incorporate an approximate member-check to give the participants an opportunity to clarify and expand upon their citizenship identities. Data collected from the follow-up study in 2014 included one semi-structured interview designed to explore how participants' understanding of citizenship had or had not grown and changed over time.

Broward County is an interesting site for the research. While there is attention regarding racial profiling of Latinas/os in areas like Arizona and Georgia, there is little attention paid to Florida despite it being a gateway state. In 2010, all Latina youth who participated in the study were juniors attending Palmetto City High School (PCHS), which was 46% Latina/o, 44% White, 6% Asian, and 4% Black Caribbean and African American.[4] The Latina/o population at the high school was predominantly middle-class, first- or second-generation, and mostly from South America. All Latina youth in the study were Spanish/English bilingual. Youths' parents generally had a bachelor's and/or master's degree. For some youth, however, their parents' educational credentials were not recognized in the United States, causing their parents to work lower-wage jobs or earn another degree. At the time of the follow-up interviews in autumn 2014, the 6 Latina youth who participated were juniors in college and attended either community college or 4-year public or private universities. Not all the Latina youth in this study were directly targeted by anti-Latina/o immigration discourses and practices, but we found that all of them had to grapple with racial surveillance of Latinas/os.

CITIZENSHIP MEANS OPPORTUNITY
AND RACIALIZED VULNERABILITY

The experiences of the Latina youth linked with practices of immigration in ways that created possibilities for citizenship marked by vulnerability, as well as citizenship imagined as opportunity. Citizenship and immigration, as political and cultural projects of the nation-state (Kearney 1995), are articulated as essentialized and exclusive practices that protect and secure the rights of some while, at the same time, ensure the vulnerability of others (Pérez Huber et al. 2008). Such vulnerability may conflict with US democratic promises of freedom, justice, and opportunity.

Many Latina youth and their families migrated to the USA for social, economic, and educational opportunities; yet, they, their parents, or friends also encountered social exclusion and limited opportunities. In 2010, Lucia, a US resident from Venezuela, and Carolina, a naturalized US citizen from Colombia, described their imaginaries of educational and economic opportunities. Lucia explained that her parents migrated to the United States for "more opportunities for us in education, future-wise." Carolina stated that her family migrated "for college and academics and jobs and things like that." As first-generation immigrants, both girls appear to draw upon an opportunity narrative that schooling will create better life chances (Michael et al. 2007). Lucia maintained her optimism in education and opportunities when, in 2014, she described the American Dream as "being able to work hard, get an education, and obtain whatever you want." However, some Latina youth described these opportunities with tempered optimism.

Gabriela, a young woman from Venezuela who had become a naturalized US citizen one week before the first interview in 2010, appeared to acutely feel the limitations of the opportunity narrative. She described these limitations in 2010 and again in 2014. For example, in 2010, while Gabriela spoke of pursuing an education as something she must embrace, she also communicated the high price her family paid by uprooting their lives in Venezuela. She and her sister, who did not work as young girls in Venezuela, both worked at her dad's watch store "every day after school, weekends, and summer vacation" when her family moved to the USA. Additionally, Gabriela heart-wrenchingly explained that her mother, who was a principal in Venezuela, had to "revalidate" her education because it was not recognized in the USA. This sentiment was echoed again in 2014 when Gabriela, then a junior in college, questioned the American Dream by stating:

> You have an opportunity here to build a future, but I've noticed that it's not really as true as people say. I think when people come to study, they can't work, or you can graduate here...and then you have to leave because you have no papers.

When asked to expand on this statement, Gabriela expounded on sacrifice and then opportunity.

In my preschool where I work, there's Hispanic women in their 30 s, 40 s. They were clinical psychologists at hospitals in Latin America and they come here and they're not even teachers; they're teacher *aides*...that's what makes the adults crash; no one's going to study again. And for the youth, it's coming here...they finish college and what do they have? They don't have papers to work...I feel like they're really set up for failure. It's *better* than studying over *there* [Latin America]; it's *something*.

The Latina youth and their families migrated to the US to seek better education and work. Yet, many might find these opportunities inaccessible. As Gabriela suggested, the state can mobilize education and employment as technologies to define Latinas/os, both documented and undocumented, as immigrants. This mobilization has the effect of coupling race and citizenship. Thus, Latinas/os can be caught in a web of work and immigration policies, and relegated to a racialized economic citizenship that is linked with immigrant labor and national exclusion (Bondy 2014; Maira 2009). While Latinas/os might perform an economic citizenship that fulfills the American ethos of hard work and opportunity, they may also "crash," "be set up for failure," and never gain full inclusion (DeJaeghere and McCleary 2010; Michael et al. 2007).

In addition to encountering limited freedom to develop their identities in the USA, Latina youth born in Venezuela—Lucia, Scarlett, and Gabriela—also expressed the vulnerabilities they experienced in their home country. For example, in 2014, Lucia explained, "The country is falling apart and the ridiculous levels of economic insecurity...it's just horrendous." Scarlett, a naturalized US citizen, echoed this sentiment in 2014 in her description of life in the US compared to Venezuela, "It's not safe at all in Venezuela. Here, you can do anything you want really and be fine. Over there, you cannot." Both girls allude to not having certain social and economic freedoms met in Venezuela; yet, as Gabriela expressed in 2014, despite "waking up to the sound of gunshots and ambulances," there was freedom to embody certain cultural identities. She explained, "In Venezuela, it's more of a community. Everyone is together...I like the culture, the *food*...the music." Gabriela later stated, "In Venezuela, *every* Friday night and *every* Saturday lunch, it would be with family. Here, you don't have that." This suggests through their family and cultural affiliations, Latina youth may see the nation as a site of familiarity and belonging, rather than as a bestower of rights. However, as Bondy (2014) has previously argued, Latina youth often negotiate social, educational, and economic opportunities in the USA while also being racially excluded.

The boundaries of citizenship can result from transnational migration and the contradictions between espoused US ideals of opportunity and experiences with racialized vulnerability. Latina youth often interrogate the technologies of citizenship by alluding to its legal dimensions and to cultural practices that racialize them as immigrants and inscribe them as citizens of differential worth (Ong 1996). For example, Viviana, a US resident from

Venezuela, explained in 2010 that if she became a US citizen, she wouldn't celebrate because people would still "treat you as different." Gabriela and Carolina, both US citizens, offered examples of this different treatment. Not only were Gabriela and her family harassed by US airport security, Carolina shared a story of racist White neighbors in Texas who attempted to shoot her cousins' cats and dogs (Bondy 2014). As Dejaeghere and McCleary (2010) argued, social groups can engage immigration as a project that constitutes race as a category of national exclusion. Rather than create opportunities, social practices related to immigration can essentialize identities thus creating racialized vulnerability around belonging.

Citizenship Means Flexibility

The data suggest that Latina youth are living a transnational adolescence where they are confronting the limits of any one nation-state to protect and provide for them (Maira 2009). Their desires for US citizenship were not seen as conflicting with their affiliations with their home countries; rather, they wanted US citizenship for the economic, social, and educational benefits (Bondy 2014). Emma, a US-born citizen whose parents were from Colombia, stated in 2010 that citizenship enabled the ability to travel freely across national borders to see her family in Colombia. Maira (2009) noted, citizenship can be understood as layered in mobility and migration, and in the transnational engagement of political, economic, and/or social resources not available in one country. In 2014, Lucia desired citizenship as a "legal status" that would enable her to vote, "have job opportunities," and protect her from "prejudice" against immigrants. Uses of citizenship as flexible (Ong 1999) not only leave open questions of national belonging, but also the strategic use of citizenship for civic and economic aims, and for a safeguard against race-based civil rights violations in anti-immigrant contexts.

Latina youth in this study seemed to enact a type of flexible citizenship. In 2010, five of the girls had been separated from their extended families in South America for at least 7 years. Three of the Latina youth had lived in the same apartment building as their cousins, aunts, and uncles; one had lived on the same street as her extended family; and, one of the Latina youth had lived with her grandparents. In 2010 and 2014, all girls spoke longingly and with great sadness about their friends and families back home, and four of the Latina youth—Carolina, Lucia, Viviana, and Gabriela—recounted the trauma they experienced in school by not speaking English when they first arrived. The Latina youth, however, appeared resigned to transnational family arrangements as a fact of life (Ek 2009; Sánchez 2007; Maira 2009). For example, in 2010 and 2014, Viviana explained that she and her family in Venezuela sustained ties by skyping together every Christmas dinner, and that this enabled her to maintain connections to home. While the re-creation of family ties is possible through technology (Ek 2009; Sánchez & Kasun 2012), cross-border physical mobility, as previously indicated by Emma, is tied to legal membership in a nation-state (Ong 1999).

It became evident that some Latina youth thought of citizenship it contextual ways. Gabriela, as the only Jewish participant, drew upon religion and language to both resist racial exclusion and claim belonging in Venezuela and the USA. In 2010, Gabriela recounted a summer camp experience in New Jersey with "White kids from the north, like Michigan," who asked her, "How can you be Venezuelan *and* Jewish?" The youth also stated, "You're from Venezuela? You don't speak English." Gabriela's response that Venezuela is a country and Judaism is a religion, and her question, "Wait. You're American *and* Catholic?" were unconvincing arguments to the White youth. Also unconvincing were her claims that she lived in the United States and spoke English. What is important, however, is that Gabriela thought through questions of belonging during an experience when Jews were being framed as non-citizens of Venezuela because of particular constructions of Latinas/os. She was also able to think through questions of belonging when Latinas/os were being framed as non-citizens of the US because of racialized constructions of an ethno-linguistic identity. Gabriela uses Judaism to counter a technology of exclusion from Venezuela and Spanish/English bilingualism to counter a technology of racialized exclusion from the USA. Her maintenance of her Jewish and bilingual identities matters because it enables her to support flexible notions of citizenship; counter racist nativist, English-only ideologies in the USA that are hostile to Latinas/os and the Spanish language; and, reconcile racialized national exclusions (Ek 2009; Maira 2009).

CITIZENSHIP MEANS CRITIQUE

Everyday experiences of citizenship and national belonging for the Latina youth were often shaped by US policies and practices on the national and global stages. Although the girls did not engage in formal political language, many offered critiques of racism, anti-Latina/o sentiments, and US foreign policy. Criticism for the US's rationale for deportation and war on immigration was pervasive. For example, in 2010, Emma emphasized respect for human rights when she condemned the "harsh" treatment of undocumented Latina/o immigrants, stating they weren't "doing anything bad" and "just wanted a better future for their families." Scarlett echoed this sentiment in 2014 when she explained, "Latino immigrants *should* get a chance to become a citizen, no matter what social situation they come from. *Anyone* who is trying to escape *should* get a chance to come into this country."

Other youth challenged rhetoric around the US as a "benevolent" immigrant nation by linking such "benevolence" to violence and colonialism. In 2010, Laura, a US resident from Colombia, spoke of the US history of colonization and conquest when asked about US perceptions of Latinas/os. After describing Latinas/os economic contributions to the US Laura stated that Europeans were immigrants who killed Native Americans and "everybody else" who would "have made another country." Scarlett also contested the benevolent narrative in 2014 when she asked, "What is an immigrant? I mean, Europeans are the first who came here and colonized America." For Laura and Scarlett, it appears their critiques of "benevolence" are partly a response to practices which locate Latinas/os (and not Europeans) as racialized immigrants and therefore outsiders.

In a climate where Latinas/os are framed as "criminals" and "illegal aliens" (Pérez Huber et al. 2008), youth may find little room to critique US politics and foreign policy in schools. Interestingly, though, school was a space where many Latina youth felt comfortable discussing politics, mainly because of the number of Latina/o students who attended the high school. In classroom conversations between teachers and students, ideals of national and global justice are inculcated. For example in 2010, Laura shared a story of a heated debate from her US history class during which a White teacher, in the midst of a lecture on immigration, condemned Mexico's president for not supporting Arizona SB1070.[5] Numerous Latina/o students, including Laura, spoke up and disagreed. The teacher, however, dismissed students' concerns by opposing Latin American intervention in the US and by supporting US intervention in other countries. Laura was upset and said,

> Isn't America the one that's all about free speech, first of all? Second of all, the United States is the one country that gets involved in every single international thing. Whether they're invited or not, or making a positive impact. They do it automatically.

Even though Latina youth may not have the validation of formal citizenship, they can take a stance in discussions about race, immigration, and global politics to publicly voice a critique.

IMPLICATIONS FOR EDUCATION FOR GLOBAL CITIZENSHIP

The voice and shared experiences included in this chapter demonstrate the powerful role race may play for young immigrants of color in the development of citizenship identities and civic understandings that bares particular significance when further considered in the context of global citizenship and education for global citizenship. The concept of race coupled with youth cultural identities provided our participants with a robust lens through which they grappled with, negotiated, and ultimately made meaning concerning citizenship—as factors including opportunity narratives (and its shortcomings) were held in tension with their own lived experiences. As such, the civic understandings articulated by participants proved highly complex and sophisticated, appearing to oscillate across conceptualizations suggestive of cultural and transnational orientations that proved both flexible in their compositions and contextually imagined. It is from these dynamic understandings and voiced experiences that we now consider further within the gaze of preparing youth for global citizenry.

The goal of global education is the preparation of responsible and effective citizens within a global society (Merryfield & Kasai 2010; Myers 2006; Noddings 2005; Nussbaum 2007). Such preparation, many global education scholars have argued, is attained through learning experiences and opportunities that foster and incorporate multiple perspectives; an awareness to the cause and effects of globalization; recognition and respect for cross-cultural commonalities and difference; and, an alertness to the interconnected nature of life and events within global society (Kirkwood-Tucker 2009). Consistently woven through global education discourse is the need to solve problems that permeate geographic boundaries while fostering common understandings and values, all the while avoiding the pitfalls of cultural absolutism—many have referred to this as balancing desires for both unity with diversity (Banks 2004; Hansen 2011). What appears missing, however, when held against the experiences of our participants, is a deeper understanding of one's self in this conversation, understandings that experiences documented here have shown are highly influenced by notions of race and racism. Without such understanding, issues of privilege and oppression may covertly operate under the auspices of universal citizenship, nationalism, and/or neoliberalism within the context of global citizenship (e.g., Gaudelli 2009; Noddings 2005). In building bridges across difference toward solving shared social problems, we suggest opportunities for students to introspectively reflect upon who they are as citizens and critically consider forces including oppression and privilege that may impact principles embedded within global education aimed at preparing future global citizens.

Such a suggestion, as our participants' experiences have shown, is underpinned with a clarion call for equal consideration of student voice and the need for intentional spaces for students to unpack emergent understandings and articulate those through co-constructed channels. The power differentials common to K-12 classrooms and domineering roles of classroom teacher ultimately served in these instances to preclude the voice of our participants and in doing so colored their civic worldviews with cynicism and an increased sense of disassociation. This was, however, in stark contrast to other shared spaces within the school campus, many spaces of which our participants freely expressed themselves, and in doing so demonstrated greater notions of political self-efficacy with their peers. Surveillance in these cases stymied the voice of our participants within the classroom context; however, youth resilience and desires to be publicly heard did not let them to go silent.

Youth resilience and voice in these instances challenges researchers and those with an interest in preparing youth for global citizenship to consider alternative spaces through which youth exercise political behavior; spaces not restricted to classroom contexts. As Marshall and colleagues (2015) reminded us, today's students are equipped with a "sophisticated storehouse of critical, nuanced, and multi-layered experientially based knowledge of what it means to be a citizen" (p. 67); knowledge that will ultimately challenge anachronistic notions of what it means to be a citizen. Capturing these new knowledge forms and political behaviors may prove insufficient however, if the locus of concentration for researchers remains the classroom, a place where students of color in particular may feel is a space where their contribution is not being heard.

FUTURE LINES OF INQUIRY

Citizenship, according to cultural citizenship scholars and critical multicultural scholars, cannot be divorced from culture (Rosaldo & Flores 1997; Urrieta, 2004)—Brown et al. (2011) argue race and culture are "inextricably embedded" (p. 295) within the concept of citizenship. Scholars from these fields have reported a love/hate relationship expressed by students of color when national citizenship identities collide with cultural identities (Maira 2009; Urrieta 2004). With this in mind and within the purview of global citizenship, future inquiries are suggested concerning the civic identities of underrepresented youth in relation to the intersection of cultural identity and global citizenship identity—or more succinctly, further exploration of the unity/diversity tension as it relates to the specific experiences and civic development of racial minorities within a global context. Studies in this area would be greatly served by drawing from the rich tradition of work in the fields of cultural and critical multicultural citizenship education.

In her study of school campus as public space Schmidt (2013), considers the impact space regulation and surveillance may bare on youth civic development. She reported new forms of resistance and re-creation of space efforts exercised by students. Schmidt's work and the experiences voiced by our participants, while suggesting the possibility and potential of re-envisioned public spaces, also forces us to consider this same logic as applicable to the shared space of the classroom and the need for re-envisioning and re-negotiating student-teacher binary. Future inquiries are suggested within the confines of re-negotiated classroom spaces, spaces that include flattening or disrupting hierarchies within the classroom context, e.g. dialogic approach to pedagogy (Fecho and Botzakis 2007) and allow for students to challenge monolithic representations of global citizenship as they are held in contrast with their lived experiences.

CONCLUSION

The purpose of this chapter was to explore how race, particularly through transnational and cultural citizenship frameworks, is central to understanding immigrant youths' of color citizenship formations. More specifically, we first examined transnationalism and cultural citizenship and why they are important for understanding how race is designed as a project that is mobilized to exclude immigrant youth of color from citizenship and from the nation. We then explored how Latina youth understand citizenship (i.e., as opportunity and racialized vulnerability, flexibility, and critique) and described the implications for education for global citizenship. Similar to Marshall and colleagues' (2015) admonition regarding citizenship education within the nation-state, education for global citizenship can never be deracialized and, at the same time, be democratic, just, and responsive to the needs and experiences of immigrant youth of color. Finally, we put forth a vision for future lines of inquiry that explore how classrooms are imbued with meanings and processes that potentially undermine racialized bodies in spaces marked by Whiteness. How do youth of color manage their positioning within universal notions of global citizenship? How do universal notions of global citizenship education become naturalized and what does it mean if such notions are disrupted?

Citizenship can be taken for granted; yet, if our goal is to move toward more just and democratic world in which youth are prepared to be global citizens, then it is imperative to consider the voices of those for whom citizenship is not a given. While perhaps not all immigrant youth of color are constructed as "illegal aliens" or "criminals," many nevertheless bear the burden of doubt that questions their right to belong. As we imagine possibilities for education for global citizenship, inquiries related to racialized inclusion and exclusion in the nation may be helpful points of departure.

NOTES

1. We use inverted commas to suggest certain terms are socially constructed, rather than natural and given.
2. First-generation refers to foreign-born youth with foreign-born parents and second-generation refers to US-born youth with at least one foreign-born parent.
3. All names for the city, school, and participants are pseudonyms. Percentages are approximated to maintain confidentiality.
4. As previously noted, all names for the city, school, and participants are pseudonyms. Additionally, percentages are approximated to maintain confidentiality.
5. Arizona SB 1070 is state legislation legitimizing the racial profiling and surveillance of Latinas/os.

REFERENCES

Abu El-Haj, T. R. (2009). Becoming citizens in an era of globalization and migration: Re-imagining citizenship as critical practice. *Theory Into Practice, 48*(4), 274–282. doi:10.1080/00405840903192714.

Banks, J. A. (2004). Teaching for social justice, diversity, and citizenship in a global world. *The Educational Forum, 68*, 289–298. doi:10.1080/00131720408984645.

Bondy, J. M. (2014). "Why do I have to pledge the U.S. flag? It's not my country!": Latina youths rearticulating citizenship and national belonging. *Multicultural Perspectives, 16*(4), 193–202. doi:10.1080/15210960.2014.952300.

Bondy, J. M. (2015). Hybrid citizenship: Latina youth and the politics of belonging. *The High School Journal, 98*(4), 353–373. doi:10.1353/hsj.2015.0012.

Bondy, J. M. (2016). Latina youth, education, and citizenship: A feminist transnational analysis. *Theory & Research in Social Education, 44*(2), 212–243. doi:10.1080/00933104.2016.1170644.

Brown, A., Crowley, R., & King, L. (2011). Black civitas: An examination of Carter Woodson's contributions to teaching about race, citizenship, and the black soldier. *Theory & Research in Social Education, 39*(2), 278–299. doi:10.1080/00933104.2011.10473455.

DeJaeghere, J. G., & McCleary, K. S. (2010). The making of Mexican migrant youth civic identities: Transnational spaces and imaginaries. *Anthropology & Education Quarterly, 41*(3), 228–244. doi:10.1111/j.1548-1492.2010.01085.x.

Ek, L. D. (2009). "Allá en Guatemala": Transnationalism, language, and identity of a Pentecostal Guatemalan-American young woman. *The High School Journal, 92*(4), 67–81. doi:10.1353/hsj.0.0033.

Fecho, B., & Botzakis, S. (2007). Feasts of becoming: Imagining a literacy classroom based on dialogic beliefs. *Journal of Adolescent & Adult Literacy, 50*(7), 548–558. doi:10.1598/JAAL.50.7.4.

Gaudelli, W. (2009). Heuristics of global citizenship discourses towards curriculum enhancement. *Journal of Curriculum Theorizing, 25*(1), 68–85.

Hansen, D. (2011). *The teacher and the world: A study of cosmopolitanism as education.* New York, NY: Routledge.

Kearney, M. (1995). The local and the global: The anthropology of globalization and transnationalism. *Annual Review of Anthropology, 24,* 547–565. doi:10.1146/annurev.an.24.100195.002555.

Kirkwood-Tucker, T. F. (2009). *Visions in global education: The globalization of curriculum and pedagogy in teacher education and schools: Perspectives from Canada, Russia, and the United States.* New York, NY: Peter Lang.

Lukose, R. A. (2007). The difference that diaspora makes: Thinking through anthropology of immigrant education in the United States. *Anthropology & Education Quarterly, 38*(4), 167–189. doi:10.1525/aeq.2007.38.4.405.

Maira, S. M. (2009). *Missing: Youth, citizenship, and empire after 9/11.* Durham, NC: Duke University Press.

Marshall, P., Manfra, M. M., & Simmons, C. (2015). No more playing in the dark: Twenty-first century citizenship, crucial race theory, and the future of the social studies methods course. In A. Crowe & A. Cuenca (Eds.), *Rethinking social studies teacher education in the twenty-first century* (pp. 61–79). New York, NY: Springer.

Merryfield, M., & Kasai, M. (2010). How are teachers responding to globalization? In W. Parker (Ed.), *Social studies today research and practice* (pp. 165–174). New York, NY: Routledge.

Michael, A., Andrade, N., & Bartlett, L. (2007). Figuring "success" in a bilingual high school. *Urban Review, 39*(2), 167–189. doi:10.1007/s11256-007-0045-y.

Myers, J. (2006). Rethinking the social studies curriculum in the context of globalization: Education for global citizenship in the U.S. *Theory & Research Social Education, 34*(3), 370–394. doi:10.1080/00933104.2006.10473313.

Noddings, N. (2005). *Educating citizens for global awareness.* New York, NY: Teachers College Press.

Nussbaum, M. (2007). *Cultivating humanity and world citizenship.* Retrieved from http://net.educause.edu/ir/library/pdf/ff0709s.pdf.

Ong, A. (1996). Cultural citizenship as subject-making: Immigrants negotiate racial and cultural boundaries in the United States. *Current Anthropology, 37*(5), 737–762. doi:10.1086/204560.

Ong, A. (1999). *Flexible citizenship: The cultural logics of transnationality.* Durham, NC: Duke University Press.

Peguero, A., & Bondy, J. M. (2015). Schools, justice, and immigrant students: Assimilation, race, ethnicity, gender, and perceptions of justice and fairness. *Teachers College Record, 117*(7), 1–42.

Pérez Huber, L., Lopez, C. B., Malagon, M. C., Velez, V., & Solórzano, D. (2008). Getting beyond the "symptom", acknowledging the "disease": Theorizing racist nativism. *Contemporary Justice Review: Issues in Criminal, Social, and Restorative Justice, 11*(1), 39–51.

Rong, X. L., & Preissle, J. (2009). *Educating immigrant students in the 21st century: What educators need to know.* Thousand Oaks, CA: Corwin Press.

Rosaldo, R., & Flores, W. V. (1997). Identity, conflict, and evolving Latino communities: Cultural citizenship in San Jose, California. In W. V. Flores & R. Benmayor (Eds.), *Latino cultural citizenship: Claiming identity, space, and rights* (pp. 57–96). Boston, MA: Beacon Press.

Sánchez, P. (2007). Urban immigrant students: How transnationalism shapes their world learning. *Urban Review, 39*(5), 489–517. doi:10.1007/s11256-007-0064-8.

Sánchez, P., & Kasun, G. S. (2012). Connecting the transnational to the classroom and to theories of immigrant student adaptation. *Berkeley Review of Education, 3*(1), 71–93.

Seidman, I. (2006). *Interviewing as qualitative research: A guide for researchers in education and the social sciences.* New York, NY: Teachers College Press.

Urrieta, L., Jr. (2004). Dis-connections in "American" citizenship and the post/neo-colonial: People of Mexican descent and whitestream pedagogy and curriculum. *Theory & Research in Social Education, 32*(4), 433–458. doi:10.1080/00933104.2004.10473264.

Villenas, S. A. (2007). Diaspora and anthropology of Latino education: Challenges, affinities, and intersections. *Anthropology & Education Quarterly, 38*(4), 419–425. doi:10.1525/aeq.2007.38.4.419.

Authors' Biography

Jennifer M. Bondy is an Assistant Professor in the School of Education and a Fellow of the Women's and Gender Studies Program in the Department of Sociology at Virginia Tech. Her research interests involve youth citizenship (with a focus on Latina youth); gender, immigration, and schooling; and, equity studies in education. Dr. Bondy serves on the Editorial Board for *Race, Ethnicity and Education, Journal of Curriculum and Pedagogy,* and *Taboo: The Journal of Culture and Education.* Her research can be found published in journals such as *Teachers College Record; Theory & Research in Social Education; Race, Ethnicity and Education;* and, *Multicultural Perspectives.*

Aaron Johnson is an Assistant Professor of Social Science Education at the University of Nebraska-Lincoln. In 2016, he received his Ph.D. in History and Social Science Education from Virginia Tech in Blacksburg, Virginia. Dr. Johnson's research interests include historical thinking and inquiry, global education, technology integration and the pedagogical locations of convergence that ultimately link these foci within the context of social studies education and teacher preparation. Dr. Johnson's scholarship has appeared in peer-reviewed journals including *Theory and Research in Social Education*, *Social Studies Research and Practice*, and *Social Studies and the Young Learner*.

CHAPTER 26

Gender, Sexuality and Global Citizenship Education: Addressing the Role of Higher Education in Tackling Sexual Harassment and Violence

Vanita Sundaram

Conceptual Underpinnings

What Is Global Citizenship Education?

This chapter explores the ways in which gender and sexualities equality links to global citizenship education, with a specific focus on sites of gender inequality in higher education in the UK. The very purpose and scope of global citizenship education have been contested. Davies et al. (2004) note that global citizenship can be conceptualised in a range of ways, from 'vague' to 'precise' (Heater 1997) or can range from what Banks (2008) has termed as 'legal' or 'mainstream' citizenship to 'transformative citizenship'. The former implies a citizen who has legal and political rights but who does not actively participate in the political system, while the latter position describes a citizen who is concerned with global connections and responsibility and who is enabled to put their values into action. Alongside the spectrum of positions on which to locate global citizens, global citizenship education has been broadly defined as covering knowledge and understanding of global issues and a sense of belonging to a global community, to having particular skills that enable action local change, to espousing values and attitudes that are explicitly

V. Sundaram (✉)
University of York, York, UK
e-mail: vanita.sundaram@york.ac.uk

I. Davies et al. (eds.), *The Palgrave Handbook of Global Citizenship and Education*, https://doi.org/10.1057/978-1-137-59733-5_26

409

aligned with a commitment to challenging injustice and inequality (Ibrahim 2005). Increasingly, non-governmental organisations, such as Oxfam, Christian Aid and Save the Children, employ an understanding of global citizenship education that assumes an understanding of a global citizen as someone who has an affective response to injustice [e.g. outrage (Davies et al. 2004, 4)], which is channelled into action to confront this injustice or inequality. This does not mean 'reducing global citizenship to international do-goodery' but to be able to influence decision-making processes at the global level; it involves understanding and potentially challenging the current distribution of power and resources to act in a globally responsible way (Ibrahim 2005, 178).

This conceptualisation of global citizenship, which emphasises values and attitudes, is more explicit than the national curriculum in England and Wales, in which a broader concern with human rights and 'a belief in human dignity and equality' (QCA 1998, 44) is foregrounded. There is an emphasis on respect for diversity, development of empathy, a commitment to social justice and a belief that people can make a difference (Oxfam 1997, 14–15 as cited in Ibrahim 2005, 180). Banks' (2008, 135) distinction between mainstream citizenship education and transformative citizenship education similarly focuses on the remit of the latter to equip students with the decision-making skills that they need to identify problems in society, recognise their values and 'take thoughtful individual or collective civic action.' Osler and Vincent (2002, 20) also suggest that global education should be based around 'pedagogical approaches based on human rights and a concern for social justice which encourage critical thinking and responsible participation'. A primary purpose of global citizenship education is thus explicitly identified as being to enable young people to expose social, political, economic (structural) inequality and to challenge this.

With such an explicit focus on recognising and challenging social injustice, exposing the links between global citizenship education and gender and sexualities equality become apparent. Unterhalter (2008) Nussbaum (2002) and have both taken the concept of *cosmopolitanism* as key to thinking about links between global citizenship education and gender equality. Unterhalter discusses the ways in which actions for gender equality can be taken globally ('thick' cosmopolitanism) if we accept that our obligations to all people in the world (Miller 1988) should outweigh our local ties. 'Thin' cosmopolitanism, on the other hand, places most weight on local ties, such as shared citizenship, community or family relations. In this sense, thin cosmopolitanism can be seen as foregrounding individuals' ties to other individuals, emphasising a more insular conception of community and necessarily involving the construction of a national, racialised and gendered hierarchy (in which we prioritise our links to some people, with whom we feel affiliated, over our links with others). In terms of fostering a collective conscience (Arnot 2009) and sense of responsibility for global relations, the emphasis on local affiliations such as shared citizenship is less helpful and may not acknowledge the creation of global hierarchies and elitism. Unterhalter (2008) argues that 'thick' cosmopolitanism would argue for the establishment of institutions, practices and cultures that recognise the gendered power dynamics of global relationships, for example, that some countries might benefit from the exploitation or discrimination perpetuated by educational institutions in other countries. Thick cosmopolitanism thus enables us to think of our responsibilities to (social justice for) others beyond national, ethnic, gender and other boundaries. As Appiah (2006, xvi, as cited in Banks 2008, 134) argues, 'no local loyalty can every justify forgetting that each human being has responsibilities to every other.'

Global Citizenship, Gender Equality and Higher Education

Nussbaum (2002, 291) has argued that universities are 'shaping future citizens in increasingly plural societies', suggesting therefore, that a core aim of higher education might be to educate global citizens, students who can critically reflect on their own positions in a global framework. If, as Unterhalter (2008) argues, global citizens should be able embody thick cosmopolitanism to recognise the ways in which gendered power relations operate on a global level, and a key aim of global citizenship education is to recognise injustice and take action to challenge it (Banks 2008), then universities must reflect on key sites of injustice within their institutions, including gender inequality. A robust body of research has looked at practices, processes and policies that are simultaneously reflective of and reproductive of gender inequality in higher education (for example, Leathwood and Read 2009; Leathwood and Francis 2006; Jackson and Dempster 2009; Reay 2001). Universities are educational spaces in which gendered ideas about valid knowledge, ability, professionalism and student experiences are formed. Higher education is frequently perceived as a feminised arena, given increasing numbers of women entering undergraduate degrees in particular (Leathwood and Read 2009; Francis et al. 2014) and entry into higher education is positioned an exemplifying case of gender equality, where 'all' citizens are capable of achieving success, free from their prior 'attachments' (Banks 2008). However, constructions of higher education as a 'rational' sphere have, in reality, served to undermine and exclude women's contributions by positioning them as 'emotional' and 'subjective' (Burke and Crozier 2014; Leathwood and Hey 2009; Morley 2013). The increasing commercialisation of higher education (Burke and Crozier 2014), as expressed *inter alia,* by an increased focus on widening participation and diversification of the student body to illustrate institutional value has been linked to concerns about gender and ethnic equality, as well as developing the global citizen. The performative framework in which higher education now operates extends to concerns with social justice, such that the performance of 'excellent inclusivity' can now be measured through student (and other) data.

Curuana (2014, 85) has argues that within higher education we might extend global citizenship as a concept to include diversity, belonging, community and solidarity, and to develop pedagogies and teaching and learning spaces (Banks 2008) which support these values. In her consideration of 'internationalisation' as a key priority that is explicitly valued by many universities (linked to the diversification agenda discussed above), she notes that social segregation between international students and home students is prevalent. In 'internationalising' themselves, are universities actively fostering global environments in which home students are explicitly positioned as 'global citizens', who should be able to recognise and challenge unequal power relations and various forms of injustice? In a market-oriented higher education climate, where 'excellence', 'competition' and 'employability' are core values, universities might be seen to be contributing to the development of more individualistic learner identities, teaching students that they are individually responsible for 'getting the most out of' their university journeys. Linked to increasing neo-liberalisation and consumerism in higher education is the reaffirmation of gendered, classed and racialised hierarchies, in which some people are viewed as more 'able' to pursue and claim success and others' seeming lack of ability is constructed as a matter of individual will/failure rather than as shaped by social, cultural, political and economic inequality. Thus, social segregation becomes an inevitable outcome of this type of stratification. Phipps and Young (2015) have also argued that neo-liberal 'rationalities' in higher education foster an individualistic, competitive, and even adversarial culture (ibid., p. 305) that may also be linked to the degradation of certain groups of students, seen not to fit the mould of the desirable (white, male) 'citizen'. This new managerialism in higher education has, indeed, been characterised as 'masculinist' (Blackmore 2004) in its emphasis on competition, dominance and establishing authority.

Phipps and Young (2015) has recently linked the neo-liberalisation of higher education to institutional cultures that are generative of structural and interpersonal violences. Cultures of higher education have been described by students and staff as hostile', (NUS 2013b) where people are continuously evaluating each other in different types of 'markets. These are educational markets, institutional markets, and sexual markets. The ongoing and shrinking allocation of resources implies that, as actors in higher education, academics are in constant competition with each other, evaluating and being evaluated against student intake numbers, research funding, teaching evaluations and so on. Phipps notes that the constant evaluation can lead to bullying and harassment; indeed, she argues that the constant evaluation *is* bullying and harassment (Phipps and Young 2015). Rather than constituting spaces for radical change and challenge to traditional hierarchies of power and knowledge, universities are becoming characterised as spaces in which we are exposed for not complying with managerialist targets for success. This culture of evaluation and targets can be read as reinforcing gendered power relations as distinct areas of our work become codified as masculine (e.g. research success) and others as feminine (e.g. teaching and administration).

However, Nussbaum (2002, 291) notes that changes to higher education curricula that *have* challenged traditional values and questioned accepted modes of thinking, including the inclusion of the experiences, histories and treatment of minority groups, have been presented as threatening (to academic excellence, as well as traditional norms for citizenship). Those subjects that explicitly teach students to recognise inequality, to reflect critically on their place in a global hierarchy, to consider ways in which they could destabilise unequal power relations, perhaps sit in tension with the strategic priorities of institutions which highlight global competitiveness, employability and (teaching and research) excellence rankings. Phipps (2016) has also noted that certain groups are also more vulnerable to being 'exposed' in the neo-liberal university where evaluations and judgements about quality are made along gendered, classed and racialised lines—this includes women, people of colour, people with disabilities, sexual minorities. A 'universal conception of citizenship' may not recognise these different identifying characteristics (Banks 2008, 131), thus erasing or marginalising the experiences and perspectives of minority groups. I argue here that university environments should arguably be actively engaged in helping students to understand how different 'attachments' shape people's experiences of citizenship and the interrelatedness of cultural, regional and global identifications.

Key Issues and Debates

Violence Against Women: A Key Issue for Global Citizenship (and Higher) Education

Feminist research has historically been concerned with exposing and critically analysing systems, processes and practices of gender inequality and injustice. It has been characterised as fundamentally being concerned with critically questioning accepted knowledge (historically based primarily or wholly on male experience), and with naming women's 'issues' with the explicit aim of improving the lives of women (e.g. Westmarland 2001). The aims of feminist scholarship therefore align closely with those of global citizenship education—to expose social and structural inequality. It could, therefore, rightly inform the work of universities, which have traditionally adopted a universalised conceptualisation of 'citizenship' and rights that can be marginalising of the experiences of cultural (and gendered) 'others' (e.g. Nussbaum 2002). While feminist scholarship has traditionally been conceptualised as 'niche' or as relevant only to the lives of women, more contemporary understandings emphasise the fundamental concern with questions of power, inequality and difference/diversity, including gender, class, race, disability and sexuality. Looking back to perspectives on the purpose of global citizenship education, then, feminist research can be seen as necessary to educate global citizens, students who adopt a 'collective conscience' in relation to gender-based injustice (as well as other forms of inequality).

Violence against women and girls is a key area of feminist research and is increasingly recognised as a pertinent global issue for higher education institutions. Arnot (2009) has argued that an aim of global citizenship education is to develop a 'global conscience collective'. This involves the major challenge of addressing inequalities faced by women as a result of global exploitation, poverty, sexual and reproductive oppression and violence against women (ibid. p. 117). She notes that,

> Global citizenship education that challenges gender violence could encourage young people to consider the ways of being men in the public, community and private domains, to acknowledge the diversity, complexity and hierarchy of masculinities [...] and the associations of violence with male power. (Arnot, 2009, 128)

Gender-based violence in higher education can be considered a pressing global issue. In the USA, sexual violence on university campuses has been the subject of ongoing national and international attention, with particular scrutiny of violent, homophobic and racist initiation practices and activities initiated by campus fraternity societies and sports teams (Armstrong and Hamilton 2015). In the UK, several studies have investigated the prevalence of sexual harassment and violence towards university students, perpetrated by fellow students and by staff. Sexual harassment, violence and abuse are reported to be widespread experiences for women students in particular (NUS 2010, 2013b, 2014). Between 15 and 25 percent of women students in the UK and the US report experiencing serious sexual and/or physical assault while at university (NUS 2010; Washington Post-Kaiser Foundation 2015). In a recent study of sexual harassment in Chinese higher education institutions, more than one in three students reported experiencing sexual violence (Jinghua 2016).

University responses to sexual violence have been found to be inadequate (UUK 2016; Westmarland 2017). Concerns to preserve 'free speech' and to uphold legal rights for perpetrators, and debates about the responsibility of universities to act in situations outside the context of the campus itself, or involving individuals unrelated to the university, have weakened the response of higher education institutions to sexual harassment and violence against women. High-profile cases in which institutional responses have been criticised include the case of Emma Sulkowicz, a Columbia University student, whose rapist was allowed to continue to live on campus and attend classes after she (and two other women) reported him to the university and had filed a police complaint against him (Gambino 2015), and the recent case of Lee Salter, a senior academic at Sussex University in the UK, who was charged with 'assault by beating' of his female partner, a student at the same university, and continued to be employed by that institution (Westmarland 2017).

The policies and processes currently followed by many higher education institutions in relation to gender violence are therefore weakly aligned to the aims of global citizenship education, to fostering institutional environments in which students or staff might be supported to challenge injustice or to develop Arnot's vision for a global conscience collective. Understanding the prevalence of gender-based violence and the necessary actions for challenging its root causes remains a pertinent issue for higher education. In the UK, the Universities UK body has set up a taskforce to look at violence against women, harassment and hate crime in higher education institutions. The task force conducted research into the scale of the problem and models of good practice for challenging sexual violence in higher education, and released a findings and recommendations report in late 2016 (UUK 2016). This report provided clear guidelines to universities in the UK regarding actions they should take to transform institutional cultures through effective prevention of and response to sexual violence.

In the US context, there is an ongoing and active debate around the obligations of universities to support survivors of sexual violence. Title IX of the Education Amendments of 1972 mandates the prohibition of gender-based discrimination in publicly funded education programmes and activities (including universities). Specific legislation requires universities to have procedures in place to respond to sexual harassment and violence against students (Violence against Women Reauthorisation Act 2013). Most universities have staff actively deployed to develop inclusive and accountable process and policies with regard to sexual violence (e.g. Title IX coordinators). Similarly, Public Sector Equality Duty (PSED) in the UK context require s all public institutions to eliminate discrimination and harassment and to foster good relations within the given community. Thus, the role of universities in challenging social injustice and to educate citizens who can critically reflect on their own position and actions within global and local frames is under increasing scrutiny.

Gender-Based Harassment and Violence in Higher Education in the UK

In the UK, gender-based harassment and violence in universities is not a 'new' issue. However, there has been a resurgence of concern around the harmful practices being enacted by some students in higher education and the negative and disproportionate impact on women students. These concerns have been linked to a range of issues, such as health, 'risky' behaviours, responsibility and accountability and resilience among young adults. The debates have thus far been characterised by a focus on the individual and the local, rather than a consideration of the structural and the global.

Media reports have tended to focus on anecdotal accounts of violent practices such as 'slut dropping' (where male students offer women lifts home after night-time socials but leave them stranded miles away from home) and 'hazing' (initiation ceremonies usually linked to male sports teams), as well as fancy dress parties with themes such as 'pimps and hoes' and 'geeks and sluts' (*The Independent*, 11/10/2012). These practices have been identified as reflecting a 'lad culture' in the press (Jackson and Sundaram 2015). Recent research in the UK has focused on the forms in which 'lad culture' manifests in universities, its impact on students, and the ways in which institutional cultures may themselves be productive of violent practices in teaching and learning contexts.

The National Union of Students (NUS) has conducted several studies since 2010, which have sought to document the extent to which sexual and physical harassment, abuse and violence exist in university contexts. The *Hidden Marks* survey (2010) found that two-thirds of women students had experienced harassment on campus and 1 in 7 had experienced sexual assault. The majority of perpetrators were reported to be students at the same institution. In 2013, the NUS commissioned a study of 'lad culture', as they termed it, in higher education. The resulting *That's What She Said* report found that 'lad culture' was widespread at UK universities. Women students narrated varying experiences of sexual violence, including 'groping' in nightclubs, rape jokes being made in on- and offline spaces, and sexist and sexualised chanting at women in sports contexts. The report concluded that 'lad culture' could be defined, on the basis of participants' responses, as '*[involving] the objectification of women and rape supportive attitudes and occasionally, spilled over into sexual harassment and violence.*' (Phipps and Young 2013, 28). A follow-up study by the NUS in 2014, which included women *and* men students, suggested that sexual harassment and abuse were quite prevalent experiences in higher education. Over one-third of women and 12% of men reported having experienced sexual harassment and two-thirds said they had witnessed other students have unwanted sexual comments made towards them.

Institutional Awareness and Attitudes to Gender-Based Violence

A key element of developing institutional cultures which can foster 'transformative citizenship' (Banks 2008) is the knowledge and awareness of university staff around key global issues of inequality. A recentcross-institutional qualitative study sought to explore staff understandings of 'lad culture' and their perceptions of sexual harassment and violence as a problem in higher education. Jackson and Sundaram's (2015) study involved six higher education institutions in England and a total of 130 staff working in these institutions. We conducted qualitative interviews and focus groups with staff in a range of positions at each of our participating institutions (for a fuller description of the study, see Jackson and Sundaram 2015) in order to explore perceptions of 'lad culture' from a variety of perspectives. We were interested in whether our participants had come across the phenomenon of 'lad culture' in their work in higher education institutions; whether they perceived sexism, sexual harassment and violence (as practices associated with 'lad culture') to be widespread and/or problematic; and whether their universities were leading initiatives to address gender-based violence and harassment among their students.

Our findings suggest that many staff were aware of practices associated with the phenomenon of 'lad culture' and that it was perceived as manifesting in a number of ways, including physical, sexualised and verbal actions, which objectified, demeaned and/or humiliated women students in particular. Examples included:

> *Recently I've seen advertising at the University for summer internships at the sports centre on campus and the advert consists of a photograph of a woman's backside in bikini bottoms, but just that, no head, no legs, nothing [...]* (HEI1, interview 7, female dean of school)

> *There was somebody who was taking these photographs, snap chat type of things of students, through the windows of the college, and then posting it to their friends as the students are walking into breakfast in their kitchens and they may just have their nightwear on and not be as fully dressed as they would be* (HEI 4, focus group 5, male welfare staff)

There was some recognition that harassment and abuse could target multiple minority groups, such as LGBTQ students or Black or minority ethnic (BME) students. While the association with social activities and heavy drinking meant that 'lad culture' was perceived to happen primarily in social spaces—and this was confirmed by previous research (NUS 2010, 2013a)—there was evidence that sexual harassment and misogynistic attitudes and practices were enacted in teaching and learning contexts also. Women staff narrated their own experiences of being routinely undermined and challenged by male students and a number of participants recounted witnessing sexist, and in some cases, racist behaviour targeted at women students in their institutions. This ranged from sexualised evaluations of women lecturers in module feedback to homophobic and sexist graffiti in lecture rooms and 'banter' between male staff and students in lectures or seminars. For example,

> *Another example for you, one of my department's lecturers was giving quite an interactive lecture on India and she said 'does anyone know how many women are in the [Indian parliament]? There was a cry from the back: 'too many'. In my department, I certainly encounter a lot of misogyny and 'jokes' about feminism and about women [...].* (HEI 4, interview 3, male welfare staff)

Unwanted sexual attention and touching were so common as to be perceived as normal and very few of our participants had reported their own experiences of harassment. The normalisation of sexism and sexual harassment among our participants was so pervasive that we could conclude that these views might be reflective of whole-institution values regarding sexual violence (Jackson and Sundaram 2015). Values, attitudes and practices associated with 'lad culture' were mainly perceived to be enacted by young men. The notion that 'lads' may not be aware of the severity of their behaviours and that they may simply see their practices as 'fun', related to bonding or friendship formation, was fairly entrenched among some staff:

> *I've tended to see it more as a, it could be a source of entertainment, it could be a source of fun, it can be a sort of joke and when they get together and there's a congregated group then they'll behave in a particular way rather than [sexism being] a reason to get together.* (HEI 2, interview 6, female)

> *I think it does bring people together though, I think it definitely brings people together because, like you say with the awards, whether that was part of lad culture or not, they were there and they all loved it. Not everyone mind, but I bet most people found it hilarious.* (HEI 4, focus group 3, male college officer)

This was one way of narrating 'laddish' behaviour as unrelated to wider, structural and systemic patterns and forms of inequality and injustice. Very few participants conceptualised the values and practices associated with 'lad culture' as connected to gender inequality more broadly, or violence against women as a specific issue. This perception of sexual violence has clear implications for how higher education institutions might foster a 'global conscience collective' (Arnot 2009) regarding violence against women among its citizens.

IMPLICATIONS FOR EDUCATION FOR GLOBAL CITIZENSHIP

University Approaches to Tackling Sexual Harassment and Violence

Our findings suggest that universities tend not to focus on challenges to social injustice or a concern with active/transformative citizenship in their approaches to dealing with attitudes and practices associated with 'lad culture' (Jackson and Sundaram 2015). Perceptions of 'lad culture' tended to centre on individual behaviours (some of which were viewed negatively) and were rarely situated in a framework of structural and cultural inequality. Most initiatives that were mentioned by our participants reflected this conceptualisation of 'lad culture'; they tended to be responsive to an individual high-profile 'incident' or to be framed as a health and safety issue that individual students (or groups of students) needed educating about. The onus was on raising awareness about (the implications of) individual behaviours, rather than a concern with inter-related arenas of inequality and the structural conditions underpinning these. Campaigns that were led by the university itself (as different to the students' union) tended to emphasise risk management to the individual student, for example, through 'responsible' drinking (*Have a Safe Night Out* campaign) or minimising risk of assault by sticking with friends on a night out.[1] This certainly leads to the question of whether universities are fostering cultures in which collective responsibility and morals are prioritised over individual responsibility, well-being or gain. I argue here that a risk management approach to addressing sexual harassment and violence foregrounds individual responsibility and choice over an understanding of the structural inequalities that may shape experiences, identities, knowledges, skills, values and practices. To return to Wringe (1999, 6 as cited in Ibrahim 2005, 178) our findings did not suggest that university initiatives were explicitly engaged with a fundamental purpose of global citizenship education: to 'ensur[e] that the collective arrangements to which we give our assent do not secure the better life of some at the expense of a much worse life for others.'

Are universities the right spaces in which to tackle gender inequality though? As discussed earlier in the chapter, universities in the UK are under pressure to perform in a number of ways, including in terms of national ratings exercises, which seek to measure performance in terms of student experience, research, and teaching. Higher education institutions are engaged in a near-constant exercise of ranking which is premised on individual institutional performance and competition, of 'beating other institutions' at the academic game. Individual academic staff are, in turn, put under pressure to contribute to a high institutional ranking through ensuring their own individual excellence in teaching, research, academic support, management and a range of other performance metrics. A culture of individualism and competition is fostered, rather than one of collaboration. Hierarchies are not destabilised; rather new ones (institutional and individual) are created. The Higher Education and Research Bill (HC Bill—4), which was recently discussed in UK Parliament, outlines a vision for quality assurance and participation in higher education that positions the student as individualised consumer rather than as global citizen. A teaching excellence exercise (Teaching Excellence Framework) which ranks universities on the basis of student feedback on their individual experiences of teaching, assessment, and personal development is due to be introduced in the UK in 2017. I follow Arnot (2009, 123) here, in arguing that in order to develop university environments in which a global or collective conscience can be created, in which hierarchies and power relations can be contested, in which the experiences of minority groups are heard, the very premises on which our national [higher] educational systems are based would have to be challenged. The individualisation and personalisation in/of education has been badged as a route to a freer and fairer educational system offering choices for 'learner citizens' (ibid., p. 118), rather than emphasising a moral collective. As Banks (2008) has argued, this assimilationist perspective understands learners as free of their hindering attachments to race, class, gender and other characteristics, in order to achieve free choice and to pursue individual success.

Curuana (2014) notes that global citizenship is often formulated in terms of international student mobility by higher education institutions. However, as she points out, this premise may be ineffective in the development of openness and the ability to engage with cultural 'others', given the elitism that is associated with travel and the various forms of engagement travellers can adopt with the local culture. Superficial contact with other cultures can, according to Curuana, simply reproduce self-indulgence and does not develop any sense of responsibility to other humans that would prompt activism (so here the links to challenge inequality and power are made) (ibid., p. 90). She argues that the higher education sector needs to think more about the ways in which identities may be formed within and by participation in higher education. Curuana's argument can be used to think about the ways in which students interact with gendered 'others' and to consider how certain 'university experiences' (including international mobility) can be used as a means for individual(istic) gain, in practice therefore, reinforcing existing social and economic hierarchies and power inequalities.

CONCLUSION AND RECOMMENDATIONS FOR FUTURE RESEARCH

Looking forward to explore positive avenues for change and progress, it has been suggested that higher education settings may be radically transformed to enable the development of truly global citizens, outraged by gender and sexual (and other) inequalities. Transformative university classrooms should create conditions in which students from different groups can interact as equals, sharing different perspectives and critically reflecting on perspectives that are different to their own. However, this does imply a reduced focus on assessment, test-passing and competitiveness. As Banks (2008, 136) puts it: 'transformative and democratic classrooms foster cooperation rather than competition among students from diverse [...] groups'. Educators should be actively involved in reflections on how truly engaging with the 'other' (in terms of gender, class, race, disability) might enable students to recognise issues of injustice, inequality and discrimination relating to these topics. Such a cultural shift might contribute to university climates in which there is a sense that it is a global responsibility rather than local (individuals or specific interest groups) responsibility for challenging inequalities, minimising marginalisation and exclusion and challenging unequal power relations. Future research in this area might therefore engage with avenues for institutional cultural change, which fosters such a conscience among staff *and* students. Whole-institution approaches such as awareness-raising about sexual violence for staff and students, training for responding to disclosures of sexual violence, engaging with active bystander education, are potential pathways for shifting the culture and identity of an institution—and the values of the individuals within it. More research is therefore needed to establish the current limitations in knowledge and factors that might prevent such cultural and value-based changes from happening in higher education.

This chapter has sought to discuss the ways in which global citizenship education might be seen as fundamentally concerned with gender in/equality and, in particular, with sites of gender inequality in higher education. The argument has focused on the specific issue of 'lad culture', which includes sexual harassment, abuse and assault, in universities in the UK. I have discussed the ways in which an explicit focus on recognising and challenging social injustice in global citizenship education means that gender equality should form a central concerns for educators. Universities tend to conceptualise global citizenship in terms of an interest in international mobility or a recognition of cultural difference; drawing on Curuana (2014), Banks (2008) and Unterhalter (2008) in particular, I suggest that a less commercialised and individualistic approach should be taken. I have argued that not only is 'lad culture' a fundamental issue for universities to address in their development of 'global citizens', but that increasingly consumerist and marketised university climates may actually be reproductive of gender inequality, including the values and practices associated with 'lad culture'. The chapter therefore critically considers the ways in which university cultures themselves might sustain gender inequality and might not adequately support the development of the global citizen.

NOTE

1. The National Union of Students has initiated a number of campaigns around sexual harassment, consent and sexual assault which have been taken on or used as inspiration by students' unions around the UK. These include Stand By Me, I Heart Consent and It Happens Here, all of which emphasise the collective responsibility that citizens of the university (students and staff) have to recognize and actively challenge gender inequality. This type of action has tended to remain de-coupled from official university policy or formalised initiatives.

REFERENCES

Appiah, K. (2006). *Cosmopolitanism: Ethics in a world of strangers.* New York: Norton.

Armstrong, E.A., & Hamilton, L.T. (2015). *Paying for the party: How college maintains inequality.* Boston: Harvard University Press.

Arnot, M. (2009). A global conscience collective? Incorporating gender injustices into global citizenship education. *Education, Citizenship and Social Justice, 4*(2), 112–132.

Banks, J. A. (2008). Diversity, group identity and citizenship education in a global age. *Educational Researcher, 37*(3), 129–139.

Blackmore, J. (2004). The Emperor has no clothes: Professionalism, performativity and educational leadership in high-risk postmodern times. In J. Collard & C. Reynolds (Eds.), *Leadership, gender and culture in education: Male and female perspectives* (pp. 173–194). Maidenhead: McGraw-Hill International.

Burke, J. P., & Crozier, G. (2014). Higher education pedagogies: Gendered formations, Mis/recognition and emotions. *Journal of Research in Gender Studies, 4*(2), 52–67.

Curuana, V. (2014). Re-thinking global citizenship in higher education: From cosmo-politanism and international mobility to cosmopolitanism, resilience and resilient thinking. *Higher Education Quarterly, 68*(1), 85–104.

Davies, I., Reid, A., & Evans, M. (2004). Globalising citizenship education? A cri-tique of 'global education' and 'citizenship education'. *British Journal of Educational Studies, 53*(1), 66–89.

Francis, B., Burke, P., & Read, B. (2014). The submergence and re-emergence of gender in undergraduate accounts of university experience. *Gender and Education, 26*(1), 1–17.

Gambino, L. (2015).*Columbia University student carries rape protest mattress to grad-uation.* The Guardian, Tuesday 2015, 19th May. https://www.theguardian.com/us-news/2015/may/19/columbia-university-emma-sulkowicz-mattress-gradua-tion.

Heater, D. (1997). The reality of multiple citizenship. In I. Davies & A. Sobsich (Eds.), *Developing European Citizens.* Sheffield: Sheffield Hallam University Press.

Ibrahim, T. (2005). Global citizenship education: Mainstreaming the curriculum? *Cambridge Journal of Education, 35*(2), 177–194.

Jackson, C., & Sundaram, V. (2015). *Is 'lad culture' a problem in higher education: Exploring the perspectives of staff working in UK universities.* Society for Research into Higher Education.

Jackson, C., & Dempster, S. (2009). 'I sat back on my computer …with a bot-tle of whiskey next to me': Constructing 'cool' masculinity through 'effortless' achievement in secondary and higher education. *Journal of Gender Studies, 18*(4), 341–356.

Jinghua, Q. (2016). *1 in 3 Chinese college students sexually harassed, survey says.* http://www.sixthtone.com/news/1-3-chinese-college-students-sexually-harassed-survey-says?platform=hootsuite.

Leathwood, C. and Read, B. (2009). *Gender and the changing face of higher educa-tion: A feminised future?* Society for Research into Higher Education/Open University Press. UK: McGraw-Hill Education.

Leathwood, C., & Francis, B. (Eds.). (2006). *Gender and lifelong learning: Critical feminist engagements.* London: Routledge.

Leathwood, C., & Hey, V. (2009). Gender/ed discourses and emotional subtexts: Theorising emotion in UK higher education. *Teaching in Higher Education, 14*(4), 429–440.

Morley, L. (2013). The rules of the game: Women and the leaderist turn in higher education. *Gender and Education, 25*(1), 116–131.

Miller, D. (1988). The ethical significance of nationality. *Ethics, 98*(4), 647–662.

National Union of Students. (2010). *Hidden marks. A study of women students' experi-ences of harassment, stalking, violence and sexual assault.* London: National Union of Students.

National Union of Students. (2013a). *That's what she said. A study of women students' experiences of harassment and sexual violence.* London: National Union of Students.

National Union of Students. (2013b). *That's what she said. Women students' experi-ences of 'lad culture' in higher education.* University of Sussex and National Union of Students.

National Union of Students. (2014). *Lad culture and sexism on campus: August–September 2014.* London: National Union of Students.

Nussbaum, M. (2002). Education for citizenship in an era of global connection. *Studies in Philosophy and Education, 21*, 289–303.

Osler, A., & Vincent, K. (2002). *Citizenship and the challenge of global education*. Stoke on Trent: Trentham Books.

Oxfam. (1997). *A curriculum for global citizenship*. Oxford: Oxfam Development Education Programme.

Phipps, A., & Young, I. (2013). *That's what she said: Women students' experiences of 'lad culture' in higher education*. London: National Union of Students.

Phipps, A., & Young, I. (2015). Neoliberalisation and 'lad cultures' in higher education. *Sociology, 49*(2), 305–322.

Phipps, A. (2016). *Reckoning up: An institutional economy of sexual harassment and violence*. https://genderate.wordpress.com/2016/06/22/reckoning-up/.

QCA. (1998). *Education for citizenship and the teaching of democracy in schools*. Sudbury: QCA Publications.

Reay, D. (2001). Finding or losing yourself?: Working-class relationships to education. *Journal of Education Policy, 16*(4), 333–346.

Universities UK. (2016). *Changing the culture: Report of the Universities UK taskforce examining violence against women, harassment and hate crime affecting university students*. Universities UK.

Unterhalter, E. (2008). Cosmopolitanism, global social justice and gender equality in education. *Compare, 38*(5), 539–553.

Violence Against Women Reauthorisation Act. (2013). 113th Congress of the United States of America.

Washington Post-Kaiser Foundation. (2015). *Survey of current and recent college students on sexual assault*. The Henry J: Kaiser Family Foundation.

Westmarland, N. (2001). The quantitative/qualitative debate and feminist research: A subjective view of objectivity. *Forum: Qualitative Social Research, 2*(1), article 13.

Westmarland, N. (2017). *Independent Review into The University of Sussex's Response to Domestic Violence*. Documentation.

Wringe, C. (1999). Issues in education for citizenship at national, local and global levels. *The Development Education Journal, 6*(1), 4–6.

Author Biography

Vanita Sundaram Vanita Sundaram is currently a Senior Lecturer in Education at the University of York. Her research broadly covers gender and education, focusing more specifically on gender-based violence and teenagers; violence prevention work in schools; addressing issues of gender, sexuality and plurality in sex and relationships education; tackling everyday sexism through education across the life course; and lad cultures in higher education. She is the author of numerous publications on these issues, including *Global debates and key perspectives on sex and relationships education: Addressing issues of gender, sexuality, plurality and power* (2016) and *Preventing youth violence: Rethinking the role of gender in schools* (2014). She is an academic member of the NUS Strategy Team on Lad Culture and serves on the Gender and Education Association executive committee and the Gender and Education journal editorial board.

CHAPTER 27

Migration and Implications for Global Citizenship Education: Tensions and Perspectives

Laura Quaynor and Amy Murillo

INTRODUCTION

Any consideration of global citizenship education in the twenty-first century is incomplete without an examination of migration as part and parcel of the contemporary world. In this chapter, we frame this discussion of migration and global citizenship education in postcolonial theory, considering these two concepts in the context of power and relationships. We highlight tensions inherent in global citizenship education in the context of migration, and then discuss what migration means for global citizenship education both in schools and in the daily lives of students.

Intensified migration is a global phenomenon, and a hallmark of contemporary globalization. Although migration and movement is a constant part of the human story, the population of migrants has increased globally, from 77 million people, or 2.6% of the world population in 1960, to 231 million people, or 3.2% of the world population in 2015 (Migration Policy Institute 2015). Although this is a minority of the current population, this increase is worldwide: post- 2010, nearly all countries report increasing numbers of migrants.[1]

L. Quaynor (✉) · A. Murillo
College of Education, Lewis University, 1 University Parkway,
Romeoville, IL 60446, USA
e-mail: quaynola@lewisu.edu

© The Author(s) 2018
I. Davies et al. (eds.), *The Palgrave Handbook of Global Citizenship and Education*, https://doi.org/10.1057/978-1-137-59733-5_27

In addition, in certain countries this fluctuation has been more dramatic. The immigrant population of the USA, for example, has changed from 14.7% of the total population in the 1910s (Gibson and Lennon 1999), to 5.8% in 1960, to 14.3% in 2015 (Migration Policy Institute 2015). The USA remains the top destination of migrants worldwide with 46.6 million immigrants, although countries such as Australia and Canada have larger shares of their population who are immigrants than the USA; in this case, 26.8 and 20.6%, respectively.

Intensified migration, developing alongside augmented global communication, is oft summarized through the term globalization, itself made possible through worldwide advances in technology and communication, collapsing barriers that may have previously constricted nations and businesses from working together more closely (Nederveen Pieterse 2009). Stemming from this political and economic globalization, there is an increasing need to understand not only what it means to be a citizen of your own nation, but also a citizen of the globe. Global citizenship education proposes the question: What is my role as a human citizen of the world? Global citizenship education is concerned with how and if people learn that they are more than a citizen of a single town, state, or county, but rather a member of a global citizenry. For our purposes, exemplary global citizenship education is a humanist pedagogy that teaches the value of human life, empathy, and an appreciation for diversity. In this chapter, we consider the ways that migration intersects with the goals for global citizenship education as set forth by United Nations Educational, Scientific, and Cultural Organization (UNESCO) in their document titled Global Citizenship Education Topics and Learning Objectives (2015). These goals prioritize the development of understandings of global national and local systems and processes; attitudes of appreciation for difference, multiple identities, and the environment; and skills for civic literacy, such as "critical inquiry, information technology, media literacy, critical thinking, decision-making, problem solving, negotiation, peace building and personal and social responsibility" (p. 16). There is also a focus on developing values of social justice, and participating in discussion and action around contemporary global issues. Migration is implicated in each of these foci and often surfaces tensions that would otherwise be invisible.

MIGRATION AND GLOBAL CITIZENSHIP EDUCATION THROUGH A POSTCOLONIAL FRAME

The ways that migration and global citizenship education are defined and intersect in the present moment are embedded in multiple social and historical contexts. To unpack these, we employ a theoretical framework addressing social cohesion and power to understand the influences of migration on global citizenship education, and vice versa. Here, we consider these two phenomena and their intersections through a postcolonial lens. Postcolonialism, discussed at length elsewhere in this volume, is a school of thought that centers the ways that the world was affected by the recent global age of European colonialism and imperialism (McEwan 2001). When we use postcolonialism to think about migration and global citizenship education, we highlight the ideas of hybridity, center/periphery, and power. Below, we discuss each of these concepts, as well as how they relate to theories of migration.

Due to the ways that the colonial enterprise of state building shaped the political and social world today, postcolonial thinkers contend that all communities and individuals exist in a state of hybridity—that the identities and experiences of individuals in Nigeria, for example, are inextricably linked to indigenous Nigerian, British colonial and postcolonial African epistemologies, and even Chinese cultural and economic experiences (Bhabha 1994; Ngũgĩ wa Thiong'o 1986; Pretorius 2013; Said 1978). As the world changes around us, we, as individuals and societies are also changed—there is no pure indigeneity (Dimitriadis and McCarthy 2001).

Hybridity applies not only to individual perspectives but communal experiences. Individuals and communities enter into the sphere of global citizenship not only as citizens of a particular nation state, but in a state of hybridity where people might be Americans and Nepalis and Buddhist and young women at the same time. Furthermore, each of these categories is itself a hybrid experience—as an example, what it means to be Nepali has been thoroughly influenced by India, America, historical events, and countless other discourses.

Hybridity is also a key feature of the migration experience, as transnational migrants engage in transnational citizenship—either in terms of official status, citizenship practices, or feelings of belonging. Often young people and their families have active hybrid identities, describing a sense of belonging to multiple places at the same time (Abu El-Haj 2015; DeJaeghere and McCleary 2010; Sanchez 2007). For example, Mexican immigrants to the USA might collect funds and implement community projects in their hometowns, such as the construction of streets, plazas, schools, or churches (Suárez-Orozco et al. 2001). Young immigrants' transnational activities do not negatively affect the acculturation of young people to American society (Chavez 2013); indeed, the hybridization and globalization of youth identities have been noted in societies worldwide (Maira 2002; Maira and Soep 2005; Aidi 2014).

In this world of hybrid societies and individuals, postcolonial scholars argue that all global ideas, goods, and services flow between centers and peripheries, and that these centers and peripheries are a source of power imbalances in the world (Spivak 1988; Patel 2015). In the field of migration, Ravenstein's inverse distance theory suggests that often, people move to the place that is the closest to them with the best perceived outcome (Skeldon 2008). Generally, demographers find that voluntary migrants engage in step migration, moving from a local periphery to a local center (Laczko 2008). For example, often rural economic migrants move to a regional or national city; urban migrants might move from a state or national capital to a global city. In order to have social capital in the receiving community, many immigrants engage in chain migration: migrants from a particular area follow others from that town to a particular city. Often an adult will immigrate first, then a spouse/children, then close relatives, then friends (Boyd 1989). Practices such as remittances demonstrate the flow of power and cash from migrant centers to countries of origin at global peripheries (Van Hear 2005).

In a postcolonial lens, power is also a key feature of the ways that individuals and communities relate to each other in a historical context; this power is organized into different center and peripheries. Although the United Nations highlights the ideals of global connectivity in the UNESCO goals mentioned previously, there are centers and peripheries of ideas and identities around the world. For example, although millions of Facebook users overlaid a picture of the French flag on their profiles following terrorist attacks in 2015 (Sanders Nov. 21 2015), international responses to terrorism in Syria and Afghanistan are more muted. In the same way, the plight of the Palestinian people gains much more attention from Arabic language media than English language media (el-Nawawy and Powers 2008). Thus, the ways that different migrant groups are connected to centers of power influences the way they experience global citizenship.

Different types of migrants have differing access to social, economic, and political power: migration can be internal or transnational; voluntary or forced; permanent, circular, or seasonal; and undertaken for economic, political, religious, or cultural reasons. Refugees, or those who move across national borders due to a "well-founded fear of persecution" (UNHCR 1967), often have less social capital than voluntary migrants, although their economic and social resources are related to the family's status before migration: often first wave refugees have more economic, political, and social power than later waves of refugees from a conflict (Kelly 1986). Voluntary, economic migrants tend to be younger individuals, as the perceived benefit of migration is higher; if these migrants have higher education or other sources of power, they will have more time to collect on the payoff of the economic benefits they may be able to access (Laczko 2008).

KEY ISSUES RELATED TO GLOBAL CITIZENSHIP EDUCATION AND MIGRATION

With recent developments in the realm of both global citizenship education and migration, many key issues in the implementation of global citizenship education in the context of human migration are still emerging. However, there are some tensions inherent in this field: first, the tensions between nationalism and globalism, second, the related separation between the ethnos, or cultural community, and demos, or citizenship community (Benhabib 2004). In addition, the economic and political status of migrants may influence the ways in which global citizenship education takes place in the host country.

Overall, in this chapter, we argue that migration has divergent and concurrent implications for global citizenship education. Although many migrants move in particular diasporic patterns, in general, migration involves the process of communities or nations becoming more culturally heterogeneous over time. This diversification as a result of global migration is an impetus for prioritizing global citizenship education, so that receiving communities may see more common bonds with both sending communities and migrants themselves. However, these implications of migration may also threaten the possibility of global citizenship education: because migration can involve competition for scarce resources (food, jobs, public goods), it is often accompanied by increased nationalism, causing calls for education in a host community to focus more strongly on nationalistic citizenship education. Globally, societies are facing the common phenomenon of most communities moving from more cultural homogeneity to being more heterogeneous culturally (Nederveen Pieterse 2009). With an increased number of migrants worldwide in contemporary years compared to preceding decades, recent political campaigns in Europe and the USA have also demonstrated an increase in isolationism or nationalism; the Brexit vote in the UK (Jackson-Preese 2016), the Modi government in India (Varshney 2014), and the Trump presidency in the USA are examples of this phenomenon (Detrow 2016).

Overall, one of the barriers to a substantial dedication to global citizenship education is the intense dedication to the philosophical institution of nationalism (Banks 2007; Osler 2011; Quaynor 2015). For example, many young people in the USA do not identify themselves as global citizens because of the focus on nationalism and societal importance of declaring themselves Americans (Banks 2007, p. 133). Images of students saying a national pledge or singing a national anthem, saluting a flag, and participating in an annual national celebration are representative of cultural dedication to nationalism. Throughout Africa, Asia, and the Americas, there is an anticolonial bent to nationalism, as in many of these areas, nationalism was developed as a spiritual and political response to colonialism and a mechanism for self-determination (Chatterjee 1993; Schmidt 2009). Despite the scholarly contention that young people are better democratic citizens when they understand the values of their nation, yet are still encouraged by that same nation to maintain a connection with their cultural and global community (Banks 2007), programs in international education may be discouraged or rejected by teachers and parents because they are seen as an affront to the nation (Parker and Camicia 2009). Another critique often heard in indigenous and African communities is that human rights laws are Eurocentric and fail to incorporate indigenous customs, practices, and values (Mutua 2013).

An additional key issue related to migration and global citizenship education is the separation between the ethnos, or cultural community, and demos, or citizenship community (Benhabib 2004). Nationalism, in its inception, focused on the unification of the ethnos and the demos, homogenizing local differences to create a sense of national belonging. For example, nation-states supplanted local languages to merge into a single national voice (May 2012). At times, global migration is an outcome of this type of nationalism; for example, Jewish people who migrate to Israel are often seeking a demos that represents their ethnos (Duvold and Bergland 2014). However, most global migration diversifies the receiving country, and so conceptually necessitates either assimilationist logic, in which the migrants must sacrifice their cultural community to become members of a new political community, or requires the acceptance of a political community that incorporates multiple cultural communities; at the same time, one cultural community may span many political communities.

In the field of global citizenship education, there are multiple theories that attempt to resolve this disconnection between the cultural and national community. Banks (2007) considers multilevel citizenship to be critical, discussing that fully developed citizens have connections to their cultural, national, and global communities. Appiah (2006) and Kymlicka (2012) consider cosmopolitan citizenship, discussed in its own chapter in this volume, in which because of the disconnect between the ethnos and the demos, individuals might have primary identification with the global sphere.

The final key issue highlighted here in the study of global citizenship education and migration is the question of the economic and political status of migrants in the host country. Theorists discuss globalization and migration from "above" or "below"—indicating that some migrants, who are members of diplomatic corps or transnational corporations, have differing experiences from those who come as refugees or who work in low-paying jobs (Apple 2011; Robinson 2004). The ways that host communities are positioned within this context of globalization appears to have implications for global citizenship education. Global cities such as Singapore and Hong Kong that have evolved in the context of migration for global capitalism promote an apolitical form of global citizenship education (Alviar-Martin and Baildon 2016; Ong 2006). In contrast, communities that have lost economic power and experience the arrival of working class migrants report anti-globalization and isolationism movements (Massey and Sanchez 2012). The social capital and economic power migrants bring with them seem to be associated with the ways that both migrant groups and host communities experience global citizenship education. For example, many teachers developed an exclusionary citizenship curriculum when working with Palestinian immigrant and Palestinian heritage students, and questioned Latino students' citizenship status, in a lower-middle-class US high school (Abu El-Haj 2015). The amount of social, cultural, and economic capital held by migrants may influence whether or not they are seen as an asset to the host community, which in turn affects the tenor of global citizenship education.

The response of the host community to migration has implications for the education of young migrants. For example, in recent years, laws have been passed in the USA that make it illegal to give a ride to undocumented people, require parents to report the residency status of their children to schools, and that allow police to demand proof of citizenship based solely on suspicion of undocumented status (Suarez-Orozco et al. 2011). Similar restrictions on full residency have been noted in Western Europe (Sergent and Larchanché-Kim 2006). In a recent research initiative with 1201 young Latino immigrants in Orange County, California, legal citizenship was an important factor in increasing interaction with society and institutions. As the rates of legal citizenship increase, so does immigrant youth's participation in society and the more likely they are to earn more income, gain more education, obtain medical insurance, and be a homeowner (Chavez 2013). Without such status, young immigrants are essentially shut out of interaction with institutions and are unable to achieve autonomy as they enter adulthood; this semi-permanent state of liminality lacks a sense of certainty, predictability, or hopefulness often present in the transition to adulthood and blocks the young person from becoming a full member of society (Suarez-Orozco et al. 2011, p. 455).

IMPLICATIONS FOR GLOBAL CITIZENSHIP EDUCATION

With increases in migration worldwide, classrooms and schools have become more heterogeneous than in recent years; in addition, teachers often come from a different culture than their students (Irvine 2003; Sleeter 2001). At the national level, many societies have reacted to this change by adapting and adopting different forms of global citizenship education curricula.

For example, although the population of South Korea is 96% ethnic Korean, the number of immigrants recently surpassed the million person mark (Sojung et al. 2016). This change was related to an initiative to revise the national curriculum, including migrants in the South Korean story (Moon 2010). When such revisions take place, nations may adopt different forms of global citizenship education curricula. A study of citizenship education curricula in France, Ireland, and the UK indicated that these three countries incorporated global citizenship education in three different ways. In France, there was an emphasis on human rights with a national lens; in Ireland, transcendental and European values, and in the UK, different ways to be a national and global citizen (O'Conner and Faas 2012). Yet, in all of the cases mentioned above, scholars note that there are failures "to include citizens of migrant origin in the contemporary 'imagined community' [of members of the nation state] articulated in civic education discourses" (O'Conner and Faas 2012, p. 51). For example, stories and experiences of historical and contemporary migration as part of national and global citizenship are excluded from the curriculum.

Another example of curricular tensions related to global citizenship education in the context of migration is the case of Syrian refugees in Turkey. Currently, Turkey's Syrian Education Commission sponsors an adapted Arabic language curriculum for refugee schools serving 40,000 students; the roughly 6000 Syrian refugees who have residence permits attend Turkish language schools offering the Turkish curriculum. There are concerns that attending Syrian language schools will not help students integrate into social life in Turkey; however, Turkey does not allow government schools to provide education in languages other than Turkish (Kirişci 2014). Western ideas of global and multicultural education have received some discussion and promotion among Turkish scholars (Açikalin 2010), and may be incorporated into Turkey's developing migrant education policies.

Despite attempts to use global citizenship education to incorporate migrant students into schools and communities, researchers conducting observations in secondary schools note tensions between exclusionary national discourse and immigrant students (Abu El-Haj 2015; Garcia-Sanchez 2013; Rios-Rojas 2014; Quaynor 2015). For example, during a class discussion of trade in Asia, an American-born student in class with Chinese-born students asked, "Aren't we at war with China?" The teacher replied, "We're not buddies, but we trade...they don't want to hurt us because we're such good customers. We don't agree with the philosophy they use to govern their country, but they wouldn't hurt us because they'd be hurting their own wallet" (Quaynor 2015, p. 9). In another study, a secondary school government teacher registered students in the general education class to vote, while talking to students in the English Learner government class as non-citizens as if they were not eligible to vote (Dabach 2014). Abu el-Haj (2015) reports ways that teachers marginalized Palestinian American youth in their school, with the principal suggesting that "Palestinian kids" had an "aggressive and kind of irreverent" posture toward the school. In one incident, a substitute teacher told a young woman, "I know how the men in your country treat you...if you talked to your family member like that he would smack you across the face" (p. 103).

These studies highlight that some teachers of social studies or citizenship education focused on the ways migrant students were different than others. Apple (2011) explains that limited information about migrant communities can cause educators to act on stereotypes of migrant communities. For example, teachers often study Spanish with the assumption that they will be able to speak to students from Latin America in their home language, despite the reality that many immigrant students speak indigenous languages that have been repressed by Spanish-speaking elites in the home country (Apple 2011). In fact, global citizenship education sometimes defines the imagined community in a particular way and educators in both Europe and the USA distinguish between appropriate and inappropriate forms of diversity; for example, in a study in Spain, students in a class for newcomers are asked to discuss native foods, customs, and clothing, but teachers do not encourage a student of Moroccan origin to progress in school because they believe she will be forced to wear a hijab and attend to domestic duties (Rios-Rojas 2011).

However, some initiatives report promising possibilities for providing a space for global citizenship education that is welcoming and relevant to migrant youth. These initiatives align with the UNESCO learning objective of cultivating attitudes of appreciation for different and multiple identities. In both New York City (Hantzopoulos 2012) and Atlanta (Quaynor 2015), studies of small schools with guiding values targeting the inclusion and support of migrant and refugee youth report both positive reports from teachers, staff, and students, as well as successful educational outcomes for students. Global citizenship education and human rights are thus institutionalized via schools that consider these values to be enacted in school culture, policies, and pedagogy, and practices (Tibbitts 2002; Hantzoupolos 2012). This outcome is reported in U.S.-based literature when there is targeted attention to creating an inclusive community for immigrant students focused on global citizenship—if it just happens that migrant students are present in schools with a nominal focus on global citizenship education, students' transnational experiences and concerns may not be highlighted by the school (Li 2008; Quaynor 2015). In a recent study of teachers of transnational students in the UK and Denmark, most educators saw transnational students' experiences as distinct assets in the classroom: "For these teachers, their transnational students made civic education topics real" (Hahn 2015, p. 114). The schools in Hahn's study were remarkably devoid of nationalism, representing both cultural norms as well as a desire by the teachers to make sure their transnational students felt included in the curriculum.

CONCLUSION AND RECOMMENDATIONS REGARDING FUTURE RESEARCH

In light of these tensions and development in global citizenship education related to migration, we recommend research foci on initiatives to ensure (im)migrant youth have the necessary documents to navigate their society, the ways in which new UNESCO-backed initiatives impact migrants, attention to global youth culture and its relationship to global citizenship education, and inclusion of transnationalism in global citizenship education.

Currently, one obstacle to global citizenship education is the stress migrant youth and families feel when interacting with institutions; this inhibits their ability to identify as a global citizen. If young immigrants do not feel a sense of belonging in their own country of residence, it is nearly impossible for them to be expected to take an interest in other nations or citizenry of the globe. Researchers might be interested in social movements and policies related to migrant documentation, and the ways this intersects with global citizenship education. Creating paths for citizenship that would increase interactions with institutions would be an effective strategy to ensure young immigrants worldwide have opportunities to fully develop into global citizens.

The United Nations' recent inclusion of global citizenship education as a priority (Tawil 2013) will be an important turn to attend to in future scholarship. The learning objectives focused on attitudes of appreciation for different and multiple identities, developing values of social justice, and skills for negotiation and peace building should be inclusive of migrants, but theory and practice in this respect sometimes differ. Specifically, researchers will want to consider the ways in which initiatives positioned under the UNESCO umbrella impact migrant communities. Does this global discourse create opportunities to increase social cohesion, or might it highlight societal divisions?

Finally, given the preponderance of nationalism in citizenship education despite its limitations, researchers should investigate how transnationalism and participation in global youth cultures are related to global citizenship education for communities and youth affected by migration. The globalization of youth identities has been noted in societies worldwide (Maira 2002; Maira and Soep 2005; Aidi 2014). As young people experience participation in transnational cultural spheres, do these feelings of belonging and connection intersection with global civic action or ideas about human rights? Given that transnationalism does not appear to affect acculturation (Chavez 2013), how can educators and educational institutions consider students' participation in transnational networks and global youth cultures in relationship to global citizenship education?

Migration has both theoretical and practical implications for global citizenship education, and is a central part of the contemporary human experience worldwide. If migration is not considered in global citizenship education, multiple outcomes are possible: instead of teaching students that they have a place in their community, students may learn to be fearful of and feared by their community. Instead of learning that all humans have the same worth, student may learn that their worth is often linked to what documents they have. Instead of learning that all cultures are significant and valuable, students can learn that their own culture is different and not as valued as a dominant culture. Educators and researchers in the realm of global citizenship education must consider the role of migration in curriculum and schooling for both migrant and non-migrant youth in the service of human rights and social cohesion in diverse communities. In all, given the growth of migrant and immigrant communities combined with different concentration of refugee populations across the globe, the task of creating a global citizenry through global citizenship education presents an urgency for leaders in the educational field.

NOTE

1. Because this chapter focuses on migration and education, we use the term migrants indicating people who have left their country or community of origin, and immigrants to indicate people who have entered a new country with intention to stay (Jensen 2015). As we cite research on both groups in this chapter, we use the term most closely aligned with each original source.

REFERENCES

Abu El-Haj, T. R. (2015). *Unsettled belonging: Educating palestinian American youth after 9/11*. Chicago: University of Chicago Press.

Açikalin, M. (2010). The influence of global education on the turkish social studies curriculum. *The Social Studies, 101*(6), 254–259. doi:10.1080/00377991003774887.

Aidi, H. (2014). *Rebel music: Race, empire, and the new Muslim youth culture*. New York: Knopf Doubleday.

Alviar-Martin, T., & Baildon, M. (2016). Context and curriculum in two global cities: A Study of discourses of citizenship in Hong Kong and Singapore. *Education Policy Analysis Archives, 24*, 58. https://doi.org/10.14507/epaa.24.2140.

Appiah, K. A. (2006). *Cosmopolitanism: Ethics in a world of strangers* (1st ed.). New York: Norton.

Apple, M. W. (2011). Global crises, social justice, and teacher education. *Journal of Teacher Education, 62*(2), 222–234.

Babha, H. (1994). *The location of culture*. New York: Routledge.

Banks, J. A. (2007). *Educating citizens in a multicultural society* (2nd ed.). New York: Teachers College Press.

Benhabib, S. (2004). *The rights of others: Aliens, residents, and citizens*. Cambridge: Cambridge University Press. Retrieved from http://ebooks.cambridge.org/ref/id/CBO9780511790799.

Boyd, M. (1989). Family and personal networks in international migration: Recent developments and new agendas. *International Migration Review, 23*(3), 638. doi:10.2307/2546433.

Chatterjee, P. (1993). *The nation and its fragments: Colonial and postcolonial histories*. Princeton, NJ: Princeton University Press.

Chavez, L. R. (2013). *The Latino threat: Constructing immigrants, citizens, and the nation* (2nd ed.). Stanford, CA: Stanford University Press.

United National High Commissioner for Refugees. (1967). *Convention and protocol relating to the status of refugees*.

Dabach, D. B. (2014). "You can't vote, right?": When language proficiency is a proxy for citizenship in a civics classroom. *Journal of International Social Studies, 4*(2), 37–56.

DeJaeghere, J. G., & McCleary, K. S. (2010). The making of Mexican migrant youth civic identities. *Anthropology & Education Quarterly, 41*(3), 228–244. doi:10.1111/j.1548-1492.2010.01085.x.

Detrow, S. (2016, June 25). From "Brexit" to Trump, nationalist movements gain momentum around world. Weekend edition saturday. *National Public Radio*. Retrieved from http://www.npr.org/2016/06/25/483400958/from-brexit-to-trump-nationalist-movements-gain-momentum-around-world.

Dimitriadis, G., & McCarthy, C. (2001). *Reading and teaching the postcolonial: From Baldwin to Basquiat and beyond*. New York: Teachers College Press.

Duvold, K., & Berglund, S. (2014). Democracy between ethnos and demos: Territorial identification and political support in the Baltic states. *East European Politics & Societies, 28*(2), 341–365. doi:10.1177/0888325413511851.

el-Nawawy, M., & Powers, S. (2008). *Mediating conflict: Al-jazeera english and the possibility of a conciliatory media*. Los Angeles: Figueroa press. Retrieved from http://stage.uscpublicdiplomacy.org/sites/uscpublicdiplomacy.org/files/userup-loads/u22281/AJERP%2520el%2520Nawawy%2520%2526%2520Powers%2520Nov%25205.2.pdf.

García-Sánchez, I. M. (2013). The everyday politics of "cultural citizenship" among North African immigrant school children in Spain. *Language & Communication, 33*(4), 481–499. doi:10.1016/j.langcom.2013.03.003.

Gibson, C. J., & Lennon, E. (1999). *Historical census statistics on the foreign-born population of the United States: 1850–1990*. Washington, DC: Population Division, U.S. Bureau of the Census. Retrieved from https://www.census.gov/population/www/documentation/twps0029/twps0029.html.

Hahn, C. L. (2015). Teachers' perceptions of education for democratic citizenship in schools with transnational youth: A comparative study in the UK and Denmark. *Research in Comparative and International Education, 10*(1), 95–119. doi:10.1177/1745499914567821.

Hantzopoulos, M. (2012). Considering human rights education as U.S. public school reform. *Peace Review, 24*(1), 36–45.

Irvine, J. J. (2003). *Educating teachers for diversity: Seeing with a cultural eye*. New York: Teachers College Press.

Jackson-Preece, J. (2016, June 29). *Is nationalism to blame for the post Brexit vote divisions? [University]*. Retrieved from http://blogs.lse.ac.uk/brexit/2016/06/29/is-nationalism-to-blame-for-the-post-brexit-vote-divisions/.

Jensen, E. (2015, August 21). "Refugee" or "Migrant": How to refer to those fleeing home. *National Public Radio*. Retrieved from www.npr.org.

Kelly, G. P. (1986). Coping with America: Refugees from Vietnam, Cambodia, and Laos in the 1970s and 1980s. *The Annals of the American Academy of Political and Social Science, 487*, 138–149.

Kirişci, K. (2014). *Syrian refugees and Turkey's challenges: Going beyond hospitality*. Washington, DC: Brookings Institution.

Kymlicka, W. (2012). *Multiculturalism: Success, failure, and the future*. Washington, DC: Migration Policy Institute.

Laczko, F. (2008). Migration and development: The forgotten migrants. In J. De Wind & J. Holdaway (Eds.), *Research and policy perspectives on internal and international migration* (pp. 7–15). Geneva: International Organization for Migration [u.a.].

Li, G. (2008). *Culturally contested literacies: America's "Rainbow underclass" and urban schools*. New York: Routledge.

Maira, S. (2002). *Desis in the house: Indian American youth culture in New York city*. Philadelphia: Temple University Press. Retrieved from http://public.eblib.com/choice/publicfullrecord.aspx?p=570543.

Maira, S., & Soep, E. (Eds.). (2005). *Youthscapes: The popular, the national, the global*. Philadelphia: PENN/University of Pennsylvania Press.

Massey, D. S., & Sánchez, M. (2012). *Brokered boundaries: Creating immigrant identity in anti-immigrant times* (1st ed.). New York: Russell Sage Foundation.

May, S. (2012). *Language and minority rights: Ethnicity, nationalism and the politics of language* (2nd ed.). New York: Routledge.

McEwan, C. (2001). Postcolonialism, feminism and development: Intersections and dilemmas. *Progress in Development Studies, 1*(2), 93–111. doi:10.1177/146499340100100201.

Migration Policy Institute. (2015). *International migration statistics.* Washington, DC. Retrieved from http://www.migrationpolicy.org/programs/data-hub/international-migration-statistics.

Moon, S. (2010). Multicultural and global citizenship in a transnational age: The case of South Korea. *International Journal of Multicultural Education, 12*(1), 1–15.

Mutua, M. (2013). *Human rights: A political and cultural Critique.* Philadelphia: University of Pennsylvania Press.

Nederveen Pieterse, J. (2009). *Globalization and culture: Global mélange* (2nd ed.). Lanham, Md: Rowman & Littlefield.

Ngũgĩ wa Thiong'o. (1986). In J. Currey & Heinemann, *Decolonising the mind: The politics of language in African literature.* London: Portsmouth, NH.

O'Connor, L., & Faas, D. (2012). The impact of migration on national identity in a globalized world: A comparison of civic education curricula in England, France and Ireland. *Irish Educational Studies, 31*(1), 51–66. doi:10.1080/03323315.2011.579479.

Ong, A. (2006). *Flexible citizenship: The cultural logics of transnationality (5th printing).* Durham: Duke University Press.

Osler, A. (2011). Teacher interpretations of citizenship education: National identity, cosmopolitan ideals, and political realities. *Journal of Curriculum Studies, 43*(1), 1–24. doi:10.1080/00220272.2010.503245.

Parker, W. C., & Camicia, S. P. (2009). Cognitive praxis in today's "international education" movement: A case study of intents and affinities. *Theory & Research in Social Education, 37*(1), 42–74. doi:10.1080/00933104.2009.10473387.

Patel, L. (2015). *Decolonizing educational research: From ownership to answerability.* New York: Routledge.

Pretorius, M. (2013). *The transnational intellectual in contemporary Nigerian literature.* University of the free state, South Africa. Retrieved from http://scholar.ufs.ac.za:8080/xmlui/bitstream/handle/11660/1917/PretoriusM.pdf?sequence=1.

Quaynor, L. (2015). Connections and contradictions in teacher practices for preparing globally minded citizenship in two IB public schools. *Teachers' College Record, 117*(9), 1–38.

Rios-Rojas, A. (2011). Beyond delinquent citizenships: Youths (re)visions of citizenship in a globalized world. *Harvard Educational Review, 81*(1), 64–94.

Ríos-Rojas, A. (2014). Managing and disciplining diversity: The politics of conditional belonging in a Catalonian Institute. *Anthropology & Education Quarterly, 45*(1), 2–21. doi:10.1111/aeq.12044.

Robinson, W. I. (2004). *A theory of global capitalism: Production, class, and state in a transnational world.* Baltimore, MD: Johns Hopkins University Press.

Said, E. W. (1978). *Orientalism.* New York: Routledge.

Sánchez, P. (2007). Urban immigrant students: How transnationalism shapes their world learning. *The Urban Review, 39*(5), 489–517. doi:10.1007/s11256-007-0064-8.

Sanders, S. (2015, November 21). Meme of the week: French flags on Facebook. *National Public Radio.* Retrieved from http://www.npr.org/2015/11/21/456820583/-memeoftheweek-french-flags-on-facebook.

Sargent, C. F. (2006). Liminal lives: Immigration status, gender, and the construction of identities among malian migrants in paris. *American Behavioral Scientist, 50*(1), 9–26. doi:10.1177/0002764206289652.

Schmidt, E. (2009). Anticolonial nationalism in French West Africa: What made guinea unique? *African Studies Review, 52*(02), 1–34. doi:10.1353/arw.0.0219.

Skeldon, R. (2008). Linkages between internal and international migration. In J. DeWind & International Organization for Migration (Eds.), *Migration and development within and across borders: research and policy perspectives on internal and international migration* (pp. 27–36). Geneva: International Organization for Migration [u.a.].

Sleeter, C. E. (2001). Preparing teachers for culturally diverse schools: Research and the overwhelming presence of whiteness. *Journal of Teacher Education, 52*(2), 94–106. doi:10.1177/0022487101052002002.

Sojung, P., Hyeon-sil, K., & Yoo-lee, S. (2016, May 10). Rising immigration pushes S. Korea toward diversity. *Yonhap.* Retrieved from http://english.yonhapnews.co.kr/.

Spivak, G. C. (1988). Can the subaltern speak? *Marxism and the interpretation of culture* (pp. 271–313). Champaign-Urbana: The University of Illinois Press.

Suárez-Orozco, C., Yoshikawa, H., Teranishi, R., & Suárez-Orozco, M. M. (2011). Growing up in the shadows: The developmental implications of unauthorized status. *Harvard Educational Review, 81*(3), 438–472.

Suárez-Orozco, M. M., Suárez-Orozco, C., & Qin-Hilliard, D. (Eds.). (2001). *Interdisciplinary perspectives on the new immigration.* New York: Routledge.

Tawil, S. (2013). Education for "global citizenship": A framework for discussion. *UNESCO.*

Tibbitts, F. (2002). Understanding what we do: Emerging models for human rights education. *International Review of Education, 48*(3), 159–171. doi:10.1023/A:1020338300881.

United Nations Educational, Scientific and Cultural Organization. (2015). *Global citizenship education topics and learning objectives.* UNESCO.

Van Hear, N. (2005). *New diasporas.* New York: Routledge.

Varshney, A. (2014). Hindu nationalism in power? *Journal of Democracy, 25*(4), 34–45. doi:10.1353/jod.2014.0071.

Authors' Biography

Laura Quaynor is an assistant professor of ESL/Bilingual education in the Division of Foundations, Leadership, and Literacy of the College of Education at Lewis University. Her work focuses on citizenship and language education in contexts of migration and conflict, particularly in West Africa and the United States. She began her professional career as an ESL and French Immersion teacher in Maryland and Virginia.

Amy Murillo is the assistant principal of talent development and student engagement at Yorkville High School in Yorkville, IL and a doctoral student at Lewis University. She has over a decade of experience working in public education, teaching Spanish, and leading world language programming.

CHAPTER 28

Social Class

Paul Wakeling

INTRODUCTION

Social class is a foundational concept in sociology, which finds some traction in other social sciences. However, its meaning is strongly contested: definitions vary considerably in what they refer to when invoking the idea, with popular or folk usages differing still further. This can make it difficult to grasp what social class actually 'is' and consequently the implications of social class for understanding global citizenship.

In essence, social class is a way of describing 'who gets what' in society, and explaining why. It refers to a dimension of social structure which is distinct from other major divisions such as gender and race/ethnicity. Social classes are usually taken to be discrete groups of people sharing similar economic position and/or status over time. But there is disagreement concerning the nature and extent of these groups, the criteria by which they ought to be identified, their degree of influence over a range of aspects of life (many of which are pertinent to global citizenship), and whether they have national or international reach. A number of scholars have even questioned the continued utility of social class.

In this chapter, I will make the case for the continued importance of the concept of social class for understanding global citizenship. I will briefly introduce foundational theories of social class, before outlining the key ideas from the classic statement on the relationship between citizenship and social class by TH Marshall (1992 [1950]). I will also rehearse some criticisms of

P. Wakeling (✉)
Department of Education, Derwent College, University of York,
Heslington, York, UK
e-mail: paul.wakeling@york.ac.uk

I. Davies et al. (eds.), *The Palgrave Handbook of Global Citizenship and Education*, https://doi.org/10.1057/978-1-137-59733-5_28

Marshall's ideas, in particular his 'methodological nationalism', a charge also directed at the use of social class more broadly within social science. I will then turn to contemporary debates about social class, particularly the 'cultural turn', to consider its role in education and educational inequalities, and in political and civic participation and engagement. Finally, I consider what this means for citizenship education and for global citizenship.

CLASSICAL THEORIES OF SOCIAL CLASS

Arguably, all complex human societies feature forms of social division which might be identified as social class. Ancient Rome was divided between slaves, plebeians and patricians; Japan had a ruling class of *daimyo*, a warrior class of *samurai* and various peasant groups; and in India there have been castes associated with particular jobs or social roles. These divisions severely proscribed people's lives, covering what they were and were not able to do, to own and the kind of life they would lead, with little or no opportunity for this to change.

Social science itself followed in the wake of the eighteenth and nineteenth-century revolutions which overthrew the European version of these ingrained social class divisions, feudalism. The most significant foundational theories of social class can be understood as attempts to explain the radically altered nature of social divisions which followed these political events. In tearing up the social and economic fabric of feudal society, social and economic divisions were not ended, but instead rewoven in new patterns. These theories stress the importance of the economic and material in defining social class. I argue below that while these are necessary components of social class, they are insufficient for a rounded and global understanding of the connection between social class and citizenship in the twenty-first century.

Karl Marx's theory of historical materialism represented an attempt to explain the changes outlined above as part of a grand history of human societies. Marx saw class conflict as the driving force of social change and inherent in the social relations of production—the way in which society is organised around economic ends and in particular, who gets to own what and who exploits whom as a result. These material relations are ideologically legitimated through culture, religion, the law and so on. Marx saw the new capitalist society emerging from the seventeenth century onwards as featuring two 'great' classes: the *bourgeoisie*; and the *proletariat*. The former comprises the owners of the means of production: factories, offices, banks, mines and so on. The proletariat, on the other hand, must sell their labour to survive. They engage in productive work, whereas the bourgeoisie simply expropriate the surplus value of proletarian labour—profit.

Key features of Marx's view of social class then are: that it is intrinsically antagonistic and exploitative; that social classes are huge, historically significant groupings; that under capitalism, membership of a social class is determined by ownership (or not) of capital; and that social class is intricately bound up with *power*. In Marx's view, classes have an 'objective' existence. Given the right conditions, these groups can also develop subjective identity, or what he labels 'class consciousness'. While the bourgeoisie tends to exhibit a high level of class consciousness, seen in terms of concerted action in its own self-interest, this is less often seen among the proletariat, since the ideological trappings of capitalism misdirect people from the 'true' organisation of society, inducing 'false consciousness'. For some Marxists, citizenship, especially as tied to the rise of nationalism and as embedded in the nation-state, is a kind of false consciousness. It promises formal equality of humans and freedom both political, through representative parliamentary democracy, and economic through the 'free market'. However, it obscures how social class in capitalism contaminates principles of moral and legal equality, which some would see as compromised by contemporary levels of social and economic equality. I expand on this argument below in discussing TH Marshall's ideas.

Marx's prediction that the contradictions inherent in capitalism would accelerate class conflict causing the overthrow of the bourgeoisie by the proletariat, the abolition of private property and the establishment of a communist society proved inaccurate. Indeed, the Marxist revolutions of the twentieth century largely occurred in agrarian societies where the industrial proletariat was a demographic minority (e.g. Russia and China). Instead, many pointed to the rise of divisions among those who worked for a living, such as between professionals, managers and workers.

The principal alternative conception of social class was put forward by the German sociologist Max Weber. Weber accepted part of Marx's view of social class: that property ownership is a key component. However, he also saw the labour contract itself as another central element of the formation of social classes in late nineteenth/early twentieth-century industrial societies. Whereas Marx saw two great classes locked in a grand historical struggle, Weber argued that social class formation and conflict is contingent, with social classes of different shapes and sizes appearing wherever there are processes of social closure. Weber pointed to essential social class differences *within* the set of individuals who needed to work for a living, which he argued could be described by their 'market situation' (pay) and 'work situation' (conditions). Finally, Weber drew a conceptual distinction between social class, which he saw as essentially economic and in contemporary capitalist societies, tied to work; and *status*, meaning an individual's standing in society independent of their wealth. While someone with high status may also be in a dominant social class (think of Bill Gates or Steve Jobs), for Weber it is possible to have high status but without an equivalent social class position. The Pope, for instance, earns no income from his job, but commands global status as head of the Roman Catholic church.

Crucially, Weber's approach acknowledged the existence of a 'middle class' as distinct from a 'working class', which together make up the majority of the population of industrial societies. The nature, location and significance of this division between middle and working classes have preoccupied sociologists following Weber. It has manifested in various ways in different societies over the course of the twentieth century, such as the division between 'salaried' and 'waged' (hourly-paid) workers (seen in the French distinction between *cadres* and *ouvriers*). Refinements and applications of Weber's concept of social class have dominated the empirical sociology of social class and its effects across the mid-late twentieth century.

I will return below to consider evidence about effects of social class on various aspects of social life, such as education and political participation. First, however, I will review the arguments put forward in TH Marshall's classic essay on the topic about the implications of social class for citizenship itself.

CITIZENSHIP AND SOCIAL CLASS

Marshall's contribution began as a set of lectures at the University of Cambridge in 1949, subsequently published as an extended essay (Marshall 1992 [1950]). He was talking in a given national context (Britain), shortly after the end of the Second World War, and when some key elements of contemporary citizenship had recently been achieved. This included universal suffrage for men and women, free and universal secondary education for boys and girls, and the establishment of the British welfare state, including free healthcare and a range of social insurance benefits.

Drawing on the ideas of social class I have outlined above, Marshall considered the relationship of citizenship to social class. He noted that in previous societies throughout history, the two have been closely tied together. Only certain social classes enjoyed something recognisable as citizenship. Most of the population did not. Tracing the historical evolution of citizenship in relation to social class in England, Marshall delineated three distinct phases, which he labelled civil, political and social and which he assigned, respectively, to the eighteenth, nineteenth and twentieth centuries. By civil rights, he meant equality before the law, property rights, free association, freedom of religion and so on. Some of these rights were won before the eighteenth century and others afterwards—long afterwards for women in certain respects (e.g. rape was not a crime within marriage in England and Wales until 1991). The establishment of these civil rights had the effect, in this sphere, of decoupling this aspect of citizenship from social class.

Political citizenship—the right to vote and stand for election—unfolded piecemeal across the nineteenth and into the early twentieth century in Britain. Beginning with the 1832 Reform Act, there was an incremental shift from electoral rights being limited by property or income towards universal male, and eventually (but not until 1928) female suffrage. Again, Marshall shows that this decoupled political rights from social class.

This leaves the 'social' aspects of citizenship. What did Marshall mean by this? The civil and political elements of citizenship would seem to capture the claims of French and American revolutionaries, British Chartists and their ilk for representative democracy and equality before the law. Marshall notes though that the formal equality which these historical changes had engendered had not, in practice, led to a workable *social* equality. He points somewhat derisively to his namesake Alfred Marshall's prediction that technological change would obviate the need for heavy and demeaning work and that socio-economic equality would consequently dwindle. For (TH) Marshall, continuing social class divisions are a barrier to the achievement of the final piece of the citizenship troika. While he saw the new welfare state having potential to foster such rights, he also recognised that it may unintentionally undermine social citizenship through stigma—a point I pick up below in discussing the moral dimensions of class.

He illustrates the effect of social class inequality on citizenship through the example of legal aid: means-tested financial support offered to litigants by the state. Citizenship civil rights give all formal equality before the law, but that is a long way from actual equality. Court time is limited and expensive, so charging to access justice helps to prevent vexatious cases and discourages speculative litigants. However, within cases which reach court, the adversarial English legal system gives an advantage to the litigant who can afford the best legal advocates. The most advantaged and powerful have the least to lose in high legal spending, where a poorer litigant could face financial ruin if losing. It is not accurate simply to claim that the law is always bought, but in marginal cases, the risk is that socio-economic inequalities override civil equality.

Marshall's account is not without its weaknesses. Other dimensions of our social being could also be seen as compromising social rights. To remain with the British case, there is almost universal civil and political equality on grounds of gender. Aspects of civil equality continue to be corrected, such as women's right to serve in the armed forces, men's right to parental leave and the extension of civil rights to consider sexuality (through marriage equality legislation, for instance). However, in practice gender has significant effects on the practice of citizenship in many spheres, especially in politics and positions of power where men continue to dominate.

The Marxist sociologist Tom Bottomore (1992), reflecting on Marshall's essay 40 years later noted that it was class conflict which gave rise to demands and agitation for citizenship rights in the first place, initially the urban bourgeoisie in the eighteenth century and then the working-class, with middle-class allies in the nineteenth. With the benefit of hindsight, he also identifies empirical examples contrary to Marshall's argument. Sweden's achievement of a relatively equal society through social democracy, while it might now be eroding, is an example of a nation approaching the achievement of citizenship with social rights, even if exceptional. The former State socialist societies of eastern Europe emphasised social rights but lost political ones along the way, and they did not eradicate social class either.

For me, there is a Whiggish whiff in Marshall's argument, with its story of incremental progress in each successive century. The global turn to inequality which scholars such as Piketty (2014) identify after the 1970s suggests that the kind of social rights Marshall projected are further away than hitherto. Political events of the last fifteen years also caution against any sort of teleology. Moreover, there is considerable scope for a feminist and post-colonial critique of his case, which foregrounds male citizenship and is written almost without reference to empire. Reading Marshall (and indeed the classical sociologists) one could be forgiven for thinking that the whole world exists only between the eastern shores of the Atlantic Ocean and the west bank of the river Oder. I shall develop this criticism in thinking about the methodological nationalism of ideas of social class.

Despite these issues, Marshall's argument about the importance of social class in realising citizenship, notwithstanding its progressive decoupling from civil and political rights in England and elsewhere, remains powerful. It has important implications for how to think about education, citizenship and social class which I shall return to below.

Contemporary Debates About Social Class

So far in this chapter, I have outlined classical definitions and concepts of social class and described Marshall's influential thesis on how social class inequalities endanger citizenship. In this section I want to bring consideration of social class up to date by reviewing social class inequalities identified by empirical research in two key fields, and by rehearsing debates about the 'death of class' and the 'cultural turn' in theories of social class. In the first part of the section then, I show how social mobility—the likelihood of movement across social classes within and between generations—has proven stubbornly stable over many decades. I will also show how political engagement and participation, such a foundational part of contemporary citizenship, shows wide variations by social class. This patterning by social class supports Marshall's thesis about the effect of social class inequalities on citizenship. Sticking with formal politics, psephologists and political sociologists have detected a decoupling of social class from voting behaviour over recent decades. Some have pointed to this—and other trends—as evidence of the 'death of class'. They argue that social class may continue to have effects 'behind our backs' (Bottero 2005), but it ceases to carry any subjective meaning for individuals in terms of identity and allegiance. While there are potential benefits here if people feel belonging as citizens of a nation, not members of a social class, there are also indications to the contrary. The 'cultural turn' in the sociology of social class highlights how cultural distinctions of taste see the return of older folk definitions of social class, where cultural practices of groups in different socio-economic circumstances are imbued with a moral value that marks some out as more worthy than others. This in turn has implications for citizenship.

Social Mobility

The main application of social class within sociology in the last half century has been to study social mobility: the relationship between the position an individual is born into and where they eventually reach. In turn, social mobility has been a recurrent concern of sociology itself during this time. Ideas of meritocracy and equality of opportunity are closely related to those of civil and political rights. In the good society, it should be possible for anyone to aspire to and achieve success, limited only by ability and effort. In the historical societies mentioned earlier, an individual's prospects were strictly limited by birth. With the dissolution of these social structures, the modernisation thesis anticipates that the link between social class origin and destination will wither away. This idea has significant political traction, through the American Dream that anyone can 'make it' with sufficient talent and application. Politicians the world over have pushed for educational expansion as a means of ensuring 'opportunity for all'.

The overwhelming consensus of 70 years of research on this topic is that such an equalisation of life chances is barely detectable. It appears perhaps in certain countries, with a very slow equalisation, but overall there is a fairly constant pattern of social mobility: some up, some down, but mostly static. Sociologists distinguish between absolute and relative social mobility. Absolute mobility—the proportion of individuals who have a different social class than their parent(s)—grew in the mid-twentieth century. However, this was due to changes in overall social structure where there was more 'room at the top', more 'white-collar' jobs and less manual work. This inevitably meant some of those from working-class origins ended up in middle-class destinations, simply because there were more such spaces to fill. *Relative* mobility showed much more consistency. That is, the chance of someone from an advantaged class background ending up in advantaged position *relative to* the chance for someone from a disadvantaged home did not change, even though more of the disadvantaged were receiving a 'leg up' (Erikson and Goldthorpe 1992). Recent research suggests that absolute mobility has levelled off and relative mobility is either stable or, for a few European countries, improving very slowly (Breen 2010). Corak (2013) has shown that the level of income mobility in a society is related to the level of inequality in that society—a pattern labelled the *Great Gatsby* curve, after the super-rich protagonist of F. Scott Fitzgerald's novel. The more unequal a society, the lower its mobility rates.

Political Engagement

The promise of equal political rights is the opportunity for all citizens to share in and contribute to decision-making. Free association and representative democracy give all citizens the formal right to express their views, form and join organisations to further their interests, to stand for public office and to cast votes of equal weight in elections and referenda.

Whether citizens in practice exercise these rights is known to vary by social class. For instance, summarising research on political participation and engagement by social class in the USA, Laurison (2016) found that those with less education, income or occupational vote less, pay less attention to political debates, engage at a lower rate with their elected representatives and are less likely to make political donations. This group also reports feeling less connected to and empowered by the political system. These findings invert for highly educated, well-paid individuals who are also more likely to believe in the efficacy of political engagement. There are very similar robust findings when considering less overtly political forms of civic engagement such as volunteering, which are also closely associated with social class. Expanding the ambit of citizenship to include partaking in public life through cultural participation, there are also very clear differences by social class (Savage et al. 2015).

At the same time, however, there is some evidence of a countervailing trend, whereby social class is decoupling from some aspects of politics, specifically political beliefs and party allegiance. A study of eight European countries found variations in the strength of the relationship between class and vote, but a common pattern of long-term declining association (Knutsen 2006). Some have pointed excitedly to the recent 'Brexit' vote in the UK and the election of Donald Trump as US president as indicative of a resurgent working-class vote, but more temperate analysis suggests a much more complicated picture, with middle-class support substantial and vital in both cases.

These two contradictory connections between social class and political participation provide the context for considering two theoretical departures from the classical ideas of social class outlined above. The two contrasting directions have opposite implications for the relationship between social class and citizenship. If, as some contend, class is dying as a meaningful social division, then perhaps Alfred Marshall's prediction beats TH Marshall's. Alternatively, according to the logic of the proponents of the cultural turn, the significance of social class for citizenship is undiminished and the role of *education* in the question of citizenship and social class returns to centre stage.

Death, Resurrection and the 'Cultural Turn'

During the 1990s, several accounts of the 'death of class' were put forward, including by some of the most prominent sociologists of the late twentieth century. A century before, the leading thinkers had latched on to class as fundamental to sociology; now the opposite was the case. While they differed in whether they emphasised the 'risk society' (Beck 1992); individualisation (Giddens 1991) or 'liquid modernity' (Bauman 2000), these arguments shared several key tenets. They did not deny the continuation of social inequality, but they suggested that such inequalities were decoupled from social-class-based divisions. The old familiarity of strong connections between social class origin, life experiences, occupation and outcomes were seen as withering away, or at least becoming more 'complex' (Pakulski 2005). A general reduction in certainty in the social world, also seen in changes in gender roles, for instance, meant that it was no longer possible to 'read off' individuals' cultural preferences, voting behaviour or even financial position from their notional social class. Moreover, this melting of the social structure meant individuals' agency took on increasing prominence as one's fortunes and lifestyle became matters of choice rather than being determined by social class. The (post)modern reflexive worker was seen as the author of their own fate, rather than following a social class script.

Such arguments have been strongly challenged. Whatever their merits for subjective social class identity, more objective measures of life chances for those from different social classes have shown consistent long-term patterns, whether the outcome be health, educational attainment, or as already seen, social mobility. But perhaps the most interesting challenge to the 'death of class' thesis is represented by the 'cultural turn' in the sociology of social stratification, which broadens out the concept of social class itself. This perspective looks beyond occupation to see other dimensions around which social class divisions cohere, which may be material, but may equally be *symbolic*. Adopting this broader idea of social class allows us to resolve a tension in Marshall's original discussion of social class and citizenship. When he talked of 'social rights' as the third part of the citizenship troika, Marshall seems mainly to have meant *economic* rights: the barriers to de facto citizenship which economic inequality erected. This is seen in his examples of exclusion of the poor from true citizenship, such as the cost of accessing the courts or healthcare. Underlying this discussion though is a subsidiary recognition of a *moral* dimension of social class, invoked in Marshall's discussion of stigma. He shows how the recipients of benefits addressed at removing economic barriers to more complete citizenship are stigmatised, whether they be residents of one of the 'workhouses' established as a poverty relief mechanism under the English Poor Law, or a patient receiving means-tested state healthcare benefits.

In Pierre Bourdieu's sociology, these sociocultural distinctions are integral to social class divisions. Bourdieu's ideas regarding social class have implications for understanding social rights beyond simply economic rights, and because of the special role played by education within his theory. In considering social class, Bourdieu breaks with Weber in two fundamental ways. First, he insists on an *inductive* approach to identifying social classes as grounded in particular social practices. Weberian social class schemes have instead identified social classes a priori, before slotting in specific occupations or individuals. Second, Bourdieu is "inclined to disallow" Weber's strict separation of class and status, meaning that symbolic divisions are not independent of or separate to social class, which instead has a simultaneously material *and* symbolic nature (Weininger 2005, p. 84).

Bourdieu takes from Marx the idea of 'capital', but points to other kinds than the economic. Individuals or groups have greater or less volumes of other capitals, which can also be deployed to secure advantage. He adds social capital, representing one's connections and contacts ('who you know'); and cultural capital, a wide-ranging concept incorporating taste, deportment, linguistic skill, accent, education, cultural participation and *savoir faire*. Relating this to specific groups, there are many among the socially advantaged who are well-connected, well-educated and have certain skills and status while lacking significant wealth or income. These capitals can be used to secure distinction and may even be 'converted' to economic benefits (as in using a university diploma to secure a high-paid job; and a high-paid job to secure a private education). Some may have substantial economic capital, yet be socially excluded in other ways—the idea of the *parvenu* for instance.

Bourdieu's ideas have inspired scholarship which points to intensification of the sociocultural cues used to assign social class identity and to ascribe *moral* value to different social classes. Thus certain cultural tastes or habits, especially those associated with the economically disadvantaged, are construed as vulgar and signals of unworthiness. Such tastes, practices and habits are then held up as causally important for material conditions, in a reinvention of nineteenth-century ideas about the poor as responsible for their own situation, rather than this being recognised as structurally constrained and conditioned. Culture itself is mobilised in inscribing these class divisions, through language (e.g. the figure of the 'chav' in Britain, 'bogan' in Australia or 'white trash' in the USA) and especially through reality television programmes sensationalising the lives of the disadvantaged.

Crucially for considering social class and citizenship, these cultural divisions become weapons not just in the drawing of moral boundaries, but also in the enactment of political decisions regarding the redistribution of resources. Discourses which emphasise the culpability of welfare claimants in their own situation are mobilised to justify stringent 'austerity' measures to cut welfare state expenditure in Britain, a process which Tyler (2015) characterises as 'social abjection'.

Until recently, the cultural turn was largely applied to close-up studies of social class, lacking a systematic social class schema with which to describe a whole society. Savage et al.'s (2015) analysis of the BBC's Great British Class Survey changes that by using the very large dataset generated by the survey (more than 160,000 respondents) to inductively construct social classes for Britain based on volumes of economic, social and cultural capital. The shape of the class structure identified differed markedly from the pyramid-shaped view of social class seen in more Marxian-inspired schemas. A diamond-shaped distribution emerged, with an Elite class of about 6% at the top possessing high levels of all three kinds of capital; a Precariat, socially, culturally, economically and spatially excluded at the bottom; and five different groups taking up the middle ground, with varying balances of the different forms of capital.

This newly revealed social class landscape gives a fresh angle on Marshall's concern with social rights, since it makes plain that these really are *socially*, and not just economically constrained. Analysis after analysis shows the huge advantages accruing to the Elite across wealth, income, political influence, housing, and education. Their geographical concentration is also evident, located around the main bases of economic and political power in the UK and most particularly, London. However, the analysis also draws out a class—labelled Emergent Service Workers—who are relatively low in economic capital, but high in social and especially cultural capital. These are well-educated, typically younger service sector workers who are civically active, whether that be politically, culturally or both and who arguably populate the new international wave of activists in urban left-wing movements such as Spain's Podemos, Greece's Syriza and the UK's Momentum.

This brings us back to education, a key source and indicator of cultural capital in Bourdieu's thinking and a vital ingredient of contemporary global citizenship. In the next, and final section, I consider how social class and education are caught up in a mutually reinforcing loop whereby social class influences one's education and one's education influences one's social class. I also reflect on how education gives access to qualitatively different citizenship, looking particularly at global citizenship as both a new opportunity but also a potential new site of social division. In doing so I note how concepts of social class tied closely to the nation-state may obscure emerging—and indeed older—global divisions and global elites.

EDUCATION, SOCIAL CLASS AND GLOBAL CITIZENSHIP

Marshall himself recognised the tightening symbiotic relationship of social class and education. "I see no signs of any relaxation of the bonds that tie education to occupation," he wrote. "On the contrary, they appear to be growing stronger" (1992 [1950], p. 38). His prediction is confirmed by later research, which shows a very close link between education and occupation throughout education systems (Goldthorpe and Jackson 2008) but also almost universal acceptance of the link's legitimacy (Baker 2011). There is abundant evidence that social class inequalities in education are not simply the working through of innate differences in cognate ability, but there are few neater examples than Marshall's own. He mentions a housing estate in Middlesbrough, north-east England, where a policy of 'slum clearance' led to relocation of one set of residents to a new estate. Among those who moved, one in eight passed the entrance examination to the academically selective grammar school; among those left behind in poor quality housing, the rate was one in 154 (1992 [1950], p. 36). Elsewhere, raw economic differences appear to contribute to educational inequalities such as those observed in the use of private tutors in countries with significant 'shadow education' markets, such as South Korea and Greece.

For Bourdieu, however, the role of cultural capital is paramount in explaining educational inequalities, and in turn formal education is pivotal in the reproduction of inequalities. Schools value and reward the pre-existing knowledge and ways of being and expression of children socialised in advantaged backgrounds, and stigmatise or at least dismiss those of others. Thus children arrive at school with different capacities to succeed not principally due to innate cognitive ability but rather as a result of the alignment of their cultural resources with those of the education system. Education objectifies this cultural capital through the award of credentials. Crucially, the resulting inequalities are seen as natural, arising from qualities which inhere in individual students rather than as a result of their social, economic and cultural circumstances, a process labelled by Bourdieu as 'symbolic violence' (Weininger 2005).

This perspective has profound consequences for thinking about citizenship education, which in turn has consequences for social justice if accepting that cultivated civility is a prerequisite for access to citizenship. If Bourdieu is right, students arrive endowed with different levels of knowledge and skills in relation to citizenship, such as their rights, the value and practice of civic and political engagement, understanding of how the political system works in their context, and indeed the embodied skills for citizenship, such as oratory, rhetoric and organisation. Formal citizenship education can potentially reinforce such inequalities, but it also offers the promise of mitigating them, through developing the cultural capital of the disadvantaged. For them, the school represents one of the main opportunities to acquire knowledge of their rights and duties, and hence some capacity for resistance.

With the possible exception of Marx, most of the analysis presented so far has stopped at the level of the nation-state. This risks a methodological nationalism, where societies are seen as tightly bounded and discrete and where the development of theory is fixated within single states only. This issue cuts two ways: it means idiosyncratic societal features may be inappropriately generalised to elsewhere, and that global patterns and trends are erroneously assumed to have causes endogenous to individual countries. This problem is endemic to contemporary social science (Bhambra 2014), but is arguably acute for theories of social class, which have been developed mainly through analysis of northern/western European countries. Whether social class has the same salience elsewhere needs to be determined empirically. In thinking about *global* citizenship education and social class one needs to look at social class formation above the level of the nation-state and how this relates to the capacity to operate as a global citizen.

While the recent surge of interest in global wealth inequalities and the '1%' has given some attention to international elites, arguably social class theories have yet to catch up. Ball and Nikita (2014) propose the idea of a post-national 'global middle class' of internationally mobile, cosmopolitan individuals who are breaking free of national citizenship. There are intimations of such a group in the Great British Class Survey, where the foreign-born and those with international higher education are massively over-represented in the Elite class (Savage et al. 2015). Sociologists of education have begun to investigate how international education is used strategically by the advantaged to seek or maintain membership of this global class. If the ingredients of global citizenship include multilingualism, cosmopolitanism and a knowledge of rights and political engagement at the global level, then certain kinds of elite education are thought to help bestow or reproduce these (Forbes and Lingard 2015). Such education requires substantial economic capital since it is usually fee-paying and comes with the high cost of international travel.

Concluding Thoughts

I have argued that, despite the absence of a consensus about its shape and extent, social class represents a fundamental form of division and inequality within contemporary societies. Following Marshall, this has consequences for citizenship, because economic and social divisions block the practical exercise of civil and political rights for the disadvantaged. It matters for citizenship *education* in that teaching about social class (alongside other structural inequalities such as gender and race/ethnicity) is one way to help students to understand their societies, the challenges they face and the distance yet to travel in achieving the good society and social justice. It matters too in that citizenship education has the potential to provide the skills and knowledge for political efficacy and civic participation which students may not be able to acquire elsewhere. But it also carries the risk that education can further entrench and reproduce social class differences: citizenship education can be part of the solution, but it can also be part of the problem.

Looking forward, the global level represents the next challenge for research and scholarship in both citizenship education and social class. Sociologists need to develop theories and concepts to describe and explain emerging transnational social classes, and to refine and test nationally focussed models of social class outside of their native context. Global citizenship education needs to reflect on how Marshall's arguments might be adapted to understand access to global citizenship and that the internationally mobile, cosmopolitan global citizen is not necessarily altruistic, but may also be engaged in class-based processes of the deployment and accumulation of advantage.

References

Baker, D. P. (2011). Forward and backward, horizontal and vertical: Transformation of occupational credentialing in the schooled society. *Research in Social Stratification and Mobility, 29,* 5–29.

Ball, S. J., & Nikita, D. P. (2014). The global middle class and school choice: A cosmopolitan sociology. *Zeitschrift für Erziehungswissenschaf, 17*(S3), 81–93.

Bauman, Z. (2000). *Liquid modernity.* Cambridge: Polity Press.

Beck, U. (1992). *Risk society: Towards a new modernity.* London: Sage.

Bhambra, G. K. (2014). *Connected sociologies.* London and New York: Bloomsbury Academic.

Bottero, W. (2005). *Stratification: Social division and inequality.* London and New York: Routledge.

Bottomore, T. (1992). Citizenship and social class, forty years on. In T. H. Marshall & T. Bottomore (Eds.), *Citizenship and social class* (pp. 53–93). London: Pluto Press.

Breen, R. (2010). Educational expansion and social mobility in the 20th century. *Social Forces, 89*(2), 365–388.

Corak, M. (2013). Income inequality, equality of opportunity, and intergenerational mobility. *The Journal of Economic Perspectives, 27*(3), 79–102.

Erikson, R., & Goldthorpe, J. H. (1992). *The constant flux: A study of class mobility in industrial societies.* Oxford: Clarendon Press.

Forbes, J., & Lingard, B. (2015). Assured optimism in a Scottish girls' school: Habitus and the (re)production of global privilege. *British Journal of Sociology of Education, 36*(1), 116–136.

Giddens, A. (1991). *Modernity and self-identity.* Cambridge: Polity Press.

Goldthorpe, J. H., & Jackson, M. (2008). Education-based meritocracy: The barriers to its realization. In A. Laureau & D. Conley (Eds.), *Social class: How does it work?.* New York: Russell Sage Foundation.

Knutsen, O. (2006). *Class and voting in Western Europe: A comparative longitudinal study.* Lanham, MD: Lexington Books.

Laurison, D. (2016). Social class and political engagement in the United States. *Sociology Compass, 10*(8), 684–697.

Marshall, T. H. (1992 [1950]). *Citizenship and social class.* In T. H. Marshall, & T. Bottomore (Eds.), (pp. 1–51). London: Pluto Press.

Pakulski, J. (2005). Foundations of a post-class analysis. In E. O. Wright (Ed.), *Approaches to class analysis* (pp. 152–179). Cambridge: Cambridge University Press.

Piketty, T. (2014). *Capital in the twenty first century.* Cambridge, MA: The Belknap Press.

Savage, M., Cunningham, N., Devine, F., Friedman, S., Laurison, D., Mckenzie, L., et al. (2015). *Social class in the 21st century.* London: Pelican Books.

Tyler, I. (2015). *Revolting subjects: Social abjection and resistance in Neoliberal Britain.* London: Zed Books.

Weininger, E. B. (2005). Foundations of Pierre Bourdieu's class analysis. In E. O. Wright (Ed.), *Approaches to class analysis* (pp. 82–118). Cambridge: Cambridge University Press.

Author Biography

Paul Wakeling is professor in the Centre for Research on Education and Social Justice, Department of Education, University of York, UK. He is a sociologist with interests in education, social inequalities and social mobility, with a particular focus on social class and higher education participation. His recent work has covered access to postgraduate study; and the association between university prestige, student characteristics and graduate outcomes. He has received research funding support from various agencies and advised numerous public bodies on postgraduate access including extensive work on the flagship Postgraduate Support Scheme initiative in England.

PART V

Key Issues in Teaching and Learning

CHAPTER 29

History Education and Global Citizenship Education

Antoni Santisteban, Joan Pagès and Liliana Bravo

INTRODUCTION

History education provides children and young people with knowledge on the past that can help them to locate themselves in the present and project their lives into the future. We understand this future to be open to different interpretations of global citizenship. But in this chapter we want to commit ourselves to a particular form of global citizenship described by Shultz (2007) as transformationalist global citizenship. We would like the new generations to take on leading roles in building a world democracy, fight imbalances and inequalities, war, violence and intolerance, and establish a real democratic system that permits peace, dialogue and mutual understanding among all women and men on Earth. As one of us wrote somewhere else (Pagès 2005), these citizens need to be able to problematize their reality considering their historical perspective; to seek interrelations over time and space; to develop critical awareness for historical accounts. They need to propose solutions to social problems, putting them into perspective, relating that which is global

A. Santisteban (✉) · J. Pagès
Facultat de Ciències de l'Educació, Universitat Autònoma de Barcelona, Edifici G-5, 08193, Bellaterra, Spain
e-mail: antoni.santisteban@uab.cat

J. Pagès
e-mail: joan.pages@uab.cat

L. Bravo
Universidad Alberto Hurtado, Santiago, Chile
e-mail: libravo@uahurtado.cl

© The Author(s) 2018   457
I. Davies et al. (eds.), *The Palgrave Handbook of Global Citizenship and Education*, https://doi.org/10.1057/978-1-137-59733-5_29

and that which is local, consider participation beyond their own borders. They need to go beyond the stereotypes in national history and construct an account of world history; to develop a historical sense of identity and otherness; to defend the principles of social justice. In many aspects, a discussion on global citizenship—at least in the form we here defend—is a discussion on social justice.

We understand history education to be essential for the education of these global citizens. History education helps students to develop historical awareness. As stated by Rüsen (2004), historical awareness builds upon the past towards an understanding of the present. Further, it provides guidance in constructing the future by putting action into practice, social commitment and responsibility. History education can also make relevant contributions towards social justice-oriented education. History education can lead to knowledge of the battles that men and women fought and continue fighting for equality, democracy, solidarity and social justice, and the implementation and furthering of human rights. History education for global citizenship, in our understanding, must denounce the hardships that happened, happen and will happen to many people and many human groups due to the egotism of those defending banking, commercial and speculative interests. Social injustices that have taken place in the history of humanity and which consequences are still extremely present today in Africa, Asia, the Americas and practically in the entire world should be denounced. History education can also help us to reflect on notions of diversity. Humanity is highly diverse and history illustrates this when revealing how different people have different responses to similar problems. All people in the world, nevertheless, have the same essential needs and also have the same desire to be alive and to fight for human dignity. In this respect, Levstik (2014) ponders what history can provide to civic education. 'Arguing for a "global citizen", she explains, "is the ultimate aim of civic education" (p. 47). For her, history can help us to reflect on and understand what makes us human, why we are human, how we have learned to get along and what responsibility we have to improve this harmonious coexistence at a global level.

In this chapter, we first discuss the links between history education and the education of the national and global citizenry. We then propose controversial issues as a way to develop a global citizenship-orientated history education. As examples, we describe some of the proposals to teach history for global citizenship that we have developed together with a group of Spanish Secondary Social Studies teachers. This is followed by an examination of how history education for global citizenship should be assessed. We conclude the chapter by identifying questions for future consideration.

HISTORY EDUCATION AND GLOBAL CITIZENSHIP

'The past is the fabric that throws citizenship into relief; it is the springboard from which citizens learn to think and act' (Arthur, Davies, Wrenn, Haydn, Kerr 2001:161).

The relations between history education and citizenship have been handled by many authors. Examples of this include the works of Arthur et al. (2001) and Davies (2000) in England, Audigier (2003) in France and Switzerland, Ávila, Borghi and Mattozzi (2009) in Italy and Spain, Charland (2003) in Canada, García Gonzalez (2016) in Chile and our own work in Spain (Pagès, 2007; Pagès and Santisteban 2010; Santisteban 2004).

For some, the differences between history and citizenship education are greater than the similarities. Harris (2011), after comparing the key concepts and processes on the English history and citizenship plans of study, states,

> "citizenship is firmly rooted in the present (although there is a need to go into the past to make sense of this) and has an explicit agenda in creating "active" citizens; whether history shares this purpose is a moot point and will be explored further below. The subjects do have a different conceptual basis and potentially very different areas of content to study." (p. 189).

In this line of thought, Lee (1992) argues that the connection between history and citizenship education is contingent. History education should exclusively aim to the acquisition of "rational knowledge and understanding of the past" (Lee 1992, p. 24).

Others, in contrast, understand that history and citizenship education are intrinsically associated. Citizenship education is here understood as the main purpose of history education (Barton and Levstik 2004). This is, however, a complex purpose. French historian Suzanne Citron (1999) evidenced some challenges when she answered the question posed by the IREHG magazine featuring "L'école du citoyen",

> "À quoi peut servir l'enseignement de l'histoire et/ou de la géographie dans une perspective de la construction citoyenne?', she asked, 'l'enseignement de l'histoire doit permettre de comprendre comment l'idée de 'droit de l'homme' a émergé dans l'humanité, quelles en furent les balbutiements et les figures (pas seulement occidentales). La lutte pour les droits de chacun et de tous est un combat nécessaire et jamais achevé: à nous par notre conviction d'en convaincre les jeunes"[1] (1999, p. 157).

"How can teaching history at our schools contribute to the education of citizens in the contemporary world?", Selva Guimarães asks (2016, p. 12), in a project that coordinates different contributions from Latin American and European authors. In Britain, Arthur, Davies, Wrenn, Haydn and Kerr argue that "both [citizenship and history education] are concerned with equipping young people with the necessary knowledge, understanding, skills, attitudes, values and experiences for life in modern society" (2001, p. 26). The knowledge and understandings that could be promoted from history lessons are essential for citizenship education: History is explicitly intended to promote citizenship through "providing opportunities for pupils to discuss the nature and diversity of societies in Britain" (DfEE/QCA 1999a: p. 8)' (p. 59). Similarly, our previous research suggests that history knowledge is not only relevant but necessary for citizenship education. In a study on the political knowledge of 461 sixteen-year-old Spaniards, we discussed how the poor students' knowledge of the history of democracy in Spain could explain, partially, the low interest on contemporary politics and national-based stereotypes (Santisteban and Pagès 2009).

There are many coincidences between these debates on citizenship and history education and possible debates on history and global citizenship education. Thus, these debates are arguably to be considered when taking decisions on the purposes and practices associated with global citizenship education. But the links between history education and global citizenship education generate additional challenges and possibilities.

History is often understood as serving national purposes (Ravitch 2006). However, Hobsbawm (Hobsbawm and Kertzer 1992) argues that the academic study of history is incompatible with nationalistic principles. In this respect, the global dimension is not only relevant but also necessary for history education. In 1967, the pioneering author American Washburne, wrote,

> "in the current interdependent world, one cannot really comprehend one's own country without understanding its past and present interrelations with other nations and cultures. Whether speaking of our country or any other, its peoples, language, customs and values have reached many other places in the world. Our culture is based on many other cultures" (1967, p. 87).

The global dimension of history is also highlighted for comparative purposes. The United States Study Commission on Global Education committed to teaching history that would devote "more attention to the development of the world's civilisations and how they are related to the history of the USA (...) [and] more attention to the diversity of cultural models both in the world and in the USA" (Gutek, 1993, pp. 29–30, cited in Dynneson, 2001, p. 463). Further, knowing about events in other countries can also contribute to indirect knowledge about ourselves. In South Africa, for instance, the Facing the Past programme, as applied to South African schools, was aimed at

> "reviewing histories related to the violation of human rights, which do not directly mention or refer to our situation (South Africa). For example, we tell them that teachers who look at the Holocaust, the case of Northern Island, and critical events in which a lack of respect of human rights was extreme" (Wray 2005, p. 41).

On the other hand, history education has lots to offer to the education of the global citizenry. The proposals made from the new conceptions of the History of Humanity are particularly relevant in this respect. For instance, Stearns (2012) understands that universal history must let citizens "access the historical context of the globalised society in which we live today", (pp. 9–10).

The universal history proposed by Stearns (2012) reviews the Eurocentric timeline with this line of reasoning: "universal history deals with the entire world and not a religious experience, no matter how undeniable its importance may be" (p. 20). He does not outline universal history as an alternative to national or regional histories, although the fields that he presents in his work could end up being questioned, at least in their most traditional school version.

History education for global citizenship education, nevertheless, faces some difficulties. First, it requires preparing teachers for this challenge. Teacher education should change so teachers become independent and socially committed. Teacher education should provide the space and resources for in service teachers and student teachers to reflect on the global dimension of the national curricula. Second, the endurance of nation-centric teaching is as an obstacle. Global citizenship, we argue, is practically the antithesis of national citizenship, which only looks at itself and looks down on others from a stance of superiority. Third, Europe-centric approaches to history education exclude the majority of the population, due to reasons of class, gender, ethnicity, age, culture, ideology or religion. Non-Western people and cultures are often used or excluded. History education for global citizenship, in our understanding, shall look at the histories of the whole humanity and challenge any narratives of Western supremacy. Fourth, the national history that is represented in teaching is far from the global world in which today's youth live (see for example, the debates in the magazine *Le Débat* (2013), on the situation of national history in France and in other European countries). When teaching history in the majority of countries, the protagonists are never normal men and women, commoners we could relate to, with whom students could identify (Barton and Levstik 2004; Pagès and Sant 2012; Pinochet 2016; Villalón and Pagès 2013). When teaching history, there are no people with problems, with feelings, with joys and heartaches, who work, fight, suffer, enjoy or pray, like the men and women who live among our students or who live anywhere in the world, now or in any other historical period. Global citizens look beyond states, nations, regions or any other entity created to organise the power and people's lives in a specific place. They place a greater emphasis on what humanity has had and has in common, and on the diversity of situations generated to resolve the same problems. From this approach, identity and diversity are considered common heritage of humanity.

Proposals for Teaching History for Global Citizenship

We propose the use of controversial issues for a history education for global citizenship. Having in mind global citizenship as a purpose of history education, we understand, that issues-centred approaches can better fulfil this purpose. Others seem to share this understanding. Numerous authors have highlighted the potential of using controversial issues in history teaching and learning. In the USA, Evans and Saxe (1996) argued for the 'issues-centred social studies'. In English-speaking journals, the term controversial issues seems to have gained primary (see e.g. Hess 2008). In the Francophile setting, the concept of 'socially alive matters' is used (Legardez 2003, Legardez and Simonnaux 2006). In the Spanish and Latin American context, the most commonly used concept is that of 'relevant social problems', problems which are considered to be contemporary relevant (Benejam 1997).

In the context of education for global citizenship, there is a wide range of controversial issues that can be selected from those affecting the majority of the world population. We understand most issues related to democracy, inequality, injustices, conflicts, social and economic segregation and so forth to be appropriate. All these issues, in our understanding, demand historical perspective, relating the past to the present and analysing future prospects (Santisteban and Anguera 2014). Without the historical component, we cannot understand today's world including how interrelations between countries and regions have been shaped.

Controversial issues are currently defined from two stances. A first stance proposes problematising history contents in relation to problematic situations in our present (e.g. Dalengueville 2001; Dalongueville and Huber, 2000). Dalongueville (2001), for example, suggests problematising the study of one aspect of the Roman Empire starting from what are known as problem situations. He suggests analysing the Latin concept of 'barbarians', which the Romans used to designate peoples in Northern Europe, as a synonym for foreigner, to compare it with the use and meaning that the term has today, as a derogatory term towards cultures different than our own. Thus, we can reflect on how our idea of foreigner has changed, to then ask ourselves the question posed, among others, by Todorov (2010): Who are the barbarians today?

This first approach is likely to be more easily selected by those working in settings where history is an independent subject area (e.g. England). In one of our studies, we required secondary students to consider a historical problem: Why did Spaniards go into exile after the Civil War? Students first interpreted primary history sources, in an initial process to construct the historical account that would respond to the question. Students then contrasted opposed historiographic sources in order to gain a more complex understanding of the historical reasons explaining the exile. This was followed by an activity in which students were expected to create an historical audiovisual account that would respond to the initial question (Santisteban, González-Monfort, Pagès 2010; González-Monfort, Pagès, Santisteban 2011).

Although drawing on controversial issues on the past, this first approach might establish clear links with the present. For instance, these activities could be perfectly linked to present debates on the Syrian refugees crisis through an examination of selected pieces from the media (for an example, see Santisteban et al. 2016). Students could compare the crisis of the Syrian refugees and the Spanish refugees after the Spanish Civil War (1936–1939) and examine the situation of the refugees after both crisis. Through this activity, students would not only gain a deeper insight about past and present refugees but they would also develop their critical literacy.

These are only some examples that could be used to problematize history education. But there are numerous examples. Historical problems can be selected in each context considering the local or regional contextualisation, but they must also have a world-wide projection for the issues analysed. Similarly, although these problems can relate to past situations, they need to allow comparison with present issues, as is the case of those in exile and refugees during wartime. Thus, the study of history lets us modify students' analysis perspective with regard to their ideas on present problems. Other examples of these type of historical problems could include a comparison of the situations of peasants in the past [for instance, the Remença conflict in Catalonia (1462–1486) or the conflict in Chiapas, Mexico (1994)] with more current rural conflicts, such as the Landless Workers' Movement (MST, for *Movimento dos Trabalhadores Sem Terra*) in Brazil (Pagès 1997; Santisteban and Pagès 2008) .

The second approach to controversial issues relates to work of some social studies and critical pedagogy authors. Following the work of Evans and Saxe (1996), some studies emphasise controversial social issues for the democratic education of citizens (Hess 2008, 2009; Legardez 2003; Pagès and Santisteban 2011). In this case, controversial issues are defined as "problematic questions that need to be addressed and answered, at least provisionally. Problematic questions are those on which well-informed people may disagree. Such disagreement, in many cases, leads to controversy and discussion marked by expression of opposing views." (Evans, Newman and Saxe 1996, p. 2). This disagreement may be about facts, definitions, values and beliefs and the problems or issues can be past, present and future.

In one of our studies, we worked with secondary students to examine a global controversial issue: 'Limits, borders and walls' (Santisteban 2012). In this study, students first took a genealogical approach to examine the notions of limit, border and wall. Students then examined historical walls in different eras (historical perspective). Examples of these include Hadrian's Wall or the Great Wall of China and. This was followed by a discussion on the social uses of walls including their role dividing, isolating, excluding and marginalizing 'others' (geographical perspective). The examples of the Berlin Wall and the walls in Belfast and Palestine were here used to illustrate this discussion. A particular feature was the discussion around 'invisible walls' such as those dividing neighbourhoods in different cities in the world. Students then conducted case studies on contemporary walls that were later presented to the rest of the class. In the end, a scenario activity took place. The question posed was, what would happen if a giant unpassable wall were constructed around the borders of Melilla (Spanish enclave in Africa) to prevent people getting into Spain from Africa? After a group role-play and a debate setting out arguments and counter-arguments, the students took decisions, putting what they have learned into practice.

ASSESSMENT

Assessment forms part of the teaching and learning process, and should be a tool for improving educational learnings and proposals. Assessing global citizenship, however, is a tricky issue. It implies the assumption that those designing the assessment strategies know better how a global citizen should look like. As we mentioned before, there are multiple understandings of global citizenship. In what follows, we describe specific learnings that history education can bring to the education of the global citizenry as we defined in the beginning of the chapter. We do not attempt to provide any guidance to measure whether students become 'good' global citizens, but to identify knowledge and skills that students might need to handle global history and social problems whilst keeping their commitment to social justice-orientated forms of citizenship.

In other works, we have tried to describe the contribution of history education to the education of citizens (Santisteban 2011). In the present paper, we expand this framework to define what we could teach and what we could evaluate in the context of history education for global citizenship. The table below summarises our proposal. The first column shows the key concepts for teaching and learning history: temporality, change/continuity, interpretation, historical problems, historical imagination, representation of history and historical awareness (Santisteban, González-Monfort and Pagès 2010; Santisteban 2011). Column two relates to the contribution of history education towards global citizenship education. Derived from the competences, column three sets out the expected learnings in education for global citizenship, from a revamped history education (Table 29.1).

Table 29.1 Contributions of history education towards global citizenship education

Key historical concept	Contribution of history education towards global citizenship education	Learnings expected
Temporality	*To value diversity in how different cultures interpret time, the different forms of historical periodisation and the simultaneity or contemporaneity of historical events in the world*	• To identify the relativity and multiplicity of time, through which each person and each culture has different conceptions and experiences of time and, consequently, also on historical time • To interpret historical periodisation, starting from the diverse cultural ways of assessing and classifying social changes • To compare the simultaneity or contemporaneity of historical events and changes at different places in the world, whether they are related or not
Change and continuity	*To assess the change and continuity processes in the global world from a view of universal history, but also by comparing the situations in different places on the planet with diverse historical developments*	• To identify change-continuity in shaping the spaces of the world and humanity's global advances • To recognise that there are and have been communities with distinct historical evolutions • To evaluate concepts related to time, such as 'modernity', 'progress' and 'decline' through historical evolution and the situations in different regions of the world
Historical interpretation	*To develop critical literacy in historical interpretation, starting by analysing primary and secondary sources, with the aim of going beyond prejudices and stereotypes, and take a position about the world's social problems*	• To interpret primary and secondary historical sources, separating facts from opinions and assessing their veracity and reliability by comparing information from diverse origins • To identify intentionality, cultural and economic values, and the political ideology of the sources of information, and their positioning with regard to the controversial issues analysed • To interpret the voids or silences in the media with regard to specific minorities, cultures and identities (invisible)

(continued)

Table 29.1   (continued)

Key historical concept	Contribution of history education towards global citizenship education	Learnings expected
Historical problems, issues-centred social studies and controversial issues	*To analyse social problems and controversial issues by looking at their historicity, in order to understand their development and alternatives, and to contribute solutions*	• To identify the similarities and differences of past and present social problems, and compare them to those in difference countries or regions of the world • To relate past and present through conceptual thought, on concepts like migrations, refugees, walls, freedom, democracy and conflict • To analyse economic, cultural, political, territorial, etc. conflicts that exist between countries, by looking at their historical development
Historical imagination	*To apply critical and creative thought to historical events, in order to contextualise them or show empathy, but also to assess and make value judgements*	• To show empathy with people from other historical eras and other cultures different from our own, from the sincerity of our own convictions • To contextualise historical events both locally and nationally, but also globally, looking for the interrelations • To make moral judgements from historical analysis, staring from an awareness of global advances in human rights and by clarifying our own values
Representation of history	*To represent history as a form of oral, written, digital or audiovisual narration, as a causal and intentional explanation, adding the perspectives of equality and cultural diversity*	• To add the multicultural, social class and gender perspectives to historical narrations • To create multicausal historical explanations, bearing in the mind the interrelation of global situations in history • To draft intentional historical explanations in order to discover the different values, ideologies and points of view of historical events

(continued)

Table 29.1 (continued)

Key historical concept	Contribution of history education towards global citizenship education	Learnings expected
Historical awareness	To reflect on the fact of being human with temporal awareness, which lets us know where we come from, where we are and what type of future we want to build	• To evaluate our belonging to the human race and reflect on what has made us and makes us humans • To relate the past to the present and to the future, understanding the historical process as a single inseparable fabric • To draft future prospects for social problems starting from our historical past, including responsibility to participate, locally or nationally, but also globally

Conclusion and Possible Future Research on History Education for Global Citizenship

We would like to conclude this chapter by setting out ten key questions on the why, what and how to teach history for global citizenship. We feel we have provided some answers here in relation to the particular form of global citizenship that we committed ourselves in the beginning of the chapter. Other educators and researchers might want to consider these questions in relation to their own approaches to global citizenship education. In addition, we understand that some new questions have arisen from the thoughts detailed in the text which further debate might be necessary. Educators, researchers and policy-makers might want to reflect about:

(1) What is teaching and learning history for in a globalised world? How does history contribute to the formation of a global democratic and critical citizenship?

(2) What history should we teach in a global world? Which social problems and which historical problems are the most suitable?

(3) What does teaching and learning world history provide to citizens? How do we relate local and national history to global history education?

(4) What does teaching multicultural history provide? How do we work with the fact that we are 'all' immigrants?

(5) Who are the protagonists in history for education for global citizenship?

(6) Which historical period for the history education of global citizenship shall we teach? Which historical periodisation should we teach? How do we teach the concepts of change, progress, decline...?

(7) What is the importance of studying contemporaneity in history education for global citizenship? How can we interrelate the histories of the world's countries and regions?

(8) What role should historical sources and ICT play in history education for global citizenship?

(9) Which historical account should we construct in global history education? What role should social justice play on this? What type of presence should human rights have in our history narrations?

(10) What does forming historical awareness mean in education for global citizenship? How do we use history to project ourselves into the future and how do we teach students to be forward-looking yet grounded in the past?

These questions could also be key to future research on the contributions of teaching history for education for global citizenship. In short, there is a need to keep researching how we can help boys and girls to shape historical thought that considers world history. A history that reveals us as human beings who are walking towards an understanding—overcoming difficulties—and towards the plenitude of human rights. As Gadamer (1993) states, human beings' most important revolution has been discovering their transient nature and their historical awareness. This cannot be either an individual project or that of a specific group. It must be a project of all human beings.

NOTE

1. "How can the teaching of history and/or geography serve in terms of citizenship construction?", she asked, "the teaching of history must guide us to understand how the idea of 'human rights' emerged in Humanity, what were the stammerings and the figures (not only the western ones). The struggle for the rights of each and every one of us is a necessary and never-ending struggle: by our conviction to convince the young".

REFERENCES

Arthur, J., Davies, I., Wrenn, A., Haydn, T., & Kerr, D. (2001). *Citizenship through Secondary History*. London: Routlegde/Falmer.

Audigier, F. (2003). Histoire scolaire, citoyenneté et recherches didactiques. In Baquès, M-C.; Bruter, A.; Tutiaux-Guillon, N. (Ed.), *Pistes didactiques et chemins d'historiens. Textes offerts à Henri Moniot* (pp. 241–263). Paris: L'Harmattan.

Ávila, R., Borghi, B., Mattozzi, I. (a cura di) (2009). *L'educazione alla cittadinanza europea e la formazione degli insegnanti. Un progetto educattivo per la "strategia di Lisboa"*. Bologna: Pàtron Editore.

Barton, K. C., & Levstik, L. S. (2004). *Teaching history for the common good*. Mahwah, NJ: Lawrence Erlbaum Associates.

Benejam, P. (1997). Las finalidades de la educación social. In P. Benejam, & J. Pagès (coord.), *Enseñar y aprender Ciencias Sociales, Geografía e Historia* (pp. 33–51). Barcelona: Horsori.

Charland, J.-P. (2003). *Les élèves, l'histoire et la citoyenneté. Enquête auprès d'élèves des régions de Montréal et de Toronto.* Québec: Les Presses de l'Université Laval.

Citron, S. (1999). À quoi peut servir l'enseignement de l'histoire et/ou de la géographie dans une perspective de la construction citoyenne? In *Revue Nationale du Réseau CNDP-CRDP pour l'enseignement de l'histoire et de la geographie*, 7, 151–161. IREHG (Information, Recherche, Education Civique, Histoire, Geographie). Monographie "L'école du citoyen".

Dalongeville, A. (2001). *L'Image du Barbare dans l'Enseignement de l'Histoire. L'Expérience de l'Altérité.* París: L'Harmattan.

Dalongeville, A., & Huber, M. (2000). *(Se) former par les situations-problèmes.* Lyon: Chronique Sociale.

Davies, I. (2000). Citizenship and the teaching and learning of history. In J. Arthur & R. Phillips (Eds.), *Issues in history teaching* (pp. 137–147). London. Routlegde.

Dynneson, T. L. (2001). *Civism. cultivating citizenship in european history.* New York: Peter Lang.

Evans, R. W., Newmann, F. M., & Saxe, D. W. (1996). Defining issues-centered education. In R. W. Evans & D. W. Saxe (Eds.), *Handbook on teaching social issues* (pp. 2–5). Washington: National Council for the Social Studies (NCSS).

Evans, R. W., & Saxe, D. W. (Eds.). (1996). *Handbook on teaching social issues.* Washington: NCSS.

Gadamer, H.-G. (1993). *El problema de la conciencia histórica.* Madrid: Tecnos.

García González, C. A. (2016). Interpretaciones y paradojas de la educación ciudadana en Chile. Una aproximación comprensiva desde las significaciones ciudadanas y pedagógicas de los profesores de historia. Tesis doctoral. Pontificia Universidad Católica de Chile. Santiago de Chile.

González-Monfort, N., Pagès, J., Santisteban, A. (2011). ¿Cómo evaluar el pensamiento histórico del alumnado? In P. Miralles, S. Molina, A. Santisteban (Eds.), *La evaluación en el proceso de enseñanza y aprendizaje de las ciencias sociales* (pp. 221–231). Murcia: AUPDCS/Universidad de Murcia.

Guimarâes, S. (Org.) (2016). *Ensino de História e cidadania.* Campinas. Papirus.

Harris, R. (2011). Citizenship and history. Uncomfortable bedfellows. In Davies, I. (Ed.), *Debates in History Teaching* (pp. 186–196). London: Routledge.

Hess, D. (2008). Controversy issues and democratic discourse. In L. S. Levstik & C. A. Tyson (Eds.), *Handbook of research in social studies education* (pp. 124–136). New York: Routledge.

Hess, D. (2009). *Controversy in the classroom. The democratic power of discussion.* New York: Routledge.

Hobsbawm, E. J., & Kertzer, D. J. (1992). Ethnicity and nationalism in Europe today. *Anthropology today, 8*(1), 3–8.

IREHG (Information, Recherche, Education Civique, Histoire, Geographie) (1999). Monographie "L'école du citoyen". *Revue Nationale du Réseau CNDP-CRDP pour l'enseignement de l'histoire et de la geographie, 7.*

Le Débat (2013/3) (n° 175). Difficile enseignement de l'histoire,

Lee, P. (1992). *The aims of school history: The national curriculum and beyond.* London: Tuffnell Press.

Legardez, A. (2003). L'enseignement des questions sociales et historiques, sociale-ment vives. *Le Cartable de* Clio, 3, 245–253.

Legardez, A. & Simonneaux, L. (coord.) (2006). *L'école à l'épreuve de l'actualité. Enseigner les questions vives.* Paris: ESF éditeur.

Levstik, L. S. (2014). What can history and the social sciences contribute to civic edu-cation? In J. Pagès & A. Santisteban (eds.). *Una mirada al pasado y un proyecto de futuro. Investigación e innovación en didáctica de las ciencias sociales* (pp. 43–51). Barcelona: Servei de Publicacions de la Universitat Autònoma de Barcelona/ AUP-DCS, Vol. 1.

Pagès, J. (1997). Los conflictos en las sociedades rurales: el conflicto Remensa (s. XV) y el conflicto de Chiapas (1994). In P., Benejam & J. Pagès (coord.), *Ciencias Sociales. Contenidos, actividades y recursos* (pp. 415–480). Barcelona: Praxis.

Pagès, J. (2005). Educación cívica, formación política y enseñanza de las ciencias sociales, de la geografía y de la historia. *Íber. Didáctica de las Ciencias Sociales, Geo-grafía e Historia, 44,* 45–55.

Pagès, J. (2007). La educación para la ciudadanía y la enseñanza de la historia: cuando el futuro es la finalidad de la enseñanza del pasado. In R. M. Avila, R. Lopez, & E. Fernández (Eds.), *Las competencias profesionales para la enseñanza-aprendizaje de las Ciencias Sociales ante el reto europeo y la globalización* (pp. 205–215). Bilbao: Asociación Universitaria del Profesorado de Didáctica de las Ciencias Sociales.

Pagès, J. (2012). Las mujeres en la enseñanza de la Historia: ¿Hasta cuando serán invisibles? *Cad. Pesq. Cdhis, 25*(1), 91–117.

Pagès, J. & Santisteban, A. (coords.) (2011). *Les qüestions socialment vives i l'ensenyament de les ciències socials.* Barcelona: Servei de Publicacions de la Univer-sitat Autònoma de Barcelona.

Pagès, J., & Santisteban, A. (2010). La educación para la ciudadanía y la enseñanza de las ciencias sociales, la geografía y la historia. *Íber. Didáctica de las Ciencias Sociales, Geografía e Historia, 64,* 8–18.

Pinochet, S. (2016). ¿Niños, niñas y jóvenes son protagonistas de la historia? Concep-ciones de profesores y estudiantes sobre la historia de niños, niñas y jóvenes. *Ense-ñanza de las Ciencias Sociales. Revista de Investigación, 15,* 49–59.

Ravitch, D. (2006). Should we teach patriotism? *Phi Delta Kappan, 87*(8), 579–581.

Rüsen, J. (2004). Historical consciousness: Narrative structure, moral function, and ontogenetic development. In P. Seixas (Ed.), *Theorizing Historical Consciousness* (pp. 63–85). Toronto: University of Toronto Press.

Santisteban, A. (2004). Formación de la ciudadanía y educación política. In M. I. Vera & D. Pérez (Eds.), *Formación de la ciudadanía: Las TICs y los nuevos problemas* (pp. 377–389). Alicante: Asociación Universitaria del Profesorado de Didáctica de las Ciencias Sociales.

Santisteban, A. (2011). La formación en competencias de pensamiento histórico. *Clío & Asociados. La Historia Enseñada, 14,* 34–56.

Santisteban, A. (2012). La investigación sobre el desarrollo de la competencia social y ciudadana para una participación crítica. In N. De Alba, F. García & Santisteban, A. (Eds.), *Educar para la participación ciudadana en la enseñanza de las ciencias sociales* (Vol. II., pp. 277–286). Sevilla: Díada.

Santisteban, A., & Anguera, C. (2014). Formación de la conciencia histórica y edu-cación para el futuro. *Clío & Asociados, 18*(19), 249–267.

Santisteban, A., González-Monfort, N., & Pagès, J. (2010). Una investigación sobre la formación del pensamiento histórico. In R. M. Ávila, P. Rivero & P.L., Domínguez (Coords.), *Metodología de investigación en Didáctica de las Ciencias Sociales* (pp. 115–128). Zaragoza: Institución Fernando el Católico. Diputación de Zaragoza. 115–128.

Santisteban, A. & Pagès, J. (2008). ¿Es posible la paz? Los conflictos internacionales en el mundo actual. In J. Pagès & A. Santisteban (coord.), *Educación para la ciudadanía*. Madrid: Wolters Kluwer. Guías para la Educación Secundaria Obligatoria.

Santisteban, A., & Pagès, J. (2009). Una propuesta conceptual para la investigación en educación para la ciudadanía. *Revista de Educación y Pedagogía, 21*(53), 15–31.

Santisteban, A. Tosar, B., Izquierdo, A., Llusà, J., Canals, R., González, N. & Pagès, J. (2016). La literacidad crítica de la información sobre los refugiados y refugiadas: construyendo la ciudadanía global desde la enseñanza de las ciencias sociales. In C.R. García Ruiz, A. Arroyo, B. Andreu (Eds.), *Deconstruir la alteridad desde la didáctica de las ciencias sociales: educar para una ciudadanía global* (pp. 550–560). Las Palmas de Gran Canaria: Universidad de Las Palmas/AUPDCS.

Shultz, L. (2007). Educating for global citizenship: Conflicting agendas and understandings. *The Alberta Journal of Educational Research, 53*(3), 248–258.

Stearns, P.N. (2012). *Una nueva historia para un mundo global. Introducción a la "World History"*. Barcelona: Crítica. Edición en inglés de 2011.

Todorov, T. (2010). *The fear of barbarians: beyond the clash of civilizations*. Chicago: University of Chicago Press.

Villalón, G., & Pagès, J. (2013). ¿Quién protagoniza y cómo la historia escolar? La enseñanza de la historia de los otros y de las otras en los textos de estudio de Historia de Chile de educación primaria. *Clío&Asociados, 17,* 119–136.

Washburne, C. (1967). *Educación para una conciencia mundial*. Buenos Aires: Losada. Edición en inglés de 1954.

Wray, D. (2005). Leer la historia y construir ciudadanía. In Arcudi. L. et al. *Comprensiones sobre ciudadanía. Veintitrés expertos internacionales conversan sobre cómo construir ciudadanía y aprender a entenderse* (pp. 39–47). Bogotá: Ministerio de Educación Nacional/ Cooperativa Editorial Magisterio.

AUTHORS' BIOGRAPHY

Antoni Santisteban Fernánde is Professor of Social Sciences Education at the Universitat Autonoma de Barcelona (Spain). He has been Principal Investigator of several research projects on history and citizenship education. He is a visiting professor in several Master's Degrees and PhD programmes in Spanish and Latin American universities. His research focuses are on the teaching of historical thinking and Historical Consciousness, controversial issues in the teaching of social studies, global citizenship education, critical literacy and the democratic participation. He has been President of AUPDCS (University Association of Social Sciences Education). He is member of different scientifics councils and he also act as evaluator for different university quality agencies. Presently, he is Deputy Dean of Quality and Innovation at the Faculty of Education of the Universitat Autonoma de Barcelona.

Joan Pages is a Professor at the Universitat Autonoma de Barcelona (Spain) and Chair for Social Science Education. He holds a degree in Philosophy and Letters (Modern and Contemporary History) and PhD in Education Sciences. He coordinates the Doctorate of Education of the Unit of Didactics of the Social Sciences and the Group of Investigation in Didactics of the Social Sciences (GREDICS) of the UAB. He was founder of the University Society of Didactics of the Social Sciences (AUPDCS). His research focuses on history education, social science education, citizenship education and teacher education. He is an expert in the curriculum of these disciplines. He has developed different projects with colleagues from Latin American and European universities.

Liliana Bravo is Associate Professor at the Department of History in the Universidad Alberto Hurtado (Chile). She lectures in the area of Social Science Didactics in the Teacher Education Programme. Her research focuses on initial teacher training, history education and the development of citizenship education competences. She has been guest lecturer in the Universitat Autonoma de Barcelona (Spain) and the Universidad Tecnológica de Pereira (Colombia). Presently, she leads the Chilean representation in the Red Iberoamericana de Didáctica de las Ciencias Sociales (Ibero-American Network on Social Science Didactics).

CHAPTER 30

Global Citizenship Education and Geography

William Gaudelli and Sandra J. Schmidt

Geography provides invaluable and unique ways of thinking the world that are very much in congress with Global Citizenship Education (GCE). This includes the fundamentally dependent nature of humanity. People are reliant upon the earth's resources and interactions with one another for survival. Geographers examine these interactions; they are specifically interested in why and how people use and transform their physical and social contexts. Geographic inquiries about people's engagement with their environments are also matters of civics. One of the foundational relationships between geography and civics is the *where* of citizenship. Because citizenship presumes a locational attachment, we might begin by contemplating how citizens articulate the places to which they claim belonging or membership. When citizenship is modified by global, global arises as a conceptual and lived space worthy of investigation. The global place is not a neutral or preexisting space but rather one heavily structured through histories and contemporary forms of slavery, patriarchy, imperialism, colonization, and heteronormativity. As an emerging field, global citizenship (education) evokes geographic questions about how people engage with global systems across the container of the nation-state and how resistances and reimaginations of these forms, through claims of global citizenship, make the global a place of becoming and possibility.

Global citizenship education is a relative newcomer in educational discourse though one with a growing body of literature around conceptions,

W. Gaudelli (✉) · S.J. Schmidt (✉)
Teachers College, Columbia University, Horace Mann 334, New York, USA
e-mail: gaudelli@tc.columbia.edu

S.J. Schmidt
e-mail: ss4146@tc.columbia.edu

473

I. Davies et al. (eds.), *The Palgrave Handbook of Global Citizenship and Education*, https://doi.org/10.1057/978-1-137-59733-5_30

approaches, and problems. Given the recency of its development, educators seek ways to draw connections between existing categories, like geography, and the innovative ethos that is GCE. These retrofittings are both necessary and problematic since the desire for a *tabula rasa* is just that. The reality of education is that repetition and continuity are the norm as compared to alteration (Cuban 1993). The retooling that we examine in this chapter is geography. How can geography be a vehicle by which GCE can manifest in schools? How can spatial theories foster the worldviews of GCE? We offer two observations regarding this change; first, we by no means seek to replace geography as a stand-alone subject which to varying degrees exists around the world. Second, we recognize that GCE will strategically seek geography and many other points of entry into schools which it should engage. Our choice to examine geography and related constructs is in recognition of the fecundity of these concepts in achieving the teaching and learning aims of GCE.

The geographic configuration most requiring destabilization in global citizenship research is the nation-state. Traditionally, citizenship and its activities are oriented around and legally granted through the nation-state (Castles and Davidson 2000). The nation-state arose as a modern and Western tool that united/protected ethnic enclaves and was later used by the same group to govern colonial outpoints (Cox 2002; Connor 1978; Moodley and Adam 2000). While global citizenship requires us to look beneath, between, and beyond the nation-state, it is not disappearing. Instead, global citizens disrupt the stability of its borders, meaning, and saliency in the contemporary world. Nation-states mount forces to secure borders, regulating bodies and their movements across those boundaries while constructing home and foreign interests, *our* people and *those* people with all of its divisive connotations. And yet the solidity of nation-states is increasingly intersected by networked global forces—from trade to communication to finance—that abide by the authority and singularity of these geographic units.

The state is invested in the political and legal activities of its citizens. Unbound from the state, global citizenship deliberates the sociological, anthropological, and economic conditions of citizenship. Scholars in these disciplines are guided by the conditions of belonging (Ong 1999; Yuval-Davis 2006). The unevenness of access implicated in raced, gendered, and sexualized exclusions has often meant that people must act properly to be fully recognized as citizens. So-called deviants to the expected norms of behavior and belonging might claim to belong, but they are situated in the margins where their forms of engagement are often under-recognized. The global citizen is one of these forms, for the very idea of a global citizen who transcends the nation-state and sees oneself in community with those who have been othered is a citizenship of deviance and marginalization, yet one clamoring for broader acceptance in a world wherein the nation-state has limited functional capacity.

The migrant is a specific othered subject and one whose position has been central to producing global citizenship discourse. Hyndman and Giles (2011) note, "the idea that mobility is the new metaphysical norm in modern social and geographical life, and therefore a critique of more static notions of society and culture, is a provocative one" (p. 365). Mobility and migration have been used to distinguish classes of people (Castles 2010). Mobility of those belonging to the professional class whose need to traverse national borders for capital production is often seen as desirable, whereas the migrant is depicted as someone who moves in search of opportunity. The migrant is often seen as an economic problem and one whose civic attachments are threatened and threatening. We find the migrant a provocative subject to interrogate in the study of geography and global citizenship. The migrant as a mobile, global citizen disrupts western and masculine orientations toward good citizenship and ways of belonging (Hyndman and Giles 2011).

This chapter proceeds from these foundational discourses—GCE and geography—to examine their points of mutuality. We begin by exploring briefly one conceptualization of GCE followed by a brief discussion of some geographic concepts that warrant attention within GCE. We then move to illustrate by way of salient example—migration and movement—how GCE might come to fruition in a geographic frame, with attention to teaching and learning strategies as well as assessment approaches for the same. We take up different spatial orientations of migration and how each interrogates global citizenship. The first is the form of coerced migration, specifically the trafficking and exploitation of women. How do migrant women, in this sexualized and exploited discourse in which they are simultaneously victim and threat, become transformed as citizens? The space of investigation here are the intersecting systems that transcend the nation-state. The second section examines how flows of resources and subsequent power are mapped and transacted in a globalized world. How does the world we create continue to inscribe an old, premodern principle of 'might makes right' when it comes to global trade? And how does geography illustrate the limitations and affordances of this Westphalian outlook? The third explores the migration of discourse, or the way in which the flow of texts in a constantly churning media space unmoors places from their enveloping stories in circulation. Here we take up the question of what it means to have texts-in-flow about issues like forced migration in the context of Syria 2015. We conclude with consideration of what future research in this nexus might be particularly attending to the compatibilies of each discourse and their mutually shared interest in developing these lines of thoughts among the next and future generations of students.

WHAT IS GLOBAL CITIZENSHIP EDUCATION?

We borrow upon UNESCO's broad articulation of global citizenship education as a starting point:

> GCE aims to empower learners to engage and assume active roles both locally and globally to face and resolve global challenges and ultimately to become pro-active contributors to a more just, peaceful, tolerant, inclusive, secure and sustainable world. (UNESCO 2014, p. 15)

This conception has a few noteworthy features. First is that it is learner focused. The empowerment referred to in the statement has a social overtone but also applies to the immediate situation of the student. This outcome orientation is noteworthy as it speaks to a paradigmatic shift in education away from inputs, or what educators do and what instructional practices and curricula are put into place, and toward a performance of learning, a way of thinking that addresses what students are able to do as a result of a set of learning experiences. The breadth of content is also significant in this conceptualization. The authors clearly had in mind a conglomeration of the various prefixed/suffixed educations that could reasonably be considered part of GCE, including human rights education, education for sustainability, intercultural education, peace education, and a variety of others. This approach, however, might be viewed as an encroachment upon or even an appropriation of long-standing educational discourses. The rhetorical argument, only an implied one in UNESCO's document, is that the need for an aggregated approach is more pervasive now given the perilous nature of impinging and interconnected global problems (Gaudelli 2016).

UNESCO's frame also points toward pedagogical practices in a digitally networked communicative space of and for learning. Multimodal forms of learning and resources are highlighted, and participatory modalities are encouraged to leverage various tools now available to connect educators and students. Too, there is recognition that tools alone will not beckon the GCE required of the current situation as they call attention to the cultivation of dispositions of openness, caring, and empathy accompanied by critical, creative, and innovative thinking. This attention to soft skills and orientations is noteworthy as it suggests a less mechanistic and formulaic approach to GCE, one that embraces the uncertain terrain of emotional and aesthetic landscapes of people's lives.

Geography informs about the foundationally material condition of all life on earth. As we invent worlds through words, it is easier to imagine ourselves as placeless, absent these material conditions and necessary connections. Yet, we are regularly reminded of how each of us generally consume goods, use materials, create waste, and exchange objects of value as part of our daily routines. That these everyday happenings occur in particular locales which are bounded by physical and social contexts is often taken for granted. Thinking geographically helps to remind and reconstitute how we realize ourselves in the world.

Geography and GCE in Migration and Mobility

We illustrate congruence between GCE and geography through contemporary issues of pressing concern: migration and mobility. Migration of various kinds is endemic in human history. We see evidence of this in the earliest speciation and centrifugal movement of hominids who left ancestral lands likely in search of greater access to food, water, and protection. More recently, the modern era of approximately 1500 C.E. onwards is perhaps best characterized by the increase and rapidity of people, materials, and ideas flowing around the world, though with particular volition from Europe outward: "Europe … began to increase its manufacturing sector, while relying on fairly traditional technologies and home-and-shop-based production. It traded these finished goods for raw materials, precious metals and spices from other parts of the world" (Stearns 2008, p. 161). These early trade patterns were a catalyst for the rapidly integrated global economy of the latter twentieth century and also created vast inequalities that were exacerbated over time.

Modernity has been characterized by migrations, as the economic growth of certain regions compelled the movement of peoples involved in the production and distribution of goods. Migration of people has many variations, of course, from the compulsory movement of sub-Saharan Africans in the Atlantic Slave Trade of the sixteenth through nineteenth centuries to the economic refugees of the late nineteenth and early twentieth centuries from agricultural areas toward industrial and urban centers to the political refugees throughout the nineteenth and twentieth centuries fleeing repressive regimes such as Nazi Germany, Czarist and Stalinist Russia to war-torn regions of Southwest Asia, namely Syria and Libya. Migrations have comingled with power and politics throughout the modern period not unlike what drives movements of people today. Too, the flow of people, materials, and texts has taken on a trenchant emotional quality in an age of mass/social mediation, as the notion of being *uprooted from home* amidst growing anxiety of a globally interconnected world, is parasitic on the anxiety induced by modernity generally.

Coerced Migration

Coerced migration, forced migration, trafficking, refugees, and asylum seekers. These terms have significant overlap in reflecting mobility, but their application depends on the gender of the migrant and the conditions of departure. The choice of language has discursive power on how mobility is experienced, specifically the extent to which the migrant is perceived as a global citizen. In GCE, women's empowered pathways toward citizenship encounter interconnected locales and oppressive social structures.

Women's movement is best understood not through local conditions at the place of departure or arrival but in nested transnational systems. Unlike men, women, particularly from the Global South, move less frequently as part of the capital class and are thereby relegated to the migrant class. The conditions confining and demanding women's movement exist at the intersection of global and local heteronormativity, patriarchy, and capital production. As activists against oppression and war, women's actions are rarely public nor direct enough to warrant asylum claims. Thus, women must await the extensive refugee resettlement process to escape sociopolitical threats in their home locales. Patriarchal systems complicate women's claims as refugees when without husband or children. These systems make it most convenient for women to follow a husband, real or necessary, or submit their bodies to traffickers. In either case, women rely on neoliberal economic systems and global cities that simultaneously rebuke migration and rely on low-skilled, imported labour to meet demand in manufacturing, food, and service/sex industries (Castles 2002). To understand women's migration, we must move beyond rational actor theories, agent/victim categories, or movement based on push/pull factors; women act at the intersection of a multitude of systems (Luibheid 2008).

Trafficking is deemed a critical problem of migration and resultant civic identity. Trafficked women are positioned as coerced and vulnerable (Andrijasevic 2003; Pickup 1998). On the one hand, international women's organizations acknowledge that the sex work often accompanying trafficking arises through a patriarchy that confines women's choices (Pickup 1998). Legislation in Sweden and elsewhere that criminalizes the demand for, rather than supply of, prostitution attacks patriarchy (FitzGerald 2016; Shifman 2003). But this approach denies the (rational) agency of women who traffic themselves and work in sex industries (Andrijasevic 2003; Pickup 1998; van Liempt 2011). In struggling with whether to take up the agent or victim position, women must consider the innocence of the victim and the immorality of the prostitute, decisions that will determine their access to citizenship (Andrijasevic 2009; Doezema 2002; van Liempt 2011). Women move in search of work, they seek out traffickers as a form of mobility, and they participate in relationships that benefit their ability to move and find a job or social community that is brighter than the one afforded to them in their home. Inscribed as a victim, the migrant woman is disempowered, dependent, and in need of protection.

The discourse that positions female migrants and the policies designed to remedy their exploited conditions have implications for the expectations of *good* citizenship associated with migration. The coerced migrant is generally perceived as a *bad* citizen, one whose actions do not allow her to be fully recognized. States enact restrictive and protective terminologies and practices to prevent the impurities from infecting their nation:

> Border controls – and the moral panics that drive them – have very little to do with stopping movements of people. Instead, they work to make those who do cross the line incredibly vulnerable within the spaces defined as belonging to members of the "nation" and protected by "their state." In other words, ever-increasing restrictive immigration policies do not work to restrict people's

movements but to create a group of people vulnerable to exploitation in the workplace; a population of workers who benefit employers by providing a cheapened and weakened alternative to legal workers. (Sharma 2003, p. 56)

Trafficking takes advantage of border insecurity. Sharma explains that this insecurity is placed upon the migrants rather than the receiving nation. Unable to control her movement into the country, the nation regulates migrant women within the country through the discourse of the good citizen. The good migrant citizen integrates into the dominant ethos and identity of the new nation. Migrants are perceived as threats when they function in ways seen as economically productive (in the formal) sector, speak the dominant language, and assimilate properly (Castles 2010). But trafficked women tend toward an identification and path consistent with what Luibheid (2008) calls the queer migrant, one who does not seek assimilation, "but to experience continued though transformed engagement with nation-states and regimes of power that have already profoundly shaped their lives" (p. 170). Their participation in sex industries and informal sector work are not productive labor. They are not invisible in these sectors. The response of most states is to view the women as victims in need of protection from exploitation (Andrijasevic 2009). In the trade-off for being allowed to stay, women must participate in social integration programs that offer them skill sets that lead to a more productive and moral means of economic productivity. These same policies recreate the female citizen, even if she is to return home as a means of escape from her exploited position (Richardson, Poudel and Laurie 2009).

The materiality of migrant women reflects the spatial constraints and possibilities of global citizenship. These women move above and beneath the nation-state, yet repeatedly find nation-states attempting to regulate their bodies. These truly global citizens penetrate porous boundaries because they recognize that the global place structured by inequities—patriarchy, heteronormativity, neoliberalism, and colonialism—transcends the nation-state. They move not because they can overcome these structural obstacles but because of promises that there are more opportunities elsewhere. Women may transport themselves between locations, but the places in which they live change little. The social systems are not confined by localities and certainly not by nation-states. By belonging when not wanted, by making choices through the construction of victim, she challenges us to rethink the parameters of the citizen.

FLOWS OF RESOURCES AND POWER

Castles' (2010) differentiation of coercive migration and the choice of movement enjoyed by those of a certain class points out the ways in which the construct *global citizenship* is layered with overtones of privilege. In this section, we consider a macro-view of movement with particular emphasis on how materials flow around the world and the ways in which we are implicated by the same. These implications are profoundly geographic concerns, as Wenar (2016) notes:

> Take a quick inventory of the objects you have touched today. Those objects are made of molecules from many countries. Perhaps you woke today in Egypt. You may be wearing a bit of Spain around your waist, some Venezuela on your feet. There might be a bit of the Congo in your pocket, and quite possibly some Oman on your nose. It's like you've circumnavigated the globe in somersaults, with soil of many countries sticking to you. (p. xxiv)

While Wenar invokes what has become an old saw in GCE—material flows in the world connecting us all—his is a bit more controversial a take. Wenar looks beneath these surfaces into the types of resource economies that create the materials of one's cell phone, describing how many rare or valuable materials are sourced in say the Congo transferred to manufacture in Taiwan later to be sold in Chicago. Yet, raw material economies—be it those focused on rare-earth metals or oil or some other valuable metals, oil or gases in global trade—are often run by despots and their gangs who abscond and sequester resources, claiming them as property and enforcing pillage by force.

And significantly, these pillaging acts are treated as legitimately owned goods in global trade. Wenar illustrates this dynamic with the case of long-standing Equatorial Guinea strongman Teodoro Obiang, whose estimated wealth of $600 million sits atop a country of oil wealth and vast poverty. Obiang presides over vast wealth amidst grinding poverty because a Westphalian principle of 'might makes right' and 'possession makes property' undergird the global economy (p. 69–71). Wenar notes that it is this global system, one that looks the other way at gross violations of human rights and rampant corruption while promoting the flow of resources from being held by the commonwealth of a country, a common law tradition, into the possession of a rapacious few, that is to blame for a bleak situation.

A confounding aspect of this dynamic is the water's edge phenomenon of international law. There are regulations and protocols for how global trade is conducted as codified by the World Trade Organization (WTO), an organization that has been both heralded as a ground rules equalizer and criticized for the way that trade is organized to the benefit of the North (Narlikar 2005). A key principle in the operation of the WTO is the sovereignty of nations, or that a trade agreement as such does not reach beyond the water's edge to determine the legitimacy of resource claims. That these boundaries are recognized by all states in the system as legitimate creates the conditions for consumers being mindlessly implicated by participating/purchasing everything from bed sheets to jewelry.

A global citizen confronted with this dilemma has few options short of pressing for a system change that adopts human rights norms in governance within societies as well as common law practices over how raw materials and resources are owned and who benefits from their distribution. Global protocols, the WTO notwithstanding, have not yet approached the issue of kleptocracies and how they function on a global scale. But global citizens, themselves aware of these norms in the flow of global trade, can advocate for greater disclosure around sourcing. We have witnessed a similar development in the sourcing of tuna when there was a public outcry around the wanton killing of dolphins with mass netting practices in the 1990s or the public relations campaign surrounding blood diamonds from Sierra Leone and elsewhere under the Kimberley Agreement of 1998.

These small-scale if egregious violations of good conscience and human rights norms set the stage for a more broad-based approach to resource flows in the twenty-first Century. Yet, it would be problematic to see these cases as symmetrical to the previously described principle of 'might makes right' in the global trade system, and perhaps this is why a more generalized address of this issue has been lacking. This is simply due to the fact that the global system of resource exploitation, distribution, and manufacture would be completely disrupted by accountability for ruthlessness and rightful/shared ownership vis-a-vis resources. The petroleum industry, which literally fuels the global economy, would need to be completely reallocated and reconstituted since it is perpetuated by 'might makes right' doctrine and is generally held in the statist hands of an elite few rather than toward the benefit of a commonwealth as a whole. Given the steepness of the challenge it is hard to imagine a reconstitution of this magnitude, so partial measures like those discussed may be an incrementalist intervention that is most optimal.

MIGRATION OF TEXTS THROUGH MEDIA

A constant in our interactions is that we are always exchanging things, be it in our individual movement from one physical location to another, either for a brief excursion, an extended duration or with some degree of permanence, or in the physical exchange of oxygen for carbon, or in the metaphysical exchange of ideas and theories about the world. The interactive processes that each of us participates in all the time has been amplified and accelerated by media technologies that connect and distribute material and discursive flows. The irony of these never-ending exchanges, particularly of ideas but increasingly of substances too, is that as they become more facile, the sense that these exchanges are without consequence has grown. Witness how media attention 'blows up' over an event, only to quickly disintegrate from view in the unending vacillation of a 24/7/365 'breaking news' media cycle. The ways in which these flows intersect and resynthesize is particularly evident in the issue of migration and movement, itself a form of movement.

The enormity of the Syrian refugee crisis caused by the civil war that began in 2011 is difficult to grasp, given its sheer scale is an illustration of this larger media dynamic. At the time of writing in January 2017, the UN Refugee Agency estimates that some 4.8 million Syrians are refugees and 6.3 million are internally displaced (IDP) (Agency, n.d.). Due to the lengthy process of resettlement and resistance in European, North American, and some Middle Eastern countries, over half of those refugees live in camps in Jordan and Turkey. Internal and external migrations have created horrific living conditions for those on the move and have led to significant political problems throughout the EU. The intensity and volume of refugees is without precedent in post-World War II Europe, which has inflamed nativist politics, creating a volatile situation in countries either serving as unwilling hosts or way stations in transit, all being picked up in a repeating media cycle of image/story (Heisbourg and François 2015).

The Syrian refugee crisis illustrates the lack of conceptual authority of global citizenship. The fact that countries like Hungary tried to deny entry of Syrians through barricades and detention suggests that global citizenship may be a construct that points to a far different, future world rather than a nation-state dominated contemporary one. The imagined citizen of nations, fabricated out of the mythos of an allegedly shared past now edified in the borders of a territorial state, is a pernicious concept that seems to rub squarely against a transcendent notion like global citizenship (Anderson 2006). So there is a sort of irony in discussing migration in the case of Syria when considering the plausibility of GCE therein. Put another way, there may be perhaps no better counter-example to the emergence of global citizenship than the lingering concept of a citizen constituted solely by the legal boundaries of a state.

And yet nations are no longer impenetrable with respect to their sovereign rights of who constitutes a citizen—national, global, or otherwise. The Refugee Convention of 1951 and subsequent related protocols stipulate the rights of people who leave their home countries for reasonable fear of their lives. Signatories to the Refugee Convention of 1951, numbering some 145 countries and including all of the European nations to which the Syrian refugees fled, are required to permit asylum for those who fit the legal definition. This is a significant legal change as prior to the establishment of a human rights regime in the post-World War II era, nation-states were inviolable with respect to making these determinations. Now, individuals have legal recognition as such given the supranational framework of international laws. In the case of migration, one's state of being human is a more significant consideration than a person's territorial status. Reconfigurations in relationship to identity, personhood, and territoriality point to the fecundity of global citizenship as a concept.

While this change is now well established in international law through mutually held treaties, perhaps more salient is the way that it has taken root in global public consciousness. At some moments—particularly in the fall of 2015—media attention was transfixed on the situation unfolding in the Middle East and Eastern and Central Europe. This attention undoubtedly affected the will of politicians throughout Europe and in other regions of the world to accept Syrian refugees as the idea, if not the reality, that the 'whole world was watching' was in evidence daily. Stories about the suffering of children, poignantly displayed in homes around the world through various media, were founded implicitly in a universal understanding of personhood. These stories contributed to a widely shared view that no one, and especially no child, should suffer the indignity of being cast out when they are escaping the ravages of a violent conflict at home.

Media images of the event—most horrifically typified in the drowned body of the three year old boy, Aylan Kurdi—circulated to make the distant seem more immediate. The power of hyper-mediated images that go viral through myriad platforms instantaneously illustrates how networks circulate image-texts to create powerful narratives about contemporary events. That media depicts particular places and events in a media space itself under erasure suggests yet another irony in thinking geographically about GCE. Flows of texts that signal particularity but work through processes of generality and ubiquity give us pause: Where is place in this circulation of texts? Is place consequential to this image-text?

Teaching Practices: Curriculum, Instruction, and Assessment

The discussions of migrations and mobility utilized congruence between CGE and geography. Coerced migration, flows of power, and migration of text each demonstrate an interconnected world in which conceptions of place are shaped by agentive and discursive plays. Coerced migrants and refugees disrupt media spaces that seek to erase the images of those who do not model idealized behaviors such as sex workers. GCE takes the global tensions of citizenship into the classroom in search of interconnected learning that implicates learners. Through geography, we seek to maintain the complexity of articulating global processes and their boundedness, use, and reconstruction of space. We have developed with colleagues in the nonprofit sector a teaching instrument called the Framework for Global Interpretation (FGI). The FGI is a process of uncovering the global and geographic connectivity of everyday materials through a series of collective inquiries. Our migration examples illuminate the need for broad inquiry; each could also be taken up by teachers seeking to understand spatial movements. The instrument is relevant in K-12 classrooms, with the opportunity for more interdisciplinary focus in elementary grades. The model remains across the grades with modifications about the depth of research, more structured categories, and appropriate presentation.

FGI begins in a small group as students are given an issue and related topics that will spark their ability to guide a deep and thoroughgoing analysis of the event/issue. Students interpreting the Syrian refugee crisis might be given categories of questions, including: perspectives, connections, media, spatial, political, economic, social, medical infrastructure, ecological, and immunology. Each of these categories is shaped into a series of questions about the nature of the issue (refugees) in light of the category (political), for example: What are the political responsibilities of nations where refugees arrive? How do receiving nations integrate refugees into their civic structure? What are the social and religious policies that threaten the safety of its citizens? How does global discourse shape the political decisions of nations where refugees arrive? What are the standards for evaluating human rights violations?

Students divide up the subtopics/questions and undertake independent or paired research on these questions, identifying relevant source material and providing heuristic summaries, or briefs, of each issue. They then return to share their insights, which contributes to developing a fuller, connected, and rounder grasp of the issues at play around a seemingly singular, place-specific event. Students present individually and work collectively to develop theories about what is happening within and among categories. The discussion across categories allows analysis of patterns, structures, and institutions that inform multiple categories. In the case of migration, the categories are not each an explanation, but a set of factors working to force people from Syria, empower some countries to refuse refugees, and dispossess Syrians of civic belonging. This may end with a brainstorming of questions, perhaps in a more specific and refined manner, to develop an even deeper grasp of what is happening with respect to this crisis.

The assessment of this learning activity germinates from the representation of outcomes. Students might prepare a multimedia presentation using a digital resource to illustrate the outcomes and processes of their inquiry. Spatial analysis programs such as Google Earth and ArcGIS offer multimodal means of situating the FGI inquiry in spatial flows. They enable opportunities to depict patterns, explore movement, and demonstrate changing place. These representations can be displayed synchronously or otherwise so that each group can learn both about the specific facets of the Syrian refugee crisis along with the way it is connected to the flow of media. The aim of the FGI is to move students toward inquiring more deeply and connectedly about what otherwise in the media are presented as momentary, placeless, and passing events, such that they begin to develop a more critical and circumspect stance about the various texts-in-flow that bombard them on a daily basis. The FGI opens up a space of inquiry and intellectual repose about seemingly fleeting episodes that make up our daily global media diet. The process of FGI inquiry supports GCE by taking existing knowledge and understandings of global problems and posing questions about them, examining them as layered, interrelated and multidimensional, and connecting them back to the learner.

Geographic analysis proposes that global citizenship education engages with how places are transformed by citizenship and how spatial analysis shapes civic engagement and efficacy. It emphasizes that places do not exist in isolation, so teaching and assessing must inquire into the interactions between and changes to places involved in a concept or event. An FGI on migrant women can bring together the policies, social environments, and economic systems of Nepal, India, England, and the United Nations. Spatial analysis simultaneously explores the implicated places for existing and transformed dynamics. The tendency is to examine each country and then make comparisons across the countries. But in trying to understand the spatial reasons for and implications of trafficking through an FGI approach, the relationship is not one of comparison or what the different economies are that would entice someone to migrate. The economies are not different but connected. Nepali people are searching for more secure incomes because England (and others) is outsourcing cheap, unskilled labor to Nepal. The policies regarding civic rights of migrants in England exist because people are migrating in undesirable manners. To account for this, spatial analysis is better done by taking a factor within the broader topic—migration policies and access—and exploring then across the places of inquiry. While students in their inquiry or the teacher when offering material will likely move from one place to another, the reflexive elements of inquiry always ask about the flows and interaction of the policy.

Conclusion and Future Research

An ongoing challenge for GCE and geography education is the relative absence of funding to support studies of implementation. The fact that schools and educators are primarily focused on practice and the students and situations immediately before them offers a significant hurdle for calls for research in education. The episodic characteristic of educational research creates a special challenge as the scope of studies makes general claims problematic. The likely future for research in these spaces is similar to the more recent past: that is, small-scale studies of cases and projects that are not necessarily commensurate with other like-studies. Spatiality is implicated in GCE; this discussion encourages more robust and explicit attention to how concepts like global are used and how specific places come into or are given meaning in the flows of people, power, and media.

References

Agency, U. N. R. (n.d.). *Protecting and supporting the displaced in Syria*. Retrieved August 9, 2016, from http://www.unhcr.org/en-us/news/editorial/2016/2/56cad5a99/unhcr-syria2015-end-of-year-report.html?query=syria.

Anderson, B. (2006). *Imagined communities: Reflections on the origin and spread of nationalism*. Verso.

Andrijasevic, R. (2003). The difference borders make: (Il)legality, migration and trafficking in Italy among Eastern European women in prostitution. In S. Ahmed, C. Castaneda, A. Fortier & M. Sheller (Eds.), *Uprootings/regroundings: Questions of home and migration* (pp. 251–272). Oxford: Berg Publishers.

Andrijasevic, R. (2009). Sex on the move: Gender, subjectivity, and differential inclusion. *Subjectivity, 29*, 389–406.

Castles, S. (2002). Migration and community formation under conditions of globalization. *International Migration Review, 36*(4), 1143–1168.

Castles, S. (2010). Understanding global migration: A social transformation perspective. *Journal of Ethnic and Migration Studies, 36*(10), 1565–1586.

Castles, S., & Davidson, A. (2000). *Citizenship and migration: Globalization and the politics of belonging.* Psychology Press.

Connor, W. (1978). A nation is a nation, is a state, is an ethnic group is a…. *Ethnic and Racial Studies, 1*(4), 377–400.

Cox, K. R. (2002). *Political geography: Territory, state, and society.* Malden, MA: Blackwell Publishers.

Cuban, L. (1993). *How teachers taught: Constancy and change in American classrooms, 1890–1990.* Teachers College Press.

Doezema, J. (2002). Who gets to choose? Coercion, consent, and the UN Trafficking Protocol. *Gender & Development, 10*(1), 20–27.

FitzGerald, S. A. (2016). Vulnerable geographies: Human trafficking, immigration and border control in the UK and beyond. *Gender, Place & Culture, 23*(2), 181–197.

Gaudelli, W. (2016). *Global citizenship education: Everyday transcendence.* New York: Routledge.

Heisbourg, F., & François, H. (2015). The strategic implications of the Syrian refugee crisis. *Survival, 57*(6), 7–20.

Hyndman, J., & Giles, W. (2011). Waiting for what? The feminization of asylum in protracted situations. *Gender, Place, and Culture, 18*(3), 361–379.

Luibhéid, E. (2008). Queer/migration: An unruly body of scholarship. *Gay and Lesbian Quarterly, 14*(2–3), 169–190.

Moodley, K. & Adam, H. (2000). Race and nation in post-apartheid South Africa. *Current Sociology, 48*(3), 51–69.

Narlikar, A. (2005). *The World Trade Organization: A very short introduction.* Oxford University Press.

Ong, A. (1999). *Flexible citizenship: The cultural logics of transnationality.* Durham: Duke University Press.

Pickup, F. (1998). More words but no action? Forced migration and trafficking of women. *Gender & Development, 6*(1), 44–51.

Richardson, D., Poudel, M., & Laurie, N. (2009). Sexual trafficking in Nepal: Constructing citizenship and livelihoods. *Gender, Place & Culture, 16*(3), 259–278.

Sharma, N. (2003). Travel agency: A critique of anti-trafficking campaigns. *Global Movements for Refugee and Migrant Rights, 21*(3), 53–65.

Shifman, P. (2003). Trafficking and women's human rights in a globalised world. *Gender & Development, 11*(1), 125–132.

Stearns, P. N. (2008). *World history in documents: A comparative reader.* NYU Press.

UNESCO. (2014). *Global citizenship education: Preparing learners for the challenges of the 21st century.* UNESCO.

Van Liempt, I. (2011). Different geographies and experiences of 'assisted' types of migration: A gendered critique on the distinction between trafficking and smuggling. *Gender, Place & Culture, 18*(02), 179–193.

Wenar, L. (2016). *Blood oil: Tyranny, resources, and the rules that run the world.* USA: Oxford University Press.

Yuval-Davis, N. (2006). Belonging and the politics of belonging. *Patterns of prejudice, 40*(3), 197–214.

Authors' Biography

William Gaudelli is Professor of Social Studies and Chair of the Department of Arts and Humanities at Teachers College, Columbia University. His research areas include global citizenship education and teacher education/development. Gaudelli has published over 50 scholarly pieces in journals, including *Teachers College Record, Teaching Education, Theory and Research in Social Education, The Journal of Curriculum Theorizing, The Journal of Aesthetic Education* and *Teaching and Teacher Education* along with two books. His third book, *Global Citizenship Education: Everyday Transcendence*, offers an analysis of global citizenship education in various locales globally, will be published in April, 2016.

Sandra J. Schmidt is an Associate Professor in the Program in Social Studies at Teachers College, Columbia University. Her research brings spatial thinking into social studies education. She explores how young people navigate and make meaning of everyday spaces. She focuses on the gendered and sexualized symbols in space.

CHAPTER 31

Intercultural Citizenship Education in the Language Classroom

Melina Porto

INTRODUCTION

This chapter describes an intercultural citizenship project in the English as a foreign language classroom (EFL) between Argentina and Italy. It combines language teaching with an intercultural orientation on the one hand and citizenship education on the other. After a general overview of this theory and its relation to global citizenship education, the project is illustrated with student samples, followed by implications for teachers.

In many parts of the world, language teaching (whether native, foreign, second or additional) is understood in linguistic and communicative terms, with an instrumental orientation. Students learn the system of a language (grammar, vocabulary, phonology, etc.), (what is known as linguistic competence), and they learn to relate linguistic expressions with functions and contexts of use in order to communicate in that language (or communicative competence). Language learning understood in this way was dominant in the 1970s and 1980s and still pervades in instrumental perspectives that see language learning as a bridge to employability, social and economic development, education, entertainment, etc.

In the late 1990s, Byram (1997) introduced his *Model of Intercultural Competence*. This model represents the shift from linguistic and communicative

M. Porto (✉)
Instituto de Investigaciones en Humanidades y Ciencias Sociales (Institute of Research in the Social Sciences and the Humanities), Facultad de Humanidades y Ciencias de la Educación (School of Humanities and Sciences of Education), Universidad Nacional de La Plata and CONICET (Consejo Nacional de Investigaciones Científicas y Técnicas), La Plata, Argentina
e-mail: melinaporto@conicet.gov.ar; M.Porto@uea.ac.uk

I. Davies et al. (eds.), *The Palgrave Handbook of Global Citizenship and Education*, https://doi.org/10.1057/978-1-137-59733-5_31

competence to intercultural communicative competence, i.e. language learning with an intercultural orientation (Liddicoat and Scarino 2013; Lu and Corbett 2011). It moved the field from the dichotomy competence–performance (knowing the language or knowing about the language vs. knowing to use the language in context) to different dimensions of knowledge, skills,[1] and attitudes called *saviors*. In this view, (foreign) language education involves the following *saviors*:

- *savoir être:* attitudes of curiosity and inquisitiveness;
- *saviors:* knowledge of the ways of life in a given society or context, for instance work, education, traditions, history, dress codes, food, etc.;
- *savoir comprendre:* skills of interpreting and relating those *saviors*;
- *savoir apprendre/savoir faire*: skills of discovery and interaction; and
- *savoir s'engager*: critical cultural awareness.

Other scholars such as Bredella, Zarate and Kramsch have developed this intercultural dimension in the last decade (Byram and Feng 2004; Kramsch 2011; Risager 2011).

A further and recent development are the axioms and characteristics of intercultural citizenship education in the language classroom initially set out in Alred et al. (2003, 2006) and later gathered under the concept of *education for intercultural citizenship in the (foreign) language classroom* (Byram 2008, 2010)—a concept that put forth a new conceptualization of language education (Byram 2012, 2014; Byram et al. 2017). In this view, language learning is pushed beyond the linguistic and the communicative, and also beyond the instrumental (learning a language for communication, employment, etc.), toward an intercultural citizenship perspective that connects the foreign language classroom with the community, whether local, national, regional, and/or global. Intercultural citizenship becomes the content of foreign language education. This link with the community makes language teaching an educational endeavor. It should be pointed out that this view focuses in particular on the ordinary (foreign) language classroom in mainstream education and is consequently different from intercultural bilingual education, which focuses on indigenous and minority languages in specific contexts (López and Sichra 2008).

Very few intercultural citizenship studies as conceptualized before exist. Byram et al. (2017) present cases in the form of curriculum development projects in eleven countries (Argentina, China, Denmark, Hungary, Italy, Japan, South Korea, Sweden, Taiwan, UK, USA), which are examples of how learners of different ages and different levels of linguistic competence in different languages can be taught on the basis of the principles of intercultural citizenship enunciated before. The project described in this chapter is one of such studies.

LANGUAGE EDUCATION IN COMBINATION WITH INTERCULTURAL CITIZENSHIP

Intercultural citizenship (Byram 2008, 2012, 2014) takes Byram's (1997) intercultural communicative competence further by giving emphasis to three dimensions, namely the relational, the critical, and the civic. The relational means that students get involved with others and become intercultural speakers or intercultural mediators (Byram 2009), i.e., they interpret linguistic and non-linguistic input critically in a comparative perspective. The critical means analyzing and reflecting on one's thoughts and actions and those of others, questioning the national basis of one's presuppositions and views (Barnett 1997; Johnston et al. 2011) through interaction in different languages and with diverse ideas, values and beliefs about a certain topic. Finally, the civic/citizenship dimension involves students acting in their communities, i.e. undertaking a civic action beyond the classroom and the school/university. This civic aspect makes language teaching educational (beyond the instrumental orientation) by involving a dimension of justice that Budd (2013, p. 18) describes in these terms: "The aim is not simply the ability of people to learn, the utility of obtaining an education, but locating learning and its outcomes in a structure of justice that extends to life within complex societies."

INTERCULTURAL CITIZENSHIP AS GLOBAL CITIZENSHIP

Here is the link with global education (Abdullahi 2010) and global citizenship education (Jackson 2014; Myers 2016). Global education, global citizenship education, and intercultural citizenship education in the language classroom aim at developing knowledge, skills, and attitudes, of a civic and social kind but also of other kinds, in order to instill change in students' views and positionings through criticality and reflexivity, aspiring at building committed, sustainable, long-lasting, and world-friendly perspectives and behaviors. The element of criticality and reflexivity aligns with the "justice-oriented citizen [who] [C]ritically assesses social, political, and economic structures to see beyond surface causes" and is different from the personally responsible citizen (an honest, integral person who recycles, gives away food to those in need, etc.) and the participatory citizen (who collectively engages in civic action) (Westheimer and Kahne 2004, p. 240). In tune with Myers and Zaman (2009), global education, global citizenship education, and intercultural citizenship education emphasize the links between globalization and cosmopolitanism and coincide in the focus on a moral dimension (students form part of, and identify with, a global community, and have ethical responsibilities toward it), an institutional dimension (learning is framed within universal bases like human rights) and a political dimension (political in the sense that learners take action to change the world).

In Oxley and Morris' (2013) typology of global citizenship, Byram's intercultural citizenship shares features with the eight types the authors identify:

political, moral, economic and cultural (as the cosmopolitan types) and social, critical, environmental and spiritual (as the advocacy types). It has strong links with "moral global citizenship," which rests on human rights frameworks such as UN conventions and declarations and embodies an "ethical positioning of individuals and groups to each other" (Oxley and Morris 2013, p. 306). Two empirical studies reported in Byram et al. (2017) embody this type of citizenship. One addressed the topic of the Malvinas war fought between Argentina and the UK in 1982 in a project between Argentinean and British language undergraduates carried out in 2012 (Porto and Yulita 2017). The project aimed at the cultivation of a culture of peace and the reconciliation of both nations through the collaborative work the students engaged in using English and Spanish as foreign languages. The other study was undertaken in the same settings but in 2013 and 2014 (Yulita and Porto 2017) and focused on the theme of human rights violations during the 1978 dictatorship period in Argentina. It aimed at raising the awareness of people today about human rights violations in the Argentinean context but also elsewhere. In both studies Osler and Starkey's cosmopolitan citizenship framework was paramount (Osler and Starkey 2010; Osler 2012) and Oxley and Morris (2013) identify these authors as key theorists and educationalists within "moral global citizenship."

Furthermore, both studies also aimed at the development of democratic competences in students on the basis of the Council of Europe's (2010) Charter on Education for Democratic Citizenship and Human Rights Education and in this sense intercultural citizenship can simultaneously be seen as "political global citizenship," with which it shares a focus on cosmopolitan democracy (Oxley and Morris 2013). In addition, students in these two projects were encouraged to critically analyze the recent historical past (Malvinas war, dictatorship period) to understand who they are individually and as a nation now (self transformation) but also to build a better future together (social transformation). This is "critical global citizenship" in Oxley and Morris' typology, which focuses on challenging inequalities, oppression and human rights abuses, in this case in the language classroom.

Intercultural citizenship can also be strongly identified as "cultural global citizenship," which addresses a "particular emphasis on globalization of arts, media, languages, sciences and technologies" (Oxley and Morris 2013, p. 306). Cultural competence, intercultural communication, and experience through travel, reading, personal contact and cultural expressions (art, music, film, etc.), and their critical evaluation, are key features in this type of citizenship. These elements are also central in intercultural citizenship as students from different countries who speak different languages engage in collaboration, become intercultural mediators (Byram 2009) and develop criticality and reflexivity through awareness of the national basis of their views and presuppositions. The comparative perspective in students' languages, beliefs and views allows for critical analysis, evaluation and reflection. The study reported in this chapter is an example of this type of global citizenship.

The civic action feature in intercultural citizenship theory resembles transnational activity in "social global citizenship" (Oxley and Morris 2013) where local, bottom-up solutions are found in collaboration with community organisations in the figure of the "participatory citizen" (Westheimer and Kahne 2004). An illustration of this element appears later in the chapter, with the caveat that the critical stance adopted by students, which inspired them to examine political, ideological and other underpinnings of street art, transformed them into "justice-oriented citizens." In addition, in this type of citizenship individuals ascribe multiple and simultaneous identities and identifications and in the case reported here, Argentinean and Italian students experienced a new sense of bonding called "transnational identification." The theoretical basis shared by intercultural and social global citizenship is multiculturalism, which in turn brings connections with "cultural global citizenship."

Intercultural citizenship addresses issues of social import in the classroom and one of those is the environment, a concern shared with "environmental global citizenship" in the typology. Both theories highlight three aspects (Dobson and Bell 2006): a focus on obligations and collective responsibilities, not only rights; importance attributed to the private world (learners instill change in the home and in their immediate surroundings), not only the public (in intercultural citizenship in the language classroom, in the form of civic action beyond the school/university); and a focus beyond the nation toward the transnational–international, accompanied by a spirit of de-territorialized well-being of the world. Reliance on UN declarations on sustainable development and similar frameworks ties this type of citizenship to the moral type. An empirical case in the primary English classroom between Argentina and Denmark is an example of "environmental global citizenship" described in Porto (2016). The love and care for a greener world that the children experienced during the project echo "spiritual global citizenship" in Oxley and Morris' typology.

Finally, a small note should be made of the fact that language learning, in its instrumental orientation, i.e. learning a language to have better opportunities for employment, access to health, education and entertainment, social mobility, coincides in its aims with "economic global citizenship" geared toward the development of human capital, labor, and resources in an international development framework.

INTERCULTURAL CITIZENSHIP PEDAGOGY

Pedagogically, Byram et al. (2017) outline the following characteristics of an intercultural citizenship project in the language classroom:

(1) citizenship is the content of language lessons through the inclusion of themes of social relevance (the environment, ecology, languages, peace and conflict, diversity, linguistic and other rights, sustainability, poverty, hunger, etc.);

(2) students who speak different native languages engage with others in intercultural communication in a transnational project and develop a sense of community called "transnational identification";
(3) students engage in criticality and reflexivity not only at the level of thought but also by taking action in the community (at local, national, regional or global levels).

These characteristics coincide roughly with the elements of globally-informed programs of citizenship education outlined by Myers (2016) and Jackson (2014), namely cross-cultural sensitivity through intercultural dialogue, service learning (what is called here "civic action"), international understanding, and global justice (here, the social justice dimension of civic action embodied in the figure of the "justice-oriented citizen"—Westheimer and Kahne 2004).

In the reality of the language classroom, intercultural citizenship can be realized through project work, content-based and task-based instruction. By addressing a theme of social import using meaningful tasks within a challenging project aimed at identifying and solving a problem in the community cooperatively, students interact with peers from another country, develop a critical understanding of life in different societies, awareness of cultural difference and awareness of the need to seek contextualized responses to specific issues on the basis of critical analysis. Involved here are the competences, abilities or skills of intercultural citizenship (Alred et al. 2003, 2006; Jackson 2014): consciousness-raising (observing, describing, analyzing, discovering), comparative interpretation (comparing, contrasting, relating, de-centering, perspective-taking, interpreting), and critical thinking (critical reflexivity and critical action in the world through community engagement). On this basis, Byram (2008) and Byram et al. (2017) argue that the foreign language classroom is well positioned in the school curriculum to educate the global citizenry.

In this view, language learning means much more than linguistic and communicative competence: it involves a multiliteracies perspective that embeds new literacies and multiple languages (García 2009), meaning negotiation through plurilingual repertoires and practices (Canagarajah 2013), in supportive, collaborative and transnational efforts "premised on the normative value of contributing to the creation of a better world, especially the responsibility to solve world problems" (Myers and Zaman 2009, p. 2595; Guilherme 2002; Witteborn 2010). In this sense, this intercultural citizenship perspective represents what may be called "ecology of language learning."

OVERVIEW OF THE PROJECT

The project was an online intervention about mural art and graffiti designed to test the theory of intercultural citizenship in practice in the language classroom. It was carried out in 2013 between second-year undergraduate students of English at *Universidad Nacional de La Plata* in Argentina and second-year bachelor's level degree students in English at *Università degli Studi di Padova* in Italy. There were 100 Argentinean students and 75 Italian students, all aged 18–22 and with a B2/C1 level of English according to the Common European Framework of Reference (Council of Europe 2001).

The project, undertaken in ordinary language courses, had linguistic and intercultural aims, for example appreciate linguistic diversity in English, Spanish and Italian; develop research skills; engage in intercultural dialogue with others using English as lingua franca; and analyze critically images, texts, practices, etc. It also had citizenship aims, something novel in both language courses, for instance allow others to express their viewpoints, avoiding hostility and confrontation and resolving conflict when necessary; develop values such as respect, mutual understanding, social awareness and openness; and engage in civic participation locally, nationally, regionally, and/or globally.

There were three phases: introductory and awareness, intercultural dialogue, and citizenship. The introductory and awareness phase involved all students researching about mural art and graffiti in their own foreign language classes without meeting online yet. They also went outside their classrooms and walked around their communities with the aim of photographing existing murals and graffiti in their towns (La Plata in Argentina and Padova in Italy) and creating a corpus of street art in each city. They uploaded their photographs to a wiki that we used following the guidelines in O'Dowd (2015). Using asynchronic communication tools such as the chat in the wiki and email, they shared their impressions about that corpus.

The online intercultural dialogue phase was undertaken using Skype in weekly meetings over 2 months, which were recorded and uploaded to the wiki. In mixed nationality groups, students described the social, cultural and historical meanings behind the murals and graffiti they had photographed in their communities and discussed whether they were a form of art or an act of vandalism, touching upon issues of freedom, police enforcement and repression, ecology, sustainable art, etc. They developed their critical understanding of those forms of expression and engaged in the collaborative design of a mural or a graffiti intended to represent their group identity and their positioning on the topic using a tool called Mural.ly.

The citizenship phase involved students taking action in their communities. Only the Argentinean students took part in this stage due to constraints at the Italian university. One group taught a lesson on mural art and graffiti in a shelter home for poor women who were victims of domestic violence; another one drew reverse graffiti in a local square (an environmentally friendly way of creating temporary images on walls or other surfaces by removing dirt from a surface); others published an article in the university newspaper; and another group drew a mural in collaboration with children from a primary state school in La Plata.

PROJECT FINDINGS

There were conversational data such as the chats in the wiki and the recorded Skype sessions between the Argentinean and Italian students. Documentary data comprised photographs of street art in La Plata and Padova, the collaboratively created murals and graffiti, student products (newspaper articles, leaflets, photos, etc.), written reflection logs, and the Autobiography of Intercultural Encounters (hereafter AIE) (Byram et al. 2009) which the Argentinean students completed individually in English. The AIE is a resource created by the Council of Europe intended to encourage intercultural reflection and critical analysis. Students participated on a voluntary basis and signed consent forms. All names are pseudonyms and the focus in on the Argentinean students.

The data were analyzed qualitatively (Cohen et al. 2011; Mertens 2015) for linguistic evidence of the three key elements of intercultural citizenship theory:

(a) a sense of community of transnational peers
(b) intercultural citizenship skills
(c) civic engagement.

Identification as a Transnational Group

Byram et al. (2017) argue and show that intercultural citizenship leads to the emergence of a sense of identification and bonding among those participants who work in collaboration across countries. This is a new identification that brings each group together. Underlying here is a conceptualization of identity as social identifications and groupings (in the plural) (Norton and Toohey 2011) which are multiple, hybrid, complex, fluid, and contradictory (Genetsch 2007; Norton and Toohey 2011) because "identity is not an essence but a positioning" (Genetsch 2007, p. 15). So this project positioned the students at La Plata university as Argentinean, middle-class, educated and Catholic, for instance, but simultaneously emphasized performativity. The transnational identification that emerged was a "temporary identification" (Butler 1997, p. 266), one of several others (Argentinean, middle-class, educated, Catholic, etc.), and was enacted simultaneously with others. In the data, this transnational identification became evident in the use of first person plural forms and expressions of communion (shown in bold), as the following extract from a reflection log shows.

We tried to show **this closeness and friendship in our final mural through images and phrases that represent our union and the feeling of growth we reached by our relationship.** That was the reason why **we thought important to write our names on it,** as well as tell the viewers through notes about **common aspects we shared as young people, like simply having fun. We, above**

everything, wanted to express the naturalness and simplicity through which we felt connected.

(Final reflection log)

Through observation and analysis, another group discovered that they shared more than they had initially thought:

Not only do we coincide in daily life matters such as habits and interests, but also in beliefs and aims concerning mostly studies. This demonstrated us that, **in spite of the distance, one can feel really close to people only by sharing opinions and feelings through communication.**

(Final reflection log)

These feelings of closeness, communion, joy and care resemble spiritual global citizenship in Oxley and Morris' typology.

Skills Involved in Intercultural Citizenship

Simultaneously, the skills involved in intercultural citizenship became evident in all data types. These skills are described in definitions of intercultural competence in language teaching theory and also in citizenship education theory (Byram 2008, 2014) and comprise the skills of observing, discovering, describing, analyzing, comparing and contrasting, relating, interpreting, perspective-taking, de-centering, critical thinking, and reflexivity.

There was an important focus on awareness of others, that is, engaging in relations with others for the sake of this project and one student expressed in his AIE (evidence in italics in the data here and elsewhere) "We did not know *who we were going to work with, how they will be*". In addition, the online communication stage fostered processes of comparing and contrasting leading to self-awareness as well as awareness of otherness. In the following AIE extract, skills are identified between brackets:

> *One of the first things that called our attention* [de-centring and perspective-taking] *was the similarities we encountered between our Italian peers and us*, as the Skype sessions went along [comparing]. *We had expected to* [de-centring and perspective-taking] *face differences other than common aspects, considering the distance that separate us, together with the well-known but still important factor of living in a community which is, in many ways (culturally, politically and socially) distinct from theirs* [comparing and contrasting].

De-centering and perspective-taking were important and involved students distancing from their own positions and becoming aware of the different perspectives of their peers. In the previous AIE, this is revealed linguistically through the expressions "One of the first things that *called our attention* was ... *We had expected to...*". At the same time, the project encouraged students to examine different perspectives through discovery, critical analysis and reflection:

> As regards the subject of the project, we found ourselves -again- learning more than we thought we would learn. *Graffiti turned out to be a mode of expression that is related with a variety of fields that does not only concern art* [discovering]. *This project opened our minds to new cultures and thoughts* [discovering], *which allowed us to know more about the world and made us eager to keep on learning about it* [analyzing critically, reflecting]

(Marina, AIE)

Marina concluded: "Fortunately, this cultural exchange brought about *unexpectedly and most interesting conclusions* about culture, art and people, which enriched us in various ways." It is clear that the skills of intercultural citizenship match cultural global citizenship in Oxley and Morris' typology.

Civic Engagement

The citizenship phase of the project involved students in planning, designing and implementing an action in the community (whether local, national, regional or global) with the aim of bringing the university and society together by applying the knowledge and skills gained through their learning in the English classroom to improve the world. This civic engagement links intercultural citizenship with social global citizenship in Oxley and Morris' typology. In addition, this citizenship element distinguishes intercultural citizenship from intercultural communication projects where the aim is only intercultural dialogue and understanding. Here the students acted critically on the world and their actions in the community were "transformatory" (Barnett 1997; Witteborn 2010). This element is totally innovative in foreign language education and criticality transforms social global citizenship into critical global citizenship (Oxley and Morris 2013).

As mentioned before, only the Argentinean students engaged in this phase due to constraints at the University of Padua. For instance, one group of three students travelled to Berazategui, a town near La Plata, and taught a lesson about mural art and graffiti to a group of women in need enrolled in a social relief governmental plan (called "Ellas hacen", ["They do"]). The government pays for their education so that they can be reinserted into society. Some of those women had many children and had been abandoned by their husbands, others were homeless and others suffered domestic violence. The students gathered the women's opinions on the lesson and concluded that it had provided a sense of fulfillment through exploration and participation. In her AIE Carla said: "They [the women] really enjoyed the class and they showed they were interested in the topic as they asked many questions about Banksy."

Two groups published articles in Utopia´s newspaper, the School of Humanities newspaper at La Plata university and evaluated the intercultural encounter with the Italian peers. They valued the possibility to learn from others, their views and their culture (cultural global citizenship):

The experience was outstanding since *we could learn from the Italian culture, we could exchange opinions.*

(Article 1)

It was a new experience for us and *we took the best of it that was getting to know new people and also learn about different cultures and how they see graffiti and mural art.*

(Article 2)

Another group created leaflets in Spanish and in English describing both types of expression, murals and graffiti, aimed at raising the awareness of people about whether they are a form of art or an act of vandalism (Fig. 31.1). They distributed them at the university and around the city. On the basis of critical analysis of and reflection on the dichotomy art-vandalism, which

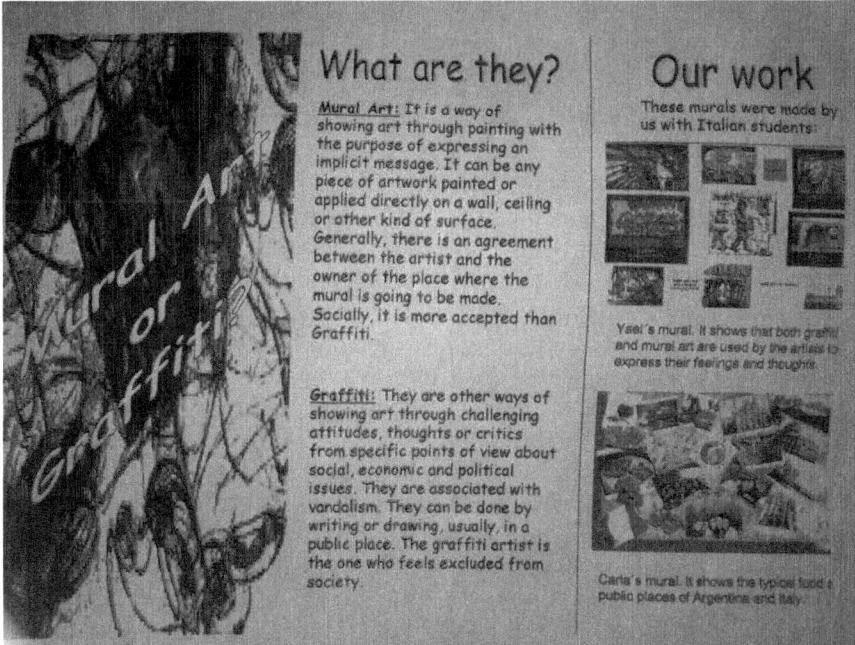

Fig. 31.1 Leaflet in English

prompted them to see the political, ideological, and social forces involved in this form of expression, they concluded that "our mural shows how street art can change people's mind and begin a revolution with its drawings. This is a way of expressing thoughts without violence" (final reflection log). The element of critical analysis of underlying forces in mural art and graffiti is a characteristic of critical global citizenship (Oxley and Morris 2013), where social transformation is important ("art can change people's mind and begin a revolution with its drawings"). Criticality turns students into justice-oriented citizens beyond the development of personal values (the personally responsible citizen) and participation in the community (the participatory citizen) (Westheimer and Kahne 2004). The values of freedom and peace ("expressing thoughts without violence") are part of the cosmopolitan democracy that political global citizenship instills.

Others carried out their own investigation, therefore engaging their research skills in this phase too (not only during the introductory phase) and they interviewed people in three different cities (La Plata, Berazategui and Quilmes) to find out how they conceived of graffiti. They put their findings and conclusions in a written report.

> From the eight interviews that we conducted, *we have arrived at the conclusion that* all the interviewees consider that GRAFFITI is an art. *However, four of the interviewees clearly said that* graffiti becomes an act of vandalism if it is sprayed over an inhabited house without the owner's permission. *Another good point that we found in the interviews is that* people pay attention to graffiti especially those which contains colourful drawings and some of the interviewees also confessed that they try to interpret the graffiti sometimes.

> (Report on action in the community)

As a further outcome of their research, they realized that "*not all the interviewees know precisely what graffiti is*" and on the basis of this small scale needs analysis, they decided to create a leaflet (Fig. 31.2) and distribute it in the area to raise awareness: "That's why we handed in leaflets on graffiti to them or explained to them the general definition of graffiti" (Report). These students diagnosed a situation using interviews, produced a report on it, conducted a needs analysis, and acted on its findings by creating a leaflet and distributing it in their town. They can therefore be seen as justice-oriented citizens (Westheimer and Kahne 2004), engaged in critical global citizenship (Oxley and Morris 2013).

In addition, one group taught a class about this theme to a group of teenagers at school No 77 in Bernal (a town 42 km away from La Plata). They discovered that these students did not take care of their school or their classroom as the classroom walls were dirty, covered in tags. The group suggested painting a mural to improve the room and offered their help. The teenagers were

Translation into English:

Graffiti project 2013
What you have to know about graffiti:
It is a text painted on walls freely and creatively.
It is a form of expression through which the artist makes a complaint or accusation, expresses a thought or a personal wish.
They are generally anonymous.
It is usually drawn on public walls without governmental permission.
Types: tags, wild style, throw ups, pompas, dirty, etc.

Fig. 31.2 Graffiti project

excited and sought permission from the headmistress. Figure 31.3 is a photograph of the outcome where we can also see students finishing up the mural. Social global citizenship in the form of the concrete action of painting the classroom walls is combined here with critical global citizenship through the participants' analysis of underlying issues affecting this school's environment.

Finally, another group considered art to be universal as it can cross cultural boundaries. They decided to convey this idea in their action in the community by painting the message on an outside wall in one of the students' house. They chose different works of art by graffiti artists from the different cultures involved in the project using the stencil technique: Italy (Kenny Random), Britain (Banksy) and Argentina (8-bit). Then the students painted a bridge to link each work of art with one another. In the middle of their work students wrote "Art = cultural bridge" and at the bottom they wrote "art is universal." The image cannot be reproduced here for copyright reasons, but it is interesting to point out that the transnational identification in this case

Fig. 31.3   Classroom mural art

transcended the group, as they conceptualized mural art and graffiti as a form of expression that can bring humankind together, highlighting the commonalities that actually bring people together in this world. This is evidence of the de-territorialized spirit of art as a language (cultural global citizenship), which in this case provided a general framework resembling moral global citizenship. The sense of communion and humankind is again an example of spiritual global citizenship.

CONCLUSIONS AND SIGNIFICANCE OF THE PROJECT

This project is an empirical investigation of intercultural citizenship in higher education using English as a lingua franca in a transnational project involving two countries. The Argentinean and Italian students engaged critically with a topic of significance to them and they developed a sense of bonding called "transnational identification." As an outcome of project work and this new sense of community, they took action in their world, gaining new experiences and building a bridge between the university and their communities. They explored the theme of mural art and graffiti with a comparative perspective, getting in contact with new ideas and views, and also a comparative perspective in the languages that the project brought together, namely English, Spanish and Italian. The civic and social actions that they carried out, conceived as citizenship involvement with their local communities, are an innovative element in foreign language education.

The starting point in an intercultural citizenship project of this kind is that language teaching has instrumental purposes but also educational purposes, among which are the development of the self and of societies. Byram (2008) recognizes the potential role of foreign language education in citizenship, political and moral education through the development of critical cultural awareness (Guilherme 2002) or *savoir s'engager* (Byram 1997). The significance of this project outside Argentina and Italy, the countries involved, lies in this educational dimension of language teaching.

Citizenship education and interculturally oriented language education, referred to by Byram (2008) as intercultural citizenship, both aim at developing learners' competences in analysis, cooperation and knowledge about societies and the socio-cultural environment through critical literacy. The basis for the development of intercultural citizenship skills and competences is the critical literacy experience that the project fostered through the engagement in multiple and varied literacy practices in the foreign language (English) as well as the native languages (Spanish, Italian). The civic actions in the community that the Argentinean students carried out are evidence of "transformatory critique in action" (Barnett 1997), i.e., criticality beyond thought realized in concrete civic and social actions. This "criticality in action," which transformed students in justice-oriented citizens (Westheimer and Kahne 2004), occurred in the English as a foreign language classroom in this Argentinean setting. The axioms and characteristics of intercultural citizenship in the language classroom link the theory with Oxley and Morris' (2013) eight types of global citizenship in various ways simultaneously as illustrated in this chapter.

This curricular innovation has shown that it is feasible to put in practice the theory of intercultural citizenship in the language classroom. The axioms, characteristics and phases of an intercultural citizenship project have been enunciated and illustrated with student data, making replication possible in other settings and contexts. The chapter has provided enough detail for the researcher interested in investigating intercultural citizenship further and it has also set the specifics for the language teacher interested in innovative practice for the classroom.

Several issues need to be considered as well, all addressed in Byram et al. (2017), such as the investment in time and resources that the project demanded, for instance in its design and piloting by teachers, technology demands (availability of computer labs, Internet connection, etc.) and the competences of the tellecollaboration teacher (O'Dowd 2015), among others.

Finally, this chapter has not addressed the issue of assessment, dealt with in another chapter of this book. It is important to mention that the question of assessment of intercultural competence or intercultural understanding alone (without the citizenship dimension) is complex and in constant development

(Bennett 2009; Scarino 2009) and to date, high-stakes testing which is feasible and acceptable in education systems remains unresolved. Assessment of intercultural citizenship is not on the language education agenda yet because curricular developments based on the theory are new. It is possible to use reflection logs and the Autobiography of Intercultural Encounters as self-assessment tools and also as tools where the teacher would look for evidence of critical reflexivity and other intercultural citizenship skills as an indication of the development of intercultural citizenship competences in students.

NOTE

1. According to the Council of Europe (2001, p. 11, their emphasis), "*[K]knowledge*, i.e. declarative knowledge (*savoir*), is understood as knowledge resulting from experience (empirical knowledge) and from more formal learning (academic knowledge) (…) *Skills* and *know-how* (*savoir-faire*) (…) depend more on the ability to carry out procedures than on declarative knowledge."

Acknowledgements I am grateful to the editors of this book for this opportunity to put intercultural citizenship in language education in the foreground. I am also indebted to Mike Byram for his continuous support and to Ana Virginia Miguel, Graciela Baum and Marta Guarda for their collaboration in this joint project.

REFERENCES

Abdullahi, S. (2010). Rethinking global education in the twenty-first century. In J. Zajda (Ed.), *Global pedagogies: Schooling for the future, globalisation, comparative education and policy research* (pp. 23–34). Springer Link: E-book.

Alred, G., Byram, M., & Fleming, M. (2003). *Intercultural experience and education.* Clevedon: Multilingual Matters.

Alred, G., Byram, M., & Fleming, M. (2006). *Education for intercultural citizenship: Concepts and comparisons.* Clevedon: Multilingual Matters.

Barnett, R. (1997). *Higher education: A critical business.* London: Open University Press.

Bennett, M. J. (2009). Defining, measuring, and facilitating intercultural learning: A conceptual introduction to the intercultural education double supplement. *Intercultural Education, 20*(sup1), S1–S13.

Budd, J. (2013). Informational education: Creating an understanding of justice. *Education, Citizenship and Social Justice, 8*, 17–28.

Butler, J. (1997). Merely cultural. *Social Text, 52*(53), 265–277.

Byram, M. (1997). *Teaching and assessing intercultural communicative competence.* Clevedon: Multilingual Matters.

Byram, M. (2008). *From foreign language education to education for intercultural citizenship.* Clevedon: Multilingual Matters.

Byram, M. (2009). Intercultural competence in foreign languages. The intercultural speaker and the pedagogy of foreign language education. In D. Deardorff (Ed.), *The SAGE handbook of intercultural competence* (pp. 321–332). California: Sage.

Byram, M. (2010). Linguistic and cultural education for Bildung and citizenship. *Modern Language Journal, 94*, 317–321.

Byram, M. (2012). Conceptualizing intercultural (communicative) competence and intercultural citizenship. In J. Jackson (Ed.), *The Routledge handbook of language and intercultural communication* (pp. 85–97). London: Routledge.

Byram, M. (2014). Twenty-five years on—from cultural studies to intercultural citizenship. *Language, Culture and Curriculum, 27*(3), 209–225.

Byram, M., Barrett, M., Ipgrave, J., Jackson, R., & Méndez García, M. C. (2009). *Autobiography of intercultural encounters*. Strasbourg: Council of Europe.

Byram, M., & Feng, A. (2004). Culture and language learning: Teaching, research and scholarship. *Language Teaching, 37*, 149–168.

Byram, M., Golubeva, I., Han, H., & Wagner, M. (Eds.). (2017). *From principles to practice in education for intercultural citizenship*. Bristol: Multilingual Matters.

Canagarajah, S. (2013). *Translingual practice: Global Englishes and cosmopolitan relations*. New York: Routledge.

Cohen, L., Manion, L., & Morrison, K. (2011). *Research methods in education* (7th ed.). London: Routledge.

Common European Framework of Reference for Languages. (2001). Strasbourg: Council of Europe.

Council of Europe. (2010). *Charter on education for democratic citizenship and human rights education*. Retrieved from http://www.coe.int/en/web/edc/charter-on-education-for-democratic-citizenship-and-human-rights-education.

Dobson, A., & Bell, D. (Eds.). (2006). *Environmental citizenship*. Cambridge, MA: MIT Press.

García, O. (2009). *Bilingual education in the 21st century: A global perspective*. West Sussex: Wiley-Blackwell.

Genetsch, M. (2007). *The texture of identity*. Toronto: TSAR Publications.

Guilherme, M. (2002). *Critical citizens for an intercultural world: Foreign language education as cultural politics*. Clevedon: Multilingual Matters.

Jackson, J. (2014). Global citizenship and intercultural (communicative) competence. In J. Jackson (Ed.), *Introducing language and intercultural communication* (pp. 297–323). London: Routledge.

Johnston, B., Mitchell, R., Miles, F., & Ford, P. (2011). *Developing student criticality in higher education*. London: Continuum.

Kramsch, C. (2011). The symbolic dimensions of the intercultural. *Language Teaching, 44*, 354–367.

Liddicoat, A., & Scarino, A. (2013). *Intercultural language teaching and learning*. West Sussex: Wiley.

López, L. E., & Sichra, I. (2008). Intercultural bilingual education among indigenous peoples in Latin America. In J. Cummins & N. Hornberger (Eds.), *Encyclopedia of language and education. Volume 5. Bilingual education* (pp. 295–309). New York: Springer.

Lu, P., & Corbett, J. (2011). An intercultural approach to second language education and citizenship. In J. Jackson (Ed.), *The Routledge handbook of language andintercultural communication* (pp. 325–339). London: Routledge.

Mertens, D. (2015). *Research and evaluation in education and psychology: Integrating diversity with quantitative, qualitative and mixed methods* (4th ed.). Los Angeles: Sage.

Myers, J. P. (2016). Charting a democratic course for global citizenship education: Research directions and current challenges. *Education Policy Analysis Archives*, *24*(55). http://dx.doi.org/10.14507/epaa.24.2174.

Myers, J. P., & Zaman, H. A. (2009). Negotiating the global and national: Immigrant and dominant culture adolescents' vocabularies of citizenship in a transnational world. *Teachers College Record*, *111*(11), 2589–2625.

Norton, B., & Toohey, K. (2011). Identity, language learning, and social change. *Language Teaching*, *44*, 412–446.

O'Dowd, R. (2015). The competences of the telecollaborative teacher. *The Language Learning Journal*, *43*(2), 194–207.

Osler, A. (2012). Teaching for inclusive citizenship, peace and human rights. In P. Cowan and H. Maitles (Eds.), *Teaching controversial issues in the classroom: Key issues and debates* (pp. 71–83). London: Continuum.

Osler, A., & Starkey, H. (2010). *Teachers and human rights education*. Stoke-on-Trent: Trentham.

Oxley, L., & Morris, P. (2013). Global citizenship: A typology for distinguishing its multiple conceptions. *British Journal of Educational Studies*, *61*(3), 301–325.

Porto, M. (2016). Ecological and intercultural citizenship in the primary english as a foreign language (EFL) classroom: An online project in Argentina. *Cambridge Journal of Education*, *46*(4), 395–415.

Porto, M., & Yulita, L. (2017). Language and intercultural citizenship education for a culture of peace: The Malvinas/Falklands. In M. Byram et al. (Eds.), *From principles to practice in education for intercultural citizenship* (pp. 199–224). Bristol: Multilingual Matters.

Risager, K. (2011). The cultural dimensions of language teaching and learning. *Language Teaching*, *44*(4), 485–499.

Scarino, A. (2009). Assessing intercultural capability in learning languages: Some issues and considerations. *Language Teaching*, *42*, 67–80.

Westheimer, J., & Kahne, J. (2004). What kind of citizen? The politics of educating for democracy. *American Educational Research Journal*, *41*(2), 237–269.

Witteborn, S. (2010). The role of transnational NGOs in promoting global citizenship and globalizing communication practices. *Language and Intercultural Communication*, *10*(4), 358–372.

Yulita, L., & Porto, M. (2017). Human rights education in language teaching. In M. Byram et al. (Eds.), *From principles to practice in education for intercultural citizenship* (pp. 225–250). Bristol: Multilingual Matters.

Author Biography

Melina Porto Ph.D., works in the Institute of Research in the Social Sciences and the Humanities, Universidad Nacional de La Plata (UNLP) and in CONICET (Consejo Nacional de Investigaciones Científicas y Técnicas). She holds a MA ELT from the University of Essex (UK) and a Ph.D. in Sciences of Education from UNLP (Argentina).

CHAPTER 32

Science Education: Educating the Citizens of the Future

David Geelan

INTRODUCTION

Many of the challenges that students at all levels of education will face in the future they will inhabit have two features in common: they have a scientific or technological dimension and they are no respecters of state boundaries. Perhaps the most immediate and obvious is the challenge presented by global climate change, but issues including energy, clean water, disease pandemics, machine intelligence, genetic engineering and other 'technologies of the body', life extension and a plethora of others face the citizens of the future. These challenges are global in scope and nature and efforts to address them must be similarly global. Many of them are also characterized by complexity and ambiguity—including the enterprise of science education itself. The rights and responsibilities of citizens of the world, therefore, require some understanding of science and technology, and their interaction with society. This chapter outlines some key issues in relation to the contribution of science education to preparing the citizens of the future and briefly reviews current efforts and approaches. It also outlines ways in which science education will need to change in order to meet these challenges, and suggests further research and theoretical work remaining to be done.

D. Geelan (✉)
Griffith University, Southport Queensland, Australia
e-mail: d.geelan@griffith.edu.au

507

I. Davies et al. (eds.), *The Palgrave Handbook of Global Citizenship and Education*, https://doi.org/10.1057/978-1-137-59733-5_32

Globalization and Citizenship

This handbook includes a range of descriptions and approaches to the term 'globalization' which also inform this chapter, but I find an approach outlined by David Smith (1999) compelling. He suggests that there are (at least) three forms of globalization, and that confusion often arises when people speak at cross-purposes because they intend different things by the term. The three forms are:

> **Globalization One** (G1)—movement for 'free trade' and free flow of global capital (with its associated growth in the power and influence of transnational corporations),
>
> **Globalization Two** (G2)—public reactions to G1, both adaptations and resistance and
>
> **Globalization Three** (G3)—global dialogues for a sustainable human future.

My gloss on Smith's scheme is as follows:

> We could say that G1 is couched in the language of economics and of rights, and that G2 tends to fall into those same ways of thinking and speaking because it is just a reaction to G1. G3, however, is about our responsibilities to the planet, to one another and to those less fortunate than us. Within this context national boundaries in particular but all political divisions increasingly seem to me to be (a) very artificial, (b) the source of more trouble than benefit, and (c) pretty much irrelevant to our lifeworlds, except rhetorically. (Geelan 2010, p. 149)

That is to say, within the context of both the global nature of many of the challenges being faced and the different forms of globalization, national boundaries and nationalism are more likely to be part of the problem than part of the solution. Approaches that emphasize our common humanity and develop an identity as global citizens are likely to be more effective in addressing these issues than focusing on competitive advantage and the interests of nation-states.

Issues Connecting Science Education and Global Citizenship

As a preliminary to the discussion of these themes, there is value in looking at work by Ian Davies (2004) that considers the relationship between science education and citizenship education. Coming from a perspective in the UK where citizenship was mandated in 2002 as a school subject area, Davies discusses the distinction between approaches that could be characterized as 'science education *for* citizenship' and 'science education *as* citizenship education'. The perspective I have taken in this chapter, and and that is taken by most of the work reviewed, is closer to the former than to the latter. The distinction is a valuable one, and there is the potential for some very interesting work in the field of 'science education as citizenship education'.

It is important, too, to acknowledge Davies' reminder that 'science education for citizenship' can be vulnerable to (a) relatively simplistic notions of what constitutes 'citizenship', not well informed by expert work in that area and (b) being subsumed by the issues, concerns and imperatives arising 'within' science and science education that can tend to marginalize concerns for citizenship.

Scientific Understanding for Facing Future Challenges

A wide variety of issues that will face the citizens of the future have a scientific dimension. They are typically not susceptible to being entirely solved by science and technology, but involve science as well as social and political issues and challenges. The Science, Technology and Society movement in education in the 1970s and 1980s (e.g., Solomon 1993) sought to contextualize science education and address social issues. Initially using the acronym STS, later writers within this tradition added an interest in the Environment to yield 'STSE' (e.g. Hodson 2003; Pedretti 2013). More recently, the terminology has shifted to 'socioscientific issues' (e.g. Kolstø 2001; Zeidler 2005), but the central concerns are similar.

Some of the issues facing citizens of the future that have a scientific component are well known—climate change is perhaps the most prominent. It is entwined with a number of other issues, such as the supply of clean fresh water (including in relation to the loss of glacial water in the Himalayas that is crucial to dry season water supply to China on one side and India on the other, the two nations with the world's largest populations) and consideration of whether or not nuclear (fission) energy should form part of meeting human energy needs.

Other issues are well known among the scientifically literate population but less so to the general populace. One example is disease pandemics. The Black Plague in Europe is quite well known, but the Spanish flu epidemic of 1918 that killed 3–5% of global population is almost forgotten. Recent epidemics that have threatened but not attained pandemic status have included bird flu, swine flu, SARS and Ebola. HIV—AIDS is a global pandemic that has killed almost 40 million people. It is now quite survivable in developed countries but still taking lives in developing countries. It is very probable that in the future there will be more large pandemics that will need to be addressed. Increasing incidence of potentially pandemic pathogens may also be linked with changing climate.

Some issues initially appear more positive, but may have a hidden sting. In 1900, mean male life expectancy in Australia was 50. In 2017 it is 82. Currently, life expectancy in developed countries is increasing at a rate of approximately 2 years every decade. This may seem positive; however, those in developed countries such as the USA, Canada, Australia, and western Europe are also the people who use a disproportionate share of the world's energy and other resources. Increasing the lifespans of these people—of whom I am very cognizant that I am one—is likely to place an increased burden on global resources, unless more sustainable life practices are adopted. The challenges may be even more complex: Bruce Sterling's novel 'Holy Fire' (1996) is set within a 'gerontocracy', a society in which falling population and increased life expectancy has led to a society ruled by and for the benefit of those approaching 200 years of age and young people struggle to find a place.

Increased life expectancy is likely to lead to increases in working age—which may be more sustainable for those engaged in office work than in hard manual labor—and to a larger pool of retirees relying on a smaller pool of workers for support. A related issue is automation and machine intelligence. We increasingly hear media reports that say "Unemployment may rise to 50% as automation, machine intelligence and robots take over human work". Yet in the Golden Age of science fiction, the foreseen future was more often one of increased leisure for everyone as work was taken over by our technologies. Neither outcome is inevitable: a future in which everyone has some work and income but also more leisure is (I would argue) strongly preferable over one in which many have no work and a few continue to have too much. These issues link science and technology with society, economics and ideology.

Also linked with life expectancy are the 'technologies of the body', such as prosthetics, transplantation (including xenotransplantation from other species), mechanical organs, human genetic engineering and gene therapies, cloning, chimeras and a very wide variety of other technologies that impact on the human body and what it means to be human. Machine intelligence (formerly called 'artificial intelligence', but the terminology has changed on the grounds that if it is actually intelligence then it is real rather than artificial, no matter whether it runs on the substrate of a brain or a silicon chip) has the potential to transform human life in ways that are difficult to predict. Given Moore's Law about the rate at which computing power increases, very shortly after our machines become *as* intelligent as us, they will become orders of magnitude *more* intelligent than us.

I could continue giving examples, but (a) I think the point is established that there are many challenges for the citizens of the future that have a scientific dimension but dramatic social and political consequences and (b) the really dramatic changes are likely to be unforeseeable. William Gibson's prescient 1984 novel 'Neuromancer' coined the term 'cyberspace' and envisaged a near future in which machine intelligences interact with and manipulate human beings, but had the ringing of pay phones as a key plot point. Gibson saw so much, but did not foresee the advent of the mobile phone. Technology and science will always surprise us. Scientists at the end of the nineteenth century thought physics was almost 'finished'... and then along came Einstein and others who introduced relativity and quantum physics and revolutionised the ways Western science sees the world. Science still has considerable work to do in coming to terms with dimensions of indigenous knowledges and other traditions such as Chinese medicine. This latter work may prove revolutionary—or the next revolution may come from some entirely unenvisaged direction.

The point is that one of the important roles of science education is to prepare students—who will be the citizens of the future—for the future they will face. Some of that preparation involves the learning of scientific concepts and theories already developed and scientific ways of thinking and approaches to evidence, but much of it must necessarily be about tolerance for and the ability to operate—without paralysis—within complexity and ambiguity, and to use a rich understanding of science and technology to inform citizenship and engagement.

Scientific Understanding for Protection from Charlatanry

Claims made in advertisements on television and in social media are often phrased in scientific terms, but are also often false or misleading. Politicians also make claims in relation to scientific issues such as energy policy and climate change that may be well or poorly founded in evidence. Lobbyists for particular corporations or industry groups both advertise to the public and lobby political leaders. The increase in the sheer volume of information with which people are confronted every day makes it even more challenging to critically judge the quality of proffered information and claims.

Various conspiracy theories—such as the claim that climate change is an anti-capitalist plot, or that chemtrails are being used to control the minds of the populace or make people sterile, or that the HAARP array is used to control the weather and caused Hurricane Katrina—typically grow in the ground of misunderstanding rather than intentional deception, but can lead to real consequences.

Some of these false claims or misunderstandings are relatively innocuous—they may lead to wasting money by purchasing a product that does not perform as advertised, for example—but some have potentially lethal consequences. Deceptive advertisements and testimonials kept people smoking—and dying of lung cancer—for decades after the connection was first understood. There have already been incidents of children dying from diseases that vaccination would have protected them from, due to fallacious anti-vaccination claims. Patients choose to discontinue chemotherapy for cancer and replace it with natural remedies that sometimes have the net effect of shortening their lives. Misinformation in relation to climate change is leading to delays in taking action to ameliorate it.

Science education has a role in protecting the citizens of the future from those who would seek to mislead and exploit them. They also need protection from self-deception. The ability to test a knowledge claim based on empirical evidence and scientific methodology, to check claims of expertise and appeals to authority, to spot when (for example) the axes of a graph have been manipulated in order to deceive, is an important part of preparing students for an increasingly complex future.

Avoiding Scientism

Susan Haack (2011) outlines an approach to the philosophy of science that she argues is 'between scientism and cynicism'. While this chapter is devoted to a passionate advocacy of the value and importance of science education, and implicitly of science itself, it is important to avoid falling into scientism. Scientism may be defined as the belief that science is the *only* source of valid human knowledge. It rejects all knowledge from sources other than empirical evidence. It rejects Habermas' (1972) 'practical' and 'emancipatory' human interests and reduces all of life to the 'technical' interest: an approach drawn by analogy from the physical sciences, particularly (classical) physics, in which controlling the initial conditions of an experiment allows the outcome to be reliably predicted.

In the face of modern physics—quantum theory, relativity and complexity theory—such a position is not tenable even in its metaphorical roots. Add to this the knowledge generated in the social sciences and humanities and other fields of endeavor, and scientism cannot be supported. Indeed, it can be argued that scientism represents the kind of retreat into an over-simplified, reductive version of reality that I am claiming science education has the power to dispel. Scientism is arguably an idolatry of science that is ironically antithetical to the inquiring spirit and openness to challenge that exemplify science at its best. A science education that fosters rather than challenges scientism has betrayed its purpose and its students.

Complexity and Ambiguity

Education is a human activity, and human systems and activities are inherently complex. By 'complex', I mean more than 'complicated' (Geelan 2003). Complicated systems are challenging to subject to reductive analysis, to the process of coming to understand the whole through understanding the large range of complicated parts making it up and their complicated relationships. Complex systems, on the other hand, at least as I use the term here, are inherently *irreducible*: not subject to reductive analysis. Biggiero (2001) outlines the ways in which human systems may be understood to be complex in this sense:

> Human systems are affected by several sources of complexity, belonging to three classes, in order of descending restrictivity. Systems belonging to the first class are not predictable at all, those belonging to the second class are predictable

only through an infinite computational capacity, and those belonging to the third class are predictable only through a trans-computational capacity. The first class has two sources of complexity: logical complexity, directly deriving from self-reference and Gödel's incompleteness theorems, and relational complexity, resulting in a sort of indeterminacy principle occurring in social systems. The second class has three sources of complexity: gnosiological complexity, which consists of the variety of possible perceptions; semiotic complexity, which represents the infinite possible interpretations of signs and facts; and chaotic complexity, which characterizes phenomena of nonlinear dynamic systems. The third class coincides with computational complexity, which basically coincides with the mathematical concept of intractability. Artificial, natural, biological and human systems are characterized by the influence of different sources of complexity, and the latter appear to be the most complex. (p. 3)

Of course, it is not only educational systems that are complex but political, economic and other human systems. Arguments can be made about whether human systems are inherently complex—impossible to ever compute—or simply beyond our present computational abilities, but for all practical purposes there is no difference. We can—and arguably must—behave as though human systems are complex. That does not lead to a philosophy of despair in which we make no effort at all to improve or govern human systems, but it does lead to humility and the recognition that unintended consequences may well overwhelm our intentions.

Similarly, life is already full of ambiguity, some of it related to complexity, some of it to the sheer volume of often-competing information to which people are subjected, and the level of ambiguity is likely to increase rather than decrease as the pace of technological change speeds up. As humanity itself is changed through technologies of the body and information technologies, ambiguity will be a persistent feature.

Within a complex and ambiguous world, a retreat into magical thinking may be tempting. Imposing a faux simplicity on the world through ideology is one possible response to complexity and ambiguity. Paul Feyerabend acknowledges the difficulty in his final (posthumous) book, 'The Conquest of Abundance' (1999), but explores approaches to living within a complex world rather than resisting it. "How is it that views that reduce abundance and devalue human existence can become so powerful?", he asks (p. 16). The answer seems to be 'as a retreat from complexity and ambiguity'.

Science education has a role, I believe, in preparing students to be able to cope with complexity, and to take the world on its own terms. Rather than seek a Procrustean reduction of the world to manageable terms, science education can help students develop their capacity to enlarge their minds and worldviews to contain more of the world, in all its complex, ambiguous glory. This requires, to some extent, a deeper understanding of more recent science including quantum, relativity, complexity, epigenetics and bioinformatics. These fields are inherently complex, probabilistic and sometimes ambiguous. These forms of science can be antidotes to a trend that also exists in society:

a kind of scientific authoritarianism (Altemeyer 2006) that draws metaphorically on classical physics to valorise reductive and mechanistic approaches to complex human challenges.

SCIENCE EDUCATION FOR GLOBAL CITIZENSHIP

A relatively small literature exists in relation to science education for global citizenship. This section of the chapter reviews that literature and explores key issues in relation to pedagogy and curricula.

The book 'Science Education for Citizenship: Teaching Socioscientific Issues' (Ratcliffe and Grace 2003) offers an excellent overview of issues and approaches. The authors are based in the UK but largely take a global perspective to citizenship. It reviews research studies to ground its claims, and offers practical suggestions for teachers in relation to planning, pedagogy and assessment. The authors also consider how to make space for socioscientific issues in crowded school curricula—a theme I will revisit later in discussing the 'curricular emphases' model.

Mannion et al. (2011) offer a critical perspective on the notion of 'global citizenship' itself, and the way in which it is used within UK curricula. They note that it combines traditions from citizenship education, environmental education and development education, but that the term also serves as a 'floating signifier' onto which different and sometimes competing interests project a range of meanings.

Jenkins (1999) links the notion of 'citizen science' into research in relation to the public understanding of science, and recommends a range of modifications to the structure and focus of school science education intended to enhance the public understanding of science. It must be said that, while these recommendations would accord with many of the things for which this chapter is arguing, in the 17 years since this article school science education has not conspicuously changed to reflect them.

Taking up this same point, Hodson (2003) issues a call to action. He surveys the various 'slogans' that have been popular in science education, and notes that:

> ... while much of value has been achieved, there is still considerable cause for concern and [ ] it is time for action in two senses. First, it is time to take action on the school science curriculum because it no longer meets the needs, interests and aspirations of young citizens. Second, it is time for a science curriculum oriented toward sociopolitical action. (p. 645).

Lim (2008) describes a research project using integrated curriculum and roleplay with primary school students in Singapore to explore global citizenship. Students played the role of 'global citizens', and explored the implications of that positioning for issues in mathematics, English and science. Students were engaged with a narrative of 'the fall of Atlantis' that drew on a range of environmental and social issues, and challenged to save their world. Lim found that engagement, motivation and social commitment on the part of students were enhanced by this activity.

Lyn Carter (2005) synthesizes a number of studies to make an argument about the centrality of globalization in science education, while acknowledging that this centrality has not yet been sufficiently researched and, more importantly, implemented. A critical approach to whether 'science education reform' movements have a credible evidence base in terms of the foci of science education and the needs of students and society, or whether it is instead based in discourses of national competitiveness and Smith's (1999) 'Globalization 1' is an important contribution of Carter's work. Jay Lemke (2001) had taken up similar issues a few years earlier, with less of a specific focus on globalization.

The common themes in the literature reviewed are that, while there is a compelling case for developing a more global and critical perspective on science education, and some well-informed perspectives and approaches, these concerns remain to some extent at the periphery of science education rather than informing the mainstream. This is a story familiar from the history of the STS(E) movement (Pedretti 2013). Perhaps the key challenge facing those of us advocating these approaches and framings of the issues is to expand our influence in science education so that global citizenship becomes a mainstream goal, to some extent against the tendencies of current 'science education reform' movements (McFarlane 2013).

PEDAGOGICAL ISSUES IN SCIENCE EDUCATION IN RELATION TO GLOBAL CITIZENSHIP

This section of the chapter does not so much offer specific examples of pedagogical approaches that have been adopted and tested in conducting science education for global citizenship. Rather, it outlines issues relevant to pedagogy and to teacher professional judgments about what is valuable and appropriate in the endeavor of better adapting science education to the goals of equipping citizens of the future for global citizenship.

Open-ended Inquiry and Open-entry Inquiry

Inquiry learning is an influential perspective in science education, mandated in syllabus documents around the world, but has been found to be more difficult to implement than to advocate (Alvermann and Moore 1996; Loucks-Horsley et al. 1988). Part of this difficulty arises from the pressures of high-stakes standardized testing and other assessment demands, part from the fact that, as Loucks-Horsley et al. (1988) noted, "it is difficult to teach in ways in which one has not learned". I would argue, however, that part of it has also arisen due to confusion about the ways in which inquiry education can and should be used in science education.

Xinxin Fan and I have outlined (Geelan and Fan 2014) a distinction between 'open-ended' and 'open-entry' inquiry. This distinction, I argue, can be helpful for science education for global citizenship. It is the former that I consider particularly appropriate to socioscientific issues (Pedretti 2013). In 'open-ended', where there is a range of social and political issues and perspectives, there is a range of legitimate positions at which students can arrive.

As an example, in response to the question "Should nuclear energy form part of our solution to moving beyond fossil fuels for energy?", students will inquire into the climate change exacerbated by emissions from fossil fuels, into renewable energy sources such as wind, tidal, solar and hydroelectricity, into the problems of dealing with radioactive waste and nuclear weapon proliferation. At higher levels, they might consider enrichment of uranium for peaceful and warlike purposes, fast breeder and thorium reactors and a range of other technologies and issues. In the end, some students may well decide, and support their position with evidence and argument, that nuclear energy should make up part of our mix of energy sources while others will decide differently. This is an example of 'open-ended' inquiry, in that students enter with a number of perspectives and exit with a range of positions.

Open-entry inquiry, on the other hand, is better adapted to studying scientific concepts. Students begin with a range of perspectives and approaches (including misconceptions, alternative conceptions, children's science or naïve conceptions (largely synonymous terms used to describe the non-scientific or pre-scientific ideas students bring to the classroom)). If the inquiry learning sequence is appropriately scaffolded and supported by the teacher and informed by experiments and experiences, the students' inquiry will converge on the canonical scientific answer to the initial question (as well as some elaborations and qualifications). The inquiry is 'open-entry' but ends at a single focused point, with non-scientific alternatives extinguished and the scientific concept well understood and well supported with evidence and arguments.

STE(A)M

The focus of this chapter is specifically on science education; however, science education is increasingly linked with technology, engineering and mathematics education and represented by the acronym 'STEM'. More recently, there has been a movement to add the arts to the blend and make the acronym 'STEAM' (e.g., Bequette and Bequette 2012; Maeda 2013).

Wolf-Michael Roth (2014) has pointed out that each of the four disciplines that make up STEM has a different epistemology: mathematics logically derives proofs from axioms, science creates and tests theories using empirical evidence and makes and tests knowledge claims, technology and engineering, in different ways, create products and technologies to enhance human life which are tested by the market for effectiveness, efficiency and attractiveness. Combining the four into a single term and using it as a unitary construct may lead to hiding differences that are important for productive framing of the problems. This may in fact be further exacerbated by adding the arts, which also have different epistemological approaches, to the mix. The addition of the arts is often promoted on the grounds that it would bring creativity to the STEM disciplines; however, the sciences, technology, engineering and mathematics are already inherently creative activities. That is not to say the arts have nothing to contribute, but the grounds on which they are introduced should be considered carefully. Recognizing the key differences between each of the STEAM disciplines is relevant to this goal.

Curricular integration (Case 1991; Morris 2003), however, is a related issue that is likely to be much more productive. Under such an approach, each of the 'STE(A)M disciplines' retains its own epistemological approach and disciplinary integrity, but the links and commonalities are addressed, and complex real-world problems explored by students using these disciplines in combination. Such an approach more authentically matches the way in which students will engage with problems during their careers and as citizens, but does not submerge the distinctive features of each discipline. Curricular integration has been extensively pursued in medical education (Goldman and Schroth 2012).

Curricular Emphases Model

I have described and illustrated elsewhere (Geelan 2009, 2010) the Curricular Emphases model, developed by Doug Roberts (1995) and refined by my colleague Frank Jenkins at the University of Alberta. In brief, this is a pedagogical approach to attending to socioscientific issues in science education. It involves each teaching unit including the scientific content (including the development of conceptual understanding as well as investigative skills) but also one of three 'curricular emphases'. A unit can have a Technology, a Nature of Science or a Science and Society emphasis. Across a year of science education, each emphasis may be used more than once, and all three should be included.

The emphasis chosen should complement the content of the unit: a unit on radio waves and the electromagnetic spectrum may have a Technology emphasis and focus on the relationship between science and technology and the various technological problem solutions founded in the science of electromagnetic waves. A unit on the water cycle may have a Science and Society emphasis and focus on water pollution and how to ensure that human populations have adequate supplies of clean fresh water, and the social consequences of water scarcity. A unit on chemical bonding may have a Nature of Science emphasis and include consideration of the inferences made about the nature of the atom, the history of atomic theories, the relationship between evidence and inference and the different levels of representation used to describe atomic phenomena and bonding.

This model offers a means to teachers to attend to socioscientific issues in a way that is authentic and connected with learning the relevant scientific content and makes it manageable to add these issues to the curriculum despite full syllabuses. It places scientific knowledge within a broader social context and involves explicit consideration of the nature of science.

CONCLUSION

This chapter has outlined issues in relation to science education for global citizenship, and sketched some preliminary pedagogical approaches, in addition to those outlined by Ratcliffe and Grace (2003). While there may be some scope for further research on methodologies, pedagogies and approaches, particularly in relation to assessment, it could be argued that the major challenges are with policy implementation (Gowlett et al. 2015). That is, it is not so much that we need a stronger and broader evidence base in relation to effective approaches to science education for global citizenship, but that these approaches have remained relatively fringe.

To some extent, this may be due to the obsession of national governments with standardized testing and 'league tables' of international rankings, which leads to inauthentic forms of assessment inimical to a more global understanding that includes tolerance for complexity and ambiguity. It may also be related to instrumental approaches to science (and STE(A)M) education that focus on entry to university courses and preparation for employment, rather than on the development of students as global citizens.

Implementing approaches to science education that foster global citizenship, then, will require action at a number of levels:

1. Individual teachers and school communities using pedagogical strategies such as open-ended and open-entry inquiry and the Curricular Emphases model to implement richer models of science education in classrooms.
2. Collaborative research on the part of academics, teachers and students to bridge the 'research-practice gap' (Hirschkorn and Geelan 2008) and implement and test new pedagogies. The inclusion of students in the research activity both enhances its authenticity and heeds Corbett and Wilson's (1995) call to 'make a difference with, not for, students'.
3. Action on the part of state, provincial and national governments, teacher registration and degree accrediting bodies and other authorities that influence syllabuses and pedagogy.
4. In accordance with Smith's (1999) 'Globalization Three', action from like-minded people focused on enhancing the effectiveness of science education for global citizenship to influence communities and political leaders.

5. Further theoretical and curricular work focused on Davies' (2004) notion of 'science education *as* citizenship education'. Exploring the implications of this approach that draws more extensively on the field of citizenship education is a largely and more challenging political task but has the potential to be transformative.

There are interesting beginnings and signs, and an urgent need but, it has to be admitted, there remains much to be done.

REFERENCES

Altemeyer, B. (2006). *The Authoritarians* (PDF). Winnipeg: University of Manitoba. OCLC 191061772.

Alvermann, D. E., & Moore, D. W. (1996). Secondary school reading. In R. Barr, M. L. Kamil, P. B. Mosenthal, & P. D. Pearson (Eds.), *Handbook of Reading Research* (Vol. 2, pp. 951–983). New York: Longman.

Bequette, J. W., & Bequette, M. B. (2012). A place for art and design education in the STEM conversation. *Art Education, 65*(2), 40–47.

Biggiero, L. (2001). Sources of complexity in human systems. *Nonlinear Dynamics, Psychology, and Life Sciences, 5*(1), 3–19.

Carter, L. (2005). Globalisation and science education: Rethinking science education reforms. *Journal of Research in Science Teaching, 42*(5), 561–580.

Case, R. (1991). The anatomy of curricular integration. *Canadian Journal of Education/Revue Canadienne de l'Education, 16*(2), 215–224.

Corbett, D., & Wilson, B. (1995). Make a difference with, not for, students: A plea to researchers and reformers. *Educational Researcher, 24*(5), 12–17.

Davies, I. (2004). Science and citizenship education. *International Journal of Science Education, 26*(14), 1751–1763. doi:10.1080/0950069042000230785.

Feyerabend, P. K. (1999). In B. Terpstra (Ed.), *Conquest of abundance: a tale of abstraction versus the richness of being.* Chicago: University of Chicago Press.

Geelan, D. (2003). The death of theory in educational research. In *Proceedings of the First Conference on Complexity Science and Educational Research* (pp. 169–185).

Geelan, D. (2009). Science education for global citizenship. *Curriculum Leadership, 7*(36).

Geelan, D. (2010). Science, technology, and understanding. *Citizenship Across the Curriculum, 147.*

Geelan, D. R., & Fan, X. (2014). Teachers using interactive simulations to scaffold inquiry instruction in physical science education. In *Science teachers' use of visual representations* (pp. 249–270). Springer International Publishing.

Gibson, William. (1984). *Neuromancer.* New York: Ace Books.

Goldman, E., & Schroth, W. S. (2012). Perspective: Deconstructing integration: A framework for the rational application of integration as a guiding curricular strategy. *Academic Medicine, 87*(6), 729–734.

Gowlett, C., Keddie, A., Mills, M., Renshaw, P., Christie, P., Geelan, D., et al. (2015). Using Butler to understand the multiplicity and variability of policy reception. *Journal of Education Policy, 30*(2), 149–164.

Haack, S. (2011). *Defending science—within reason: Between scientism and cynicism.* Amherst, NY: Prometheus Books.

Habermas, J. (1972). Knowledge *and Human Interests.* London: New Left Books.

Hirschkorn, M., & Geelan, D. (2008). Bridging the research-practice gap: Research translation and/or research transformation. *Alberta Journal of Educational Research, 54*(1), 1–13.

Hodson, D. (2003). Time for action: Science education for an alternative future. *International Journal of Science Education, 25*(6), 645–670.

Jenkins, E. W. (1999). School science, citizenship and the public understanding of science. *International Journal of Science Education, 21*(7), 703–710.

Kolstø, S. D. (2001). Scientific literacy for citizenship: Tools for dealing with the science dimension of controversial socioscientific issues. *Science Education, 85*(3), 291–310.

Lemke, J. L. (2001). Articulating communities: Sociocultural perspectives on science education. *Journal of Research in Science Teaching, 38*(3), 296–316.

Lim, C. P. (2008). Global citizenship education, school curriculum and games: Learning mathematics, english and science as a global citizen. *Computers & Education, 51*(3), 1073–1093.

Loucks-Horsley, D., Hewson, P., Love, N., & Stiles, K. (1988). *Designing professional development for teachers of science and mathematics.* Thousand Oaks: Corwin Press.

McFarlane, D. A. (2013). Understanding the challenges of science education in the 21st century: New opportunities for scientific literacy. *International Letters of Social and Humanistic Sciences, 4*(1), 35–44.

Maeda, J. (2013). STEM + Art = STEAM. *The STEAM Journal, 1*(1), 34.

Mannion, G., Biesta, G., Priestley, M., & Ross, H. (2011). The global dimension in education and education for global citizenship: Genealogy and critique. *Globalisation, Societies and Education, 9*(3–4), 443–456.

Morris, R. C. (2003). A guide to curricular integration. *Kappa Delta Pi Record, 39*(4), 164–167.

Pedretti, E. (2013). Teaching science, technology, society and environment (STSE) education. *The role of moral reasoning on socioscientific issues and discourse in science education* (pp. 219–239). Dordrecht, Netherlands: Springer.

Ratcliffe, M., & Grace, M. (2003). *Science education for citizenship: Teaching socioscientific issues.* London: McGraw-Hill Education.

Roberts, D. A. (1995). Building companion meanings into school science programs: Keeping the logic straight about curriculum emphases. *Nordisk Pedagogik (Journal of Nordic Educational Research), 15*(2), 108–124.

Roth, W-M. (2014). *STEM Curriculum through the Eyes of the Learner: The unseen and therefore unforeseen.* Keynote presentation, STEM Conference 2014, July 12–15, 2004, University of British Columbia, Vancouver, Canada.

Smith, D. G. (1999). *Pedagon: Interdisciplinary essays in the human sciences, pedagogy, and culture.* New York: Peter Lang.

Solomon, J. (1993). *Teaching science, technology and society. Developing science and technology series.* Briston, PA: Taylor and Francis.

Sterling, B. (1996). *Holy Fire.* New York: Bantam Spectra.

Zeidler, D. L., Sadler, T. D., Simmons, M. L., & Howes, E. V. (2005). Beyond STS: A research-based framework for socioscientific issues education. *Science Education, 89*(3), 357–377.

AUTHOR BIOGRAPHY

David Geelan has taught science in 4 Australian states, been a teacher educator in Papua New Guinea, Australia and Canada and worked with science teachers in South Africa. His research interests span research methodology and educational technology, and he is a Carnegie Scholar on the scholarship of teaching and learning. His current research focus, with collaborators in Chile and Germany, is on the ways in which teachers explain concepts in physics. David has an on-going interest in the dynamic interplay of science education and citizenship education.

CHAPTER 33

Drama Education and Global Citizenship and Education

Norio Ikeno and Jun Watanabe

INTRODUCTION

In this chapter we build on previous work (e.g., Ikeno et al. 2015) to make the case for strong links between drama education and citizenship education to be recognized and enhanced. We make this argument by exploring elements that are essential to both drama education and citizenship education. In relation to public context, relevant content, and appropriate process, we feel that drama and citizenship are strongly linked. Both fields deal with events occurring in, and that are defined by, public spaces. Drama is something that may be personally experienced but it is usually publically enacted. Citizenship connects strongly with personal and individual matters and is a key element of the public space which we inhabit. Drama and citizenship, separately and jointly, deal with similar content. It may be that that content is institutionally framed allowing for understanding about, for example, political frameworks, but more generally there is the potential for work in both areas that aims to develop "cultural capital for future leaders" (Ikeno et al. 2015, p. 243). Furthermore, common to drama education and citizenship education is participation in the process of education, that is, the process that requires students "to think, to express their points of view and generally to develop the skills of informed and responsible participation"

N. Ikeno (✉)
Nippon Sport Science University, Tokyo, Japan
e-mail: norioikeno@gmail.com

J. Watanabe
Nihon University, Tokyo, Japan
e-mail: jun-w@ar.ejnet.ne.jp

© The Author(s) 2018
I. Davies et al. (eds.), *The Palgrave Handbook of Global Citizenship and Education*, https://doi.org/10.1057/978-1-137-59733-5_33

(Ikeno et al. 2015, p. 244). The skills and attributes that are developed in both fields have much educational potential.

In this chapter we draw attention to the connections between drama education and citizenship education, describe and discuss the expansion of research and teaching, and explore the shared spaces for research, teaching and learning. The potential contribution that drama education as a method could make to citizenship education will be clarified.

CONNECTING CITIZENSHIP EDUCATION AND DRAMA EDUCATION

In this section of the chapter, we discuss the ways in which citizenship education has developed by drawing attention to its expansion into new geographical areas, by extending the types of content that it covers and by using a greater range of teaching methods.

Spatial expansion. Citizenship education received worldwide attention when it was introduced into a number of individual countries. Its introduction to the school curriculum in England was an example of relatively early implementation (Holden and Clough 1998; Davies, Gregory and Riley 1999). In addition to this, research and teaching in the field of citizenship education have been given importance in the European Union, in its function of creating European citizens, and have been adopted as education policy (Ross 1999, 2002). In Germany, the development of multicultural and intercultural education has taken place in the context of reunification as well as longstanding and recent migrations of people (Cogan and Derricott 1998). In these contexts debates about citizenship and citizenship education are major issues in the formulation and implementation of state policy.

Over the past 20 years, the idea that it is necessary to develop active citizenship collaboratively and proactively at the national and local levels and, beyond that, at the level of global society, has become a worldwide trend. Because of this, academic and professional handbooks (e.g., Isin and Turner 2002; Arthur et al. 2008) and related collections of papers (Arthur and Davies 2008) have been published, indicating the expansion of interests in citizenship education and research about it. In the early days of the most recent development of citizenship education, a good deal of relevant was undertaken by researchers and educators in English-speaking countries (Cogan and Derricott 1998; Engle and Ochoa 1998; Ichilov 1998; Kerr 2000). Very recently that work has now spread to Asia (Cogan et al. 2002; Lee et al. 2004; Benei 2005; Mohanty and Tandon 2006). There is, for example, significant work in Japan, with many authors emerging and many lively debates in both spheres of research and education (Kodama 2003; Naganuma 2003; Suzuki 2005; Usui 2006; Hirata 2007; Minei 2007; Muto and Arai 2007; Ninomiya 2007; Mizuyama 2008; Ikeno 2011; Mochizuki 2012; Ikeno 2014).

Expansion of scope. Citizenship education has expanded its scope from a strong focus on the political and social aspects of citizens and their rights to the cultural sphere, and from issues of rights as a citizen (principally civil rights) to a concern with individuals' inner selves, particularly, issues relating to individual existence in the contexts of diversity, empathy and identity, such as language, religion, customs, habits and morals (Osler 2000; Mohanty and Tandon 2006; Kiwan 2008; Lin 2008; Davies 2011).

The extension and expansion of the space and scope of citizenship education (and the research associated with these things) are due in large part to growing societal and cultural diversity, within the context of globalization of economics and other spheres, whereby society becomes plural and diverse rather than uniform and definitive (Shafer 1998; Edwards 2004). Members of society have always been diverse and there is now an increasing awareness of and acceptance of 'race' and ethnicity, and the plurality of cultures, religions, and customs. This societal diversity leads to the development of cultural plurality and complexity. When we see society not as a homogenous group of members but rather as something that comprises a group of multiple ethnicities and cultures, we will see the development of diversity and complexity within and across ethnicities, cultures, and religions. Added to this is the emergence of individual plurilingualism, pluriculturalism, and multiple identities (Semprini 2003). The inner complexity of individuals requires the management, revision, and integration of multiple identities (Kennedy 1997; Alred, Byram and Fleming 2006; Garratt and Piper 2008; Zajda and Daun 2009; Reid, Gill and Sears 2010).

Citizenship education assumes that citizens have the responsibility to learn about rights and the attributes of society and to learn about cultures and identities. Citizenship education is necessary as education for learning to be a new member of particular societies and organizations. It requires learning not only about rights and duties in the political sphere, but also about societal and cultural perspectives on empathy, tolerance and identities.

Expansion of teaching methodology. In the International Civic and Citizenship Education Study (ICCS) conducted by the International Association for the Evaluation of Educational Achievement (IEA) in 1971, 1999, 2009 and 2016, citizenship is understood in relation to students' knowledge and understandings of concepts as well as their beliefs, attitudes, and behaviors with respect to this cognitive domain. The study understands citizenship education in a complex way that includes the organization and content of civic and citizenship education in the curriculum, teacher qualifications and experiences, teaching practices, school environment and climate, and home and community support (Schultz et al. 2016).

In England, citizenship education is promoted not only as a subject, but also through various school and community activities (Wales and Clarke 2005; Gearon 2015), and the subject of citizenship has been taught in conjunction with other subjects starting in elementary school, rather than being treated as a stand-alone subject (Gearon 2015). Specifically, it requires various forms of collaboration in relation to teaching methods. Citizenship education is designed and implemented using a range of activities, including discussion, debate, surveys, role play, group activities, presentations, simulation activities and the use of ICT (Wales and Clarke 2005).

As teaching methods have expanded, the central focus of citizenship education has changed from teaching to learning and has moved from knowledge and understanding of citizenship to an emphasis on attitudes and motivation. This comes from the fact that citizenship education and its content have become ever more diverse, moving from political, economic and social issues involving rights as a citizen to issues related to individuals' inner diversity and plurality, complexity and multiplicity, involving culture and religion. In terms of goals, too, citizenship as a school subject now needs to be expanded beyond the initial topics of social and moral responsibility, political literacy and community involvement to address diversity and identity.

This characterization of citizenship connects directly with drama. One teaching method that can be used in coordination with citizenship education is drama education (Taylor and Leeder 2001). Drama education can be an effective method of realizing the goals of citizenship education and addressing its content (Neelands and Goode 2000; O'Conner 2010).

Exploring Drama Education for Citizenship Education

The Origins of Drama Education in Japan

There is a long tradition of drama education in Japan. This is seen in the tradition of theater education, the two pillars of which are drama performances by students in cultural festivals, and appreciation education in the form of viewing performances by professional theater groups. This is, however, seen by some as a rather narrow definition of drama education, and Tomita (1993) has argued for a wider approach, emphasizing the significance of using drama methods in subject learning and educational guidance. This, it was argued could be labeled "dramatic education". The first edition of Tomita's book was published in Japan in 1958, and reissued in 1993. However, even though Tomita raised these issues as a trailblazer, hardly any research into drama education using drama in subject teaching and everyday educational activities was conducted until the 1980s.

Claiming that "dramatic methods" should be used across all educational activities, including subject teaching and educational guidance, Tomita (1993) stated the following:

Acting means spurring on the self, both body and mind, to take on the role of another person, and the effects of this performance can be used positively as dramatic methods in a range of educational activities.

For example, in impromptu dramatization in social studies education, playing a specific role can extend experience in terms of understanding the position and viewpoint of the person in the role, and help to deepen understanding of key issues. Role playing as an aspect of educational guidance or similar activities can exert positive stimulation on children as they assume a role other than themselves, enabling them to see themselves more objectively, deepen their understanding of the perspectives of self and others, and develop socially (pp. 63–64).

This statement is very relevant to (and to some extent, anticipates) the contribution that drama education could make to citizenship education.

The Influence of British Drama Education in Japan

The turning point for the diffusion of drama work in school education in Japan occurred in 1964. This was the year that Akira Okada and others began to attend meetings and other events of the International Association of Theatre for Children and Young People (ASSITEJ), which in turn led them to introduce global trends in drama education to Japan, translating and publishing work on drama education. In particular, the translation and introduction of Brian Way's work entitled "Development through Drama" (1977) had a major impact as a key source of reference in drama education.

In response to the idea that theater was mainly "communication between actors and spectators", Way (1977) argued that drama was "the experience of the individual participant" and, based on the definition of the differences embedded there, emphasized the magnitude of the role of drama in the following way:

> In every meaning, drama is education method. It is a method of living. It helps rather than hinders other subjects, promoting achievement (p. 19).

However, it was only in the latter half of the 1980s that a wide variety of activities began to spread across education in schools in Japan. This coincides with the period when attention turned to 'internationalization of teaching methods', in line with growing public awareness of internationalization in Japanese society—the borderlessness of people, goods, money and information. This trend is perhaps best symbolized by the focus on the 'debate boom' and the increased emphasis on communicative education as a social phenomenon in the 1990s. The spread of drama work is an element of these wider movements.

This greater emphasis on drama education in schools accelerated as the twenty-first century began, and this, again, was due in part to British influence. For example, influential leaders in the field of drama education visited Japan, and Japanese teachers were able to participate in their workshops. Since 2004, workshops have been conducted in various regions of Japan by Ken Taylor (Middlesex University) and Jonothan Neelands (Warwick University). Being able to experience workshops through physical presence rather than just through the written word had a major impact on the understanding of the nature and potential of drama work.

However, even though drama education is beginning to spread in Japan, the fact remains that the level of awareness of drama activities generally remains low, and there are still relatively few cases of dramatic methods being introduced into classes in schools. Consequently, there is a need to introduce drama work and spread activities simultaneously and in parallel from now on.

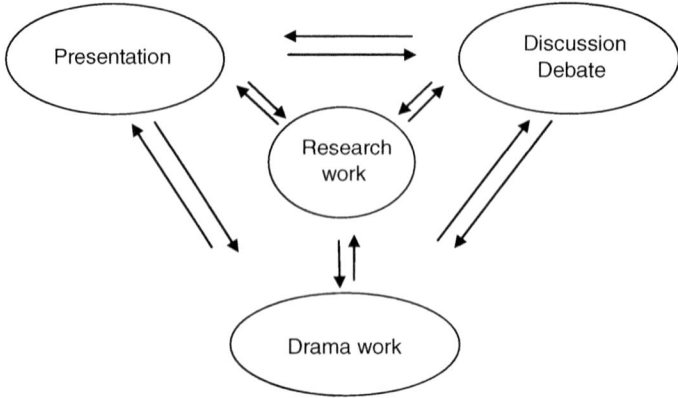

Fig. 33.1 Acquisition-oriented learning model

The Effectiveness of Introducing Drama Techniques in Classes

There are different approaches possible to the teaching of drama. Drama specialists may teaching drama workshops and teachers may incorporate drama into the context of other subject teaching. There is, of course, potential to do good work in both discrete lessons on drama and by means of infusing drama through other subjects. Recognizing the existence of relatively few discrete drama lessons in schools, the absence from almost all schools of a subject titled 'drama' and very few trained teachers, Watanabe et al. (2010, 2011) has developed a series of activities as learning tools and worked hard to disseminate the results of that work. He is keen to make the point that drama techniques are learning tools that can be used for all ages and in all types of schools, from elementary schools to universities.

In acquisition-oriented learning which is based on student autonomy, three types of activities, i.e., discussion/debate, presentation and research work, are considered to be particularly important, and drama work can be positioned alongside these as a fourth category (Fig. 33.1).

Putting it simply, drama techniques are a tool for becoming "something" other than oneself, and thinking and acting in this role. Learning through drama work fully operationalizes the imagination, as it is learning that requires transitioning back and forth between the fictional world and the real world, and it is only through freely using drama techniques that we are able to access "another world" in addition to the real world.

Watanabe (2007) has highlighted the following five points as ways in which dramatic activities may influence the quality of learning:

- Drama as the transmission of a message (i.e., in the development of a creative act)
- Drama as a method of understanding the content of research
- Drama as a method of embodying learning
- Drama as a way of "savouring" learning and its outcomes
- Drama as a way of making learning collaborative

Watanabe has suggested that in order to introduce drama methods into classes successfully the following three matters are important. Firstly, he suggests that there is hidden potential for the development of rich expressive activities in school. Expressive activities take place in the three modes of "words," "things," and "body," and drama techniques integrate these in the form of practical action. In particular, the substantial weight given to the physical mode is a key feature. In the Japanese educational setting, which is prone to depend on the "words" mode, this has significant potential and could provide the key to revising the very quality of learning itself. Secondly, he argues that drama techniques are compatible with subject learning. This applies not only to humanities and social science subjects such as "Japanese" and "Social Studies", but also to science subjects. For example, it is possible for students to engage in physical expression by "becoming" molecules that bond and split, taking on the roles of things themselves. Thirdly, he suggests that not only is there a rich variation of techniques already available in drama education, but that new techniques are being developed and introduced on an ongoing basis. This development of a large number of techniques means that a range of possibilities for lesson design is available even when dealing with the same topic.

An example of successful drama education can be given by referring to history learning. "The assassination of Caesar" is a standard example of a lesson in which dramatization can be used to act out the Roman era in costume. This plan requires a lot of advance planning, but there are simple techniques that can also stimulate deep learning. For example, after casting the parts of Caesar and other characters and going through the flow of the scene, an impromptu "role play" may be carried out, followed by techniques of reflection on inner changes. Alternatively, the expression of a series of "freeze frames" can be done for a number of selected symbolic scenes, like a series of photos. For Japanese students who are not used to being watched or acting, it is often more effective to use this freeze frame method rather than acting in motion. By combining this with the thought tracking method, for example by focusing the spotlight on the student posing as Brutus and asking why he decided to engage in the act of assassination, it is possible to make students think about the meaning of actions taken by characters from their perspectives.

CONNECTING DRAMA EDUCATION AND CITIZENSHIP EDUCATION

Methodology of Drama Education

One specific characteristic of drama education is that it raises the possibility of studying the possibilities associated with acting. O'Conner explains this in the following way.

> All drama education involves people learning how to act. It would be a very limited view of drama education to suggest this was only about acting on the stage. A wider view is that in drama in education, students learn to be actors in and for the real world. In creating fictional worlds in classrooms young people take on a wide range of imagined roles to explore what it might be like in different circumstances. These fictional worlds are created not merely to learn the skills and techniques necessary to construct them, but also to understand their own and other's lives better by trying out real solutions to real issues, looking at the world through different eyes and safely enquiring into issues of deep significance (2010, p. xxiii).

O'Conner points out that the core essence of drama education is "learning how to act", and that seeing issues with different eyes and thinking differently in a fictional world, a world of the imagination, in contrast to the real world, may lead to deeper exploration of the issues. O'Conner's view is that this is possible not only in theater, but also in school classrooms.

If drama education is perceived as the promotion of learning how to act, then it can be situated as something that promotes deep learning. Through the creation of drama, drama education facilitates an educational process of going between the two worlds of reality and fiction, and between self and other, between one's own view of things and someone else's view of things, and between a solution being proposed and other possible solutions, where students transcend the boundaries of their own knowledge and selves to create an imaginary world with other possibilities, finding possible ways of acting and making them significant.

If drama education adopts such goals and methods, and is actually carried out by teachers and others in this way, this process of learning how to act can lead to citizenship education. This is done by making the classroom the stage, making it a learning space in which all students learn in collaboration, and creating a public space where everyone thinks and participates. In terms of content, students may not only address people's ways of acting, but also learn about the enacted world of people. Furthermore, there is commonality with citizenship as far as methods are concerned, as students engage in a learning process of going back and forth between the real world and an imagined fictional world, or between the actual world as reality and the potential world of possibilities.

Of course, drama education has its own unique features. These include selecting and reading a text, role creation, performance on the stage, relationships with spectators, and communication. Going beyond these specific characteristics, drama education can create connections and commonalities with other subjects and forms of education, making it likely to enrich both forms of education. For example, Neelands describes role creation in the following way,

> Encouraging students to work through dramatic situations, in fictitious roles, enables them to view their own behaviour, and other people's, from unfamiliar perspectives. The emotional experience is real for the students even through the activity (think, for example, of the real sadness that may move us when we read a story). As a consequence, the students can be helped to reflect on their behaviour in the drama from 'another' person's point of view. The right choice and management of situations, contexts and stories relating to the environment, for instance, can provide young people with authentic experiences of what it would be like to be in a threatened environment which may be far removed in time and place from their own immediate and protected environment. This is useful in overcoming the detached climate of the classroom by helping students: to see the underlying human significance and themes in their learning; to explore prejudices and stereotype; and to develop empathy and respect for others who are culturally, historically or socially different from themselves (O'Conner 2010, p. 38).

Through role creation, drama education enables students to take on roles, and adopt a different way of seeing through that dramatic experience.

Let us take as an example a case from the school subject of social studies, where students see and engage seriously with problems occurring in reality. Students think about the reasons why a situation has arisen, and discuss possible types of solutions. However, this may not be very effective. Students are seeing the problematic situation from the outside. They see it only through their own eyes, and are unable to go beyond this. Drama education repositions this situation as drama, placing students into roles, enabling them to acquire a different way of seeing than they had from outside of the situation, and encouraging greater diversity of options and ways of resolving the situation.

In the book "Drama in Education", Neelands and Watanabe raise the following issues (Neelands and Watanabe 2009, pp.54–55).

1. How can group work be effectively organized?
2. How can discussion be facilitated?
3. How can questioning skills be used?
4. How can boys and girls be encouraged to work together cooperatively?
5. How can student activities be controlled in an open space such as a hall?
6. How should responsibility be given to learners so that they can evaluate their own learning?
7. How can the subject be integrated to be meaningful?
8. How can wider-ranging evaluation tools than traditional tests be found?

In order to teach drama, all of these issues have to be resolved and, of course, these kinds of issues have to be resolved by anyone who wants to become a good teacher in any field in the twenty-first century. Drama teachers are good teachers in accordance with many existing general criteria. As such learning to teach drama may be linked to becoming a good teacher in other specialized areas.

Issues Shared by Citizenship Education and Drama Education

- Connecting Citizenship and dramatic intelligence

Watanabe (2007) has pointed out that "becoming independent as a learner is linked to becoming independent as a citizen" (p. 28). Being an independent learner is related to being an active, autonomous citizen. There is a mutual link between the minimum level of learning skills and the minimum level of citizenship skills. The process by which children acquire learning skills through engaging in activities, including drama techniques, is the process by which they develop independence as a learner. At the same time, they are becoming members of a society of citizens. These citizens are, in the words of J.J. Rousseau, citizens who are "open-minded, intelligent, ready for anything" (Emile), and able to renew their own intelligence ceaselessly.

Here, it is worth using "Emile" as a key to citizenship development. Individuals who are engaging in acquisition-oriented learning, i.e., those who have acquired learning skills, consensus-building ability, and skills of understanding situations critically and questioning frameworks, have the basic grounding of citizenship skills. The fact that the quality of collaborative learning improves through drama work means that constructive relationships can be formed (learning socialization) concurrently with the development of individual skills reflected in the learning group. In this way, learning "how to learn" goes beyond simple mastery of how to behave in the classroom, but rather forms the premise of acquiring social experience. Rousseau conceived Emile to be "large-minded, not through knowledge, but through the power of acquiring it". Translated into more modern terms, this means having the openness of spirit to "learn how to learn".

Given this, what are the attributes required of citizens capable of choosing their own course through the web of strained relations between society and individuals and groups? What is required is the ability to link people with different skills through networks, organizing and reorganizing in such a way as to cover weaknesses and maximize strengths. By mutually recognizing and maximizing the unique goodness and strengths of each member, latent potential can be realized. This, simply put, is centrally about the development of competence. The implication of Emile for the twenty-first century may be in the search for networked intelligence and the creation of collective reasoning.

The experience of participative learning through drama work also serves as operational experience in a participatory democracy. The constituent elements of democracy comprise not only democratic thought and a democratic system, but also "procedures and operationalization" as means of putting principles into practice. Experience in participatory democracy can be broadly classified into categories such as experience in creating rules collaboratively, experience in putting those rules into operation autonomously, and experience in revising frameworks, with the act of communication permeating through all of these. As agents of communication, it is desirable that individuals have the coolness to be able to think about rights and wrongs in line with different matters (distinguishing between personalities and issues), have the strength of spirit to gauge harmony in public while controlling individual desires and self-interest (self-restraint), and are aware of the roles of individuals in public spaces and proactively contribute (volunteer spirit).

Watanabe (2001) defined dramatic intelligence as "the active and creative intelligence created inside the learner through coordinated activities focused on developing a performance from activities of intellectual pursuit—the whole form of awareness and learning involving the body, the structure of knowledge and way of understanding" (p. 170). Two things need to be examined here. The first is the problem of how to act as citizens in public spaces. In public spaces, people cannot just reveal their inner selves and feelings directly. Rational and composed expression is required. In such situations, what is required is not supposition that the actions of the speaker will accord perfectly with what she/he thinks, but rather the intelligence of being able to distinguish between different personas. The second is the orientation in which imagination works. This is related to the way individuals can construct relationships of mutual support in public spaces. Rousseau wrote that, "It is man's weakness which makes him sociable; it is our common miseries which turn our hearts to humanity" (Book IV). The key idea is that the cause of social bonds can be found in human "weakness," and that the world can be seen as "a community of suffering". The basic thinking here is that not only is intrinsic motivation of human action sought for self-preservation, but that the "compassionate feeling" that arouses empathy for other humans who are suffering is innate to the true character of human beings. This can be seen as a complementary relationship between reason and imagination.

- Connecting dramatic intelligence and citizenship attributes

We would now like to return briefly to the connection between dramatic intelligence and citizenship attributes. As stated above, the experience of collaborative learning is linked to self-awareness as active, autonomous citizens. But we, of course, accept that one important viewpoint provided by dramatic intelligence is that every individual sees himself/herself from his/her own perspective, while simultaneously transcending self and seeing self from the outside. Watanabe (1995) elaborated on the following way of thinking when defining international perspective as a citizenship attribute. That is to say, he explained that people who have an international perspective or perspective as a global citizen in the widest sense "are people who have a perspective on the world from their own position, while simultaneously having a perspective on their own way of living and thinking within the movement of the world" (p. 208).

This perspective, whereby self-formation occurs within relations with others, is also prevalent in international documents. For example, the UNESCO Delors Report states that "individual development, which begins at birth and continues throughout life, is a dialectical process which starts with knowing oneself, and then opens out to relationships with others" (p. 95). In relation to the OECD-DeSeCo, Matsushita (2010) explained as follows: "Key competencies involve interacting with the environment using a range of tools, interacting with heterogeneous others, and orienting self within the big picture of space and time to construct a life narrative. ... The skills involved emerge within relationships, but are owned by individuals, that is, they appear at the intersection of relationship theory and ownership theory" (p. 22).

CONCLUSION

In this chapter, we have examined connections between drama education and citizenship education, identifying points of commonality. In conclusion:

- Drama education deals with the fictional world, while citizenship education deals with the real world. However, it is possible to connect drama education and citizenship education.
- Although there are differences in the aims and content of drama education and citizenship education, it is possible to go beyond those differences and broadly apply drama as a method in citizenship education. For example, by perceiving another person's different way of seeing through drama work, it is possible to use this experience usefully in citizenship education.
- By incorporating drama techniques into the implementation of citizenship education:
  (1) It becomes possible to provide breadth and depth in the development of the attributes and skills of each individual.
  (2) The experience of subtly appreciating the inner self of an imaginary individual in a fictional world helps to promote understanding of the inner selves of others and oneself in the real world.
  (3) Options and ways of seeing things in the real world are expanded, which facilitates problem-solving.

While these tentative conclusions can be offered, the next step is that these conclusions have to be tested in reality by creating collaborative spaces for drama education and citizenship education, and confirming their validity.

REFERENCES

Alred, G., Byram, M., & Fleming, M. (Eds.). (2006). *Education for intercultural citizenship: Concepts and comparisons.* Clevedon, Buffalo and Toronto: Multilingual Matters.

Arthur, J., Davies, I., & Hahn, C. (Eds.). (2008). *The sage handbook of education for citizenship and democracy.* London: Sage.

Arthur, J., & Davies, I. (Eds.). (2008). *Citizenship education* (4 Vols.). London: Sage.

Benei, V. (Ed.). (2005). *Manufacturing citizenship: Education and nationalism in Europe, South Asia and China.* London & N.Y.: Routledge.

Cogan, J., & Derricott, R. (Eds.). (1998). *Citizenship for the 21st century: An international perspective on education.* London: Kogan Page.

Cogan, J. C., Morris, P., & Print, M. (Eds.). (2002). *Civic education in their Asia-pacific region: Case studies across six societies.* N.Y. & London: Routledge Falmer.

Davies, I. (2011). *100+ideas for teaching citizenship* (2nd ed.). London & N.Y.: Continuum.

Davies, I., Gregory, I., & Riley, S. C. (1999). *Good citizenship and educational provision.* London & N.Y.: Falmer.

Edwards, M. (2004). *Civil society Policy.* Cambridge: MIT Press.

Engle, S. H., & Ochoa, A. S. (1998). *Education for democratic citizenship: Decision making in the social studies.* New York: Teacher College Press.

Garratt, D., & Piper, H. (2008). *Citizenship education, identity and nationhood: Contradictions in practice?.* New York: Continuum International Pub.

Gearon, L. (2015). *Learning to teach citizenship in the secondary school: A companion to school experience* (3rd ed.). Abingdon: Routledge.

Hirata, T. (Ed.). (2007). *Comparative study of citizenship education in Japan and Thailand.* Tokyo: Toshindo. [in Japanese].

Holden, C., & Clough, N. (Eds.). (1998). *Children as citizens: education for participation.* London: Jessica Kingsley.

Ichilov, O. (Ed.). (1998). *Citizenship and citizenship education in a changing world.* Abington: Woburn Press.

Ikeno, N. (Ed.). (2011). *Citizenship Education in Japan.* London & N.Y.: Continuum, Bloomsbury Publishing.

Ikeno, N. (2014). Citizenship education in the global age: Issues and possibilities from the perspectives of democracy and the logic of the public sphere. Japan educational research association (ed.) *Educational Studies in Japan, 81*(2), 138–149 [in Japanese].

Ikeno, N., Fukazawa, H., Watanabe, J., Elliott, V., Shawyer, C., Olive, S., et al. (2015). Putting the case for building a bridge between drama and citizenship education. *Citizenship Teaching and Learning, 15*(3), 237–250. doi:10.1086/ctl.10.3.237_1.

Isin, E. F., & Turner, B. S. (Eds.). (2002). *Handbook of citizenship studies.* London: Sage Publishing.

Kennedy, K. (Ed.). (1997). *Citizenship education and the modern state*. London & Washington D.C.: Falmer.

Kerr, D. (2000). Citizenship education: An international comparison. In D. Lawton, J. Cairns, & R. Gardner (Eds.), *Education for citizenship*. London: Continuum.

Kiwan, D. (2008). *Education for inclusive citizenship*. London: Routledge.

Kodama, S. (2003). *Educational thought of citizenship*. Tokyo: Hakutakusha. [in Japanese].

Lee, W. O., Grossmann, D. L., Kennedy, K. J., & Fairbrother, G. P. (Eds.). (2004). *Citizenship education in Asia and the Pacific: Concepts and issues*. Norwell, Mass: Kluwer Academic.

Lin, A. M. Y. (2008). *Problematizing identity: Everyday struggles in language, culture, and education*. N.Y. & London: Routledge.

Matsushita, K. (2010). *Will "new skills" change education? Academic achievement, literacy, competencies*. Kyoto: Minerva Shobo. [in Japanese].

Minei, A. (Ed.). (2007). *Citizenship education in a global age: Comparative and transnational perspectives*. Tokyo: Toshindo. [in Japanese].

Mizuyama, M. (2008). Citizenship education: Developing "public nature" and "democracy". In A. Sugimoto, H. Takanori & M. Mizuyama (Eds.), *The 3C era of education: Culture, carrier, citizenship*. Kyoto: Sekaishisosha [in Japanese].

Mochizuki, K. (2012). *Citizenship education and teacher positionality: Focus on home economics and educational guidance practice*. Tokyo: Keisoshobo. [in Japanese].

Muto, T. & Arai, A. S. (Eds.). (2007). *The development of personal and social education and citizenship in European schools: The situation in France, Germany and Britain*. Tokyo: Toshindo [in Japanese].

Mohanty, R., & Tandon, R. (Eds.). (2006). *Participatory citizenship: Identity exclusion, inclusion*. New Delhi, London: Thousand Oaks, Sage.

Naganuma, Y. (2003). *What is citizenship education? Possibilities for volunteering study*. Tokyo: Hituzi Syobo. [in Japanese].

Neelands, J., & Goode, T. (2000). *Structuring drama work: A handbook of available forms in theatre and drama*. Cambridge: Cambridge University Press.

Neelands, J., & Watanabe, J. (2009). *Using drama as a medium of instruction*. Tokyo: Bansei Shobo. [in Japanese].

Ninomiya, A. (Ed.). (2007). *Theories of citizenship formation*. Tokyo: Foundation for the Promotion of the Open University of Japan. [in Japanese].

O'Conner, P. (2010). *Creating democratic citizenship through drama education: The writing of Jonathan Neelands*. Stoke on Trent: Trentham Books.

Osler, A. (Ed.). (2000). *Citizenship and democracy in schools: Diversity, identity, equality*. Stoke on Trent & Sterling: Trentham Books.

Reid, A., Gill, J., & Sears, A. (Eds.). (2010). *Globalization, the national-state and the citizen: Dilemmas and directions for civics and citizenship education*. N.Y. & London: Routledge.

Ross, A. (Ed.). (1999). *Young citizens in Europe*. London: CiCe & University of North London.

Ross, A. (Ed.). (2002). *Future citizens in Europe*. London: CiCe & London Metropolitan University.

Schulz, W., Ainley, J., Fraillon, J., Losito, B., & Agrusti, G. (2016). *IEA international civic and citizenship education study 2016 assessment framework*. Amsterdam: IEA.

Semprini, A. (2003). *What is multiculturalism?* (Nobutaka Miura and Hideki Hasegawa Trans.). Tokyo: Hakusuisha. [in Japanese].

Shafer, G. (Ed.). (1998). *The citizenship debates*, Minneapolis: University of Minnesota Press.

Suzuki, T. (2005). *Citizen literacy.* Tokyo: Kyouiku-shuppan. [in Japanese].

Taylor, K., & Leeder, J. (2001). *GCSE drama for edexcel.* London: Hodder & Stoughton.

Tomita, H. (1993). Drama education. Tokyo: Kokudosha. [in Japanese].

Usui, Y. (Ed.). (2006). *Prospects for citizenship education: Rugg's philosophy and core curriculum.* Tokyo: Gakubunsha. [in Japanese].

Wales, J., & Clarke, P. (2005). *Learning citizenship: Practical teaching strategies for secondary schools.* London & N.Y.: Routledge Falmer.

Watanabe, Jun. (1995). *What is an international perspective?* Tokyo: Iwanami Shoten. [in Japanese].

Watanabe, J. (2001). *Dramatic intelligence in education.* Tokyo: Kashiwashobo. [in Japanese].

Watanabe, J. (2007). *Teacher: Director of learning.* Tokyo: Junposha. [in Japanese].

Watanabe, J. (2011). An adventure around educational methods: Teachers' explorations for application of dramatic activities. *Educational Studies in Japan: International Yearbook, 6,* 33–45.

Watanabe, J., & Kakutokugata K. K. (Eds.). (2010). *Change the way you teach with dramatic conventions.* Tokyo: Junposha [in Japanese].

Way, B. (1977). *Development through Drama.* (Akira O. & Mika T. Trans.). Tokyo: Tamagawa University Press. [in Japanese].

Zajda, J., & Daun, H. (Eds.). (2009). *Global values education: Teaching democracy and peace.* Heidelberg. London & N.Y.: Springer.

Authors' Biography

Norio Ikeno Ph. D. was Professor of the Graduate School of Education at Hiroshima University and from April 2017 he is Professor of School of Childhood Sport Education at Nippon Sport Science University, Japan. His main research interests are international comparisons and new approaches to citizenship/social studies education. His most influential publication is *Citizenship Education in Japan* (Continuum, 2011).

Jun Watanabe is Professor of Education at Nihon University, College of Humanities and Sciences, Japan. His main research interests are drama education and the paradigm shift of learning styles in Japan. He founded the Society of Acquisition-Oriented Learning (SAOL) in 2006. His most influential publication is *Teacher: director of learning* (Tokyo: Junposha, 2007)

CHAPTER 34

Social Media and Youth: Implications for Global Citizenship Education

Manisha Pathak-Shelat

INTRODUCTION

The transformations that we see in our world today, largely brought about by the processes of globalization and the rapid spread of the digital media, have brought into the focus two concepts connected to citizenship: global citizenship and digital citizenship. In this chapter, I address the possibilities and challenges of citizenship education, highlighting both these concepts. I begin with an overview of evolution of social media and their affordances, analyze briefly the scholarly construct and contemporary practices of global citizenship, then trace their implication on educational practices, and finally, outline the role of social media in global citizenship education (GCE) with the help of empirical examples.

SOCIAL MEDIA, CIVIC ENGAGEMENT AND CITIZENSHIP EDUCATION

Along with globalization, social media are certainly one of the larger forces defining the current generation of millennials and its lived experiences. Social media allow the users to generate and share content, interact in real time with fellow users, and build online communities and network. We can credit Usenet in 1979 as an early usher of the social media era and should take a note of the bulletin boards and chat groups of the 1980s; it was, however, not until the new millennium that the social media blossomed

M. Pathak-Shelat (✉)
MICA, Ahmedabad, India
e-mail: manisha@micamail.in; manishashelat@gmail.com

© The Author(s) 2018
I. Davies et al. (eds.), *The Palgrave Handbook of Global Citizenship and Education*, https://doi.org/10.1057/978-1-137-59733-5_34

into their current forms and popularity. Unlike the earlier Web 1.0 that was dominated by static information posting, the Web 2.0 offered rich possibilities for sharing user generated content. In 2001, Wikipedia, the free online encyclopedia exposed the world to the power of crowdsourcing. In a rapid succession, the second half of the first decade of the millennium saw social media platforms such as Friendster, Hi5, MySpace, Orkut, Facebook, Twitter, and Tumblr that allowed an ordinary individual to not only access information from global sources but also interact and network with individuals, groups, and organisations across the world. New features and possibilities such as the options for video sharing, live streaming, and multiplayer gaming are being added with every passing year to the already vast repertoire of the social media platforms and thereby generating new possibilities for their application.

Notwithstanding the impressive possibilities offered by social media, the question is why we are even connecting them to either global citizenship or education. To answer this question, we must pay attention to some contemporary social and technological shifts that accompany the rapidly increasing transnational flows of people, media, money, information, and ideas. Two of these shifts are the most relevant to our present discussion: one, shift in our notions of citizenship and civic engagement, and two, shift in our notion of valid pedagogical spaces and practices. I discuss these shifts briefly.

To begin with, our definitions of civic engagement and citizenship practices are changing. Scholars like Bennett et al. (2011), Friedland (1996), and Papacharissi (2010) have urged us to not overlook citizen practices that may appear unfamiliar but may be equally valid for democratic participation in the new contexts. Most theories and language often used in citizenship studies were formulated when digital media were not even considered a possibility. Social media's many unique affordances have opened our eyes to their potential for facilitating knowledge production and people-to-people connectedness beyond the national borders, but we are still struggling to understand their implications for civic practices.

My research on transcultural citizenship (Shelat 2014) endorsed the claims of scholars such as Beck (1998), Bennett (2008), Friedland (1996), Giddens (1998), Howard (2011), Papacharissi (2010), Shirky (2008) and Stevenson (2001) who identify some of the changes associated with new forms of civic engagement. In contemporary times, mediated discursive practices are considered as important civic practices, the boundaries between private and public are becoming blurred, and the relational dimension of citizenship (that is relationship with other human beings) is being considered as important as the relationship with the governments through voting or paying taxes.

The unprecedented affordances of the Web 2.0 have made possible a new kind of public sphere facilitated by global social networks. I have identified a set of seven interconnected affordances of the Web 2.0-driven social media. These are:

1. Sharing of user-generated content
2. Ease of multimodal expression, publication, and distribution
3. Trans-border networking
4. Flexibility to choose real-time or asynchronic communication
5. Efficient and low-cost many-to-many communication
6. Vast storage and archiving capacities
7. Hyperlinks.

Together, these affordances facilitate diverse and non-traditional sources of information production and acquisition, transnational connections, sharing of resources, real-time conversations, collaborations, and to some extent, collective action. Social media have the potential to help amplify the scope and scale of an individual's civic experience across physical and cultural boundaries to an extent that can shape new civic cultures in themselves (Dahlgren 2011; Shelat 2014).

The second major shift we have experienced is that with our notions of acceptable spaces, tools, and practices for education. Informal, peer-led and out-of-classroom experiences are now considered valid educational experiences. The digital native youth today use networked platforms to voice their opinions, host discussions and share content of public concern with other civic participants (Jenkins et al. 2016; Bennett et al. 2009). There are immense learning opportunities in such spontaneous, quotidian activities.

Both the shifts discussed above compel us to take a fresh look at social media going beyond just the "social" and exploring the "civic" and the "political" dimensions of these media. We must, however, take into consideration that the potential of social media to become a vehicle for global citizenship is not always fully realized in practice. Several scholars have cautioned against celebrating this potential by driving our attention to multiple challenges. Bimber (2000) and Dahlgren (2007), for example, warn that the mere availability of communication technology is no guarantee that it will be used for civic/political purposes. It has also been observed that most of the use of new media by young people has been banal more than transformative and that youth use new media to connect with those who are familiar rather than with those in different sociocultural locations (Boyd 2008; Buckingham 2008; Livingstone 2009; Watkins 2009). Internet-based civic engagement has also been dismissed as a low-risk, low-engagement version of civic engagement—more like a pseudo-engagement (Cornelissen et al. n.d.). There is also the risk of polarization and extremism as Dahlberg observes, "despite the enormous diversity of views and identities on the Internet, online participants generally seek out information and interaction that reinforces their private positions, avoiding meaningful engagement with difference" (2008, p. 829). For many activists and publishers on social media, especially women and transgender, social media mobbing, trolling, and bullying have unfortunately been a regular experience. Saleh (2014) and

Pathak-Shelat and DeShano (2013), within the contexts of South Africa and India respectively, show how digital inequalities produce uneven media participation leading to uneven civic participation. Also, the mere provision of technology without appropriate media and information literacies serve little purpose for youth.

When we evaluate the contribution of social media to global citizenship education, we have to weigh their potential with the above reservations. The challenge, then, is twofold. First, to facilitate civic experiences that can optimally use young people's informal and spontaneous participatory digital cultures. And second, to design non-formal and classroom-based educational experiences using social media that can bring about civic learning not produced by the typical informal social media use. The underlying prerequisite, of course, is that we bridge the digital inequalities.

GLOBAL CITIZENSHIP

For the time being, I will bracket the discussion on social media and shift the attention to global citizenship education (henceforth GCE). Global citizenship is a buzzword today. One only has to glance at the websites of colleges and universities, the vision statements of non-profits and civic initiatives, and the claims made by corporates to grasp the centrality of global citizenship as an important goal in the fields as diverse as education, development, social change, marketing, and corporate management. The United Nations Secretary General's Global Education First Initiative (2012), for example, clearly gives prominence to fostering global citizenship by including it in their three priority areas.

Before assigning a place of honor to any idea in education, however, it is very important to understand and operationalize it fully. What is global citizenship and more importantly how do you operationalize it in terms of educational outcomes? Educational initiatives for global citizenship require clarity about not just the values but also the practices we associate with this orientation to citizenship. Besides, how fair it is for these practices to be universally prescriptive? As Coleman and Blumler argue, political citizens "are constituted through complex interactions between their own life experiences, traditions to collective action, structures of opportunity, and available discourses of thinking and acting politically" (2009, p. 5). Different geo-political locations engender different civic cultures and identities including those associated with and made complicated by social media. Such differences have to be accounted for in educational initiatives. It is, therefore, helpful here to briefly examine different perspectives on global citizenship and arrive at a pragmatic framework for GCE.

Interestingly, global citizenship is not a new concept at all. Versions of this idea have been proposed time and again starting with the Stoics and the Cynics in the ancient Greco-Roman period, continuing through the eighteenth and nineteenth centuries, and more recently in the debates of the 1990s. Global citizenship has captured our attention once again in the new millennium because of several ongoing contemporary transformations—more and more people now live outside their countries of origin and the increasing interconnectedness has opened our eyes to the fact that global challenges like terrorism, climate change, and growing inequalities require a global response. Besides, never before we have seen the kind and scale of exchanges of people, money, ideas, and information that we see today. This is the first time in history that ordinary individuals can access each other around the world in a genuine dialogue thanks to easier travel options and new media technologies. At the same time, the current refugee crisis engulfing the Middle East and Europe (and also several other parts of the world) and the rising calls to patriotism in many parts of the world have drawn our attention to the discontents, the limits, and the tricky questions of national and ethnic identities made trickier under economic pressures. Each one of us is living a life transformed by globalization whether willingly or unwillingly. Education today would not be relevant if it does not address citizenship practices that respond to our new realities and help us lead our lives with agency and meaning.

Defining Global Citizenship

The conventional notion of citizenship is predominantly associated with the nation-state. The scholarly literature on global citizenship focuses on juxtaposing global citizenship against national citizenship, which in the conventional sense valorizes one's national identity and revolves around loyalty to one's nation and fellow national citizens. Dower (2002), Falk (2002) and Appiah (2010), for example, capture the essence of global citizenship by emphasizing the primacy of universal moral rights of all human beings. They valorize the commitment to a larger, many a times imagined, human community of the present and the future. Despite their valorization of a universal human community, none of the scholars imply that for becoming a global citizen, one has to relinquish one's national citizenship. In fact, Dower (2003) argues that one of the best hopes for cosmopolitanism is reorienting national priorities from within. Held offers a valid observation that political communities can be reconceptualised as "multiple overlapping networks of interaction" (2002, p. 93). In this sense, Tarrow's (2005) conceptualization of rooted cosmopolitanism or Parekh's (2003) argument of not global but globally oriented citizenship provide a more achievable goal for citizenship education because they both acknowledge the continued importance of the local and the national in citizenship experience.

In the deliberations about global citizenship, however, we notice the desire to free citizenship from a strictly people–government equation and legal–formal arrangements. My research (Shelat 2014) with women of 15 different countries also showed a striking similarity about the core values these women associated with being a global citizen despite being situated in vastly different geo-political and cultural locations. Care, love, respect, tolerance, awareness, understanding, solidarity, and engagement were the words mentioned the most frequently when women spoke about the qualities of a global citizen. These women also value the people-to-people bonds much more than those with the government in their daily practice of civic engagement. Interestingly, but not surprisingly, all of the women ascribed a considerable value to social media in their citizenship practice. This was not only because of the increased opportunities for direct people-to-people bonding but also due to the perceived freedom to engage in civic activities beyond those sanctioned by their respective governments.

Based on their conceptualization of global citizenship various scholars and educators have attempted to develop guidelines about the roles and responsibilities of such citizens. For example, Kung (2002), sees intercultural communication and dialogue as the most important responsibility of global citizens and outlines some actions including clearing up misunderstandings, reflecting on things that are held in common and taking concrete initiatives for reconciliation. We can clearly see that these actions also revolve around people-to-people engagement rather than government–people engagement. In practice, a global citizen according to Dower (2003), would engage in a number of activities including: the pursuit of global causes, democratic engagement in global issues through national political parties, NGOs, networking and so on and the development of particularistic transnational solidarities for the protection of group rights and identities. Later in the chapter, we will revisit some of these ideas to outline the contribution of social media in fulfilling these civic roles. Of course, the notion of global citizenship attracts equally strong criticism. The criticism merits close attention in the process of designing GCE programs that promote meaningful, and culturally sensitive citizenship practices.

CRITICAL REFLECTIONS ON GLOBAL CITIZENSHIP

Chandhoke (2002), Chandler (2004), Keohane (2003), Mouffe (2005), and Scholte (2002) are among the critical voices that caution us about the practical challenges inherent in practicing global citizenship. The four main criticisms of the notion of global citizenship are based on their following observations. One, we have not had any success, so far, with global institutions of governance. Without such institutions, global citizenship cannot be managed. Moreover, even if such a world state exists, it will be dominated by one or two most powerful nations. Two, interpretation and practice of ethics are culture sensitive and hence it is not possible to have uniform global ethics. Three, primordial ties still engender very strong passions. Individuals would have a natural affinity to those closer to them, relationally and geographically. Besides, nations and national identities are far from disappearing.

In fact, tribal, caste-based, racial, and national affinities are getting stronger as a backlash to globalization. And four, global citizens are like rootless nomads with no local ties, interest, or influence and hence are not really effective as citizens. In citizenship practice and education, the tricky questions of loyalty, responsibility, and solidarity would surface again and again in the case of migrant populations or refugees or when citizens might find their national interests conflicting with interests of other nations or a larger transnational population.

Tawil correctly points out, "Any attempt to transpose the notion of citizenship beyond the nation-state to the global level thus becomes even more problematic, particularly from a legal perspective" (2013, p. 2), but at the same time argues that even if global citizens do not exist legally, they do exist in practice. This is very much evident in the findings of my research on women, Internet, and global citizenship (Shelat 2014). Based on these findings, I have proposed the concept of transcultural citizenship that offers us an alternative (but not a substitute) way to experience citizenship that reflects our global and convergent lives. Transcultural citizenship is relational in that it is built or performed in relation with defined others through the process of communication across cultures. Interpersonal relations and cultural experiences are more important here than legal–political institutional governance. The civic practices of actors, however, are embedded in their local cultures. They have strong local ties and intimate knowledge about their local histories and cultures. The articulation of transcultural citizenship, at the same time, recognizes that these local cultures are also transcultural because of the constant and complex multidirectional flows of people, images, information, and goods in the world today.

Transcultural citizens rely heavily on the affordances of the Internet because of the predominant role of the discursive practices and communication across cultures in their civic practices. In the past two decades, Internet has provided a valuable support to those desiring to participate in civic causes beyond their close geographic boundaries. The transnational civic engagement online ranges from signing petitions, donating to causes, sharing information, joining civic movements, or advocating for the rights of the marginalized. Much of online civic engagement today takes place using social media. Such online engagement, especially the symbolic and expressive engagement such as sharing images, updating profile pictures to endorse a cause, and liking someone else's status, however, is often looked down upon as an inferior version of engagement identified as slacktivism, clicktivism, or armchair activism that is high on "talk" and lip service and low in commitment and actual impact. I am not willing to dismiss all online engagement as slacktivism but I do agree that a certain level of media and information literacy, and commitment are necessary for using online platforms effectively for civic engagement.

Transnational civic engagement in practice also poses several dilemmas for well-meaning and sensitive citizens who struggle with questions such as: who can and should intervene in a conflict situation, when to intervene in issues of those geographically and culturally distant, how best to show solidarity, and when to withdraw or support from outside are some questions that such citizens struggle with. Citizens with geo-political, class, educational or linguistic privileges are often accused of "speaking for others" and thus further silencing the voice of the marginalized (Alcoff 1991–1992; Mohanty 2003; Tripp 2006). These dilemmas, therefore, become more acute in the case of citizens from the locations of privilege and power. Tripp discusses some of these questions in detail with respect to international feminist activism. Tripp observes, "When international support is extended it is not always offered in ways that reflect an understanding of other women's movements, their local contexts, and their needs" (2006, p. 296). Social media are likely to amplify these risks when the so-called global citizens substitute sporadic engagement with a website for a deep engagement with an issue.

When local cultural sovereignty is given supreme importance, however, there emerges a risk of extreme moral relativism. Should we valorize local cultural practices that violate basic human dignity and life in GCE? Such questions bring us again to the recurring debates over universal versus culture-specific human rights and the feasibility of global ethics. Though there are no easy answers to such dilemmas, sensitization about these issues should be an important part of the GCE. In the following section, I discuss the implications of the above discussion for designing citizenship centered educational programs.

SHAPING GLOBAL CITIZENS: DESIGNING THE EDUCATIONAL INITIATIVES

The United Nations Secretary General's Global Education First Initiative (2012) summarizes well the larger goal of citizenship education: "Education must fully assume its central role in helping people to forge more just, peaceful, tolerant and inclusive societies. It must give people the understanding, skills, and values they need to cooperate in resolving the interconnected challenges of the twenty-first century" (Davies 2006). National-oriented citizenship education has a remarkable emphasis on understanding the government formation and functions and participating in them as dutiful national citizens. As educators of global or rather, transcultural citizens, our concern, however, is with developing certain qualities and competencies that we should address in our pedagogy and also with defining the specific learning outcomes.

Scholarly and field-based literature make several observations related to desirable cognitive, affective, and practice-based attributes of global citizens that are helpful in designing learning experiences for shaping such citizens. Falk (2002, p. 27), for example argues that global citizens have "allegiance to values and not to states." Dahlberg (2008) brings to our attention the centrality of 'respect for difference' in democracy. He also argues that public sphere is "a space constituted through discursive contestation" thus highlighting the communication dimension. Kung (2003) emphasizes citizen responsibility with a critical observation that there was no declaration of human responsibilities with the declaration of human rights in 1948. Intercultural understanding and communication are the most frequently highlighted area of education for global citizenship while UNESCO (2014) clearly emphasizes the participation, practice, and problem-solving dimensions in GCE.

Andreotti (2006) provides a crucial consideration for educators by outlining two different ethical approaches—soft and critical—to envision GCE. In the "soft" approach there is an emphasis on the global human community, global ethics, intercultural communication, and care. The "critical" approach examines global issues from a post-colonial standpoint and considers it important to examine the global power relations. Social justice is the ultimate goal toward which the critical global citizens are expected to act.

These are all very valuable observations from the pedagogical point of view. From these observations, we can cull out the key areas for GCE even when we are sensitive to cultural differences in the ideals and practices of global citizenship. Through a review of the previous approaches on GCE, I identify the five following learning outcomes—(1) democratically and respectfully understanding and negotiating differences; (2) understanding the cultural–historical and geo-political contexts of globalization, nationalism, and civic engagement; (3) developing a public voice along with other core competencies in media and information literacy; (4) exercising one's political agency to ensure social justice; and (5) making critical reflection a part of one's civic practice. These learning outcomes would guide the learning experiences including those available via social media and also the assessment criteria in formal contexts. The affordances of social media can certainly facilitate these outcomes but not without critical social media literacy and geo-political and historical awareness of the global power dynamics.

SOCIAL MEDIA AS THE SPACE FOR CITIZENSHIP EDUCATION

As we have discussed earlier, social media can facilitate GCE in two ways: one, through everyday informal and spontaneous social use, and two, through carefully designed pedagogic experiences. In either case, media and information literacy, competency in agonistic negotiations/contestations, and public engagement skills are crucial for an effective use of social media for civic purposes.

Several empirical studies, albeit most with relatively small samples, indicate that when combined with critical media and information literacy, and reflective thinking, use of social media enhances civic engagement and may prove to be useful media for GCE. Some studies show that social media enhance civic collaboration and participation and contribute to developing civic skills. For example, a quick scan analysis and case studies conducted on aid organizations and the activities of young people aged 12–25 years in Belgium concluded that new media platforms help the youth form collaborative projects for participating in civic issues and aid organisations use social networking platforms for mobilizing their traffic (Baeldenet al. 2013, pp. 181–206). In Singapore, a study was conducted through the designing of a digital game called "Statecraft X" which utilized interactive digital gaming to engage 15-year-old students in the subjects of governance and citizenship. The study showed that the civic engagement skills of students increased as opposed to the traditional classroom social studies teaching (Chee et al. 2013). A study was conducted on Australian students who were granted digital affordances to help them create campaigns for an NGO in India. Results showed how for digitally abled youth the online space provides them both with familiarity and the opportunity to engage in transnational civic activities. Online platforms in such cases also facilitated global partnership and intercultural dialogue (Harris 2014). Somus Project in Finland shows how social media provide the users with the affordances for civic engagement (Näkki et al. 2011). The Somus Project, with the focus on the dynamics between "information, knowledge and citizenship" draws the attention to the idea of using the various kinds of social media platforms like Twitter, Facebook, YouTube, Skype, and Wiki to participate in global civic collaborations. A 5-month study of the technology usage of 12 high school students of social studies in USA showed how students used the digital space in order to engage in global civic activities like acquiring access to international news, participating in global networks and producing content for global audiences. In USA, where social studies are one of the major vehicles of civic education, the study points out how digital intervention is the need of the hour for effective GCE (Maguth 2012).

Some other studies have drawn our attention to social media's role in providing liberating spaces for youth civic engagement. For example, Social media platforms like Facebook, Twitter, YouTube and other blogging sites that are essentially non-political in nature, provided the much-needed liberation sought after by the youth civic activists of Egypt whose traditional Mediascape had fallen victim to State ownership and control (Khamis and Vaughn 2011). After the uprising, Egypt faced the challenge of not having sustainable developmental programs in place and training youth to think critically when it came to engaging in civic activities. In order to foster GCE, a new path was being sought. A survey of 200 university students shows how online participatory video making and sharing platforms of the likes of You-Tube acted as an effective media literacy tools to help percolate GCE to the youth, helping them build their civic skills (Gomaa 2014). A study on young Canadians investigated the role played by the Internet in Canadian children's lives (Wilson and Johnson 2014). According to the report even if these platforms do not have a direct impact on the level of civic participation of Canadian youth, they provide the opportunities for communal interaction on civic issues and generation of online content of the same genre through concientization techniques.

For the moment, I would like to connect the above review to the five key learning outcomes for GCE previously outlined and to the two approaches—soft and critical suggested by Andreotti (2006). Social media lend themselves easily to following the soft approach where the emphasis is on the global human community and intercultural communication. The "critical" approach asks for the examination of the global power relations with an ultimate goal of social justice. Such an approach requires careful intervention, guidance, and critical literacy on part of the mentors. The following section is devoted to discussing how different social media may be used for civic learning experiences with the help of the examples of some global initiatives. Again, most of these global civic initiatives tend to lean toward the soft approach to global citizenship but critical intervention is possible using appropriate learning experiences.

It is helpful to categorize social networking sites according to the functions they serve for an easy grasp of their wide range. All of these platforms, however, are founded on similar grounds of user-generated content (UGC) which marks the basic nature of Web 2.0 (Kaplan and Haenlein 2010). The potential to share and publish content by the participants encourage interactivity on these sites and makes education a participatory process. The following table outlines how various types of social media can facilitate different learning experiences that can together contribute to the five global citizenship learning outcomes.

Table 34.1 Classification of social media and their potential use in GCE. Adapted from http://www.fredcavazza.net/2010/12/14/social-media-landscape-2011/ Retrieved on January 27, 2017.

There are, of course, a number of limitations in the use of these platforms for GCE. Besides the limitations of social media themselves I have already outlined, there is also a question of the knowledge competence that it is expected from teachers. The trainings for teachers and students designed by several organizations (see Shelat 2014 for a comprehensive list of these organizations) can be helpful in this respect.

Table 34.1 Social media and global citizenship education

Function/use	Examples of social media	Examples of popular social media players	Examples of learning experiences	Examples of social media spaces that offer the global civic experience
Publish (publicly)	Blogs, microblogs, stream services, wikis	WordPress, Twitter, Tumblr, Wikipedia, YouTube	Reading or watching narratives from other locations and cultures; commenting; writing personal narratives (both audio-visual and text-based); interesting and readable reports of projects, or analytical commentaries	Global Voices Online; UNICEF Voices of Youth; Youth Ki Avaaz; Plural+
Share (with a selected group of people or organisations)	Services allowing to share videos, photos, music, or documents	YouTube, Flickr, Instagram, Spotify, SlideShare, Scribb	Producing and sharing videos on local contexts and issues and also on local-global connections; producing visual essays; Critically watching others' work	Plural+; TakingITGlobal
Discuss	Bulletin boards, chat groups, comment management systems, social research tools	Phorum, Gravity, IntenseDebate, Disqus, Quora	Initiate and join discussion threads; analytically and critically follow discussion threads	Soliya Connect Program; TakingITGlobal
Network	Personal and professional social networks and network creation tools	Facebook, LinkedIn, Ning	Join identity or issue based networks; collaborate on international projects; critically observe global online civic communities	Peace x peace; UNOY Peace Builders
Games	Traditional, virtual worlds, social and mobile	Pogo, Habbo, Zynga, ngmoco	Participating in games-both popular and those developed for civic education; developing games;	iCivics; SimCity, and Civilisation; Tropico5

(continued)

Table 34.1 (continued)

Function/use	Examples of social media	Examples of popular social media players	Examples of learning experiences	Examples of social media spaces that offer the global civic experience
Location based community building	Social location platforms, mobile social networks, local social networks, event sharing	Foursquare, Mig33, Loopt, Upcoming	Creating and sharing cause-led events; publicizing events; participating in events	Ethical consumer
Commerce	Review and feedback tools, recommendation and inspiration communities	BazaarVoice, Weardrobe, LivingSocial	Explore ethical buying communities and their work; participate in such communities to critically understand ethical buying; insert labor right and environment conservation discussion in a product review and monitor the ensuing discussion; trace the global footprints of the things we use daily	

CONCLUSION

There exists a tendency to look at GCE in a utopian, celebratory, and over-simplified manner ignoring the historical and geo-political complexities of the world and also the complexities of the human mind. A critical, rather than, neutral understanding of the processes and impacts of globalization, the connections between local and global, and the histories of structural inequalities between and within nations should be an integral component of GCE. At the same time, I would caution against such critical approaches that leave the youth either with a crippling guilt about their privilege or a crippling anger at the history of injustice. These emotions rob individuals of the will to exert their political agency because of the overwhelming feeling of "nothing can be done." I argue that GCE should prepare the learners to contribute constructively to the global causes in such a manner that the patterns of injustice do not repeat themselves. The form of transcultural citizenship here presented can respond, in my understanding, to these challenges.

Social media can be particularly helpful to the education of this transcultural citizenship as specified in the key learning outcomes previously outlined. The possibilities offered by social media in terms of their web 2.0 supported affordances, interactivity, and global networking nature are huge. However, limitations such as the real civic impact in absence of commitment, geopolitical understanding, and critical media literacy need to be acknowledged. I understand critical and transcultural media and information literacy (MIL) education and geo-political literacy might be necessary to address this limitation. An education that encompasses both a reasonable use of social media together with media literacy, in my understanding, can ensure that students recognize the civic potential of social media and use them appropriately in their road to acting as global citizens.

Acknowledgements I thank Devpriya Chakravarty, research scholar with the FPM-C program at MICA for her extensive literature review and copy editing support.

REFERENCES

Alcoff, L. (1991–1992). The problem of speaking for others. *Cultural Critique, 20*, 5–32.

Andreotti, V. (2006). Soft vs. critical global citizenship education. *Policy and Practice: A Development Education Review, 3*, 40–51.

Appiah, K. A. (2010). *Cosmopolitanism: Ethics in a world of strangers (Issues of our time)*. New York: W.W. Norton & Company.

Baelden, D., Audenhove, L. V., & Jehaes, E. (2013). New and social media for strengthening the public support among young people for development cooperation: Instant karma. In I. Pollet & J. V. Ongevalle (Eds.), *The Drive to global citizenship: Motivating people, mapping public support, measuring effects of global education* (pp. 183–192). Belgium: Maklu.

Beck, U. (1998). *Democracy without enemies*. Cambridge, UK Malden, MA: Polity Press.

Benett, L. (2008). *Changing citizenship in the digital age. Civic life online: Learning how digital media can engage youth*. Cambridge, MA: MIT Press.

Bennett, L., Wells, C., & Freelon, D. (2011). Communicating civic engagement: Contrasting models of citizenship in the youth web sphere. *Journal of Communication, 61*(5), 835–856.

Bennett, W. L., Wells, C., & Rank, A. (2009). Young citizens and civic learning: Two paradigms of citizenship in the digital age. *Citizenship Studies, 13*(2), 105–120.

Bimber, B. (2000). The study of information technology and civic engagement. *Political Communication, 17*(4), 329–333.

Boyd, D. (2008). *Taken out of context: American teen sociality in networked places*. Berkeley: University of California.

Buckingham, D. (2008). *Youth, identity, and digital media*. In D. John & T. Catherine (Eds.), Cambridge. MA: The MIT Press.

Chandhoke, N. (2002). The limits of global civil society. In H. Anheier, M. Kaldor, & M. Glasius (Eds.), *Global civil society*. Oxford: Oxford University Press.

Chandler, D. (2004). Building global civil society from below? *Millennium-Journal of International Studies, 33*(2), 313–339.

Chee, Y. S., Mehrotra, S., & Liu, Q. (2013). Effective game based citizenship education in the age of new media. *The Electronic Journal of e-Learning, 11*(1), 16–28.

Coleman, Stephen, & Blumler, J. G. (2009). *The Internet and democratic citizenship: Theory, practice, and policy*. Cambridge: Cambridge University Press.

Cornelissen, G., Karelaia, N., & Soyer, E. (n.d.). Clicktivism or slactivism? Impression management and moral licensing.

Dahlberg, L. (2008). Rethinking the fragmentation of the cyberpublic: From consensus to contestation. *New media and society, 9*(5), 827–847.

Dahlgren, P. (2007). Youth, civic engagement and learning via new media. In P. Dahlgren (Ed.), *Young citizens and new media: Learning for democratic participation* (pp. 1–18). New York: Routledge.

Dahlgren, P. (2011). Young citizens and political participation: Online media and civic cultures. *Taiwan Journal of Democracy, 7*(2), 11–25.

Davies, L. (2006). Global citizenship: Abstraction or framework. *Educational Review, 58*(1), 5–25.

Dower, N. (2002). Global citizenship: Yes or no? In N. Dower & J. Williams (Eds.), *Global citizenship: A critical introduction* (pp. 30–40). New York: Routledge.

Dower, N. (2003). *An Introduction to global citizenship*. Edinburg: Edinburg University Press.

Falk, R. (2002). An emergent matrix of citizenship: Complex, uneven and fluid. In N. Dower & J. Williams (Eds.), *Global citizenship: A critical introduction*. New York: Routledge.

Friedland, L. (1996). Electronic democracy and the new citizenship. *Media, Culture & Society, 18*(2), 185–212.

Giddens, A. (1998). *The third way: The renewal of social democracy*. Cambridge: Polity, Global Education First Initiative.

Gomaa, E. H. (2014). Video production as a tool to reinforce media literacy and citizenship in Egypt. In S. H. Culver & P. Kerr (Eds.), *Global citizenship in a digital world* (pp. 33–43). Sweden: NORDICOM.

Harris, U. (2014). Virtual partnerships implications for mediated intercultural dialogue in a student-led online project. In S. H. Culver & P. A. Kerr (Eds.), *Global citizenship in a digital world* (pp. 177–184). Sweden: NORDICOM.

Held, D. (2002). The transformation of political community: Rethinking democracy in the context of globalization. In N. Dower & J. Williams (Eds.), *Global citizenship: A critical introduction* (pp. 92–100). New York: Routledge.

Howard, R. (2011). *Digital Jesus: The making of a New Christian fundamentalist community on the Internet.* New York: New York University Press.

Jenkins, H., Shresthova, S., Gamber-Thompson, L., Kligler-Vilenchik, N., & Zimmerman, A. (2016). *By any media necessary: The new youth activism.* New York: NYU Press.

Kaplan, A. M., & Haenlein, M. (2010). Users of the world, unite! The challenges and opportunities of social media. *Business Horizons, 53,* 59–68.

Keohane, R. (2003). *Global governance and democrat.* Retrieved on January 27, 2017 from http://unpan1.un.org/intradoc/groups/public/documents/apcity/unpan034133.pdf.

Khamis, S., & Vaughn, K. (2011). Cyberactivism in the Egyptian revolution: How civic engagement and citizen journalism tilted the balance. *Arab Media and Society* (14).

Kung, H. (2002). A global ethic for a new global order. In N. Dower & J. Williams (Eds.), *Global citizenship: A critical introduction* (pp. 133–145). New York: Routledge.

Livingstone, S. (2009). *Children and the Internet.* Cambridge: Polity.

Maguth, B. M. (2012). Investigating student use of technology for engaged citizenship in a global age. *Education Science, 2,* 57–76.

Mohanty, C. T. (2003). *Feminism without borders: Decolonizing theory, practicing solidarity.* Delhi: Zubaan.

Mouffe, C. (2005). *On the political.* London: Taylor & Francis.

Näkki, P., Bäck, A., Ropponen, T., Kronqvist, J., Hintikka, K. A., Harju, A., et al. (2011). *Social media for citizen participation: Report on the Somus project.* Helsinki: JULKAISIJA—UTGIVARE.

Papacharissi, Z. (2010). *A private sphere: Democracy in a digital age.* Cambridge: Polity.

Parekh, B. (2003). Cosmopolitanism and global citizenship. *Review of International Studies, 19,* 3–17.

Pathak-Shelat, M., & DeShano, C. (2013). Digital youth cultures in small town and rural Gujarat India. *New Media and Society, 16*(6), 1–19.

Saleh, I. (2014). Whatever happened to South African youth? New media, new politics and new activism. In S. H. Culver & P. A. Kerr (Eds.), *Global citizenship in a digital world* (pp. 203–2013). Sweden: NORDICOM.

Scholte, J. (2002). Civil society and democracy in global governance. *Global Governance, 8,* 281–304.

Shelat, M. (2014). Global civic engagement on online platforms: Women as transcultural citizens. Unpublished doctoral dissertation. University of Wisconsin-Madison. Retrieved on January 27, 2017 from http://gradworks.umi.com/36/24/3624233.html.

Shirky, C. (2008). *Here comes everybody: The power of organizing without organizations.* London: Penguin.

Stevenson, N. (2001). *Culture and citizenship.* Thousand Oaks, London: Sage.

Tarrow, S. (2005). *The new transnational activism*. Cambridge: Cambridge University Press.

Tawil, S. (2013). Education for global citizenship: a framework for discussion. UNESCO.

Tripp, A. (2006). Challenges in transnational feminist mobilization. In M. Ferree & A. Tripp (Eds.), *Global feminism: Transnational women's activism, organizing, and human rights* (pp. 296–312). New York, London: New York University Press.

UNESCO (2012). Global Education First Initiative. Retrieved on January 27, 2017 from http://www.unesco.org/new/en/education/global-education-first-initiative-gefi/.

UNESCO. (2014). *Global citizenship education: Preparing learners for the challenges of the 21st century*. Paris: UNESCO.

Watkins, C. (2009). *The young and the digital: What the migration to social network sites and anytime anywhere media means for our future*. Boston: Beacon Press.

Wilson, C., & Johnson, M. (2014). Media literacy, digital technologies and civic engagement: A Canadian perspective. In S. H. Culver & P. A. Kerr (Eds.), *Global citizenship in a digital world* (pp. 95–105). Sweden: NORDICOM.

Author Biography

Manisha Pathak-Shelat is Professor of Communication and Digital Platforms & Strategies at MICA, India. She has a doctorate in Mass Communication from the University of Wisconsin-Madison, USA and in Education from the Maharaja Sayajirao University of Baroda, India. Her research concerns transcultural citizenship, media literacy, youth media cultures, digital media, and gender. She is the Editor, Journal of Creative Communications and Vice-Chair of the Media Education Research section of the International Association for Media and Communication Research (IAMCR). Awards and fellowships include the Shastri Indo-Canadian Faculty Research Award, The Salzburg Seminar Fellowship, and the TATA Fellowship for the Study of Contemporary India.

CHAPTER 35

Seeking Global Citizenship Through International Experiential/Service Learning and Global Citizenship Education: Challenges of Power, Knowledge and Difference for Practitioners

Allyson Larkin

The affects of globalization, including increasing mobilities of people and rapid transfer of information, are part of the phenomena driving notions of global citizenship education (GCE) in contemporary higher education. Advocates for global citizenship education acknowledge that there is no agreed upon definition for global citizenship, rather it is described as an "ethos or metaphor, rather than a formal membership" (UNESCO 2016, p. 1). In a recent publication by UNESCO (2016), global citizenship is conceptualized as a "sense of belonging to the global community and a common sense of humanity, with its presumed members experiencing solidarity and collective identity among themselves and collective responsibility at the global level" (p. 1). The universal sense of hope and responsibility for humanity and the planet embodied in this approach to GCE appeals to educators who seek to inspire their students to make a difference or respond to global crises. Taking action in and on the world is a logical response to the ideals of GCE, and indeed, UNESCO's (2016) resources for global citizenship education require that knowledge acquired by learners must be combined with "actual experiences and opportunities to develop, test and build their

A. Larkin (✉)
Western University, London, ON, Canada
e-mail: alarkin2@uwo.ca

© The Author(s) 2018   557
I. Davies et al. (eds.), *The Palgrave Handbook of Global Citizenship and Education*, https://doi.org/10.1057/978-1-137-59733-5_35

own views, values, and attitudes and to learn how to take actions responsibly" (p. 4). It is at the intersection of cognitive and behavioral learning that the practice of international experiential or service learning (IESL) is often included in GCE programs.

The influences of globalization in higher education are also linked to intensifying calls for university students to be prepared to be globally competent citizens, which translates into globally competent workers (Beck 2012). To produce such individuals, universities turn to global programming to provide students with firsthand experience of other cultures. In this chapter, I am particularly concerned with the ways in which narratives of global citizenship and international learning experiences reflect, affirm, and construct hierarchies of power and knowledge. The asymmetry of power and knowledge, located within the university and represented by its students, sets up a challenging relationship in the context of global learning that brings students into globally marginalized communities to provide service or for experience. The universalizing discourse that runs through global citizenship narratives is difficult to reconcile with efforts by educators who are working toward pluralizing and decolonizing knowledge and global relationships. Calls for a universal humanity are particularly thorny, according to Didier Fassin (2010), an anthropologist researcher in the field of humanitarianism. He observes that persistent tensions exist in humanitarian endeavors, between an "ideal of universality" and "practices of difference (p. 239)." These tensions between the aspirational desire for a human universal and the more real production difference within humanity are key concerns within the research and theory examining both GCE and IESL.

At this contemporary time of global crisis, there are approximately 66 million people now displaced by violent conflict, chronic poverty or environmental degradation (UNHCR 2016). The UNHCR reports that nearly 34,000 people per day are now forced to flee their homes due to violence or chronic poverty and according to the United Nations' (UN), statistics, 1 in every 113 people in the world is now a displaced person; the population of displaced people and refugees is larger than the total population of the UK (UNHCR 2016). With the number of refugees expected to increase again in 2016, to speak of a global citizenship in universal terms must be challenged by the globally uneven distribution of power and authority, which provides protection to some and renders others disposable. Bound up in this process which distinguishes among valued and discarded humans are hierarchies of knowledge, power, and authority which inform, legitimize and obscure whose rights count and whose do not. Questions of who has the right to claim status as a (global) citizen, or who has the right to have rights, are at the core of critical scholarship on global citizenship.

In this chapter, I am approaching the challenges of working with the concept of global citizenship education (GCE) in the context of international experiential learning (IESL) practices that attempt to put global citizenship education into action. IESL is a pedagogy closely linked to and aligned with the formation of global citizens in the context of higher education (Cameron 2014; Jefferess 2012). My goal here is to highlight key controversies and to provide critical insights from a practitioner's point of view. IESL and GCE are two concepts which are often linked in the higher education narratives and imaginaries that inform and promote each practice; global citizenship discourses are taken up in IESL literature as one of the outcomes from participation in such programs, while university internationalization strategies point to the number of participants in global programming as representative of achievement for institutional metrics. In the space between institutional policy and practice, critical researchers continue to raise questions related to global citizenship's epistemological grounding, (Andreotti 2011; Shultz 2007), the possibility for global social justice within higher education, (Shultz and Viczko 2016; Cameron 2014) and the privileging of some racialized identities over others (Andreotti 2016; Mahrouse 2014).

First, I will highlight diverse epistemic positions within the notion of global citizenship in the context of higher education internationalization; next I will move to consider the ways GCE informs the practice of IESL. Critical research in IESL and GCE continues to call attention to the oppressive impacts of IESL practices for host communities, what Tuck (2009) calls the "hidden costs" of research or pedagogical strategies on "depleted communities" (p. 412). In response, a number of contemporary researchers are developing pedagogical strategies to mitigate these effects through the development of collaborative standards for practice or intellectual strategies which work from a critique of global structures of power and knowledge. I will take up three such approaches to IESL and GCE in this chapter: Fair Trade Learning practices, (Hartman and Kiely 2014; Hartman et al. 2014); structural critique of knowledge production through IESL (HEADS UP) (Andreotti 2016), and the GlobalPov Project which seeks to reframe the way researchers, educators and students understand their relationships to 'the poor' (Roy et al. 2016).

ACADEMIC PRACTICE OF IESL AND GLOBAL CITIZENSHIP EDUCATION

Combining some measure of traditional academic/classroom learning with travel and service to international communities, IESL is generally defined as

> a course-based, credit-bearing educational experience in which students (a) participate in an organized service activity that meets identified community needs, and (b) reflect on the service activity in such a way as to gain further understanding of course content, a broader appreciation of the discipline and an enhanced sense of personal values and civic responsibility. (Bringle et al. 2012, p. 5)

The emphasis in this definition on increasing civic engagement and the influ-ence of neoliberalism through the promotion of personal values, reiterates the notion that a universal set of moral values and knowledge may be called upon to build a foundation for IESL practice. The notion of the universal, how-ever, continues to call into question the development of a hierarchy among those with the power and resources to be in service in contrast to those who are damaged or in need.

An additional complication arises from the affective experience gained from being in the position of one who is able to help others, which reaffirms a benevolent and generous identity. In tandem with the growing popularity of voluntourism as a form of leisure and entertainment, the combination of service and travel is a powerful draw for youth in higher education (Simpson 2004; Heron 2007; Vrasti 2013). The desire to 'make a difference' or to 'be the change' is reflected in recruiting materials and integrated into curricula and syllabi through competitions and campaigns to use learning material and to apply it to contemporary global crises (Stein and Andreotti 2016). The contagious optimism embedded in benevolent identities associated with those who participate in global service is in sharp contrast to the critical arguments that foreground the element of complicity attributed to IESL participants in the production of ongoing marginalization of some communities (Andreotti 2016; Tuck 2009).

The degree to which IESL actually produces transformation within stu-dent participants is an ongoing debate and results from empirical research are ambiguous (Kiely 2004). Recent research on the attitudes of youth partici-pants in volunteer abroad programs suggests the motives are often unclear to participants themselves; on a more cynical note, some students report a more self-serving motive for participation, including the opportunity to seek adven-ture, or to add experience to develop a personal *curriculum vitae* (Tiessen 2012; Andreotti and de Souza 2012).

The reproduction of power relations over and development of privileged knowledge on or about host communities are key concerns for critical prac-titioners of IESL. Tiessen and Huish (2014), challenge the privilege of travel that may initially draw students to IESL programs (Tiessen 2012). Tiessen and Huish (2014) ask three pointed questions of GCE and IESL. First, "is global competency and cross-cultural understanding facilitated through international experiential learning and second, why does the quest for global citizenship matter? Three, does international experiential learning produce globe trot-ters or global citizens?" (p. 3). Practices that position some as the bestowers of benevolence on communities constructed as needy or making a difference in the world by spending thousands of dollars to travel across the world sug-gest that it is the student experience that is valued versus focused attention on the root causes of inequality or global poverty (Vrasti 2013; Jefferess 2012). Additionally, the uneven and uncritical approaches to IESL and the growing practice of decoupling IESL from any course-based content, for example in "alternative reading week" or "spring break" programs, exempts participants from engaging in an analysis of the historical, ethnocentric, apolitical implications for education travel (Andreotti 2006, 2016; Biccum 2010). In response to random exercise of IESL, several research practitioners advocate an ethics based approach to programming.

Internationalizing the University: Global Citizenship Narratives

In the context of contemporary North American universities, global citizenship narratives closely align with institutional goals for internationalization and intersect with calls to increase student participation in global learning opportunities (Shultz 2007). Shultz and Jorgenson (2012) contend that the growth in global citizenship education programs are deployed as part of marketing strategies to attract students who want global experiences to complement their education and to add to their desirability in an increasingly competitive global workforce (p. 6). The role that neoliberal, private sector interests play in higher education, specifically in relation to institutional goals to increase internationalization, is well documented in the research literature (Beck 2012; Shultz and Viczko 2016). As an extension of globalization, higher education internationalization continues to operate as a source of power which reshapes the space, scale, form and context of human interactions. The debate over global citizenship education and the practice of international experiential/service learning speaks to the ways in which higher education is influenced by diverse, often antagonistic, interests (Pashby 2011, 2012).

There is a lack of consensus on what or who defines global citizenship and its relationship to the nation-state (Cameron 2014; Roy et al. 2016; Pashby 2014). Conceptually, there is a twofold paradox: First, if the nation-state is the protector of citizens' rights, how is a global state to come into existence and provide protection and accountability for citizens' rights? Second, given the growing gulf of inequalities that exist across the world, is it even possible to imagine how there could exist social and political conditions that qualify one as a global citizen without it being a highly privileged and exclusive class? (Balibar 2012). Balibar contends that conceptual ambiguities have challenged notions of democratic citizenship throughout the history of western civilization. Even within the context of the nation-state, equitable participation in citizenship rights and privileges is uneven (Balibar 2012).

Despite the conceptual and political constraints identified by philosophers on the notion of citizenship, the imaginary global citizen remains a popular leitmotif in marketing literature in higher education. This image is aimed at inspiring youth who may pursue higher education and desire to make a difference in the world. Key challenges from researchers persist: how can one aspire to be a global citizen in the context of exclusion, displacement and violence?

What knowledge claims are made by global citizenship narratives (Shultz and Jorgenson 2012; Langdon and Agyeyomah 2014)?

Despite challenges to the epistemological foundations for global citizenship, the number of international education programs designed to engage youth in travel to communities to gain an experience of poverty or to provide service is increasing. There are consequences for youth educational travel to communities identified as marginal. Tuck (2009) challenges the practice of education and research that focuses on communities' deficiencies and labels it "damage-centred" research/education (p. 410). Engaging the term "damage-centred," Tuck references the increasing number of researchers and faculty who actively seek out disenfranchised communities to produce knowledge on their condition. She strongly urges researchers to consider the long-term repercussions that result from the need to document or experience the effects of oppression within these communities, and to acknowledge the consequences for these individuals reiterating an identity that frames some communities and their residents as broken (Tuck, p. 209). The impact on communities is so powerful, that in an absence of radically reforming current practices, she calls for a moratorium for communities from engaging with researchers. Similar concerns are raised by critical researchers on IESL and GCE (Larkin 2015; Tiessen and Huish 2014).

Tuck's argument is grounded against the trend to identify disenfranchised communities by their perceived deficits. She argues that damage-centered approaches to research, and subsequently teaching, "emphasize what a particular student, family or community is lacking … it looks to historical exploitation, domination and colonization to explain contemporary brokenness, such as poverty, poor health, and low literacy" (p. 413). In contrast, IESL and GCE narratives position those outside of damage-centered communities in a position of strength and benevolence. Further, appeals to global citizenship in higher education work may actually work against the damaged community. Tuck argues that "for many well-meaning people, it is actually a de facto reliance on a potentially problematic theory of change that leads to damage-centred research" (p. 413), or, in the case of GCE or IESL, pedagogical practice.

Two problematic narratives drive notions of GCE and IESL in contemporary higher education. First, GCE narratives project the image of an active citizenry, intellectually prepared and endowed with rights and responsibilities to care for a single planet that is increasingly under threat from environmental degradation and regionalized violence (Lewin 2009). Second, global citizenship discourses in higher education typically respond to an economic imperative based on the need for the nation-state to produce a globally competent workforce through the practices and technologies of the university (Shultz and Jorgenson 2012). The tension between the two identities demonstrates the power relations and hierarchical difference produced by narratives of the global citizen and which Other the citizen from a community perceived as damaged.

Identifying the roots of the exceptionality of the global citizen establishes a foundation from which to critique approaches to IESL and GCE practices.

The Idealized Global Citizen: Complicit in the Production of Power and Privilege?

Narratives of global citizenship promote an image of an idealized individual whose personal/social responsibilities extend well beyond the local and expand the boundaries of an individual's identity to include the values of an imaginary global community (Jefferess 2012). This imagined borderless identity, in the context of open mobility and increasing financial support, informs much of the creation and promotion of programming aimed at providing students with opportunities to immerse themselves in communities, cultures, and contexts different from their own. Indeed, one of the most commonly cited goals for international experiential or service learning is to produce students whose subjectivities are rooted in an awareness and practice of global citizenship (Cameron 2014, p. 21). Yet critical researchers argue that practitioners and participants in IESL too often overlook the power and privilege that structure relations between the communities who host IESL programs and the institutional as well as student participants' complicities in maintaining those systems.

The production of an idealized global citizen identity reinforces and legitimizes uncritical practices in higher education. Although acknowledging that critical researchers are quick to point to neo-colonial practices as something to be avoided and shunned, Andreotti (2016), contends that clinging to notions of exceptionalism has meant that the role of the state in the reproduction of coloniality through education practices has evaded critique. Speaking specifically to the role of exceptionalism in Canadian higher education, she argues, "these tendencies mobilise (in different ways and degrees) identities that dissociate the creation of the Canadian state and Canadian nationalism from the historical and systemic reproduction of injustices locally and abroad" (p. 102). Grounded in a notion of Canadian identity linked to innocence and benevolence, Andreotti builds a critique of the practice and research of IESL, derived from Thobani's (2007 in Andreotti 2016) work on Canadian citizenship. The production of an innocent or "exalted" Canadian citizen

> relies on the concealment of the colonial violence at the core of the national project that also marks the origin of the national subject. In other words, for Canadians to be produced as naturally benevolently superior, the national master narrative necessarily needs to foreclose its own construction as well as the violence it engenders. (Thobani in Andreotti 2016, p. 103)

Key to Andreotti's (2016) analysis of global citizenship education and IESL is its epistemological links to the ongoing expansion of global capitalism as an extension of western modernity. She argues that,

> if the darker side of modernity, nationalism and development are forgotten in our accounts of local and global belonging, the result is a modern subject who uncritically celebrates the progress and evolution that they represent, and who believes and affirms their own neutrality and innocence in the face of injustice. (p. 104)

Andreotti (2016) further stresses that the persistence of global citizenship narratives promoted within higher education or in transnational organizations such as UNESCO reinforces "ethnocentric, paternalistic, ahistorical and depoliticised" practices in education (p. 105). Additionally, the mediatization of distant suffering has positioned response to suffering as a matter of individual choice (Chouliaraki 2013). The shift to entrepreneurial humanitarian efforts has created distance between affected communities and those with the resources to respond to need. Response has become a matter of choice (Chouliaraki 2013). Thus Andreotti's critique challenges approaches to IESL practices that are contingent on an acceptance of some notion of common humanity and a thin understanding of a universal moral obligation to respond to the suffering of others. Her approach to rethinking global citizenship education and IESL practices through the HEADS UP framework is discussed later in this chapter.

Theorizing International Experiential Learning as a Practice of Global Citizenship Education

The diversity of global communities' particular situatedness, lived-experiences, culture, and knowledge poses challenges to institutional attempts to universalize identities through concepts such as global citizenship. Seeking unity amidst diversity, cosmopolitanism has emerged as one way to frame a common humanity as a starting point to develop an equitable notion of global citizenship. Cameron (2014) sees an opportunity to engage in a rigorous analysis of global citizenship through this framework. Cosmopolitanism is founded on a belief that there are common bonds of humanity, rooted in a moral relationship, that link communities and individuals together. He argues that the absence of "any serious analysis of normative ethics … (or) consideration of the moral considerations that should guide human behaviors in the first place" is a serious gap in IESL practices (p. 26). Considerations in any practice or theory for IESL or global citizenship education should challenge participants and practitioners to consider

- What rights do human beings possess by virtue of their being human?
- What obligations do those rights impost on others?

- How far do those obligations extend?
- What specific actions do those obligations require? (p. 26)

Cameron's emphasis on a moral grounding for IESL and GCE, as a way to move beyond the paralysis of critique that emphasizes difference, is valuable contribution to rethinking GCE and IESL, yet the challenge to synthesize plurality with universality remains. Overstating the universality of humanity continues to privilege the role of western values in the development of the moral universal to the exclusion of others (Shultz 2007).

Critical GCE researchers contend that attempts to construct a universal notion of citizenship (un)intentionally continues a colonizing process begun centuries ago that seeks to subjugate knowledges outside of Western traditions. Pashby (2012) argues that a critical approach to global citizenship education can become a provocative educational space to disrupt hegemonizing and universalizing notions of history, politics, economics and social relations. This critique opens the field of critical global citizenship education as a space to challenge dominant historical narratives by interrogating mere 'good intentions,' implied within notions of global citizenship and to set down to the 'messy' work of thoroughly decolonizing higher education. Pashby (2011) contributes valuable insights into the tensions and contradictions within global citizenship education. She argues that the very exceptionalism and universalism implied in the notion of global citizenship provides the avenue to begin to deconstruct its implications and is an opportunity for educators to potentially move forward and rethink pluralistic notions of "the global" and "citizenship."

IESL: Practitioners' Approaches to Ethical Practices

Acknowledging the gaps and critiques raised by critical researchers, Hartman and Kiely (2014), identify tensions between narratives of global citizenship and global service learning. In their research, they identified an ongoing attempt by educators "aimed at disrupting, decolonizing and transforming historic, linguistic, structural, cultural and institutional arrangements that cause harm" (p. 32), yet the authors also suggest that student participants in their programs have not consistently found global citizenship theories relevant to their experiences. In contrast, Hartman and Kiely (2014) found that their student participants resisted the identity of global citizens, and preferred reporting their approach to IESL as "humble, careful and ongoing action to better acknowledge human dignity" and that actions were designed to "remind of us the possibility of our own, perhaps unintentional or unwitting complicity in perpetuating structures of exclusion ... and patterns of oppression" (p. 32). In their practice and research, they sought to engage students within a pedagogy of global service learning frameworks that attempt to integrate "intellectual, political, moral, social, cultural and personal outcomes" with critical concern for the impact of their actions (p. 32).

Although inculcating a sense of humility is a valuable step toward recognizing the hegemonic and power asymmetries that persist in IESL practices, programs and pedagogies that do not engage in a critique of the socioeconomic systems and institutions that sustain global inequality through IESL practices risk being complicit with them.

THE TURN TO ETHICS: FAIR TRADE LEARNING APPROACHES TO IESL

The critical objections raised above have been framed by some practitioners and researchers as ethical dilemmas that may be addressed through the development of standards that guide practitioners and mitigate the oppressive impacts of IESL. Recognizing that the global market for youth travel and educational tourism is enormous, ($173 billion/year) (Hartman 2014, p. 108), and unlikely to respond to the claims of critical research, Hartman (2014) advocates for 'Fair Trade' practices to guide university and host participants through the process of IESL programming. His work draws on the commercial model of Fair Trade products and adapts the framework to reflect the concerns raised by researchers. His intention is "to direct attention to the most important issues, imply the most compelling questions and drive continuous improvements for individuals and organizations approaching this practice with conscientiousness and care" (Hartman 2014, p. 114).

Hartman turned to the Fair Trade Learning construct, developed by Amazide Global Service Learning and its host partner, the Association of Clubs in Jamaica, a framework jointly developed to assist the two partners to "stay honest" with one another, to "work to uphold ethical, community-centered principles despite market pressures to do otherwise" (Hartman 2014, p. 114). The Fair Trade Learning model is built on an understanding of 'reciprocity,' analyzed across the fields of service learning and civic engagement, philosophy, evolutionary biology, leadership and indigenous meaning making (Hartman, 2014, pp. 14–15). He identifies key fields of interaction where the exercise of power or operational assumptions may be made that privilege the resource-holding partner over local interests. Transparency, participation, sustainability, diversity, reflection and community building are all goals incorporated into the core principals of the Fair Trade Learning approach. The turn to ethics in education practices, to guide and mitigate practices, however, raises criticisms. The deferral of work on systems institutions that structure power and knowledge inequities appear as accommodation and acceptance of contemporary hierarchies.

Hartman's analysis can be seen as a first step to mitigating the consequences of oppressive IESL practices. Although engaging with the interests of the host community, it is an accommodation of contemporary practices that, while acknowledging power asymmetries, does not deconstruct the embedded power within the social systems and institutions that sustain inequality and epistemic privilege. Critics may dismiss the production of a set of best practices as potentially an act of appeasement that will please administrators and practitioners who are unwilling to engage in the deeper epistemological investigation called for by Andreotti (2016), however, as Hartman clearly notes, the Fair-Trade standards are intended as aspirational guidelines, not as "limiting proscriptions" (p. 14).

HEADS UP: Interrogating the Structures of Power and Knowledge that Produce Oppression

Not content to merely identify the gaps within IESL practices that gloss over ongoing oppression, Andreotti (2016) developed a heuristic to engage educators in critical analysis of non-Western experiences and knowledges. HEADS UP is an acronym for hegemony, ethnocentrism, ahistorical, depoliticized, salvific, uncomplicated and paternalistim, that effectively identifies seven fields which practitioners may use to frame critical engagements with students and to imagine the world through different epistemological lenses (Andreotti 2016). By de-centering the role not only of Western knowledge, education practices and innocent identities, those perceived to be benevolent international helpers, Andreotti calls for a holistic rethinking of the role of history, colonialism and ongoing socioeconomic exploitation that underlies the privileges of IESL/GCE practices.

A Pedagogy of Praxis: Bringing Together Critique and Practice

The GlobalPov Project, out of the University of California, Berkeley, creatively engages critical global poverty scholarship and is developing new conceptual frameworks to think about global citizenship, inequalities and youth engagement. Roy and Kalir (2016), creators of the GlobalPov Project bring together a multi-disciplinary group of scholars and students to think and teach about social justice, development and inequalities from diverse perspectives to engage what she terms a pedagogy of praxis, rooted in a strong critical analysis of the roots of poverty and inequality. Drawing on the experiences and history of social movements, she challenges practitioners to reconceptualise anti-poverty education, to place it "in a different category—that of anti-colonial struggles, civil rights campaigns and grassroots efforts to bring about social change" (p. 175). This model rethinks 'the poor,' as the 'damaged-centred' community site for IESL practice and asks:

> What if rather than seeing the 'poor' as outside of the project of development, we acknowledge that they are a product of these very modes of intervention? What if we understand the poor as the revolutionary subject—not the disenfranchised in need of intervention and help, but the marginalized and oppressed poised to make history? (Roy et al. 2016, p. 175)

Perhaps Roy and her collaborators' perspective can be thought of as post-critical. Their analysis engages deeply with critical theories and histories that document relations in the production of global poverty while simultaneously recognizing the potentially positive impact that the millennial generation, informed and critical, could have on global campaigns designed to end poverty. Although not explicitly oriented to IESL, Roy's approach to anti-poverty education addresses both the need for a rigorous critical investigation of the socioeconomic relations that produce sustain and make invisible the sources of poverty, and the development of relationships that resist and reform harmful practices.

Through a series of short videos produced by the #GlobalPOV Project, Roy and her team creatively engage students in a critique of the approaches to poverty alleviation that have failed to acknowledge or address the drivers of poverty. In the short film, "Can experts solve poverty?" Roy and Kalir, (#GlobalPov Project 2016), problematize the failures of poverty experts who frame social issues as isolated problems that have technical solutions. By isolating social issues, whether it is malaria, unemployment, or the environment, Roy and Kalir (2016) argue that poverty experts tend to describe problems as if they are natural phenomena. In this film, they theorize that the solutions they (poverty experts), propose tend not only to "ignore the political foundations that lie beneath the problems, but in fact they help prevent challenges to the status quo" (Roy and Kalir 2016).

Drawing attention to the historical legacies of colonialism and the interconnectedness between industrial, social and environmental development, the GlobalPov Project creatively illustrates how poverty experts have managed to evade the political complexities that sustain poverty. Roy and Kalir (2016) conclude, "by separating who can help from those who are subject to help, the poor. Experts see poverty as deficiencies of the poor. They have the problems. The other side of the equation is "we don't have the poverty, so we must have the solutions'" (#GlobalPov Project 2016). The silos of academic disciplines act as blinders to those experts who seek to address serious problems yet do not address the political structures that produce and maintain poverty.

Roy et al. (2016) recognize that the numbers of millennial youth who want to get engaged in global anti-poverty actions continues to grow exponentially. She argues that youth from this generation

are the ubiquitous presence in the global conscience that is marshalled to attend to each new global crisis, each new human disaster…new scripts for global citizenship and person hood are being negotiated at the site of such encounters…(She) argues that this new articulated and young global citizenry must be seen as a new type of poverty expert, one that is producing distinctive forms of poverty knowledge in the crucible of volunteerism, charity, aid advocacy and humanitarian engagement. (p. 5)

This analysis acknowledges a powerful role that youth are playing and will continue to play as producers of knowledge on and about global poverty, and seeks to direct their desire to effect change. By reframing the role of youth, not as passive participants in a neo-colonial project to spread western hegemonic values through IESL, Roy challenges educators to recognize the potential power embedded in IESL. It is simultaneously a critical interrogation of higher education practices and a call to subvert superficial notions of global citizenship that are self-serving, both for institutions seeking to benefit through the appeal of youth volunteering abroad, and students, whose inchoate desires to 'be the change' needs to be rigorously informed by the broader discourses of history, politics, economy and culture.

MOVING FORWARD: TOWARD PEDAGOGIES OF SURVIVANCE & RENEWAL

Critical research continues to raise concerns over claims to universal global citizenship, particularly in an age marked by growing discourses of fears of Others, particularly refugees, amid escalating racial tensions across North America and Europe. The reproduction of hierarchies of power and accentuation of difference through education is key to the critique of GCE and IESL. Global education practices which ignore very real ongoing power asymmetries and historical colonial legacies, "very often foreclose the complex historical cultural and political natures of the issues, identities and perspectives embedded in global/local process and events and in the production of knowledge about the self, the other and the world" (Andreotti and de Souza 2011). This chapter sought to outline active pedagogies and practices that acknowledge the criticisms of IESL and GCE education and seek to do education otherwise.

WORKS CITED

Andreotti, V. (2006). Soft versus critical global citizenship education. *Policy & Practice: A Development Education Review, 3*(3), 40–51.

Andreotti, V. (2016). The educational challenges of imaging the world differently. *Canadian Journal of Development Studies, 37*(1), 101–112.

Andreotti, V. D. O., & De Souza, L. M. T. (2011). *Postcolonial perspectives on global citizenship education*. Routledge: Routledge Research in Education.

Andreotti, V. O., & de Sousza, L. M. (2012). Towards global citizenship otherswise. In V. O. Andreotti & L. M. de Souza (Eds.), *Postcolonial perspectives on global citizenship education* (pp. 1–8). New York: Routledge.

Balibar, E. (2012). *Citizenship*. Malden, MA: Polity Press.

Beck, K. (2012). Globalization/s: Reproduction and resistance in the internationalization of higher education. *Canadian Journal of Education, 35*(3), 133–148.

Biccum, A. (2010). *Global citizenship and the legacy of empire*. London: Routledge.

Bringle, R. G., Hatcher, J. A., & Jones, S. G. (Eds.). (2012). *International service learning: Conceptual frameworks and research.* Stylus Publishing, LLC.

Cameron, J. (2014). Grounding experiential learning in "thick" conceptions of global citizenship. In R. Tiessen & R. Huish (Eds.), *Global learning or globetrotting? Perils and potential of international experiential learning* (pp. 21–42). Toronto, ON: University of Toronto Press.

Chouliaraki, L. (2013). *The Ironic spectator: Solidarity in the age of post-humanitarianism.* London, UK: Polity Press.

Fassin, D. (2010). Inequality of lives, hierarchies of humanity. In I. Feldman & M. Ticktin (Eds.), *The name of humanity: The Government of threat and care.* Durham, NC: Duke University Press.

Hartman, E., & Kiely, R. (2014). A critical global citizenship. In P. Green & M. Johnson (Eds.), *Crossing boundaries: Tension and transformation in international service-learning.* Sterling, VA: Stylus.

Hartman, E., Paris, C. M., & Blache-Cohen, B. (2014). Fair trade learning: Ethical standards for community-engaged international volunteer tourism. *Tourism and Hospitality Research, 14*(1–2), 108–116.

Heron, B. (2007). *Desire for development: Whiteness, gender, and the helping imperative.* Wilfrid Laurier University Press.

Jefferess, D. (2012). Unsettling cosmopolitanism: Global citizenship and the cultural politics of benevolence. In V. O. Andreotti & L. M. de Souza (Eds.), *Postcolonial perspectives on global citizenship education* (pp. 27–46). New York: Routledge.

Kiely, R. (2004). A chameleon with a complex: Searching for transformation in international service-learning. *Michigan Journal of Community Service Learning, 10*(2).

Langdon, J., & Agyeyomah, C. (2014). Critical hyper-reflexivity and challenging power: Pushing past the dichotomy of employability and global citizenship in development studies experiential learning contexts. In R. Tiesssen & R. Huish (Eds.), *Globetrotting or global learning? Perils and potential of international experiential learning.* Toronto, ON: University of Toronto Press.

Larkin, A. (2015). North-South partnerships in Canadian higher education. In L. Shultz, A. Abdi, & T. Pillay (Eds.), *Decolonizing global citizenship education* (pp. 141–155).

Lewin, R. (2009). The quest for global citizenship through study abroad. In R. Lewin (Ed.), *The handbook of practice and research in study abroad* (pp. xii–xxii). New York: Routledge.

Mahrouse, G. (2014). *Conflicted commitments: Race, privilege and power in transnational solidarity activism.* Montreal, CA: McGill-Queen's Press.

Pashby, K. (2011). Cultivating global citizens: Planting new seeds or pruning the perennials? Looking for the citizen-subject in global citizenship education theory. *Globalisation, Societies and Education, 9*(3–4), 427–442.

Pashby, K. (2012). Questions for global citizenship education in the context of the 'New Imperialism': For whom, by whom? In V. O. Andreotti & L. M. de Souza (Eds.), *Postcolonial perspectives on global citizenship education* (pp. 9–26). New York: Routledge.

Pashby, K. (2014). Discovering, recovering, and covering-up Canada: Tracing historical citizenship discourses in K-12 and adult immigrant citizenship education. *Canadian Journal of Education, 37*(2), 1.

Roy, A., & Kalir, K. (2016). *The #GlobalPOV project: "Can experts solve poverty?"* Retrieved on November 22, 2016 from https://www.youtube.com/watch?v=8jqEj8XUPlk.

Roy, A., Negrón-Gonzales, G., Opoku-Agyemang, K., & Talwalker, C. (2016). *Encountering poverty: Thinking and acting in an unequal world*. Berkeley, CA: University of California Press.

Simpson, K. (2004). Doing development: The gap year, volunteer-tourists and a popular practice of development. *Journal of International Development, 16*, 681–692.

Shultz, L. (2007). Educating for global citizenship: Conflicting agendas and understandings. *Alberta Journal of Educational Research, 53*(3), 248–258.

Shultz, L., & Jorgenson, S. (2012). Global Citizenship Education (GCE) in postsecondary institutions: What is protected and what is hidden under the umbrella of GCE? *Journal of Global Citizenship & Equity Education, 2*(1), 1–22.

Shultz, L., & Viczko, M. (2016). Global social justice, democracy and leadership of higher education: An introduction. In *Assembling and governing the higher education institution* (pp. 1–7). UK: Palgrave Macmillan.

Stein, S., & de Andreotti, V. O. (2016). Cash, competition, or charity: International students and the global imaginary. *Higher Education, 72*(2), 225–239.

Tiessen, R. (2012). Motivations for learn/volunteer abroad programs: Research with Canadian youth (Special Edition). *Journal of Global Citizenship & Equity Education, 2*(1), 1–21.

Tiessen, R., & Huish, R. (Eds.). (2014). *Globetrotting or global citizenship?: Perils and potential of international experiential learning*. Toronto, ON: University of Toronto Press.

Tuck, E. (2009). Suspending damage: A letter to communities. *Harvard Educational Review, 79*(3), 409–428.

UNESCO. (2016). *The ABCs of global citizenship education*. Retrieved on January 15 from https://en.unesco.org/system/files/abcs_of_gced.pdf.

UNHCR. (2016). *Global trends: Forced displacement in 2015*. Retrieved on November 1, 2016 from http://www.unhcr.org/statistics/unhcrstats/576408cd7/unhcr-global-trends-2015.html.

Vrasti, W. (2013). *Volunteer tourism in the global south: Giving back in neoliberal times*. New York: Routledge.

Author Biography

Allyson Larkin is an assistant professor in the Social Justice and Peace Studies Program at King's University College at Western University. She is currently involved in research that investigates the impact of higher education partnerships with community organizations in the Caribbean and Sub-Saharan Africa. Her work focuses on the ways in which power, knowledge and difference are negotiated across transnational boundaries through practices of international experiential/service learning, research partnerships and social activism.

CHAPTER 36

Study Abroad and Global Citizenship: Paradoxes and Possibilities

Graham Pike and Mackenzie Sillem

At first glance, a study abroad experience would seem an ideal pathway on the journey to becoming a global citizen. What better way to develop intercultural competence and a global mindset than to fully immerse oneself as a student in another country, with all the associated demands of having to live, work and play amidst cultural, educational and social systems that are different from one's own? For some students, study abroad can indeed be a 'life-changing' experience, a transformative journey that triggers a period of self-reflection and analysis thereby fomenting the development of skills and understanding necessary for global citizenship. For others, study abroad is far from transformational and can, at worst, lead to a reaffirmation of the superiority of one's own cultural viewpoints. In this chapter, we will examine some paradoxes of the study abroad experience and suggest some possible strategies for enhancing the likelihood of a pathway to global citizenship. In so doing, we acknowledge that the concept of global citizenship is complex and contested. To provide context for this chapter, we offer Byers' (2005, 9) definition:

> Global citizenship empowers individual human beings to participate in decisions concerning their lives, including the political, economic, social, cultural and environmental conditions in which they live. It includes the right to vote, to express opinions and associate with others, and to enjoy a decent and dignified quality of life. It is expressed through engagement in the various communities of which the individual is a part, at the local, national and global level. And

G. Pike (✉) · M. Sillem
Vancouver Island University, Nanaimo, Canada
e-mail: Graham.pike@viu.ca

it includes the right to challenge authority and existing power structures – to think, argue and act – with the intent of changing the world.

The term "study abroad" is generally understood around the world but is subject to a range of meanings and interpretations. For the purpose of this chapter, we are adopting the Canadian Bureau for International Education's definition:

Study Abroad: An umbrella term referring to any for-credit learning activity abroad including full degree, exchange and Letter of Permission programs as well as experiential or service learning abroad for credit (CBIE 2016).

Included in this definition would be internships, practicums, field schools and study tours of any length, as long as they are for credit, but not volunteer or work placements or independent travel experiences. Even within this definition the range of possible experiences is vast, in terms of factors such as duration, degree of challenge and potential outcomes, adding to the complexity of determining the relationship between study abroad and global citizenship. Discussion of these, and other, factors will form the basis of this chapter, with a principal focus on study abroad in higher education.

Implicit in this definition is the idea that students will study abroad for a relatively short time and transfer the credits gained back to their home institution, from where they will graduate; it does not refer to the increasing number of students worldwide who decide to leave their home country and pursue their education elsewhere. The former is principally a global North phenomenon, while the latter is largely a movement from the global South—an issue to which we will refer later in the chapter.

Journey Outwards, Journey Inwards

Support for the value of study abroad is growing among leaders in education, government, business, and commerce, not only for the perceived development of global citizens but, more practically, for the enhancement of a wide range of desired employability skills. In many countries, the message is being heard. A recent report (Gribble and Tran 2016) commissioned by Universities Australia claims that 16.5% of the 2015 graduating domestic undergraduate cohort have studied abroad, up from 12.3% in 2011. Among some European nations, study abroad rates are even higher, fueled by ERASMUS—the world's largest student mobility program, launched in 1987—and facilitated by the introduction of the Bologna Declaration in 1999. In Germany, 29% of all undergraduate students and 41% of all masters students had participated in a study abroad experience on completion of their degrees in 2013 and the government has set a target of 50% participation among university students by 2020 (Gribble and Tran 2016). In Canada where, by comparison, the number of study abroad participants remains low at about 3.1% of university students per year, the Canadian Bureau for International Education is garnering support from government and the private sector to implement the recommendation of the government's International Education Advisory Panel to provide 50,000 study abroad awards annually (McBride 2016).

Beyond the rhetoric and the numbers, questions abound regarding the true value of a study abroad experience, especially in terms of its relationship to global citizenship. In addition to the issues addressed in this chapter, other pertinent questions include:

- How does a student's motivation to study abroad, embedded in a complex web of personal, family and socioeconomic factors, impact their learning from the experience?
- What is the impact of study abroad marketing, often couched in terms of exotic adventures and 'doing good' in the world, on participants' attitudes, perceptions and eventual learning (Zemach-Bersin 2009)?
- What kind of preparatory learning is required to equip students with the ability to transform a fleeting emotional response to cultural difference into a more refined and reflective platform for intercultural understanding?
- What should be the key components of a study abroad experience in order to engage students' critical thinking skills and nurture a commitment towards responsible social action?
- How, in short, can we best ensure that the journey outwards, to a new nation, culture and landscape, becomes also a journey inwards, to a deeper understanding of self and one's relationship to the wider world (Pike and Selby 1988)?

Perhaps an even more critical question is whether study abroad is defensible, from a global citizenship perspective, if it is available only to an elite, and privileged, minority (Picard et al. 2009; Green et al. 2015). While governments and international education advocacy organizations continue to promote study abroad, many higher education institutions are turning their attention and resources to 'internationalization at home' on the grounds that the majority of students—even in the most optimistic study abroad growth scenarios—will probably not be able to enjoy a study abroad experience. Is study abroad a twenty-first century manifestation of the seventeenth century Grand Tour, undertaken by aristocratic Europeans to further their liberal education and reaffirm their position in society? We shall return to the issue of privilege later in the chapter.

Sense of Belonging

Global citizenship education is an ontological activity (Lilley et al. 2015), and study abroad experiences are unique in their potential as opportunities for students to define who they will become. Whether or not a student resists or embraces global citizenship will depend on their development readiness

(Jones 2008). During their sojourn, students may begin to question their identity and discover that they are unprepared to shift their social identification from their in-group (nationality, or home culture) to an outgroup (host culture or global community). At a memorable study abroad debrief one of our students responded to the question "What did you learn?" by replying: "I learned I do not belong here and I really only belong at home." (personal communication, May 17, 2001) Her statement demonstrates that rather than finding their place in the world, students can return from study abroad with a stronger sense of identification with their home culture (Savicki 2012).

The word 'belong' describes the affinity a person has for a specified location or environment. It implies a relationship with a place or, in the context of a study abroad experience, a cultural identity. Paradoxically, the challenge of fitting in with cultures different from those we were raised in can strengthen a sense of belonging to one's own culture(s) (Osland 2000). Through immersion in another culture, study abroad requires students to relate themselves to a group or a nation to which they do not belong (Allport 1954). This experience of marginality is a critical foundation for intercultural empathy. It is also necessary to develop the ability to construct an identity for oneself that is flexible enough to accommodate a pluralistic existence, a hallmark of a global citizen (Bennett 2012; Lilley 2014). However, if students do not understand their own cultural identity as part of the fabric of a global community prior to their study abroad experience, the challenge to become a member of what was previously an outgroup can confuse their development of self-identity. Rather than embrace their newly expanded vision of the world, students may conclude they do not belong and reject engagement beyond the cultural borders of "home."

A student's sense of marginality, more often described as culture shock or cultural transition, is constructive in the sense that the student is actually experiencing the dissonance created by exposure to other ways of existing in the world. As students move through their experience abroad and reach out to develop relationships with cultural others, those relationships can act as a mirror, reflecting back an image of oneself in addition to an image of how one is seen by others (Killick 2012). This reflection can also reveal cultural differences previously unseen or deemed insignificant. However, if students are unable to grasp more than a shallow understanding of cultural differences, the cultural commonalities that allow students to see themselves in the other may be obscured. Overwhelmed by their perception of the threat that differences pose to their identity, the cultural immersion of a study abroad experience can lead students to develop a more polarized view of the world (Hammer et al. 2003).

A study abroad experience allows for the development of a more ethnorelative (Bennett 2012) mindset which can lead students to struggle to find an authentic cultural home in a global community (Coryell et al. 2014). Students who have previously had a monocultural socialization and then experience alternative ways of knowing and being (Hammer et al. 2003) through study abroad may develop a more sophisticated view of the world that brings about the need to make choices, potentially changing their cultural identity. In the ongoing process of becoming, students have to decide which values, ideas and behaviors of their home culture need to be challenged and which elements of their host culture they would be well served to adopt (Osland 2000).

Those who identify strongly with a nation may wonder how they can maintain their allegiance to their national community (Davies and Pike 2009) in light of an expanded view of the world and a newly formed relationship with another or multiple nations. To acknowledge that other ways of knowing and being in the world have validity can threaten a sense of nationalism. Students coming to a study abroad experience steeped in messaging about the superiority of their own culture may not be motivated to give up their allegiance to a nation that they believe to be the best. For study abroad to be a transformative experience, students must first be motivated to move beyond their comfort zones and step outside established communities in order to experience disequilibrium and develop synergy with their new environment (Kolb 2015). For study abroad to provide global citizenship education, students' efforts to cultivate relationships with a global community need to be both supported and legitimized (Killick 2012).

MANAGING RISK, CONTROLLING LEARNING

In a world in which threats to personal safety and security have become increasingly unpredictable, it is not surprising that educational institutions are devoting more attention to risk management and mitigation in their study abroad programs. While the concern for personal well-being is of paramount importance, the impact of risk management strategies on students' learning needs to be explored if the potential of study abroad for global citizenship education is to be fully understood. Learning theories, within and beyond the student mobility literature, suggest that more profound personal learning happens when the learner is in intellectually or emotionally challenging situations, where she finds herself outside her comfort zone (Killick 2012; Lilley et al. 2015). Study abroad has significant potential for giving rise to a vast array of challenging situations, from the mild to the severe, simply due to the fact that participants are living and working daily outside their comfort zone. To some extent, the degree of challenge will be mitigated by participants themselves, depending on their preparedness to take personal risks in the choices they make in any situation: the student who ventures off alone to explore an unknown city neighborhood will expose herself to potentially greater challenges than her peers who stick together as a group in the city center. However, the degree of challenge will also be established through key decisions made by administrators and organizers in the home institution, including such factors as the location and duration of the study abroad experience as well as the level of preparedness of participants, the degree to which they are supervised and the sophistication of emergency plans.

Study abroad research reports consistently show that students from OECD countries have a strong preference for study abroad destinations in similarly developed countries (Macready and Tucker 2011). There are many reasons for such choices, including the similarity of academic programs and ease of credit transfer, fewer communication challenges (especially the likelihood of one's own language or English being understood), familiarity with the logistics and services available in the country (e.g., travel systems, standards of accommodation, leisure opportunities), and perceived levels of safety and security. Such choices generally limit the degree of emotional and intellectual dislocation that participants are likely to experience. The field school or field study experience, in which groups of students are led on study tours by their professors, add further layers of comfort through creating a group of like-minded traveling companions to whom one can retreat when the sense of dislocation becomes too severe. Duration is another key factor: despite research to indicate that short-term experiences can be as effective in achieving certain goals, such as intercultural development and personal growth, as semester- or year-long study abroad experiences (Chieffo and Griffiths 2009), the full impacts of culture shock are more likely to be felt during a longer period abroad when the comforting thought of returning home remains in the distant future.

If deep learning requires a feeling of disequilibrium (Killick 2012), the paradox would seem to be that a stronger focus on personal safety, security, and support will limit the personal insights to be gained from addressing the mental destabilization that helps us to reshape our understanding of the world. As Barnett (2004) suggests, as we encounter more descriptions of the world, often in conflict with the stereotypes we hold, we become less certain about our prior interpretations and begin to see our vision of the world as fragile and always contestable. Such uncertainty is a precursor to the intellectual adjustment that needs to take place in the emotional transition from national to global citizenship, the shifting of allegiance and identity from a single country focus to a framework that views that country and all its values in a broader context.

It is generally accepted that the purpose of higher education is to promote deeper learning, including analytical and critical thinking. Students are encouraged to experiment with ideas, to take risks and develop more sophisticated insights into self and society. Study abroad would certainly be considered by most to contribute to that purpose. However, the increasing focus on risk management, alongside the growing trend in higher education toward the development of measurable learning outcomes (Barnett 2004), would seem to limit the learning potential of study abroad experiences. Profound learning often comes from the unplanned encounter, the multisensory onslaught for which no pre-departure briefing can adequately prepare.

Such encounters cannot be predicted, but their likelihood can be enhanced or diminished through the decisions taken in planning and implementing the study abroad experience. Of course personal safety has to be a primary consideration and sound planning and preparation are vital in order to mitigate the risks; however, the study abroad experience that incorporates higher levels of personal comfort and security, perhaps in order to attract greater participation, is less likely to achieve the depth of learning, or the sense of social responsibility, that the global citizen requires.

This paradox generates some awkward decisions for study abroad administrators. While it would be irresponsible for any educational institution to condone a study abroad program that knowingly places participants at risk of personal harm, a primary focus on risk management can severely limit participants' learning potential. Gorski (2008) argues that few administrators are likely to make choices that will leave themselves and their institutions vulnerable but, in choosing the more secure options, they fail in their duty as intercultural educators to challenge existing norms and dominant power structures. The fact that study abroad mobility patterns show a majority of students moving from North to North (Macready and Tucker 2011) is disappointing; the likely impact of an increased focus on risk management reinforcing this trend is troubling for the development of future global citizens.

REPRODUCING PRIVILEGE

In societies where the dominant educational paradigm is to graduate students to compete in the global marketplace and where travel is seen as a leisure activity or as an opportunity to enhance their employability profile, study abroad may be catering to students as global consumers rather than developing them as global citizens (Lewin 2009; Lilley 2014). From the perspective of global citizenship, we are obligated to explore the question of how study abroad programs engage students in critical thinking and nurture a commitment toward responsible social action, ultimately contributing to a more just global community. Unfortunately, students' sense of superiority of one culture over another may not be challenged and study abroad curricula are often silent on issues of systemic discrimination against non-Western ways of knowing and being. Despite the fact that a majority of study abroad participants come from white, privileged backgrounds (Green et al. 2015), students often do not expect to analyze, nor are they asked to become more aware of and understand, the implications of their own power and privilege through their study abroad experience. The focus on increasing study abroad participation rates in developed countries may, in fact, lead to a sense of justification, and a reproduction, of existing patterns of power and privilege in the global community (Gorski 2008).

Study abroad is built upon the premise that the "other" exists primarily outside of the boundaries of one's own country. As previously discussed, one of the strengths of study abroad is that it provides students exceptional opportunities to "become" themselves. However, those who come from more powerful and privileged backgrounds tend to be in control of the rules for engagement in a cross-cultural interaction, which may require already disenfranchised participants to render themselves even more vulnerable. While engaging in cross-cultural dialogue seems to be a logical and beneficial activity during a study abroad program, the opportunity for learning from that dialogue is often not equal (Gorski 2008). Research indicates that participation in cross-cultural interactions can result, in the short term, to changes in attitudes (Dessel et al. 2006); however, absent from this scholarship is evidence that cross-cultural dialogue contributes to, or even mitigates, systemic inequities (Gorski 2008). In some cases, it may be that study abroad perpetuates a discourse where only less-developed nations are home to poverty or social injustice and a belief that these things could not be experienced in one's home country (Jorgenson 2014). This lays the foundation for the neo-colonial belief that study abroad students are somehow helping developing countries to make progress. Thus, the dogma about the superiority of developed country ideologies and values systems endures, unchallenged.

A prevailing belief among well-meaning attempts to increase study abroad participation rates in developed countries is that the key impediment to involvement in higher education student mobility is a lack of adequate financial resources. This would seem a reasonable assumption, given the evidence to indicate that study abroad participants come disproportionately from privileged backgrounds. Indeed, a national survey of Canadian higher education students found that 70% of respondents who had not participated in study abroad listed a lack of funding as a barrier (Academica Forum 2016). However, the survey data revealed that concerns about study abroad costs did not vary considerably between low and high household income groups. Other research suggests that the profile of a 'typical' study abroad participant is a white female from a middle to upper-middle-class home background (Picard et al. 2009; Green et al. 2015). The disproportionately low representation of minority students in study abroad stems, arguably, from the mix of personal and social resources that participants already have packed in their bags as they begin their journeys. Financial security is certainly among these resources, but so too are parental support, international travel experience, personal confidence and resilience, and a belief—though not always well-informed—in the intrinsic value of engaging in an experiential encounter with the "other". Such resources, as a whole package, are more likely to be found among students from privileged backgrounds than among the more disadvantaged, suggesting that increasing funding for study abroad is just one of several initiatives that need to be undertaken in order to ensure equitable access. A report on the US State Department's Gilman International Scholarship program, which awards study abroad funding for traditionally underserved undergraduate students, indicates that targeted programs for such minority groups can have a significant long-term impact on participants' intercultural understanding and career aspirations (Association of American Colleges and Universities 2016). While increasing participation in study abroad would seem to be a worthy goal, it appears that a more nuanced and strategic vision is required if the impact of larger numbers of mobile students is to avoid the pitfalls of reproducing existing power dynamics and further advantaging the already privileged.

Possibilities—Reconciling Paradoxes

Despite the challenges and paradoxes highlighted in this chapter, study abroad professionals, motivated by their responsibility to prepare students for a globalized world, have continued efforts to understand and experiment with program design that activates global citizenship development. Educators may not agree on the exact recipe, but there is consensus that program design must be integrated and that students need to be prepared and supported (Lilley 2014; Vande Berg et al. 2012). While more research is required on why some interventions are more or less effective than others, the following paragraphs highlight promising practices that may allow paradoxes around belonging, risk, and privilege to be reconciled in order for study abroad to be a more effective vehicle for global citizenship education.

Integrated Experiences

Passareli and Kolb (2012) suggest that student learning would be better served if a study abroad experience were considered but one part of a process of global citizenship education rather than being the sole or key means to that end. Immersed and supported in a teaching and learning environment where global citizenship values are embedded throughout their university experience, students are encouraged to think beyond personal experiences, fostering the development of a more than superficial understanding of global values, beliefs and meanings (Tarrant 2010). Scaffolding on this internationalized experience at home, study abroad can be better integrated into the curriculum so that students have the opportunity to apply the learning they have acquired through both coursework and experiential activities (Loberg and Rust 2014).

Theoretical Grounding

As a critical element of international education scholarship and practice, study abroad programs should be underpinned by relevant theories (Deardorff 2016). Often a study abroad program is designed with an itinerary or course content as the predominant consideration. However, adult learning, intercultural competence development, and global citizenship education theories can strengthen program design. Grounding a study abroad program in developmental theories can allow for more personalized learning through acknowledging discrete and measurable levels of learning progress (Bennett 2012; Stuart 2012) and provide structure for the development of personal learning goals in an experiential setting (Kolb 2015; Passareli and Kolb 2012). Students not only have the opportunity to learn at a deeper level and increase their knowledge, they also have the opportunity to apply their learning and practice skill development (Deardorff 2016).

A key area for further research relates to the use of theories from non-Western epistemologies that can be used to provide a solid foundation for study abroad programs. Non-western theoretical foundations not only can expose blind spots in Western ways of knowing and being, they can also broaden the possibilities for the interpretation of concepts to the advantage of study abroad students (Deardorff 2016).

RELATIONSHIPS WITH ROLE MODELS

In her comparison of the expatriate experience to a fabled "hero's journey," Joyce Osland (2000) describes the critical role of "magical friends" (guides, teachers, country nationals or fellow expats). These role models provide moral support and guidance to expatriates through relationships that involve sharing of questions and information. While different from expatriates, study abroad students likewise need supportive and motivational relationships. As mentors to students for whom the goal is the development of global citizens, educators in these roles must be motivated by social and ethical values (Lilley 2014). Also required are skills in creating a safe space within which to challenge students to consider and imagine alternate paradigms and perspectives. Continuous professional development is needed for educators to be as prepared and effective as possible in facilitating the process of global citizenship learning (Vande Berg, et al. 2012).

Not all "magical friends" of study abroad participants will be educational institution employees. In his study of outbound students, Killick (2012) notes the importance of a "significant other" in several students' experiences. While the relationships students formed with these "significant others" could not be predicted, they were critical in enabling students to be able to see-themselves-in-the-world.

REFLECTIVE PRACTICE

Increasingly, educators are integrating reflective practice into study abroad programs (Biagi et al. 2012; Vande Berg et al. 2012). Students have been shown to learn and develop more as a result of a sojourn when they have been prepared to be more self-reflective and are provided consistent opportunities for reflection (Vande Berg et al. 2012). To make meaning of their experiences study abroad students need opportunities to explore and question their preconceptions and to revisit experiences in light of additional context and knowledge (Kolb 2015; Bennet 2012). Whether reflective practice needs to be primarily formal (e.g. reflective writing, structured debriefs) or a mix of formal and informal (e.g. blogs and serendipitous conversations) will depend on the program structure and educational context, as will the timing of reflection opportunities. How we process, and what we learn from past experiences determines how future choices and decisions are made (Kolb 2015). Therefore, reflective practice during study abroad can provide critical starting points that direct students toward future global citizenship learning opportunities.

Provide Global Citizenship and Intercultural Competence Language and Concepts

In the fields of both global citizenship education and intercultural competence development, there is a call for educators to provide students with language and concepts, a schema or lens, they can use to make meaning of their study abroad experience (Bennet 2012; Lilley 2014). This schema provides the hooks on which learners can hang their study abroad experiences and interpret them at increasing levels of complexity (Passareli and Kolb 2012). Learning outcomes often use explicit language about (for example) intercultural awareness or global citizenship, yet students are often not provided a definition of such terms, nor the context within which the definitions were created. Similarly, students are left to organize the perception of their experiences informed only by the schemata of their own culture or one haphazardly created through previous experience (Bennett 2012). Students need to receive explicit information before, during and after their study abroad experience that allows them to develop an understanding of terminology and key concepts for intended learning outcomes to have a greater probability of leading to the transformative learning they describe.

Acknowledging Power and Privilege at Play in the Study Abroad Experience

If a goal of study abroad is to play a part in developing a global citizen who is inspired to engage in responsible social action, then programs must involve opportunities for students to critically analyze power and privilege in the context of their experience. To achieve this, educators and administrators who provide support to students need to be socially and ethically motivated and articulate (Lilley 2014) and must be aware of their own power and privilege (Gorski 2008). How students are prepared to conceptualize the other needs to be considered. For example, are students expecting to make the world a better place through showing the other supposedly "better" ways of doing something? Or are they expecting to learn from the relationships they develop with cultural others? In addition to how the other is presented and perceived, Gorski (2008) advocates for facilitating an anti- hegemonic discourse and helping students develop critical thinking skills by analyzing global systems that perpetuate the dominance of Western values and beliefs.

ASSESSMENT

Assessment of global citizenship learning can be overwhelming and is fraught with challenges (Deardorff 2009). Driven by a general trend toward assessment in higher education and specific needs to improve programming, to link study abroad activities to intended learning outcomes, and to promote student-centered learning through reflective feedback, administrators and educators are beginning to integrate purposeful assessment into study abroad (Vande Berg et al. 2012).

To begin the assessment process, there needs to be clarity on the purpose of the assessment and confidence in the appropriateness of the learning outcomes. The goals of the assessment and how it will be used/shared will also provide direction as to what kind of assessment techniques to employ. While the reliability of various assessment methods is not always agreed upon, research suggests that using multiple methods, including both quantitative and qualitative assessment, is the most effective (Deardorff 2009). An increasingly common practice is the use of psychometric tools with pre- and post-test timing to measure student development of particular mindsets or competencies.[1] Additional forms of assessment used in study abroad include reflection papers, journaling, capstone projects, portfolios, focus groups, interviews (in person and via Skype), and documentation of discussions and observations of student behavior (Deardorff 2009).

Integrating assessment into study abroad requires time and resources, both in the planning and implementation as well as in analyzing and sharing the data collected. Putting such effort into developing and sharing effective assessment is critical to improving study abroad programs and to documenting their role in developing global citizens (Deardorff 2009).

NOTES

1. A list of instruments is in Paige, M. (2004) Instrumentation in intercultural training. In D. Landis, J.M. Bennett, and M.J. Bennett. (Eds.) *Handbook of Intercultural Training.* CA: Sage.

REFERENCES

Academica Forum. (2016). *Why don't more Canadian students study abroad?* Retrieved from: http://forum.academica.ca/forum/why-dont-more-canadian-students-study-abroad.

Allport, G. W. (1954). *The nature of prejudice*. Mass: Addison-Wesley. Association of American Colleges & Universities (2016). Facts & figures—International experiences have lasting impact on traditionally underserved students. *AAC&U News*, June/July. Retrieved from: https://www.aacu.org/aacu-news/newsletter/facts-figures-international-experiences-have-lasting-impact-traditionally.

Barnett, R. (2004). Learning for an unknown future. *Higher Education Research & Development, 23*(3), 247–260.

Bennett, M. (2012). Paradigmatic assumptions and a developmental approach to intercultural learning. In M. Vande Berg, R. M. Paige, & K. H. Lou (Eds.), *Student learning abroad: What our students are learning, what they're not, and what we can do about it* (pp. 90–114). Sterling, VA: Stylus.

Biagi, F., Bracci, L., Filippone, A., & Nash, E. J. (2012). Instilling reflective intercultural competence in education abroad experiences in Italy: The FICCS approach + reflective education. *Italica, 89*(1), 21–33.

Byers, M. (2005). Are you a 'Global Citizen'? *The Tyee*. Retrieved from: https://thetyee.ca/Views/2005/10/05/globalcitizen/.

CBIE. (2016). *Canada's education abroad lexicon*. Retrieved from: http://cbie.ca/media/policy-statements/canadas-education-abroad-lexicon/.

Chieffo, L., & Griffiths, L. (2009). Here to stay: Increasing acceptance of short-term study abroad programs. In R. Lewin (Ed.), *The handbook of practice and research in study abroad higher education and the quest for global citizenship* (pp. 365–380). N.Y: Routledge.

Coryell, J. E., Spencer, B. J., & Sehin, O. (2014). Cosmopolitan adult education and global citizenship: Perceptions from a european itinerant graduate professional study abroad program. *Adult Education Quarterly, 64*(2), 145–164.

Davies, I., & Pike, G. (2009). Global citizenship education: Challenges and possibilities. In R. Lewin (Ed.), *The handbook of practice and research in study abroad higher education and the quest for global citizenship* (pp. 61–78). N.Y: Routledge.

Deardorff, D. K. (2009). Understanding the challenges of assessing global citizenship. In R. Lewin (Ed.), *The handbook of practice and research in study abroad higher education and the quest for global citizenship* (pp. 346–364). N.Y: Routledge.

Deardorf, D. K. (2016). Key theoretical frameworks guiding the scholar-practitioner. In B. Streitweiser & A. Ogden (Eds.), *International education, in international education's scholar-practitioners bridging research and practice* (pp. 241–261). Oxford: Symposium.

Dessel, A., Rogge, M., & Garlington, S. (2006). Using intergroup dialogue to promote social justice and change. *Social Work, 51*(4), 303–315.

Green, W., Gannaway, D., Sheppard, K., & Jamarani, M. (2015). What's in their baggage? The cultural and social capital of Australian students preparing to study abroad. *Higher Education Research & Development, 34*(3), 513–526.

Gorski, P. C. (2008). Good intentions are not enough: A decolonizing intercultural education. *Intercultural Education, 19*(6), 515–525.

Gribble, C., & Tran, L. (2016). *International trends in learning abroad*. International Education Association of Australia.

Hammer, M. R., Bennett, M. J., & Wiseman, R. (2003). Measuring intercultural sensitivity: The intercultural development inventory. *International Journal of Intercultural Relations, 27*(4), 421–443.

Jones, S. (2008). Student resistance to cross-cultural engagement. In S. R. Harper (Ed.), *Creating inclusive campus environments for cross-cultural learning and student engagement* (pp. 67–86). USA: NSPA.

Jorgenson, S. R. (2014). *(De)Colonizing global citizenship: A case study of north american study abroad programs in Ghana* (Unpublished Doctoral Thesis). Retrieved from: https://era.library.ualberta.ca/files/gm80hw49z/JorgensonShelane_Spring%202014. pdf.

Killick, D. (2012). Seeing-ourselves-in-the-world: Developing global citizenship through international mobility and campus community. *Journal of Studies in International Education, 16*(4), 372–389.

Kolb, D. (2015). *Experiential learning: Experience as the source of learning and development.* Retrieved from: http://ptgmedia.pearsoncmg.com/images/9780133892406/samplepages/9780133892406.pdf.

Lewin, R. (2009). The quest for global citizenship through study abroad. In Lewin, R. (Ed) *The handbook of practice and research in study abroad higher education and the quest for global citizenship* (pp. xiii–xxii). NY: Routledge.

Lilley, K. (2014). *Education global citizens: Translating the idea into university organisational practice.* International Education Association of Australia, Discussion Paper 3.

Lilley, K., Barker, M., & Harris, N. (2015). Exploring the process of global citizen learning and the student mind-set. *Journal of Studies in International Education, 19*(3), 225–245.

Loberg, L., & Rust, Val D. (2014). Key factors of participation in study abroad: Perspectives of study abroad professionals. In B. Stretwieser (Ed.), *Internationalisation of higher education and global mobility* (pp. 301–311). Oxford: Symposium.

Macready, C., & Tucker, C. (2011). *Who goes where and why? An overview and analysis of global educational mobility.* New York: The Institute of International Education.

McBride, K. (2016). The state of internationalization in Canadian higher education. *International Higher Education, 86*, 8–9.

Osland, J. S. (2000). The journey inward: Expatriate hero tales and paradoxes. *Human Resource Management, 39*(2–3), 227–238.

Passareli, A., & Kolb, D. (2012). Using experiential learning theory to promote student learning and development in programs of education abroad. In Vande Berg, et al. (Eds.), *Student learning abroad: What our students are learning, what they're not, and what we can do about it* (pp. 137–161). Sterling, VA: Stylus.

Picard, E., Bernadino, F., & Ehigiator, K. (2009). Global citizenship for all: Low minority student participation in study abroad—seeking strategies for success. In R. Lewin (Ed.), *The handbook of practice and research in study abroad higher education and the quest for global citizenship* (pp. 321–345). N.Y: Routledge.

Pike, G., & Selby, D. (1988). *Global teacher, global learner.* London: Hodder and Stoughton.

Savicki, V. (2012). The psychology of student learning abroad. In Vande Berg et al. (Eds.), *Student learning abroad: What our students are learning, what they're not, and what we can do about it* (pp. 215–237). Sterling, VA: Stylus.

Stuart, D. (2012). Taking stage development theory seriously implications for study abroad. In Vande Berg et al. (Eds.), *Student learning abroad: What our students are learning, what they're not, and what we can do about it* (pp. 61–89). Sterling, VA: Stylus.

Tarrant, M. A. (2010). A conceptual framework for exploring the role of studies abroad in nurturing global citizenship. *Journal of Studies in International Education, 14*(5), 433–451.

Vande Berg, M., Paige, R. M., & Lou, K. H. (2012). Student learning abroad paradigms and assumptions. In Vande Berg, M., et.al. (Eds.) *Student learning abroad: What our students are learning, what they're not, and what we can do about it.* Sterling (pp. 3–28). Sterling, VA: Stylus.

Zemach-Bersin, T. (2009). Selling the world: Study abroad marketing and the privatization of global citizenship. In R. Lewin (Ed.), *The handbook of practice and research in study abroad higher education and the quest for global citizenship* (pp. 303–320). N.Y: Routledge.

AUTHORS' BIOGRAPHY

Graham Pike is Dean of International Education at Vancouver Island University (VIU). Previously, as Dean of Education at the University of Prince Edward Island, he launched an international practicum program for pre-service teachers. He has also held positions at the University of Toronto and the University of York (UK). He has published widely in global education and has consulted on curriculum development and school improvement projects around the world.

Mackenzie Sillem is the Coordinator for International Student Retention in the Faculty of International Education at Vancouver Island University (VIU), on the traditional territory of the Coast Salish. In her current position she is working to promote and facilitate intercultural learning to support change towards a more inclusive and accepting community.

CHAPTER 37

Activism as/in/for Global Citizenship: Putting Un-Learning to Work Towards Educating the Future

Stephanie Curley, Jeong-eun Rhee, Binaya Subedi
and Sharon Subreenduth

INTRODUCTION

The editors' charge to connect global citizenship education and the theme of activism—as a key issue in learning and teaching about and for global citizenship—presents us with an imperative to theorize how we act and become global rather than just learning about it. Thus, we explore activism as/in/for global citizenship theoretically, historically, and in practice. However, as education can be overly practice-based and under-theorized, we do not offer a curriculum guide, "what works", or a "to do" list of best practices (Daza 2013b). In our view, there is no magical formula for educating the future—no one,

S. Curley (✉)
Manchester Metropolitan University, Manchester, UK
e-mail: S.curley@mmu.ac.uk

J. Rhee
College of Education Information & Technology, New York, NY, USA
e-mail: jeong-eun.rhee@liu.edu

B. Subedi
The Ohio State University, Columbus, OH, USA
e-mail: Subedi.1@osu.edu

S. Subreenduth
Bowling Green State University, Bowling Green, OH, USA
e-mail: ssubree@bgsu.edu

© The Author(s) 2018   589
I. Davies et al. (eds.), *The Palgrave Handbook of Global Citizenship and Education*, https://doi.org/10.1057/978-1-137-59733-5_37

simple or best way of teaching and learning activism and global citizenship education because contexts, histories, and socio-political dynamics complicate them both (Maira 2009; Verma 2010). Instead, we focus on the long-term project of 'decolonising the mind' (wa Thiong'o 1986) towards more complex, nuanced and critical global citizenships (Subedi and Daza 2008).

To become an educated human, including an educator, one necessarily learns hierarchical violences that disconnect the world and self from the so-called Other. Therefore, to think more relationally and outside of regimes of truth requires a radically different way of knowing, that does not simply follow our usual habits of thinking (Foucault 1980; Spivak 2012). Therefore, we argue that un-learning is an important *activism* for educating a future global imaginary—for inculcating authentic global-thinking citizens. Un-learning is activism because it implies educators' bringing the un-learning into educational practice, and it further implies the 'self-transformation' of the educator, the students and the field and actions of education. We argue that activism as/in/for global citizenship asks educators and students to be unlearners—because to interrogate their location within the global power structure and requires radically different ways of thinking about self, world, other.

What Does It Mean to Un-Learn to Think Differently?

As we write this chapter in 2016, "Black Lives Matter" (BLM)[1] banners and die-in demonstrations block major motorways and access to airports across the USA and the UK. Arguably, BLM has grown into a trans/national movement (McKenzie 2016), and serves as a visible, albeit North/West example, of *activism as/for/in global citizenship education*. BLM, and our use of it as an example here marks how what might be considered global is simultaneously limited by localities, as well as English-language—and USA—centrism.[2]

Additionally, our use of BLM shows how *activism, global, education*, and *citizenship* are entangled and complicated by sense-making that emerges from who and where we are and can be. Because we are always inside our own sense-making, it is difficult to see how we make sense of the world. We argue that un-learning can help us see our habitual ways of thinking and thus how thinking, habitualized through power-laden frameworks, goes on to shape our relationships with people and the world. In contrast to un-learning, the concepts of *activism, global, and citizenship* are used widely in societal and educational (policy) practices, often in neutral, apolitical and ahistorical ways that erases, both intentionally and unintentionally, the traces of power relations from which they emerge (de Oliveira Andreotti and de Souza 2012). As we have written elsewhere, salient models of nation-building and democracy (Daza 2013c), global education curriculum (Subedi 2013) and social justice (Subreenduth 2013a, b) may be well-intentioned but ultimately undermined by the habitualized thinking that undergirds them (Spivak 2012).

Unfortunately, many salient forms of thinking are inherently hierarchical and insidiously laden with a humanism that actually de-humanizes us (discussed in the next section). And too often, narratives on citizenship privilege human lives and discount the violence against ecology and non-human subjects, as well as forget the interdependent relationship between social and ecological justice (Martusewicz, Edmundson and Lupinacci 2015).

For example, one's entry point may make it easier to recognise BLM as *activism* than as *education* and *citizenship*, but BLM educates and illustrates different citizenships and learned frames of references. In a "Herstory" (not *his*tory) of BLM, Alicia Garza explains why Black freedom is world freedom:

> When we are able to end hyper-criminalization and sexualization of Black people and end the poverty, control, and surveillance of Black people, every single person in this world has a better shot at getting and staying free. When Black people get free, everybody gets free... (http://www.thefeministwire.com/2014/10/blacklivesmatter-2/)

Under the learned ideology of white supremacy, making sense of the BLM logic, which puts Black people at the center, not at the margin, requires un-learning white-black hierarchy (Daza 2009, 2013d; Merryfield and Subedi 2001) and ways in which the world has been divided (Willinsky 1998). Because of this lack of un-learning we see that a dominant response has been "all lives matter" (May 2016).

What we can learn from the plethora of articles and blogs trying to interpret, explain and analyze the hashtag "all lives matter" in response to BLM is that the distinction is not simply linguistic[3] but deeply onto-epistemological and difficult to address across and beyond the varying frames of belief (e.g., learned regimes of truth) that shape our thinking and being. In our view, ontology and epistemology cannot be separated (Daza and Gershon 2015); while space disallows a full discussion, onto-epistemology in a nutshell is how our sense of sense is generated: how we come to know/understand what world/beings/objects/selfs are, or what we think they are through our specific being/existence. This shows the immense challenge of translating across onto-epistemologies boundaries and the unlearning required to recognise multiple worlds (Spivak 2012). To understand the meaning of both thinking and being at the same time is to keep in tension simultaneously multiple ways of being and imagining/knowing the world, and relationships to it and within it—as in our example above of BLM, where alternate world views animate two phrases "black lives matter" and "all lives matter." The chapter brings forth these issues of onto-epistemological differences as we theorize global citizenship education through activism.

Although in our view we can never fully grasp all the frameworks within which we live and work, efforts to make our learning visible are not in vain (Kumashiro 2015). To be able to learn, un-learn, and re-learn is to notice, even if only sometimes and partially, how thinking, being, and imagining is being learned, both somatically/physically and socially. Keeping with Gregory Bateson (b. 1904–d. 1980), we learn to learn; so, thinking, being and acting is not neutral, ahistorical, linear, or simply natural—but learned. In this same way, we cannot simply, linearly, or completely un-learn who we are, where and when we live, or how we think. Nevertheless, to notice these onto-epistemological dilemmas is education. When we can notice that there is no non-complicitous subject position, then we can better notice our interdependent relationships (e.g., why Black lives must matter for all lives to matter) and thus understand the limits and possibilities of global—this is *activism*.

Global citizen/ships are not outside of learned ways of being in (and dividing) the world (Willinsky 1998). In particular, it is a challenge to think citizenships outside of "nation"—Spivak (2012) refers to this as "nation-think". And we must remember that nation-states privilege certain identities/markers of citizenship (Banks 2004). Thus, our move is to engage with the current debates on citizenship in transnational (and unavoidably international) contexts and foreground how we un-learn to become global-national-local with tensions, privileges, and contradictions. To do this, we begin by outlining some of the assumptions that inform global citizenship education, such as humanism and nation-think. We also explain what we mean by "activism as/in/for global citizenship", reflected in our chapter's title. Then, our section on learning and teaching offers three frameworks that shape what activism looks like and the meaning or purpose of global citizenship. Each framework offers a different engagement with curricula material, concepts, and pedagogy.

Education as Becoming Human

Education may have many guises and it may play out differently in different geographies, but often formal education in the global North/West (USA, UK and Europe), and elsewhere via (neo)colonialism and globalization, is rooted in humanism, produced by Enlightenment/colonial ideas. Consequently, the production of the knowing/knowable subject (i.e., an educated subject) has a strong relationship with "becoming human"—developing, transmitting, training, and educating what is/can be cognitive, social, political, moral/ethical, physical/biological, and so on. This "becoming human" project, or the project of civilization, has served as the epistemological foundation of European coloniality: racism, capitalism, heteropatriarchy, etc. Therefore, while education is often touted as "the great equalizer", we ask readers to remember that it has served as a tool of both liberation and oppression (Subreenduth 2013a). Now, in the regime of a global capitalist economy, which some call "new imperialism" (Rhee 2009; Tikly 2004), nation-states educate citizens for the global market; becoming human means being consumers (Black 2010). The importance of these old and new histories cannot be overstated in global citizenship education, as we underline how the analytical category of citizenship is not natural/neutral. Global citizenship education, akin with other attempts to educate differently (See Daza 2013a; Merryfield and Subedi 2001), is complicit with nation-think and the imperial legacy of becoming human.

Thus, we take up Spivak's charge: "we must learn to do violence to the epistemological difference and remember that this is what education 'is'" (2012, p. 10). Our task here is to displace such underpinnings and re-imagine what it means to be a human citizen subject (before Enlightenment dictated humanism). We are very concerned with noticing and un-learning deeply embedded and largely elusive transcendentalized frameworks, such as nation-think, as a means towards activism. Spivak (2012) argues that nation-think always already worlds spaces, bodies, and imaginaries. In the continuing yet new process of (post)colonial[4] worlding (Spivak 1985; Willinsky 1998; Coloma 2013), through the establishments of the Bretton Woods Agreements, the United Nations, and General Agreement of Tariffs and Trade (Read these examples not only as institutional, but also at the level of episteme.), we have learned to divide the world. For recent examples, Scotland is already its own nation with its own citizens but yet Scotland's referendum to become a separate nation-state from the UK failed, while the UK's referendum to withdraw from the European Union succeeded. The irony of these examples show the epistemic depth of nation-think in practice and that the nation is still prominent in understanding global citizenship and activisms.

For postcolonial nation-states, nation-think has been a way towards decolonizing and claiming their independence (e.g., Bandung Conference). However, as Tuhiwai Smith (1999) argues, in the context of Maori Indigenous knowledge, the very concept of "global citizenship" can easily recolonize those who are marginalized in society, such as Indigenous people who often are not included in conversations about "global". Likewise, refugee subjects, often seen as non-citizens of the world (or as stateless), are not part of the conversation on citizenship or global citizenship. Thus, we, as people and educators, often make sense of global citizenship education through nation-think. Rather, we argue for de-transcendentalizing "nation" and working through the politics on who and how we speak about global citizenship. Otherwise "global" risks being a new name for old (colonial, imperial, national) violences.

However, to de-transcendentalize modern notions of "citizen" and "nation" through which we have to think can prove impossible. Yet, being able to notice the limits helps us imagine different ways to think global and citizen, as you can't imagine what you already know (Spivak 2012). Also, foregrounding complicity moves towards un-learning habitual thinking, doing, and dividing (Daza 2012). In the face of the imperial legacy of becoming human, our central query is: How can we mobilize global citizenship to promote decolonization? For us, activism as/in/for global citizenship education is about engaging in anti-oppressive practices that can create a more equitable world (Kumashiro 2015). As demonstrated in BLM, when Black Lives Matter, all lives can matter, because being as free as we can be is through interconnection, not individualism (see also Relativist section). Heeding to the historical understanding of how education has always been part of nation-state building projects, we invite readers in diverse geographies to work with questions: when educational institutions include global citizenship education, how does it work and what does it look like vis-a-vis its nation-state building project? How can activism be a new imagination for (making) global citizens? What are the limitations and dangers of activism as/for global citizens? What are other ways we can think of activism as/in/for learning? And in doing so, what possibilities emerge for making different global citizens differently? Rather than try to get away from complicity and contradictions, we embrace a more complicated sense of *activism*, *global citizenship*, and *education*.

Why 'as/in/for'

Most discussions in the public domain assume there is one, best/right/real truth to be told, but when relationships and meanings are "on the move"—fluid, multiple, contested—then activism and global citizenship education may imply, as well as mobilize, different educations: different learning, teaching, curricula, and assessment for different purposes. In this way, "global citizens" themselves and the processes of engaging with global citizenship, including in/formal education, *are* activism—actors shaping an interdependent society, whether within or beyond formal/State structures governing citizenship.

Activism *within* global citizenship and education often focuses on specific issues, such as immigration, aid, equity and access, climate change, literacy, BLM in itself and so on, that are transnational. In this way, people and groups in different geographies are not simply showing solidarity with, and support for, the issues of others, but the issue itself is transnational. In this case, structural racism does disproportionate violence to Black Lives. Although minoritized, people of colour are the majority of the world's population. The UK BLM movement is NOT about the USA but about State sponsored violence against Black lives that has deep roots in colonial white supremacy and anti-black racism. Social movements that desire to be heard in the global context can be seen as an exercise to claim citizenship rights that have been violated, whether historically or presently. They are often organized around how the everyday citizenship rights are being suppressed by people or organizations in power, as well as by epistemic regimes of power (e.g., white supremacy, heteronormativity, androcentrism, anthropocentrism, etc. (Martusewicz, Edmundson and Lupinacci 2015). Like the call to de-transcendentalize nation-think, identity politics offer both limits and possibilities. Consider how BLM's explicit support of Palestinian sovereignty can be seen as a way to ally with struggles of people of colour globally, especially against States that use language, religion, white supremacy and other markers to suppress citizenship rights. (Un)Learning (about) oppression within and beyond nation-states can be useful sites to engage with different meanings and impossibilities of global citizenships, as well as how to become a critical ally, rather than a so-called liberator or white saviour, in global contexts across the planet (Rhee 2009, 2013; Subedi 2013).

Finally, activism *for* global citizenship might best be understood as a double desire for people to be both more planetarity and more worldly. According to Spivak (2012, p. xiv), global citizenship presents a double-bind between 'the uselessness of human life (planetarity) and the push to be useful (worldliness)':

> If we imagine ourselves as planetary accidents rather than global agents, planetary creatures rather than global entities, alterity remains underived from us, it is not our dialectical negation, it contains us as much as it flings us away—and thus to think of it is already to transgress, for, in spite of our forays into what we metaphorize, differently, as outer and inner space, what is above and beyond our own reach is not continuous with us as it is not, indeed, specifically discontinuous. (p. 339)

In other words, "to re-imagine the subject as planetary accident" (p. 339) interrupts "globalization [a]s achieved by the imposition of the same system of exchange everywhere," as well as us/them (self/Other) binaries (p. 335). In the planetary–global bind, the Other and self contain and repel each other equally, which provides a different onto-epistemological engagement (Thinking with our previous onto-epistemological example; "All Lives Matter" is imposed as origin/al in response to BLM). In contrast, often what/who is imagined as Other in our habitual thinking is positioned as derived from the self and in a deficit-bind with what/who is imagined as the original source. In this way, the Other is falsely disconnected from the self as the self is positioned as superior, more advanced, civilized (human), normal, and/or the animator and standard-bearer. The following section addresses how educators can put unlearning to work vis-à-vis activism as/in/for global citizenship in education.

THREE FRAMEWORKS THAT SHAPE WHAT ACTIVISM LOOKS LIKE AND THE MEANING AND PURPOSE OF GLOBAL CITIZENSHIP IN TEACHING, LEARNING, AND ASSESSMENT

In this section, we present three major ways that activism as/in/for global citizenship is approached in classrooms (Subedi 2013; Subreenduth 2013a). It is important to emphasize that the first two dominant frameworks are discussed through our critiques as they rarely involve unlearning. The third framework offers our possibility for activism through global citizenship education. We utilize Marjane Satrapi's (2003) graphic novel *Persepolis* as an example of how we can do un-learning by providing different ways of inquiry into a curricular text, which may offer opportunities of un-learning habitualized thinking. While thinking with theoretical frameworks has limits, including the pretense of seeming more complete, distinct, and straightforward than they actually are, we believe providing analytical frames of inquiry through which to engage curricula material, concepts, and pedagogy can help educators and students notice how and what we learn.

Deficit Model

As discussed at the end of the last section, otherness (alterity) is precisely when an Other is imagined as derived from a source (e.g., the self as origin/al, superior, standard-bearer) and consequently is subordinate, deviant, isolated, and disconnected. The deficit model rests on these taken-for-granted assumptions about so-positioned original sources of animation against which anything else is positioned as deficient. The Other becomes a problem to be fixed and the solution is to be more like its source. However, like a vicious circle, the Other can never be the source within this overriding deficit framework. Unlearning deficit-thinking is to think the Other is already whole, complete and connected.

Under the deficit model, activism is not focused on unlearning frameworks or changing systems and societal structures. Rather, it is myopically focused on helping, liberating, civilizing/humanizing, or saving deficient Others (cultures, groups, individuals). For example, rather than examining how a problem in a particular local setting interconnects with structural issues or with other communities and societies, a deficit approach treats each problem as if it is contained and often self-inflicted. Then, the deficient, undeveloped or underdeveloped, uncivilized, and/or undemocratic Other (individual, nation-state, etc.) is viewed as the root cause for the problem. Under a linear model of development and a modern discourse of progress, this deficit approach sees "whiteness" and North/Western, English-speaking, and capitalist/industrial-ized societies as more progressive and democratic. Consequently, the global majority is positioned as less civilized (Subedi 2013). Under a deficit framework, the solution is to be more like the so-positioned originals, in this case North/West societies, and to take up Euro-American (colonial/imperial) notions of becoming human. For example "universal human rights" are part and parcel of the Enlightenment project: rights, human, individual, and constitutional are differently operating, and interweaved with local–national–international–global histories and politics that deny and grant humanity, rights, land, and status such as citizen (Spivak 2012).

Because people and groups endowed with full humanity as agency (can) act on problems (Martusewicz, Edmundson and Lupinacci 2015; Subreenduth 2013a, b), under the deficit model, the activist struggle is to gain human, individual, and civil rights to protect the Other, rather than questioning how these concepts exclude vast peoples in the first place. It may include the desire to save the Other or make the Other a (lesser) version of the self: a thinking that is deeply implicated in colonial racial discourse, civilizing missions, etc. When activism is approached as a rescue, charity, service, aid, or development project, Freire (1970/2000) has warned that "one cannot expect positive results from an educational or political action program which fails to respect the particular view of the world held by the people. Such a program constitutes cultural invasion, good intentions notwithstanding" (p. 95).

We return to BLM for another example of how the deficit model works. As justifications for police killing black people or State violence against Black people, one of the dominant counter arguments against BLM includes high black-on-black crime rates and Black people's non-compliant attitudes and behaviors toward law enforcement. This deficit approach works by trying to make State violence against Black people their own fault and by consequently implying that it is something Black people can fix themselves, if they change themselves, which is sometimes referred to among people of colour as "acting white." However, a deeper analysis can reveal how inherently biased societal institutions disproportionately target and impact Black people because they are Black; e.g., US Department of Justice report (2015) on the Ferguson Police Department shows racial bias and revenue generation were integral to institutions.

The deficit model is well entrenched. Most of us must actively and continuously un-learn deficit-thinking. In this way, un-learning is pedagogical and activism. In teaching and learning, we can start by imagining Others as complete and not problems to be fixed. We can notice issues are rarely isolated but rather local-national-global all at once. We can notice deficit-thinking in ourselves and the world by examining current and historical events and asking who/what is Othered/centered. We can refuse binaries and static categories. We can engage in broader structural analyses that do not blame victims and survivors for their own oppression. We might better question how humanism mobilizes benevolence and other activisms based on deficit-thinking about humans and localities.

Relativist–Pluralist–Neoliberal Multiculturalist Model

In attempts to move away from a deficit model, the relativist, pluralist, or neoliberal multiculturalist approach emphasizes understanding the existence of different solutions, perspectives, and approaches to a problem. It seeks to include as diverse perspectives as possible in the process of inquiring an issue, soliciting ideas and solutions, and making decisions about how to bring changes. However, this approach misses how our habit of thinking, in which we do not examine our own habit of thinking (Spivak 2012), contributes to ever-increasing inequality.

A simple move for inclusion and plurality, which appears to be a new (and thus better) thinking, has become a new habit of thinking (and neoliberalism thrives on proliferation). Yet, this valorization for diversity that pretends to redress the existing unequal structures of differences such as race, gender, and nation-state cunningly masks how it supports and rationalizes neoliberal (or new imperial) violence (see below and Rhee 2013, for theorizing neoliberal multiculturalism). The binary between self and Other is often indeterminate, economic, political, and cultural; inequality and discrimination continue. By assuming "we are all the same" or "we are all different but the same," Western orientation toward universal human rights (Subedi 2013, p. 630) and individualism based in humanism is reinscribed. Through this inclusive model—fixated with an individual/private self as a choice maker with free wills—certain members of our planet are systematically excluded and become disposable. We lose the ability to account for historical and structural matrices that allow the existence of such a self who is responsible only for one's self. Individual freedom of choice, disguised as a tool for achieving global equity, is in fact a neoliberal concept that plays a pivotal role in managing difference through subjectification, humanization, and dehumanization (Subreenduth 2013a).

Under this framework, global citizenship becomes a "neoliberal racial project" (Rhee 2013); individuals and/or national citizens, as markers and extensions of nation-states—being able to compete and consume (the Other) in the global market. Often, becoming global is to consume or exploit in order to benefit the individual self (and this happens at different levels of self, i.e., individuals, institutions, and States). Un-learning this framework is crucial for educators like us, who work in institutions that promote global citizenship education, sometimes as a way to learn how to compete and exploit rather than be more planetary and interconnected.

For example, when Western liberal discourse problematically equates African female genital mutilation with female cosmetic surgeries in Western (industrialized) societies and then both of these phenomena are framed simply as individual choices, this logic presents neoliberal individualism (Sensoy and Marshall 2010). When consuming/appropriating/eating the Other's culture and traditions including spiritualities is considered as activism for self-salvation from capitalism's malaise (e.g., the popularity and Westernisation of yoga), it perpetuates neocolonial individualism (Rhee and Subedi 2014). Neoliberal individualism is epitomized when an elite from any cultural/ethnic group marketises one's cultural identity to claim a Self that automatically generates the Other, e.g., "Tiger Mother" (Rhee 2013) or erase/denies historically and structurally institutionalized conditions of life to claim "we are (all different but) all the same" [e.g., Prince Ea's (2017) music video and Ko and Ko's critique (2017)]. What binds the above examples is that they reinforce a habit of thinking through which we learn to think that individuals can make different choices and triumph anything and everything (history, institutionalized power differences, materiality, policies, international politics, military violences, climate change, etc.). This puts individuals as primarily responsible for our condition of life but inevitably sustains hierarchical, deficit-thinking. Due to space limitations, we refer readers to the above references that work to un-learn neoliberal/multiculturalist thinking rather than delineating those critiques here. Below, we take up Marjane Satrapi's (2003) *Persepolis* to present a decolonising approach for activism as/in/for global citizenship education.

Decolonising Pedagogy

A decolonising framework queries how histories shape the present articulations of (global) citizenship. It also provides anti-essential perspectives on how we have come to understand concepts such as culture, nation, and citizenship through how the Other has been written in dominant imagination (Subedi 2013). By sharing the value of contrapuntal reading (Said 1993), educators can help students unlearn the complex relationship between local and global and how politics shape the articulations of global citizenship.

As a way to discuss this approach, we use Marjane Satrapi's (2003) *Persepolis*[5] to explore the complex meanings of national and global citizenships as analytical categories. Written as a memoir of growing up in Iran, the author as narrator is a 13-year-old girl who shows how the political events and the socialization of children in schools/society cannot be separated from broader historical events that are integral parts of colonial and neocolonial formation. Educators/students may notice how they, too, cannot be separated from historical formation. By touching upon national and international citizenship politics and power differences, sex/gender, and religion, the text can enable readers to see the realm of international in contrapuntal ways and un-learn how one is situated in local–national–global citizenship narratives. In this way, the memoir offers a way to examine how global citizenship is a contradictory identity/category: it is both inclusionary and exclusionary and has the potential to critique nationalistic and oppressive ways of conceptualizing citizenship ideals.

Persepolis is a text that can enable students to think through how one is situated in the broader colonial and neocolonial history and contemporary white politics on racism and Islamophobia. A postcolonial (un-learning) pedagogical approach is not simply about understanding a text but using the text to understand one's own self, world, and Other, as habitualized through nation-think, race/identity politics, etc. This is a project of deep un-learning. As Satrapi explores how she is situated and shaped, educators/students can explore their own habitualization. When used as a decolonizing pedagogy, *Persepolis* enables students to do the following:

1. Engage the inter/national realm of activisms, politics, cultures, educations, and citizenships, and particularly explore how the concept of "local" in a given place is complexly intertwined with the national and global;

2. Un-learn how one has learned global, especially about other societies, and particularly about Iran, a nation-state that has been consistently demonized in US textbooks and media;

3. Notice how complex citizenship narratives are and particularly how this story about growing up in Iran disrupts stereotypes of culture and religion;

4. Explore complicity through the characters, particularly regarding socioeconomics, gender, religion and State/political oppression and violence;

5. Study ourselves and critique our own learning and positionality in the world and particularly notice our complicities, whether or not intentional, in local/global oppressions.

Below we outline a decolonising (un-learning) pedagogical approach using *Persepolis*. What we highlight here is that readers may engage the text in different ways, while the text itself may NOT do the work of unlearning (*activism*) unless educators and learners interrogate their own self-other-world relationships, assumptions, sense making, and participation in the realms of activism as/in/for global citizenship. Thus, while we offer how *Persepolis* as sample material can be used for decolonising and un-learning, we do not suggest prescribed curricula or offer any specific lesson plans or other prescriptive methods of teaching. Rather, questions are posed as a potential means for un-learning to take place. In our view, activism cannot be prescribed. As we discuss in the BLM example at the beginning of the chapter, one's entry point may make it easier to recognise BLM as *activism* than as *education* and *citizenship*, but BLM educates and illustrates different citizenships and learned frames of references. Similarly, one's entry point may make it easier to recognise *Persepolis* as education (and global citizenship education, in particular). However, as we posit herein, a decolonising approach to unlearning offers the means of activism, precisely because we cannot fully untangle activism as/in/for global citizenship education. Once we approach the concepts as if they have their own territory—metaphorically—we risk falling into our habitual thinking. Below, we try to show how the concept of global citizenship (education) has more critical pedagogical usefulness when it is theorized as an act of engaging how one is implicated in inter/national history and contemporary political formations (e.g., globalization, Islamophobia, etc.) and as a practice of a complex identity that enables the self to critique how, and what, one has learned what s/he knows and who s/he becomes (Table 37.1).

Table 37.1 Teaching and learning pedagogy/possibilities

The text can offer analytical inquiries into the following:	*Teaching and learning pedagogy/possibilities*
How citizenship narratives are influenced by both colonial and neo-colonial discourses	Citizenship politics in Iran are addressed, particularly the rule of fundamentalist governments in the 1980s; how authoritarian regimes deploy State sanctioned surveillance mechanisms; the use military and police to suppress dissents; and how various political propaganda discipline people and daily life. Satrapi frames the suppression of rights in relation to broader struggles to critique Arab, European (particularly British) and US economic and political interventions in Iraq. The text enables readers to recognise how internationals in Iran focus on Iranian resources (oil) to enrich international corporations and international governments. Educators might ask: What are the histories and politics of one's own self/citizenship? What does international mean in different localities?
The relationship between gender and citizenship	The text serves as a critique of citizenship that is shaped by patriarchal values. Satrapi examines questions of gender by noting how over centuries men have yielded power by engaging in various wars. Aligned with war narratives (described later), she examines how men in power "play" the politics of the State to discipline people on ways to perform citizenship. Women are used by the State to discipline other women on citizenship, e.g., during the Khomeini era, women teachers mandated girls to wear a headscarf as a way to show allegiance to the State; serving the patriarchal State, women tell other women how to be patriotic and how not to protest the State. Yet, notably, gender is not a monolithic category in the text. Women of various social and political beliefs negotiate different forms of citizenship and contest the politics of the State differently. Educators can ask: What are markers of citizenship and patriotism from one's own experience? How do these markers discipline women and men? How are citizenships gendered/sexed?
The relationship between religion and citizenship	The text shows how State politics and religious dogmatism shape socialisation and schooling. It demonstrates how family lives are regulated, and how State sponsored political activities encourage fundamentalism. Educators and students can explore how their socialisation, schooling, and family life are influenced. The text also examines ways in which people question and resist State sponsored religious citizenship practices. Students can examine in their own localities ways in which religion, whether openly or sublimely, enters State and school cultures; and how (quasi-governmental) organizations may attempt to influence school policies or practices that support their agenda. Students may recognise and critique how marginalized religious backgrounds are silenced; e.g., often in US and Western contexts, what counts as "authentic" religion is conflated with brands of Christianity, whereas Islam or Hinduism is racialized (Rizvi 2004). The text generates discussion on Islamophobia; educators could extend via comparisons with anti-Semitism, etc.

(continued)

Table 37.1   (continued)

The text can offer analytical inquiries into the following:	Teaching and learning pedagogy/possibilities
Critical consciousness and the value of questioning people in power	Satrapi questions social norms, especially taboos that impose restrictions on what can/not be said or done. Educators using the text can help students understand how Satrapi does/ not conform to socialization and dominant habits of thinking inculcated by schools. The text offers examples of how labels (communist, hijab, etc.) are used as markers of who/ what is il/legitimate; students can un-learn by questioning what marks "real" citizenship, and one as "stranger" and "foreigner" (Ahmed 2000) in different localities. The text asks students to constantly interrogate how one is asked to be loyal citizen and raises questions over the value of questioning or resisting practices that are imposed in society. Questioning power, the text also examines how torture is a way to control/ discipline subversive subjects to State mandates. Educators can ask how torture has been justified by their own State and its implication to how (national) citizenship discourses are mobilized within the rhetoric of "protecting" the nation-state (US war-on-terror, etc.). The text also critiques war and ways in which wars are waged in the name of protecting economic and political interests. *Persepolis* asks who supported the regime of Saddam Hussein and then invaded Iraq? By examining who supports and invades, educators/students can examine the degree and consequences of different complicities, as well as critique the concept of "ally". Satrapi notes the impact of Iraq and Iran wars and how people coped with being at war. Educators can ask how war impacts different peoples/ places differently, e.g., as death of people and infrastructure, im/migration, military service, economic gains/losses, etc.
Relationship between privilege and citizenship	Educators can explore how individuals and families from different circumstances (socioeconomic, etc.) encounter or perform citizenship differently. Because of her middle class family privilege, Satrapi and her family have access to mobility (passport, travel to Europe, etc.), economic resources (work, car, apartment, etc.) and the ability to change schools and study abroad. Contrariwise, Mehri, a maid/nanny, has lived with Satrapi's family since Mehri was eight years old (p. 34). Mehri, is not formally educated in school and does not learn to read and write. Mehri's character is a reminder of different citizenships and that global citizenship is not accessible for many, e.g., women who are poor, not formally educated, and who sacrifice living with their own families in order to make a living in cities. Educators might ask how citizenship is classed?

CONCLUSION AND FUTURE RESEARCH

No lives matter, until black lives matter...when black lives matter, then all lives matter....

When we can begin to imagine the Other as not from the self (e.g., 'them' as not from 'us') is to begin to un-learn agency and activism underpinned by the becoming human project that can reinforce us/them and deficit-thinking about the Other. However, planetary subjectivity is not to become one whole or be the same as, neither is it to be separated and disconnected (i.e., the impossibility of non-complicity is not homogenization or the reduction of difference) nor is it neoliberal individualism. Activism as an inherent part of educating for, and unlearning as an inherent part of activism for global citizenship, is to rethink agency, activism, and education regarding who can act, how and what it means. Global citizenship in such (post)Enlightenment ruins is necessarily within nation-think but must also transgress it—to interrogate the taken-for-granted and critically engage with global histories, politics, structures.

Activism in this chapter presents (un/re)learning as transgressive. Thus, this chapter emphasizes if (and how) we might engage people in learning to learn doubly—being, thinking, and acting both planetary and worldly. Part of this work is helping educators and young people notice how we are always already local, national, and global. When we notice the relationship among our local selves/lives, the planet, and the local-national-global, then we have the chance to learn doubly or otherwise. This chapter suggests how we might learn and teach this "peculiar mind-set" (Spivak 2012, p. 339) by approaching global citizenship education as/in/for activism and vice versa by approaching activism as/in/for global citizenship education.

NOTES

1. In 2012, the hashtag "#BlackLivesMatter" was created in response to the acquittal of George Zimmerman, the man who killed Trayvon Martin, a Black teenager, in the US. BLM has continued to grow through social media as a response to racist policing and violences against Black lives (see blacklivesmatter. com). It also has entered formal political dialogue on the national stage, inciting the US presidential race, for example (Rosier et al. 2016).
2. We might discuss "bring back our girls" in Nigeria (http://www.bringbackourgirls. ng/), the Arab Spring (see Jamshidi 2013), or other trans/national projects on which we publish (See Daza 2006, 2007, 2013a; Rhee 2009, 2013; Subedi 2013; Subreenduth 2013a, b).
3. Yet, we can see at surface-level how concepts are elusive and shaped. Pearce's (2015) article "Why the term 'Black Lives Matter' can be so confusing" states: "the words could be serving as a political rallying cry or referring to the activist organization. Or it could be the fuzzily applied label used to describe a wide range of protests and conversations focused on racial inequality" (n.p.). According to BLMs Wikipedia entry "The phrase 'Black Lives Matter' can refer to a

Twitter hashtag, a slogan, a social movement, or a loose confederation of affiliated groups and organizations that advocate for multiple causes related to racial injustice" (BLM, n.d.).

4. Read the postcolonial as not after the colonial era but as "a reminder of continuously changing, adapting, persistent colonial and neocolonial structures and relations that have chained all of us (Rhee and Subedi 2014).

5. Providing alternative access to the curricular material, in 2007, Marjane Satrapi and Vincent Paronnaud directed a film based on the graphic novel.

REFERENCES

Ahmed, S. (2000). *Strange encounters: Embodied others in post-coloniality*. London: Psychology Press.

Banks, J. A. (Ed.). (2004). *Diversity and citizenship education: Global perspectives*. San Francisco: Jossey-Bass.

Black, C. (2010). *Schooling the world (2010): The white man's last burden*. Lost People Films.

BLM. (n.d.). In Wikipedia. Retrieved August 22, 2016, from https://en.wikipedia.org/wiki/Black_Lives_Matter.

Coloma, R. S. (2013). Empire: An analytical category for educational research. *Educational Theory, 63*(6), 639–658.

Daza, S. L. (2006). Local responses to globalizing trends: Student-produced materials at a Colombian public university. *International Journal of Qualitative Studies in Education, 19*(5), 553–571.

Daza, S. L. (2007). Student activism (Latin American). In G. L. Anderson & K. G. Herr (Eds.), *Encyclopedia of activism and social justice* (pp. 1347–1349). Thousand Oaks, CA: Sage.

Daza, S. L. (2009). The Non-innocence of recognition: subjects and agency in education. In R. S. Coloma (Ed.), *The postcolonial challenge in education* (pp. 326–343). New York: Peter Lang.

Daza, S. L. (2012). Complicity as infiltration: The im/possibilities of research with/in NSF engineering grants in the age of neoliberal scientism. *Qualitative Inquiry, 18*(8), 773–786.

Daza, S. L. (2013a). Reading texts, subtexts, and contexts: Effects of (post)colonial legacies in/on curricular texts in different contexts. Special issue. *Qualitative Research in Education, 2*(3), 206.

Daza, S. L. (2013b). Putting Spivakian theorizing to work: Decolonizing neoliberal scientism in education. *Educational Theory, 63*(6), 601–619.

Daza, S. L. (2013c). Storytelling as methodology: Colombia's social studies textbooks after La Constitución de 1991 *Qualitative. Research in Education, 2*(3), 242–276. doi:10.4471/qre.2013.28.

Daza, S. L. (2013d). A promiscuous (feminist) look at grant-science: How colliding imaginaries shape the practice of NSF policy. *International Journal of Qualitative Studies in Education, 26*(5), 580–598.

Daza, S. L. & Gershon, W. (2015; 20th Anniversary Issue). Senses beyond the Eye/I: Sound, silence and sonification as inquiry. *Qualitative Inquiry*. doi:10.1177/1077800414566692.

de Oliveira Andreotti, V., & de Souza, L. M. T. (Eds.). (2012). *Postcolonial perspectives on global citizenship education*. New York: Routledge.

Foucault, M. (1980). *Power/knowledge: Selected interviews and other writings 1972–1977*. New York: Pantheon Books.

Freire, P. (1970/2000). *Pedagogy of the oppressed*. New York: Continuum.

Jamshidi, M. (2013). *The future of the Arab spring: Civic entrepreneurship in politics, art, and technology startups*. Oxford: Elsevier.

Ko, A., & Ko, S. (2017, January 29). Reasons why the "I am not a label" video makes no sense. Retrieved from http://www.4synapses.com/education/i-am-not-a-label-labels-were-made-up-to-divide-us/.

Kumashiro, K. (2015). *Teaching and learning Toward Social Justice*. New York: Routledge.

Maira, S. (2009). *Missing: Youth, citizenship and empire after 9/11*. Durham, NC: Duke University Press.

Martusewicz, R. A., Edmundson, J., & Lupinacci, J. (2015). *Ecojustice education: Toward diverse, democratic, and sustainable communities*. New York: Routledge.

May, S. (July 13, 2016). #AllLivesMatter hashtag is racist, critics say. USA TODAY. Retrieved from http://www.usatoday.com/story/news/nation-now/2016/07/13/why-saying-all-lives-matter-opposite-black-lives-matter/87025190/.

McKenzie, S. (5 August 2016). Black lives matter block London's Heathrow Airport. *CNN*. Retrieved from http://edition.cnn.com/2016/08/05/europe/black-lives-matter-uk-heathrow-shutdown/.

Merryfield, M. M., & Subedi, B. (2001). Decolonizing the mind for world-centered global education. *The social studies curriculum: Purposes, problems, and possibilities*, (pp. 277–290).

Pearce, M. (October 20, 2015). "Why the term 'Black Lives Matter' can be so confusing". *Los Angeles Times*. Retrieved July 13, 2016 from http://www.latimes.com/nation/la-na-black-lives-matter-explainer-20151020-story.html.

Prince E. (2017, Jan 29). I am Not Black, You are NOT White. [video file] Retrieved from https://www.youtube.com/watch?v=q0qD2K2RWkc.

Rhee, J. (2013). The neoliberal racial project, governmentality, and the Tiger mother. *Educational Theory, 63*(6), 561–580.

Rhee, J. (2009). International education, new imperialism, and technologies of self: Branding the globally educated self. *Multicultural Education Review, 1*(1), 55–81.

Rhee, J., & Subedi, B. (2014). Colonizing and decolonizing project of re/covering spirituality. *Educational Studies, 50*, 340–357.

Rizvi, F. (2004). Debating globalization and education after September 11. *Comparative Education, 40*(2), 157–171.

Rosier, S., Aubert, E., Aull, C. Coyle, K. Eirich, K. Haas, J., & Hilton, S. (2016). 2016 presidential candidates on the Black Lives Matter movement. *Ballotpedia*. Retrieved from https://ballotpedia.org/2016_presidential_candidates_on_the_Black_Lives_Matter_movement.

Said, E. (1993). *Culture and imperialism*. Cambridge, MA: Harvard University Press.

Satrapi, M. (2003). *Persepolis*. New York: Pantheon.

Sensoy, Ö., & Marshall, E. (2010). Missionary girl power: Saving the third world one girl at a time. *Gender and Education, 22*(3), 295–311.

Spivak, G. (2012). *An aesthetic education in the era of globalization*. Cambridge, MA: Harvard University Press.

Spivak, G. (1985). Three women's texts and a critique of imperialism. *Critical Inquiry: Race, writing, and difference, 12*(1), 243–261.

Subedi, B. (2013). Decolonizing the curriculum for global perspectives. *Education Theory, 63*, 621–638. doi:10.1111/edth.12045.

Subedi, S. & Daza, S. L. (Eds). (2008). *Postcolonial Perspectives on Education: A Special Issue. Race Ethnicity and Education*, 11(1).

Subreenduth, S. (2013a). Theorizing social justice ambiguities in an era of neoliberalism: The case of post-apartheid South Africa. *Educational Theory, 63*, 581–600.

Subreenduth, S. (2013b). Insidious colonialism in post-apartheid education: Interplay of black teacher narratives, educational policy, and textbook analysis. *Qualitative Research in Education, 2*(3), 213–241.

Tikly, L. (2004). Education and the new imperialism. *Comparative education, 40*(2), 173–198.

Tuhiwai Smith, L. (1999). *Decolonizing methodologies: Research and indigenous peoples.* London; New York: Zed Books; University of Otago Press; Distributed in the USA exclusively by St Martin's Press.

United States Department of Justice (USDOJ) Civil Rights Division. (2015). Investigation of the Ferguson Police Department. Retrieved from https://www.justice.gov/sites/default/files/opa/press-releases/attachments/2015/03/04/ferguson_police_department_report.pdf.

Verma, R. (Ed.). (2010). *Be the change: Teacher, activist, global citizen.* NY: Peter Lang Publishing.

wa Thiong'o, Ngũgĩ. (1986). *Decolonizing the mind.* London: James Currey.

Willinsky, J. (1998). *Learning to divide the world: Education at empire's end.* Minneapolis: University of Minnesota Press.

AUTHORS' BIOGRAPHY

Stephanie (Daza) Curley is re-searcher of interdependence and social-somatic processes of learning to learn. Her research falls across four areas: (1) Local Responses to Global Policy Practice Trends in Education and Society; (2) Social Science Research Methodology; (3) STEM Culture and Philosophies; and (4) Difference. Steph is editor of *Educational Studies*, the official journal of the American Education Studies Association and Research Fellow in the Education and Social Research Institute at Manchester Metropolitan University, where she also directs the Masters in Research.

Jeong-eun Rhee is a professor of education at Long Island University, New York. Her scholarship focuses on anti-oppressive education through the lens of race, class, gender, immigration and other socially constructed differences; qualitative research methodology; and international education, empire, and politics of knowledge. Her commitment has been to opening up a space for the unsayable, silenced, and marginalized in the production of knowledge to delineate historical, material, and spiritual interdependence.

Binaya Subedi teaches classes on diversity and equity, global education, race, poverty and immigration at the Ohio State University. He has published articles in a number of journals and is editor of the journal *Educational Studies*. Professor Subedi has conducted community work in Nepal and in urban areas of the Midwest. His current research examines the identities and experiences of refugee/immigrant youth in mid-western U.S. cities.

Sharon Subreenduth's research and scholarship locate the historical and contemporary context of curriculum production and practice and interconnect local and global knowledge, responsibility and accountability, while addressing issues of cultural identity, power, race, gender, class, and colonialism and imperialism.

CHAPTER 38

Global Citizenship Education—Assessing the Unassessable?

Alicia Prowse and Rachel Forsyth

INTRODUCTION

In this chapter, we explore the role of formal assessment of curriculum activity in GCE, with a focus on Higher Education (HE), although much of the discussion could also be applied with some modification to other educational levels and types of institution. In particular, we focus on summative assessment (resulting in the award of grades), and the questions raised by what some may see as its intrusion into education for GC. Should Global Citizenship (GC) itself be assessed? How might we assess it? How might we mitigate the effects of power relationships in designing assessment for GC?

As a working definition of GCE, we use the one provided by UNESCO:

> Global Citizenship Education ... is a framing paradigm which encapsulates how education can develop the knowledge, skills, values and attitudes learners need for securing a world which is more just, peaceful, tolerant, inclusive, secure and sustainable (UNESCO 2014, p. 9)

Critiques of global citizenship education, while not the focus of this chapter, have often centred on the emphasis some conceptions of GC place on an *individual's* attributes. Biesta and Lawy (2006), for example, have highlighted the dangers of decontextualizing the individual and spoken of the

A. Prowse (✉) · R. Forsyth
Manchester Metropolitan University, Manchester, UK
e-mail: a.prowse@mmu.ac.uk

R. Forsyth
e-mail: r.m.forsyth@mmu.ac.uk

I. Davies et al. (eds.), *The Palgrave Handbook of Global Citizenship and Education*, https://doi.org/10.1057/978-1-137-59733-5_38

need to shift from 'teaching citizenship to learning democracy' and of this learning to be something that is done in society, not just by educators (Biesta and Lawy 2006, p. 65).

The UNESCO definition suggests that an education for GC is more about re-focusing the purpose to which education is put, rather than simply another "item" to be included. Thus, assessment for GCE might be more concerned with the intentions of the curriculum than with the measurement of the performance of the emergent global citizens.

In this chapter, we take the position that some assessment of GC in education *is* desirable, as discussed by Jerome (2008). If this is accepted, then there is a practical need for students to be able to demonstrate that they have indeed developed knowledge, skills, values and attitudes, and to be able to articulate their achievements.

Students may re-examine and change their values as a result of education but a GC-focussed curriculum would concentrate on encouraging students' willingness to consider that values other than their own exist and have validity, as this a core feature of GCE. This is, of course, a value in itself and exposes the extent to which a curriculum reflects the values of those involved in its design. The values of an institution, discipline, or a teacher are more or less explicit in the design of a curriculum, and may be modelled rather than taught, but are nonetheless inescapable.

At the level of assessment design within the modules of an HE curriculum, it is important that GC is foregrounded in order to ensure its place. It is also important to acknowledge the differences in having a system of graduate outcomes that relates strongly to 'employability' but is potentially disempowering, as opposed to developing the attribute of global citizenship with the agency that this implies. This difference is an important pre-requisite for developing assessments in relation to GCE.

In terms of activities to support GC in tertiary education, there have been moves towards inclusion of such curriculum items as study abroad programmes, language learning, volunteering, engagement with theoretical aspects, and reflective engagement (Stearns 2009). These kinds of curriculum items may tend to become standalone instances of where GCE is "done", whether or not they are formally assessed. If the aim is to focus on the overall intention of the curriculum, and a wider integration of GCE, this separation itself may still be seen as problematic.

The challenge is to find ways to design GCE-related assessments that can be integrated effectively with disciplinary requirements at a particular level of education. Stearns (2009) for example, discusses the difficulties of integrating appropriate outcomes into the curriculum, suggesting that insisting on assessment of GC may seem like "one obligation too many" (Stearns 2009, p. 9). Seeing GCE as somehow fundamental rather than an 'added extra' may help teachers and curriculum designers with the task of integrating GCE into their assessment planning.

In this chapter we explore three key challenges in approaching this task:

1. To consider what GCE means in relation to a discipline and therefore, what could be assessed.
2. To integrate the assessment of GC with disciplinary requirements at a particular level of education.
3. To encourage assessors to themselves model the characteristics of GC in designing and managing the assessment process.

This chapter will consider each of these issues in turn, before providing some practical examples of designing GC assessment in specific contexts.

GLOBAL CITIZENSHIP EDUCATION AND ASSESSMENT

Assessment Design as a 'Wicked' Problem

As Boud (2000) pointed out, assessment in formal education always has to do "double duty". There are multiple purposes associated with any single assignment task, and these purposes may sometimes appear contradictory. For instance, a task is usually designed to enable teachers to measure performance whilst also providing developmental feedback. The performance being measured is traditionally situated in a disciplinary (subject) context, but the task may also require the demonstration of generic skills, attributes or values. Some tasks may require the grader to attribute similar importance to both the product submitted and to the process of production. Any individual task will almost certainly require students to work with the fact of a specific, and perhaps personally inconvenient, time of submission with the need to situate that significant piece of work in a continuum of personal and professional development and to be able apply the learning from that task in future contexts.

In addition to these multiple purposes, the complexities of student assignments increase as students progress through education and are expected to synthesise information and opinion from a wider range of sources and in a wider range of contexts. In general, the higher the award, the greater the value and significance of each individual assignment.

The pressure to get the design and management of the assessment 'right' can be very high, which may in turn reduce teachers' appetites for risk-taking in assessment. At the authors' institution, 40% of final year assignment tasks are essays or examinations; it is difficult to know whether these choices are made because they are the best way to assess specific outcomes, or because they are familiar to assessors. Any discussion of the assessment of Global Citizenship must be in the context of these existing complexities which already affect decision-making around assessment.

Assessment design can be considered as a 'wicked problem': according to Rittel and Webber (1973), this is a problem which, among other characteristics, is unique, poorly defined, has many stakeholders with potentially conflicting values, and has no single correct solution. Addressing a wicked problem requires the practitioner to continually monitor what is happening, to continue to consult with stakeholders, to work with others to make sense of the problem, and to adapt behaviours and actions to reflect the current situation (Jordan et al. 2014).

Accepting the concept of assessment design as a wicked problem may be difficult in the context of assessment, where there is a culture of expectation of certainty and objectivity. There is a growing literature to counteract this expectation, and in relation to marking criteria in tertiary education, Bloxham et al. point out that "assessment decisions at this level are so complex, intuitive and tacit that variability is inevitable." (2015, p. 1)

What might be assessed? In seeking to assess education for Global Citizenship, we may, as Stearns (2009) suggested, appear to be adding another "burden" to the assessor who is already wrestling with a plethora of requirements and disciplinary expectations. An education for global citizenship focusses on the purposes of the education that is being assessed, and the challenge is to design assessments with this in mind. Taking the view that GCE is somehow fundamental, rather than an "added extra", may help teachers to integrate GCE into their assessment planning more readily.

The focus of many of the definitions of GC is on attributes and values, so the potential assessment of these is a good place to begin thinking about what might be assessed. This focus relates to what Oxley and Morris (2013) defined in their typology of GC as an approach based on attributes (rather than on rights, identities, practices or status). The eight GC types that these authors delineated could relate more or less closely to particular disciplines: for example the focus on 'economic' global citizenship may fit more easily into the curriculum of say, business disciplines as opposed to 'moral' global citizenship that could be related quite readily to say, philosophy or other humanities. The GC types may also have differing implications for assessment and this is often underplayed in discussion of the possible approaches.

There has been recent interest in the measurement of attributes and values from employers and policy makers, particularly in healthcare science {"values-based recruitment"; see, for example, Miller and Bird (2014) and in business (e.g. Ralston et al. 2011)}. Although a full discussion of the measurement of values or personality traits is outside the scope of this chapter, it may be useful to consider briefly some of the approaches that have been used.

One of the most commonly used measures of personal values, the Schwartz Values Survey and the Portrait Values Questionnaire, have developed as instruments that ask a series of questions designed to assess individuals' motivations towards perceived desirable ends. They measure the relative importance of ten value-types distinguished by Schwartz (2012). Schwartz's value model, developed from this work and usually shown as a wheel, has these ten value-types representing the interrelationship of adjacent concepts.

The contribution of personality traits to an individual's values and attributes is also of interest here. The Big Five personality scale is one method of measuring an individual's personality traits (Digman 1990). The scale includes an assessment of: openness to experience, conscientiousness, extraversion, agreeableness, and neuroticism. This scale and its derivatives have been widely used in different forms, for example, to predict employment performance (Judge and Zapata 2015).

Although the relationship between values and personality traits is still the subject of debate, there is some agreement that these are separate constructs, with traits being largely descriptive and values being motivational (Olver and Mooradian 2003; Parks-Leduc et al. 2014).

Personality traits are generally said to be endogenous, and stable across cultures and even across species, while values are characterised as learned adaptations (Olver and Mooradian 2003). Further, the personality trait with the strongest cognitive component (openness to experience) is said to be the one most closely linked to a portion of Schwartz's values model (openness to change).

The use of the term 'openness' in both the language of values, and personality traits might therefore suggest that the concepts of both personality traits and values have some bearing on the way in which a Global Citizen may develop, and therefore upon the concept of 'assessing' that development. In the language of personality traits for example, an individual who has a high 'openness to change' tends to be:

> curious, intellectual, imaginative, creative, innovative, and flexible (vs. closed-minded, shallow, and simple) (Parks-Leduc et al. 2014)

Schwartz's values model, on the other hand, groups the ten value-types so that eventually two bipolar dimensions emerge: (1) self-enhancement vs. self-transcendence; and (2) openness to change vs. conservation. Self-transcendence and openness to change are of particular interest in relation to GC as self-transcendence includes:

> enhancement of others and transcendence of selfish interests (Schwartz 2012, p. 9)

while openness to change is characterised by:

> values that emphasize independence of thought, action, and feelings and readiness for change (Schwartz 2012, p. 8).

Given the UNESCO definition, we might consider then, that individuals who subscribe to these values are more likely to display attributes relating to GCE. Values themselves are said to have a more cognitive base, whereas traits—thinkings, feelings and behaviours—have a more emotional one, although this distinction is still under scrutiny (Parks-Leduc et al. 2014).

Research on both values and personality is still very active, for example in the validity and reliability of measurement of personality, Dobewall (2014) has found that reliability is improved by adding assessment via an 'other'-someone well-known by the candidate. This perhaps indicates the need for peer- as well as self-assessment in attempts to measure the complex attributes associated with GCE.

Terminology

This discussion helps us to establish 'what' we are seeking to assess, however, we also need to navigate the wide variety of language that HE institutions use in relation to the graduates they seek to educate. There has been a general shift towards the use of terms such as graduate outcomes, attributes or competencies to describe the 'product' of tertiary education, as well as 'core capabilities', 'soft skills' or 'transferable skills'—often in relation to the 'employability' agenda. There is sometimes a tension around these discussions and HEIs are still seeking to resolve use of these terminologies (see Hill et al. 2016 for further discussion of this).

The term 'graduate outcomes' usually describes a general skill (such as critical analysis) and examples adopt the language of learning outcomes or abilities, for example, graduates are able to: critically analyse real-world situations. This suggests that these outcomes can be assessed, or at least 'measured' in some way. 'Competencies' generally describe various levels of particular skills (which can also be assessed) but when partnered with 'global' this becomes a much wider idea of education for professionals with the skills, knowledge, attributes, and perhaps values to transform rather than just to interpret the world (Reimers 2013).

Many universities now use the term 'graduate attributes'. Some would argue these ultimately have use only as a marketing exercise. However, where these attributes have values-based elements, they could be useful as the basis for discussion of values and motivations towards developing skills or practising desired behaviours and of the various circumstances of their deployment. For example: if I value self-advancement, I may display this by attaining and practicing the skill of being a negotiator. I may have developed this considerably during my time on a business management course. The attribute of being an empathetic negotiator, however, may also be developed in someone with the value of 'openness to change' and who may display this in the context of a more self-transcendent mode of looking to enrich the lives of others (Table 38.1). Thus, the attribute of being an empathetic negotiator may be put to various uses, some indicative of a global citizen, but others perhaps less so.

Measurement of attributes *with context* may thus help in direct assessment of GCE as this becomes about more than simply the skill (in this example) of negotiation. If the development of the attribute of good negotiator has occurred within a context of ethical practice, which underpins the curriculum, then this may more reliably form part of an assessment of GCE. Therefore, we use the term 'attributes' in this chapter in the same way as

Table 38.1 'Assessability' of skills, values and attributes (All definitions from Oxford English Dictionary)

Term	Definition	Example	Deployed as	Assessable?
Skill	An ability to perform a function, acquired or learnt with practice	Negotiation	Being able to influence or change people's behaviours.	Yes
Attribute	A quality or character ascribed to a person	Empathetic negotiator	Being able to influence other's behaviours whilst being mindful of other's values.	Yes
Value	The principles or moral standards held by a person or social group	Openness to change; Self-advancement; Self-transcendence	Use of the skill of negotiation for ends that are congruent with an indivdual's own values.	No

Spronken-Smith et al. (2015), to articulate the full range of skills, knowledge, attitudes and values in a broad all-encompassing sense whilst acknowledging that whole curricula are essentially values-based as discussed earlier.

If ultimately we seek to embed within HE programmes an orientation towards GCE, some attention to the wording of learning outcomes to enable a focus on GC in a discipline may be desirable and is discussed further in section "GC Assessment in Practice".

The Role of the Assessor

The validity of the design of assessment, the judgements made, and the power relations involved in the process of assessment may be affected significantly by stakeholder perceptions of the role of "assessor". The identity of a teacher is often entwined strongly with that of 'expert' (McNaughton and Billot 2016) and making critical judgement of the work of others is very much a part of what is expected of the role. Assessors need to act as global citizens in designing and managing their assessments: we will use the term 'GC assessor' to describe someone who is aiming to demonstrate the aims and values of a global citizen in their assessment practice.

One of the strong threads that exist in any definition of GCE is that of social justice, equity and plurality. The power relations that are implicit in the whole process of assessment are potentially problematic in bringing the process of assessment together with the process of becoming, or being, a global citizen. Having the power to award grades, which may have a profound impact on an individual's self-esteem and future prospects, may seem contradictory to the aim of encouraging a plurality of perspectives and approaches to problems.

Boud (1990), writing generally about the dissonance between academic values and the power relations associated with assessment, suggested that assessors could mitigate this kind of situation by developing a more critical approach to their own assessment practice, by encouraging more peer- and self-assessment, and by setting assessment tasks such as reflective writing and the setting of open problems to solve. We will consider the practicalities of setting tasks later in this chapter, but will consider first how the GC assessor might articulate their role.

Assessors need to situate themselves. As we form communities, whether they be personal or professional, there is a natural tendency to look inwards at a social, community or discipline level, but engagement with GCE requires us to broaden our perspectives and to question our own assumptions:

> Global citizenship is about recognizing and thus acknowledging how limited our perspective of the world truly is, and how our limited perspective signifi-cantly informs our actions or lack thereof. (Scott Belt 2016, p. 6)

A critical self-dialogue on the GC assessor's own perceptions of their 'exper-tise' and identity is thus important.

Assessors also need to be able to situate their students and have some idea of what students will bring to their interpretation of the assessment task.

> Every act of assessment gives a message to students about what they should be learning and how they should go about it. The message is coded, is not eas-ily understood and often it is read differently and with different emphases by staff and by students. The message is always interpreted in context and the cues which the context provides offer as much or more clues to students than the intentions of staff, which are rarely explicit (Boud 1995, p. 2)

Sambell and McDowell (1998) provide a good overview of the ways in which students construct their own meanings around assignment requirements and expectations, and are strongly influenced by their previous experiences. We know that assessment is motivating for students; the GC assessor needs to help them to direct their efforts to the intended outcomes, rather than to a perceived or hidden curriculum. This is more likely to happen if the assessor shares clear information about what is expected and how it will be graded and checks with students that they have understood. In doing this, the assessor may need to seek out regular peer review. Such review may come from col-leagues, but also from students.

In a recent critique of the 'neoliberal university', Burdon and Heath (2015) suggest that one way of resisting the default position of 'teacher as expert' is to empower students. This helps academics to look outside their familiar com-munities and to increase empowerment of students as collaborators. For the GC assessor, encouraging student partnership has the added benefit of devel-oping student agency, which is an integral part of the concept of GC.

The idea of student collaboration in assessment is a clear challenge to the conventional power relationships and individual assessors and their institutions are likely to find the idea unsettling. Low-risk examples from the literature include the co-creation of marking criteria and formative self-assessment (Deeley and Bovill 2015), perhaps using exemplars to support this as suggested by Orsmond et al. (2002) or by encouraging students to create a module feedback strategy (Nixon et al. 2016). Falchikov (2013) provides a very wide range of examples of developing student participation in assessment, based mainly on peer and self-assessment.

Another possible way of thinking about assessment and GCE is using the Human Capabilities Approach (HCA). This approach was first proposed by Sen (1980, 1999) and developed by others, particularly by Nussbaum, over the last 30 years. Sen's model acknowledges that the social context and the resources that an individual can access can affect how those resources are converted to capabilities. Capabilities are the freedoms to achieve sets of functionings, where functionings are the beings and doings that a person values and has reason to value. In Sen's own words, capabilities are:

> the substantive freedom he or she enjoys to lead the kind of life he or she has reason to value (Sen 1999, p. 87)

Authors such as Walker (2008) have used the HCA to explore the way individual students assess their own learning and capability development although Sen's work is sometimes critiqued for the focus on the individual rather than the collective (i.e. it tends to foreground the wellbeing of the individual) which chimes with the critiques noted earlier in terms of the individualising nature of some GC discourses.

One possibility for a more collective approach in an HE context might be provided by a consideration of how individuals contribute both to their own wellbeing and to the wellbeing of their communities, a key facet of an outlook based on GC. Walker also hints at how the use of an HCA in evaluating the success of a university in achieving its learning and teaching aims might also be undertaken:

> From the perspective of university teaching and learning, we ought to ask who has the power to develop valued education capabilities, and who has not? If there is inequality in learners' wellbeing we might wish to raise questions as to why some students can promote all their ends while others face barriers, whether of social class, race, gender, culture or disability. (Walker 2008, p. 484)

However, the eventual focus of most assessment at present is on achievement of an individual. The following section provides practical ideas for ways in which module specific assignments may demonstrate elements of GCE.

GC Assessment in Practice

Planning for Assessment

If we accept the premise that GC should be integrated into existing assessment structures, then it follows that there is no need for a special process of assessment design. Rather, it may be useful to consider opportunities for checking the integration of GC at each stage of the usual process. The assessment lifecycle (Forsyth et al. 2015) is a visual representation of these stages, and Fig. 38.1 adds to it some prompt questions for the GC assessor.

In the UK, the Quality Assurance Agency has produced a framework for the inclusion of Education for Sustainable Development and Global Citizenship in Higher Education curricula (Longhurst 2014) which draws heavily on the UNESCO framework for global citizenship. We have used this framework, and the elements of guidance it includes, to develop a series of generic learning outcomes that might be used to provide ideas for GC learning outcomes which could be readily adapted to disciplinary contexts (Fig. 38.2).

If we consider that everyone engaged in assessment is making a contribution to the community of learners, the GC assessor may also have some additional considerations when designing their assignment task, such as:

- Does the task take account of the diverse experiences and attributes students bring to it, and allow them to integrate these into their submissions?
- Will students feel motivated to perform this task well?
- Will I enjoy assessing the students' work?
- Will students feel able to self- and peer-assess their work?

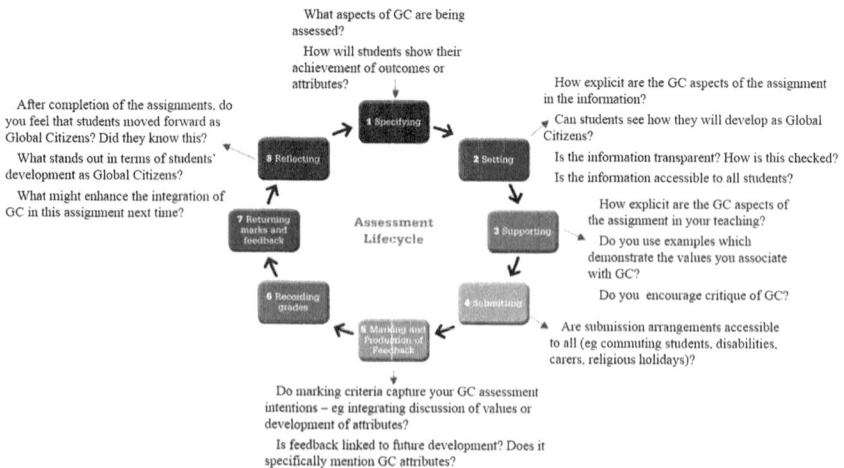

Fig. 38.1   Assessment lifecycle

Element 1: Consider what the concepts of global citizenship and environmental stewardship mean in the context of a discipline and in students' future professional and personal lives	**Sample outcomes**
	Identify assumptions in relation to diverse values, norms and beliefs
	Justify the selection of an approach, as a global citizen, to a real world problem [in discipline]
	Contribute positively to a team task
	Recognise, respect, and evaluate team members' (including own) contributions
	Listen to, support and encourage others
	Consider the effects of the study of [discipline] on the United Nations Sustainable Development Goals
	Identify personal strengths and weaknesses in relation to ideas of global citizenship
	Reflect on (global, local) inequalities in relation to power relations [in the discipline]

Element 2: Consider issues of social justice, ethics and wellbeing, and how these relate to ecological and economic factors	**Sample outcomes**
	Produce a professional [discipline specific] report including contexts of social justice in relation to [discipline].
	Construct and pursue a line of argument in relation to ethics in [discipline].
	Evaluate the impact of the study of [discipline topic] on human wellbeing/social justice
	Justify a particular viewpoint or course of action in [discipline topic] in relation to ecological or economic factors
	Persuade [a defined audience] of the value of a wellbeing focus in relation to [the discipline]
	Evaluate arguments for and against a discipline-related issue using an explicit ethical focus.
	Describe and exhibit ethical behaviour [in disciplinary context]

Element 3: Develop a future-facing outlook; learning to think about the consequences of actions, and how systems and societies can be adapted to ensure sustainable futures	**Sample outcomes**
	Consult widely with [relevant stakeholders] to predict and mitigate the consequences of actions in a [discipline-related] context.
	Evaluate sources of [discipline-related] information and data in the context of global power relations.
	Use a 'systems' approach to problem-solving [discipline-related] issues.
	Evaluate the authority and accuracy of sources of information (Whose authority, whose accuracy? Recognise and interrogate power relationships)
	Critically reflect on the core of [discipline]. What is learned and what is not learned? Who decides?
	Consider the future of the discipline – what are the future effects of [discipline] on society?
	Describe, analyse or evaluate social or community aspects of [discipline]
	Justify actions planned for an intervention in [disciplinary context] in terms of environmental sustainability
	Reflect on intercultural contexts of work in [disciplinary context].

Fig. 38.2   Sample generic outcomes

- Will the assessment process be manageable for this task?
- Could any assessor look at the outcomes in Fig. 38.1 and self-assess against these?

Figures 38.3, 38.4 and 38.5 provide notional examples of how these generic learning outcomes may be used in idealised worked examples to show how assessment could be aligned within a particular disciplinary context and how the assessment lifecycle may be used to ensure a focus on GCE is maintained.

Commentary on Fig. 38.3
The example of Fig. 38.3 uses the outcomes linked to Element 1 in Fig. 38.2. The students will be in the last year of their undergraduate courses, and most of them will go on to marketing positions in organisations like the ones mentioned in the assignment. As well as giving them an opportunity to work on a real-world scenario, which may give them something to talk to potential

---

Unit Learning Outcomes (ULO). At the end of this unit students will be able to:

1. Consider the effects of the study of Marketing on one of the United Nations Sustainable Development (UNSD) Goals
2. Recognise and evaluate team members' (including own) contributions
3. The UNSD goal selected by the team for this assessment is: *Ensure sustainable consumption and production patterns*

Assessment task: In teams, you will imagine a marketing context in a fictitious company, social enterprise, charity, public sector organisation, or other context of your own choice. Within this context, you will design a process for monitoring the contribution of marketing to the selected UNSD goal of *ensuring sustainable consumption and production patterns*. You might include regular consultations, specific projects, engagement with a variety of local, regional, national or international bodies and so on. Your submission will be a summary of this process for the management board of your chosen organisation.

The assignment submission is divided into three sections:

1) 200 word individual statement of each participant's assessment of own contribution – peer marked (10% of total)
2) 300 word collaborative statement summarising group process – tutor marked (10% of total, each member of the group gets the same mark)
3) 3000 word team report describing and explaining the planned process – tutor marked (80% of total, each member of the group gets the same mark)

Feedback plan: You will receive feedback from each of your peers in the group on your individual statement, as well as a summary comment from your tutor with some suggestions for your future team-working development. You will receive collective feedback on your collaborative statement and on your team report, which will comment on the feasibility of the process you propose and give you some suggestions for future team-working development.

Fig. 38.3 Assessment for responsible marketing unit (Business marketing degree, final year)

employers about, it covers explicitly one of the UNSD goals (UNDP 2015) and it recognises the importance of team-working by offering grades both for the description of the process and for the final product. The students have some agency, in selecting their own context for the assignment development.

Commentary on Fig. 38.4

An early introduction to a real-world problem is one of the techniques mentioned earlier to engage students with the curriculum and with ideas about their own agency. It may also introduce students to peer-learning and self-assessment, which, given the emphasis of UNESCO and other frameworks (e.g. QAA) on equalities, are important skills for GCE, and provides opportunities for some of the challenges mentioned earlier: negotiation of criteria can take up considerable tutor and student time and create anxiety amongst team members. There is an argument for saying that this may be a good thing to do at this level of study, when the stakes of assessment are relatively low, and students can develop skills in relative safety.

Unit Learning Outcomes (ULO). At the end of this unit students will be able to:

1. Justify the selection of an approach, as a global citizen, to a real world problem in Zoology
2. Contribute positively to a team task

Students are asked to consider the real world problem of: decline in populations of pollinating insects

Assessment task: Work as a team to produce a report in a response to a government report that suggests the population of pollinating insects in the UK is in serious decline.

Your report should include a plan to engage relevant stakeholders: alternative methods of measurement of population size: indices of species richness and community composition: your team's argument for a course of action.

Assessment marking:
 Completion of grid showing peer input contribution agreed between team members – peer marked (20% of total: each member of the group gets the same mark)
1) Formative assessment and negotiation of criteria between tutor and team. Subsequent summative self-assessment of own performance by each team member - self-marked. (30% of total):
2) Report (2000 words) – tutor marked (50% of total: each member of the group gets the same mark)

Feedback:
You will receive the peer feedback grid summarising your contribution to the task and suggesting areas to develop for your next group task: you will complete your own feedback on your own performance overall, and you will share written feedback from the tutor to the whole group on the final report. This feedback will focus on the overall structure and findings of the report, and the apparent coherence of the team work.

Fig. 38.4 Assessment for ecology unit (Ecology and wildlife conservation degree, year one)

Commentary on Fig. 38.5
The example in Fig. 38.5 demonstrates some of the features of assessment design for a module in a geography curriculum with a focus on education for GC. In the second year of an undergraduate degree, we expect students to be in transition towards a range of professional behaviours and to have developed a facility with assessing each other's contributions and presentations.

CONCLUSION AND FUTURE RESEARCH

It is clear that there are potential difficulties if we simply seek to apply traditional assessment methods to the assessment of GCE. This is primarily due to the complexity of assessing attributes and the self-awareness that comes with the acknowledgement of the power relations inherent in any assessment process. However, the first of these difficulties is at least partly addressed by careful attention to the stages of an assessment lifecycle: good assessment practice

---

Unit Learning Outcomes (ULO). At the end of this unit students will be able to:

1. Evaluate the urban development plans of a local council in terms of environmental sustainability and social justice
2. Persuade local representatives of the value of consideration of a citizenship focus in relation to the urban development plans
3. Identify assumptions in relation to diverse values, norms and beliefs

Assessment task (ULO1):
Collaborative report to provide an analysis of the urban development plans of a selected council in relation to environmental sustainability and social justice. Guide length: 1500-2000 words; can be presented as a traditional document, or as a web page, or a video (guide length 10 minutes). Tutor marked (50% of total; each member of the group gets the same mark)

Assessment task (ULO 2):
10-minute presentation produced collaboratively and presented by members of the team (in any medium suitable for a boardroom scenario). Peer and tutor marked (30% of total; each member of the group gets the same mark, arrived at by negotiation with tutor and peers)

Assessment task (ULO 3):
500 word team reflection on the process of working on this project. All team members to contribute and include reflection on the strengths and areas for improvement in own and other team members' contributions. Peer marked (20% of total; each member of the group gets the same mark)

Assessment Marking and Feedback
The 500 words provides part of the portfolio for assessment in the professional development unit.

The presentations are watched by all. There is opportunity to contribute online as these are given – the audience are asked to pick out one strength and one area for development – training in giving and receiving feedback provided in advance.

Formative feedback is provided at three set points. A final summative mark is negotiated with the tutors.

Fig. 38.5 Assessment for shaping the community unit (Geography diploma/degree, Year 2)

can provide fair and reliable ways of doing the double duty that assessment of attributes for GC can achieve. The second is addressed primarily through a consideration of the role of the assessor—modelling values that ensure that the assessors themselves deploy characteristics of a global citizen as they design and manage the assessment process.

As future research develops in the domains of both personality and values, this will continue to inform assessment practice in GCE. There is also potential for ideas from development education, such as the Human Capabilities Approach to be applied to this area.

REFERENCES

Biesta, G., & Lawy, R. (2006). From teaching citizenship to learning democracy: Overcoming individualism in research, policy and practice. *Cambridge Journal of Education, 36*(1), 63–79.

Bloxham, S., den-Outer, B., Hudson, J., & Price, M. (2015). Let's stop the pretence of consistent marking: Exploring the multiple limitations of assessment criteria. *Assessment & Evaluation in Higher Education*, 1–16.

Boud, D. (1990). Assessment and the promotion of academic values. *Studies in Higher Education, 15*(1), 101–111.

Boud, D. (1995). Assessment and learning: Contradictory or complementary? In P. Knight (Ed.), *Assessment for learning in higher education* (pp. 35–48). London: Kogan Page.

Boud, D. (2000). Sustainable assessment: Rethinking assessment for the learning society. *Studies in Continuing Education, 22*(2), 151–167.

Burdon, P. D., & Heath, M. (2015). Academic resistance to the neoliberal university. *Legal Education Review, 23*(2), 379–401.

Deeley, S. J., & Bovill, C. (2015). Staff student partnership in assessment: Enhancing assessment literacy through democratic practices. *Assessment & Evaluation in Higher Education*, 1–15.

Digman, J. M. (1990). Personality structure: Emergence of the five-factor model. *Annual Review of Psychology, 41*(1), 417–440.

Dobewall, H. (2014). A comparison of self-other agreement in personal values versus the Big Five personality traits. *Journal of Research in Personality, 50*, 1–10.

Falchikov, N. (2013). *Improving assessment through student involvement: Practical solutions for aiding learning in higher and further education*. London: Routledge.

Forsyth, R., Cullen, R., Ringan, N., & Stubbs, M. (2015). Supporting the development of assessment literacy of staff through institutional process change. *London Review of Education, 13*, 34–41.

Hill, J., Walkington, H., & France, D. (2016). Graduate attributes: Implications for higher education practice and policy. *Journal of Geography in Higher Education, 40*(2), 155–163.

Jerome, L. (2008). Assessing citizenship education. In J. Arthur, I. Davies & C. Hahn (Eds.), *Sage handbook of education for citizenship and democracy*. London: Sage.

Jordan, M. E., Kleinsasser, R. C., & Roe, M. F. (2014). Wicked problems: Inescapable wickedity. *Journal of Education for Teaching, 40*(4), 415–430.

Judge, T. A., & Zapata, C. P. (2015). The person–situation debate revisited: Effect of situation strength and trait activation on the validity of the Big Five personality traits in predicting job performance. *Academy of Management Journal, 58*(4), 1149–1179.

Longhurst, J. (2014). *Education for Sustainable Development: Guidance for UK Higher Education providers.*

McNaughton, S. M., & Billot, J. (2016). Negotiating academic teacher identity shifts during higher education contextual change. *Teaching in Higher Education, 21*(6), 644–658.

Miller, S., & Bird, J. (2014). Assessment of practitioners' and students' values when recruiting: Sam Miller and Jim Bird explain how values-based recruitment is being used to create a workforce that is suitable to provide the care required by the NHS. *Nursing Management, 21*(5), 22–29.

Nixon, S., Brooman, S., Murphy, B., & Fearon, D. (2016). Clarity, consistency and communication: Using enhanced dialogue to create a course-based feedback strategy. *Assessment & Evaluation in Higher Education*, 1–11.

Olver, J. M., & Mooradian, T. A. (2003). Personality traits and personal values: A conceptual and empirical integration. *Personality and Individual Differences, 35*(1), 109–125.

Orsmond, P., Merry, S., & Reiling, K. (2002). The use of exemplars and formative feedback when using student derived marking criteria in peer and self-assessment. *Assessment & Evaluation in Higher Education, 27*(4), 309–323.

Oxley, L., & Morris, P. (2013). Global citizenship: A typology for distinguishing its multiple conceptions. *British Journal of Educational Studies, 61*(3), 301–325.

Parks-Leduc, L., Feldman, G., & Bardi, A. (2014). Personality traits and personal values: A meta-analysis. *Personality and Social Psychology Review*. doi:10.1177/1088868314538548.

Ralston, D. A., Egri, C. P., Reynaud, E., Srinivasan, N., Furrer, O., Brock, D., et al. (2011). A twenty-first century assessment of values across the global workforce. *Journal of Business Ethics, 104*(1), 1–31.

Reimers, F. M. (2013). Education for improvement: Citizenship in the global public sphere. *Harvard International Review, 35,* 56+.

Rittel, H. W., & Webber, M. M. (1973). Dilemmas in a general theory of planning. *Policy Sciences, 4*(2), 155–169.

Sambell, K., & McDowell, L. (1998). The construction of the hidden curriculum: Messages and meanings in the assessment of student learning. *Assessment & Evaluation in Higher Education, 23*(4), 391–402.

Schwartz, S. H. (2012). An overview of the Schwartz theory of basic values. *Online Readings in Psychology and Culture, 2*(1), 11.

Scott Belt, A. A. (2016). *Does global citizenship education predict identification with all humanity?* Bowling Green, Kentucky: West Kentucky University.

Sen, A. (1980). *Equality of what?* Paper presented at The Tanner Lecture on Human Values.

Sen, A. (1999). *Development as freedom*. Oxford: Oxford Paperbacks.

Spronken-Smith, R., Bond, C., McLean, A., Frielick, S., Smith, N., Jenkins, M., et al. (2015). Evaluating engagement with graduate outcomes across higher education institutions in Aotearoa/New Zealand. *Higher Education Research & Development, 34*(5), 1014–1030.

Stearns, P. N. (2009). *Educating global citizens in colleges and universities: Challenges and opportunities*. London: Routledge.

UNDP. (2015). *United nations development programme sustainable development goals*.

UNESCO. (2014). *Global citizenship education: Preparing learners for the challenges of the 21st century*. Paris.

Walker, M. (2008). A human capabilities framework for evaluating student learning. *Teaching in Higher Education, 13*(4), 477–487.

Authors' Biography

Alicia Prowse is a Principal Lecturer in the Centre for Excellence in Learning and Teaching at Manchester Metropolitan University, UK. Her background includes a PhD in Plant Ecology, teaching in Higher Education (Biology and Research Methods), Teaching English to Speakers of Other Languages (TESOL), as well as having worked as an actor and collaborated with an artist. Her present role includes formal and informal academic staff development and her research interests include: Global Citizenship; Interdisciplinarity and Student Transition to Higher Education.

Rachel Forsyth is Associate Head of the Centre for Excellence in Learning and Teaching at Manchester Metropolitan University, UK. She began her career as a lecturer in physics and then moved into educational development. At the moment, she works mainly in the area of curriculum design and assessment in higher education, and teaches on the PGC in Learning and Teaching in Higher Education. She is a Senior Fellow of the UK Higher Education Academy.

Index

© The Editor(s) (if applicable) and The Author(s) 2018
I. Davies et al. (eds.), *The Palgrave Handbook of Global Citizenship and Education*, https://doi.org/10.1057/978-1-137-59733-5

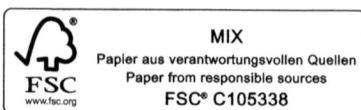

Printed by Books on Demand, Germany